1/5 7/07

Moh

# Solid State Physics

## Structure and Properties of Materials

### Second Edition

# Solid State Physics

## Structure and Properties of Materials

### Second Edition

**M A Wahab**

Alpha Science International Ltd.
Harrow, U.K.

**Mohd. Abdul Wahab**
Department of Physics
Jamia Millia Islamia (Central University)
New Delhi, INDIA

Copyright © 1999, 2005
Second Edition 2005


Alpha Science International Ltd.
Hygeia Building, 66 College Road
Harrow, Middlesex HA1 1BE, U.K.

ISBN 1-84265-218-4


Printed in India.

# Preface to the Second Edition

I am grateful to the readers for the encouraging response to the first edition. Based on their suggestions, revisions have been made in this second edition.

The whole book can be conveniently divided into two parts, the structural part and the properties part. A number of physical properties of materials have been discussed in Chapters 9 to 17. In general, they can be understood in terms of tensors of different rank. Consequently, it was felt desirable to add a new chapter at the end in the form of *anisotropic properties of materials*. The concept of tensor has been introduced to visualize the inherent macroscopic symmetries of physical properties. It has been observed that the number of property tensor decreases with the increase of crystal symmetry. This chapter has been added for the benefit of readers to understand the crystal properties (anisotropic) in terms of some simple mathematical formulations such as tensor and matrix.

Any omissions, errors, suggestions brought to the knowledge of the author will be gratefully acknowledged.

M A Wahab

# Preface to the First Edition

This book intended as a textbook for B.Sc. (H) and M.Sc. (General) courses in Solid State Physics will also be helpful to the students of Chemistry, Materials Science, Engineering and those appearing for National Eligibility Test (NET) conducted by UGC/CSIR.

The present work is the outcome of lectures delivered by the author to the undergraduate and postgraduate students during the last 23 years. The aim of the book is to provide a comprehensive introduction to the subject of Solid State Physics to the students related to the above mentioned areas. In preparation of the text, the author has taken special care to present the topics in a coherent, simple and straightforward manner. This book contains a total of eighteen chapters and broadly deals with the topics related to structural aspects and various physical properties of crystalline solids. The chapter number eight particularly deals with the experimental methods to determine the crystal structures of materials. On the other hand, the chapter number eighteen deals with the anisotropic properties of materials and their representations in terms of tensors of different types and ranks. MKS (SI) system of units has been used throughout this book. Assuming that the students are familiar with vector quantities, the use of arrow sign ($\rightarrow$) on the top of them has been avoided except on the unit vectors. The main features are:

1. Solved examples for a better understanding of the text,
2. Brief summary at the end of each chapter for a quick review,
3. Definitions of important terms at the end of each chapter for further enrichment of knowledge,
4. Problems and exercises.

Although proper care has been taken during the preparation and proofreading of the manuscript, still some errors are expected to creep in. Any omissions, errors and suggestions brought to the knowledge of the author will be gratefully acknowledged.

I sincerely express my deep sense of gratitude to my Research Guide, Professor G.C. Trigunayat, Department of Physics, Delhi University from whom I have learnt a lot including the art of writing and I would like to thank my colleagues from Departments of Physics, Chemistry and Mechanical Engineering and friends for their valuable suggestion and encouragement during the preparation of the manuscript.

I am indeed grateful to all the authors and publishers of Books and Journals mentioned in the bibliography for freely consulting them and even borrowing some ideas during the preparation of the manuscript. I am also grateful to M/s Narosa Publishing House, New Delhi, for the timely publication of this book.

My special thanks to Mr. Ghayasuddin and Mr. Salahuddin for preparing the diagrams in the shortest possible time. Last, but not the least, my family members who continuously supported and encouraged me during the entire writing period. I particularly thank my daughter Dr. Shadma Wahab for helping me in proofreading of the entire manuscript.

M A Wahab

# Units of Measurements

| Quantity | SI UNITS | | Other Units |
|---|---|---|---|
| | Written as | Read as | |
| Temperature | K | kelvin | °C, °F |
| Pressure | MPa or $MNm^{-2}$ | Megapascal meganewton per square meter | atmosphere, Psi $kg/cm^2$, $dyne/cm^2$ mm of Hg |
| Internal energy, E<br>External energy, PV<br>Enthalpy, H<br>Enthalpy of formation, $\Delta H_F$<br>Gibbs Free energy, G<br>Thermal energy, RT<br>Activation Energy, Q | $Jmol^{-4}$ | joule per mole | cal/mol |
| Entropy, S<br>Specific heat, $C_v$, $C_p$ | $Jmol^{-1}k^{-1}$ | joule per mole per kelvin | cal/mol/°C cal/gm/°C |
| Frequency of radiatition, shear strain rate, $v$ | $s^{-1}$ or Hz | Hertz or per second | — |
| Electron energy level<br>Kinetic Energy, E<br>Fermi energy, $E_F$<br>Energy gap, $E_g$<br>Contact potential, $eV_0$ | J | Joule | eV, erg |
| Ionization potential<br>Electron affinity<br>Bond energy | $kJmol^{-1}$ | kilo joule per mole | eV/atom, kcal/mole |
| Lattice parameter, a<br>Atomic diameter, Interplanar spacing, d | | | |

| Quantity | SI UNITS | | Other Units |
|---|---|---|---|
| | Written as | Read as | |
| Wavelength of radiation, $\lambda$ Bond length, Jump distance, $\delta$ | mm | nanometer | Å |
| Dipole moment | Cm | coulomb meter | debye |
| Density | $kgm^{-3}$ | kilogram per cubic meter | $g/cm^3$ 1b/cu.in. |
| Dislocation density, $\rho$ | $mm^{-3}$ or $m^{-2}$ | meter per cubic-meter, or per square-meter | per square inch |
| Dislocation energy, E | $Jm^{-1}$ | joule per meter | erg/cm eV/plane |
| Shear modulus, $\mu$ Young's modulus, Y | $GNm^{-2}$ | giganewton per square meter | $dyne/cm^2$ psi |
| Energy of surface imperfection, $\gamma$ | $J/m^2$ | joule per square meter | $erg/cm^2$ |
| Surface tension, $\gamma$ | $Nm^{-1}$ | newton per meter | dyne/cm |
| Flux, J | $mol\ m^{-2}\ s^{-1}$ | mole per square meter per second | no. of atoms/ $cm^2/s$ |
| Concentration, c | $mol\ m^{-3}$ | mole per cubic meter | no. of atoms/ $cm^3$ |
| Concentration of electrons and holes, $n_c$ or $n_h$ | $m^{-3}$ | per cubic meter | — |
| Mobility, $\mu_c$ or $\mu_h$ | $m^2V^{-1}s^{-1}$ | meter squared per volt per second | — |
| Concentration gradient, (dc/dx) | $mol\ m^{-4}$ | mole per cubic meter per meter | no. of atoms/ $cm^4$ |
| Diffusion coefficient, D Diffusion constant, $D_0$ | $m^2\text{-}s^{-1}$ | square meter per second | — |
| Vibration frequency, $v$ or $v'$ Strain rate, $\dot{\varepsilon}$ | $s^{-1}$ | per second | — |
| Strain energy, $\varepsilon$ | $Jm^{-3}$ | Joule per cubic meter | $erg/cm^{-3}$ |

| Quantity | SI Unit | Name | Other Units |
|---|---|---|---|
| Interatomic force, F<br>Applied force | N | newton | kgf, lb, dyne |
| Uniaxial stress, $\sigma$<br>and<br>Shear stress | $MNm^{-2}$<br>or<br>$MP_a$ | Meganewton per<br>square meter or<br>mega pascal | $kgf/mm^2$, psi<br><br>$dyne/cm^2$ |
| Current density, J | $Am^{-2}$ | ampere per<br>square meter | $mA/cm^2$ |
| Electrical<br>  conductivity, $\sigma$ | $\Omega^{-1}m^{-1}$ | per ohm<br>per meter | mho/cm |
| Standard electrode<br>  potential, V | V | volt | — |
| Capacitance, C | F or $CV^{-1}$ | farad or coulomb<br>per volt | — |
| Dielectric constant<br>  of free space, $\varepsilon_0$ | $Fm^{-1}$ | farad per meter | — |
| Polarization, P<br>Saturation Pol., $P_0$ | $Cm^{-2}$ | coulomb per<br>square meter | — |
| Collision time, $\tau$ | s | second | — |
| Dislocation velocity, $v_d$<br>Drift velocity, $v_d$ | $ms^{-1}$ | meter per second | — |
| Field gradient, $\varepsilon$<br>Electric field<br>  strength, E | $Vm^{-1}$ | volt per meter | — |
| Resistivity, $\rho$ | ohm m | ohm meter | $\mu\Omega$-inch.<br>ohm-cm |
| Wave number, k | $m^{-1}$ | per meter | — |
| Magnetic Induction, B | $Wm^{-2}$ | weber per<br>square meter | gauss |
| Magnetic field<br>  strength, H<br>Coercieve field, $H_c$<br>Magnetization, M | $Am^{-1}$ | ampere per meter | oersted |
| Magnetic Permeability | $Hm^{-1}$ | oersted | |
| Magnetic Permeability | $Hm^{-1}$ | henery per meter | — |
| Magnetic moment, $\mu_m$ | $Am^2$ | ampere meter<br>squared | — |

## BASE UNITS

| Quantity | Unit | Symbol |
|---|---|---|
| Length, L | metre | m |
| Mass, M | kilogram | kg |
| Time, t | second | s |
| Electric current, I | ampere | A |
| Temperature, T | kelvin | K |
| Amount of substance, n | mole | mol |
| Luminous Intensity | candela | cd |

## SUPPLEMENTARY UNITS

| Plane angle, $\theta$ | radian | rad |
|---|---|---|
| Solid angle, $\Omega$ | steradian | sr |

## DERIVED UNITS

| Quantity | Special name | Symbol | Equivalence in | |
|---|---|---|---|---|
| | | | Other derived units | Base units |
| Frequency | hertz | Hz | — | $s^{-1}$ |
| Force, weight | newton | N | — | $kg\,ms^{-2}$ |
| Stress, strength, & pressure | pascal | Pa | — | $kgm^{-1}s^{-2}$ |
| Energy, work, quantity of heat | joule | J | Nm | $kgm^2s^{-2}$ |
| Power | watt | W | $Js^{-1}$ | $kgm^2s^{-3}$ |
| Electric charge | coulomb | C | — | As |
| Electric potential | volt | V | $WA^{-1}$ | $kgm^2s^{-3}A^{-1}$ |
| Resistance | ohm | $\Omega$ | $VA^{-1}$ | $kgm^2s^{-3}A^{-2}$ |
| Capacitance | farad | F | $CV^{-1}$ | $kg^{-1}m^{-2}s^4A^2$ |
| Magnetic flux | weber | Wb | Vs | $kgm^2s^{-2}A^{-1}$ |
| Magnetic flux density | tesla | T | $Wbm^{-2}$ | $kgs^{-2}A^{-1}$ |
| Inductance | henry | H | $WbA^{-1}$ | $kgm^2s^{-2}A^{-2}$ |

## PREFIX, MULTIPLES AND SUBMULTIPLES

| Factors by which the unit is multiplied | Name | Symbol |
| --- | --- | --- |
| $10^{12}$ | tera | T |
| $10^{9}$ | giga | G |
| $10^{6}$ | mega | M |
| $10^{3}$ | Kilo | k |
| $10^{2}$ | hecto | h |
| $10^{1}$ | deka | da |
| $10^{-1}$ | deci | d |
| $10^{-2}$ | centi | c |
| $10^{-3}$ | milli | m |
| $10^{-6}$ | micro | μ |
| $10^{-9}$ | nano | n |
| $10^{-12}$ | pico | p |
| $10^{-15}$ | femto | f |
| $10^{-18}$ | atto | a |

# Physical Constants

| | |
|---|---|
| Avogadro's number | $N = 6.023 \times 10^{23}$ mol$^{-1}$ |
| | $= 6.023 \times 10^{26}$ kmol$^{-1}$ |
| Boltzmann's constant | $k = 1.380 \times 10^{-23}$ JK$^{-1}$ |
| | $= 8.614 \times 10^{-5}$ eVK$^{-1}$ |
| Gas constant | $R = 8.314$ Jmol$^{-1}$K$^{-1}$ |
| | $= 1.987$ cal mol$^{-1}$K$^{-1}$ |
| Planck's constant | $h = 6.626 \times 10^{-34}$ Js |
| | $= 6.626 \times 10^{-27}$ ergs |
| Electronic charge | $e = 1.602 \times 10^{-19}$ C |
| | $= 4.8 \times 10^{10}$ esu |
| Electron rest mass | $m_o = 9.11 \times 10^{-31}$ kg |
| | $= 9.11 \times 10^{-28}$ g |
| Proton rest mass | $m_p = 1.673 \times 10^{-27}$ kg |
| | $= 1.673 \times 10^{-24}$ g |
| Neutron rest mass | $M_n = 1.675 \times 10^{-27}$ kg |
| | $= 1.675 \times 10^{-24}$ g |
| Velocity of light | $c = 2.998 \times 10^8$ ms$^{-1}$ |
| | $= 2.998 \times 10^{10}$ cms$^{-1}$ |
| Bohr magneton (magnetic moment) | $\mu_B = 9.273 \times 10^{-24}$ Am$^2$ |
| | $= 9.273 \times 10^{-21}$ erg. gauss$^{-1}$ |
| Permitivity of free space | $\varepsilon_o = 8.854 \times 10^{-12}$ Fm$^{-1}$ |
| Coulomb force constant | $1/4\pi\varepsilon_o = 9 \times 10^{-9}$ Nm$^2$C$^{-2}$ |
| Permeability of free space | $\mu_o = $ lesu |
| | $= 4\pi \times 10^{-7}$ Hm$^{-1}$ |
| | $= 1.257 \times 10^{-6}$ Hm$^{-1}$ |
| Faraday's constant | $F = 96.49$ kC mol$^{-1}$ |
| | (of electrons) |
| Atomic mass unit (amu) | $(1/10^3 N) = 1.660 \times 10^{-27}$ kg |
| Acceleration due to gravity | $g = 9.81$ ms$^{-2}$ |
| Ice point | $0°C = 273.15$ K |

# Conversion Factors

$$1 \text{ micron} = 10^{-6} \text{ m}$$

$$1 \text{ nm} = 10^{-9} \text{ m}$$

$$1 \text{ Å} = 10^{-10} \text{ m}$$

$$1° = 1/57.3 \text{ rad}$$

$$1 \text{ eV} = 1.602 \times 10^{-19} \text{ J}$$

$$1 \text{ erg} = 10^{-7} \text{ J}$$

$$1 \text{ eV/entity} = 96.49 \text{ kJ mol}^{-1} \text{ of (entities)}$$

$$1 \text{ calorie} = 4.18 \text{ J}$$

$$1 \text{ atmosphere} = 0.101325 \text{ MPa}$$

$$1 \text{ torr (= 1 mm of Hg)} = 133.3 \text{ Nm}^{-2}$$

$$1 \text{ bar} = 105 \text{ Nm}^{-2} = 10^{-1} \text{ MPa}$$

$$1 \text{ Psi} = 6.90 \text{ kNm}^{-2}$$

$$1 \text{ dyne/cm}^2 = 0.1 \text{ Nm}^{-2}$$

$$1 \text{ Poise} = 0.1 \text{ Pa s}$$

$$1 \text{ mol/cm}^2/\text{sec} = 10^4 \text{ mol m}^{-2}\text{s}^{-1}$$

$$1 \text{ mol/cm}^3 = 10^6 \text{ mol m}^{-3}$$

$$1 \text{ mol/cm}^4 = 10^8 \text{ mol m}^{-4}$$

$$1 \text{ cm}^2/\text{sec} = 10^{-4} \text{ m}^2\text{s}^{-1}$$

$$T\,°C = (T + 273.15) \text{ K}$$

$$1 \text{ erg/cation} = 1.43933 \times 10^{13} \text{ kCal/mol}$$

$$1 \text{ electronic charge} = 1.6 \times 10^{-19} \text{ C}$$

$$1 \text{ Wb} = 10^8 \text{ Maxwell}$$

$$1 \text{ Tesla} = 1 \text{ Wb/m}^2$$

$$= 10^4 \text{ Mx/cm}^2$$

$$= 10^4 \text{ Gauss}$$

$$1 \text{ A/m} = 4\pi \times 10^{-3} \text{ Oe}$$

$$= 1.26 \times 10^{-2} \text{ Oe}$$

# Contents

# Chapter 1

# Atoms in Crystals

## 1.1  THE SOLID STATE

Matter is usually regarded to exist in the solid state or the fluid state, the latter being subdivided into the liquid and gaseous states. However, on the basis of modern concept, the matter is more conveniently divided into the condensed state and the gaseous state, the former being subdivided into the solid and the liquid states. It is not easy to give a completely satisfactory definition of a solid; a "borderline" material can always be found. We shall use "solid" to mean any material whose constituent particles (atoms, ions or molecules) are relatively fixed in position, except for thermal vibration. "Fluid" on the other hand will mean a material whose particles are in a state of constant translational motion.

In order to understand various states of solid, it is useful to consider the process of growth. The growth could be either from solution, melt or vapour, or from a suitable combination of these. If the growth process is slow, then the constituent particles have a tendency to settle down in positions for which the free energy of the configuration is minimum. This leads to an arrangement of long-range order in the solids. However, in certain extreme cases when the growth process or the phase change is rather rapid, the constituent particles do not have sufficient time to achieve minimum energy configuration. Consequently a long-range order is not obtained in such cases. Nevertheless, there is evidence for the preferential ordering of neighbouring atoms around a particular atom or ion and hence a short-range order is still preserved.

In the following section, an attempt will be made to classify solids in terms of their degree and type of order. It is convenient to think of three broad classes: crystalline, semi-crystalline and non-crystalline. It is to be pointed out here that the extremes such as perfect order or perfect disorder are rare and are of theoretical interest only.

### Crystalline Solids

A solid in general is said to be a crystal if the constituent particles (atoms, ions or molecules) are arranged in a three dimensional periodic manner, or simply if it has a reticular structure. The regularity in the appearance of crystals found in nature (Fig. 1.1) or grown in laboratory has led us to believe that crystals are formed by a regular repetition of identical building blocks in three dimensional space (Fig. 1.2). When a crystal grows under constant environment, the external geometrical shape of the crystal often remains unchanged. The shape is a consequence of internal arrangement of constituent particles of which it is build up.

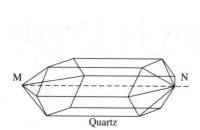

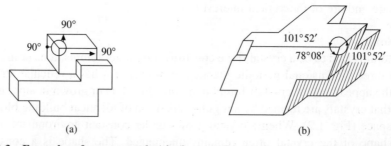

**Fig. 1.1 External forms of the crystal found in nature**

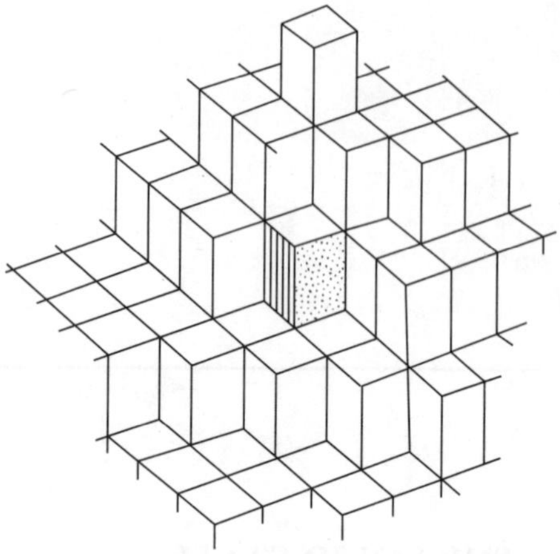

**Fig. 1.2 Formation of crystals by regular repetition of identical building blocks**

Observations show that crystals are bounded by optically plane faces, sharp straight edges and interfacial angles. A relationship among these elements can be expressed by the formula

$$f + c = e + 2 \qquad (1)$$

where $f$ is the number of faces, $c$ is the number of angles and $e$ is the number of edges. Out of the three elements in eq. 1, if two are known then the third can be easily obtained.

*Example*: Determine the number of edges in a quartz crystal, if there are 18 faces and 14 angles in it.

*Solution:* Given: $f = 18$, $c = 14$ (also refer Fig. 1.1).
Using eq. 1, number of edges

$$e = 18 + 14 - 2 = 30.$$

This can be verified from Fig. 1.1
A crystal if more or less regular in shape is called a monocrystal or a single crystal. Quite common crystals such as rock salt, calcite, quartz, etc. (Fig. 1.3) are some examples of this class. A typical feature of a single crystal is its anisotropy, i.e. the difference in its physical properties in different directions. In addition, a crystalline solid has a sharp melting point.

**Fig. 1.3 Examples of monocrystals (single crystals), (a) Common salt (b) Quartz crystal**

### Semicrystalline (Polycrystalline) Solids

A solid consisting of many crystallites grown together in the form of an interlocking mass, oriented randomly and separated by well defined boundaries is said to be a polycrystalline solid (Fig. 1.4). In general, the grains in such a solid are not related in shape to the crystal structure, the surface being random in shape rather than well defined crystal planes. A great majority of solids occurring in nature such as rock, sand, metals, salts, etc. are of polycrystalline structure. However, they can be grown as a single crystal under suitable conditions. Due to random distribution of crystallites, a polycrystalline solid is isotropic, i.e. its properties are same, on an average in all directions.

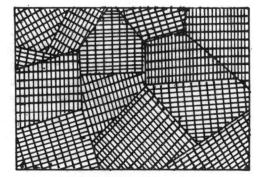

**Fig. 1.4 Polycrystalline aggregates separated by well defined boundaries**

### Noncrystalline (Amorphous) Solids

A class of solids showing neither reticular nor granular structure is termed as noncrystalline or amorphous solid. In other words, an amorphous solid is the opposite extreme of a single crystal. Glass and plastic are common examples of this class. Other common substances include, resin, pitch, sugar candy, etc. A typical feature of these substances is that they have no definite melting points. As their temperature is raised, they gradually become soft, their viscosity drops, and begin to behave like ordinary viscous liquids. Observations reveal that an amorphous body may get crystallized with the passage of time. For instance, crystals of sugar are formed in sugar candy after a certain time has passed. In exactly the same way, glass "ages" i.e. polycrystalline grains are formed in it. When this happens, the glass loses its transparency and becomes brittle.

## 1.2 PERIODICITY IN CRYSTALS

### Space Lattice and Translation Vectors

The property that distinguishes crystals from other solids is that the constituent particles (atoms, ions or molecules) in crystals are arranged in a three dimensional periodic manner. In order to describe the periodicity in crystals, in 1848 Bravais introduced the concept of space lattice. To understand the concept clearly, let us consider the translation of an object (symbolized by the letter J) to a finite distance (say $a$) and then repeated systematically along three crystallographic directions, $x$, $y$ and $z$ to obtain three dimensional space lattice. Since a translation operation repeats an object infinite number of times in one direction, therefore using such an operation a one dimensional periodic array (infinite linear array) of J's can be obtained (Fig. 1.5a). Further, since the nature of the repeated object in Fig. 1.5a does not affect the translational periodicity,

**Fig. 1.5 One dimensional array of: (a) objects, (b) points; a linear lattice**

therefore, it is easy to represent this periodicity by replacing each object in the array with a point. The resulting collection of points in Fig. 1.5b is called a lattice, in this case, a one dimensional or a linear lattice. It should be remembered that a point is an imaginary infinitesimal spot in space, and consequently a lattice of points is imaginary also. On the other hand, the array of J's in Fig. 1.5a is real. Thus, it is not a lattice of J's, instead it is correctly called a lattice array of J's.

If the translation $a$ is combined with another noncollinear translation $b$, then a two dimensional array (Fig. 1.6a) is obtained and the corresponding collection of points shown in Fig. 1.6b is called a two dimensional or a plane lattice.

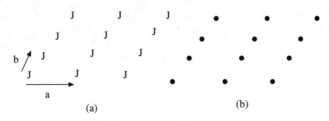

(a)           (b)

**Fig. 1.6**   **Two dimensional array of: (a) objects, (b) points; a plane lattice**

Finally, if the plane pattern having repetition intervals, $a$ and $b$ is combined with a third noncoplanar translation $c$, then a three dimensional array (Fig. 1.7a) is obtained. In a similar way as mentioned above, the corresponding collection of points shown in Fig. 1.7b is called a three dimensional or a space lattice.

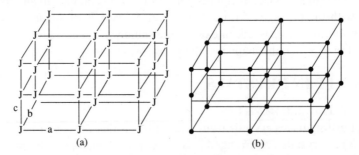

(a)           (b)

**Fig. 1.7**   **Three dimensional array of: (a) objects, (b) points; a space lattice**

The characteristic feature of the space lattice is that the environment around any one point is identical with the environment around any other point in the lattice. This can be visualized by considering $a$, $b$ and $c$ as translation vectors and three translation directions $x$, $y$ and $z$ as crystallographic axes with respect to any lattice point as the origin, then the location of any other lattice point can be defined as

$$T = n_1 a + n_2 b + n_3 c \qquad (2)$$

where $n_1$, $n_2$ and $n_3$ are arbitrary integers.

*Example*: A crystal has a basis of one atom per lattice point and a set of primitive translation vectors are (in Å):

$$a = 3i, \quad b = 3j, \quad c = 1.5 \, (i + j + k)$$

where *i*, *j* and *k* are unit vectors in *x*, y and z direction of a cartesian system. What is the lattice type of this crystal? Calculate the volume of the conventional unit cell and the primitive unit cell.

*Solution:* If we take $c' = 3k$, then

$$c = 1.5 \, (a + b + c')$$

which is the body centred position of a cubic unit cell defined by the primitive translation vectors *a*, *b*, *c'*.

The conventional unit cell volume $a^3 = 3^3 = 27$ Å$^3$

The primitive unit cell volume = half the conventional unit cell volume

$$= 13.5 \text{ Å}^3$$

## Basis and the Crystal Structure

As it has been pointed out in the preceding section that a lattice of points is an imaginary concept and therefore, it is essential to distinguish a lattice from a crystal. A crystal structure is formed only when a group of atoms or molecules is attached identically to each lattice point. This group of atoms or molecules is called basis, the basis is identical in composition, arrangement and orientation which is repeated periodically in space to form the crystal structure (Fig. 1.8). The logical relation is

Lattice + Basis = Crystal Structure

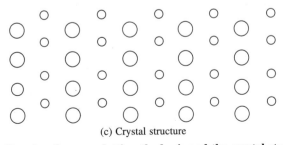

(a) Space Lattice

(b) Basis containing two different ions

(c) Crystal structure

**Fig. 1.8   Showing the space lattice, the basis and the crystal structure**

## 1.3 CHOICE OF A UNIT CELL

It has been shown above that two noncollinar translations define a plane lattice and three noncoplanar translations define a space lattice. Now the question arises that which pair (or triplet) of translations does one choose to describe it? In fact, there is an infinity of choices for each translation, because a line joining any two lattice points is a translation of the lattice. Fig. 1.9 shows a plane lattice and some of the choices that can be made.

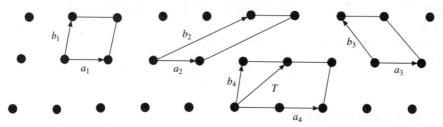

**Fig. 1.9    Different combinations of unit translations in a plane lattice**

In three dimensions, it is convenient to consider simplest parallelepiped formed by the primitive translation operation $T$ and is known as unit cell. The entire lattice then can be considered as an infinite collection of such unit cells repeated by its translations in all directions. The unit cell thus can be defined as the smallest volume which when repeated in all directions builds the crystal.

The choice of the unit cell is not unique. According to the requirement of the case, either a primitive or a non primitive cell, can be selected as a unit cell. The parallelepiped defined by translations $a$, $b$, $c$ as the shortest possible sides along three crystallographic axes $x$, $y$, $z$ is called a "primitive cell". A primitive cell is a minimum volume unit cell (Fig. 1.10) and has only one lattice point in it. The volume $V_c$ of a primitive cell defined by primitive translation $a$, $b$, $c$ is

$$V_c = |\, a \times b \cdot c|  \qquad (3)$$

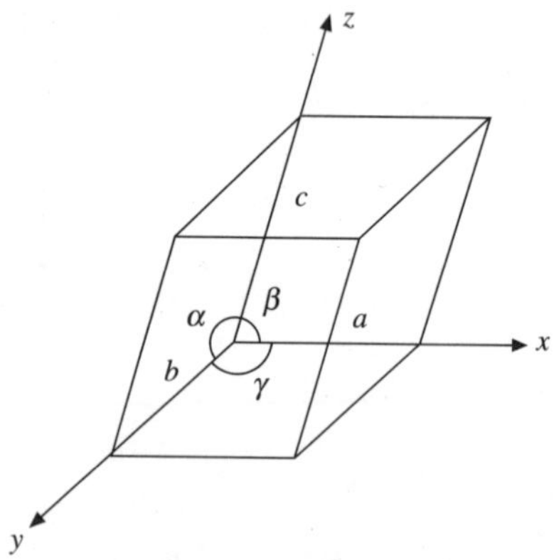

by elementary vector analysis. The primitive unit cell volume of different lattice types are provided in Table 1.1

**Fig. 1.10    A primitive cell**

Sometimes, it is more convenient to choose a non primitive unit cell depending upon the symmetry of the lattice. These cells contain more than one lattice points per unit cell (Fig. 1.11)

## 1.4 WIGNER-SEITZ UNIT CELL

Another way of choosing a primitive cell of equal volume as given by eq. 3 has been suggested by E.P. Wigner and F. Seitz and hence is known as Wigner-Seitz primitive unit cell. The Wigner-Seitz unit cell about a lattice point is the region of space that is closer to that particular point than to any other lattice point. It conforms with the translational symmetry and hence when translated

**Table 1.1   Unit cell volume of different lattice types**

| Lattice type | Volume |
|---|---|
| Cubic | $a^3$ |
| Orthorhombic | $abc$ |
| Tetragonal | $a^2c$ |
| Hexagonal | $\dfrac{3\sqrt{3}a^2c}{2}$ |
| Rhombohedral | $a^3\sqrt{1 - 3\cos^2\alpha + 2\cos^3\alpha}$ |
| Monoclinic | $abc\,\sin\beta$ |
| Triclinic | $abc\sqrt{1 - \cos\alpha - \cos\beta - \cos\gamma + 2\cos\alpha\cos\beta\cos\gamma}$ |

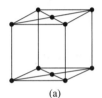 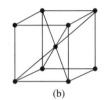 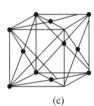

(a)          (b)          (c)

**Fig. 1.11   Some non-primitive cells**

through all lattice vectors, the space will just be filled, leaving no empty space in between, nor there is any overlapping. The method of construction of Wigner-Seitz primitive cell is same for both two and three dimensional lattices. The following procedure is adopted.

1. For a given lattice, select a reference point and draw lines to connect this point to all nearby lattice points.

2. Draw new lines (in a plane lattice) or planes (in a space lattice) bisecting each of the previous lines (or planes). The smallest area (in two dimensions) or volume (in three dimesnsions) enclosed in this way gives the Wigner-Seitz primitive cell.

Following the above mentioned procedure, the Wigner-Seitz unit cell for a two dimensional oblique lattice is found to be a hexagon. Similarly, for a three dimensional body centred cubic lattice, it is a truncated octahedron and for a face centred cubic lattice, it is a rhombic dodecahedron, respectively. They are shown in Fig. 1.12.

## 1.5   NUMBER OF LATTICE POINTS PER UNIT CELL

From above discussion, it is clear that the number of lattice points in a unit cell depends on its nature and in a crystal structure each point is occupied by a group of atoms or molecules. In a primitive cell, lattice points are located only at the corners, while each corner of the cell is common to eight neighbouring unit cells and the contribution towards the unit cell per corner is only one-eighth. Since the cell has eight corners, therefore the number of lattice point per unit cell is only one.

In a bcc unit cell, the lattice points are located at the eight corners and at the body centre, therefore it has two lattic points per unit cell. Similarly, an fcc unit cell will have four lattice

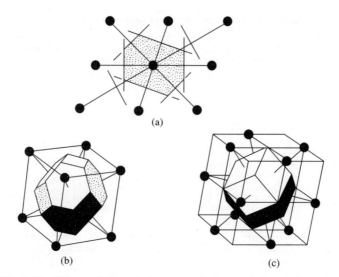

**Fig. 1.12** **Wigner-Seitz primitive cells in two and three dimensions**

points per unit cell. All possible cells along with their symbols, location of additional points and total number of lattice points contained by them are given in Table 1.2

**Table 1.2** **Primitive and nonprimitive cells**

| Symbol | Name | Additional points (Location) | Total number of Lattice Points |
|--------|------|------------------------------|-------------------------------|
| p | Primitive | — | 1 |
| I | Body centred | centre of the cell | 2 |
| A | Base centred | centre of (100) face | 2 |
| B | | centre of (010) face | 2 |
| C | | centre of (001) face | 2 |
| F | Face centred | centre of all faces | 4 |
| R | Rhombohedral | Two points along the body diagonal of the cell | 3 |

The number of lattice points (precisely the number of atoms or molecules) can also be determined if we know the volume, density and molecular weight of the constituent atom of the cell. For the purpose, let us consider a cubic unit cell of lattice constant $a$ (in m). Let $n$ be the number of atoms per unit cell, $\rho$ be the density of the crystal material, M be the atomic (or molecular) weight of the material and $N$ (= $6.023 \times 10^{26}$) the Avogadro's number. Now as per the Avogadro's hypothesis, we know that one kg-mole of crystalline material contains $6.023 \times 10^{26}$ atoms or molecules. Therefore,

Mass of $N$ atoms or molecules = $M$ kg, and

Mass of the unit cell containing $n$ atoms or molecules = $M \dfrac{n}{N}$

Hence, density of the unit cell

$$\rho = \frac{\text{Mass of the unit cell}}{\text{Volume of the unit cell}}$$

or

$$\rho = \frac{Mn}{NV} = \frac{Mn}{Na^3} \quad \text{or} \quad n = \frac{a^3 \rho N}{M}$$

or

$$a^3 = \frac{Mn}{N\rho} \tag{4}$$

For convenience, Appendix 1 enlists the values of density and atomic weight of various elements.

*Example:* Calculate the number of atoms per unit cell for an fcc lattice of copper crystal. It is given that $a = 3.60$ Å, at. wt. of Cu = 63.6, density of Cu = 8960 kg/m$^3$ and the Avogadro's number, $N = 6.023 \times 10^{26}$

*Solution:* Using eq. 4, we have

$$n = \frac{a^3 \rho N}{M}$$

$$= \left( \frac{(3.60 \times 10^{-10})^3 \times 8960 \times 6.023 \times 10^{26}}{63.6} \right)$$

$$= 3.959 \cong 4, \text{ since } n \text{ must be a whole number}$$

$\Rightarrow$ fcc lattice of copper contains four atoms per unit cell.

*Example*: Calculate the lattice constant for a rock salt crystal (density = 2180 kg/m$^3$), assuming that it has fcc lattice. Mol. wt of NaCl = 58.5.

*Solution:* For an fcc lattice, $n = 4$ and $V = a^3$. Therefore, using eq. 4, we have

$$a^3 = \frac{Mn}{\rho N} = \frac{58.5 \times 4}{2180 \times 6.023 \times 10^{26}} = 178.22 \times 10^{-30} \text{ m}^3$$

This gives $a = 5.63$ Å

*Example:* The lattice parameter and the atomic mass of a diamond crystal are 3.57 Å and 12, respectively. Calculate the density of the same.

*Solution:* Given: $a^3 = (3.57 \times 10^{-10})^3$, $M = 12$

The effective number of atoms, $n$ in the DC (Diamaond Cubic) unit cell = $\frac{1}{8} \times 8$ (corner atoms) + $\frac{1}{2} \times 6$ (face centered atoms) + $1 \times 4$ (atoms completely within the unit cell) = 8

From eq. 4, we have

$$\rho = \frac{Mn}{Na^3} = \frac{8 \times 12}{6.023 \times 10^{26} \times (3.57 \times 10^{-10})^3}$$

$$= 3540 \text{ kg/m}^3$$

*Example:* Aluminium has an fcc structure. Its density is $2.7 \times 10^3$ kg/m$^3$. Calculate the unit cell dimensions and the atomic diameter.

*Solution:* Given: atomic wt. = 26.98, $\rho = 2.7 \times 10^3$ kg/m$^3$. Since aluminium has an fcc structure, $n = 4$.

From eq. 4, we have

$$a^3 = \frac{Mn}{\rho N} = \frac{26.98 \times 4}{2.7 \times 10^3 \times 6.023 \times 10^{26}} = 66.36 \times 10^{-30} \text{ m}^3$$

This gives $a = 4.05$ Å

Now for fcc crystals, we know that $\sqrt{2}a = 4R = 2D$

Therefore, $$D = \frac{a}{\sqrt{2}} = 2.86 \text{ Å}$$

## 1.6   SYMMETRY ELEMENTS

In section 1.2, we observed that the repetition of an object (or a lattice point) by a translation leaves the environment around that object (or lattice point) unchanged. In an extended array, such as atomic pattern of a crystal, symmetries involving translation, rotation, reflection, inversion or their combinations are found to occur. The characteristic feature of these symmetries is that the translaton operation repeats an object infinite number of times, while other operations (such as rotation, reflection, inversion or their combinations) repeat it only a finite number of times (Fig. 1.13). Further, the operations like translation or proper rotation leave the 'motif' (a fundamental group of atoms or molecules) unchanged whereas the operations like reflections, inversion or improper rotation change the character of the motif from a right handed to a left handed one and vice versa. The geometrical locus about which a group of finite operations act is known as 'symmetry element'. Thus in Fig. 1.13, the line normal to the page about which a rotation takes place, the plane about which the reflection occurs and the centre about which the inversion takes place are simple examples of symmetry elements and are called, a rotation axis, a reflection or a miror plane and an inversion centre, respectively.

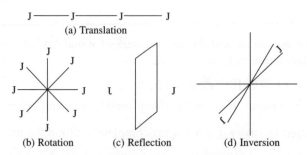

J————J————J————J
(a) Translation

(b) Rotation          (c) Reflection          (d) Inversion

**Fig. 1.13   Simple symmetry operations**

A crystalline solid can have the following symmetry elements:

(i)  Pure translation: ($T$) defined by eq. 2

(ii) Proper rotation: through an angle $\phi$

(iii)  Reflection: across a line (in two dimensions) or a plane (in three dimensions)
(iv)  Inversion: through a point
(v)  Improper rotation: Rotoreflection/Rotoinversion.

However, it may be easily verified that the above symmetry elements are not all independent but are interconnected to each other. We have already discussed the translation operation and derived plane and space lattices earlier in section 1.2. In the following, we shall discuss about other symmetry elements.

## Proper Rotation

The simplest way of representing the operation for proper rotation is shown in Fig. 1.13b. One can think of a line or axis passing through the centre and normal to the figure so that the J's (or in general any geometrical figure) are represented by a rotation through any angle $\phi = 2\pi/n$ about the axis of rotation, the axis is said to have $n$-fold symmetry. However, because of the reticular structure of crystals, only 1-, 2-, 3-, 4- and 6- fold rotational symmetries (Fig. 1.14) are possible. They are known as symmetry elements corresponding to proper rotation, consequently, it means that a crystalline solid can not possess either 5-fold or any other rotational symmetry higher than 6-folds. They are being demonstrated in Fig. 1.14e, 1.14g and 1.14h.

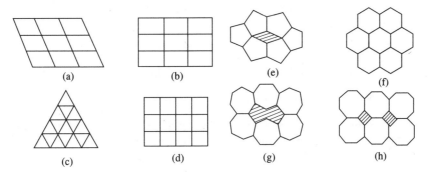

**Fig. 1.14  Possible and non-existent symmetry axes**

For $n = 1$ in equation $\phi = 2\pi/n$ means that the crystal must be rotated through $2\pi$ (360°) to achieve congruency. Such an axis is also called as identity axis. Every crystal possesses an infinite number of such axes. Further, $n = 2$ means the crystal is rotated through $\pi$ (180°) and the axis is said to have 2-fold symmetry. Such an axis is termed as a diad axis and symbolically represented as (). In a similar way for $n = 3$, 4 and 6 the corresponding angles of rotation are 120°, 90° and 60°, respectively. They are said to have 3-fold, 4-fold and 6-fold symmetry, the axes are termed as triad, tetrad and hexad and symbolically represented as $\triangle$, $\square$ and $\bigcirc$ respectively.

In order to check the permissible rotational symmetry elements in a crystal, one may start with the fundamental requirement that all crystals must have periodic structure, that is the symmetry elements present in the crystals must conform to their translational periodicities. This is the reason why the number of symmetry elements found in crystals is limited. Now, let us consider the combination of $n$-fold axis of rotation $A_n$ with a translation $t$ as shown Fig. 1.15. As we have already seen that a rotation axis repeats the translation $\phi°$ (= $2\pi/n$) away, and hence $n$ such rotations will bring back the object into its initial position (it is immaterial whether the rotation is clockwise or counter clockwise). Therefore, starting from the linear array as in Fig. 1.15, two such rotations will produce new lattice points $p$ and $q$ as shown in Fig. 1.16. Since they are equidistant from the original lattice row by construction, the two lattice points $p$ and $q$ must be connected by the same translation $t$ or some integral multiple of it say $mt$, depending upon the magnitude of $\phi$. Consequently, the allowed values of $\phi$ can be determined from the construction shown in Fig. 1.16. From simple geometrical consideration, we have

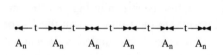

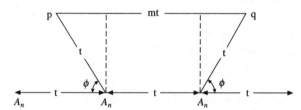

**Fig. 1.15**   *n*-fold axis of rotation with a
translation *t*

**Fig. 1.6**   **Two dimensional array of: (a) objects, (b) points;
a plane lattice**

$$mt = t + 2t \cos \phi, \text{ where } m = 0, \pm1, \pm2, \ldots \tag{5}$$

$\pm m$ is used depending whethr the rotation is clockwise or counterclockwise. Dividing both sides by $t$, eq. 5 can be written as

$$m = 1 + 2 \cos \phi \quad \text{or} \quad m - 1 = 2 \cos \phi \tag{6}$$

Since $m$ is an integer, $(m - 1)$ will also be an integer. Taking $(m - 1) = N$, we have

$$N = 2 \cos \phi \quad \text{or} \quad \cos \phi = N/2, \text{ where } N = 0, \pm 1, \pm 2, \ldots \tag{7}$$

Since all possible values of $\cos \phi$ lie between $\pm1$, corresponding possible values of $N$, $\phi$ and $n$ can be easily obtained and are given in Table 1.3. This table clearly shows the non existence of symmetry axes other than 1-, 2-, 3-, 4- and 6-fold.

**Table 1.3 Allowed rotational axis in a crystal lattice**

| $N$ | $\cos \phi$ | $\phi$ | $n$ allowed rotational axes |
|:---:|:---:|:---:|:---:|
| −2 | −1 | 180 | 2 |
| −1 | −1/2 | 120 | 3 |
| 0 | 0 | 90 | 4 |
| +1 | +1/2 | 60 | 6 |
| +2 | +1 | 360 or 0 | 1 |

*Example:* Construct a two dimensional pentagonal and octagonal lattice.

*Solution:* Since each interior angle of a pentagon is 108°, which is not a quotient of 360°. So, if we try to construct a periodic array having 5-fold symmetry, we can see that the resulting pentagons do not fit together neatly and leave empty spaces in between as shown by the shaded region in Fig. 1.14e. Similarly, in an octagon each interior angle is 135°, which again is not a quotient of 360°. In this case too, the octagons cannot fill the whole space without leaving gaps

(Fig. 1.14h). Both considerations indicate that neither 5-fold nor 8-fold symmetries can exist. In fact, all symmetries higher than 6-fold are not possible.

### Reflection (Mirror Plane or Symmetry Plane)

If we look at Fig. 1.13c, we find that a plane transforms left handed object into a right handed one and vice-versa. The element of symmetry in this case is known as a symmetry plane or a mirror plane and symbolically represented by the letter $m$. Mirror coincident figures of this type are known as enantiomorphous pairs and are related by reflection across a plane passing half way between them. If a crystal is cut along symmetry plane and put on a mirror, the image will produce the other half of the crystal.

### Inversion Centre (Centre of Symmetry)

This is a symmetry operation similar to reflection, with the difference that reflection occurs in a plane of mirror, while inversion is equivalent to reflection through a point called inversion centre or centre of symmetry. In other words, the enantiomorphous pair of figures in this case is related by inversion centre lying half way between the two (Fig. 1.13d). Each point of one figure is obtained from the other by reflection through centre and is symmetrically inverted. The complete figure thus obtained is inverted completely. Thus the inversion centre or the centre of symmetry has the property of inverting all space (at present the letter J) through a point.

### Improper Rotations

Symmetry operations encountered above, i.e. reflection and inversion, produce enantiomorphous sets of objects. However, it is also possible to have a rotational operation relating enantiomorphous objects. Such an operation is called improper rotation. The corresponding symmetry element is known as improper rotation axis. There exist two improper rotations, they are rotoreflection and rotoinversion.

### Rotoreflection

If a rotation and a reflection is combined to form a single hybrid operation, the resulting operation is called rotoreflection. The corresponding symmetry element is called rotoreflection axis. For each proper rotation axis, there exists a corresponding rotoreflection axis. To distinguish the two kinds of axes, a tilde symbolically represented as (~) is placed over the numerical symbol of the corresponding rotationa axis, e.g. $\tilde{1}, \tilde{2}, \tilde{3}$, etc. For a better understanding, let us see the following examples.

*Example:* Show that $\tilde{1}$ (one "tilde") is equivalent to a mirror plane.

*Solution:* It is a combined operation of rotation and reflection. In this case, the proper 1-fold rotation will rotate the motif representing all space (here it is taken as *J*) through an angle of $0°$ or $360°$, i.e. leaving it unchanged. Combining this with reflecting plane perpendicular to the rotation axis to produce a configuration as shown in Fig. 1.17a, which is identical to the configuration already encountered in Fig. 1.13c. Thus, the operation $\tilde{1}$ is equivalent to a reflection through a plane (specifically a mirror plane).

*Example*: Show that $\tilde{2}$ is equivalent to an inversion centre.

*Solution:* In this case, the proper 2-fold rotation will rotate the object (through an imaginary axis) through an angle 180° and then reflected across an imaginary plane placed at right angle to the imaginary rotation axis, the resulting configuration (Fig. 1.17b), is identical to the configuration shown in Fig. 1.13d. Thus, the operation $\tilde{2}$ is equivalent to an inversion centre.

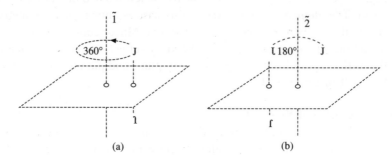

**Fig. 1.17 Improper rotation axes (a) $\tilde{1}$, (b) $\tilde{2}$**

**Rotoinversion**

As we stated above that an inversion is equivalent to a reflection through a point, therefore it is possible to combine an inversion with a rotation axis to produce a rotoinversion axis in a manner similar to the formation of a rotoreflection axis. Consequently, there exist five rotoinversion axes corresponding to five proper rotation axes. Again, to distinguish these axes, both from pure rotation and rotoreflection, a bar (–) is plaed over the numerical symbol of the corresponding rotational axis, e.g. $\bar{1}, \bar{2}, \bar{3}$ etc.

When these rotoinversion axes are compared with the corresponding rotoreflection axes, they are found to be equivalent in pairs and therefore, it is sufficient to adopt only one kind to represent these symmetry operations. Table 1.4 enlists the conventional symbols used to represent the improper axes.

**Table 1.4 Conventional symbol for improper axes**

| Rotoinversion axes | Rotoreflection axes | Conventional symbol | |
|:---:|:---:|:---|:---:|
| $\bar{1}$ | $\tilde{2}$ | Centre of symmetry | $\bar{1}$ |
| $\bar{2}$ | $\tilde{1}$ | Mirror Plane | $m$ |
| $\bar{3}$ | $\tilde{6}$ | 3-fold rotoinversion | $\bar{3}$ |
| $\bar{4}$ | $\tilde{4}$ | 4 " " | $\bar{4}$ |
| $\bar{6}$ | $\tilde{3}$ | 6 ' ' | $\bar{6}$ |

*Example:* Find the total number of symmetry elements that exist in a cube.

*Solution:* Looking at the Fig. 1.18, we find that there exist

  (i) 2-fold axes parallel to the face diagonal and passing through the centre of the cube. There are six such axes.

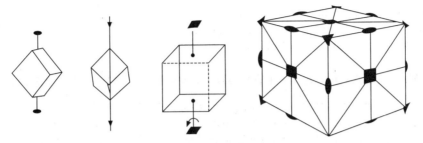

**Fig. 1.18   Showing various symmetries of a cube**

(ii)  3-fold rotoinversion axes passing through the body diagonal. There, are four such axes.

(iii)  4-fold symmetry about an axis passing through the centre of two opposite faces. There are three such symmetry axes.

(iv)  Nine mirror planes bisecting the parallel faces, and connecting diagonal edges. All of them passing through the centre of the cube.

(v)  One centre of symmetry at the centre of the cube

Thus, there are: 6-diads + 4-triads + 3-tetrads = 13 axes, 3 surface planes + 6 diagonal planes = 9 planes, and 1 centre of symmetry. Therefore, the total symmetry elements in a cube = 13 + 9 + 1 = 23

## 1.7   COMBINATION OF SYMMETRY ELEMENTS (POINT GROUP)

In the preceding section, we discussed about various symmetry elements and their relationships. It was found that the symmetry elements are interlinked to each other and are not independent. In other words, a given symmetry element could be obtained from suitable combinations (if they are compatible) of other symmetry elements. Such a combination forms a group and gives rise to different symmetry points called point groups. Thus, a point group in the lattice is defined as the collection of symmetry operations which when applied about a lattice point, leave the lattice invariant. In other words, in point groups all possible symmetry elements must pass through a point. Suitable combinations of various symmetry elements give rise to thirty two (32) allowed point groups. Since crystals belonging to different crystal systems show different point group symmetries and therefore the classification of crystal systems can be easily made on the basis of point groups. A few examples illustrating the locations of equivalent positions forming groups are shown in Fig. 1.19.

Here, the dots represent equivalent points. The point group 1 has no symmetry elements and hence the single isolated point has no other point equivalent to it. For 1m, there is a mirror plane, one dot on reflection across the mirror

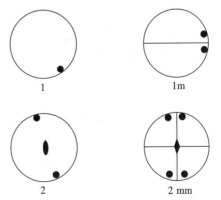

**Fig. 1.19   Locations of equivalent positions for four point groups**

plane becomes the second dot. With a 2-fold axis 2, a rotation of $\pi$ takes one dot into the other. With 2-fold axis and one mirror plane there is automatically a second mirror plane normal to the first and we have the point group 2 mm with four equivalent points.

## 1.8 BRAVAIS LATTICE IN TWO DIMENSIONS: PLANE LATTICE

In general, unlimited number of lattices are possible since there is no restriction on the length $a$, $b$ of the lattice translations and on angle $\phi$ between them. Such a lattice drawn earlier in Fig. 1.9 for an arbitrary $a$, $b$, and $\phi$ is known as oblique lattice. An oblique lattice is invariant only under the rotation $2\pi/n$ (with $n = 1$ and 2) about any lattice point. However, this can also be made invariant under the rotation $2\pi/n$ with $n = 3, 4, 6$ or mirror reflection if some suitable restrictions are imposed on $a$, $b$ and $\phi$. These symmetry elements in turn put restrictions on the shape of the lattice (precisely the shape of the unit cell). The resulting latices are known as special lattices. They are obtained as follows.

We know that we need two repeat distances (noncollinear translations) $a$ and $b$ and an angle $\phi$ to form a two dimensional or plane lattice. Clearly there exist two possibilities $a = b$, or $a \neq b$. Further, the angle $\phi$ between the two vectors may take any value including that of $\phi = 90°$. A suitable combination of these possibilities leads to four possible planar lattices filling the plane space completely. They are represented by the square, rectangle, rhombus and parallelogram, as shown in Figs. 1.20a-d.

It is to be mentioned here that in general it is convenient to work with a cell of higher

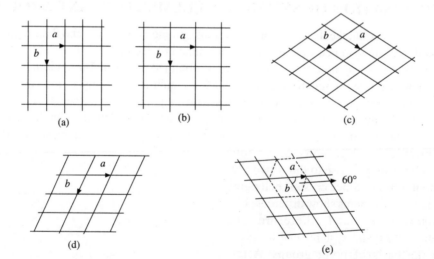

**Fig. 1.20**  **The five possible plane lattices: (a) Square, $a = b$ and $\phi = 90°$, (b) Rectangular, $a \neq b$ and $\phi = 90°$, (c) Rhombus, $a = b$ and $\phi = \phi°$ (d) Oblique, $a \neq b$ and $\phi = \phi°$, (e) Hexagonal, $a = b$ and $\phi = 60°$**

symmetry which may not always be primitive and therefore an alternative cell in place of a plane rhombohedral lattice (Fig. 1.20c) may be used because the choice of the unit cell is not unique (as discussed in section 1.3). One such cell is marked out as a centred rectangular lattice shown in Fig. 1.21. In addition to the above, plane space can also be filled by hexagonal or triangular figures. However, an equilateral triangle cannot be used as the basis of a lattice because its representation in filling a plane would involve a change of orientation in addtion to its translation. Further, an assembly of equilateral triangles is clearly equivalent to a rhombus with $a = b$, $\phi = 60°$) as repeat unit (Fig. 1.22a, b). There are thus only five plane lattices, one general and four special. A detailed description of two dimensional Bravais lattice is given in Table 1.5.

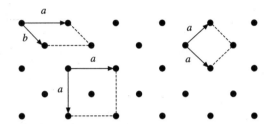

**Fig. 1.21   Three alternative unit cells for a two-dimensional lattice**

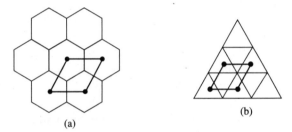

(a)                                                                    (b)

**Fig. 1.22   Demonstration of: (a) The equivalence of filling space with 60° rhombuses, and with hexagons, (b) The repetition of this pattern to one based upon equilateral traingles in which, by joining centres of triangles of equivalent orientation, the same rhombohedral lattice is chosen**

**Table 1.5   Bravais lattice in two dimensions**

| Sl. No. | Lattice Type | Conventional Unit cell | Axes and Angles | Point groups symmetry about lattice point |
|---------|--------------|------------------------|-----------------|-------------------------------------------|
| 1. | Oblique | Parallelogram | $a \neq b$; $\phi = \phi°$ | 2 |
| 2. | Square | Square | $a = b$; $\phi = 90°$ | 4 mm |
| 3. | Hexagonal | 60° rhombus | $a = b$, $\phi = 120*$ | 6 mm |
| 4. | Primitive rectangular | Rectangle | $a \neq b$, $\phi = 90°$ | 2 mm |
| 5. | Centred rectangular | Rectangle | $a \neq b$, $\phi = 90°$ | 2 mm |

## 1.9   BRAVAIS LATTICE IN THREE DIMENSIONS: SPACE LATTICE

In the preceding section, we observed that in two dimensions suitable restrictions on lattice translations and angles allow only five types of lattices. Extending the same idea to a three dimensional case and applying similar restrictions on the lattice translations $a$, $b$, $c$ and angles

$\alpha$, $\beta$, $\gamma$, one can verify that only fourteen types of lattices are possible in three dimensions, one general (triclinic) and thirteen special. They are collectively known as Bravais lattices—named after the nineteenth century French crystallographer who worked them out first or simply space lattices.

In order to specify the given arrangement of points in a space lattice or of atoms in a crystal, it is customary to define its coordinates with reference to a set of axes chosen with its origin at a lattice point. The three axes $a$, $b$, and $c$ and the opposite angles $\alpha$, $\beta$ and $\gamma$ are defined as shown in Fig. 1.23. Further, each space lattice has a convenient set of axes, however, only seven different system of axes have been found to be sufficient for representing all Bravais lattices. Accordingly, fourteen space lattices are divided into seven crystal systems. They are triclinic, monoclinic, orthorhombic, tetragonal, trigonal, hexagonal and cubic. A brief explanation of each crystal system is given below:

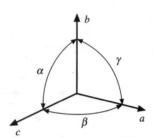

**Fig. 1.23   The crystallographic axes and the corresponding angles**

If a crystal has no symmetry (point group 1), or a centre of symmetry $\bar{1}$ only, then there is no restriction on the shape of the unit cell; all three angles $\alpha$, $\beta$ and $\gamma$ have to be specified and hence the system is called triclinic or occasionally called anorthic (i.e. non-orthogonal). A monoclinic crystal has 2-fold symmetry in one direction only. One crystallographic axis is taken parallel to the direction of 2-fold symmetry axis, and the other two axes must therefore be perpendicular to it. The choice of the cell is thus restricted to a parallelepiped having two right angles; one angle has to be specified, hence the name monoclinic.

An orthorhombic crystal has 2-fold symmetry in three mutually perpendicular directions. The crystallographic axes are taken parallel to the symmetry directions, so that the unit cell is orthogonal. Higher symmetry involving axes of order greater than 2, impose more stringent restrictions on the shape of the unit cell. The trigonal, tetragonal or hexagonal systems are characterized by a single 3-, 4-, or 6-fold axis, respectively. One crystallographic axis, always designated $c$, is taken parallel to this unique axis (except for primitive setting of rhombohedral cells), the other two must be perpendicular to it and equal to each other.

The highest symmetry among all is that of cubic system. The three crystallographic axes are orthogonal and equivalent. In the cubic system there are three lattices; the simple cubic (sc) lattice, the body centred cubic (bcc) lattice and the face centred cubic (fcc) lattice. The characteristics of the three cubic lattices are summarized in Table 1.6.

A detailed description of three dimensional Bravais lattices is given in Table 1.7, while they have been shown diagrammatically in Fig. 1.24.

*Example*: Show that each of the 14 Bravais lattices possess a centre of symmetry.

*Solution*: If we look at Fig. 1.24, in each case the lattice arrangement is such that for each lattice point on one side of the unit cell there exists a corresponding lattice point on the diametrically opposite side, and at the same distance.

*Example*: Show that 13 out of 14 Bravais lattices possess at least one reflection plane.

**Table 1.6  Characterstics of cubic lattices**

|  | Simple | Body centered | Face centered |
|---|---|---|---|
| Volume of conventional unit cell | $a^3$ | $a^3$ | $a^3$ |
| Lattice points per unit cell | 1 | 2 | 4 |
| Volume, primitive cell | $a^3$ | $\dfrac{a^3}{2}$ | $\dfrac{a^3}{4}$ |
| Lattice points per unit vol. | $\dfrac{1}{a^3}$ | $\dfrac{2}{a^3}$ | $\dfrac{4}{a^3}$ |
| Number of nearest neighbours (coordination number) | 6 | 8 | 12 |
| Nearest neighbour distance | $a$ | $\dfrac{a\sqrt{3}}{2} = 0.866a$ | $\dfrac{a}{\sqrt{2}} = 0.707\,a$ |
| Number of 2nd neighbours | 12 | 6 | 6 |
| Second neighbour distance | $\sqrt{2}\,a$ | $a$ | $a$ |
| Packing factor | $\dfrac{\pi}{6} = 0.52$ | $\dfrac{\sqrt{3}\pi}{8} = 0.68$ | $\dfrac{\sqrt{2}\pi}{6} = 0.74$ |

**Table 1.7  Bravais lattice in three dimensions**

| Crystal system | Restrictions on conventional cell; axes and angles | Associated lattice | | Characteristic symmetry elements | To be specified | | |
|---|---|---|---|---|---|---|---|
| | | Number | Symbol | | Axes | Angle | Total para-meter |
| Triclinic | $a \neq b \neq c$ $\alpha \neq \beta \neq \gamma \neq 90°$ | 1 | P | None | $a, b, c$ | $\alpha, \beta, \gamma$ | 6 |
| Monoclinic | $a \neq b \neq c$ $\alpha = \gamma = 90° \neq \beta$ | 2 | P, C | one 2-fold rotation axis or $m$ ($\equiv \bar{2}$) | $a, b, c$ | $\gamma$ | 4 |
| Orthorhombic | $a \neq b \neq c$ $\alpha = \beta = \gamma = 90°$ | 4 | P, C, F, I | three 2-fold rotation axis or $m$ (mutually perpendicular) | $a, b, c$ | — | 3 |
| Tetragonal | $a = b \neq c$ $\alpha = \beta = \gamma = 90°$ | 2 | P, I | one 4-fold rotation axis or $\bar{4}$ | $a, c$ | — | 2 |
| Trigonal (Rhombo-hedral) | $a = b = c$ $\alpha = \beta = \gamma < 120°$ $\neq 90°$ | 1 | P | one 3-fold rotation axis or $\bar{3}$ | $a$ | $\alpha$ | 2 |
| Hexagonal | $a = b \neq c$ $\alpha = \beta = 90°$ $\gamma = 120°$ | 1 | P | one 6-fold rotation axis or $\bar{6}$ | $a, c$ | — | 2 |
| Cubic | $a = b = c$ $\alpha = \beta = \gamma = 90°$ | 3 | P or sc I or bcc F or fcc | four 3-fold rotation axis or $\bar{3}$ (parallel 1 to cube diagonal) | $a$ | — | 1 |

* Lattice symbol:
P - Primitive (Lattice points are at the corners of the unit cell only)
C - Side centred or Base centred (Lattice points are at the corners and at two face centres opposite to each other)
I - Body centred (Lattice points are at the corners and at the body centre)
F - Face centred (Lattice points are at the corners and at the six face centres)

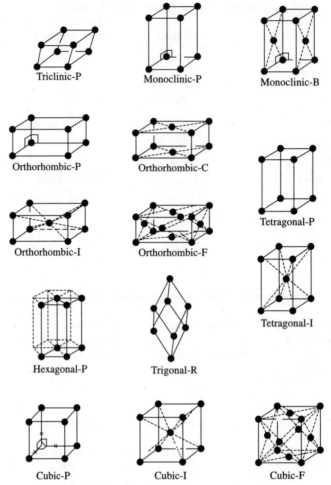

**Fig. 1.24  The fourteen Bravais or space lattices**

*Solution*: It is the triclinic lattice only which does not possess, the mirror plane.

*Example:* If the object or motif itself has a reflection plane (or centre of symmetry), show that it cannot have enantiomorphs.

*Solution:* Consider a motif ⟨⟩, its mirror image will be identical to it. They are indistinguishable from each other. Such objects or arrangements may be called self enantiomorphs.

*Example:* Show that a face-centred tetragonal lattice does not exist.

*Solution:* Draw two face centred unit cells side by side as shown by dotted lines in Fig. 1.25. Inside these cells, draw a new tetragonal

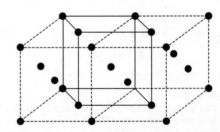

**Fig. 1.25  Non-existence of face centred tetragonal lattice**

cell of half the volume. This turns out to be a body-centred tetragonal unit cell. This implies that face-centred tetragonal lattice does not exist.

## 1.10  RATIONAL FEATURES OF A CRYSTAL AND MILLER INDICES

The geometrical features of a crystal which are represented by lattice points are called rational. Thus a lattice point (site) with respect to another lattice point (site) is a rational point, a row of lattice points is rational line and a plane defined by the lattice points is a rational plane. All other features are irrational. It is necessary to have appropriate notations to represent their rational features. A notation conventionally used to describe lattice points (sites), directions and planes is known as Miller indices.

### Site Indices

The position of any lattice site relative to a chosen origin is defined by three of its coordinates $x, y, z$ as shown in Fig. 1.26. These coordinates in general can be expressed in the following forms; $x = ma$, $y = nb$, $z = pc$, where $a$, $b$ and $c$ are the lattice parameters and $m$, $n$ and $p$ are integers. However, if the lattice parameters are used as the units of length along the respective axes then the lattice coordinates will be obtained simply in the form of numbers

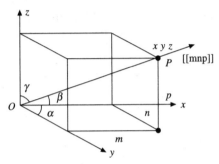

**Fig. 1.26  Indices of crystal lattice site and direction**

$m$, $n$ and $p$. These numbers are then termed as site indices and are written in the form of $[[m \ n \ p]]$. For a negative index the minus sign is written above the index. As an example, for a site with coordinates $x = -2a$, $y = 1b$, $z = -3c$, the site indices are written as $[[\bar{2} \ 1 \ \bar{3}]]$.

### Indices of Direction

To describe a direction in a crystal lattice, a straight line passing through the origin is chosen. It is defined by the indices of the first lattice site (point) through which the line passes (Fig. 1.26). In other words, it is defined by the three smallest integers that describe the position of the site nearest to the origin which lies on the given direction. Therefore, the site indices are at the same time the indices of direction (Fig. 1.27a). The indices of direction are calculated by adopting the following procedure:

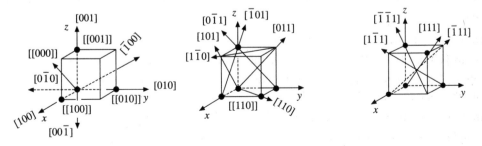

**Fig. 1.27  Indices of principal directions in a cubic crystal**

(i) Note down the coordinates of the lattice site nearest to the origin in a given direction.
(ii) Divide the coordinates by appropriate unit translations.
(iii) If fractions result, multiply each of them by smallest common divisor.
(iv) Put the resulting integers in a set of square brackets, i.e. [hkl] to get the required indices of that and all parallel directions.

It should be noted that the indices of direction are quite independent of the actual geometry of the unit cell and are determined solely by the ratios of the coordinates of any point on the given direction to the appropriate unit translations.

In a crystal, there exists an infinite number of families of directions. Out of these, there are sets of directions having identical spacing between the atoms (i.e. same unit translations) are called equivalent directions. Such sets of directions are always related by a symmetry operation. The shortened notation used to specify a family of directions, is a set of angled brackets i.e. <hkl>. For example (in the cubic system): the family <100> comprises the directions [100], [$\bar{1}$00], [010], [0$\bar{1}$0], [001] and [00$\bar{1}$]. Fig. 1.27 shows all the principal directions (crystallorgraphic orientations) in a cubic crystal alongwith their notations. The unit translations for the low index directions in the three Bravais lattices of cubic system are given in Table 1.8

**Table 1.8 The unit translation for low index directions of a cubic system**

| Family | Unit translation | | |
|---|---|---|---|
| | **P** | **I** | **F** |
| <100> | $a$ | $a$ | $a$ |
| <110> | $\sqrt{2}\,a$ | $\sqrt{2}\,a$ | $\dfrac{a}{\sqrt{2}}$ |
| <111> | $\sqrt{3}\,a$ | $\dfrac{\sqrt{3}a}{2}$ | $\sqrt{3}\,a$ |

*Example:* Write all directions from the family <110> and <111>.

*Solution:* The family <110> comprises the directions [110], [$\bar{1}$10], [1$\bar{1}$0], [$\bar{1}\bar{1}$0], [101], [$\bar{1}$01], [10$\bar{1}$], [$\bar{1}$0$\bar{1}$], [011], [0$\bar{1}$1], [01$\bar{1}$], and [0$\bar{1}\bar{1}$]. Similarly, the family <111> comprises the directions [111], [$\bar{1}$11], [1$\bar{1}$1], [11$\bar{1}$], [$\bar{1}\bar{1}$1], [$\bar{1}$1$\bar{1}$], [1$\bar{1}\bar{1}$] and [$\bar{1}\bar{1}\bar{1}$].

*Example:* Classify the members of <100>, <110> and <111> families of direction in the tetragonal system.

*Solution:* For a tetragonal system, we know that $a = b \neq c$. Thus, the unit translation for the directions [100], [$\bar{1}$00], [010] and [0$\bar{1}$0] is the same as $a$, whereas for the directions [001] and [00$\bar{1}$] is $c$. Consequently the first four directions are the members of <100> family and the last two are the members of <001> family.

Similarly, <110> family has four members, i.e. [110], [$\bar{1}$10], [1$\bar{1}$0] and [$\bar{1}\bar{1}$0], while the other eight directions [101], [$\bar{1}$01], [10$\bar{1}$], [$\bar{1}$0$\bar{1}$], [011], [0$\bar{1}$1], [01$\bar{1}$] and [0$\bar{1}\bar{1}$] are the members of <101> family or equivalently the <011> family.

Since all <111> directions have the same unit translation in the tetragonal system and therefore the family contains the same eight members as it does in the cubic system.

In certain calculations (e.g. in resolved shear stresses, Ch. 5), it is necessary to determine the angle between two different crystal directions. The formula for a general case like triclinic is very complicated. Therefore in Table 1.9, we enlist the formulae for some crystal systems which may be frequently used in calculations. The formula for cubic system is the simplest of all which can be determined by dot product.

**Table 1.9 Angle between two crystal directions $[h_1k_1l_1]$ and $[h_2k_2l_2]$**

| Crystal system | Cos $\phi$ |
|---|---|
| Cubic | $\dfrac{h_1h_2 + k_1k_2 + l_1l_2}{(h_1^2 + k_1^2 + l_1^2)^{1/2} (h_2^2 + k_2^2 + l_2^2)^{1/2}}$ |
| Tetragonal | $\dfrac{a^2(h_1h_2 + k_1k_2) + c^2(l_1l_2)}{\sqrt{\{a^2(h_1^2 + k_1^2) + c^2l_1^2\}\{a^2(h_2^2 + k_2^2) + c^2l_2^2\}}}$ |
| Orthorhombic | $\dfrac{a^2h_1h_2 + b^2k_1k_2 + c^2l_1l_2}{\sqrt{(a^2h_1^2 + b^2k_1^2 + c^2l_1^2)(a^2h_2^2 + b^2k_2^2 + c^2l_2^2)}}$ |
| Hexagonal | $\dfrac{h_1h_2 + k_1k_2 - \dfrac{1}{2}(h_1k_2 + h_2k_1) + \dfrac{c^2}{a^2}l_1l_2}{\sqrt{\left(h_1^2 + k_1^2 - h_1k_1 + \dfrac{c^2}{a^2}l_1^2\right)\left(h_2^2 + k_2^2 - h_2k_2 + \dfrac{c^2}{a^2}l_2^2\right)}}$ |

*Example:* Calculate the angle between [111] and [001] directions in a cubic crystal.
*Solution:* From Table 1.9, we have

$$\cos\phi = \frac{h_1h_2 + k_1k_2 + l_1l_2}{\sqrt{(h_1^2 + k_1^2 + l_1^2)}\sqrt{(h_2^2 + k_2^2 + l_2^2)}} = \frac{0 + 0 + 1}{\sqrt{3} \times \sqrt{1}} = \frac{1}{\sqrt{3}}$$

so that $\phi = 54.75°$

*Example:* Calculate the angle between [111] and $[\bar{1}\,\bar{1}1]$ directions in a cubic crystal.

*Solution:* From Fig. 1.28, we observe that [001] direction bisects the angle between [111] and $[\bar{1}\,\bar{1}1]$. Therefore, the angle $\phi$ between them is $2 \times 54.75° = 109.5°$. This can be verified from the dot product as mentioned above.

$$\cos\phi = \frac{-1 -1 + 1}{\sqrt{3} \times \sqrt{3}} = -\frac{1}{3}$$

so that $\phi = 109.5°$

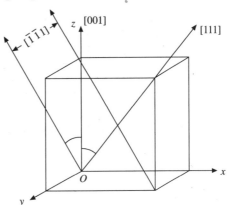

**Fig. 1.28 Angles made by [111] and $[\bar{1}\,\bar{1}1]$ directions with respect to [001] in a cubic crystal**

## Indices of Lattic Plane

A crystal lattice may be considered as an assembly of a number of equidistant parallel planes passing through the lattice points and are called lattice planes. For a given lattice, these sets of planes can be selected in a number of ways. The interplanar spacing for a given set of parallel planes is fixed but for different sets of planes the interplanar spacing vary as also the density of lattice points. For simplicity, let us start with a 2-dimensional lattice and then generalise to a three dimensional case. A 2-dimensional lattice is considered to be made up of a number of rows of atoms. In this case, the set of rows of atoms can be selected in a number of ways as shown in Fig. 1.29. Now, if we fix the coordinate axes, then any given line (particular row of atoms) will intercept the coordinate axes $x$ and $y$ at "$a$" and "$b$" units, respectively (Fig. 1.30a). From simple geometry, the equation of this line is given as

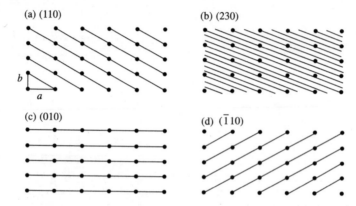

Fig. 1.29   Miller indices of some planes in a two-dimensional lattice

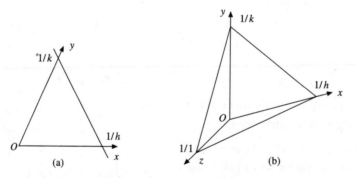

Fig. 1.30   Intercepts along (a) x and y axes (b) x, y and z axes

$$\frac{x}{a} + \frac{y}{b} = 1 \tag{8}$$

Similarly, the equation of plane in three dimensions having the intercepts $a$, $b$ and $c$ (Fig. 1.30b) along the axes $x$, $y$ and $z$, respectively will be

$$\frac{x}{a} + \frac{y}{b} + \frac{z}{c} = 1 \tag{9}$$

In describing crystallographic planes, the axes are taken along three non parallel edges of the unit cell, and the intercepts are measured in term of respective unit length, which is assigned to each of the cell regardless of its actual dimension. The use of the intercepts *a*, *b* and *c* to represent a crystallographic plane has the disadvantage that the intercepts are often fractions (less than 1) and may be infinite (for a plane parallel to an axis). For this reason, it is now common practice to use the reciprocal of the intercepts to designate a crystallographic plane. Therefore, suppose $h = 1/a$, $k = 1/b$, and $l = 1/c$ so that eq. 9 becomes.

$$hx + ky + lz = 1 \tag{10}$$

Equation 10 describes the first lattice plane, nearest to the origin, in a set of parallel, identical and equally spaced planes. The resulting set of three integers *h*, *k* and *l* are conventionally enclosed in parentheses (*hkl*), called the Miller indices and describe the lattice plane in question. Equation10 can also be written as

$$\frac{x}{1/h} + \frac{y}{1/k} + \frac{z}{1/l} = 1 \tag{11}$$

where 1/*h*, 1/*k* and 1/*l* are intercepts along the *x*, *y* and *z* axes, respectively. This implies that the (*hkl*) plane divides "*a*" into *h* parts, "*b*" into *k* parts and "*c*" into *l* parts. Therefore, to obtain the Miller indices of a plane, we adopt the following procedure:

(i)   Determine the intercepts of the plane along *x*, *y*, and *z* axes in terms of lattice parameters.
(ii)  Divide these intercepts by the appropriate unit translations.
(iii) Note their reciprocals.
(iv)  If fractions result, multiply each of them by the smallest common divisor.
(v)   Put the resulting integers in parenthesis (*hkl*) to get the required Miller indices of that and all parallel planes.

*Example*: In a crystal, a plane cuts intercepts of 2*a*, 3*b* and 6*c* along the three crystallographic axes. Determine the Miller indices of the plane.

*Solution:* Following the above procdure, we have

| | 2*a* | 3*b* | 6*c* |
|---|---|---|---|
| (i) Intercepts | 2*a* | 3*b* | 6*c* |
| (ii) Division by unit translations | $\frac{2a}{a} = 2$ | $\frac{3b}{b} = 3$ | $\frac{6c}{c} = 6$ |
| (iii) Reciprocals | $\frac{1}{2}$ | $\frac{1}{3}$ | $\frac{1}{6}$ |
| (iv) After clearing fraction | 3 | 2 | 1 |

⇒   The required Miller indices of the plane are (321)

*Example:* Determine the Miller indices of a plane which is parallel to *x*-axis and cuts intercepts of 2 and 1/2, respectively along *y*- and *z*-axes.

*Solution:* Following the same procedure, we have

| | | | |
|---|---|---|---|
| (i) Intercepts | $\infty$ | $2b$ | $\frac{1}{2}c$ |
| (ii) Division by unit translations | $\frac{\infty}{a} = \infty$ | $\frac{2b}{b} = 2$ | $\frac{(1/2)c}{c} = \frac{1}{2}$ |
| (iii) Reciprocals | $\frac{1}{\infty}$ | $\frac{1}{2}$ | $2$ |
| (iv) After clearing fraction | $0$ | $1$ | $4$ |

$\Rightarrow$ The required Miller indices of the plane are (014).

*Example*: An orthorhombic crystal whose primitive translations are $a = 1.21$Å, $b = 1.84$Å and $c = 1.97$Å, respectively. If a plane with Miller indices $(23\bar{1})$ cuts an intercept of 1.21Å along the x-axis, find the length of intercepts along y- and z-axes.

*Solution:* We have $p^{-1}: q^{-1} : r^{-1} = h : k : l = 2 : 3 : -1$

Therefore

$$p:q:r = \frac{1}{2} : \frac{1}{3} : -1$$

The ratio of actual lengths of the intercepts are

$$l_1 : l_2 : l_3 = pa : qb : rc$$

$$= \frac{1.21}{2} : \frac{1.84}{3} : -1.97$$

Since $l_1$ is given as 1.21 Å, we therefore multiply the right hand side by 2, so that

$$l_1 : l_2 : l_3 = 1.21 : \frac{3.68}{3} : -3.94$$

$\Rightarrow l_2 = 1.23$Å and $l_3 = -3.94$Å

*Example:* Determine the Miller indices of a plane that makes intercepts of 2 Å, 3 Å, 4 Å on the coordinate axes of an orthorhombic crystal with $a : b : c = 4 : 3 : 2$.

*Solution*: Here the unit translations are $a = 4$, $b = 3$ and $c = 2$.
Following the same procedure as above, we have

| | | | |
|---|---|---|---|
| (i) Intercepts | $2$ | $3$ | $4$ |
| (ii) Division by unit translations | $\frac{2}{4} = \frac{1}{2}$ | $\frac{3}{3} = 1$ | $\frac{4}{2} = 2$ |
| (iii) Reciprocals | $2$ | $1$ | $\frac{1}{2}$ |
| (iv) After clearing fraction | $4$ | $2$ | $1$ |

$\Rightarrow$ The required Miller indices of the plane are (421)

*Example*: Find the Miller indices of a plane that makes intercepts on $a$, $b$, and $c$, axes equal to 3 Å, 4 Å and 3 Å in a tetragonal crystal with $c/a$ ratio as 1.5.

*Solution*: For a tetragonal system we have $a = b \neq c$. Since $c/a = 1.5$, therefore $c = 1.5a$ or $c = 1.5$ if $a = 1$. Following the above procedure, we have

|  |  |  |  |
|---|---|---|---|
| (i) Intercepts | 3 | 4 | 3 |
| (ii) Division by unit translations | $\frac{3}{1} = 3$ | $\frac{4}{1} = 4$ | $\frac{3}{1.5} = 2$ |
| (iii) Reciprocals | $\frac{1}{3}$ | $\frac{1}{4}$ | $\frac{1}{2}$ |
| (iv) After clearing fraction | 4 | 3 | 6 |

$\Rightarrow$ The required Miller indices of the plane are (436)

### Representation of Planes of Known Miller Indices

In the preceding section, we learnt the procedure for determining the Miller indices of an atomic plane when the intercepts made by it along the three crystallographic axes are known. In the present case, the problem is of opposite nature and hence to represent a given plane of known Miller indices in a unit cell, the following procedure is adopted.

(i) Take the reciprocals of the given Miller indices. They represent the intercepts in terms of axial units.

(ii) Mark the length of the intercepts on the respective coordinate axes. Join the end points, the resulting sketch will represent the required plane.

*Example*: Draw ($\bar{1}$11) and (1$\bar{1}$1) planes inside the unit cell of a cubic crystal. Determine the Miller indices of the direction that is common to both planes.

*Solution*: Consider the conventional orthogonal axes and construct a cubic unit cell with O as the origin (Fig. 1.31). Now by imagining the origin to be at O′, draw ($\bar{1}$11) plane. Similarly, imagining the origin to be at O″, draw (1$\bar{1}$1) plane. Common direction of these planes is also shown.

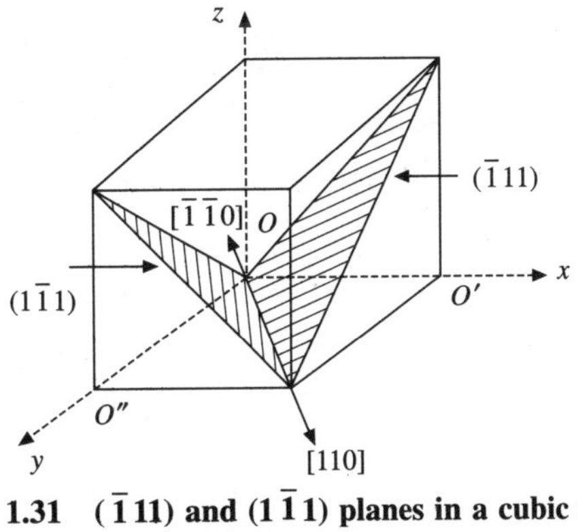

**Fig. 1.31** ($\bar{1}$11) and (1$\bar{1}$1) planes in a cubic unit cell, with the common direction [110] or [$\bar{1}$$\bar{1}$0]

In a crystal, there exists a group of planes having identical arrays of atoms and consequently have the same $d$-spacing. They are crystallographically equivalent planes. Such sets of planes are always related by a symmetry operation. The shortened notation used to specify a family of planes is a set of braces or curly brackets {$hkl$}. In this notation, the {100} family consists of six planes, i.e. (100), ($\bar{1}$00), (010), (0$\bar{1}$0), (001) and (00$\bar{1}$) bounding the unit cell of crystal of cubic system (Fig. 1.32). Similarly, the {110} family consists of twelve planes (110), ($\bar{1}$10), (1$\bar{1}$0), ($\bar{1}$$\bar{1}$0), (101), ($\bar{1}$01) (10$\bar{1}$), ($\bar{1}$0$\bar{1}$), (011), (0$\bar{1}$1), (01$\bar{1}$) and (0$\bar{1}$$\bar{1}$) and the {111} family consists of eight planes (111), ($\bar{1}$11), (1$\bar{1}$1), (11$\bar{1}$), ($\bar{1}$$\bar{1}$1), (1$\bar{1}$$\bar{1}$), ($\bar{1}$1$\bar{1}$) and ($\bar{1}$$\bar{1}$$\bar{1}$). In the cubic crystals, indices of some principal planes are shown in Fig. 1.33.

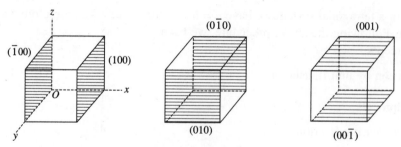

**Fig. 1.32  Indices of six faces of a cube**

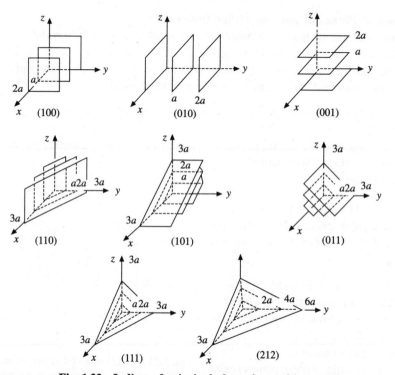

**Fig. 1.33  Indices of principal planes in a cubic crystal**

## Miller-Bravais Indices

As discussed above, for all crystal systems except hexagonal three noncoplanar axes are sufficient to describe a plane or a direction. However, for a hexagonal system, four index notation is required: three coplanar axes $a_1$, $a_2$, $a_3$ in the basal plane of the hexagon and an axis $c$ perpendicular to the hexagonal prism as shown in Fig. 1.34. This is known as Miller-Bravais system of notation. Miller-Bravais indices are obtained exactly as before and for a plane (in hexagonal system) it is given by ($hkil$). Since the three coplanar axes $a_1$, $a_2$ and $a_3$ are related to one another by a rotation of 120° about $c$-axis, so the indices $h$, $k$ and $i$ are also related to one another. From a simple geometrical consideration the relationship is found to be:

$$i = -(h + k)$$

or $\qquad h + k + i = 0 \qquad$ (12)

The indices $h$ and $k$ on the axes $a_1$, and $a_2$ respectively, determine the third index $i$ on the axis $a_3$ simply as $-(h + k)$. Thus it is often omitted from the notation and is replaced by a dot. For example, a plane $(11\overline{2}0)$ in full notation can be written as $(11.0)$ in shortened notation with exactly the same meaning. The existence of above relationship provides a very simple means of conversion from Miller indices to Miller-Bravais indices and vice versa.

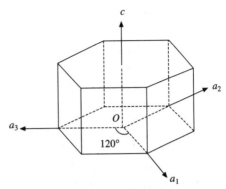

**Fig. 1.34  Miller-Bravais axes**

*Example*: Convert the Miller indices $(110)$, $(1\overline{1}0)$, $345)$, and $(3\overline{45})$ into Miller-Bravais indices.

*Solution*: The value of $i$ is obtained from eq. 12 and hence the Miller-Bravais indices. They are shown on the right column.

| Miller indices | Miller-Bravais Indices |
|---|---|
| $(110)$ | $(11\overline{2}0)$ or $(11.0)$ |
| $(1\overline{1}0)$ | $(1\overline{1}00)$ or $(1\overline{1}.0)$ |
| $(345)$ | $(34\overline{7}5)$ or $(34.5)$ |
| $(3\overline{4}5)$ | $(3\overline{4}15)$ or $(3\overline{4}.5)$ |

*Example*: Replace the dots by numerals from the following shortened Miller-Bravais notations:
$(11.2)$, $(10.3)$, $(1\overline{1}.4)$, $(12.6)$, $(2\overline{4}.5)$, $(21.3)$ $(01.2)$, $(03.5)$, $(\overline{1}3.2)$, $(\overline{1}\,\overline{1}.2)$, $(2\overline{2}.3)$ and $(1\overline{4}.4)$

*Solution:* Using the relationship $i = -(h + k)$, we write full notation of the above as:
$(11\overline{2}2)$, $(10\overline{1}3)$, $(1\overline{1}04)$, $(12\overline{3}6)$, $(2\overline{4}25)$, $(21\overline{3}3)$, $(01\overline{1}2)$, $(03\overline{3}5)$, $(\overline{1}3\overline{2}2)$, $(\overline{1}\,\overline{1}22)$, $(2\overline{2}03)$ and $(1\overline{4}34)$,

The advantage of four index (Miller-Bravais) system of notation over three index system can be seen when we index the prismatic faces of a hexagonal prism (Fig. 1.35). Miller indices have different forms, e.g. $(100)$ and $(\overline{1}10)$, for different planes of the same crystallographic type. On the other hand, in Miller-Bravais notation, these planes become $(10\overline{1}0)$ and $(\overline{1}100)$, respectively, and their crystallographic equivalence, as members of the $\{10\overline{1}0\}$ family, is then quite clear.

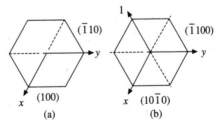

**Fig. 1.35  Prismatic planes in: (a) Miller notation and (b) Miller-Bravais notation**

A direction in this notation is obtained by constructing four vectors, in the order $a_1$, $a_2$, $a_3$, $c$ along the four axes, which combine to give a vector in the required direction. These four vectors must be chosen so that the length of third, in the cell edge units, is always equal to the negative sum of the first two. The four vector lengths are then reduced to smallest integers and written as [*hkil*]. Fig. 1.36 shows some crystallographic directions in the basal plane of the hexagonal system.

The conversion from Miller indices to Miller-Bravais indices for a crystallographic direction is not as simple as it is for a crystal plane. We know that for planes the conversion from one notation to another is carried out simply by insertion or removal of the index $i = -(h + k)$. However, for directions, the relationships are not so simple. The three Miller indices [HKL] and the four Miller-Bravais indices [*hkil*] are connected as given below:

$$H = h - i \qquad\qquad h = (2H - K)/3$$
$$K = k - i \qquad \Rightarrow \qquad k = (2K - H)/3$$
$$L = l \qquad\qquad i = -(h + k) \text{ and } l = L$$

*Example:* Obtain Miller-Bravais indices of the three equivalent directions shown in Fig. 1.37.

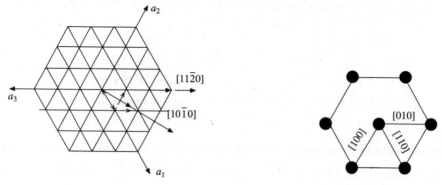

**Fig. 1.36**  **Miller-Bravais indices of some directions**       **Fig. 1.37**  **Miller-Bravais indices of three equivalent**
  **in the basal plane**                                                         **directions**

*Solution*: Case I: Given: [*HKL*] ≡ [100]. Making use of the above conversion formula, the corresponding Miller-Bravais indices can be obtained as:
Miller-Bravais indices

| $h$ | $k$ | $i$ | $l$ |
|---|---|---|---|
| $\dfrac{2}{3}$ | $-\dfrac{1}{3}$ | $-\dfrac{1}{3}$ | $0$ |
| $2$ | $-1$ | $-1$ | $0$ |

⇒ The required Miller Bravais indices are [$2\,\bar{1}\,\bar{1}\,0$].

Case II: For [*HKL*] ≡ [010]. Similar to the above the Miller-Bravais indices are:
Miller-Bravais indices

| $h$ | $k$ | $i$ | $l$ |
|---|---|---|---|
| $-\dfrac{1}{3}$ | $\dfrac{2}{3}$ | $-\dfrac{1}{3}$ | $0$ |
| $-1$ | $2$ | $-1$ | $0$ |

$\Rightarrow$ The required Miller Bravais indices are [$\bar{1}\,2\,\bar{1}\,0$]

Case III: For [$HKL$] $\equiv$ [110]. The Miller-Bravais indices are:

Miller-Bravais indices

| $h$ | $k$ | $i$ | $l$ |
|---|---|---|---|
| $\dfrac{1}{3}$ | $\dfrac{1}{3}$ | $-\dfrac{2}{3}$ | $0$ |
| $1$ | $1$ | $-2$ | $0$ |

$\Rightarrow$ The required Miller-Bravais indices are [11$\bar{2}$0].

It is clear from the above calculations that all the three Miller-Bravais indices are the members of the same family, <11$\bar{2}$0>.

## 1.11 INTERPLANAR SPACING

With the knowledge of indexing crystal planes and directions it is now possible to derive formula for the spacing between two consecutive parallel planes in a given unit cell. We shall limit our discussion to the unit cells which are expressed in terms of the orthogonal coordinate axes, so that simple cartesian geometry is applicable. Thus, let us consider three mutually perpendicular coordinate axes, ox, oy and oz, and assume that a plane (*hkl*) parallel to the plane passing through the origin makes intercepts *a/h*, *b/k* and *c/l* on the three axes at A, B and C respectively as shown in Fig. 13.8. Further, let OP (= *d*, the interplanar spacing) be normal to the plane drawn from the origin

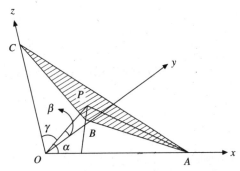

**Fig. 1.38** (*hkl*) **plane intercepting** *x, y,* **and** *z* **axes at** *A, B* **and** *C,* **respectively**

and respectively make angles $\alpha$, $\beta$ and $\gamma$ with the three axes. Therefore, *OA = a/h*, OB = *b/k*, OC = *c/l* and OP = *d*.

From triangle OPA etc., we have

$$\cos\alpha = \frac{OP}{OA} = \frac{d}{(a/h)}, \quad \cos\beta = \frac{OP}{OB} = \frac{d}{(b/k)}$$

$$\cos\gamma = \frac{OP}{OC} = \frac{d}{(c/l)}$$

Now, making use of the direction cosine, which states that

$$\cos^2\alpha + \cos^2\beta + \cos^2\gamma = 1 \tag{13}$$

and substituting the values of cos $\alpha$, cos $\beta$, and cos $\gamma$ in eq. 13, we obtain

$$\frac{d^2}{(a/h)^2} + \frac{d^2}{(b/k)^2} + \frac{d^2}{(c/l)^2} = 1$$

or

$$d^2 \left[ \frac{h^2}{a^2} + \frac{k^2}{b^2} + \frac{l^2}{c^2} \right] = 1$$

So that

$$d = \left[ \frac{h^2}{a^2} + \frac{k^2}{b^2} + \frac{l^2}{c^2} \right]^{-1/2} \tag{14}$$

This is a general formula and is applicable to the primitive lattice of orthorhombic, tetragonal and cubic systems.

(i) Tetragonal system : $a = b \neq c$, eq. 14 reduces to

$$d = \left[ \frac{h^2 + k^2}{a^2} + \frac{l^2}{c^2} \right]^{-1/2} \tag{15}$$

(ii) Cubic system $a = b = c$, eq. 14 reduces to

$$d = a(h^2 + k^2 + l^2)^{-1/2}$$

or

$$d = \frac{a}{(h^2 + k^2 + l^2)^{1/2}} \tag{16}$$

For convenience, the interplanar spacing for all simple lattices are provided in Table 1.10.

**Table 1.10  Interplanar spacings of various crystal systems**

| System | $d_{hkl}$ |
|---|---|
| Cubic | $a(h^2 + k^2 + l^2)^{-1/2}$ |
| Tetragonal | $\left[ \dfrac{h^2 + k^2}{a^2} + \dfrac{l^2}{c^2} \right]^{-1/2}$ |
| Orthorhombic | $\left[ \dfrac{h^2}{a^2} + \dfrac{k^2}{b^2} + \dfrac{l^2}{c^2} \right]^{-1/2}$ |
| Hexagonal | $\left[ \dfrac{4/3(h^2 + hk + k^2)}{a^2} + \dfrac{l^2}{c^2} \right]^{-1/2}$ |
| Rhombohedral | $\dfrac{a(1 + 2\cos 3\alpha - 3\cos^2 \alpha)^{1/2}}{[(h^2 + k^2 + l^2)\sin^2 \alpha + 2(hk + kl + lh)(\cos^2 \alpha - \cos \alpha)]^{1/2}}$ |
| Monoclinic | $\left[ \dfrac{h^2/a^2 + l^2/c^2 + (2hl \cos \beta)/ac}{\sin^2 \beta} + \dfrac{k^2}{b^2} \right]^{-1/2}$ |
| | $\left[ \dfrac{h}{a} \begin{vmatrix} h/a & \cos\gamma & \cos\beta \\ k/b & 1 & \cos\alpha \\ l/c & \cos\alpha & 1 \end{vmatrix} + \dfrac{k}{b} \begin{vmatrix} 1 & h/a & \cos\beta \\ \cos\gamma & k/b & \cos\alpha \\ \cos\beta & l/c & 1 \end{vmatrix} + \dfrac{l}{c} \begin{vmatrix} 1 & \cos\gamma & h/a \\ \cos\gamma & 1 & k/b \\ \cos\beta & \cos\alpha & l/c \end{vmatrix} \right]^{-1/2}$ |
| Triclinic | $\begin{vmatrix} 1 & \cos\gamma & \cos\beta \\ \cos\gamma & 1 & \cos\alpha \\ \cos\beta & \cos\alpha & 1 \end{vmatrix}^{-1/2}$ |

*Example*: The distance between consecutive (111) planes in a cubic crystal is 2 Å. Determine the lattice parameter.

*Solution*: For cubic crystals, we have

$$d = \frac{a}{(h^2 + k^2 + l^2)^{1/2}}$$

Substituting different values, we get

$$d = \frac{a}{(1 + 1 + 1)^{1/2}} = \frac{a}{\sqrt{3}}$$

or
$$a = 2\sqrt{3} \text{ Å} = 3.46 \text{ Å}.$$

*Example:* In a tetragonal crystal, the lattice parameters $a = b = 2.42$ Å, and $c = 1.74$ Å. Deduce the interplanar spacing between consecutive (101) planes.

*Solution*: From Table 1.10 or from eq. 15, we know that the interplanar spacing for a tetragonal system is given by

$$d_{hkl} = \left[ \frac{h^2 + k^2}{a^2} + \frac{l^2}{c^2} \right]^{-1/2}$$

and
$$d_{101} = \left[ \frac{1^2 + 0^2}{(2.42)^2} + \frac{1^2}{(1.74)^2} \right]^{-1/2}$$

$$= 1.41 \text{ Å}.$$

## Interplanar Spacing in sc, bcc and fcc Lattices

*Simple Cubic Lattice*
In a simple cubic system, the lattice parameters $a = b = c$ but the lattice points are situated only at the corners of the unit cell. Thus the interplanar spacings can be determined by simply using eq. 16. The interplanar spacings corresponding to three low index planes (100), (110) and (111) shown in Fig. 1.39 are:

$$d_{100} = a, \quad d_{110} = \frac{a}{\sqrt{2}} \quad \text{and} \quad d_{111} = \frac{a}{\sqrt{3}}$$

Hence their ratio is

$$d_{100} : d_{110} : d_{111} : = 1 : \frac{1}{\sqrt{2}} : \frac{1}{\sqrt{3}}$$

*Body Centred Cubic Lattice*
In this case, the lattice points are situated at the eight corners and at the body centre of the unit cell. Because of the presence of an additional point at the body centre, the interplanar spacings for three low index planes (100), (110) and (111) give slightly different results. There appears an

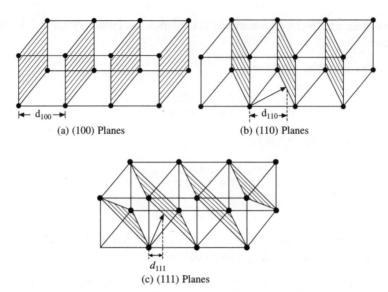

(a) (100) Planes          (b) (110) Planes

(c) (111) Planes

**Fig. 1.39 Low index planes in simple cubic crystal: (a) (100) planes (b) (110) planes (c) (111) planes**

additional plane half way between (100) and (111) planes as shown in Fig. 1.40, while no new planes appear in between (110) planes when compared to simple cubic system. Therefore, the interplanar spacings for the low index planes in the body centred cubic system are:

$$d_{100} = \frac{1}{2}(d_{100}) \text{ simple cubic lattice} = \frac{a}{2}$$

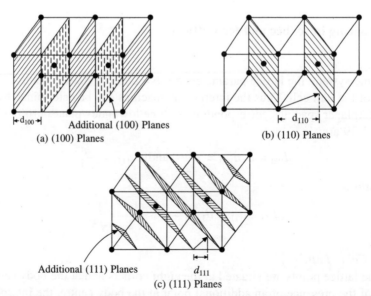

(a) (100) Planes          (b) (110) Planes

(c) (111) Planes

**Fig. 1.40 Low index planes in bcc crystal: (a) (100) planes (b) (110) planes (c) (111) planes**

$$d_{110} = (d_{110}) \text{ simple cubic lattice} = \frac{a}{\sqrt{2}}$$

$$d_{111} = \frac{1}{2}(d_{111}) \text{ simple cubic lattice} = \frac{a}{2\sqrt{3}}$$

Hence their ratio is

$$d_{100} : d_{110} : d_{111} = 1 : \sqrt{2} : \frac{1}{\sqrt{3}}$$

*Face Centred Cubic Lattice*

In this case, the lattice points are situated at eight corners and at the six face centres of the unit cell. Fig. 1.41 shows the appearance of additional planes halfway between (100) and (110) planes, while no new planes appear in between (111) planes. Therefore, the interplanar spacings for three low index planes are given as:

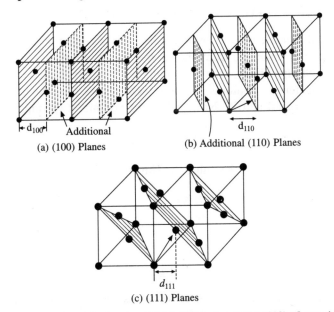

(a) (100) Planes

(b) Additional (110) Planes

(c) (111) Planes

**Fig. 1.41   Low index planes in fcc crystal (a) (100) planes (b) (110) planes (c) (111) planes**

$$d_{100} = \frac{1}{2}(d_{100}) \text{ simple cubic lalttice} = \frac{a}{2}$$

$$d_{110} = \frac{1}{2}(d_{110}) \text{ simple cubic lattice} = \frac{a}{2\sqrt{2}}$$

$$d_{111} = (d_{111}) \text{ simple cubic lattice} = \frac{a}{\sqrt{3}}$$

Hence their ratio is

$$d_{100} : d_{110} : d_{111} = 1 : \frac{1}{\sqrt{2}} : \frac{2}{\sqrt{3}}$$

From above discussion, we find that the low index planes have the widest spacings, e.g. {100} planes in simple cubic, {110} planes in body centred cubic and {111} planes in face centred cubic systems, respectively. Further, since there is a fixed total number of lattice points in a given volume of crystal lattice and since every point belongs to some crystal plane, the planes of the widest spacings are also the planes of the closest packing.

*Example*: Calculate the interplanar spacing for (321) plane in simple cubic lattice with interatomic spacing a = 4.21 Å.

*Solution*: For a simple cubic system, $d_{hkl} = a(h^2 + k^2 + l^2)^{-1/2}$
Substituting different values, we have

$$d = 4.12 \times (9 + 4 + 1)^{-1/2} = \frac{4.12}{\sqrt{14}} = 1.01 \text{ Å}$$

## 1.12  DENSITY OF ATOMS IN A CRYSTAL PLANE

We know that a crystal is made up of a large number of equidistant parallel planes. Let "*N*" be the total number of planes separated from one another by an interplanar spacing *d* and the area of cross-section of each plane be *A*, then the volume of this part of the crystal is *AdN*.

Further, Let $\delta$ be the density of atoms in one of these planes, then the total number of atoms in the same part of the crystal is $A\delta N$. Now, if *V* is the volume of the unit cell, then

$$A\delta N = \frac{AdN}{V} \cdot n$$

where *n* is the number of atoms in the unit cell. Thus the density of atoms in a plane is

$$\delta = \frac{nd}{V} \tag{17}$$

For a primitive lattice *n* = 1. So that

$$\delta = \frac{d}{V} \tag{18}$$

*Example*: Calculate the atomic density (number of atoms per unit area) in (100), (110) and (111) planes of simple cubic, body centred and face centred cubic systems as a function of lattice parameter *a*.

*Solution*: *Case I—Simple cubic system*
From section 1.11, we know that the interplanar spacings in terms of *a* for the above planes are given as

$$d_{100} = a, \ d_{110} = \frac{a}{\sqrt{2}} \text{ and } d_{111} = \frac{a}{\sqrt{3}}$$

The volume of a simple cubic cell = $a^3$ and *n* = 1

$$\Rightarrow \quad \delta = \frac{d}{V} = \frac{d}{a^3}$$

so that,

$$\delta_{100} = \frac{d_{100}}{a^3} = \frac{a}{a^3} = \frac{1}{a^2}$$

$$\delta_{110} = \frac{d_{110}}{a^3} = \frac{a}{\sqrt{2}\,a^3} = \frac{1}{\sqrt{2}\,a^2}$$

$$\delta_{111} = \frac{d_{111}}{a^3} = \frac{a}{\sqrt{3}\,a^3} = \frac{1}{\sqrt{3}\,a^2}$$

*Case II—Body centred cubic system*
In this case, the interplanar spacings are given as

$$d_{100} = \frac{a}{2}, d_{110} = \frac{a}{\sqrt{2}} \text{ and } d_{111} = \frac{a}{2\sqrt{3}}$$

Volume is the same as $a^3$ but $n = 2$

$$\Rightarrow \quad \delta = \frac{nd}{V} = \frac{2d}{a^3}$$

so that

$$\delta_{100} = \frac{2 \times d_{100}}{a^3} = \frac{2a}{2a^3} = \frac{1}{a^2}$$

$$\delta_{110} = \frac{2 \times d_{110}}{a^3} = \frac{2a}{\sqrt{2}\,a^3} = \frac{\sqrt{2}}{a^2}$$

$$\delta_{111} = \frac{2 \times d_{111}}{a^3} = \frac{2a}{2\sqrt{3}\,a^3} = \frac{1}{\sqrt{3}\,a^2}$$

*Case III—Face centred cubic system:*
In this case, the interplanar spacings are given as

$$d_{100} = \frac{a}{2}, d_{110} = \frac{a}{2\sqrt{2}} \text{ and } d_{111} = \frac{a}{\sqrt{3}}$$

Volume is same as $a^3$, but $n = 4$

$$\Rightarrow \quad \delta = \frac{nd}{V} = \frac{4d}{a^3}$$

so that

$$\delta_{100} = \frac{4 \times d_{100}}{a^3} = \frac{4a}{2a^3} = \frac{2}{a^2}$$

$$\delta_{110} = \frac{4 \times d_{110}}{a^3} = \frac{4a}{2\sqrt{2}\,a^3} = \frac{\sqrt{2}}{a^2}$$

$$\delta_{111} = \frac{4 \times d_{111}}{a^3} = \frac{4a}{\sqrt{3}a^3} = \frac{4}{\sqrt{3}a^2}$$

## Density of Atoms in a Crystal Plane (Alternative Method)

The density of atoms in a crystal plane is defined as the ratio of number of atoms to the area of that plane i.e.

$$\text{Density of atoms in a plane} = \frac{\text{No. of atoms in the given plane}}{\text{Area of the given plane}}$$

Let us obtain the density of atoms in cubic crystals.

*Case I—Simple cubic system*

Fig. 1.42 (a) and (b), respectively give the actual and cross-sectional view of (100) plane. From these figures we can find,

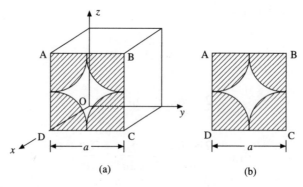

(a)                      (b)

**Fig. 1.42** **Showing (a) actual view and (b) cross-sectional view of (100) plane in a simple cubic structure**

No. of atoms contained in the plane $ABCD = 4 \times \dfrac{1}{4} = 1$

Area of the plane $ABCD = a \times a = a^2$. Therefore,

$$\delta_{(100)} = \frac{\text{No. of atoms in (100) plane}}{\text{Area of (100) plane}} = \frac{1}{a^2}$$

Similarly, from Fig. 1.43 (a) and (b), one can easily determine

No. of atoms contained in the plane $AFDG = 4 \times \dfrac{1}{4} = 1$

Area of the plane $AFDG = a \times a\sqrt{2} = a^2\sqrt{2}$

so that
$$\delta_{(110)} = \frac{1}{a^2\sqrt{2}}$$

Again from Fig. 1.44 (a) and (b), we find

No. of atoms contained in the plane $ABC = 3 \times \dfrac{1}{6} = \dfrac{1}{2}$

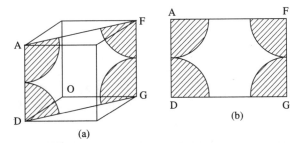

**Fig. 1.43**  **Showing (a) actual view and (b) cross-sectional view of (110) plane in a simple cubic structure**

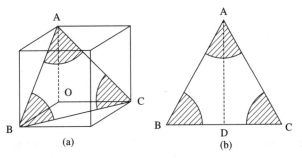

**Fig. 1.44**  **Showing (a) actual view and (b) cross-sectional view of (111) plane in a simple cubic structure**

Area of the (equilateral triangle) plane $ABC = \frac{1}{2} \times BC \times AD$

$$= \frac{1}{2} \times a\sqrt{2} \times a\sqrt{2} \sin 60° = \frac{a^2 \sqrt{3}}{2}$$

so that

$$\delta_{(111)} = \frac{\frac{1}{2}}{\frac{a^2 \sqrt{3}}{2}} = \frac{1}{a^2 \sqrt{3}}$$

*Case II—Body centred cubic system*

Since, (100) plane of a bcc structure is similar to the (100) plane of a simple cubic structure with the only difference that in the case of bcc, the corner atoms do not touch each other. For a comparison, the actual and the cross-sectional views are shown in Fig. 1.45.

Therefore, the density remains same as simple cubic case, i.e.

$$\delta_{(100)} = \frac{1}{a^2}$$

Fig. 1.46 (a) and (b), respectively give the actual and cross sectional view of (110) plane. In this case,

No. of atoms contained in the plane $AFDG = \left[ 4 \times \frac{1}{4} \right] + 1 = 2$

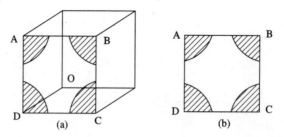

**Fig. 1.45** **Showing (a) actual view and (b) cross-sectional view of (100) plane in a body centred cubic structure**

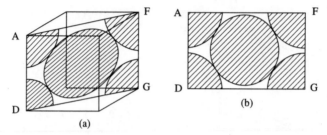

**Fig. 1.46** **Showing (a) actual veiw and (b) cross-sectional view of (110) plane in a body centred cubic structure**

Area of the plane $AFDG = a \times a\sqrt{2} = a^2\sqrt{2}$

so that
$$\delta_{(110)} = \frac{2}{a^2\sqrt{2}} = \frac{\sqrt{2}}{a^2}$$

Like (100) plane, (111) plane of a bcc structure is also similar to the (111) plane of a simple cubic structure and hence the density remains same, i.e.

$$\delta_{(111)} = \frac{1}{a^2\sqrt{3}}$$

*Case III—Face centred cubic system*
Fig. 1.47 (a) and (b), respectively give the actual and cross-sectional view of (100) plane. In this case,

No. of atoms contained in the plane $ABCD = \left[4 \times \frac{1}{4}\right] + 1 = 2$

Area of the plane $ABCD = a^2$. Therefore,

$$\delta_{(100)} = \frac{2}{a^2}$$

Fig. 1.48 (a) and (b), respectively give the actual and cross sectional view of (110) plane. In this case,

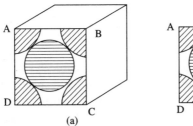
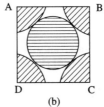

(a)   (b)

**Fig. 1.47   Showing (a) actual view and (b) cross-sectional view of (100) plane in a face centred cubic structure**

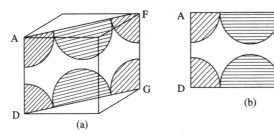

(a)   (b)

**Fig. 1.48   Showing (a) actual view and (b) cross-sectional view of (110) plane in a face centred cubic structure**

No. of atoms containd in the plane $AFDG = \left[4 \times \frac{1}{4}\right] + \left[2 \times \frac{1}{2}\right] = 2$

Area of the plane $AFDG = a \times a\sqrt{2} = a^2 \sqrt{2}$

so that
$$\delta_{(110)} = \frac{2}{a^2 \sqrt{2}} = \frac{\sqrt{2}}{a^2}$$

Fig. 1.49 (a) and (b), respectively give the actual and cross sectional view of (111) plane. In this case,

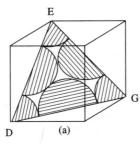
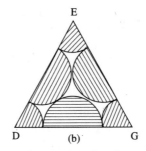

D   (a)       D   (b)   G

**Fig. 1.49   Showing (a) actual and (b) cross-sectional view of (111) plane in a face centred cubic structure**

No. of atoms contained in the plane $EDG = \left[3 \times \frac{1}{6}\right] + \left[3 \times \frac{1}{2}\right] = 2$

Area of the plane $EDG = \dfrac{a^2 \sqrt{3}}{2}$

so that
$$\delta_{(111)} = \frac{2}{\dfrac{a^2 \sqrt{3}}{2}} = \frac{4}{a^2 \sqrt{3}}$$

If we compare the densities calculated above for three cubic systems, we find that the planes of widest spacings (100) of sc, (110) of bcc and (111) of fcc respectively correspond to highest densities in their own category, while the (111) planes of fcc correspond to highest density of all. It is because of this, (111) planes of the fcc lattice are called the close packed planes.

*Example*: Give the Miller indices of the family of close packed planes and directions in sc, bcc, fcc and diamond crystal.

*Solution*: From above calculations of the densities and the idea of indices of directions discussed in section 1.10, we can write

|  | sc | bcc | fcc | Dc |
|---|---|---|---|---|
| Family of close packed planes | {100} | {110} | {111} | none |
| Family of close packed directions | <100> | $<\bar{1}11>$ | $<1\bar{1}0>$ | none |

## 1.13   SOME SIMPLE AND COMMON CRYSTAL STRUCTURES

As we shall see later that many properties of solids can be explained only if the detail crystal structure of the substance is taken into account. We shall, therefore, give a brief description of some of the very common and simple crystal structures.

Out of over hundred elements in the periodic Table, only one element (polonium) is known to crystallize in the simple cubic form. The geometry of this structure is easy and is very helpful in understanding other structures. A large number of other elements are found to crystallize in the form of fcc, bcc, hcp and the derivatives of the basic cubic structures.

### Simple Cubic Structure

In this structure the atoms are situated only at the corners of the cube touching each other along the edges (Fig. 1.50). This is a very open and loosely packed structure, i.e. there is much empty space in it. This structure is introduced mainly because of its simple geometry. However, as we shall see in the following that many other crystal structures bear a simple relationship to this structure.

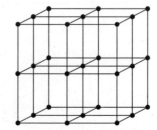

**Fig. 1.50   The simple cubic structure**

### Body Centred Cubic Structure

As a rule, atoms tend to pack more closely and therefore if we examine the simple cubic arrangement to see how it might accommodate more atoms, the most obvious empty space is that at the centre of the cube. If this space is filled, we can obtain a body centred cubic (bcc) structure (Fig. 1.51a). It is to be noted that it can be considered as if two simple cubic structures interpenetrated along the body diagonal of one cube by half the length of the diagonal (Fig. 1.51b). Many metals are found to have bcc structure,

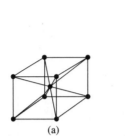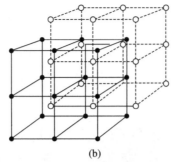

(a)                 (b)

**Fig. 1.51**   **(a) Body centred cubic structure, (b) Body centred cubic structure may be considered to be two interpenetrated simple cubic structures**

most important is iron while some others are Cr, Mo, W and also the alkali metals Li, K, Na, Rb and Cs.

Certain simple binary compounds essentially have the bcc arrangement in which the centre of the cube is occupied by one type of atoms and the corners are occupied by the others. This is usually called cesium chloride structure.

### Close Packed Structures

If the atoms are considered as hard spheres then the most efficient packing of these atoms in a plane is the close packed arrangement as shown in Fig. 1.52. There are two simple ways in which such planes can be stacked on top of one another to form a three dimensional structure. They are hexagonal close packed (hcp) structure (Fig. 1.53) and the face centred cubic (fcc) structure or equivalently the cubic close packed (ccp) structure.

In a single close packed layer, the spheres (atoms) may be arranged by placing each sphere in contact with six others, say all at positions A (Fig. 1.52). Such a layer can either be the basal plane of hcp structure or the (111) plane of the fcc structure. A second similar layer can be

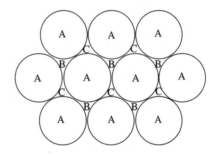

**Fig. 1.52**   **Close packed array of spheres. Note the three different possible positions, A, B and C for the successive layers**

placed above the A layer either in the space marked B or in those marked C. Let us suppose that the second layer is a B layer. Where can the third succeeding layer be placed? There are two possible arrangements each of which is an important representative structure.

### Hexagonal Close Packed Structures

Simplest arrangement for the third layer to be placed is the layer position A, i.e., immediately above the atoms in the first layer, and the fourth layer to be placed at B and so on. This gives a stacking of the type ABABAB . . . (or equivalently as ACACAC . . .) as shown in Fig. 1.53b. It has a hexagonal primitive cell in which the basis contains two atoms, one at the origin, 0 0 0 and

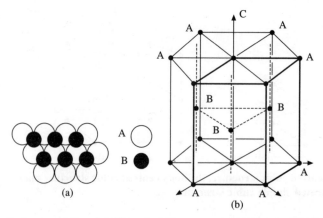

**Fig. 1.53   Hexagonal close packing. (a) The stacking sequence of layers ABABA . . . (b) The three dimensional arrangement of atoms which shows the hexagonal pattern more clearly**

the other at 2/3 1/3 1/2 as shown in Fig. 1.54. Many metals such as Mg, Zn, Cd, Ti, Ni, etc. have hcp structure.

### Face Centered Cubic Structure

There is another way in which successive close packed planes of the type shown in Fig. 1.52 can be stacked. The first two layers remain in positions A and B as before, but the third layer instead of reverting to the A positions as in hcp arrangement, can be placed on the C positions. The fourth layer is then put on the A positions which are immediately above the atoms in the lowest plane. This gives a stacking of the type ABC ABC . . . , with the pattern repeating at every third layer and is called the face centred cubic structure (Fig. 1.55a).

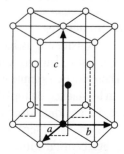

**Fig. 1.54   The hexagonal primitive cell. The two atoms of one basis are shown as solid in the figure. One atom of the basis is at the origin, 000; the other atom is at $\frac{2}{3} \frac{1}{3} \frac{1}{2}$, which means at $T = \frac{2}{3}a + \frac{1}{3}b + \frac{1}{2}c$**

At first sight there seems to be nothing cubic in it. This is because the close packed layers which have been discussed above do not correspond to the ordinary faces of a cube. A face centred cubic unit cell drawn with conventional cube axes is shown in Fig. 1.55b. As its name implies the structure is the same as the ordinary simple cubic (Fig. 1.50) with the addition of an extra atom at the centre of each cube face. The close packed layers are the body diagonal planes of the cube and one of these is shown in Fig. 1.55c. The fcc structure has in all four equivalent close packed planes as compared to hcp which has only one (basal plane). However, the actual fraction of space filled in fcc and hcp is the same (detail calculation is given in chapter 3). Table 1.11 provides a simple comparison between the two close packed arrangements.

Face centred cubic structures are typical of many metallic elements e.g., Cu, Ag, Au, Al, Ni, Pd and Pt.

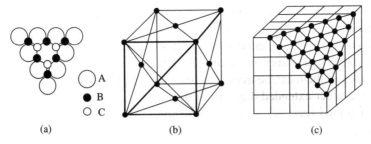

**Fig. 1.55** The face centred cubic structure. (a) Stacking sequence of layers ABCABCA . . . (b) Unit cell based on a cube. (c) Close packed planes of (a) are the body diagonal planes

**Table 1.11** Comparision between two close packed arrangements

| Lattice Type | Equivalent Structure | Efficiency | # of possible polytypes | Close Packed planes | Close Packed directions |
|---|---|---|---|---|---|
| HCP | 2H | 74% | Theoretically Infinite | {0001} | <11$\bar{2}$0> |
| FCC | 3C | 74% | Only one (3C) | {111} | <110> |

## Other Cubic Structures

We saw above that many metallic elements solidify in one of the structures described above. However, there are several other elements, e.g. As, Sb, Bi, S, Se, Te, I and Mn and many compounds, e.g. InSb, GaAs and GaP which are found to have other structures. Some of these structures are derivatives of the cubic structures and are briefly discussed in the following.

## Diamond Structure

The crystal structure of diamond can be derived from the fcc lattice although the structure itself is not a close packed one. Formally it may be described as being built up from two interpenetrating fcc lattices which are displaced with respect to one another along the body diagonal of the cube by one quarter of the length of the diagonal (Fig. 1.56a). While this definition accurately describes the position of the atoms, it is not very useful when one actually visualizes the

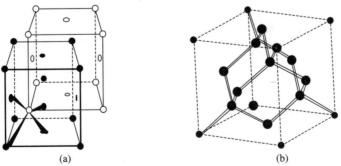

**Fig. 1.56** The diamond lattice showing (a) How it is formed from two interpenetrating fcc lattices. (b) The tetrahedral arrangement of atoms

structure. A more useful model for all practical purposes is to consider each atom to be at the centre of a tetrahedron with its four nearest neighbours at the four corners of that tetrahedron (Fig. 1.56b). From Fig. 1.56a it can be seen that if the central atom of the tetrahedron is on one fcc sublattice then the four corner atoms are all on the other sublattice. Further, since all atoms are equivalent, each of them can be treated as being the centre atom of the tetrahedron, although it would require a rather extended diagram to show this.

Apart from diamond (carbon), silicon, germanium, and grey tin crystallize in the form of diamond structure.

### Zinc Blende Structure

If the two interpenetrating lattices (as considered for the formation of diamond structure) are of two different elements, the atoms on different sublattices are no longer equivalent. However, they still produce a similar tetrahedral arrangement. This is then called the zinc blende (ZnS) structure (Fig. 1.57). Thus zinc blende has equal number of zinc and sulfur ions distributed on a diamond lattice so that each has four of the opposite kind as nearest neighbours. It is typical of the 3–5 semiconducting crystals such as InSb, GaAs, GaP.

### Sodium Chloride Structure

Sodium chloride (NaCl) consists of equal number of sodium and chlorine ions placed at alternate points of a simple cubic lattice (Fig. 1.58) in such a way that each ion has six of the other kind of ions as nearest neighbours. This structure can be described as a face centred cubic lattice with a basis consisting of a sodium ion and a chlorine ion separated by one half the body diagonal of a unit cube. There are four units of NaCl in each cube, with ions in the positions:

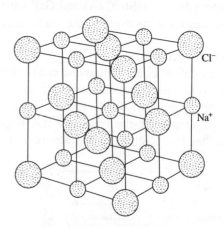

Fig. 1.58   The sodium chloride structure. Na$^+$ and Cl$^-$ are shown by small and big circles respectively. Big and small circles from interpenetrating fcc lattice

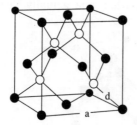

**Fig. 1.57   Crystal structure of cubic zinc sulfide**

Na : 0 0 0 , 1/2 1/2 0, 1/2 0 1/2, 0 1/2 1/2
Cl : 1/2 1/2 1/2, 0 0 1/2, 0 1/2 0, 1/2 0 0

Large number of compounds including other alkali halides crystallize in this form and are said to have rock salt structure.

## Cesium Chloride Structure

Like sodium chloride, cesium chloride (CsCl) also consists of equal number of cesium and chlorine ions. However, in this case, one type of ions are situated at the body centred positions (Fig. 1.59) so that each ion has eight other ions as nearest neighbour. The translational symmetry of this structure is the same as that of simple cubic lattice and therefore cesium chloride structure can be described as a simple cubic lattice with a basis consisting of a cesium ion at the origin (000) and a chlorine ion at the cube centre (1/2 1/2 1/2). The cesium chloride structure is shared by cesium bromide and cesium iodide.

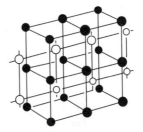

**Fig. 1.59** **The cesium chloride structure ● and O represents two different ions which form interpenetrating simple cubic lattice**

In Table 1.12, we enlist for convenience the most common crystal structures and the lattice constants of various elements.

**Table 1.12** **Crystal structures and lattice parameters**

| Element | Symbol | Crystal structure | Lattice Parameters a (Å) | c (Å) |
|---|---|---|---|---|
| Actinium | Ac | fcc | 5.31 | |
| Aluminium | Al | fcc | 4.05 | |
| Americium | Am | hex | | |
| Antimony | Sb | rhomb. | | |
| Argon | Ar | fcc | 5.31 | |
| Arsenic | As | rhomb. | | |
| Astatine | At | | | |
| Barium | Ba | bcc | 5.02 | |
| Berkelium | Bk | | | |
| Beryllium | Be | hcp | 2.27 | 3.59 |
| Bismuth | Bi | rhomb. | | |
| Boron | B | rhomb. | | |
| Bromine | Br | complex | | |
| Cadmium | Cd | hcp | 2.98 | 5.62 |
| Calcium | Ca | fcc | 5.58 | |
| Californium | Cf | | | |
| Carbon | C | diamond | 3.567 | |
| Cerium | Ce | fcc | 5.16 | |
| Cesium | Cs | bcc | 6.045 | |
| Chlorine | Cl | complex | | |
| Chromium | Cr | bcc | 2.88 | |
| Cobalt | Co | hcp | 2.51 | 4.07 |
| Copper | Cu | fcc | 3.61 | |
| Curium | Cm | | | |

*(Contd.)*

| Element | Symbol | Crystal structure | Lattice Parameters | |
|---|---|---|---|---|
| | | | *a* (Å) | *c* (Å) |
| Dysprosium | Dy | hcp | 3.59 | 5.65 |
| Einsteinium | Es | | | |
| Erbium | Er | hcp | 3.56 | 5.59 |
| Europium | Eu | bcc | 4.58 | |
| Fermium | Fm | | | |
| Fluorine | F | | | |
| Francium | Fr | | | |
| Gadolinium | Gd | hcp | 3.63 | 5.78 |
| Gallium | Ga | complex | | |
| Germanium | Ge | diamond | 5.658 | |
| Gold | Au | fcc | 4.08 | |
| Hafnium | Hf | hcp | 3.19 | 5.05 |
| Helium | He | hcp | 3.57 | 5.83 |
| Holmium | Ho | hcp | 3.58 | 5.62 |
| Hydrogen | H | hcp | 3.75 | 6.12 |
| Indium | In | tetr. | 3.25 | 4.95 |
| Iodine | I | complex | | |
| Iridium | Ir | fcc | 3.84 | |
| Iron | Fe | bcc | 2.87 | |
| Krypton | Kr | fcc | 5.64 | |
| Lanthanum | La | hex. | 3.77 | |
| Lawrencium | Lw | | | |
| Lead | Pb | fcc | 4.95 | |
| Lithium | Li | bcc | 3.491 | |
| Lutetium | Lu | hcp | 3.50 | 5.55 |
| Magnesium | Mg | hcp | 3.21 | 5.21 |
| Manganese | Mn | cubic complex | | |
| Mendelevium | Md | | | |
| Mercury | Hg | rhomb. | | |
| Molybdenum | Mo | bcc | 3.15 | |
| Neodymium | Nd | hex. | 3.66 | |
| Neon | Ne | Fcc | 4.46 | |
| Neptunium | Np | complex | | |
| Nickel | Ni | fcc | 3.52 | |
| Niobium | Nb | bcc | 3.30 | |
| Nitrogen | N | cubic | 5.66 | |
| Nobelium | No | | | |
| Osmium | Os | hcp | 2.74 | 4.32 |
| Oxygen | O | complex | | |
| Palladium | Pd | fcc | 3.89 | |
| Phosphorous | P | Complex | | |
| Platinum | Pt | fcc | 3.92 | |
| Plutonium | Pu | complex | | |
| Polonium | Po | sc | 3.34 | |
| Potassium | K | bcc | 5.225 | |
| Praseodymium | Pr | hex. | 3.67 | |

*(Contd.)*

| Element | Symbol | Crystal structure | Lattice Parameters | |
|---|---|---|---|---|
| | | | $a$ (Å) | $c$ (Å) |
| Promethium | Pm | | | |
| Protactinium | Pa | tetr. | 3.92 | 3.24 |
| Radium | Ra | | | |
| Radon | Rn | | | |
| Rhenium | Re | hcp | 2.76 | 4.46 |
| Rhodium | Rh | fcc | 3.80 | |
| Rubidium | Rb | bcc | 5.585 | |
| Ruthenium | Ru | hcp | 2.71 | 4.28 |
| Samarium | Sm | complex | | |
| Scandium | Sc | hcp | 3.31 | 5.27 |
| Selenium | Se | hex. chains | | |
| Silicon | Si | diamond | 5.430 | |
| Silver | Ag | fcc | 4.09 | |
| Sodium | Na | bcc | 4.225 | |
| Strontium | Sr | fcc | 6.08 | |
| Sulfur | S | complex | | |
| Tantalum | Ta | bcc | 3.30 | |
| Technitium | Tc | hcp | 2.74 | 4.40 |
| Tellurium | Te | hex. chains | | |
| Terbium | Tb | hcp | 3.60 | 5.70 |
| Thallium | T1 | hcp | 3.46 | 5.52 |
| Thorium | Th | fcc | 5.08 | |
| Thulium | Tm | hcp | 3.54 | 5.56 |
| Tin | Sn | diamond | 6.49 | |
| Titanium | Ti | hcp | 2.95 | 4.68 |
| Tungston | W | bcc | 3.16 | |
| Uranium | U | compex | | |
| Vanadium | V | bcc | 3.03 | |
| Xenon | Xe | fcc | 6.13 | |
| Ytterbium | Yb | fcc | 5.48 | |
| Yttrium | Y | hcp | 3.65 | 5.73 |
| Zinc | Zn | hcp | 2.66 | 4.95 |
| Zirconium | Zr | hcp | 3.23 | 5.15 |

## 1.14  SUMMARY

1. Based on the degree and type of order, solids are conveniently divided into three classes: Crystalline, Semicrystalline (Polycrystalline) and Noncrystalline (Amorphous)
2. A space lattice is an array of points related by the translation $T = n_1a + n_2b + n_3c$, where $n_1$, $n_2$, $n_3$ are integers and $a$, $b$, $c$ are primitive translations along $x$, $y$, $z$ axes.
3. A crystal structure is formed when a group of atoms (or molecules) called basis is attached to each lattice point. The basis is identical in composition, arrangement and orientation.
4. The volume $V_c$ of a primitive unit cell defined by the primitive translations $a$, $b$, $c$ is $V_c = |a \times b \cdot c|$

5. Unit cells may be conveniently chosen as primitive (containing one lattice point per unit cell) or non-primitive (containing more than one lattice points per unit cell).
6. In a crystalline solid, symmetries such as translation, rotation, reflection, inversion or their suitable combinations (if they are compatible) are found to occur.
7. Space lattices are limited to fourteen, but crystal structures run into thousands.
8. Crystal lattice sites, directions and planes are represented by the Miller indices [[*hkl*]], [*hkl*] and (*hkl*), respectively. They include all possible positive and negative indices.
9. Low index planes are found to have widest spacings. The planes of widest spacing are also the planes of the closest packing.
10. Important simple structures include the simple cubic, bcc, fcc hcp, diamond, ZnS, NaCl and CsCl structures.

## 1.15 DEFINITIONS

*Amorphous:* A solid in which the component atoms are randomly distributed.

*Anisotropic:* Having different properties in different directions.

*Atomic mass unit (amu):* One twelfth of the mass of $C^{12}$ (1 amu = $1.6605 \times 10^{-27}$ kg $\cong$ 931 MeV).

*Atomic number:* Number of electrons possessed by an uncharged atom. The number of protons in an atom.

*Atomic weight:* Atomic mass expressed in atomic mass units, or grams per mole.

*Avogadroe's number (N):* Number of amu's per gram; hence the number of molecules per mole.

*Basis:* It is the identical group of atoms (molecules) associated with each lattice point.

*Centre of symmetry:* A body has a cente of symmetry if for every point in it there is an identical point equidistant from the centre but on the opposite side.

*Crystal:* A crystal is a solid in which the component atoms are arranged in a three dimensional periodic manner.

*Crystal structure:* Logically when identical group of atoms (molecules) are attached to each lattice point; A mathematical representation of the relative position of all atoms or ions in an ideal crystal.

*Family of directions < hkl>:* Crystal directions that are identical except for our arbitrary choice of the axes.

*Family of planes {hkl}:* Crystal planes that are identical except for our choice of axes.

*Indices of direction:* The indices of a direction are those integers in square brackets which identifies the particular direction and distinguishes it from all others.

*Indices of plane:* The indices of a plane are those integers in parentheses which identify the particular plane and distinguishes it from all others.

*Lattice point:* One point in an array, all the points of which have identical surroundings.

*Lattice translation:* A vector connecting any two lattice points in the same lattice.

*Long range order:* A periodic pattern over many atomic distances.

*Miller-Bravais indices:* The Miller-Bravais indices is a four index system of notation based on four axes in the hexagonal system.

*Miller indices (hkl):* Index relating a plane to the reference axes of a crystal. Reciprocal of axial intercepts, cleared of fractions and of common multiples.

*Mirror plane:* It is a plane which divides a body into two halves that are mirror images of one another across a plane.

*Molecular weight:* Mass of one molecule (expressed in amu), or mass of $0.6 \times 10^{24}$ molecules (expresed in grams). Mass of one formula weight.

*Plane lattice:* A plane lattice is an infinite array of points in two dimensions such that every point of it has identical surroundings.

*Poly crystal:* A poly crystal is an aggregate of small crystallites (grains), which might or might not be of different kinds, generally irregularly shaped and interlocked together at the boundaries of contact.

*Primitive cell:* A unit cell which has lattice points only at its corners; equivalently, a unit cell which contains only one lattice point.

*Rotational symmetry*: It is the symmetry operation of a body about any line (axis) to one or more positions of self coincidence.

*Rotoinversion*: A body has rotoinversion axis if it can be transformed to self coincidence by the combined effect of rotation and inversion.

*Single crystal*: A single crystal is an isolated piece of one crystal of a crystalline solid.

*Space lattice*: A space lattice is an infinite array of points in three dimensions such that every point is absolutely indistinguishable from every other point; also called Bravais lattice.

*Symmetry operation*: It is an operation that can be performed on a body to transform it to self coincidence.

*Unit cell*: It is a convenient repeating parallelepiped unit of a space lattice having three noncoplanar unit translations as its edges.

# REVIEW QUESTIONS AND PROBLEMS

1. Define the following terms in relation to crystal structure: (i) Crystalline, Polycrystalline and amorphous state of matter. (ii) Lattice, basis and crystal structure.

2. What do you understand by a crystal lattice and the unit cell? In an fcc lattice each unit cell has a lattice point at the centre of each face in addition to those at the corners.

   (i)    Write down the position of atoms.
   (ii)   What will be the primitive cell for the space lattice?
   (iii)  How large is the fcc cell as compared to the primitive cubic cell?

3. What are Bravais lattices and crystal system? Explain why the base centred tetragonal, the face centred tetragonal and the face centred rhombohedral have not been included in the Fig. 1.24.

4. Prove that if a Bravais lattice has a reflection plane, it is possible to choose one primitive vector perpendicular to the plane and two others parallel to it. Is this choice unique?

5. Construct two different sets of primitive translation vectors for the simple cubic lattice. Verify explicitly that the volume $a_1 a_2 \times a_3$ is the smae for both.

6. Distinguish between the coordination number and the number of atoms per unit cell. Find both these numbers for; (i) a simple cubic lattice, (ii) a body centred cubic lattice and (iii) a face centred cubic lattice?

7. Calculate the number of atoms per unit cell for rock-salt crystal. Given $a = 5.63$ Å, Mol. wt. of NaCl = 58.5 and the density is 2180 kg/m$^3$
   *Ans.* 4 Atoms.

8. Platinum (at. wt. = 195.1) crystallizes in the fcc form and has the density of $21.4 \times 10^3$ kg/m$^3$. Calculate the side of the unit cell. *Ans.* 3.93Å.

9. The density of bcc iron is $7.9 \times 10^3$ kg/m$^3$ and the atomic weight is 56. Calculate the size of the unit cell.
   *Ans.* 2.86Å

10. Find the total number of symmetry elements in each of the fourteen Bravais lattices.

11. Name the Bravais lattice to which the following geometrical figures belong to: a brick, a prism, a cubiod deformed by unequal angles and a book. Write down their total symmetries.

12. Consider a face centred cubic unit cell. Construct a primitive unit cell within this and compare the two. How many atoms are there in the primitive cell and in the original cell?

13. Demonstrate that if an object has two reflection planes intersecting at $\pi/4$, it also posssses 4-fold axis lying at their intersection.

14. Show analytically that five fold rotation axis does not exist in a crystal lattice.

15. Draw a (11$\bar{1}$) plane in the unit cell of a cubic crystal. Find the <110> directions that lie on this plane.
    *Ans.* [$\bar{1}$10], [011], [101] and three opposite directions [1$\bar{1}$0], [$\bar{1}$0$\bar{1}$], [$\bar{1}$0$\bar{1}$].

16. Draw a (110) plane in the unit cell of a cubic crystal. Find the <111> directions that lie on this plane.
    *Ans.* [1$\bar{1}$1] or [$\bar{1}$1$\bar{1}$] and [$\bar{1}$11$\bar{1}$], [1$\bar{1}$1$\bar{1}$]

17. What is the Miller index of the line of intersection of (110) and ($\bar{1}$$\bar{1}$1) planes in a cubic system?
    *Ans.* [1$\bar{1}$0] or [$\bar{1}$10]

18. What do you understand by Miller indices of a lattice plane? Find the Miller indices of a plane that makes an intercept of $3a$, $2b$ and $c$ along the three crystallographic axes, where $a$, $b$, $c$ being the primitive vectors of the lattice.
*Ans.* (236)

19. In an orthorhombic cell, the primitive vectors are 1.27Å, 2.14Å and 1.51Å. Deduce the intercepts of $x$ and $y$ axes if (213) plane cuts an intercept of 1.51Å along the z-axis.
*Ans.* $l_1 = 1.90$Å, $l_2 = 6.42$Å.

20. Find the Miller indices of a plane that makes an intercept of 1 on $a$-axis and 2 on $b$-axis and is parallel to $c$-axis.
*Ans.* (210)

21. Determine the Miller indices of a plane that makes an intercept of 3Å, 4Å, and 5Å on the coordinate axes of an orthorhombic crystal with $a : b : c = 1 : 2 : 5$.
*Ans.* (236)

22. Find the Miller indices of a plane that makes intercepts on $a$, $b$ and $c$ axes equal to 4Å, 6Å and 4Å in a tetragonal crystal with the $c/a$ ratio as 2.
*Ans.* (326).

23. Calculate the lengths of intercepts made by planes of Miller indices (111) and (123) in $BaCl_2$ crystal with primitive translation vectors $a = 6.69$Å, $b = 10.86$Å and $c = 7.15$Å, if both the planes cut an intercept 7.15Å along z-axis.
*Ans.* (i) $l_1 = 6.69$Å, $l_2 = 10.86$Å, $l_3 = 7.15$Å and (ii) $l_1 = 20.07$Å, $l_2 = 16.29$Å, $l_3 = 7.15$Å

24. Change the following Miller indices: (210), ($\bar{1}$13), (011), (246) and ($4\bar{2}3$) into Miller-Bravais indices.
*Ans.* ($21\bar{3}0$), ($\bar{1}103$), ($01\bar{1}1$), ($24\bar{6}6$) and ($4\bar{2}\,\bar{2}3$).

25. Determine the value of "$i$" in the following Miller-Bravais indices: (10.3), (11.3), (01.4), ($1\bar{1}.4$), (10.4), ($2\bar{2}.4$), ($2\bar{2}.3$) (11.0), (32.5) and ($3\bar{4}.2$)
*Ans.* $\bar{1}$, $\bar{2}$ $\bar{1}$, 0, $\bar{1}$, 0, 0, $\bar{2}$, $\bar{5}$ and 1.

26. Show that in a cubic lattice the distance between the successive planes of indices ($hkl$) is given by

$$d_{hkl} = \frac{a}{(h^2 + k^2 + l^2)^{1/2}}$$

Find the interplanar spacing for the lattice planes of Miller indices (321), (210) and (111) for a cubic lattice with $a = 5.62$Å
*Ans.* 1.50Å, 2.51Å and 3.25Å.

27. Show that the ($hkl$) plane is perpendicular to the [$hkl$] direction in a cubic lattice.

28. Interatomic spacing of silicon (dimond lattice) is 2.35Å. Calculate the density (at. wt. = 28).
*Ans.* 2320 kg/m$^3$.

29. Calculate the atomic density in (100), (110) and (111) planes of copper (fcc) with the lattice parameter of 3.61Å. Can you pack atoms more closely than in (111) plane?
*Ans.* $1.53 \times 10^{19}$, $1.08 \times 10^{19}$ and $1.77 \times 10^{19}$ atoms/m$^2$.

- 30. Calculate the number of atoms per unit area in (100), (110) and (111) plane of a bcc crystal with the lattice parameter of 2.5Å.
*Ans.* $16.00 \times 10^{18}$, $22.63 \times 10^{18}$ and $9.24 \times 10^{18}$ atoms/m$^2$.

# APPENDIX 1

| Element | Symbol | Atomic number | Atomic weight (atomic units) | Density ($10^3$ kg/m$^3$) |
|---|---|---|---|---|
| Actinium | Ac | 89 | 227.0278 | — |
| Aluminium | Al | 13 | 26.98154 | 2.70 |
| Americium | Am | 95 | 243 | 11.7 |
| Antimony | Sb | 51 | 121.75 | 6.62 |
| Argon | Ar | 18 | 39.948 | — |
| Arsenic | As | 33 | 74.9216 | 5.72 |
| Astatine | At | 85 | 210 | — |
| Barium | Ba | 56 | 137.33 | 3.5 |
| Berkelium | Bk | 97 | 247 | — |
| Beryllium | Be | 4 | 9.01218 | 1.85 |
| Bismuth | Bi | 83 | 208.9804 | 9.80 |
| Boron | B | 5 | 10.81 | 2.34 |
| Bromine | Br | 35 | 79.904 | 3.12 |
| Cadmium | Cd | 48 | 112.41 | 8.65 |
| Calcium | Ca | 20 | 40.08 | 1.55 |
| Californium | Cf | 98 | 251 | — |
| Carbon | C | 12 | 12.011 | 2.25 (gr.) |
| Cerium | Ce | 58 | 140.12 | 2.25 |
| Cesium | Cs | 55 | 132.9054 | 1.90 |
| Chlorine | Cl | 17 | 35.453 | — |
| Chromium | Cr | 24 | 51.996 | 7.19 |
| Cobalt | Co | 27 | 58.9332 | 8.85 |
| Copper | Cu | 29 | 63.546 | 8.96 |
| Curium | Cm | 96 | 247 | — |
| Dysprosium | Dy | 66 | 162.50 | 8.55 |
| Eiensteinium | Es | 99 | 254 | — |
| Erbium | Er | 68 | 167.26 | 9.15 |
| Europium | Eu | 63 | 151.96 | 5.25 |
| Fermium | Fm | 100 | 257 | — |
| Fluorine | F | 9 | 18.99840 | — |
| Francium | Fr | 87 | 223 | — |
| Gadolinium | Gd | 64 | 157.25 | 7.86 |
| Gallium | Ga | 31 | 69.72 | 5.91 |
| Germanium | Ge | 32 | 72.59 | 5.32 |
| Gold | Au | 79 | 196.9665 | 19.32 |
| Hafnium | Hf | 72 | 178.49 | 13.09 |
| Helium | He | 2 | 4.00260 | — |
| Holmium | Ho | 67 | 164.9304 | 6.79 |
| Hydrogen | H | 1 | 1.0079 | — |
| Indium | In | 49 | 114.82 | 7.31 |
| Iodine | I | 53 | 126.9045 | 4.94 |
| Iridium | Ir | 77 | 192.22 | 22.5 |
| Iron | Fe | 26 | 55.847 | 7.87 |
| Krypton | Kr | 36 | 83.80 | — |
| Lanthanum | La | 57 | 138.9055 | 6.19 |

*(Contd.)*

| Element | Symbol | Atomic number | Atomic weight (atomic units) | Density ($10^3$ kg/m$^3$) |
|---|---|---|---|---|
| Lawrencium | Lw | 103 | 260 | — |
| Lead | Pb | 82 | 207.2 | 11.36 |
| Lithium | Li | 3 | 6.941 | 0.53 |
| Lutetium | Lu | 71 | 174.97 | 9.85 |
| Magnesium | Mg | 12 | 24.305 | 1.74 |
| Manganese | Mn | 25 | 54.9380 | 7.43 |
| Mendelevium | Md | 101 | 258 | — |
| Mercury | Hg | 80 | 200.59 | 13.55 |
| Molybdenum | Mo | 42 | 95.94 | 10.22 |
| Neodymium | Nd | 60 | 144.24 | 7.00 |
| Neon | Ne | 10 | 20.179 | — |
| Neptunium | Np | 93 | 237.0482 | — |
| Nickel | Ni | 28 | 58.70 | 8.90 |
| Niobium | Nb | 41 | 92.9064 | 8.57 |
| Nitrogen | N | 7 | 14.0067 | — |
| Nobelium | No | 102 | 259 | — |
| Osmium | Os | 76 | 190.2 | 22.57 |
| Oxygen | O | 8 | 15.9994 | — |
| Palladium | Pd | 46 | 106.4 | 12.02 |
| Phosphorous | P | 15 | 30.97376 | 1.83 |
| Platinum | Pt | 78 | 195.09 | 21.45 |
| Plutonium | Pu | 94 | 244 | 19.5 |
| Polonium | Po | 84 | 209 | — |
| Potassium | K | 19 | 39.0983 | 0.86 |
| Praseodymium | Pr | 59 | 140.9077 | 6.77 |
| Promethium | Pm | 61 | 145 | — |
| Protactinium | Pa | 91 | 231.0359 | 15.4 |
| Radium | Ra | 88 | 226.0254 | 5.0 |
| Radon | Rn | 86 | 222 | — |
| Rhenium | Re | 75 | 186.207 | 21.04 |
| Rhodium | Rh | 45 | 102.9055 | 12.44 |
| Rubidium | Rb | 37 | 85.4678 | 1.53 |
| Ruthenium | Ru | 44 | 101.07 | 12.2 |
| Samarium | Sm | 62 | 150.4 | 7.49 |
| Scandium | Sc | 21 | 44.9559 | 2.99 |
| Selenium | Se | 34 | 78.96 | 4.79 |
| Silicon | Si | 14 | 28.0855 | 2.33 |
| Silver | Ag | 47 | 107.868 | 10.49 |
| Sodium | Na | 11 | 22.98977 | 0.97 |
| Strontium | Sr | 38 | 87.62 | 2.60 |
| Sulfur | S | 16 | 32.06 | 2.07 |
| Tantalum | Ta | 73 | 180.9479 | 16.6 |
| Technitium | Tc | 43 | 97 | — |
| Tellurium | Te | 52 | 127.60 | 6.24 |
| Terbium | Tb | 65 | 158.9254 | 8.25 |
| Thallium | Tl | 81 | 204.37 | 11.85 |
| Thorium | Th | 90 | 232.0381 | 11.66 |

*(Contd.)*

| Element | Symbol | Atomic number | Atomic weight (atomic units) | Density $(10^3 \text{ kg/m}^3)$ |
|---|---|---|---|---|
| Thulium | Tm | 69 | 168.9342 | 9.31 |
| Tin | Sn | 50 | 118.69 | 7.30 |
| Titanium | Ti | 22 | 47.90 | 4.51 |
| Tungston | W | 74 | 183.85 | 19.3 |
| Uranium | U | 92 | 238 | 19.07 |
| Vanadium | V | 23 | 50.9414 | 6.1 |
| Xenon | Xe | 54 | 131.30 | — |
| Ytterbium | Yb | 70 | 173.04 | 4.47 |
| Yttrium | Y | 39 | 88.9059 | 4.47 |
| Zinc | Zn | 30 | 65.38 | 7.13 |
| Zirconium | Zr | 40 | 91.22 | 6.49 |

# Chapter 2

# Atomic Bonding

## 2.1 FORCES BETWEEN ATOMS

Matter can exist in solid state only because there are forces of interaction acting between the atoms when they are brought close to each other. For a solid to have stable structure, the forces of interaction between the atoms should be of two types: attractive, to prevent the atoms from moving away from each other, and repulsive, to prevent the atoms from merging.

In the previous chapter, we observed that the atoms in a crystalline solid are arranged in a well ordered manner. In this chapter, we shall discuss about the nature of forces which hold them together. For the purpose, let us consider the general situation of two identical atoms in their ground states with an infinite separation (having interaction potential energy equal to zero). Let the atoms consist of moving electrical charges and will either attract or repel each other when they are brought close together. As the atoms approach, the attractive forces increase and the potential energy increases in a negative sense (the energy of attraction is negative since the atoms do work of attraction). When they are at a separation of a few atomic diameters, repulsive forces begin to assert themselves (the repulsive energy is positive because external work must be done to bring two such atoms close together). This is short range in nature which prevents the crystal from collapsing indefinitely. Actually the attractive forces between the atoms bring them close together until the individual electron clouds begin to overlap and a strong repulsive force arises to comply with Pauli's Exclusion Principle. At a certain separation, called the equilibrium separation, $R_e$, at which the attractive and repulsive forces are equal, the two atoms are in a stable situation and have minimum potential energy. At the equilibrium position, the potential energy of either atom is given by

$U$ = Decrease in potential energy due to attraction + Increase in potential energy due to repulsion.

So, for a simple type of interatomic potential, it can be written as

$$U = -\frac{A}{R^n} + \frac{B}{R^m} \tag{1}$$

where $R$ is the distance between the nuclei of the two atoms: $A$, $B$, $m$ and $n$ are constants characteristics for the MX molecule. The force of interaction between the two atoms as a function of $R$ is given by

$$F = -\frac{dU}{dR} \tag{2}$$

or
$$F = -\frac{nA}{R^{n+1}} + \frac{mB}{R^{m+1}} \qquad (3)$$

Equations 1 and 3 can be represented graphically as shown in Fig. 2.1. At the equilibrium separation ($R = R_e$), the net force is zero. Therefore,

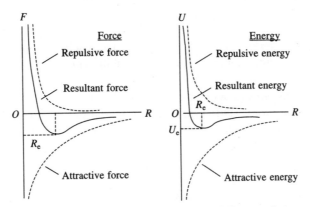

**Fig. 2.1   Force and potential energy as a function of distance between two atoms**

$$F = -\left(\frac{dU}{dR}\right)_{R=R_e} = 0$$

or
$$\frac{nA}{R_e^{n+1}} = \frac{mB}{R_e^{m+1}} \qquad (4)$$

$$(5)$$

so that

Substituting the value of $R_e$ from eq. 5 into eq. 1, the energy corresponding to the equilibrium state can be obtained as

$$U_e = U_{R=R_e} = -\frac{A}{R_e^n}\left(1 - \frac{n}{m}\right) \qquad (6)$$

The minimum value of energy $U_e$ is negative. A positive quantity $D = -U_e$ is the dissociation energy of the molecule, i.e. the energy required to separate the two atoms. Here, it is to be noted that although the attractive and repulsive forces are equal in equilibrium, the attractive and repulsive energies are not equal since $n \neq m$. In fact, if $m >> n$, the total binding energy is essentially determined by the energy of attraction. i.e. the first term in eq. 6.

Looking at Fig. 2.1, it is evident that a minimum in the energy curve is possible only if $m > n$. Consequently, the formation of a chemical bond requires that the repulsive force must be of shorter range than the attrative ones. This may be shown readily by employing the conditions that

$$\left(\frac{\partial^2 U}{\partial R^2}\right)_{R=R_e} > 0$$

if $U$ must have a minimum at $R_e$. This condition leads to

$$\frac{-n(n+1)A}{R_e^{n+2}} + \frac{m(m+1)B}{R_e^{m+2}} > 0$$

Substituting the value of $R_e$ from eq. 5, we obtain the condition

$$m > n \tag{7}$$

Although the energy in general cannot be represented accurately by a power function as in eq. 1, the above treatment provides some useful qualitative information which may be extended to solids.

The above discussion is quite general and does not take into account the detailed nature of the charge distribution in the atoms. Different charge distributions give rise to different types of bonding. They are conveniently divided into five classes, although the boundaries between them are not always distinct. They are: (i) ionic bonding, (ii) covalent bonding, (iii) metallic bonding, (iv) hydrogen bonding, (v) van der Waals bonding.

Based on the bond strength, atomic bondings can be grouped into primary and secondary bondings. Primary bondings have bond energies in the range of 0.1–10 eV/bond. Ionic, covalent and metallic bondings are examples of primary bondings. However, among these, ionic and covalent bondings are generally stronger than the metallic bonding. On the other hand, secondary bondings have energies in the range 0.01–0.5 eV/bond, one or two orders of magnitude smaller than those of primary bondings. Hydrogen bonding and van der Waals bonding are examples of secondary bondings. Generally, van der Waals bonding is the weakest of all. Let us now discuss them in some detail.

## 2.2  IONIC BONDING

An ionic bonding can only be formed between two different atoms, one electropositive and the other electronegative. Electropositive elements readily give up electrons and are usually Group I or II elements, e.g. Na, K and Ba, whereas electronegative elements readily take up electrons and are typically Group VI or VII elements, e.g. Cl, Br and O.

As an example of ionic bonding, consider a molecule of common salt, NaCl. When neutral atoms of Na and Cl are brought close together it is easy for the outer valence electron of the sodium atom to be transferred to the chlorine atom so that both of them acquire a stable inert-gas electronic configuration as shown in Fig. 2.2. Such configurations will have nearly

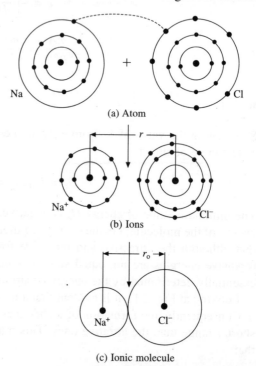

(a) Atom

(b) Ions

(c) Ionic molecule

**Fig. 2.2   Schematic representation of the formation of an ionic molecule of sodium chloride**

spherically symmetric charge distribution around the ions with some distortion near the region of contact between neighbouring atoms. This is confirmed by *X*-ray studies of electron distributions (Fig. 2.3)

**Fig. 2.3    Electron density distribution in base plane of sodium chloride, after *X*-ray studies by G. Schoknecht, Z. Naturforschg, 12, 983 (1957)**

Since the sodium cation carries a positive charge and the chlorine anion a negative charge there exists an electrostatic attraction between the two ions. However, it is incorrect to expect that sodium ions by ($Na^+$) and chlorine ions ($Cl^-$) would link up in pairs as shown, because then there would be a strong attractive force within the paired ions of a sodium chloride crystal while negligible attraction between the pairs. As a result, solid sodium chloride would not exist.

Actually, a negative charge attracts all positive charges in the neighbourhood, and vice versa. Consequently, in the crystalline solid $Na^+$ ions will be surrounded by $Cl^-$ ions and $Cl^-$ ions by $Na^+$ ions in such a way that the attraction between the neighbouring unlike charges exceeds the repulsion due to like charges. The resulting sodium chloride structure is shown in the Fig. 2.4.

## 2.3 BOND DISSOCIATION ENERGY OF NaCl MOLECULE

NaCl is considered to be the ideal representative of ionic compound. In order to calculate the bond dissociation energy corresponding to a single NaCl molecule, let us begin with the consideration that the sodium and chlorine atoms are initially free when they are at infinite distance of separation. The energy required to remove the outer electron from the Na atom is equal to its ionization potential. When this energy is absorbed by the sodium atom, it gets ionized and a positively charged $Na^+$ ion is formed. The ionization process of a Na atom is represented by the reaction

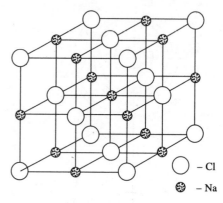

$$Na(g) + I.P. \text{ (energy)} \rightarrow Na^+(g) + \bar{e}(g)$$

Similarly, when an electron is taken from infinity and added it to a neutral chlorine atom to form a negatively charged chlorine ion, an energy

**Fig. 2.4  Sodium chloride crystal structure**

equivalent to its electron affinity is released. The formation of chlorine ion is given by the reaction

$$Cl(g) + \bar{e}(g) \rightarrow Cl^-(g) + E.A. \text{ (energy)}$$

The net amount of energy absorbed (spent) in the process of formation of positive sodium ion and a negative chlorine ion at infinity is thus given by

$$\Delta E = I.P. - E.A.$$

Combining the above two reactions, we have

$$Na(g) + Cl(g) + \Delta E \rightarrow Na^+(g) + Cl^-(g)$$

In the above reactions, the ions are infinitely separated, but now let, the Coulomb attraction between them bring the two ions closer together so that an ion-pair is formed. When the two ions are at an equilibrium separation, a stable NaCl molecule is formed. In the process, an energy equal to the potential energy is released at equilibrium separation, i.e.

$$U_e = -\frac{e^2}{4\pi\varepsilon_0 R_e}$$

where $\varepsilon_0$ is the absolute permittivity of free space and air. Its numerical value is given by

$$\varepsilon_0 = 8.854 \times 10^{-12} \, C^2 N^{-1} m^{-2}, \text{ and } \frac{1}{4\pi\varepsilon_0} = 9 \times 10^9 \, Nm^2 C^{-2}$$

Since, the entire process (starting from neutral Na and Cl atoms till the formation of NaCl molecule) consists of three steps: (i) removal of an electron from Na atom (first ionization energy), (ii) the addition of an electron to the Cl atom (electron affinity of Cl), and (iii) the

Coulomb attraction between the two molecules, the net energy released is equal to the bond dissociation energy and is given by

$$D.E. = U_e + I.P - E.A.$$

This is the amount of energy required to dissociate one NaCl molecule into $Na^+$ and $Cl^-$ions.

*Example*: Given the following data, determine whether a gaseous molecule $A^+ B^-$ will be stable with respect to the separated $A$ and $B$ gaseous atoms:

First ionization energy of $A$          = 502 kJ/mol

Electron affinity for $B$ atom          = 335 kJ/mol

Interionic $(A^+ - B^-)$ separation          = 3 Å = $3 \times 10^{-10}$m

*Solution :* Making use of the potential energy expression and substituting the values of constants, we have

$$U_e = -\frac{e^2}{4\pi\varepsilon_0 R_e} = -\frac{(1.6 \times 10^{-19})^2 \times 9 \times 10^9}{3 \times 10^{-10}}$$

$$= -7.673 \times 10^{-19} \text{ J/ion pair}$$

$$= -7.673 \times 10^{-19} \times 6.023 \times 10^{-23} \text{ kJ/mol}$$

$$= -463 \text{ kJ/mol}.$$

From above consideration, the bond dissociation energy is given by

$$D.E. = U_e + I.P. - E. A. = -463 + 502 - 335$$

$$= -296 \text{ kJ/mol}.$$

Since the bond dissociation energy is negative, the molecule $A^+B^-$ will be stable.

## 2.4 COHESIVE ENERGY OF IONIC CRYSTALS

The cohesive energy of ionic crystals is mainly due to electrostatic interaction and can be calculated on the basis of point charge model. This is possible, if we assume that there is a complete transfer of the outer valence electrons (from the metal atom to the halogen atom in the alkali halides), the resulting ions then will have spherically symmetric charge distribution which in turn can be treated as a point charge lying at the center of the distribution. Following Born, the cohesive energy $(U)$ of a crystal containing oppositely charged ions with charges $Z_1$ and $Z_2$ is written as the sum of two terms, one due to attraction and the other due to repulsion:

$$U = -\frac{AZ_1Z_2e^2}{4\pi\varepsilon_0 R} + B\exp\left(-\frac{R}{\rho}\right) \qquad (8)$$

Here, $A$, is known as the Madelung constant and depends only on geometrical arrangement of ions in the crystal (i.e. the crystal structure); $B$ is the repulsion constant, $\rho$ is the repulsion exponent and $R$ is the distance between the two oppositely charged ions. The repulsion term in eq. 8 accounts for the stability of ionic crystals without collapsing and arises from the fact that the ions with closed electron shells resist overlap of their electron clouds with neighbouring ions. The constants $B$ and $\rho$ are respectively a measure of the strength and the range of repulsive interaction.

For a uni-univalent crystal like NaCl ($Z_1 = Z_2 = 1$), eq. 8 becomes

$$U = -\frac{Ae^2}{4\pi\varepsilon_0 R} + B\exp\left(-\frac{R}{\rho}\right) \tag{9}$$

and the total energy per kmol of the crystal is

$$U = N\left[-\frac{Ae^2}{4\pi\varepsilon_0 R} + B\exp\left(-\frac{R}{\rho}\right)\right] \tag{10}$$

where $N$ ($= 6.023 \times 10^{26}$) is the Avogadro's number. The repulsion constant $B$ can be evaluated from the fact that the potential energy $U$ is minimum at the equilibrium separation $R_e$ between the oppositely charged ions. Therefore,

$$\left(\frac{dU}{dR}\right)_{R=R_e} = N\left[\frac{Ae^2}{4\pi\varepsilon_0 R_e^2} - \frac{B}{\rho}\exp\left(-\frac{R_e}{\rho}\right)\right] = 0,$$

or

$$\frac{B}{\rho}\exp\left(-\frac{R_e}{\rho}\right) = \frac{Ae^2}{4\pi\varepsilon_0 R_e^2}$$

so that from eq. 10, the potential energy at equilibrium separation is given by

$$U_e = -\frac{Ae^2 N}{4\pi\varepsilon_0 R_e}\left(1 - \frac{\rho}{R_e}\right) \tag{11}$$

Equation 11 gives us the cohesive energy (also called lattice energy) of an ionic solid like NaCl, first derived by Born and Mayer. This is the amount of energy released during the formation of NaCl crystal or the energy spent to separate the solid ionic crystal into its constituent ions. If $A$ and $\rho$ are known, the cohesive energy of ionic solids can be directly calculated using this equation. The value of $\rho/R_e$ for the alkali halides can be obtained experimentally from compressibility measurement of the crystal as follows: The bulk modulus of a solid is obtained as

$$\beta = -V\left(\frac{dP}{dV}\right)$$

where $V$ is the volume and $P$ is the pressure. The compressibility is defined as the reciprocal of the bulk modulus, i.e.

$$\frac{1}{K} = \beta = -V\left(\frac{dP}{dV}\right) \tag{12}$$

From the first law of thermodynamics, we know that $dQ = dU + dW$. Near absolute zero, $dQ = 0$, so that we have $dU + PdV = 0$. This gives us

$$\frac{dU}{dV} = -P \text{ and } \left(\frac{d^2U}{dV^2}\right) = -\left(\frac{dP}{dV}\right) \tag{13}$$

From eqs. 12 and 13, the compressibility at *OK* becomes

$$\frac{1}{K_0} = V_e \left( \frac{d^2 U}{dV^2} \right) \tag{14}$$

where $V_e$ is the volume of the crystal corresponding to the equilibrium separation $R_e$. For sodium chloride structure, the nearest neighbour distance is

$$R = R_{Cl} + R_{Na} = \frac{a}{2}, \text{ and the volume per molecule is } \frac{a^3}{4}$$

Therefore, the volume of a kmol of the solid is

$$V = \frac{a^3}{4} N = \frac{N}{4} (2R)^3 = 2NR^3$$

or

$$\frac{dV}{dR} = 6NR^2 \quad \text{or} \quad \frac{dR}{dV} = \frac{1}{6NR^2} \tag{15}$$

Now $\dfrac{dU}{dV}$ can be written as

$$\left( \frac{dU}{dV} \right) = \left( \frac{dU}{dR} \right) \cdot \left( \frac{dR}{dV} \right)$$

or

$$\frac{d}{dV} \left( \frac{dU}{dV} \right) = \left( \frac{dU}{dR} \right) \cdot \frac{d}{dV} \left( \frac{dR}{dV} \right) + \left( \frac{dR}{dV} \right) \cdot \frac{d}{dV} \left( \frac{dU}{dR} \right)$$

or

$$\left( \frac{d^2 U}{dV^2} \right) = \left( \frac{dU}{dR} \right) \cdot \left( \frac{d^2 R}{dV^2} \right) + \left( \frac{dR}{dV} \right) \frac{d}{dR} \left( \frac{dU}{dR} \right) \cdot \left( \frac{dR}{dV} \right)$$

or

$$\left( \frac{d^2 U}{dV^2} \right) = \left( \frac{dU}{dR} \right) \cdot \left( \frac{d^2 R}{dV^2} \right) + \left( \frac{dR}{dV} \right)^2 \cdot \left( \frac{d^2 U}{dR^2} \right) \tag{16}$$

At equilibrium separation $R = R_e$, $U$ is minimum and hence

$$\left( \frac{dU}{dR} \right) = 0 \text{ and } V = V_e = 2NR_e^3$$

Thus eq. 16 becomes

$$\left( \frac{d^2 U}{dV^2} \right) = \left( \frac{dR}{dV} \right)^2 \cdot \left( \frac{d^2 U}{dR^2} \right)$$

and making use of eq. 15, eq. 14 becomes

$$\frac{1}{K_0} = 2NR_e^3 \left( \frac{dR}{dV} \right)^2 \cdot \left( \frac{d^2 U}{dR^2} \right)$$

$$= \frac{2R_e^3}{36NR_e^4}\left(\frac{d^2U}{dR^2}\right) = \frac{1}{18NR_e}\left(\frac{d^2U}{dR^2}\right) \tag{17}$$

Further, differentiating eq. 10 twice, and setting $R = R_e$ we have

$$\left(\frac{d^2U}{dR^2}\right) = \frac{Ae^2N}{R_e^3}\left(\frac{R_e}{\rho} - 2\right)$$

Thus eq. 17 becomes

$$\frac{1}{K_0} = \beta = \frac{Ae^2}{18R_e^4}\left(\frac{R_e}{\rho} - 2\right)$$

and hence

$$\frac{R_e}{\rho} = \frac{18R_e^4\beta}{Ae^2} + 2 \tag{18}$$

For alkali halide crystals, the ratio $\rho/R_e$ is found to lie between 0.09 and 0.12. The low value of $\rho/R_e$ means that the repulsive interaction is steep and has a very short range.

For NaCl, $\beta = 2.4 \times 10^{10}$ N/m$^2$ and $R_e = 2.282$ Å, the ratio $R_e/\rho$ can be calculated using eq. 18, i.e.

$$\frac{R_e}{\rho} = \frac{18R_e^4\beta}{Ae^2} + 2 \cong 8.78 \quad \text{or} \quad \rho \cong 0.32 \text{ Å}$$

However, a value of $\rho = 0.345$Å fits quite well for all 20 alkali halides in cohesive energy calculation.

*Example*: Show that 1 eV is approximately equal to 23 kcal/mol.

*Solution*: As we know that the value of the electronic charge is given by $e = 1.6 \times 10^{-19}$C. Therefore

$$1 \text{ eV} = 1.6 \times 10^{-19}\text{CV} = 1.6 \times 10^{-19}\text{J}$$

Further, we know that the above value of electron-volt is per particle, which may be an atom, molecule, ion, etc. Therefore

$$1 \text{ eV per mole} = 1.6 \times 10^{-19} \times 6.023 \times 10^{23}\text{J}$$

$$= 9.635 \times 10^4\text{J}$$

$$= \frac{9.635 \times 10^4}{4.184 \times 10^3} \text{ kcal} = 23.029 \text{ kcal/mol}$$

In the earlier calculations for cohesive energy of ionic solids, the repulsion energy was assumed to vary as an inverse power of the distance between the ions, $(B/R^n)$. Like $\rho/R_e$ the value of repulsive exponent $n$ can be obtained from compressibility measurement of the crystal. Thus making use of eq. 14 and proceeding as above, we can obtain.

$$n = 1 + \frac{72\pi\varepsilon_0 R_e^4}{K_0 A e^2} \qquad (19)$$

Hence, the cohesive energy $U$ becomes

$$U = -\frac{NAe^2}{4\pi\varepsilon_0 R_e}\left(1 - \frac{1}{n}\right) \qquad (20)$$

where $N$ is the Avogadro's number.

The value of $B$ and $U$ can be obtained if $n$ is known. Pauling (1960) suggested different values of $n$ for various closed shell electronic configurations and are given in Table 2.1. The value of $n$ for an alkali halide crystal is taken as the average between the values for the two ions. For example, $n$ for NaCl according to this method is 8. However, except for the crystal containing very light ions the value of $n \cong 9$ is common.

**Table 2.1  Values of the Born exponent for various ion types**

| Ion type | $n$ |
|----------|-----|
| He | 5 |
| Ne | 7 |
| Ar | 9 |
| Kr | 10 |
| Xe | 12 |

The cohesive energy expression (eq. 11) refers to a static crystal and does not include the contributions from van der Waals forces (which are responsible for the binding in the crystalline inert gases) and the correction for zero-point energy. These are, actually minor terms accounting for a small percentage of the total lattice energy and are normally ignored. However, for an accurate calculation, the modified expression for the lattice energy of MX-type solids incorporating all the four terms is given as

$$U_c = \left[ -\frac{Ae^2}{4\pi\varepsilon_0 R_e} + B\exp\left(-\frac{R_e}{\rho}\right) - \left(\frac{C}{R_e^6} + \frac{D}{R_e^8}\right) + \frac{9}{4}h\nu_{max} \right] \qquad (21)$$

where the terms on the right hand side represent respectively the Madelung energy, the repulsion energy, the van der Waals contribution and the zero-point correction, $\nu_{max}$ being the highest frequency of the lattice vibrational mode. In the van der Waals term, the $R_e^{-6}$ and $R_e^{-8}$ terms represent dipoledipole and dipole-quadrupole interactions respectively (quadrupole-quadrupole term can be neglected). Cohesive energies of ionic solids have been extensively reviewed in literature (Tosi, 1964). Cohesive energies of the alkali halide crystals computed from eqs. 11 and 21, the experimentally observed values and other parameters are given in Table 2.2. The agreement between the experimental and theoretical values of lattice energies is good, thereby lending suport to the ionic model for alkali halides and other similar solids. The ionic model, is, however, a poor approximation for crystals containing large anions and small cations, where the covalent contribution to the bonding becomes significant.

Cohesive energy of an ionic crystal can also be determined with the help of Kapustinskii

**Table 2.2   Cohesive energy and other parameters**

| Compounds | $R_e$ in Å | Bulk modulus (K) in $10^{10}$ N/m$^2$ | (n) | Cohesive energy in (kJ/kmol) $\times 10^3$ Exp. | Cohesive energy in (kJ/kmol) $\times 10^3$ Calculated | (M.P.) in °C |
|---|---|---|---|---|---|---|
| NaCl | 2.820 | 2.40 | 8.0 | 788 | 747 | 800 |
| NaBr | 2.989 | 1.99 | 8.5 | 736 | 708 | 742 |
| NaI | 3.237 | 1.51 | 9.5 | 673 | 655 | 662 |
| NaF | 2.317 | 4.65 | 7.0 | 923 | 900 | 992 |
| KCl | 3.147 | 1.74 | 9.0 | 717 | 676 | 770 |
| KBr | 3.298 | 1.48 | 9.5 | 673 | 646 | 742 |
| KI | 3.533 | 1.17 | 10.5 | 617 | 605 | 682 |
| KF | 2.674 | 3.05 | 8.0 | 820 | 791 | 857 |
| LiCl | 2.570 | 2.98 | 7.0 | 862 | 807 | 614 |
| LiBr | 2.751 | 2.38 | 7.5 | 803 | 757 | 552 |
| LiI | 3.000 | 1.71 | 8.5 | 732 | 695 | 440 |
| LiF | 2.014 | 6.71 | 6.0 | 1038 | 1031 | 870 |
| RbCl | 3.291 | 1.56 | 9.5 | 687 | 650 | 717 |
| RbBr | 3.445 | 1.30 | 10.0 | 636 | 636 | 677 |
| RbI | 3.671 | 1.06 | 11.0 | 597 | 626 | 628 |
| RbF | 2.815 | 2.62 | 8.5 | 761 | 767 | 833 |

equation. This is particularly useful because it can be used even if the crystal structure is not known. Kapustinskii noted an empirical increase in the value of Madelung constant, $A$, as the coordination number of the ions in the molecular formula of the compound, e.g. in the series ZnS, NaCl, CsCl (Table 2.3). Any deviation in this rule is compensated by a consequent change in the value of $R_e$ for two given ions when they change their lattice symmetry. Thus one can use a standard $R_e$ (the sum of the ionic radii for the cation and anion) and the reduced Madelung constant proposed by Kapustinskii ($A$ divided by the number of ions in the formula) to calculate the lattice energy of an ionic crystal to a good approximation, no matter what its geometry may be.

**Table 2.3   Madelung constants**

| Structure | Madelung constant |
|---|---|
| Sodium Chloride | 1.74756 |
| Cesium Chloride | 1.76267 |
| Fluorite | 2.51939 |
| Zinc blende | 1.63805 |
| Wurtzite | 1.64132 |

Kapustinskii collected the reduced Madelung constant, the length conversion factor, and the energy conversion factor into a simple form of the lattice energy equation:

$$U = \frac{287.2 v Z_c Z_a}{r_c + r_a}\left(1 - \frac{0.345}{r_c + r_a}\right) \text{kcal/mol} \qquad (22)$$

where $Z_c$ is the charge on cation in multiples of electronic charge, $Z_a$ is the charge on anion in the same unit, $r_c$ and $r_a$ are the ionic radii of the cation and anion in angstrom units and $v$ is the number of ions (not atoms) in the molecules. For example, ammonium perchlorate $NH_4\,ClO_4$ has 10 atoms but only two ions. So $v$ will be equal to 2 in this case.

*Example*: Assume that the potential energy of two particles in the field of each other is given by

$$U(R) = -\frac{A}{R} + \frac{B}{R^9}$$

where $A$ and $B$ are constants.

(a) Show that the particles form a stable compound for

$$R = R_c = \left(\frac{9B}{A}\right)^{1/8}$$

(b) Show that for stable configuration, the energy of attraction is nine times the energy of repulsion.

(c) Show that the potential energy of the system under stable configuration is

$$\frac{8A}{9R_e}$$

*Solution:* (a) Since we know that the potential energy $U\,(R = R_e)$ is minimum, therefore differentiating the given potential energy and setting it equal to zero, we have

$$\left(\frac{dU}{dR}\right)_{R=R_e} = \frac{A}{R_e^2} - \frac{9B}{R_e^{10}} = 0$$

This gives us

$$R_e = \left(\frac{9B}{A}\right)^{1/8} \tag{a}$$

(b) For stable configuration,

the attraction energy, $\qquad\qquad \phi_a = \dfrac{A}{R_e}$

and the repulsive energy, $\qquad\qquad \phi_r = \dfrac{B}{R_e^9}$

Thus $\qquad\qquad\qquad\qquad \dfrac{\phi_a}{\phi_r} = \dfrac{A}{B} \times R_e^8$

Substituting the value of $R_e$ from eq. (a) we get

$$\phi_a = 9\phi_r \tag{b}$$

(c) For stable configuration, the potential energy expression becomes

$$U_{min} = -\frac{A}{R_e} + \frac{B}{R_e^9}$$

Substituting the value of $B$ from eq. (a) and then simplifying, we get

$$U_{min} = -\frac{8A}{9R_e}$$

*Example*: Calculate the potential energy of the system of $Na^+$ and $Cl^-$ ions when they are at a distance of 2Å.

*Solution*: Given: $R_e = 2\text{Å} = 2 \times 10^{-10}$m. Since we know that at equilibrium distance, the potential energy is minimum and for one NaCl molecule it is given by

$$U = -\frac{e^2}{4\pi\varepsilon_0 R_e} \text{ in joules} = -\frac{e}{4\pi\varepsilon_0 R_e} \text{ in eV}$$

Substituting different values, we get

$$U = -\frac{1.6 \times 10^{-19} \times 9 \times 10^9}{2 \times 10^{-10}} = -7.2\text{eV}$$

*Example*: (a) Calculate the compressibility of NaCl crystal assuming the repulsive potential of the type $B/R^9$, the equilibrium separation $R_e = 2.81\text{Å}$, the Madelung constant $A = 1.7496$.

    (b) Also calculate the cohesive energy per atom (ion) if the ionization potential of the sodium is 5.14 eV and electron affinity of chlorine is 3.61 eV.

*Solution*: Given: $R_e = 2.81\text{Å} = 2.81 \times 10^{-10}$m, $A = 1.7476$, and $n = 9$. (a) From eq. 19, the expression for compressibility can be written as

$$K_0 = \frac{72\pi\varepsilon_0 R_e^4}{(n-1)Ae^2} = \frac{18 \times 4\pi\varepsilon_0 R_e^4}{(n-1)Ae^2}$$

Substituting different values, we obtain

$$K_0 = \frac{18 \times (2.81 \times 10^{-10})^4}{8 \times 1.7476 \times 9 \times 10^9 \times (1.6 \times 10^{-19})^2} = 3.48 \times 10^{-11} \text{ m}^2 \text{ N}.$$

(b) Given: I.P. (of Na) = 5.14 eV, E.A. (of chlorine) = 3.61 eV. As we know that the equilibrium potential energy per ion-pair is given by

$$U = -\frac{Ae^2}{4\pi\varepsilon_0 R_e}\left(1 - \frac{1}{n}\right) \text{ in Joules} = -\frac{Ae}{4\pi\varepsilon_0 R_e}\left(1 - \frac{1}{n}\right) \text{ in eV}$$

$$= -\frac{8 \times 1.7476 \times 1.6 \times 10^{-19} \times 9 \times 10^9}{9 \times 2.81 \times 10^{-10}} = -7.96\,\text{eV}$$

Hence, the potential energy per ion = $-3.98\text{eV}$. Further, the energy required to produce the ion-pair is

$$\Delta E = \text{I.P.} - \text{E.A.} = 5.14 - 3.61 = 1.53 \text{ eV}$$

and the contribution per ion (1.53)/2 = 0.76 eV. Hence, the cohesive energy per ion (atom) is

$$-3.98 + 0.76 = -3.22 \text{ eV}$$

*Example*: The potential energy of a diatomic molecule in terms of the interatomic separation $R$ is given by

$$U(R) = -\frac{A}{R^2} + \frac{B}{R^{10}}$$

where $A = 1.44 \times 10^{-39}$ Jm$^2$ and $B = 2.19 \times 10^{-115}$ Jm$^{10}$. Calculate the equilibrium spacing $R_e$ and the dissociation energy.

*Solution*: Given: $A = 1.44 \times 10^{-39}$ Jm$^2$, $B = 2.19 \times 10^{-115}$ Jm$^{10}$, the exponents $n = 2$ and $m = 10$.

We know that the potential energy $U(R = R_e)$ is minimum, therefore differentiating the given potential energy equation and setting it equal to zero, we have

$$\left(\frac{dU}{dR}\right)_{R=R_e} = \frac{2A}{R_e^3} - \frac{10B}{R_e^{11}} = 0$$

This gives us $R_e = \left(\dfrac{5B}{A}\right)^{1/8} = \left(\dfrac{5 \times 2.19 \times 10^{-115}}{1.44 \times 10^{-39}}\right)^{1/8} = 4.08 \times 10^{-10}$ m

Now, making use of the eq. 6, the dissociation energy can be obtained as

$$D = \frac{A}{R_e^2}\left(1 - \frac{n}{m}\right) = \frac{4A}{5R_e^2} = \frac{4 \times 1.44 \times 10^{-39}}{5 \times (4.08 \times 10^{-10})^2} \text{ in Joules}$$

$$= \frac{4 \times 4.144 \times 10^{-39}}{5 \times (4.08 \times 10^{-10})^2 \times 1.6 \times 10^{-19}} \text{ in eV} = 4.33 \times 10^{-2} \text{ eV}$$

*Example*: The potential energy of a diatomic molecule in terms of the interatomic separation $R$ is given by

$$U(R) = -\frac{A}{R^2} + \frac{B}{R^{10}}$$

Calculate the value of constants $A$ and $B$ when the equilibrium spacing $R_e = 3$Å and the dissociation energy is 4 eV. Also calculate the force required to break the molecule and the critical separation between the nuclei.

*Solution:* Given: $R_e = 3$Å $= 3 \times 10^{-10}$m, $D = -U_e = 4$ eV $= 4 \times 1.6 \times 10^{-19}$J, $n = 2$, $m = 10$. Substituting the values of $m$ and $n$ in eq. 6 and solving for $A$, we obtain

$$A = \frac{5R_e^2 \times D}{4} = \frac{5 \times (3 \times 10^{-10})^2 \times 4 \times 1.6 \times 10^{-19}}{4} = 7.2 \times 10^{-38} \text{ Jm}^2$$

Further, we know that at equilibrium separation, the net force is zero, i.e.

$$F = -\left(\frac{dU}{dR}\right)_{R=R_e} = -\frac{2A}{R_e^3} + \frac{10B}{R_e^{11}} = 0$$

This gives

$$B = \frac{A \times (R_e)^8}{5} = \frac{7.2 \times 10^{-38} \times (3 \times 10^{-10})^8}{5} = 9.44 \times 10^{-115} \text{ Jm}^{10}$$

Further, we know that $F(R) = -\dfrac{dU}{dR} = 0$ will be minimum or maximum when $\dfrac{dF}{dR} = 0$, and $R = R_c$ (called the critical separation). Thus,

$$\frac{dF}{dR} = \frac{d^2U}{dR^2} = +\frac{6A}{R_c^4} - \frac{110B}{R_c^{12}} = 0$$

Substituting the value of $B/A$ from above and simplifying this, we have

$$R_c = \left(\frac{22}{6}\right)^{1/8} \times R_e = \left(\frac{22}{6}\right)^{1/8} \times 3 \times 10^{-10} = 3.53 \text{ Å}$$

Now, $F(R) = -\dfrac{dU}{dR} = -\dfrac{2A}{R^3} + \dfrac{10B}{R^{11}}$ is minimum when $R = R_c$, therefore

$$F_{min} = -\frac{2A}{R_c^3} + \frac{10B}{R_c^{11}} = -\frac{2A}{R_c^3}\left(1 - \frac{10B}{2AR_c^8}\right)$$

Substituting the value of $(B/A) = (R_e^8)/5$, the above eq. becomes

$$F_{min} = -\frac{2A}{R_c^3}\left[1 - \left(\frac{R_e}{R_c}\right)^8\right]$$

Further, substituting the values of $A$, $R_c$ and $R_e$, we have

$$F_{min} = -\frac{2 \times 7.2 \times 10^{-38}}{(3.53 \times 10^{-10})^3}\left[1 - \left(\frac{3}{3.53}\right)^8\right] = -0.238 \times 10^{-8} \text{ J/m} = -0.238 \times 10^{-8} \text{ N}$$

This is the force needed to dissociate the molecule.

*Example*: (a) How much energy is required to form a $K^+$ and $Cl^-$ ion pair from a pair of K and Cl atoms? (b) What must be the separation between $K^+$ and $Cl^-$ ion pair if their total energy is to be zero? Given: ionization energy of K = 4.1 eV and the electron affinity of Cl is 3.6 eV.

*Solution*: Given: I.P. (of K) = 4.1 eV, E.A. (of Cl) = 3.6 eV. We know that the net energy required to produce the ion pair is

$$\Delta E = \text{I.P.} - \text{E.A.} = 4.1 - 3.6 = 0.5 \text{ eV}$$

Now, if their total energy is to be zero, $\Delta E = E_c$, the Coulomb energy.
Therefore,

$$E_c = 0.5 = -\frac{e^2}{4\pi\varepsilon_0 R} \text{ in joules} = -\frac{e}{4\pi\varepsilon_0 R} \text{ in eV}$$

Therefore,

$$R = -\frac{e}{4\pi\varepsilon_0 \times 0.5} = \frac{1.6 \times 10^{-19} \times 9 \times 10^9}{0.5} = 28.8 \times 10^{-10} \text{ m} = 28.8 \text{ Å}$$

*Example*: In an *MX* molecule, suppose *M* atom has an ionization potential energy 5 eV and *X* atom has an electron affinity of 4 eV. What is the energy required to transfer an electron from *M* to *X* when they are at a distance of 5Å?

*Solution*: Given: $R = 5$Å $= 5 \times 10^{-10}$m, I.P. (of *M*) = 5 eV, E.A. (of *X*) = 4 eV. The potential energy of *MX* system is

$$U = -\frac{e^2}{4\pi\varepsilon_0 R_e} \text{ in joules} = -\frac{e}{4\pi\varepsilon_0 R_e} \text{ in eV}$$

Substituting different values, we get

$$U = -\frac{1.6 \times 10^{-19} \times 9 \times 10^9}{5 \times 10^{-10}} = -2.88 \text{ eV}$$

Now the energy required to transfer an electron from *M* to *X* atom is

$$E_r = \Delta E + U = \text{I.P.} - \text{E.A.} + U = 5 - 4 - 2.88 = -1.88 \text{ eV}.$$

## 2.5 EVALUATION OF MADELUNG CONSTANT FOR NaCl STRUCTURE

The Madelung constant, *A* is a function of crystal structure and can therefore be calculated from the geometrical arrangement of ions in the crystal. Fig. 2.5 shows the equilibrium positions of ions in NaCl structure. In this diagram, let us consider a central $Na^+$ ion as the reference ion having a single positive charge on it. This ion is surrounded by 6 $Cl^-$ ions as first nearest neighbours, 12 $Na^+$ ions as second nearest neighbours, 8 $Cl^-$ ions as third nearest neighbours and so on. Calculations of distance between the ions are made in terms of the equilibrium separation and are straight forward (Fig. 2.6). Thus, the Madelung constant for the NaCl structure can be written as a summation series.

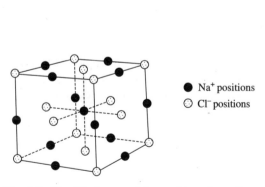

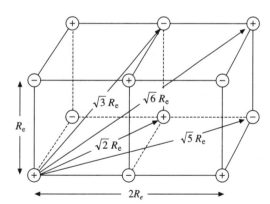

**Fig. 2.5 Equilibrium positions of ions in sodium chloride crystal**

**Fig. 2.6 Distances of neighbouring ions in the NaCl lattice**

$$A = \frac{6}{1} - \frac{12}{\sqrt{2}} + \frac{8}{\sqrt{3}} - \frac{6}{\sqrt{4}} + \frac{24}{\sqrt{5}} - \frac{24}{\sqrt{6}} + \dots \tag{23}$$

which converges to a value of 1.74756. The series is, however, only conditionally convergent because the summation can be stopped at any finite point. The value obtained at finite point is characteristic of a finite crystal. The value of $A$ quoted above for NaCl structure is obtained for nearly infinite crystals. Madelung constants of some typical ionic crystals are given in Table 2.3.

*Example*: Calculate the Madelung constant for an infinite linear chain of ions of alternating unit charge (i.e. one dimensional NaCl crystal) at a separation $R_e$.

*Solution*: Consider one dimensional chain of ions shown in Fig. 2.7. Let us take sodium ion as the reference ion and then following the above procedure, we can immediately write

$$A = 2\left(\frac{1}{1} - \frac{1}{2} + \frac{1}{3} - \frac{1}{4} + \ldots\right)$$

Making use of the series

$$\ln(1 + x) = x - \frac{x^2}{2} + \frac{x^3}{3} - \frac{x^4}{4} + \ldots$$

it follows that
$$A = 2 \ln 2$$

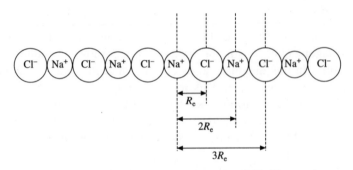

**Fig. 2.7   Geometry of a one dimensional NaCl crystal**

## 2.6   MADELUNG POTENTIAL

The electrostatic (Madelung) part of the lattice energy (MAPLE) has been employed to define Madelung potentials of ions in crystals (Hope, 1975). MAPLE of an ionic solid is regarded as the sum of contributions of cations and anions; the Madelung constant, $A$, of a crystal would then be the sum of partial Madelung constants of cation anion subarrays.
Thus,

$$A(\text{NaCl}) = A_c(\text{Na}^+) + A_a(\text{Cl}^-)$$

$$1.74756 = 1 \times 0.87378 + 1 \times 0.87378$$

$$A(\text{CaF}_2) = A_c(\text{Ca}^{2+}) + 2 A_a(\text{F}^-)$$

$$5.03878 = 3.27612 + 2 \times 0.88133$$

where $A_c$ and $A_a$ are the partial Madelung constants of cation and anion subarrays, respectively. Madelung potentials are nearly independent of the crystal structure and MAPLE values for the different polymorphic modifications of a given composition differ only by about 1%. Calculation based on the ionic model indeed predict wrong structures in certain cases; for example, LiF was predicted to have wurtzite structure instead of the rock salt structure.

## 2.7 THE BORN-HABER CYCLE

The lattice energy which we have discussed above is the amount of work which must be done to disperse a crystal into an assemblage of widely separated ions. As such it cannot be immediately compared with any readily measurable quantity, and, in particular, is not to be identified either with heat of sublimation (except for hydrogen-bonded materials), which is the energy necessary to disperse the crystal into a molecular gas, or with the chemical heat of formation, which is the energy released when the crystal is formed from metal atoms and diatomic halogen molecules. In some cases, lattice energies have been measured directly (see Table 2.2), however, in majority of the cases an indirect estimate can be made in terms of a cyclic process known as Born-Haber cycle and is represented in Fig. 2.8 for NaCl. The formation of NaCl molecule from its constituent atoms can be regarded as a result of many step process, where in each step energy is either absorbed or released. In the following, the energy absorptions are taken as positive and energy release as negative. The cycle may be summarised as follows:

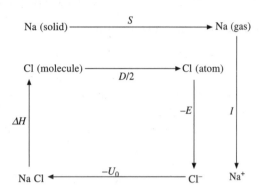

**Fig. 2.8   The Born-Haber cycle applied to sodium chloride**

(i)   In the first stage, the solid sodium and the chlorine molecules are dissociated into constituent atoms. The solid sodium is vaporized by supplying an energy equal to its sublimation energy ($S$), while chlorine molecule is dissociated by supplying an energy equal to the dissociation energy ($D$), where $D/2$ is the energy per chlorine atom.

(ii)  In the second stage, the gaseous sodium and chlorine atoms are ionized. This requires an ionization energy ($I$) to remove the outer-most electron from a Na atom. When this energy is added to a Cl atom, an energy ($E$) equivalent to its electron affinity is released.

(iii) In the third stage, the two ions ($Na^+$ and $Cl^-$) are allowed to arrange in the lattice. In the process, the lattice energy ($U_0$) is released.

(iv)  In the fourth stage, we come back to the starting point by breaking the lattice into solid sodium and chlorine molecules by supplying an energy $\Delta H$, known as heat of dissociation. The cycle is perfectly reversible.

Since according to the laws of thermodynamics, the total internal energy change during a cyclic operation must be zero, therefore from the above steps we have

$$S + \frac{D}{2} + I - E - U_0 + \Delta H = 0$$

so that

$$U_0 = S + \frac{D}{2} + I - E + \Delta H \qquad (24)$$

In eq. 24, all quantities on the right hand side are experimentally determinable, hence the lattice energy $U_0$ can be calculated. For solid sodium chloride, the values of various quantities experimentally found are:

$$S = 108.8 \times 10^3 \text{ kJ/kmol}$$

$$D = 242.8 \times 10^3 \text{ kJ/kmol}$$

$$I = 494.0 \times 10^3 \text{ kJ/kmol}$$

$$E = 364.2 \times 10^3 \text{ kJ/kmol}$$

$$\Delta H = 410.2 \times 10^3 \text{ kJ/kmol}$$

Substituting the above mentioned numerical values in eq. 24, we obtain

$$U_0 = (108.8 + 121.4 + 494.0 - 364.2 + 410.2) \times 10^3 \text{ kJ/kmol} = 770.2 \times 10^3 \text{ kJ/kmol}$$

For some ionic solids, values of lattice energies estimated through Born-Haber cycle are provided in Table 2.2. It is seen that the agreement between the theoretically calculated and experimental values is on the whole very satisfactory. A study of the Table 2.2 shows that the lattice energy (arithmetical value of this –ve quantity) increases as interionic distance decreases. Other properties also show a systematic dependence on this distance. Thus, as the distance between the ions increases and the lattice energy is reduced, the melting point and hardness of the crystal fall progressively, or conversely the coefficients of thermal expansion and of compressibility increases.

## 2.8   COVALENT BONDING

Elements from the central groups of the periodic Table, notably Group IV, are not readily reduced to a closed shell electronic configuration because the energy required to remove all the valence electrons is too large, and so ionic bonding is unlikely. Also, when atoms in a crystal have similar electronegativities, bond formation occurs through the sharing of valence electrons (not through transfer of electrons as in ionic case), each atom contributing one electron or more to the bond. This sharing of electrons gives rise to covalent bonding. The simplest case of covalent bonding occurs in the hydrogen molecule in which two hydrogen atoms contribute their $1s^1$ electrons to form an electron-pair covalent bond (Fig. 2.9a). This is indicated by the electron-dot notation reaction as:

| $\downarrow$   1s electrons | | | Electron pair covalent bond |
|:---:|:---:|:---:|:---:|
| H   . | + | H   . | $\rightarrow$     H : H |
| Hydrogen atom | | Hydrogen atom | Hydrogen molecule |

Thus, when the two atoms which are involved in the bond formation process and share a single pair of electrons, the resulting bond is known as a single covalent bond. Similarly, when the two coordinating atoms share two or three pairs of electrons, a double or a triple bond results. The formation of single, double and triple bonds in chlorine, oxygen and nitrogen, respectively are shown in Fig. 2.10. Sometimes, a covalent bond is also formed when two or more atoms of different non-metals share one or more pairs of valence electrons. Formation of HCl, $H_2O$, $CO_2$, $NH_3$ molecules are some examples of this category.

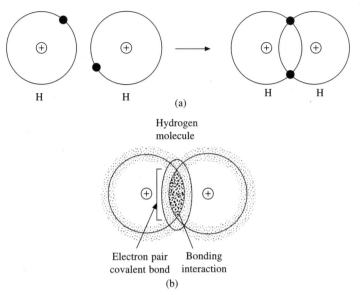

Fig. 2.9   Covalent bonding in the hydrogen molecule showing: (a) combination of valence elections (b) electron density distribution

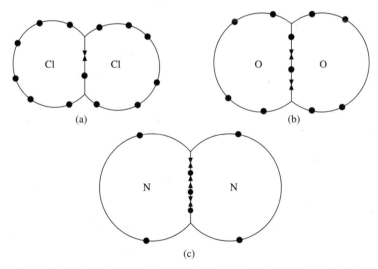

Fig. 2.10   Covalent bonds: (a) single bond (b) double bond (c) triple bond

Although the electron-dot notation is useful to represent the covalent bond, it does not take into consideration the valence-electron density distribution. When the two atoms come together to form hydrogen molecule, their electron clouds interact and overlap. The probability of finding the $1s^1$ electrons of the atoms is maximum between the two nuclei in the hydrogen molecule as shown in Fig. 2.9b. Since Pauli's exclusion principle cannot be violated, the shared electrons therefore must have opposite spins. The force of attraction between the atoms arises from the interaction of these antispin electrons. The electrostatic reulsion between the electrons keeps the atoms at an equilibrium distance where the two forces are equal, or the potential energy is minimum. A hydrogen molecule formed under this situation will have stable configuration and the bond between the two hydrogen atoms is said to be saturated. If a third hydrogen atom is brought near the $H_2$ molecule, the exchange of electron spin of hydrogen (atom) with the parallel spins of hydrogen molecule produces repulsion. On the other hand, the exchange of electron spin of hydrogen (atom) with antiparallel spins of hydrogen molecule is disallowed by the Pauli's exclusion principle. Accordingly, molecules like $H_3$, $H_4$, etc. are improbable to be formed with covalent bonding.

The directional nature of the covalent bond results from the restricted orbital motion of the electrons. The shapes of atomic orbitals $s$ $(l = 0)$ and $p(l = 1)$ are shown in Fig. 2.11. In $p$-orbitals, the shapes represent the angular dependence (directional) distribution of electron density. As a consequence of this, covalent crystal structures tend to be more open than ionic structures.

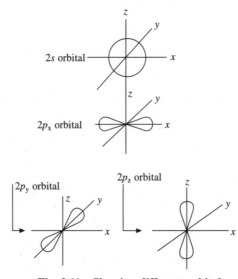

**Fig. 2.11    Showing different orbitals**

Covalent bonds are formed not only due to the overlap of pure $s$ orbitals or pure $p$ orbitals but also due to the overlap of $s$ and $p$ orbitals, called hybrid bonding. Carbon exhibits such a bonding. The electronic configuration of normal carbon atom is $1s^2\, 2s^2\, 2s^2$ and the electron spin distribution is

$$\underline{\downarrow\uparrow} \qquad \underline{\uparrow\downarrow} \qquad \underline{\uparrow} \qquad \underline{\uparrow} \qquad \underline{\phantom{\uparrow}}$$
$$1s \qquad\quad 2s \qquad\quad 2p_x \qquad 2p_y \qquad 2p_z$$

where the electron spins are paired in $1s$ and $2s$ orbitals only while $2p$ electrons remain unpaired. It is these unpaired electrons which are available for bond formation. Accordingly, the carbon atom is expected to form only two bonds. However, when the carbon atoms approach each other one electron from $2s$ orbital is excited to the $p$ level and the resulting configuration becomes $1s^2\, 2s^1\, 2p^3$ and the electron spin distribution as

$$\underline{\downarrow\uparrow} \qquad \underline{\uparrow} \qquad \underline{\uparrow} \qquad \underline{\uparrow} \qquad \underline{\uparrow}$$
$$1s \qquad\quad 2s \qquad 2p_x \qquad 2p_y \qquad 2p_z$$

This configuration shows that there are four unpaired electron spins. The favourable bonding directions of these orbitals are disposed towards four corners of a regular tetrahedron with the bond angles 109.5° (Fig. 2.12). This arrangement of orbitals is called hybridization and the four orbitals are called $sp^3$ hybrids. The schematic representation of hybridization process of carbon orbitals is shown in Fig. 2.13.

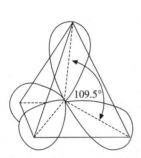

**Fig. 2.12 $sp^3$ orbitals directed symmetrically towards the corners of a tetrahedron**

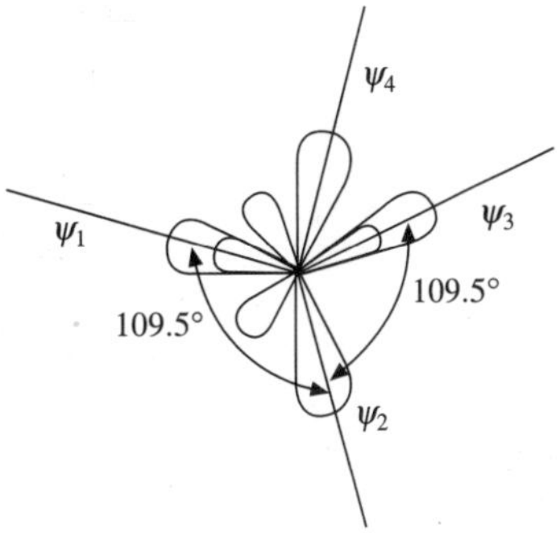

**Fig. 2.13 $sp^3$ hybrid waves functions**

Carbon in the form of diamond, $CCl_4$, $CH_4$, etc exhibits $sp^3$ tetrahedral covalent bonding. However, carbon is usually found as graphite rather than as diamond. The graphite structure results from the $sp^2$ hybrid in which three bonds are formed in a plane with interbond angles of 120° and the fourth $p$ orbital forms a bond in a direction perpendicular to the $sp^2$ bonds. The perpendicular bond is weak and hence graphite has layered structure as shown in Fig. 2.14.

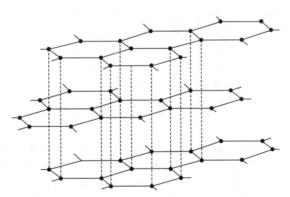

**Fig. 2.14 The layer structure of a graphite**

Typical covalent solids are formed by elements of Group IV in the periodic Table such as carbon, silicon and germanium. These elements crystallize in the diamond structure, where each atom is bounded to four others through covalent bonds. For example, consider germanium which has four electrons in the outer shell. This can acquire a closed shell electronic configuration by sharing an electron with each of the four neighbours as shown in Fig. 2.15. The valence shell around each atom is thus complete with eight electrons. A large number of binary *AB* (or *MX*) compounds formed by elements of group IIIA and VA or IIA and VIA (the so called III-V and

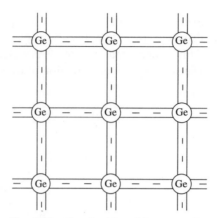

**Fig. 2.15   Covalent bond in germanium**

II-VI compounds) also crystallize in diamond-like structures. Among the I-VII compounds, copper (I) halides and AgI crystallize in this structure. Unlike in diamond, the bonds in such binary compounds are not entirely covalent because of the difference in electronegativity between the constituent atoms. This can be understood in terms of fractional ionic character or ionicity of bonds in these crystals.

Pauling (1960) expressed the ionicity of a covalent bond *A-B* in terms of the difference between the electronegativities of these two atoms:

$$f_i = 1 - \exp\left(\frac{(X_A - X_B)^2}{4}\right) \tag{26}$$

where $f_i$ is the fractional ionic character of the bond while $X_A$ and $X_B$ are the Pauling electronegativities of the elements *A* and *B*. It is seen that $f_i = 0$ when $X_A = X_B$ and $f_i = 1$ when $X_A - X_B \gg 1$. In crystals, this expression is modified to account for the fact that an atom forms more than one bond and the number of bonds formed is not always equal to its formal valence. For $A^N B^{8-N}$ crystals, the expression for ionicity reads as

$$f_i^c = 1 - \left(\frac{N}{M}\right) + \left(\frac{Nf_i}{M}\right) \tag{27}$$

where *M* is the number of nearest neighbours. Pauling's scale of ionicity explains the structures of many binary compounds. Mooser and Pearson (1959) have similarly shown that a plot of the average principal quantum number against the difference in electronegativity clearly separates the differently coordinated structures of binary compounds.

Philips (1973) proposed a new scale of ionicity for *AB*-type crystals based on the assumption that the average band gap, $E_g$, of these crystals consist of both covalent and ionic contributions as expressed by $E_g^2 = E_h^2 + E_i^2$, where $E_h$ and $E_i$ are the homopolar and ionic parts. The ionicity parameter is given by

$$f_i^c = \frac{E_i^2}{E_g^2} \tag{28}$$

The Philips' parameter is obtained by relating the static dielectric constant to $E_g$ and taking $E_h$

in such crystals to be proportional to $a^{2.5}$, where $a$ is the lattice constant. Philips' parameters for a few crystals are listed in Table 2.4. Philips has shown that all crystals with a $f_i^c$ below the critical value of 0.785 possess the tetrahedral diamond (or wurtzite) structure: when $f_i^c \geq 0.785$, six fold coordination (rocksalt structure) is favoured. Pauling's ionicity scale also makes such structural predictions, but Philips' scale is more universal. Accordingly, MgS ($f_i^c \geq 0.786$) shows a borderline behaviour. Cohesive energies of tetrahedrally coordinated semiconductors have been calculated making use of the ionicity parameters. It should be noted that the Born model of ionic solids would not be applicable to such partly ionic solids.

**Table 2.4   Philips and Pauling ionicity parameters for some $A^N B^{8-n}$ crystals**

| Crystal* | $E_n(eV)$ | $E_i$ | $f_i^c$ (Philips) | $f_i^c$ (Pauling) |
|---|---|---|---|---|
| Si (D) | 4.77 | 0 | 0 | 0 |
| BN (Z) | 13.10 | 7.71 | 0.256 | 0.42 |
| GaAs (Z) | 4.32 | 2.90 | 0.310 | 0.26 |
| ZnO (W) | 7.33 | 9.30 | 0.616 | 0.86 |
| CuBr (Z, W) | 4.10 | 6.90 | 0.735 | 0.80 |
| MgS (Z, W) | 3.71 | 7.10 | 0.786 | 0.67, 0.78 |
| NaCl (R) | 3.10 | 11.8 | 0.935 | 0.94 |
| RbI (R) | 1.60 | 7.1 | 0.951 | 0..92 |

*Crystal structures are given in parentheses:
D—diamond; Z—zin blende; W—wurtzite; R—rocksalt.

## 2.9   METALLIC BONDING

It is not easy to describe metallic bonding in terms of a simple model consisting of pairs of atoms as discussed above for ionic and covalent bondings. The bonding in a metal must be thought of in terms of all the atoms of the solid taken together, with the valence electrons from all the atoms belonging to the crystal as a whoole, i.e. no valence electrons are associated to a specific atom and they are free to move throughout the structure. Materials bound in this manner are good conductors of electricity and heat, and are invariably metals; hence the term metallic bonding.

The metallic bonding can be considered as a limiting case of the ionic bonding in which the negative ions are just electrons. For example, sodium chloride contains equal numbers of $Na^+$ and $Cl^-$, while metallic sodium contains equal numbers of $Na^+$ and $e^-$. The crucial difference is that the mass of an electrons is very small as compared to the mass of $Cl^-$ ion. As a result of this, its zero-point motion is large so that it is not localized on a lattice site and is considered to be free. Based on this, we may think of metal crystal as an array of positive metal ions embedded in a "cloud" or "sea" of free electrons (Fig. 2.16). They are held together by the resulting electrostatic interaction between the

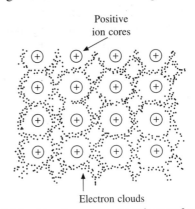

Positive ion cores

Electron clouds

**Fig. 2.16   Atomic arrangement in metal crystals**

positively charged metal ions and the cloud of negative electrons. A metallic structure is therefore determined largely by the packing of the positive ions alone; the electron fluid is just a sort of negatively charged glue.

Alternatively, the metallic bonding may be regarded as a special case of covalent bonding. In sodium, for example, each atom contributes only one valence electron, from the $3s$ shell, and the crystal structure is such that each atom is surrounded by eight nearest neighbour atoms. The valence electrons available from this arrangement are sufficient to form one closed shell. However, there will then be insufficient electrons to fill all the possible orbits around the eight atoms, effectively each atom contributes only one eighth of an electron to each bond. Such covalent bonds are unsaturated. One representation of the metallic bonding is of a time averaged fluctuating covalent bond, i.e. the valence electron of each atom spends only part of the time forming a bond between any two given atoms and with the other atoms during rest of the time. Since each valence electron is not localized between only two ion cores, as in covalent bonding, the metallic bonding is nondirectional. A metallic bonding can exist only among a large aggregate of atoms, while a covalent bonding can occur between as few as two atoms.

In general, the fewer valence electrons an atom has and more loosely they are held, the more metallic is the bonding. These elements, like sodium, potassium, copper, silver, and gold, have high electrical and thermal conductivities because their valence electrons are very mobile. They are opaque because these free electrons absorb energy from the light photons and they have high reflectivity because the electrons re-emit this energy as they fall back to lower energy levels. As the number of valence electrons and the tightness with which they are held to the nucleus increases, they become more localized in space, increasing the covalent nature of bonding. The transition metals (metal atoms with incomplete $d$ shells, such as iron, nickel, tungsten, and titanium) have a significant fraction of covalent bonding. The competition between covalent and metallic bonding is particularly evident in the fourth column of the periodic Table. Diamond exhibits almost pure covalent bonding; tin actually exists in two modifications, one mostly covalent and another mostly metallic; and lead is mostly metallic.

The unsaturated nature of metallic bonding accounts for the alloying properties of metals. When two metals such as copper and nickel are mixed together, each atom reacts fairly unspecifically to the other since they are held together by the common free electron cloud to which both have contributed. It is thus possible to make alloys over wide range of composition by randomly replacing atoms of one metal by those of another, so forming "substitutional solution". The insensitivity of the metallic bonding to the particular metal atom involved is also responsible for the ability of metals to be joined by welding and soldering. In principle, it is sufficient merely to bring clean metal surfaces into contact to form a bond. Similarly, the nondirectional nature of metallic bonding influences the surface and mechanical properties of metals. If a metal is cut into two pieces along some surface, the bonds which previously crossed that surface transfer themselves to atoms within each of the new surfaces so created. The surface energy of a metal is thus rather smaller than might be expected purely from the number of bonds intersected by the cut. As far as the mechanical properties are concerned, it is easier in metals than most other substances for atoms to slide over one another without breaking bonds. The ductility and toughness of the metals are due to this property, although their explanation requires a detailed analysis of the way the atoms move.

## 2.10  HYDROGEN BONDING

Covalently banded atoms often produce a configuration that behaves like an electric dipole (Fig. 2.17). Several such dipoles may be bonded together as a result of electrostatic attraction between them. The dipole bonds in which hydrogen atom acts as the positive end of the dipole is known as hydrogen bonding. Consider, for example, the water molecule $H_2O$, where the electrons shared between the oxygen and hydrogen atoms tend to stay closer to the oxygen atom than the hydrogen atoms because of the greater

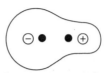

**Fig. 2.17  An electric dipole**

electronegativity of the oxygen (Fig. 2.18a). As a result, the oxygen atom acts as the negative end of the dipole and the hydrogen atoms act as the positive end. The positive end can then attract the negative end of another water molecule and thus bonding the molecule together (Fig. 2.18b). Since the proton in the hydrogen atom is not shielded by other surrounding electrons, it can be attracted quite strongly to the negative end of another dipole, and so the bond is relatively strong as compared to other dipole—dipole interactions. Like covalent bonding, this is directional in nature.

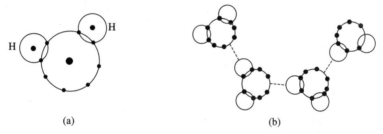

(a)                                                        (b)

**Fig. 2.18  (a) Sharing of electrons between the hydrogen and oxygen atoms in a water molecule (b) Scheme of bonding in different molecules**

Hydrogen bonding is usually formed between the most electronegative atoms like fluorine, oxygen and nitrogen because these atoms produce strong dipoles. The hydrogen bonding is important in many biological molecules such as DNA, where it helps to control the possible pairing between the two strands of the molecule, and in certain ferroelectric crystals.

## 2.11  VAN DER WAALS BONDING

Permannent dipole bonds as in hydrogen bonding are directional while temporary and weak dipole bonds are nondirectional. These are fluctuating dipole bonds and are usually known as van der Waals bonding. A van der Waals bonding arises when at any instant of time there are more electrons on one side of the nucleus of the atom than on the other side; the centres of positive and negative charges do not coincide at that moment and thus a weak fluctuating dipole is produced (Fig. 2.19). A weak attractive force exists between the opposite ends of the dipoles in the neighbouring atoms. It is this force which is responsible for the deviation from ideal gas behaviour studied by van der Waals. It is also the force which allows inert gas atoms to condense (liquefy and crystallize) at low temperatures.

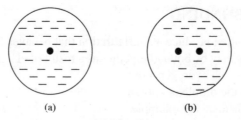

**Fig. 2.19  Distribution of electrons in a noble gas atom (a) idealized symmetrical distribution (b) Real unsymmetrical distribution**

Like metallic bonding, van der Waals bonding is nondirectional and unsaturated and is typically an order of magnitude weaker than the hydrogen bonding. The inert gas solids are therefore, like metals, largely determined by the packing of spheres.

Classification of crystals in terms of bonding is useful in understanding structure-property relations in solids. Important characteristics of five types of bondings are presented in Table. 2.5.

**Table 2.5  Types of solids**

| Type | Units present | Characteristic properties | Representative crystals | Approximate cohesive energy |
|---|---|---|---|---|
| Ionic | Positive and negative ions | Brittle, insulating and fairly high melting | NaCl LiF | 184 244 |
| Covalent | Atomic (bonded to one another) | Hard, high melting, non conductcting (in pure) | Diamond | 170 |
| Metallic | Positive ions in a cloud of electron gas | High conductivity | Na Fe | 26 94 |
| Hydrogen | Molecules held by hydrogen bond | Low melting insulators | $H_2O$ (ice) HF | 12 7.0 |
| van der Waals (Molecular) | Molecules or atoms | Soft, low melting, violatile and insulating | Argon | 2.0 |

*Example*: Given a solid made up of molecules possessing permanent dipoles and another made up of molecules possessing only induced dipoles, which will show the most dependent properties.

*Solution*: The solid containing the permanent dipoles will be more affected by temperature than will the induced dipoles, since the degree of polarization is temperature dependent in the former but not in the latter.

## 2.12  SUMMARY

1. In solids, forces between the atoms are of two types: attractive to prevent them from moving away from each other, and repulsive to prevent them from collapsing. These forces are equal at equilibrium separation (minimum potential energy configuration).

2. Based on charge distribution in the atoms, atomic bondings can be conveniently divided into five classes.

3. Based on bond strength, atomic bondings can be grouped into primary and secondary

bondings. The bond energies of these bondings are in the range of 0.1–10 and 0.01–0.5 eV/bond, respectively.

4. Ionic bonding can be formed when the outer valence electrons are transferred from an electropositive atom to an electronegative atom.
5. The cohesive energy of ionic solids can be calculated on the basis of point charge model.
6. The Madelung constant is a function of crystal structure and can be calculated from the geometrical arrangement of ions in the crystal.
7. In ionic crystals, Madelung potential is defined as the electrostatic part of the lattice energy. This is nearly indepenndent of crystal structure.
8. An indirect estimate of lattic energy can be made in terms of a cyclic process known as Born-Haber cycle.
9. Sharing of electrons between neighbouring atoms results in a covalent bonding.
10. A metal is an arrary of positive metal ions embedded in a cloud of free electrons.
11. Permanent dipole bonds in which hydrogen acts as the positive end of the dipole is known as hydrogen bonding. On the other hand, a fluctuating dipole bond is known as the van der Waals bonding.

## 2.13  DEFINITIONS

*Bonding force:* The force that holds the atoms together; it results from a decrease in the energy when two atoms are brought close to one another.

*Cohesive energy:* The cohesive energy is the amount of work which must be done to disperse a crystal into an assemblage of widely separated atoms (ions).

*Covalent bonding:* A primary bonding arising through the sharing of valence electrons.

*Directional bonds:* Bonds for which the bonding force is greater in particular direction, e.g. all covalent bonds except those involving *s* orbitals, and all permanent dipole bonds.

*Electron shell:* A group of electrons having the same principal quantum number, *n* often designated by capital letters, as K shell for *n* = 1, L shell for *n* = 2, etc.

*Electronegativity:* A numerical system describing the relative tendencies of atoms to acquire electrons.

*Equilibrium distance:* The interatomic distance at which the force of attraction equals the force of repulsion between two atoms.

*Hydrogen bonding:* A secondary bonding arising from diploe attractions where hydrogen acts as the positive end of the dipole.

*Ion core:* An atom without its valence electron or electrons.

*Ionic bonding:* A primary bonding arising from the electrostatic interaction between two positively charged ions.

*Metallic bonding:* A primary bonding arising from the electrostatic interaction between the positively charged metal ions and the cloud of negatively charged electrons.

*Nondirectional bonds:* Bonds for which no preferred bond directions exist, e.g. metallic bonds, ionic bonds, covalent bonds involving *s* orbitals, and van der Waals bonds.

*Orbitals:* The quantum mechanical description of the state of an electron, including its energy and its time-averaged spatial distribution.

*Pauli's exclusion principle:* The statement that no two electrons can occupy the same orbital, and that these two must have opposite spins.

*Permanent dipole bonding:* A primary bonding arising from attraction between dipoles, the oppositely charged ends of which are electronegative and electropositive atoms.

*Valence electrons:* Outer shell electrons which take part in bonding.

*Van der Waals bonding:* A secondary bonding arising from the fluctuating dipole nature of an atom with all electron shells filled.

## REVIEW QUESTIONS AND PROBLEMS

1. Deduce the nature of chemical bonding in the following crystals from the position of their constituent atoms in the periodic Table.
   (i)    GaAs (ii) Ne (iii) K (iv) NiO
2. Describe the ionic bonding process between a pair of Na and Cl atoms. Which electrons are involved in the bonding process?
3. (i)    How does the Madelung constant vary with the number of nearest neighbour? Would you expect this?
   (ii)    Assuming that the repulsive potential is unchanged in NaCl, what is the effect on $A$, $R_e$, $K_0$ and $U$ of doubling the charges on all the ions? Determine the total energy for one dimensional ionic crystal. Why is the result same as equation 21.
4. Discuss the Born-Haber cycle from which we may determine the lattice energy of alkali halide crystals.
5. The potential energy of a diatomic molecule in terms of interatomic distance $R$ is given by

$$U(R) = -\frac{a}{R^m} + \frac{b}{R^n}$$

   (a)    Derive an expression for the equilibrium spacing of the atoms and hence obtain the dissociation energy.
   (b)    Explain the importance of equilibrium spacing as the configuration of lowest potential energy and hence obtain an expression for the dissociation energy of the atoms.
   (c)    Prove n > m for $U(R)$ to be minimum at $R = R_e$
6. Calculate the attractive force between a pair of $Li^+$ and $Cl^-$ ions that just touch each other. Assume the ionic radius of the $Li^+$ ion to be 0.60Å and that of the $Cl^-$ ion to be 1.81Å.          *Ans.* $3.96 \times 10^{-9}$ N.
7. Calculate the atractive force between a pair of $Mg^{2+}$ and $O^{2-}$ ions that just touch each other. Assume the ionic radius of the $Mg^{2+}$ ion to be 0.65Å and that of the $O^{2-}$ ion to be 1.40Å.

    *Ans.* $2.19 \times 10^{-8}$ N.
8. What is the potential energy of CsCl at equilibrium, if the separation between cesium and chlorine atoms is 3.56Å and n is 11.5?          *Ans.* −6.50 eV
9. Calculate the value of constant $n$ for NaCl with the lattice parameter as 5.63Å. Measured binding energy for this crystal is 1.83 kcal/mol (or 7.95 eV/molecule), and $A = 1.75$.          *Ans. 9.*
10. Describe the covalent-bonding process between a pair of hydrogen atoms. What is the driving energy for the formation of a diatomic molecule?
11. Describe the covalent-bonding electron arrangement in the following diatomic molecules: (a) fluorine, (b) oxygen, (c) nitrogen.
12. Describe the metallic bonding process among an aggregate of copper atoms.
13. Define an electric dipole moment. Describe fluctuating dipole bonding among the atoms of the noble-gas neon. Of a choice between the noble gases krypton and xenon, which noble gas would be expected to have the strongest dipole bonding and why?
14. What is Madelung constant? Show that the Madelung constant for an infinite linear chain of ions of alternating unit charge at an equilibrium separation is 21n2.
15. What are ionic crystals? Explain the formation of an ionic crystal and obtain an expression for its cohesive energy.
16. Explain the term binding energy. How would you claculate the binding energy for an ionic crystal having sodium chloride structure?
17. Distinguish between ionic and covalent bonds. Explain the metallic bonds. What is the nature of bonds in NaCl and diamond?
18. Explain with suitable examples the ionic, covalent, metallic and molecular type of bonding in solids.
19. The potential energy of a diatomic molecule in terms of interatomic distance $R$ is given by

$$U(R) = -\frac{a}{R^2} + \frac{b}{R^{10}}$$

Calculate (i) the equilibrium spacing $R_e$ and the dissociation energy when $a = 1.44 \times 10^{-39}$ $Jm^2$ and

$b = 2.19 \times 10^{-115}$ Jm$^{10}$ (ii) $a$, $b$ and the force required to break the molecule and the critical distance between the nuclei for which this occurs when the two atoms form a stable molecule with an internuclear distance of 3Å and have dissociation energy of 4 eV.

*Ans.* (i) $R_e$ = 4.08 Å and $D$ = 3.18 × 10$^{-3}$ eV
(ii) $a$ = 7.2 × 10$^{38}$ jm$^2$, $b$ = 9.4 × 10$^{-115}$ Jm$^{10}$.

20. If an atom $A$ has an ionization energy 5 eV, and another atom $B$ has an electron affinity 4 eV and they are 5Å apart, calcuate the energy required to transfer an electron from $A$ to $B$.

*Ans.* –1.9 eV.

21. Calculate the potential energy of the system of Na$^+$ and Cl$^-$ ions when they are 2 Å apart.

*Ans.* –7.2.eV.

22. How much energy is required to form a K$^+$ and Cl$^-$ ion pair from a pair of these atoms? What must be the separation between a K$^+$ and Cl$^-$ ion pair if their total energy is zero? Given that the ionization energy of K = 4.1 eV and the electron affinity of Cl = 3.6 eV

*Ans.* 0.5 eV and 29 Å.

23. Calculate the cohesive energy of NaCl from the following data: $A$ = 1.748, $n$ = 9, $R_e$ = 2.81 Å, ionization energy of Na = 5.14 eV and electron affinity of Cl = 3.61 eV.

*Ans.* – 3.22 eV/atom

24. Calculate the compressibility of sodium chloride assuming a repulsive potential of the form B/R$^9$ to act between the nearest neighbours. The nearest neighbour distance $R$ = 2.81Å and the corresponding Madelung constant $A$ = 1.7476.

*Ans.* 3.49 × 10$^{-11}$ m$^2$N.

**Chapter 3**

# Atomic Packing

In the preceding chapter, we studied about different types of bonding that exist between the atoms which hold them together. In this chapter, we shall study about the atomic packing in solids, which is a consequence of the atomic bonding.

The arrangement of atoms that we observe in different solids depends partly on whether the bonding is directional (i.e. covalent and permanent dipole bonding) or non—directional (i.e. metallic, ionic, and van der Waals bonding). Atoms bonded by directional bonds are packed in a way that satisfy the bond angles. On the other hand, atoms bonded by non-directional bonds arrange in general as closely packed spheres and obey certain geometrical rules governed by their difference in size. However, it should be remembered that the division between directional and non-directional nature of bonding is simply a matter of convenience because bonding in actual material is often a mixture of both. In the following, we shall limit our discussion only to the nondirectionally bonded atoms which we expect to be as closely packed as possible. In the process, we shall find the efficiency with which the available space is being filled, i.e. the relative packing density (also known as packing factor or filling factor) in two and three dimensions. This is a dimensionless quantity and is defined as the ratio of the volume of the atoms occupying the unit cell to the volume of the unit cell relating to that structure. Thus,

$$\text{Efficiency} = \frac{\text{Volume of the atoms (in the unit cell)}}{\text{Volume of the unit cell}}$$

## 3.1 PACKING OF EQUAL SPHERES IN 2-DIMENSIONS

It is well known that the atoms or ions in a crystal can be regarded as rigid spheres of definite radii, packed together and are held by inter-atomic forces. The crystal structure can thus be regarded as the packing of spheres with radii corresponding to that of its constituent atoms. In order to ascertain this, let us analyse two different packing arrangements of spheres of radius $R$ in a plane. Fig. 3.1a shows a layer of spheres arranged on the points of a square lattice, the coordination number in this case is 4. Since in two-dimensions, the spheres become circles, the area associated with each circle is a square and equals $4R^2$, while area of the circle equals $\pi R^2$. Hence, the efficiency with which the available space is filled is given by the ratio of these two areas, i.e.

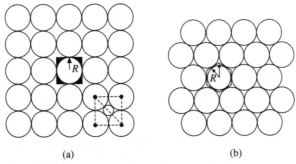

**Fig. 3.1**  **Two-dimensional arrangements of equal spheres: (a) on a square lattice, (b) on a triangular lattice**

$$\frac{\text{Area of the circle}}{\text{Area of the square}} = \frac{\pi R^2}{4\,R^2} = \frac{\pi}{4}$$

$$\text{so that, efficiency} = 78.5\% \tag{1}$$

Fig. 3.1b shows a layer of spheres arranged on the points of a triangular lattice, the coordination number in this case is 6. The area associated with each circle is a hexagon consisting of six equilateral triangles of the type ABC (Fig. 3.2), i.e.

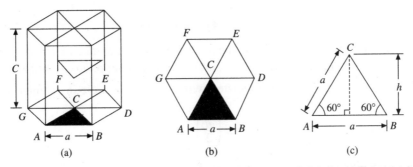

**Fig. 3.2**  **(a) The hcp unit cell, (b) base of hcp unit cell, and (c) one of the six equilateral triangles of the base**

$$\text{Area of the triangle } ABC = \frac{1}{2} \times \text{base} \times \text{height}$$

$$= \frac{1}{2} \times a \times a \sin 60° = \frac{1}{2} \times a^2 \times \sin 60°$$

where height $h = R = a \sin 60°$ and $a$ is the side of the equilateral triangle. Therefore the area of the hexagon base is six times the area of the triangle ABC, i.e.

$$6 \times \frac{1}{2} \times a^2 \times \sin 60° = 6 \times \left(\frac{R}{2 \sin 60°}\right) \times R = 2\sqrt{3}R^2.$$

The efficiency with which the available space is filled in this case is given by

$$\frac{\text{Area of the circle}}{\text{Area of the hexagon}} = \frac{\pi R^2}{2\sqrt{3}\,R^2} = \frac{\pi}{2\sqrt{3}}$$

$$\text{so that, efficiency} = 90.7\% \tag{2}$$

From the above simple calculations, it is clear that Fig. 3.1b represents the closest packing in two dimensions, since the maximum coordination number a two dimensional arrangement can have is 6.

*Example*: Determine the radius of the sphere that will just fit into the void produced by the packing of spheres of radius $R$ on a square lattice of side "a". Also determine the free area per unit cell.

*Solution*: Let a sphere of radius $r$ is introduced within the void produced by the packing of equal spheres on square lattice and is just touching the coordinating spheres (Fig. 3.1a).
In this case,

$$2(R + r) = \text{Diagonal of the square} = \sqrt{2}a$$

or
$$R + r = \frac{a}{\sqrt{2}}, \quad \text{but } 2R = a$$

so that,
$$R + r = \sqrt{2}R$$

or
$$r = (\sqrt{2} - 1)\,R = 0.414R.$$

This is the radius of required sphere. Now, the area of the square unit cell $= (2R)^2 = a^2$ and since each sphere is contributing one-fourth to the unit cell, the number of atoms in the unit cell well be $= \frac{1}{4} \times 4 = 1$. Therefore, the area associated with a sphere (a circle in 2-dimension) is

$$\pi R^2 = \pi \left(\frac{a}{2}\right)^2 = \frac{\pi a^2}{4}$$

and hence the free area is

$$a^2 - \frac{\pi a^2}{4} = a^2 \left(1 - \frac{\pi}{4}\right) = 0.215a^2$$

If $a = 1$(i.e. a square of unit length), the free area $= 21.5\%$.

Now, let us make similar calculations in 3-dimensions for the arrangement of spheres on some simple lattices.

## 3.2 PACKING OF EQUAL SPHERES IN 3-DIMENSIONS

### Simple Hexagonal Lattice

Consider a hexagonal lattice as shown in Fig. 3.3. Replace each point by a hard sphere of radius $R$ such that they touch each other (otherwise the lattice would collapse). The bottom layer of the atoms will look like Fig. 3.4a. Here, $a = 2R$. Since the two layers touch, therefore, $c = 2R$. Now the question is how many atoms are there in the unit cell? In Fig. 3.3, we can see that the twelve atoms at the corners are equally shared between six unit cells and therefore the number of atoms belonging to a unit cell is 2. Further, the atoms at the centres of the top and bottom of the cell contribute one atom to the cell, making the total number of atoms in the unit cell as 3. Now, the volume of the unit cell is

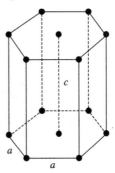

$c \times$ area of the hexagon

$$= c \times 6 \times \frac{1}{2} \times a^2 \times \sin 60°$$

$$= c \times a^2 \times \frac{\sqrt{3}}{2} \times 3$$

**Fig. 3.3 Simple hexagonal lattice**

Substituting for $a$ and $c$ is terms of $R$, we get the volume of the unit cell

$$= 12\sqrt{3} \times R^3. \text{ So that,}$$

$$\text{efficiency} = \frac{3(4\pi R^3)/3}{12\sqrt{3}R^3} = \frac{\pi}{3\sqrt{3}} = 60\% \tag{3}$$

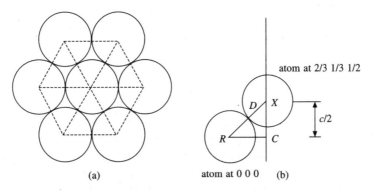

(a)

atom at 0 0 0   (b)

**Fig. 3.4 Packing of equal spheres in hexagonal close packed lattice**

### The Hexagonal Close Packed Lattice

This has a conventional unit cell as shown in Fig. 3.5a. Replace each point by a hard sphere of radius $R$. In order that this lattice should be truly close packed we need a special relationship between $c$ and $a$. Here, $a = 2R$ as before but $c$ is limited by the fact that the distance between the two basis atoms—one at 000 and the other at 2/3 1/3 1/2—must be equal to $2R$. This distance is marked as $D$ in Fig. 3.4b.

$$D = (RC)^2 + \left(\frac{c}{2}\right)^2$$

From Fig. 3.5c, we have

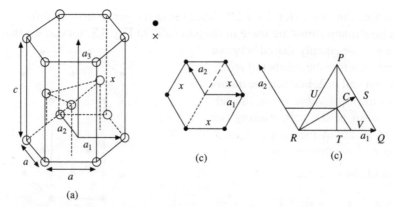

(a)

(c)

(c)

**Fig. 3.5** **(a) conventional unit cell for hexagonal close packed structure. (b) The unit cell viewed from top. (c) The position of the "centre" of a triangle**

$$(RC)^2 = \left(\frac{2}{3} RS\right)^2 = \left(\frac{2}{3} a \sin 60°\right)^2 = \frac{1}{3} a^2$$

Therefore,

$$D^2 = \frac{a^2}{3} + \frac{c^2}{4}$$

As $D = 2R$ and $a = 2R$ we can write $D = a$. So that,

$$a^2 = \frac{a^2}{3} + \frac{c^2}{4} \quad \text{or} \quad c^2 = \frac{8}{3} a^2$$

Therefore,

$$\frac{c}{a} = 1.633 \qquad (4)$$

This value of $c/a$ corresponds to an ideal close packing. However, c/a in most real hexagonal crystals is greater than 1.633 but they are referred to as hexagonal close packed (hcp) provided that the ratio does not exceed by more than 10%.

For an hcp lattice, the number of atoms in the conventional unit cell is three atoms of the simple hexagonal lattice plus three at the centre, i.e. six in all. The volume of the cell is $(ca^2 3 \sqrt{3})/2$. Here, $c = a\sqrt{8/3}$ and $a = 2R$. Therefore, the volume of the unit cell is $24\sqrt{2}R^3$. Thus,

$$\text{efficiency} = \frac{6(4\pi R^3)/3}{24\sqrt{2}R^3} = \frac{\pi}{3\sqrt{2}} = 74\% \qquad (5)$$

### Face Centred Cubic Lattice

Here, the limiting factor is that the face diagonal of the conventional unit cell must be equal to $4R$ (Fig. 3.6a). Accordingly, $\sqrt{2}a = 4R$.

The atoms on the faces of the cube contribute half their volumes to the unit cell and the atoms at the corners contribute one-eighth of their volume. Therefore, the volume of atoms within the unit cell is

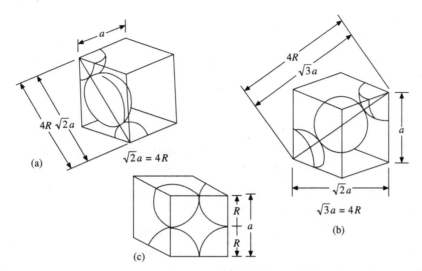

**Fig. 3.6** Sectional view of conventional cubic unit cells showing relationship between the lattice constant *a* and the atomic radius *R* in: (a) a face centred unit cell, (b) a body centred unit cell, (c) a simple cubic unit cell

$$\left(6 \times \frac{1}{2} + 8 \times \frac{1}{8}\right) \frac{4}{3} \pi R^3 = \frac{16}{3} \pi R^3$$

The volume of the cell is $a^3$ or $16\sqrt{2}R^3$. Therefore,

$$\text{efficiency} = \frac{16\pi R^3/3}{16\sqrt{2}R^3} = \frac{\pi}{3\sqrt{2}} = 74\% \tag{6}$$

which is exactly the same as for the hcp structure.

### Body Centred Cubic Lattice

Here, the limiting factor is that the body diagonal of the cube must be equal to $4R$ (Fig. 3.6b). Accordingly, $\sqrt{3}a = 4R$. The volume of atoms (one at the centre and one-eighth from each corner of the cube) within the unit cell is

$$\left(1 \times 1 + 8 \times \frac{1}{8}\right) \frac{4}{3} \pi R^3 = \frac{8}{3} \pi R^3$$

Volume of the cell is $a^3 = \dfrac{64R^3}{3\sqrt{3}}$. Therefore,

$$\text{efficiency} = \frac{8\pi R^3/3}{64R^3/(3\sqrt{3})} = \frac{\sqrt{3}}{8} \pi = 68\% \tag{7}$$

### Simple Cubic Lattice:

In this case, the side of the cube, *a*, must be equal to $2R$ (Fig. 3.6c). The volume of atoms (one-eighth from each corner of the cube) within the unit cell is

$$8 \times \frac{1}{8} \times \frac{4\pi R^3}{3} = \frac{4\pi R^3}{3}$$

Volume of the cell is $a^3 = 8R^3$. Therefore,

$$\text{efficiency} = \frac{4\pi R^3/3}{8R^3} = \frac{\pi}{6} = 52\% \tag{8}$$

It is evident from above efficiency calculations that in three dimensional packing of equal spheres, the hcp and the fcc are equally and the most closely packed arrangements. Many pure metals crystallize in one or the other of these two forms.

*Example*: Determine the packing efficiency in diamond structure. Assuming the radius of the diamond atoms as $R$ and the lattice parameter as "$a$".

*Solution*: Following the above mentioned procedure, the effective number of atoms in the diamond structure (refer Fig. 1.56b) can be found as $\frac{1}{8} \times 8$ (corner atoms) + $\frac{1}{2} \times 6$ (face centred atoms) + $1 \times 4$ (atoms completely within the unit cell) = 8.

Therefore, volume of atoms within the unit cell is

$$8 \times \frac{4}{3}\pi R^3 = \frac{32}{3}\pi R^3$$

Since the space lattice of diamond cubic crystal is fcc, with two atoms per lattice point. Therefore, the limiting factor in this case is $8R = \sqrt{3}a$. The volume of the cell is $a^3$ or $(8R/\sqrt{3})^3$. Therefore,

$$\text{efficiency} = \frac{32\pi R^3/3}{512R^3/3\sqrt{3}} = \frac{\sqrt{3}\pi}{16} = 34\%.$$

## 3.3 CLOSE PACKING OF EQUAL SPHERES IN 3-DIMENSIONS

The close packed arrangements of equal spheres in a plane is shown in Fig. 3.7 where each sphere is in contact with six other spheres. Since, the symmetry of this layer is 6 mm, such a layer is called hexagonal close packed layer. Let, this layer be called an $A$ layer. It contains two types of triangular voids, one with the apex of the triangle upwards in the diagram and labelled $B$, and the other with apex downwards and labelled $C$.

In a three dimensional packing, the next hexagonally close packed layer of spheres can occupy either the sites $B$, or $C$, but not both at the same time. Similarly, layer above a $B$ layer can be either $C$ or $A$ and that above a $C$ layer either $A$ or $B$. No two successive layers can be alike in a close packed structure. The positions

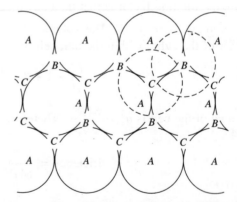

**Fig. 3.7** **The close packing of spheres. There are three possible positions for a layer: A, B and C**

*B* and *C* are displaced with respect to *A* by vectors +S and –S respectively, where $S = \frac{a}{3} \langle \bar{1}010 \rangle$ in the Miller-Bravais system of notation.

Any sequence of letters, *A*, *B*, and *C* with no successive layers alike represents a possible manner of close packing of equal spheres. The number of possible structures increases rapidly with the size of the unit cell. In such three dimensional close packings, each sphere is in contact with 12 other spheres - six in its own layer (plane), three in the layer just above it and three in the layer just below it. This is the maximum number of spheres that can be arranged to touch a given sphere and thus provides maximum packing density for an infinite lattice arrangement. There are however, other arrangements of a finite number of equal spheres which have a higher packing density.

It is clear from above discussion that the number of different possible close packed structures in three dimensions is theoretically infinite. The two most common close packed structures generally encountered are (i) the hexagonal close-packed (hcp) *ABAB*... and (ii) the cubic close packing (ccp) with a layer stacking *ABC*....

*Example*: Assuming that the lattice points of a body centred cubic crystal of lattice parameter "*a*" are occupied by spherical atoms of radius $R_L$, determine the free volume per unit cell.

*Solution*: Volume of the bcc unit cell = $a^3$. Since there are two atoms per unit cell ($8 \times \frac{1}{8}$ for the corner atoms and $1 \times 1$ for the centre atom).

Therefore, volume occupied by the atoms is

$$2 \times \frac{4}{3} \pi R_L^3$$

Since the body diagonal atoms touch one another, so that

$$4R_L = a\sqrt{3}$$

The volume of atoms in terms of "*a*" $= \frac{8\pi}{3} \left( \frac{a\sqrt{3}}{4} \right)^3$

Thus, free volume $= a^3 - \frac{8}{3} \times \frac{\pi a^3 3\sqrt{3}}{64}$

$$= a^3 \left[ 1 - \frac{\sqrt{3}\pi}{8} \right]$$

## 3.4 CLASSIFICATION OF CLOSE PACKINGS

Close packed structures can be classified (distinguished from one another) in two different ways:

(i) On the basis of symmetries and space groups, and
(ii) On the basis of identity period

### Symmetry and Space Groups

We know that the symmetry of a single close-packed layer of equal spheres is 6 mm. It has

2–, 3– and 6–fold axes of rotation normal to its plane as shown in Fig. 3.8. In addition, it has three symmetry planes one perpendicular to *x*-axis, another perpendicular to *y*-axis and the third equally inclined at *x* and *y*-axes. When two or more layers are stacked over one another in a close packing the resulting structure retains all the three symmetry planes and has at least a 3-fold axis

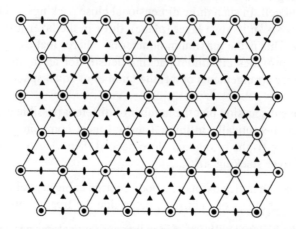

Fig. 3.8   Symmetry elements of a single layer of close packed spheres

parallel to [00.1] through the points 000, 1/3 2/3 0 and 2/3 1/3 0 as shown in Fig. 3.9. Such a structure belongs to the trigonal system and has a space group P3 ml or R3 ml, accordingly as the lattice is hexagonal or rhombohedral. This represents the lowest symmetry of a close packing of spheres comprised of a completely arbitrary periodic stacking sequence of close packed layers. If the arbitrariness in the stacking of successive layers in the unit cell is limited then higher symmetries can also result. It can be shown that it is possible to have three dimensional symmetry elements, namely a centre of symmetry $\bar{1}$, a mirror plane perpendicular to [00.1] and a screw axis $6_3$. It was shown by Belov (1947) that compatible

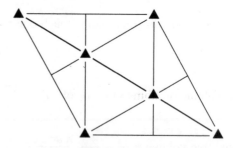

Fig. 3.9   The minimum symmetry of a three-dimensional close packing

combinations of these symmetry elements can give rise to only 8 possible space groups:

$$P3\,ml,\ P\bar{3}ml,\ P\bar{6}m2,\ P6_3\,mc$$

$$P6_3/mmc,\ R3m,\ P\bar{3}m\ \text{and}\ F\bar{4}\,3m.$$

Of these eight space groups, F$\bar{4}$3m is the only one that is cubic and corresponds to the cubic close packed structure *ABCABC* ... All others belong to hexagonal close packings.

**Identity Period**

The height or *c* dimension of the hexagonal unit cell depends on the number of layers required to complete the stacking sequence in the unit cell. The number of layers, $n$ is called the identity period (or the repeat period) of the unit cell. The smallest value that $n$ can have in a close packing is 2, which is the identity period of hexagonal close packing. Similarly, the cubic close packing is the only possible stacking sequence for $n = 3$. Next, *ABCD* (or *ABAC* ...) is the only close packing possible for $n = 4$, it is sometimes called as topaz because it occurs in the mineral topaz. It can be shown that for $n = 5$ also, there is only one possible close packed sequence, i.e. *ABCAB* ..., but for $n = 6$, there are two possible close packed sequences; *ABCACB* ... and *ABCBAB* ... Further, it can be verified that as the identity period $n$ increases, there is a rapid increase in the number of possible close packed sequences for each value of $n$.

## 3.5 AXIAL RATIO AND LATTICE CONSTANTS

The extent to which a real crystal structure approximates to a close packing can be determined from its lattice constants. As seen above, any close packing can be conveniently referred to hexagonal axes. If $c$ denotes the height of the hexagonal unit cell, $n$ the identity period, and $h$ the separation between successive close packed layers then $c = nh$. Also, we know that in a close packing, any sphere in a layer is in contact with three spheres in the layer below it (Fig. 3.10a). The centres of these spheres lie at corners of a regular tetrahedron, as shown in Fig. 3.10b. The height of this tetrahedron, is $h$, while the side equals the lattice constant "$a$", of the hexagonal unit cell (equals the diameter of the sphere). For a regular tetrahedron of side "$a$", $a \sin 60°$ is the median of any of the four bounding faces. Let BP is the median of a side face, drawn from the apex $B$ of the tetrahedron and BQ be the perpendicular from $B$ to the base of the tetrahedron. The triangle *BPQ* is shown in Fig. 3.10c. As $P$ is the mid point of one side of the base and $Q$ is its centroid,

$$PQ = \frac{1}{3} a \sin 60°$$

and

$$(BP)^2 = (BQ)^2 + (QP)^2$$

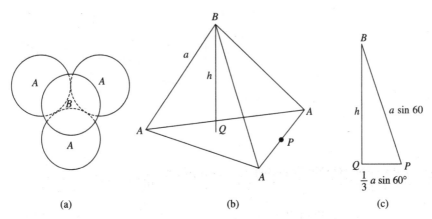

**Fig. 3.10** (a) Tetrahedral voids in a close packing (b) Tetrahedron formed by the centres of the spheres (c) Section BPQ of Fig. 3.10(b)

or
$$a^2 \sin^2 60° = h^2 + \frac{a^2}{9} \sin^2 60°$$

or
$$\frac{h}{a} = \frac{\sqrt{2}}{\sqrt{3}} = 0.8165 \tag{9}$$

so that,
$$\frac{c}{a} = \frac{nh}{a} = 0.8165 \times n \tag{10}$$

The ratio $c/a$ is known as axial ratio, for an ideal close packed structure its value must be an integral multiple of 0.8165.

In cubic close packing, we know the layers...*ABC*... are stacked along [111] direction (body diagonal) of the unit cell. Therefore, the body diagonal of the cubic unit cell must be equal to $3h$. If the side of the cube is $a_c$ then the body diagonal will be $\sqrt{3}a_c$ (which is equal to $3h$). Therefore, $a_c = \sqrt{3}h = \sqrt{2}a$ from eq. 9, where $a = 2R$ = the diameter of the sphere. Thus, the lattice parameter of an fcc unit cell is $\sqrt{2}$ times the diameter of the sphere.

## 3.6   VOIDS IN CLOSE PACKING

### Classification of Voids

There are two kinds of voids that occur in close packing. If the triangular void in a close packed layer has a sphere directly above it, the resulting void will have four spheres around it as shown in Fig. 3.11a. These spheres are arranged on the corners of a regular tetrahedron (Fig. 3.11b), such a void is called tetrahedral void. On the other hand, if a triangular void pointing up in one close packed layer is covered by a triangular void pointing down in the next layer, the resulting void will be surrounded by six spheres (Fig. 3.12a). These spheres are arranged on the corners of an octahedron, such a void is known as an octahedral void and is shown in Fig. 3.12b. Thus in three dimensions, where the possible close packed sequences are theoretically infinite, there are two kinds of possible voids.

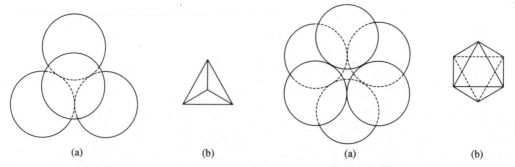

Fig. 3.11   (a) A tetrahedral void (b) Projection of    Fig. 3.12   (a) An octahedral void (b) Projection of
centre of spheres                                        centre of spheres

The number of these voids in a three dimensional close packing of sphere is surrounded by three *B* voids and three *C* voids (Fig. 3.7). When the next layer is placed on the top of this, three voids of one kind are occupied and the other three are not. Thus first three become tetrahedral voids and the other three become octahedral voids. Similarly, the close packed layer below the *A* layer gives rise to three tetrahedral and three octahedral voids. Further, the reference sphere also covers a triangular void in layer above it and another in the layer below it. There are thus two more tetrahedral voids. Each sphere is therefore surrounded by 3 + 3 + 2 = 8 tetrahedral voids and 3 + 3 = 6 octahedral voids. Since the total number of spheres and voids in a close packing is very large and difficult to calculate. However, it is possible to find the average number of voids of each kind belonging to a sphere.

As we know that each octahedral void is surrounded by six spheres and each sphere in turn is surrounded by six voids, therefore, the number of octahedral voids belonging to a sphere is given by the ratio,

$$\frac{\text{Number of octahedral voids around a sphere}}{\text{Number of spheres around an octahedral void}} = \frac{6}{6} = 1$$

Similarly, each tetrahedral void is surrounded by four spheres and each sphere is surrounded by eight tetrahedral voids. Therefore, the number of tetrahedral voids belonging to a sphere is given by the ratio,

$$\frac{\text{Number of tetrahedral voids around a sphere}}{\text{Number of spheres around a tetrahedral void}} = \frac{8}{4} = 2$$

This follows that:

(i) There are as many octahedral voids as there are spheres, and (ii) There are twice as many tetrahedral voids as there are spheres.

## 3.7   SIZE AND COORDINATION OF THE VOIDS

**In Two Dimensions**

Referring to the close packed arrangement of equal spheres in a plane as shown in Fig. 3.7, we find that one particular void (*B* or *C* type) is surrounded by three spheres and hence its coordination number is 3. The size of the planar void can be determined simply by measuring the radius of the sphere that would just fit into the void. Consider one such arrangement as shown in Fig. 3.13. Let *r* be the radius of the central sphere which just fits into the void and *R* be the radius of the coordinating spheres. From the simple construction in Fig. 3.13, we have

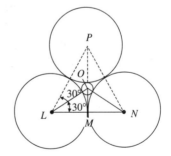

**Fig. 3.13   A planar void**

$$\frac{LM}{LO} = \frac{R}{R + r} = \cos 30°$$

or

$$r = \frac{R}{\cos 30°} - R = \frac{2}{\sqrt{3}} R - R = 1.155R - R$$

or

$$r = 0.155 \, R \qquad\qquad (11)$$

This gives the radius of the sphere representing the planar void.

### In Three Dimensions

As we have seen earlier that there exist two kinds of voids viz. tetrahedral and octahedral voids in three dimensional close packings. The size of these voids can be found in a manner similar to that discussed above. Further, these voids in a close packing can be described in terms of the number of spheres that are arranged about each void. The number of spheres surrounding a void is called the coordination number of that void. Accordingly, the coordination number of a tetrahedral void is 4 and that of an octahedral void is 6. A close packing can therefore be represented by the packing of coordination tetrahedra and octahedra (or in general coordination polyhedra) of voids as is done by the packing of spheres themselves. Size of these voids can be found as follows:

### Tetrahedral Void

Consider a tetrahedral void surrounded by four spheres of radius $R$. The centres of these spheres lie at the corners of a regular tetrahedron of side $a = 2R$. Let $r$ be the radius of the sphere that just fits into this void whose centre is at $P$ and is equidistant from all corners of the tetrahedron (Fig. 3.14a). Let the bond length $p = r + R$. As shown earlier, the height $BQ = h$ is related to the side of the tetrahedron "$a$" as

$$h = \frac{\sqrt{2}}{\sqrt{3}} a$$

Hence, from the right angled triangle $PQR$ shown in Fig. 3.14b, we have

$$PQ = BQ - BP = h - p$$

Here, $\qquad PR = p$ and $QR = \frac{2}{3} a \sin 60° = \frac{h}{\sqrt{2}}$

Therefore, $\qquad (PR)^2 = (h - p)^2 + (QR)^2$

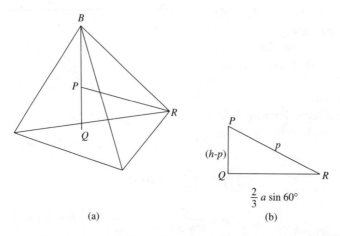

(a)                                          (b)

**Fig. 3.14   (a) A tetrahedron (b) Section PQR of Fig. 14(a)**

or
$$p^2 = (h - p)^2 + \frac{h^2}{2}$$

so that,
$$p = \frac{3}{4}h = 0.75h \tag{12}$$

The bond length for an atom placed in a tetrahedral void in a close packing is thus equal to three-fourth the layer spacing. Substituting for $p$ and $h$ in terms of $r$ and $R$, we have

$$r + R = \frac{3\sqrt{2}}{4\sqrt{3}} 2R = \frac{\sqrt{3}}{\sqrt{2}} R$$

Therefore,
$$r = \frac{\sqrt{3} - \sqrt{2}}{\sqrt{2}} R = 0.225R \tag{13}$$

This gives the radius of the sphere representing the tetrahedral void.

**Octahedral Void**

In an octahedral void the sphere that could just fit in would touch six spheres, three in the layer below and three in the layer above. The projection of the centres of the six spheres is shown in Fig. 3.15a. The point $O$ represents the centre of the sphere fitted within the void. Again the bond length $OR = p = R + r$. Now from the right-angled triangle $OO'R$ shown in Fig. 3.15b (where $O'$ lie in the plane of upper layer), we have

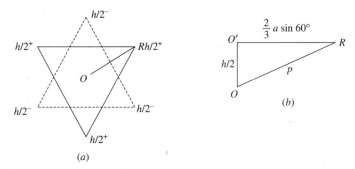

Fig. 3.15   **Projection of centres of spheres with their position coordinates**

$$(OR)^2 = (OO')^2 + (O'R)^2$$

or
$$p^2 = \left(\frac{h}{2}\right)^2 + \left(\frac{2}{3} a \sin 60°\right)^2$$

Therefore,
$$p = \frac{\sqrt{3}h}{2} = 0.88h \tag{14}$$

The bond length for an atom placed in an octahedral void in a close packing is thus 0.88 time the layer separation. Substituting $p = r + R$, $h = (\sqrt{2} / \sqrt{3})a$ and $a = 2R$ we have,

$$r + R = \sqrt{2}\,R$$

Therefore,
$$r = (\sqrt{2} - 1)R = 0.414R \qquad (15)$$

This gives the radius of the sphere representing the octahedral void.

*Example*: Determine the radius of the largest sphere that can be placed at the centre of a cube face of a body centre cube of lattice parameter $a$ and the radius of the lattice atom $R$.

*Solution*: In Fig. 3.16, we can see that the face centre of the cube is located at $\frac{1}{2}\,\frac{1}{2}\,0$. This is an octahedral void as six lattice atoms are surrounding it. Let the largest sphere placed at this position just touching the two body centre atoms of the adjacent cube has a radius $R_x$. Then from simple geometry, the distance between the two body centre atoms is given by

$$2R + 2R_x = a$$

or
$$R + R_x = \frac{a}{2}$$

But for a bcc lattice,

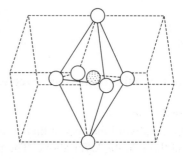

**Fig. 3.16   An octahedral void in bcc lattice**

$$4R = a\sqrt{3}$$

Therefore,
$$R + R_x = \frac{a}{2} = \frac{4}{2\sqrt{3}}R = 1.154R$$

so that,
$$R_x = 1.54R - R = 0.154R.$$

*Example*: Determine the radius of the largest sphere that will fit into the void produced by the bcc packing of atoms of radius $R_L$.

*Solution*: The largest void in the body centred crystal is located at the position $\frac{1}{2}\,\frac{1}{4}\,0$ as shown in Fig. 3.17. This is a terahedral void as four lattice atoms are surrounding it. (Note that there are several other equivalent points in each cell.) If a new spherical atom of radius $R_x$ is introduced at this point, then from simple geometry we have

$$(R_L + R_x)^2 = \left(\frac{a}{4}\right)^2 + \left(\frac{a}{2}\right)^2$$

$$= \frac{5a^2}{16}$$

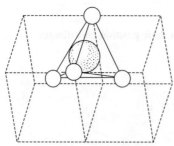

**Fig. 3.17   A tetrahedral void in bcc lattice**

or
$$R_L + R_x = \frac{\sqrt{5}\,a}{4}$$

But
$$4R_L = a\sqrt{3}$$

Substituting the value of $a$ and rearranging the terms, we have

$$R_x = \frac{4R_L}{4\sqrt{3}} \left[ \sqrt{5} - \sqrt{3} \right] = 0.291 R_L$$

*Example*: Find the diameter of the largest atom that would fit into the void in fcc nickel without distortion.

*Solution*: For Ni, the lattice parameter $a = 3.52$Å. Also for an fcc lattice, we have $\sqrt{2}a = 4R$. So that,

$$R = \frac{\sqrt{2} \times 3.52}{4} = 1.2445\text{Å}.$$

Since, the largest void in a close packing is an octahedral void (equivalent to the largest atom in question), therefore,

$$R_{oct} = 0.414R = 0.414 \times 1.2445 = 0.515\text{Å}.$$

Thus, the diameter of the largest atom, $D_{LA}$ will be equal to the diameter of the octahedral void in the structure. Therefore,

$$D_{LA} = D_{oct} = 2R_{oct} = 1.03\text{Å}$$

*Example*: Calculate the void space in a close packing of $n$ spheres of radius 1.000, $n$ spheres of radius 0.414 and $2n$ spheres of radius 0.225.

*Solution*: Let us consider the case of cubic close packing. In this case, side of the unit cell and the radius of the sphere is related as $\sqrt{2}a = 4R$, or $a = 2\sqrt{2}R$. Therefore, the volume of the unit cell

$$V = a^3 = 16\sqrt{2}R^3 = 16\sqrt{2} \text{ (for } R = 1)$$

Since an fcc unit cell contains 4 lattice points in it, therefore $n = 4$. So that the occupied volume is

$$4 \times \frac{4}{3} \times \pi \left[ (1.000)^3 + (0.414)^3 + 2 \times (0.225)^3 \right] = 18.319$$

and the void space becomes

Total volume – occupied volume = $16\sqrt{2} - 18.319 = 4.308 = 19\%$

## 3.8 SIGNIFICANCE OF VOIDS

Voids in two and three dimensional close packings of spheres are of great significance, because smaller spheres can be placed within them. In fact in many inorganic compounds, one kind of atoms are arranged in a close packed manner (not necessarily touching each other) while the other atoms present are distributed among the voids. For example, many oxides consist of oxygen atoms arranged in a hexagonal or cubic close packing with the smaller metal atoms occupying the voids. Also the voids have the capacity to hold interstitial atoms, which may be an impurity atom either added intentionally (or accidentally) or atoms of the parent structure itself accidentally displaced from the original positions. Such imperfections are known to play a very important role in influencing the properties of crystals. However, it is to be pointed out that in actual structures not all voids can be occupied. In most inorganic close packed structures only certain voids related by symmetry are occupied.

## 3.9 PACKING OF UNEQUAL SPHERES IN 3-DIMENSIONS AND EFFECT OF RADIUS RATIO

In the preceding sections we have seen that the planar voids (in 2-dimensions), and tetrahedral and octahedral voids (in 3-dimensions) in close packing differ in size which increases in the order, octahedral > tetrahedral > planar voids. Therefore, in actual crystal structures a particular atom can best fit into one or the other kind of void depending on its size relative to that of the close packed atoms. Consequently, other packing arrangements of nondirectionally bonded atoms become possible when the sizes of the atoms are appreciably different (ionic solids provide the best example of such packings). The size of an atom depends on the size and the number of its coordinating atoms. In other words, the coordination number is a function of the difference in size of the central atom and the coordinating atoms. The greater the size difference, the smaller is the coordination number. The possible coordination numbers in a three-dimensional array are 1, 2, 3, 4, 6, 8 and 12. However, the coordination numbers of cations most frequently encountered in actual structures are 3, 4, 6, 8 and 12. Out of these, 4 and 6 are most common in structures having anions in close packing and either 4, 6, or 8 in almost all close packed structures. The coordination number 3 occur in planar complexes, while 12 is the coordination number in close packing of like atoms. Each value of coordination number is found to be stable within a certain range of radius ratio (the ratio of the radius of the central atom to the atoms coordinating it).

As an example, let us consider the compound $AB$ composed of equal numbers of $A$ atoms and $B$ atoms whose atomic radii are given by $r_A$ and $r_B$, respectively. Since the number of each type of atoms present in the structure is the same, they will have same coordinations, namely 1:1, 2:2, 3:3, 4:4 etc. The above calculated radius ratios for coordination numbers 3 (planar) 4 (tetrahedral) and 6 (octahedral) show that the coordination number imposes a limitation on the radius ratio and vice-versa. Here, the coordinations 1:1 and 2:2 impose no limitations since the atoms can have any relative size and still have 1-fold or 2-fold coordination. Let us see the limitations imposed by other coordinations. According to eq. 11 obtained in section 3.7, $r_A/r_B$ must be at least 0.155 if the $A$ atom is to touch the three $B$ atoms coordinating it. Similarly, $r_B/r_A \geq 0.155$ if $B$ atom is to touch the three $A$ atoms coordinating it. Thus a 3-fold coordination would require the radius ratio to lie between the limit 0.155 and 1/0.155. Let us analyse three different situations as illustrated in Fig. 3.18. Under the limiting situation when the central atom touches the three coordinating atoms, the radius ratio ($r_A/r_B = 0.155$) is said to have a critical value. This is shown in Fig. 3.18a. When the radius ratio varies in the range $0 < r_A/r_B < 0.155$, the central atom will "rattle" in the void and do not touch the three coordinating atoms at the same time. This configuration is said to be unstable and is shown in Fig. 3.18b. Under this situation, the configuration can be made stable only if the coordination is reduced to 2. Finally, when the radius ratio $r_A/r_B > 0.155$, all the coordinating atoms touch the central atom but do not touch one another as shown in Fig. 3.18c. This is a stable configuration. Identical arguments will be applicable to other coordination numbers also.

As far as the coordination is concerned, a given coordination number will be stable between that radius ratio at which the coordinating (close packed) atoms touch each other as well as the

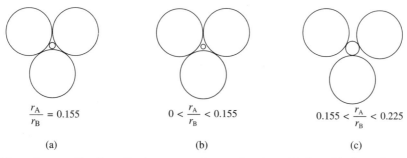

$$\frac{r_A}{r_B} = 0.155 \qquad\qquad 0 < \frac{r_A}{r_B} < 0.155 \qquad\qquad 0.155 < \frac{r_A}{r_B} < 0.225$$

(a) (b) (c)

**Fig. 3.18** **Triangular coordination of anions around central cations (a) the critical configuration, (b) the unstable configuration, and (c) stable but not critical configuration**

central atom, and that the radius ratio at which the next higher coordination number is possible. For example, a coordination of 4 (or tetrahedral coordination), will be stable between the radius ratios of 0.225 and 0.414. Below the lower limit a triangular coordination is possible and above the upper limit an octahedral coordination results. The permissible range of radius ratio in *AB* compounds for coordination numbers most frequently encountered are given in Table 3.1. A geometrical representation of these ranges is given in Fig. 3.19.

**Table 3.1 Coordination number as a function of radius ratio in *AB* compounds**

| Coordination number | Range of radius ratio | Coordination polyhedron | Packing |
|---|---|---|---|
| 1:1 | 0–∞–0 | point | point |
| 2:2 | 0–∞–0 | line | linear |
| 3:3 | 0.155–1/0.155 | triangle | triangular |
| 4:4 | 0.255–1/0.225 | tetrahedron | tetrahedral |
| 6:6 | 0.414–1/0.414 | octahedron | octahedral |
| 8:8 | 0.732–1/0.732 | cube | cubic |
| 12:12 | 1.0 | twined cubo-octahedron (hcp) | hcp and |
|  |  | cubo-octahedron (fcc) | fcc |

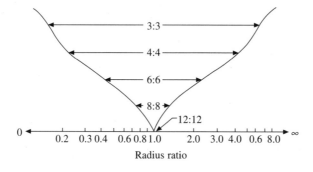

**Fig. 3.19** **A geometrical representation of radius ratio range**

The radius ratio limits for possible coordinations in compounds of the type $A_n B_m$ may be similarly determined. The composition here requires that:

$$\frac{\text{Coordination number of } A}{\text{Coordination number of } B} = \frac{m}{n} \tag{6}$$

Thus the possible coordinations in a close packed $AB_2$ structure are 2 : 1, 4 : 2, 6 : 3 etc. The coordination 2 : 1 imposes no limitation as discussed above. The coordination 4 : 2 arise if $A$ atoms lie in the tetrahedral voids between close packed $B$ atoms and 6 : 3 arise if $A$ atoms are distributed among the octahedral voids. The radius ratio limits would accordingly be $0.225 < r_A/r_B < \infty$ for 4 : 2 coordination and $0.414 < r_A/r_B < 1/0.155$ for 6 : 3 coordination. In a similar way, the possible coordinations for $A_2 B_3$ compounds are 3 : 2, 6 : 4 ... etc. Table 3.2 gives the actual radius ratios of a few ionic solids and metals alongwith their predicted and observed coordination numbers.

*Example*: Show that the minimum value of $R_A/R_X = 0.154$ will provide a 3 : 3 coordination for $A$ and $X$ ions in $AX$-compound.

*Solution*: Let $R_x$ be the radius of $X$ ions representing the bigger spheres. They touch each other and their centres lie on the corners of an equilateral triangle ABC as shown in Fig. 3.20. Also, let $R_A$ be the radius of $A$ ion representing the smaller sphere which is lying at the centre of the void produced by the $X$ ions. The $A$ ion touches the three coordinating $X$ ions, so that from Fig. 3.20 which shows various bond lengths, we have

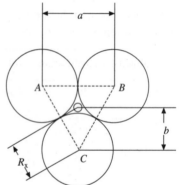

$$a = 2R_x, \ b = \frac{2}{3} a \sin 60° = \frac{2}{3} \times \frac{\sqrt{3}}{2} a = \frac{2}{\sqrt{3}} R_x$$

**Fig. 3.20   Showing various bond lengths**

Also

$$b = R_A + R_x = \frac{a}{\sqrt{3}}$$

Therefore,

$$R_A = \frac{a}{\sqrt{3}} - \frac{a}{2} = 0.0773a$$

and

$$R_x = 0.5a$$

so that

$$\frac{R_A}{R_x} = \frac{0.0773a}{0.5a} = 0.155$$

The radius ratio 0.155 corresponds to 3: 3 coordination (as can be seen in Table 3.1).

## 3.10   REPRESENTATION OF CLOSE PACKINGS

From the discussions so far we have had for the close packing of equal and unequal spheres, it is obvious that a close packing can equally well be represented by the packing of coordination

**Table 3.2**  **Predicted and observed coordination numbers for different ionic radius ratio for some ionic solids and metals**

| Compound or metal | $r_c/r_a^*$ | Coordination number predicted | Coordination number observed |
|---|---|---|---|
| $B_2O_3$ | 0.14 | 2 | 3 |
| BeS | 0.17 | 3 | 4 |
| BeO | 0.23 | 3 to 4 | 4 |
| $SiO_2$ | 0.29 | 4 | 4 |
| LiBr | 0.31 | 4 | 6 |
| MgO | 0.47 | 6 | 6 |
| $MgF_2$ | 0.48 | 6 | 6 |
| $TiO_2$ | 0.49 | 6 | 6 |
| NaCl | 0.53 | 6 | 6 |
| CaO | 0.71 | 6 | 6 |
| KCl | 0.73 | 6 to 8 | 6 |
| CaF | 0.73 | 6 to 8 | 8 |
| CsCl | 0.93 | 8 | 8 |
| bcc metal | 1.0 | 8 to 12 | 12 |
| fcc metal | 1.0 | 8 to 12 | 12 |
| hcp metal | 1.0 | 8 to 12 | 12 |

$*r_c$ and $r_a$ are the radii of cation and anion, respectively.

polyhedra of voids in lieu of the spheres themselves. In fact, such a representation may have certain advantages in regard to display the symmetry in proper manner. Fig. 3.21 shows the exploded view of the sequence of polyhedral layers in a cubic close packing. For convenience, this shows successive layers normal to [100], not [111], which is the actual stacking direction for close packed layers. The layers of tetrahedra lie within one-half of the interpenetrating octahedral layers above and below. When the layers are collapsed only the octahedral can be seen. Fig. 3.22 shows such a representation for cubic close packing. For a comparison, an exploded view of a hexagonal close packing is also shown in Fig. 3.23. There are two tetrahedral layers that fit inside two adjacent layers; the two similar layers in each case are related by a mirror plane lying between the layers. This representation of close packing is also physically more meaningful. As stated earlier that in many inorganic compounds, one kind of atoms are arranged in a close packed manner while the other atoms (metal atoms) are distributed among the voids. Thus, the coordination polyhedra of metal atoms can be used in a manner analogous to the packing

**Fig. 3.21**  **An exploded view of polyhedral layers in cubic close packing**

Fig. 3.22    **An octahedral representation of cubic close packing**

Fig. 3.23    **An exploded view of a hexagonal close packing**

scheme shown above. This kind of representation was first employed by Pauling, who showed that definite rules govern the packing of such polyhedra. These rules are called Pauling's rule and are discussed below.

## 3.11   PAULING'S RULE

In section 3.9, we discussed the effect of radius ratio on coordination numbers and vice-versa. In fact, a definite relationship between the ionic sizes and the coordination numbers of ions have been found to hold in many compounds occurring in nature. Thus certain cation-anion combinations always form similar arrangements which persist with little change from one compound to another. Therefore, one can think of many such compounds as being composed of coordination polyhedra of anions surrounding a cation at their centres. For example, the largest single group of naturally occurring compounds are silicates, having structures that are based on packing arrangements of $SiO_4$ polyhedra. Based on the observation of such packing arrangements, Pauling postulated a set of rules that determine the nature of possible arrangements. Although these rules apply strictly to ionic compounds only, they can be applied to other compounds also with slight modifications. Notable exceptions are metals and organic compounds. Pauling's rules are as follows:

1. A coordination polyhedra of anion is formed about each cation. The cation-anion distance is determined by the sum of the respective radii, and the coordination number is determined by the radius ratio.
2. In a stable structure, the total strength of the valency bonds that reach an anion in a coordination polyhedron, from all neighbouring cations, is equal to the total charge of the anion.
3. The polyhedra in a structure tend not to share edges, and in particular not faces, common to two polyhedra. If edges are shared, the shared edges are shortened.

4. Since sharing of polyhedron elements decreases the stability of a structure, cations with high valency and small coordination numbers tend not to share polyhedron elements with each other.

5. The number of essentially different kinds of atoms in a structure tend to be small. This is so called rule of parsimony.

The polyhedra which result from connecting the centres of the anions surrounding a central cation are called anion polyhedra, or in the more general case of atoms (instead of ions), it is called simply coordination polyhedra. The limiting case, i.e., the close packing of equal spheres (equal size atoms) has been discussed in the previous section. The coordination polyhedra for hcp and fcc arrangements are shown in Fig. 3.24. The coordination polyhedron for both bcc packing and cubic coordination is simply a cube. However it should be remembered that, by convention, the description, bcc is reserved when all atoms are of equal size.

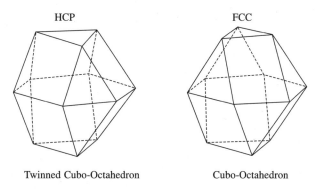

HCP — Twinned Cubo-Octahedron

FCC — Cubo-Octahedron

**Fig. 3.24   Coordination polyhedra for hcp and fcc packing**

## 3.12   APPLICATION OF PAULING'S RULE TO ACTUAL STRUCTURES

Let us apply the above rules to ionic structures. It is possible to gauge the ionic nature of a structure by the extent to which Pauling's rules are satisfied. Rule 1 is simply a concise statement of the radius ratio effect already discussed. Rule 2 can be equivalently stated as: In a stable structure, local charge neutrality must be maintained. In ionic crystals, we observe that the anions are surrounded by the cations and vice-versa. In this situation, it is necessary to estimate the amount of positive charge that is effectively associated with each cation-anion bond. For a cation $M^{m+}$ surrounded by $n$ anions, $X^{x-}$, the electrostatic bond strength (e.b.s.) of the cation-anion bond is defined as

$$e.b.s = \frac{m}{n} \qquad (17)$$

Further, for each anion, the sum of the electrostatic bond strengths of the surrounding cations must balance the negative charge on the anion, i.e.

$$x = \Sigma \frac{m}{n} \qquad (18)$$

For example, let us consider the compound $MgAl_2O_4$, which has a spinel structure. In this compound, each $Al^{3+}$ ion is coordinated octahedrally, while each $Mg^{2+}$ and $O^{2-}$ ion are coordinated tetrahedrally. We can verify them to be so, as follows:

$$\text{For } Mg^{2+}: \qquad e.b.s = \frac{2}{4} = \frac{1}{2}$$

$$\text{For } Al^{3+}: \qquad e.b.s = \frac{3}{6} = \frac{1}{2}$$

Therefore, $$\Sigma \, e.b.s \, (3 \, Al^{3+} + 1 \, Mg^{2+}) = 2$$

This must be balanced by the negative charge on oxygen which is equal to $-2$.

This shows that the charge neutrality is preserved. This analysis is diagrammatically represnted in Fig. 3.25.

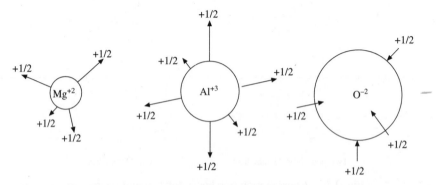

**Fig. 3.25 Bond strengths and directions in various components of $MgAl_2O_4$**

Rules 3 and 4 can be considered jointly. The reason that cation tend not to share polyhedron elements can be seen is Fig. 3.26, which shows two cube units sharing a corner, an edge and a face. The separation between the two positively charged cations at the centre of the cubes successively decreases from $\sqrt{3}$ to $\sqrt{2}$ to 1 respectively, in these cases. Since the two positively charged cations repel each other, they naturally tend to be as far apart as possible. The higher the charge on the cation and the smaller its coordination number, the greater this tendency becomes. Generally, tetrahedra can share only corners; octahedra can share corners and edges; and cubes can share corners, edges and faces, although the number of structures in which cubes share faces is small, because the cubic coordination is not very stable in itself.

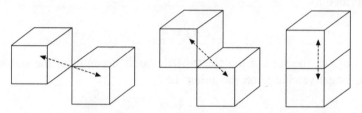

**Fig. 3.26 Sharing of corner, edge and face in two cubic units**

It logically follows from the above that, if an edge is shared, the mutual repulsion of the two cations will shorten the shared edge. Two octahedra sharing an edge are shown in Fig. 3.27. A typical example of such sharing in nature is seen in the structure of rutile, a stable modification of $TiO_2$. The oxygen octahedra coordinating $Ti^{4+}$ form rows in which opposite edges are shared, and the shared edges are shortened.

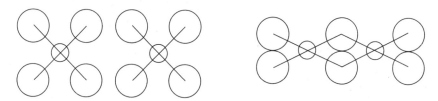

**Fig. 3.27   Situation resulting from the sharing of an edge by two octahedra**

# 3.13   EXAMPLES OF SOME CLOSE PACKED STRUCTURES

## Atomic Packings in Elements

Structures of many metallic and non-metallic elements can be described in terms of close packing of equal spheres. There is a definite relationship between the structure and the position of an element in the periodic Table. Elements in the same group tend to have the same structure at room temperature, e.g. the alkali metals and Be, Mg, Zn and Cd (group IIA and IIB) are hcp; Cu, Ag and Au (group IB) are ccp. The elements of rare-earth series crystallize in the ccp structure, the hcp structure or the 4H (*ABCB*) structure (i.e. Sm). The stable modification of Co at room temperature is probably hcp but it undergoes transformation to a ccp structure at high temperature.

## Atomic Packing in AB (or Mx-type) Compounds

### NaCl Structure

This is one of the simplest compounds of MX-class, composed of equal numbers of Na and Cl atoms. The coordination numbers of these atoms are determined by their radius ratios. According to the radii listed in Table 4.1 the radius ratio $r_{Na}/r_{Cl} = 0.525$ and corresponding coordination numbers of these ions are 6:6 (from Table 3.1) i.e. they are octahedrally coordinated to each other. Now, let us consider a collection of octahedra with sodium at the centres (Fig. 3.28), to find out the possible ways of their packings. It can be easily shown that the cubic close packing (Fig. 3.21) is the only way to pack such polyhedra. An attempt to form the hexagonal close packing leads to the sharing of faces by the adjacent octahedra, in direct violation of Pauling's rules. Thus, unless the coordination numbers of Na and Cl are changed the only stable structure that NaCl can assume is that of a cubic close packing of larger chlorine ions with the smaller sodium ions occupying the octahedral voids. This structure is shown in Fig. 1.58.

### ZnS Structure

Another simple *MX*-type compound is zinc sulfide. From Table 4.1 the radius ratio of zinc and sulfur is $r_{Zn}/r_S = 0.402$. The corresponding coordination numbers of zinc and sulfur are 4:4 (from Table 3.1), i.e. they are tetrahedrally coordinated to each other. Now, keeping in view the

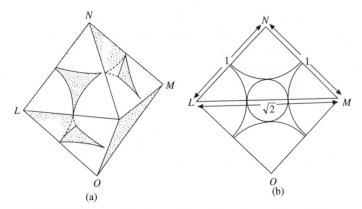

Fig. 3.28    an octahedron with sodium atom at the centre

Pauling's rule (i.e. the tetrahedra can share corners only), let us see how these tetrahedra can be arranged in space?

Consider a collection of tetrahedra with Zn atom at the centres and sulfur atoms at the corners as shown in the Fig. 3.29. A single layer of tetrahedra is shown in Fig. 3.30. Then in a plane, at each corner where three tetrahedra meet, a sulfur atom has three tetrahedrally disposed zinc

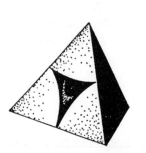

Fig. 3.29    A tetrahedron with zinc atom
at the centre

Fig. 3.30    A tetrahedral layer

neighbours. The above question, therefore, now becomes: How can such layers be stacked so that four tetrahedra share each corner and each corner atom has tetrahedral coordination? This can be achieved in two simple ways which are shown in Figs. 3.31 and 3.32, respectively.

Same result could be obtained by considering sulfur atoms at the centres and zinc atoms at the corners of the tetrahedra. The reason that these two different kinds of packings are possible is that the larger atoms can pack in either of the two close packings. Thus, any AB (or MX) compound having tetrahedral coordination can, in principle assume either of these two forms, accordingly as to which close packing the larger atoms assume. Such different structural arrangements of the same kind and number of atoms are called polymorphs or polymorphic modifications of a compound.

## Polymorphism

Two possible polymorphs of ZnS shown in Figs. 3.31 and 3.32 have been found to occur in nature. The hexagonal polymorph is the mineral wurtzite, and the cubic one is called the sphalarite or zinc blende. Polymorphism is exhibited by a number of substances.

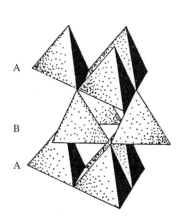

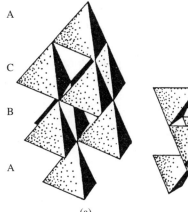

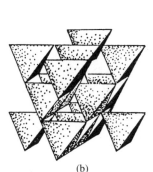

**Fig. 3.31   Packing of zinc tetrahedra in $\alpha$-ZnS (wurtzite)**

**Fig. 3.32   Packing of zinc tetrahedra in $\beta$-ZnS (sphalerite). (a) [111] vertical (b) [001] vertical**

Any substance in general, can exist in the solid, liquid, or the gaseous state, depending on the conditions of temperature and pressure. Similarly, a chemical substance grown from solution, melt or vapour can crystallize in more than one possible structural modifications, depending on the conditions of temperature and pressure prevailing at the time of growth. This phenomenon of the same chemical substance crystallizing in more than one structure (crystallographic modifications) is known as polymorphism. The different modifications are called the polymorphs or polymorphic modifications of that substance. They can be obtained from solid state phase transformations also. Polymorphism therefore includes every possible difference in the crystalline structures of a substance of constant chemical composition, except homogeneous deformations.

Since the different modifications have the same chemical composition they have similar chemical properties; but their physical properties, like density, specific heat, conductivity, melting point, and optical behaviour, which depend on the arrangement of atoms in the structure may be widely different.

## Atomic Packings in AB₂ (or MX₂ – type) Compounds:

### Cadmium Iodide Structure:

Cadmium iodide is known to be an ionic compound, the ionic radii of Cd and I being 0.97Å and 2.16Å, respectively. The structure consists of a close packing of the I ions with the Cd ions distributed among the voids. The radius ratio $r_{Cd}/r_1 = 0.45$ permits the Cd ions to occupy the octahedral voids, the composition then requires a 6 : 3 coordination of Cd and I ions. Since there are only half as many Cd ions as I ions in the structure, only one-half of the total voids are occupied. The Cd ions form close packed layers, occupying alternate layers of octahedral voids between I ions, i.e., there is one Cd layer after every two I layers (Fig. 3.33). The structure therefore consists of extended molecular sheets (called minimal sandwiches) with a layer of Cd ions sandwiched between two close packed layers of I ions. The structure of minimal sandwich is shown in Fig. 3.34 in projection on (0001) plane. The binding within the minimal sandwich is ionic in character and is much stronger than the binding between successive sandwiches which is of van der Waals type. Because of the weak van der Waals bonding between the sandwiches, the material possesses the cleavage characteristic of a layer structure. Cadmium iodide structure can have a centre of symmetry in octahedral voids but cannot have a symmetry plane perpendicular to [00.1]. Cadmium iodide can therefore have five possible space groups-P3ml, P$\bar{3}$ml, R3m, R$\bar{3}$m and $P6_3mc$. Cubic symmetry is not possible in $CdI_2$ on account of the presence of Cd atoms. The most common modifications of $CdI_2$ are 4H and 2H structures with the stacking sequences $A\gamma B$ $C\alpha B$ ... and $A\gamma B$ ..., where the Greek letters denote the positions of Cd ions. In addition, this material also displays a large number of modifications with different repeat periods known as "polytypes".

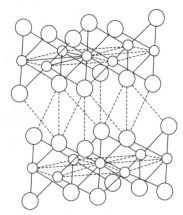

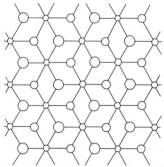

**Fig. 3.33** **The layer structure of cadmium iodide. Small circles represent Cd ions and larger ones represent the I ions**

**Fig. 3.34** **The structure of a "miniml sandwich" of CdI$_2$ in projection on (0001). Small circles (Cd ions) are in one plane and larger circles (1 ions) are in the plane above and below**

## Polytypism

The phenomenon of polytypism may be defined, in general, as the ability of a substance to crystallize into a large number of different crystallographic modifications, which differ in the number and manner of stacking of layers in the unit cell in a particular direction. The two unit cell dimensions parallel to the close packed layers are same for all modifications. The third dimension depends on the stacking sequence, is always an integral multiple of the layer spacing. As a result, the polytypism, sometimes referred to as one-dimensional polymorphism. A little consideration, however, reveals that the phenomenon of polytypism is quite distinct from polymorphism. The polymorphic modifications of a compound normally formed under different thermodynamic conditions of temperature and pressure, each having its own range of thermodynamic stability and differing from others in its physical properties. On the other hand, polytypes grow under the same conditions of temperature and pressure and have very nearly equal densities and internal energies.

The different polytypic modifications of $CdI_2$ consist of different manner of close packing the I ions, the positions of the Cd ions being then automatically determined. The coordination polyhedra in all these are octahedra with a Cd ion at the centre and I ions at the comers. The arrangement of the coordination polyhedra for the simplest structure (2H) |AB| ..., is shown in Fig 3.35, and the corresponding hexagonal unit cell is shown in Fig. 3.36. In this, the basal triangles of the octahedra in successive layers are oriented parallel to one another. For 4H |ABCD| ... structure, they would be rotated through 60° relative to each other. The coordination octahedra in the structure are almost regular, three of the I-I distances being 4.21Å and the other three 4.24Å. Moreover, these distances are nearly equal to the sum of the ionic radii of I indicating that the I ions are almost in contact with each other. The observed Cd-I distance is, however, only 2.99Å, while the sum of the ionic radii is 3.13Å. The separation, $h$ between the successive layers of iodine ions is equal to 3.42Å, and therefore an ideally octahedral bonding would require the Cd-I distance to be $(\sqrt{3}/2)\, h = 2.96$Å. The observed value of 2.99Å is slightly higher which indicates that the actual arrangement is slightly different from the ideal one.

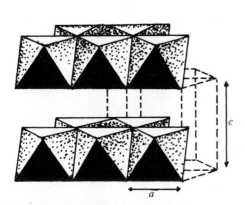

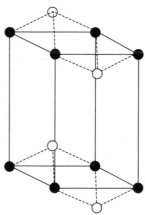

**Fig. 3.35** **The packing of coordination octahedra in CdI₂ for a 2H structure**

**Fig. 3.36** **The hexagonal unit cell of the two layered CdI₂ polytype. Open axis circles represent I ions and the black circle the Cd ions**

## 3.14 NOTATIONS USED FOR REPRESENTING CLOSE PACKED STRUCTURES

Different notations employed to distinguish various close packed structures have been described in detail by Verma and Krishna, Trigunayat and Chadha, Palosz and Fichtner. A few of them have been developed specially for describing $CdI_2$ structures, while others can describe both *MX*- and $MX_2$-structures. These existing polytype notations can be put into two different categories: (a) General notations, and (b) Special notations.

**General Notations**

The notations belonging to this group are applicable to both *MX*- and $MX_2$-type close packed structures. We shall give a brief description of only those notations which are more commonly used.

## Ramsdell's Notation

Close packed polytypic structures can be described by specfying the total number of layers in the hexagonal unit cell followed by the letter *H*, *R* or *C* to indicate the lattice type. Thus a symbol nH represents a structure with *n* layers in the primitive hexagonal unit cell while *mR* denotes a structure whose primitive lattice is rhombohedral and contains *m* layers in its hexagonal unit cell. In order to distinguish polytypes having same periodicity and lattice type but distinct layer stacking sequences, subscripts like *a*, *b*, *c*, or 1, 2, 3, are often used. This scheme of notation is applicable to all (including non-close-packed) structures, but it does not reveal the actual arrangement of layers in the unit cell.

## The Classical ABC Notation

The classical *ABC* notation provides the most exhaustive manner of describing close packed sequences. When a close packed structure is projected normally on a plane parallel to the layer, the layers (the atomic planes) fall into three possible positions, denoted by *A*, *B* and *C* (Fig. 3.37). As an example, the four layered polytype is represented by the stacking sequence *ABCB*...

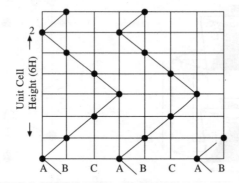

**Fig. 3.37   Ramdell's zig-zag sequence of Si (or C) atoms in the $(11\bar{2}0)$ plane of 6H (ABCACB)**

The classical *ABC* notation is well suited to small period polytypes, however, the representation becomes more and more difficult for long period polytypes. Also it does not reveal the symmetry very quickly. However, it provides a complete and unambiguous representation of various close packed polytypic structures.

## The Zhdanov Notation

The Zhdanov notation is a numerical form of the classical *ABC* notation. The symbol consisting of digits in succession, representing the numbers of consecutive cyclic and anticyclic layers in the *ABC* sequence. In this notation, the 4H structure *ABCB/A*... is denoted by the numerical sequence (22).

Ramsdell interpreted the Zhdanov symbol in terms of zig-zag sequence of atoms in the $(11\bar{2}0)$ planes of close packed polytypic structure. Fig. 3.37 illustrates the meaning of the zig-zag sequence, taking 6H (33) structure of *MX*-type as an example. If an *M* or *X* atom lies on *A* positions in one layer, the next atom must be either on the right in *B* positions, or on the left in *C* positions in the neighbouring layers. If the third layer has its atom on the right, it will continue to move on the right or it may change its direction and go to the left. Because of these repeated changes, a zig-zag pattern results. Such an arrangement can be described in terms of the number of layers added in each direction in succession and it is called zig-zag sequence. The unit cell is completed after arriving at an identical atom having the same environment as the atom from which we started. Thus in Fig. 3.37 the unit cell of 6H is completed at 2 and not at 1.

To find whether two or more similar looking Zhdanov symbols represent the same or different structures, one has simply to examine if they are *TC* (translationally congruent) or *RC* (reversely congruent). If they are so, the structures are congruent; otherwise they are non congruent. Jain and Trigunayat evolved some simple practical criteria to decide the congruence of *MX*$_2$-and *MX*-type polytypic structures. (i) For close packed *MX*$_2$-type structures, two Zhdanov symbols are *TC* if one is obtainable from the other by an "even shift" (including zero shift) of the starting point, i.e. 2211→2112 represent the same structure. For *MX*-type structures, two Zhdanov symbols are *TC* if one is obtainable from the other by any shift of the starting point. (ii) For *MX*$_2$-type structures, two Zhdanov symbols are *RC* if one is obtainable from the other by literally reversing the sequence plus rewriting it after an "odd shift" of the starting point i.e.

| 1232 | $\rightarrow$ | 2321 | $\rightarrow$ | 2123 |
|:---:|:---:|:---:|:---:|:---:|
| (True seq.) | | (Reverse seq.) | | (After odd shift) |

This implies that the symbols 1232 and 2123 represent the same structure. For *MX*-type structures, no two Zhdanov symbols are *RC*. Any ambiguity if present in the symbols, can be removed by employing the forgoing practical rules. Having done this, the Zhdavov symbol is able to represent all close packed polytypic structures uniquely and unambiguously. This is a very concise notation and being numerical in nature this is most easy to handle.

### The h-c Notation
A notation based on the relative position of atomic layers has been independently employed by Pauling, Wyckoff and Jagodzinski. This notation takes into account the orientations of layers in the immediate neighbourhood of the reference layer. A layer is said to be in the hexagonal orientation if it is surrounded by similar layers on its two sides i.e. *BAB*, *CAC*, etc. and is denoted as "h" while a layer is said to be in cubic orientation if it is surrounded by different layers on its two sides, i.e. *BAC*, *CAB*, etc. and is denoted as "c". Thus the 4H structure with the stacking sequence *ABCB* /*A*... can be written as hchc... in the *h-c* notation. This notation is particularly useful in describing the faulted structures and in calculating the stacking fault energies.

It is quite easy to transform from one notation to another. For this purpose, it is convenient to write the complete *ABC* sequence of the structure first and then express it in the desired notation. Some close packed structures expressed in different notations are listed in Table 3.3.

### Special Notations
In the recent past, some special notations have been proposed by Palosz and Przedmojski, Palosz, and Fichtner for the representation of *CdI*$_2$ (*MX*$_2$-type) structures. They are as follows:

**Table 3.3   Different notations for describing some close-packings**

| Ramsdell notation | ABC sequence | Zhdanov sequence | hc-notation |
|---|---|---|---|
| 2H | AB | (11) | h |
| 3C | ABC | ($\infty$) | c |
| 4H | ABCB | (22) | hc |
| 6H$_1$ | ABCBAB | (2211) | hchchh |
| 6H$_2$ | ABCACB | (33) | hcc |
| 9R | ABACACBCB | (12)$_3$ | hhc |

### The xyz Notation

Assuming the triple layers ($X$-$M$-$X$) as the basic structural units, Palosz and Przedmojski proposed *xyz*-notation to describe uniquely the $MX_2$-type polytypes with special reference to cadmium iodide. The six possible types of triple layers have been defined as: $x \equiv A\ \gamma B$, $y \equiv B\ \alpha\ C$, $z \equiv C\ \beta A$, $\bar{x} \equiv C\ \alpha\ B$, $\bar{y} \equiv A\ \beta\ C$ and $\bar{z} \equiv B\ \gamma A$, respectively. Thus, each polytypic structure can be written as a sequence of symbols x y z $\bar{x}$ $\bar{y}$ $\bar{z}$, e.g. the structure 6H$_2$ (represented as 33 in the Zhdanov symbol) is written as $\bar{x}$ $\bar{y}$ z. The shortened notation corresponding to *xyz*-notation is obtained in the form of a sequence of numbers, i.e. $n$, $\bar{n}$, $n'$, $\bar{n}'$, $n''$, $\bar{n}''$. In the shortened form the 6H$_2$ structure is written as $\bar{1}'1\bar{1}$.

As far as the orientations of different ($M$- and $X$-) layers are concerned, the *xyz*-notation is able to describe them uniquely. However, if the corresponding shortened form is considered (which is generally used in such representations), handling becomes very difficult particularly for the polytypes belonging to group III and IV (as classified by the authors) because of the involvement of primes, double primes, and bars etc., alongwith the numbers. Also the symmetry operations used to find the equivalent structures are equally cumbersome. The authors seem to have felt this difficulty, as one of them proposed another notation (i.e. t–o–f) for representing the CdI$_2$ structures very soon after the *xyz*-notation.

### The t-o-f Notation

Palosz proposed the t-o-f notation to describe the observed CdI$_2$ polytypes as a mixture of 2H, 4H and the faulted units. In this notation, he proposed ten different sequences of three neighbour layers in the *xyz*-notation, they correspond to *t*, *o*, f1, f2, ... f8 in the t-o-f notation. As an example, the polytype 8H$_2$ can be represented as *t* f2 *o* f1. According to this notation, many observed polytypes contain high percentage of faults, sometimes even 100 percent as in the case 6H$_2$ (f3 f3 f5), 8H$_2$ (f1 f2), 12R (f4 f5) and 18R (f1 f1 f5), which seems to be quite unreasonable.

Recently, Wahab and Rajni Kant have shown that 2H and 4H units are sufficient to describe the structure of CdI$_2$ polytypes. Accordingly, the consideration of faulted units is not required for the purpose of representation of the ordered polytypic structures.

### The $\alpha\beta\gamma$-Notation

The $\alpha\beta\gamma$-notation proposed by Fichtner is a modified form of the *xyz*-notation, proposed by Palosz and Przedmojski. The six possible triple layers defined in this case are: $\alpha \equiv C\alpha B$, $\beta \equiv A\beta C$, $\gamma \equiv B\gamma A$, $\bar{\alpha} \equiv B\alpha C$, $\bar{\beta} \equiv C\beta A$, $\bar{\gamma} \equiv A\gamma B$.

The $\alpha\beta\gamma$- and *xyz*-notations differ only in the choice of letters used to denote the triple layers (or sandwiches) as $\alpha\beta\gamma$... in one case while *xyz*... in the other. Therefore, the applicability and acceptability of this notation is the same as that of the *xyz*-nottion

**The thr-Notation**

Fichtner proposed yet another notation, known as thr-notation assuming the 2H, 4H and 6R as the basic structural units. As an example, the polytype $8H_1$ can be represented as $h_2 \, t_2$ in this notation.

We know that the polytype 6R has not been observed so far in $CdI_2$ crystals. Moreover, like t-o-f notation the inclusion of 6R in this case is not required for representation of $CdI_2$ polytypes. Zhdanov notation along with some special notations, for a few known $CdI_2$ polytypes are given Table 3.4.

**Table 3.4 Notations of some known polytypes of $CdI_2$.**

| Ramsdell notation | Zhdanov notation | xyz-notation shortened form | t-o-f notation | thr-notation |
|---|---|---|---|---|
| 2H | 11 | $\infty$ | o | t |
| 4H | 22 | $\bar{1}1$ | tt | $(h)_2$ |
| $6H_1$ | 2211 | $\bar{2}1$ | tf2f1 | $h_2 t$ |
| $6H_2$ | 33 | $\bar{1}'1\bar{1}$ | f3f3f4 | hhr |
| $8H_1$ | $22(11)_2$ | $\bar{3}1$ | tf2 of1 | $h_2 t_2$ |
| $8H_2$ | $(112)_2$ | $\bar{2}2$ | $(f1 \, f2)_2$ | htht |
| $8H_3$ | 1232 | $\bar{1}'1\bar{1}1$ | tf4 tf5 | $h_2 \bar{h}_2$ |
| $10H_1$ | $(22)_2 \, 11$ | $2\bar{1}1\bar{1}$ | $(t)_3 \, f4tf5$ | $h_4 t$ |
| $10H_2$ | $(221)_2$ | $\bar{1}'2\bar{1}1$ | tf1f1tf5 | $h_2 th_2$ |
| $12H_1$ | 222123 | $\bar{1}'(1\bar{1})_2 1$ | $(t)_3 \, f4tf5$ | $h_4 \bar{h}_2$ |
| $12H_2$ | 22121121 | $\bar{2}'2\bar{1}$ | tf5f1f2f1f1 | $h_2 th t\bar{h}$ |
| $12H_3$ | $(22)_2 \, (11)_2$ | $\bar{3}1\bar{1}1$ | $(t)_3 \, f2 \, of1$ | $h_4 t_2$ |
| $12H_4$ | 22211211 | $2\bar{2}1\bar{1}$ | $(t)_2 \, (f1f2)_2$ | $h_3 tht$ |
| $12H_5$ | $(11)_2 1232$ | $\bar{1}'1\bar{1}3$ | tf4tf2of2 | $h_2 \bar{h}_2 t_2$ |
| $12H_6$ | 22111221 | $\bar{1}'2\bar{1}2$ | $t(f2)_2 \, t(f1)_2$ | $h_2 t\bar{h}_2 t$ |
| 12R | $(13)_3$ | $\bar{1}1$ | f4f5 | $h\bar{h}$ |

## 3.15 SUMMARY

1. The fcc and the hcp are the most efficient way of packing the atoms.
2. Close packed arrangements can be differentiated form one another in the number and manner of packing of atomic planes.
3. Degree of close packing of a structure is a function of *c/a*. For an ideal close packed structure $c/a = 0.8165n$, where *n* is any integer.
4. Close packed structures are theoretically infinite, but there are only two kinds of voids in close packing; i.e. tetrahedral and octahedral.

5. There are as many octahedral voids (and twice as many tetrahedral voids) as there are spheres.

6. Relative sizes of atoms present in a crystal impose limitations on the coordination that they can have in real structure. Conversely, the coordination number of an atom imposes a limitation on the radius ratio.

7. Close packing of spheres can equally well be represented by the packing of coordination polyhedra of voids. Such representation display symmetries more clearly.

8. Pauling postulated a set of rules that could determine the nature of arrangement of ions in the structure. With suitable modifications, they can be applied to other compounds.

9. Many metallic and non-metallic elements and compounds of $MX$- and $MX_2$-classes assume close packed structures.

10. ZnS and SiC of $MX$-class and $CdI_2$ and $PbI_2$ of $MX_2$-class exibit polytypism.

## 3.16 DEFINITIONS

*Anion:* A negatively charged ion: the result of an electronegative atom's having acquired one or more extra electrons.

*Axial ratio:* The ratio $c/a$ of lattice parameters in the unit cells of a given structure.

*Cation:* A positively charged ion; the result of an electropositive atom's having lost one or more of its valence electrons.

*Close packing:* An extended three dimensional packing arrangement in which equal size atoms are packed as closely together as possible.

*Coordination:* The packing of atoms around another atom.

*Coordination number:* The number of first nearest neighbour atoms (or ions) surrounding and touching a central atom (or oppositely charged ions).

*Coordination Polyhedra:* A polyhedron resulting from joining the centres of all atoms which are touching a central atom; each vertex represents one of the surrounding atoms; the polyhedron usually called an anion polyhedron if it represents anion surrounding cation.

*Critical radius ratio:* The ratio of cation radius to anion radius for the condition where the surrounding anions are touching each other as well as the central cation.

*Identity period:* The number of layers required to complete the unit cell, also called repeat period.

*Polymorphism:* The phenomenon that a chemical substance crystallizes in more than one structure at different thermodynamical conditions of temperature and pressure.

*Polytypism:* The phenomenon that a chemical substance crystallizes in more than one structure (theoretically infinite) at the same thermodynamical conditions of temperature and pressure.

*Radius ratio:* The ratio of the radius of the central atom to the atoms surrounding it.

*Void:* The vacant interstitial space between the close packed atoms.

## REVIEW QUESTIONS AND PROBLEMS

1. How many atoms are there in sc, bcc and fcc unit cells? Calculate the packing efficiencies for these structures.

   *Ans.* 1, 2, and 4 atoms. 52%, 68% and 74%.

2. Determine the packing efficiency of equal spheres located at the points of simple hexagonal and hexagonal close packed lattices.

   *Ans.* 68% and 74%.

3. Compare the packing efficiency of spheres of equal size in a hexagonal close packing with that of cubic close packing.

   *Ans.* Both structures have 74% efficiency.

4. Determine the magnitude of the closest distance of approach between the neighbouring atoms in sc, bcc, fcc and diamond cubic crystals in terms of their lattice parameter $a$.

   *Ans.* $a, a\sqrt{3}/2, a/\sqrt{2}, a\sqrt{3}/4$.

5. Determine the packing efficiency in the diamond structure.

   *Ans.* 34%.

6. Calculate the void space in a close packing of $n$ spheres of radius 1.000, $n$ spheres of radius 0.414 and $2n$ spheres of radius 0.225.

   *Ans.* 19%

7. Find the diameter of the largest atom that would fit into the void in fcc nickel without distortion.

   *Ans.* 1.03 Å.

8. Find the diameter of the largest sphere that will fit into the void produced by the bcc packing of atoms of radius $R$. The void is located at (0 1/2 1/4) and other equivalent positions.

   *Ans.* 0.29R.

9. By using plane geometry calculate cation-anion radius ratio for a triangular arrangement in which cation is in contact with the anion but does not push them apart.

   *Ans.* 0.155.

10. Calculate the ratio of cation-anion distance to anion-anion distance in an anion coordination tetrahedron.

    *Ans.* 0.604.

11. Calculate the ratio of the volumes of a tetrahedron and an octahedron having the same edge length.

    *Ans.* 0.216.

12. What factors other than radius ratio might determine the coordination of one atom by another in a crystal?

13. What is the nearest neighbour distance in bcc and fcc structures when the atomic radius is taken as 10 Å?

    *Ans.* 20 Å in each case.

14. Show that the critical radius ratio for a triangular coordination is 0.155.

15. Show that the critical radius ratio for a tetrahedral coordination is 0.225.

16. Show that the critical radius ratio for an octahedral coordination is 0.414.

17. Show that the critical radius ratio for a cubic coordination is 0.732.

18. Calculate the $c/a$ ratio for the hcp lattice and compare this with actual values for hcp elements.

    *Ans.* 1.633.

19. Show that for an ideal hcp structure, where the atomic spheres touch each other, the ratio $c/a$ is given by

$$c / a = (8/3)^{1/2} = 1.633.$$

20. Calculate the limit of ionic radius ratio for stability of NaCl structure, and compare this with the actual radius ratio for other ionic crystals having NaCl structure.

    *Ans.* 0.414 – 1/0.414.

21. What is the coordination number of Manganese in MnO structure if $r_{Mn} = 0.80$Å and $r_o = 1.40$Å?

    *Ans.* 6:6.

22. What is the coordination number of iron in $Fe_2O_3$ structure if $r_{Fe} = 0.64$Å and $r_o = 1.40$Å.

    *Ans.* 6:6.

23. What are permissible ranges of radius ratio in $MX_2$-type compounds? Prepare a Table similar to Table 3.2 in the text.

24. Prepare a graph like Fig. 3.19, showing the permissible ranges of radius ratio for $MX_2$-type compounds.

25. Determine the identity period $n$ from the following stacking formula:
    (a) . . . . . . hhchcchc . . . .
    (b) . . . . hc . . ..
    (c) . . . . hhcc . . .
    by converting them to *ABC* notation.

    *Ans.* 8H, 4H and 12R.

# Chapter 4

# Atomic Shape and Size

## 4.1 INTRODUCTION

In earlier chapters we studied about the role of atoms in building crystals, bond formation and their packing in actual structures. However, in this chapter we shall study about the shape and size of the atom.

The ideas expressed by scientists during the early years of the 20th century regarding the structure of the atom were not unanimous. J.J. Thomson (1899) proposed the atoms as uniform spheres of positively charged matter in which electrons are embedded like plums in a pudding as shown in Fig. 4.1, and hence sometimes called as plum-pudding model. On the other hand, Earnest Rutherford (1911) proposed that the atoms are composed of tiny nucleus, in which all its positive charge and almost all its mass are concentrated at the center, and that the negative charge (electrons) are distributed throughout the atomic volume (Fig. 4.2). In order to confirm his model, Rutherford bombarded $\alpha$-particles (doubly charged helium nuclei) on a thin gold foil and observed that a number of $\alpha$-particles pass through the foil without any appreciable deflection, but some of them were deflected through large angle and a few of them even rebounded from the foil suffering a deflection of nearly 180°. The observations made from his $\alpha$-particle scattering experiments led him to suggest the following.

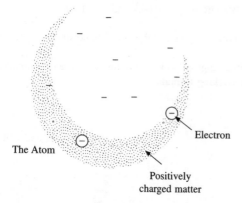

Fig. 4.1   The Thomson model of the atom

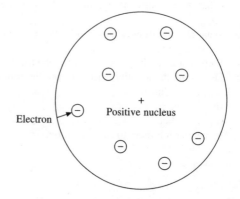

Fig. 4.2   The Rutherford model of atom

1. An atom has a central core where almost the entire mass and all its positive charge is concentrated. The core is called the nucleus of the atom. The size of the nucleus is about $10^{-15}$ m.
2. The remaining part of the atom contains electrons which surround the nucleus. The size of the atom is about $10^{-10}$ m.
3. The total negative charge of the electrons is equal to the charge on the nucleus because the atom as a whole is electrically neutral.
4. The electrons are not at rest but revolve round the nucleus in various orbits in the same way as the planets revolve around the sun (Fig. 4.3). The necessary centripetal force is being provided by the electrostatic force of attraction between the nucleus and the electrons.

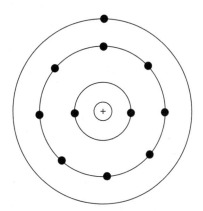

**Fig. 4.3 Showing various electronic orbits in Na atom**

The main drawback in the Rutherford model is that it is unable to explain the stability of an atom. According to the model, the electrons revolve round the nucleus in fixed orbits and are continually accelerated (because of change of direction at every instant of motion). Further, according to classical electrodynamics, an accelerating charge must radiate energy in the form of electromagnetic radiations. As a result, an orbitting electron should keep on losing its energy and thus move along a spiral path of decreasing radius till it falls into the nucleus. Thus, the atom would become unstable. this is contrary to the experimental observations. Another drawback of the model is that an atom should emit continuous energy spectrum (because according to this model all electron orbits are possible), but a hydrogen atom emits a line spectrum.

## 4.2 BOHR MODEL OF THE HYDROGEN ATOM

In 1913, Neils Bohr proposed a model particularly for hydrogen atom, but it is valid for all other atoms. He retained the essential features of Rutherford model. In addition, he introduced the concept of stationary orbits to explain the stability of the atom. Bohr suggested the following postulates to explain the electron motion in an atom and the observed spectral lines.

1. The electrons in an atom continue to revolve round the uncleus under the influence of Coulomb's force of attraction between them and the nucleus. This force is balanced by the Newtonian centrifugal force. i.e.

$$\frac{(Ze)(e)}{4\pi\varepsilon_0 r^2} = \frac{mv^2}{r} \tag{1}$$

2. The electrons cannot move in all possible orbits allowed by classical theory but they are permitted to have only those orbits for which the angular momentum of the electon is an integral multiple of $h/2\pi$, where $h$ is Planck's constant. Thus for any permitted orbit,

$$I\omega = n\left(\frac{h}{2\pi}\right)$$

or

$$mr_n^2 \times \frac{v_n}{r_n} = n\left(\frac{h}{2\pi}\right)$$

or

$$mr_n v_n = n\left(\frac{h}{2\pi}\right) \tag{2}$$

This equation is called the Bohr's quantum condition.

3. The electrons continue to revolve in their respective permitted orbits without radiating any energy. Such orbits are called the stationary orbits. The nearest orbit from the nucleus (i.e. the innermost orbit) has the least energy and the farthest (outermost) orbit has the maximum energy.

4. The atom can absorb or radiate energy if the electron jumps from an inner orbit to an outer orbit or falls from an outer orbit to inner orbit. If $E_i$ and $E_f$ are energies associated with the orbits of principal quantum number $n_i$ and $n_f$ respectively ($n_i < n_f$), the frequency of the radiation emitted is given by

$$h\nu = E_i - E_f \tag{3}$$

This equation is called Bohr's frequency condition.

In order to calculate the radius of an orbit and corresponding energy, let us consider the case of hydrogen atom, where a single electron revolves in a circular orbit of radius $r$ as shown in Fig. 4.4. From the above mentioned postulate 1, we have

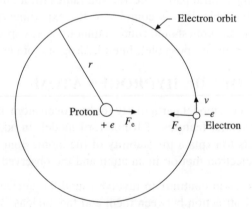

**Fig. 4.4   The hydrogen atom**

$$\frac{mv_n^2}{r_n} = \frac{Ze^2}{4\pi\varepsilon_0 r_n^2} \tag{4}$$

or

$$mr_n v_n^2 = \frac{Ze^2}{4\pi\varepsilon_0} \tag{5}$$

Now dividing eq. 5 by eq. 2, we obtain the velocity of the electron in the nth orbit as

$$v_n = \frac{Ze^2}{2nh\varepsilon_0} \tag{6}$$

Since the veocity is inversely proportional to the principal quantum number $n$, the electron moves at a lower speed in the higher orbits and vice-versa. Further, substituting the value of $v_n$ in eq. 2, we obtain

$$r_n = \frac{n^2h^2\varepsilon_0}{\pi mZe^2} \tag{7}$$

where $m$ is the mass of the electron, $e$ is its charge, $h$ is Planck's constant, $\varepsilon_0$ is the permittivity in the free space and $n$ is the principal quantum number which can assume only the integral values, e.g. $n = 1, 2, 3, \ldots$ and the corresponding permitted orbits are K, L, M, $\ldots$ respectively. From eq. 7, it is clear that $r_n \propto n^2$, i.e. the radii of stationary orbits increase with $n^2$. The total energy of the electron in the nth orbit is given by

$$E_n = \text{K.E.} + \text{P.E.} = \frac{mv_n^2}{2} - \frac{Ze^2}{4\pi\varepsilon_0 r_n}$$

$$= \frac{1}{2}\left(\frac{Ze^2}{4\pi\varepsilon_0 r_n}\right) - \frac{Ze^2}{4\pi\varepsilon_0 r_n} = -\frac{Ze^2}{8\pi\varepsilon_0 r_n}$$

Substituting the value of $r_n$ from eq. 7, we have

$$E_n = -\left(\frac{Ze^2}{8\pi\varepsilon_0}\right) \times \left(\frac{\pi mZe^2}{n^2h^2\varepsilon_0}\right) = -\left(\frac{mZ^2e^4}{8\varepsilon_0^2n^2h^2}\right) \tag{8}$$

where the negative sign indicates that the electron is bound to the nucleus and some work must be done to knock it away. Equation 8 further indicates that as n increases, $E_n$ becomes less negative and hence its algebric value increases. The electron therefore has the minimum energy when it is in its innermost orbit, i.e. $n = 1$. Now if an electron jumps from an outer (initial) orbit $n_2$ of higher energy to an inner (final) orbit $n_1$ of lower energy, then from eq. 3 the frequency of radiation emitted will be givne by

$$hv = (E_i - E_f) = -\left(\frac{mZ^2e^4}{8\varepsilon_0^2n_2^2h^2}\right) + \left(\frac{mZ^2e^4}{8\varepsilon_0^2n_1^2h^2}\right)$$

$$= \frac{mZ^2e^4}{8\varepsilon_0^2h^2}\left(\frac{1}{n_1^2} - \frac{1}{n_2^2}\right) \tag{9}$$

## 4.3 ATOMIC SHAPE

The most stable state of an atom is that in which all the electrons occupy orbits of the lowest permitted energy, i.e they are in the normal state or the ground state. This arrangement is slightly disturbed if the atom is not electrically neutral. For example, an atom can lose one or more electrons and becomes positively charged. The electrons lying in the outermost orbit (called the valence electrons) of the atom can be removed most easily. The energy required to remove one valence electron from a neutral atom is called its first ionization potential, the energy required to remove the second valence electron is called the second ionization potential, and so on. The resulting positive ions have higher energies (they are said to be in the excited states) than the neutral atom and acquire a valence of +1, +2 etc. On the other hand, if one or more electrons are added to an atom, this becomes negatively charged and the resulting ions aquire a valence of –1, –2, etc. Most positive ions are stable, unless brought in the vicinity or other electrons with which they neutralize their netgative charge, while most negative ions are unstable, the negatively charged ions repel the negatively charged electrons. However, there are some exceptions to this, notably the halogens, oxygen, and sulfur. These elements actually lose energy on becoming negatively charged. The energy difference between the state of a neutral atom (ground state) and the state of a negative ion is called electron affinity and is used as a measure of the electronegativity of an atom. Similarly, the ease with which an atom gives up its valence electrons determines how much electropositive it is. The loss or gain of one or more electrons does not greatly affect the spherical shape of an atom. Actually if an atom loses electrons, the positively charged uncleus tends to draw in the remaining electrons more tightly. Conversely, if electrons are added to an atom, the repulsive forces tend to push the outer electrons farther away. This, however, generally affects the size and not the shape of an atom.

## 4.4  WAVE MECHANICAL CONCEPT OF ATOM

Some insight into the possibilities of the wave mechanical approach to atomic structure is obtained by considering the Bohr quantum conditions. They define the stationary states which correspond to definite energy levels of the atom. However, from Heisenberg's uncertainty principle, we know that

$$\Delta E \cdot \Delta t \geq \frac{h}{2\pi} \tag{10}$$

where $\Delta E$ and $\Delta t$ are the uncertainties in measuring energy and time, respectively. If the energy is known exactly, then $\Delta E \to 0$ and therefore $\Delta t \to \infty$, implying that the error in measuring time will be extremely large. It follows that the motion of electron around the orbit will be unobservable in terms of time and hence the precise electron orbits become rather meaningless. Therefore the whereabouts of an electron at a given instant of time was replaced by the probability picture by Born who associated probability with wave amplitude to resolve the wave particle dualism. To do this we must replace the electron motion in permissible orbits by imagining them to be associated with a series of waves of wavelengths given by de Broglie equation

$$\lambda = \frac{h}{p} = \frac{h}{mv} \tag{11}$$

In order that the waves should not cancel each other by interference in any permissible orbit, the electron must move in such a manner as to produce a standing wave in the orbit. This can happen only if the permissible orbits contain an integral number of waves as shown in Fig. 4.5. This means that

$$2\pi r = n\lambda \tag{12}$$

where $r$ is the radius of the permitted orbit and $n$ is an integer. Substituting the value of $\lambda$ from eq. 11 into eq. 12, we obtain

$$2\pi r = n\,\frac{h}{mv}$$

or
$$mvr = n\,\frac{h}{2\pi} \tag{13}$$

This is just the Bohr condition for a stationary orbit which appeared so arbitrary from the old quantum theory, but now comes quite logically from the wave mechanical model.

According to the wave mechanical concept, the electron possesses a wave like nature and can no longer be pictured as particle moving in an orbit of definite radius. Instead, we can speak of a probability distribution of electron density. Thus in the case of hydrogen atom which has a single electron in its ground state, the circular orbit of the Bohr theory is replaced by a spherical probability distribution in which there is a finite probability of finding the electron at large

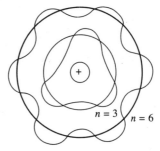

**Fig. 4.5  De Broglie's stationary wave quantized orbits**

distances from the nucleus, the most probable distance proves to be exactly equal to the radius of the Bohr orbit. Thus the orbits representing excited states of the hydrogen atom are spheres of corresponding larger radii. The experimental proof that atoms are nearly spherical is given by the results of X-ray diffraction investigation of crystal structures. Because X-rays are scattered by the electrons in each atoms, it is possible to synthesize a picture of distribution of electron density directly from the experimentally observed intensities, after their relative phases have been determined. One such synthesis is shown is Fig. 4.6, which is an electron density map of cubanite, $Cu_2FeS_3$, projected on the $xy$ plane. The contours of the figure join the points having same electron density. Such structural studies are useful in determining the effective radii of the spherical atom.

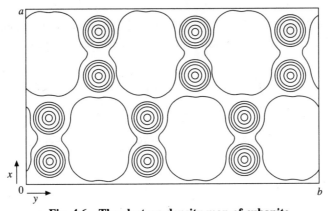

**Fig. 4.6  The electron density map of cubanite**

*Example:* Calculate the radius of the first orbit for the hydrogen atom. Also give a general expression for calculating other radii.

*Solution:* Given: $n = 1$ (the ground state orbit) and $Z = 1$. Now, using eq. 7 and substituting the values of constants, we have

$$r_n = \frac{n^2 h^2 \varepsilon_0}{\pi m Z e^2}$$

or

$$r_1 = \frac{1 \times (6.626 \times 10^{-34})^2 \times 8.85 \times 10^{-12}}{\pi \times 9.1 \times 10^{-31} \times (1.6 \times 10^{-19})^2}$$

$$= 0.529 \times 10^{-10} \text{ m} = 0.529 \text{ Å} = r_B$$

The radius of the first orbit of the hydrogen atom is known as Bohr radius ($r_B$). This can also be written as

$$r_1 = (1)^2 r_B$$

Similarly

$$r_2 = (2)^2 r_B$$

$$r_n = (n)^2 r_B$$

*Example:* Calculate the first three ionization potentials of the hydrogen atom (where $Z = 1$).

*Solution:* Using eq. 8 and substituting the values of constants, we obtain

$$E_n = -\left(\frac{m Z^2 e^4}{8 \varepsilon_0^2 n^2 h^2}\right) = -\frac{9.1 \times 10^{-31} (1.6 \times 10^{-19})^4}{n^2 \times 8(8.85 \times 10^{-12})^2 (6.626 \times 10^{-34})^2}$$

$$= -\frac{2.18 \times 10^{-18}}{n^2} \text{ Joules}$$

$$= -\frac{2.18 \times 10^{-18}}{n^2 (1.6 \times 10^{-19})} = -\frac{13.6}{n^2} \text{ eV}$$

Now, substituting $n = 1$, we have $E_1 = -13.6$ eV. This corresponds to the ground state energy of the atom, and is called the first ionization potential of the hydrogen atom. Similarly, for $n = 2$, we have

$$E_2 = -\frac{13.6}{4} = -3.4 \text{ eV (second ionization potential)}$$

and for $n = 3$.

$$E_3 = -\frac{13.6}{9} = -1.511 \text{ eV (third ionization potential)}$$

## 4.5  ATOMIC SIZE

Truly speaking no precise physical significance can be attached to the concept of atomic or ionic radius since the electron density associated with atomic wave functions approach zero assymptotically. However, common sense suggests that the observed interatomic distances may be divided according to some formula giving at least a relative scale of sizes. Starting from simple considerations, we find that there exist two distinctly different situations. Firstly, there are atoms or ions which acquire closed shell electronic configuration while forming molecular and ionic crystals. Cationic sizes will definitely be smaller than those of neutral atoms due to orbital contraction resulting from Coulombic attraction, and anions will be correspondingly larger. Secondly, the formation of bonds by overlap of atomic orbitals on different atoms is resulting in build-up of electron density between the atoms. This situation corresponds to bonding in covalent crystals and in metals. In the second situatin, the problem is much more difficult than in the first because there is no any obvious way of dividing the interatomic distances (except in pure element structures) between the constituent atoms. On the other hand, this difficulty is to some extent compensated by the relative unimportance of size considerations in understanding metallic and covalent structures.

Actually, the size of an atom depends on many factors, the coordination number, radius ratio and the types of forces existing between the atoms, where these forces may differ in different compounds or even different structural arrangements of the same compound. It is therefore definite that the absolute value of atomic size are only approximately known. However, the knowledge of atomic size in a crystal is helpful in predicting the structure of other crystals or to ascertain whether an atom will fit into the voids of parent structure. To understand further, let us consider the following cases in somewhat detail.

## 4.6   IONIC RADII

In an ionic crystal, the attractive Coulomb force is counterbalanced by a repulsive force due to interaction of the outer electron clouds of the ions, resulting in an equilibrium internuclear distance. As we have seen earlier, these outer electrons are responsible for the size of the ions, then it may be assumed that these electrons are attracted towards the nucleus by the charge $Ze$ except for the screening of this charge by the inner electrons. The effective charge may be written as $(Z - S)e$, where $S$ is a screening constant. The radius of an ion may then be written as

$$r_{ion} = \frac{C_n}{Z - S} = \frac{C_n}{Z_{eff}} \tag{14}$$

where $C_n$ is a constant determined by the quantum number and $Z_{eff}$ is the effective nuclear charge. Pauling obtained a set of values for $S$ by theoretical methods combined with other experimental data obtained from molar fraction and X-ray term values. $C_n$ takes the same value for all members of an isoelectronic series (ions having identical electronic structures). For ions with neon configuration, $S = 4.52$ per electron charge, and for argon, $S = 11.25$ per electron charge. Thus for KCl, we have

$$r_{K^+} = \frac{C_n}{19 - 11.25} \text{ and } r_{Cl^-} = \frac{C_n}{17 - 11.25}$$

or

$$\frac{r_{K^+}}{r_{Cl^-}} = \frac{17 - 11.25}{19 - 11.25} = \frac{5.75}{7.75} = 0.74 \tag{15}$$

From experiment $r_{K^+} + r_{Cl^-} = 3.14\text{Å}$. Solution of these equations yield $r_{K^+} = 1.33$ Å, and

$r_{Cl^-}$ = 1.81 Å. Similar calculations can be made on different alkali halides. The radii obtained by this process are known as univalent radii. Pauling obtained the radii of multivalent ions having rock salt structure in two stages. In the first stage, the univalent radii of multivalent ions was determined as if the ions have rock salt structure. Next the ratio of such univalent radii and the ionic radii of the isoelectronic alkali metals or halides are then taken to be equal to the inverse ratio of the corresponding effective nuclear charges. These radii are then transformed into the real multivalent radii (also called crystal radii) by means of a factor which follows readily from the Born model (as discussed in chapter 2). This suggests that the repulsive effect must be taken into account for such calculations.

Considering the Born repulsive energy term as an inverse power of the distance between the ions, $BR^{-n}$ in eq. 8 (Ch. 2), the equilibrium distance $R_e$ can be found to be

$$R_e = \left( \frac{4\pi\varepsilon_0 nB}{AZ_1Z_2e^2} \right)^{1/(n-1)}$$ (16)

This gives the interionic distance in the real crystal formed by multivalent ions ($Z_1 \neq 1$, $Z_2 \neq 1$). This distance can be represented in terms of the equilibrium interionic distance in the crystal formed by univalent ions ($Z_1 = Z_2 = 1$) having the same Born repulsive energy, by the equation

$$R_{\text{multivalent}} = R_{\text{univalent}} \times Z^{-2/(n-1)}$$ (17)

As an example of the Pauling procedure, the univalent radius of the $O^{2-}$ion is equal to $(9 - 4.5)/(8 - 4.5)$ times the standard crystal radius of $F^-$ ion. To obtain the radius of $O^{2-}$ appropriate to an alkaline-earth oxide with the NaCl structure, strictly the radius of $O^{2-}$ appropriate to MgO crystals, the univalent radius is divided by $2^{1/3}$, since for MgO $Z$ is equal to 2 and n is chosen by Pauling equal to 7. This yields the value 1.40 Å for the standard crystal radius of $O^{2-}$. A list of Pauling's crystal radii is given in Table 4.1.

**Table 4.1 Crystal radii of Pauling (in angstroms)**

| -4 | -3 | -2 | -1 | 0 | +1 | +2 | +3 | +4 | +5 | +6 | +7 |
|----|----|----|----|----|----|----|----|----|----|----|----|
|    |    |    | H  | He | Li | Be | B  | C  | N  | O  | F  |
|    |    |    | 2.08 | 0.93 | 0.60 | 0.31 | 0.20 | 0.15 | 0.11 | 0.09 | 0.07 |
| C  | N  | O  | F  | Ne | Na | Mg | Al | Si | P  | S  | Cl |
| 2.60 | 1.71 | 1.40 | 1.36 | 1.12 | 0.95 | 0.65 | 0.50 | 0.41 | 0.34 | 0.29 | 0.26 |
| Si | P  | S  | Cl | Ar | K  | Ca | Sc | Ti | V  | Co | Mn |
| 2.71 | 2.12 | 1.84 | 1.81 | 1.54 | 1.33 | 0.99 | 0.81 | 0.68 | 0.59 | 0.52 | 0.46 |
|    |    |    |    |    | Cu | Zn | Ga | Ge | As | Se | Br |
|    |    |    |    |    | 0.96 | 0.74 | 0.62 | 0.53 | 0.47 | 0.42 | 0.39 |
| Ge | As | Se | Br | Kr | Rb | Sr | Y  | Zr | Nb | Mo |    |
| 2.72 | 2.22 | 1.98 | 1.95 | 1.69 | 1.48 | 1.13 | 0.93 | 0.80 | 0.70 | 0.62 |    |
|    |    |    |    |    | Ag | Cd | In | Sn | Sb | Te | I  |
|    |    |    |    |    | 1.26 | 0.97 | 0.81 | 0.71 | 0.62 | 0.56 | 0.50 |
| Sn | Sb | Te | I  | Xe | Cs | Ba | La | Ce |    |    |    |
| 2.94 | 2.45 | 2.21 | 2.16 | 1.90 | 1.69 | 1.35 | 1.15 | 1.01 |    |    |    |
|    |    |    |    |    | Au | Hg | Tl | Pb | Bi |    |    |
|    |    |    |    |    | 1.37 | 1.10 | 0.95 | 0.84 | 0.74 |    |    |

Equation 16 also show that the equilibrium distance is a function of the type of crystal lattice. For example, if $Z_1$, $Z_2$ and $n$ are constants, the ratio of equilibrium interionic distance for CsCl to NaCl or ZnS (zinc blende) to NaCl lattices are given by

$$\frac{R_e(\text{CsCl})}{R_e(\text{NaCl})} = \left( \frac{B(\text{CsCl}) \, A(\text{NaCl})}{B(\text{NaCl}) \, A(\text{CsCl})} \right)^{1/(n-1)} \simeq \left( \frac{8}{6} \cdot \frac{1.7476}{1.7627} \right)^{1/(n-1)} \tag{18}$$

$$\frac{R_e(\text{ZnS})}{R_e(\text{NaCl})} = \left( \frac{B(\text{ZnS}) \, A(\text{NaCl})}{B(\text{NaCl}) \, A(\text{ZnS})} \right)^{1/(n-1)} \simeq \left( \frac{4}{6} \cdot \frac{1.7476}{1.6381} \right)^{1/(n-1)} \tag{19}$$

Here, the repulsive parameter $B$ is approximately taken as proportional to the coordination number. For $n = 9$, a reasonable "universal" value, the above ratios are approximately equal to 1.03 and 0.96, respectively. Thus, the equilibrium spacing and hence the effective radii of the ions change as the crystal type changes.

The accuracy of the calculated radii of multivalent ions is questionable, especially for those having charges 3 and greater. Actually, any radius for a multivalent ion (charges greater than 2) may be regarded as a sheer formalism because higher the formal charge on an ion the greater will be the covalent bonding between them (as discussed below). However, they may be used to give approximate internuclear distances only.

Historically, several different sets of ionic radii have been compiled by various investigators using different methods and are given in Table 4.2. Although, the most widely used continue to be those of Goldschmidt (1927), Pauling (1927) often with some later corrections, and Arhens (1952). General agreement between these is good, however, there exist some significant

**Table 4.2    Ionic radii (Å) from various sources**

| | Waddington | Shannon & Prewitt[1] | Pauling[2] | Goldschmidt | Ahrens |
|---|---|---|---|---|---|
| $Li^+$ | 0.739 | 0.74 | 0.60 | 0.78 | 0.68 |
| $Na^+$ | 1.009 | 1.02 | 0.95 | 0.98 | 0.97 |
| $K^+$ | 1.320 | 1.38 | 1.33 | 1.33 | 1.33 |
| $Rb^+$ | 1.460 | 1.49 | 1.48 | 1.49 | 1.47 |
| $Cs^+$ | 1.718 | 1.70 | 1.69 | 1.65 | 1.67 |
| $Tl^+$ | 1.449 | 1.50 | 0.95 | 1.05 | 1.47 |
| $F^-$ | 1.322 | 1.33 | 1.36 | 1.33 | 1.33 |
| $Cl^-$ | 1.822 | | 1.81 | 1.81 | 1.81 |
| $Br^-$ | 1.983 | | 1.95 | 1.96 | 1.96 |
| $I^-$ | 2.241 | | 2.16 | 2.20 | 2.20 |

1 Based upon $O^{2-} = 1.40$Å

2 Crystal radii

discrepancies in certain cases. The most recent among these, and relatively more accurate ionic radii have been compiled by Shannon and Prewitt (1969, 1970) and are given in Table 4.3. These were determined on the basis of a very large number of crystal data involving more than a thousand interatomic distances. Crystal radii for ions compiled by them are in the formal valence states and coordination environments based upon $r(F^-) = 1.19$Å. "SQ" in the coordination number column refers to the square-planar coordination; "PY" refers to pyramidal coordination; and others have the same meaning as in Table 4.1.

Certain general points which emerge from the data in this table need specific mention:

(a) Within Groups, Ia, IIa, IIIb-VIIb, radii increase with atomic number simply because extra electron shells are added.

(b) Across each period of the Periodic Table, ionic radii decrease with increasing charge and atomic number, e.g.

| Ion | $Na^+$ | $Mg^{2+}$ | $Al^{3+}$ | $Au^+$ | $Hg^{2+}$ | $Tl^{3+}$ |
|---|---|---|---|---|---|---|
| radius(Å) | 1.16 | 0.86 | 0.67 | 1.51 | 1.16 | 1.02 |

This is because of the increasing effect of the nucleus on the outer electrons, coupled with some contraction in bond length due to the greater Coulomb attraction associated with multivalent ions.

(c) Increase in valency of a cation decreases its size (Å). For example, $Cr^{2+}$ 0.94, $Cr^{3+}$ 0.75, $Cr^{4+}$ 0.69, $Cr^{6+}$ 0.58. In this case, one has to take into account the doubts expressed above regarding multivalent ions.

(d) A series of ions of increasing atomic number but same ionic charge shows a steady decrease in size. This is due to the steadily increasing effective nuclear charge. The electrons in the *d*- and especially *f*-orbitals do not shield the nucleus very effectively, resulting in the steady contraction observed in each of the three d-block transition metal series and in the Lanthanides. Since similarities in crystal structure, as we shall see, are closely associated with similarities on ionic size, the Lanthanide contraction is largely responsible for the remarkable chemical resemblances between such pairs of elements as zirconium and hafnium, or niobium and tantalum. A similar decrease in ionic radii with increasing atomic number is found in the limited number of ions of the actinide series of which the radii are known.

*Example:* Calculate the univalent radii of $Na^+$, $F^-$ and oxygen, when internuclear separation in NaF is 2.31Å.

*Solution:* For neon like configurations $S = 4.52$. Thus, for NaF

$$r_{Na^+} = \frac{C_n}{11 - 4.52} \text{ and } r_{F^-} = \frac{C_n}{9 - 4.52}$$

or

$$\frac{r_{Na^+}}{r_{F^-}} = \frac{9 - 4.52}{11 - 4.52} = 0.69$$

However, it is given that $r_{Na^+} + r_{F^-} = 2.31$Å. Solving these equations, we have

$$r_{Na^+} = 0.95\text{Å and } r_{F^-} = 1.36\text{Å}$$

Further, we know that $C_n$ is same for all isoelectronic series and therefore from above $C_n = 6.1$.

so that,

$$r_o = \frac{C_n}{8 - 4.52} = \frac{6.1}{3.48} = 1.75\text{Å}$$

*Example:* Crystabolite ($SiO_2$) crystallizes with the Si ions in the diamond structure and with O atoms tetrahedrally surrounding each silicon atom. If the ionic radius of $O^{2-}$ is 1.40Å and the lattice parameter as 7.12Å, what is the radius of $Si^{4+}$?

*Solution:* Si-Si distance (from 000 to 1/4 1/4 1/4) $= \left( 3 \times \dfrac{a^2}{16} \right)^{1/2}$

Distance of oxygen ions between the two Si ions is

$$2R_{Si} + 2R_o = \left[ 3 \left( \frac{7.12}{4} \right)^2 \right]^{1/2} = 3.08$$

or $$2R_{Si} = 3.08 - 2.80 = 0.28Å$$

This is much smaller than the value given in Table 4.3, indicating that the bonding in $SiO_2$ is probably not ionic but rather covalent in character. When the covalent radius of oxygen is substituted in the above problem, a value of 0.88Å is obtained for the radius of silicon.

## 4.7  EMPIRICAL IONIC RADII

Experimentally determined maps (Fig. 4.7) for NaCI and LiF shows that the electron density rises towards each nucleus but falls approximately to zero in between the ions. A plot of this function in Fig. 4.8 shows this minimum very clearly for LiF. A few compounds like LiF, NaCl, KCl, $CaF_2$, MgO, etc. have been examined so far (Table 4.4) by this technique. However, their radii do not reproduce the internuclear separations for all the alkali halides to the desired accuracy. It is believed that there is some mutual interpenetration of $Li^+$ and $F^-$ ions, the radii necessary to reproduce the crystal distances for other alkali halides are actually larger, e.g. $Li^+$ 0.94, $F^-$ 1.16 Å. Taking these values together with a marginally different one for $Na^+$, Gourary and Adrian (1960) obtained the correct ionic radii for some alkali metal and halide ions (Table 4.5). They reproduced the intermolecular separation for all alkali halides (other than LiF) within about one percent. The discrepancy in LiF is explained on the basis of the observed deviation

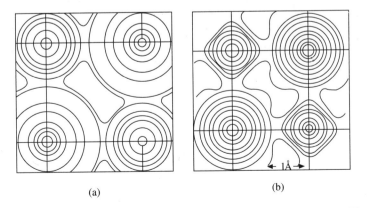

(a)  (b)

**Fig. 4.7  The electron density map (a) Rocksalt, NaCl, and (b) LiF**

**Table 4.3   Ionic Radii (Å)**

| Ion | Coordination Number | Crystal Radius | Ion | Coordination Number | Crystal Radius |
|---|---|---|---|---|---|
| $Ag^+$ | 4 | 1.14 | $Ce^{3+}$ | 6 | 1.15 |
| | 4SQ | 1.16 | | 8 | 1.283 |
| | 5 | 1.23 | $Ce^{4+}$ | 6 | 1.01 |
| | 6 | 1.29 | | 8 | 1.11 |
| $Al^{3+}$ | 4 | 0.53 | $Cl^-$ | 6 | 1.67 |
| | 5 | 0.62 | $Co^{2+}$ | 4 HS | 0.72 |
| | 6 | 0.675 | | 5 | 0.81 |
| $As^{3+}$ | 6 | 0.72 | | 6 LS | 0.79 |
| $As^{5+}$ | 4 | 0.475 | | 6 HS | 0.885 |
| | 6 | 0.60 | | 8 | 1.04 |
| $Au^+$ | 6 | 1.51 | $Co^{3+}$ | 6 LS | 0.685 |
| $Au^{3-}$ | 4SQ | 0.82 | | 6 HS | 0.75 |
| | 6 | 0.99 | $Cr^{2+}$ | 6 LS | 0.87 |
| $B^{3+}$ | 3 | 0.15 | | 6 HS | 0.94 |
| | 4 | 0.25 | $Cr^{3+}$ | 6 | 0.755 |
| | 6 | 0.41 | $Cr^{4+}$ | 4 | 0.55 |
| $Ba^{2+}$ | 6 | 1.49 | | 6 | 0.69 |
| | 7 | 1.52 | $Cr^{6+}$ | 4 | 0.40 |
| | 8 | 1.56 | | 6 | 0.58 |
| $Be^{2+}$ | 3 | 0.30 | $Cs^+$ | 6 | 1.81 |
| | 4 | 0.41 | | 8 | 1.88 |
| | 6 | 0.59 | $Cu^+$ | 2 | 0.60 |
| $Bi^{3+}$ | 6 | 1.17 | | 4 | 0.74 |
| | 8 | 1.31 | | 6 | 0.91 |
| $Br^-$ | 6 | 1.82 | $Cu^{2+}$ | 4 | 0.71 |
| $Ca^{2+}$ | 6 | 1.14 | | 4 SQ | 0.71 |
| | 8 | 1.26 | | 5 | 0.79 |
| $Cd^{2+}$ | 4 | 0.92 | | 6 | 0.87 |
| | 5 | 1.01 | $Cu^{3+}$ | 6 LS | 0.68 |
| | 6 | 1.09 | $F^-$ | 2 | 1.145 |
| | 7 | 1.17 | | 3 | 1.16 |
| | 8 | 1.24 | | 4 | 1.17 |
| $F^-$ | 6 | 1.19 | $Ir^{4+}$ | 6 | 0.765 |
| $Fe^{2+}$ | 4 HS | 0.77 | $Ir^{5+}$ | 6 | 0.71 |
| | 4SQ HS | 0.78 | $K^+$ | 4 | 1.51 |
| | 6 LS | 0.75 | | 6 | 1.52 |
| | 6 HS | 0.920 | | 7 | 1.60 |
| | 8 HS | 1.06 | | 8 | 1.65 |
| $Fe^{3+}$ | 4 HS | 0.63 | $La^{3+}$ | 6 | 1.172 |
| | 6 LS | 0.69 | | 8 | 1.300 |
| $Fe^{4+}$ | 6 | 0.725 | $Li^+$ | 4 | 0.730 |
| $Fe^{6+}$ | 4 | 0.39 | | 6 | 0.90 |
| $Fr^+$ | 6 | 1.94 | | 8 | 1.06 |
| $Ga^{3+}$ | 4 | 0.61 | $Lu^{3+}$ | 6 | 1.001 |

*(Contd.)*

| Ion | Coordination Number | Crystal Radius | Ion | Coordination Number | Crystal Radius |
|-----|---------------------|----------------|-----|---------------------|----------------|
| | 6 | 0.760 | | 8 | 1.117 |
| $Ge^{2+}$ | 6 | 0.87 | $Mg^{2+}$ | 4 | 0.71 |
| $Ge^{4+}$ | 4 | 0.530 | | 5 | 0.80 |
| | 6 | 0.670 | | 6 | 0.860 |
| $H^+$ | 1 | −0.24 | | 8 | 1.03 |
| | 2 | −0.04 | $Mn^{2+}$ | 4 HS | 0.80 |
| $H^-$ | 4 | 1.22 | | 5 HS | 0.89 |
| | 6 | 1.40 | | 6 LS | 0.81 |
| $Hf^{4+}$ | 4 | 0.72 | | 6 HS | 0.970 |
| | 6 | 0.85 | | 7 HS | 1.04 |
| $Hg^+$ | 3 | 1.11 | | 8 | 1.10 |
| | 6 | 1.33 | $Mn^{3+}$ | 5 | 0.72 |
| $Hg^{2+}$ | 2 | 0.83 | | 6 LS | 0.72 |
| | 4 | 1.10 | | 6 HS | 0.785 |
| | 6 | 1.16 | $Mn^{4+}$ | 4 | 0.53 |
| | 8 | 1.28 | | 6 | 0.670 |
| $I^-$ | 6 | 2.06 | $Mo^{3+}$ | 6 | 0.83 |
| $In^{3+}$ | 4 | 0.76 | $Mo^{4+}$ | 6 | 0.790 |
| | 6 | 0.940 | $Mo^{5+}$ | 4 | 0.60 |
| $Ir^{3+}$ | 6 | 0.82 | | 6 | 0.75 |
| $Mo^{6+}$ | 4 | 0.55 | $Pt^{4+}$ | 6 | 0.755 |
| | 6 | 0.73 | $Ra^{2+}$ | 8 | 1.62 |
| $N^{3-}$ | 4 | 1.32 | $Rb^+$ | 6 | 1.66 |
| $Na^+$ | 4 | 1.13 | | 7 | 1.70 |
| | 5 | 1.14 | | 8 | 1.75 |
| | 6 | 1.16 | $Re^{4+}$ | 6 | 0.77 |
| | 7 | 1.26 | $Rh^{3+}$ | 6 | 0.805 |
| | 8 | 1.32 | $Rh^{4+}$ | 6 | 0.74 |
| $Nb^{3+}$ | 6 | 0.86 | $Rh^{5+}$ | 6 | 0.69 |
| $Nb^{4+}$ | 6 | 0.82 | $Ru^{3+}$ | 6 | 0.82 |
| $Nb^{5+}$ | 4 | 0.62 | $Ru^{4+}$ | 6 | 0.760 |
| | 6 | 0.78 | $Ru^{5+}$ | 6 | 0.705 |
| | 8 | 0.88 | $S^{2-}$ | 6 | 1.70 |
| $Ni^{2+}$ | 4 | 0.69 | $Sb^{3+}$ | 4PY | 0.90 |
| | 4 SQ | 0.63 | | 5 | 0.94 |
| | 5 | 0.77 | | 6 | 0.90 |
| | 6 | 0.830 | $Sc^{3+}$ | 6 | 0.885 |
| $Ni^{3+}$ | 6 LS | 0.70 | | 8 | 1.010 |
| | 6 HS | 0.74 | $Se^{2+}$ | 6 | 1.84 |
| $Ni^{4+}$ | 6 LS | 0.62 | $Si^{4+}$ | 4 | 0.40 |
| $O^{2-}$ | 2 | 1.21 | | 6 | 0.540 |
| | 3 | 1.22 | $Sn^{2+}$ | 8 | 1.36 |
| | 4 | 1.24 | $Sn^{4+}$ | 4 | 0.69 |
| | 6 | 1.26 | | 6 | 0.830 |
| | 8 | 1.28 | $Sr^{2+}$ | 6 | 1.32 |

*(Contd.)*

| Ion | Coordination Number | Crystal Radius | Ion | Coordination Number | Crystal Radius |
|---|---|---|---|---|---|
| $Os^{4+}$ | 6 | 0.770 | | 7 | 1.35 |
| $Pb^{2+}$ | 6 | 1.33 | | 8 | 1.40 |
| $Pb^{4+}$ | 6 | 0.915 | $Ta^{3+}$ | 6 | 0.86 |
| $Pd^{2+}$ | 4SQ | 0.78 | $Ta^{4+}$ | 6 | 0.82 |
| | 6 | 1.00 | $T^{5+}$ | 6 | 0.78 |
| $Pd^{3+}$ | 6 | 0.90 | | 8 | 0.88 |
| $Pt^{2+}$ | 4SQ | 0.74 | $Te^{4+}$ | 6 | 0.785 |
| | 6 | 0.94 | $Te^{2-}$ | 6 | 2.07 |
| $Th^{4+}$ | 6 | 1.08 | $W^{4+}$ | 6 | 0.80 |
| | 8 | 1.19 | $W^{5+}$ | 6 | 0.76 |
| | 9 | 1.23 | $W^{6+}$ | 4 | 0.56 |
| $Ti^{2+}$ | 6 | 1.00 | | 5 | 0.65 |
| $Ti^{3+}$ | 6 | 0.810 | | 6 | 0.74 |
| $Ti^{4+}$ | 4 | 0.56 | $Xe^{8+}$ | 4 | 0.54 |
| | 6 | 0.745 | | 6 | 0.62 |
| $Tl^{+}$ | 6 | 1.64 | $Y^{3+}$ | 6 | 1.040 |
| $Tl^{3+}$ | 4 | 0.89 | | 8 | 1.159 |
| | 6 | 1.025 | $Zn^{2+}$ | 4 | 0.74 |
| $U^{3+}$ | 6 | 1.165 | | 5 | 0.82 |
| $U^{4+}$ | 6 | 1.03 | | 6 | 0.88 |
| | 8 | 1.14 | $Zr^{4+}$ | 4 | 0.73 |
| | 9 | 1.05 | | 6 | 0.86 |
| $V^{2+}$ | 6 | 0.93 | | 7 | 0.92 |
| $V^{3+}$ | 6 | 0.780 | | 8 | 0.98 |
| $V^{4+}$ | 6 | 0.72 | polynuclear ions | | |
| $V^{5+}$ | 4 | 0.495 | $IO_3^-$ | | 1.68 |
| | 6 | 0.68 | $IO_4^-$ | | 2.35 |
| Polynuclear ions | | | $BF_4^-$ | | 2.14 |
| $NH_2^-$ | | 1.16 | $CNO^-$ | | 1.45 |
| | | | $CNS^-$ | | 1.81 |
| $OH^-$ | 2 | 1.21 | $CO_3^{2-}$ | | 1.71 |
| | 3 | 1.20 | $BO_3^{3-}$ | | 1.77 |
| | 4 | 1.21 | $NO_2^-$ | | 1.75 |
| | 6 | 1.23 | $NO_3^-$ | | |
| $SH^-$ | | 1.81 | $PO_4^{3-}$ | | 2.24 |
| $HCOO^-$ | | 1.44 | $O_2^{2-}$ | | 1.66 |
| $CH_3COO^-$ | | 1.45 | $SO_4^{2-}$ | | 2.16 |
| $HCO_3^-$ | | 1.49 | $ClO_3^-$ | | 1.86 |
| $CN^{3-}$ | | 1.68 | | | |
| $ClO_4^-$ | | 2.22 | | | |
| $BrO_3^-$ | | 1.77 | | | |

**Table 4.4    Ionic radii determined from electron density maps**

|      | Cation (Å) | Anion (Å) |
|------|------------|-----------|
| LiF  | 0.92       | 1.09      |
| NaCl | 1.18       | 1.64      |
| KCl  | 1.45       | 1.70      |
| CaF$_2$ | 1.26    | 1.10      |
| MgO  | 1.02       | 1.09      |

**Table 4.5    Corrected ionic radii (in Å) from electron density maps**

|         | 'Corrected' radius | Waddington radius |
|---------|--------------------|-------------------|
| Li$^+$  | 0.94               | 0.74              |
| Na$^+$  | 1.17               | 1.01              |
| K$^+$   | 1.49               | 1.32              |
| Rb$^+$  | 1.63               | 1.46              |
| Cs$^+$  | 1.86               | 1.72              |
| F$^-$   | 1.16               | 1.32              |
| Cl$^-$  | 1.64               | 1.82              |
| Br$^-$  | 1.80               | 1.98              |
| I$^-$   | 2.05               | 2.24              |

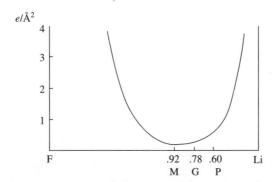

**Fig. 4.8    Variation of experimentally measured electron density with internuclear positions for LiF. M is the minimum measured electron density. G and P represent ionic radius of Li$^+$ according to Goldschmidt and Pauling respectively**

from spherical symmetry for Li$^+$ in the electron density map. Also the value of F$^-$ found in LiF and CaF$_2$ is appreciably different, which may be explained on the basis of its coordination number discussed below.

## 4.8    VARIATION OF IONIC RADII

The variation of ionic radius with coordiantion number may be represented as follows:

| Coordination number | 8    | 6    | 4    |
|---------------------|------|------|------|
| Radius              | 1.03 | 1.00 | 0.95 |

Thus, if the radii corresponding to sodium chloride structure are taken as standard, then the radii in the 8-coordinated cesium chloride structure are about 3% larger and in 4-coordinated zinc blende structure are about 5% smaller. On the basis of this, a simple conversion relation $1.052R_{CN} = 4$, $R_{CN} = 6$ and $0.97R_{CN} = 8$, may be used for calculation. It is therefore, desirable that the ionic radii should be expressed in a form appropriate to some particular coordination, and that of sodium chloride structure is conventionally chosen as standard. The crystal radii should be appropriately corrected on the basis of coordination before use in actual structure.

Another factor which influences ionic radii is the value of the radius ratio. At this stage, a natural question arises that why different MX-compounds should exist in different structural forms, such as rock salt, cesium chloride or zinc blende, in general, and why CsCl, CsBr and CsI should have a structure different from that of other alkali halides, in particular? In order to arrive at a satisfactory answer to this, we assume that:

1. the ions behave as hard spheres, the radii are fixed and independent of coordination number, and
2. the bonding between the ions is purely ionic and the cohesive energy is expressed in the form

$$U = -\frac{Ae^2 N}{4\pi\varepsilon_0 R_e}\left(1 - \frac{\rho}{R_e}\right)$$

Now, the crystal will be as tightly bound as possible if $A$ is large and $R_e$ is small. the largest value of $A$ (for the three structures mentioned above) is that of cesium chloride structure, e.g. $A = 1.763$. Practically in all cases, anions are larger than cations. Accordingly, let us assume that $R_m < R_x$ and that $R_x$ is fixed. As $R_m/R_x$ decreases from unity, $R_e = R_m + R_x$ decreases until a critical value is reached when all the anions are in contact with the cations and touch each other as shown in Fig. 4.9a for the case of cesium chloride structure. this happens when

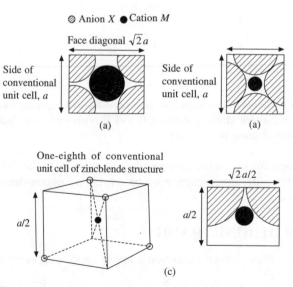

**Fig. 4.9** Critical conditions in (a) Cesium chloride structure (b) Rocksalt structure, and (c) Zincblende structure

$$R_m + R_n = \text{half the body-diagonal of cube}$$

$$= \frac{\sqrt{3}}{2} \times \text{side of the cube}$$

$$= \frac{\sqrt{3}}{2} \times 2R_x = \sqrt{3}R_x$$

The interionic spacing $R_c = R_m + R_x$ is now fixed at $\sqrt{3}R_x$ and as $R_m$ is made smaller the binding energy will not be affected. The critical radius ratio becomes

$$\frac{R_x}{R_m} = \frac{1}{\sqrt{3} - 1} = 1.37, \quad \text{or} \quad \frac{R_x}{R_m} = 0.732$$

No further increase in cohesive energy is possible with this structure. For the sodium chloride structure (Fig. 4.9b) the limiting value of $R_e$ occurs when the ions touch (in this case the face diagonal of the cube is equal to $4R$), i.e. when

$$R_m + R_x = \text{half the side of the cube}$$

$$= \frac{1}{2} \times \frac{2R_x}{\sqrt{2}} = \sqrt{2}R_x$$

An interionic spacing of $\sqrt{2}R_x$ is smaller than $\sqrt{3}R_x$. Therefore, despite the small difference in the Madelung constant, the cohesive energy for a crystal with rock salt structure can be greater than that for cesium chloride type crystals, if $R_x/R_m$ is large enough. However, the cohesive energy cannot increase further when the radius ratio becomes equal to the critical value for rock salt structure, i.e.

$$\frac{R_x}{R_m} = \frac{1}{\sqrt{2} - 1} = 2.42 \quad \text{or} \quad \frac{R_m}{R_x} = 0.414$$

As $R_m$ decreases still further, the zinc blende structure becomes energetically most favourable despite its small madelung constant. The limiting value of $R_x/R_m$ (when the anions touch) is not reached until (Fig. 4.9c)

$$2R_x = \frac{\sqrt{2}a}{2}, \text{ and } R_m + R_x = \frac{\sqrt{3}a}{2} \times \frac{1}{2}$$

so that,

$$\frac{R_x}{R_m} = \frac{1}{\sqrt{(3/2)} - 1} = 4.45, \text{ or } \frac{R_m}{R_x} = 0.225$$

These ratios must be taken with a pinch of salt. Near the critical ratios the stability of one structure as compared with another may be strongly influenced by the coordination number and its effect on the radius, which we have ignored for this calculation. Polarization effects may also be important enough to alter the above predictions. Some compounds can even change from one crystal structure to another as temperature and pressure are varied. However, it is found that generally when MX-compounds have ions with nearly equal radii, the cesium chloride structure is favoured; when the ionic radii differ by a factor of two or more the zinc blende structure is favoured; and in the intermediate cases the rock salt structure results. Table 4.6 gives the actual radius ratio in cesium chloride, sodium chloride and zinc sulfide-the compounds after which the crystal types are named.

**Table 4.6   Actual radius ratio in three leading MX-compounds (after Pauling)**

| Radius of cation $r_m$ in Å | Radius of anion $r_x$ in Å | $r_x/r_m$ | Approx. range expected from calculations |
|---|---|---|---|
| $Cs^+$ 1.69 | $Cl^-$ 1.81 | 1.1 | 1.00 – 1.37 |
| $Na^+$ 0.95 | $Cl^-$ 1.81 | 1.9 | 1.37 – 2.42 |
| $Zn^{2+}$ 0.74 | $S^{2-}$ 1.84 | 2.5 | 2.42 – 4.45 |

*Example:* Determine the radius of a cation occupying an octahedral position in an $M^+X^-$ ionic solid, when all anions are in contact with the cation and touch each other. The critical radius of anion is 2.5Å.

*Solutions:* We know that for an octahedral case, the radius ratio is given by the relation

$$\frac{R_m}{R_x} = 0.414$$

Substituting the value of $R_x$, we can find

$$R_m = 2.5 \times 0.414 = 1.035\text{Å}$$

## 4.9   COVALENT RADII

The covalent radius in a covalent molecule is only half of the bond length (the distance between two bonded atoms) and is often called the atomic radius in the case of nonmetals. This suggests that covalent radii are simply additive, provided the bonding between atoms is a single electron pair bond. On the other hand, when atoms from multiple electron pair bonds with each other, the bond lengths depend on the number of electron pair bonds formed. Further, in case of hybrid bond formation, they also depend on the type of orbitals used. It should also be remembered that most atoms do not form purely covalent bonds in crystals. From these, it appears that the concept of characteristic covalent radii is subject to a number of qualifications:

(i) That the covalent radius of an atom (unlike its ionic radius) must not be interpreted as implying that the atom is a sphere of that size. The covalent radii are applicable only to the calculation of bond lengths between atoms joined by purely covalent bonds, and tells nothing about the distances between atoms of the same kind when not so bonded. Thus the single-bond radius of chlorine (i.e. 0.99Å) is in perfect agreement with the observed Cl–Cl distance of 1.988Å in the chlorine molecule. In the crystal structure of solid chlorine, however, the interatomic distance between contiguous chlorine atoms of different molecules, which are bound together only by van der Waals forces, is about 3.6Å. Thus the van der Waals radius of the chlorine atom is about 1.8Å (nearly double the covalent radius) and consequently the $Cl_2$ molecule is pictured as having the form shown in Fig. 4.10.

(ii) That the bond length depends upon the bond number. Single bonds are the largest one and the length decreases with the increase of number of bonds. The effect of multiple bonding can be produced fairly well by a simple observation. A double bond is about 0.86 as long as a single bond for first row elements, and a triple bond is about 0.78 as long as a single bond. For second row and heavier elements (where multiple bonds are much rarer), the inner core electrons are less compressible and the factors are 0.91 for a double bond and 0.85 for a triple bond. For this reason separate radii are required for single, double and triple bonds, respectively. We must, however, also remember that a bond will not necessarily have an integral bond number (sometimes may have fractional) if the bond involves resonance. These intermediate bond lengths can be obtained by interpolation between the lengths corresponding to integral bond numbers, but with proper caution.

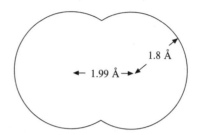

**Fig. 4.10   the dimensions of chlorine molecule**

(iii) That we must consider resonance not only between covalent bonds of different bond number but also between covalent and ionic bonds because many covalent bonds do in fact have considerable ionic character. The effect of this covalent/ionic resonance may be considerable, and in some cases reduces the length of a bond as much as 0.1Å or more. Attempts have been made to apply necessary correction in terms of difference in electronegativity of the atoms involved. Schomaker and Stevanson observed that the degree of electron transfer (cause of ionic character) in a bond is roughly proportional to the electronegativity difference between the two atoms involed, and hence they proposed an empirecal correction to the predicted bond length:

$$r_{AB} = r_A + r_B - 0.09 \, (| \, x_A - x_B \, |) \tag{20}$$

where $r_A$ and $r_B$ are covalent radii, $x_A$ and $x_B$ are electronegativity values, and the sign of electronegativity difference is disregarded. A somewhat better fit is provided by adjusting for the square of the electronegativity difference:

$$r_{AB} = r_A + r_B - 0.07 \, (x_A - x_B)^2 \tag{21}$$

It should be noted that the above correction predicts the bond length corresponding to a single bond only. When observed bond lengths are shorter than the predicted values in covalent molecules, it is usually assumed that some deree of multiple bonding is involed.

In some cases the "corrections" so applied increase the discrepancy between predicted and observed bond lengths. Therefore, the effect of covalent/ionic resonance may be better ignored while calculating bond lengths.

Based on similar argument, Pauling (1960) proposed an empirical formula for determining the percentage ionic character of the bond:

$$p = 16 \, | \, x_A - x_B \, | + 3.5 \, | \, x_A - x_B \, |^2 \tag{22}$$

The values of electronegativity calculated recently by Husain et al. (1989) alongwith the values of Pauling are provided in Table 4.7. Some important conclusions drawn from these data are summarized below:

**Table 4.7   The electronegativities of the elements**

| Z | Element | $\chi_{cal.}$ | $\chi_p$ |
|---|---------|---------------|----------|
| 3 | Li | 0.88 | 1.0 |
| 4 | Be | 1.84 | 1.5 |
| 5 | B | 2.02 | 2.0 |
| 6 | C | 2.60 | 2.5 |
| 7 | N | 3.06 | 3.0 |
| 8 | 0 | 3.13 | 3.5 |
| 9 | F | 3.60 | 4.0 |
| 11 | Na | 0.83 | 0.9 |
| 12 | Mg | 1.17 | 1.2 |
| 13 | Al | 1.34 | 1.5 |
| 14 | Si | 1.69 | 1.6 |
| 15 | P | 2.04 | 2.1 |
| 16 | S | 2.17 | 2.5 |
| 17 | Cl | 2.54 | 3.0 |
| 19 | K | 0.66 | 0.8 |
| 20 | Ca | 0.92 | 1.0 |
| 21 | Sc | 1.27 | 1.3 |
| 22 | Ti | 1.49 | 1.5 |
| 23 | V | 1.69 | 1.6 |
| 24 | Cr | 1.79 | 1.6 |
| 25 | Mn | 1.90 | 1.5 |
| 26 | Fe | 1.95 | 1.8 |
| 27 | Co | 1.89 | 1.8 |
| 28 | Ni | 1.98 | 1.8 |
| 29 | Cu | 1.93 | 1.9 |
| 30 | Zn | 1.87 | 1.6 |
| 31 | Ga | 1.52 | 1.6 |
| 32 | Ge | 1.81 | 1.8 |
| 33 | As | 2.05 | 2.0 |
| 34 | Se | 2.14 | 2.4 |
| 35 | Br | 2.45 | 2.8 |
| 37 | Rb | 0.69 | 0.8 |
| 38 | Sr | 0.92 | 1.0 |
| 39 | Y | 1.25 | 1.2 |
| 40 | Zr | 1.53 | 1.4 |
| 41 | Nb | 1.76 | 1.6 |
| 42 | Mo | 1.88 | 1.9 |
| 43 | Te | 1.98 | 1.9 |
| 44 | Ru | 2.05 | 2.2 |
| 45 | Rh | 2.06 | 2.2 |
| 46 | Pd | 1.71 | 2.2 |
| 47 | Ag | 1.84 | 1.9 |

*(Contd.)*

| Z | Element | $\chi_{cal.}$ | $\chi_p$ |
|---|---------|---------------|----------|
| 48 | Cd | 1.66 | 1.7 |
| 49 | In | 1.45 | 1.7 |
| 50 | Sn | 1.68 | 1.8 |
| 51 | Sb | 1.80 | 2.0 |
| 52 | Te | 1.93 | 2.4 |
| 53 | 1 | 2.14 | 2.6 |
| 55 | Cs | 0.68 | 0.7 |
| 56 | Ba | 0.96 | 0.9 |
| 57 | La | 1.27 | 1.1 |
| 58 | Ce | 1.33 | 1.1 |
| 59 | Pr | 1.32 | 1.1 |
| 60 | Nd | 1.33 | 1.1 |
| 61 | Pm | 1.35 | 1.1 |
| 62 | Sm | 1.37 | 1.1 |
| 63 | Eu | 1.11 | 1.1 |
| 64 | Gd | 1.42 | 1.1 |
| 65 | Tb | 1.40 | 1.1 |
| 66 | Dy | 1.43 | 1.1 |
| 67 | Ho | 1.47 | 1.1 |
| 68 | Er | 1.48 | 1.1 |
| 69 | Tm | 1.89 | 1.1 |
| 72 | Hf | 1.89 | 1.3 |
| 73 | Ta | 2.20 | 1.5 |
| 74 | W | 2.33 | 1.7 |
| 75 | Re | 2.38 | 1.9 |
| 76 | Os | 2.54 | 2.2 |
| 77 | Ir | 2.58 | 2.2 |
| 78 | Pt | 2.46 | 2.4 |
| 79 | Au | 2.35 | 2.4 |
| 80 | Hg | 2.05 | 1.9 |
| 81 | Tl | 1.65 | 1.8 |
| 82 | Pb | 1.81 | 1.8 |
| 83 | Bi | 1.82 | 1.9 |
| 84 | Po | 1.94 | 2.0 |
| 85 | At | 2.05 | 2.2 |
| 90 | Th | 1.55 | 1.3 |
| 91 | U | 2.01 | 1.5 |

(a) An electronegativity difference of about 2.1 corresponds to a bond which is 50 per cent ionic. Bonds with a larger electonegativity difference are therefore primarily ionic, those with smaller difference are primarily covalent.

(b) Beryllium and aluminium have the same electronegativity. Bonds from these elements to fluorine are essentially ionic, to other elements essentially covalent.

(c) Bond between boron and hydrogen is almost purely covalent, between boron and other more electronegative elements is partially ionic with predominantly covalent character.

(d) Bonds between silicon and all other elements (except perhaps fluorine) are primarily covalent.

(e) Fluorine and oxygen are the most electronegative elements. Bonds between these elements and all the metals have considerable ionic character, and in most cases predominantly ionic.

(f) That even if a bond is purely covalent, its character and strength are not uniquely determined unless we know the orbitals involved in its formation. We must therefore use different effective radii in calculating the lengths of different types of hybrid bond. Tetrahedral radii are applicable when $sp^3$ hybridization takes place, octahedral radii correspond to $d^2sp^3$ and $sp^3d^2$ hybrids, square radii are those which apply when a $dsp^2$ hybrid is formed and linear radii are those appropriate to the limited number of elements which form two $sp$ hybrid bonds oppositely directed along a straight line. The square radii and the octahedral radii are numerically indistinguishable, however, they have been tabulated separately because in some cases the valency states corresponding to the types of coordination are not the same; for example, $Pt^{IV}$ forms a $d^2sp^3$ hybrid whereas $Pt^{II}$ is $dsp^2$ hybridized. Values for the covalent radii of a number of atoms are given in Table 4.8.

*Example:* Determine the percentage of ionic character in HF molecule, the electronegativities of the hydrogen and fluorine atoms are 2.1 and 4.0, respectively.

*Solution:* Using eq. 22 and substituting the values of electronegativity given by Pauling, we obtain

$$P = 16\,(4.0 - 2.1) + 3.5\,(4.0 - 2.1)^2 = 43\%$$

**Table 4.8   Covalent radii (in Angstrom units)**

(a)   Normal radii

|              | H    | C    | N    | O    | F    |
|--------------|------|------|------|------|------|
| Single bond  | 0.30 | 0.77 | 0.74 | 0.74 | 0.72 |
| Double bond  | —    | 0.67 | 0.62 | 0.62 | —    |
| Triple bond  | —    | 0.60 | 0.55 | —    | —    |

|              | Si   | P    | S    | Cl   |
|--------------|------|------|------|------|
| Single bond  | 1.17 | 1.10 | 1.04 | 0.99 |
| Double bond  | 1.07 | 1.00 | 0.94 | —    |
| Triple bond  | 1.00 | 0.93 | —    | —    |

|              | Ge   | As   | Se   | Br   |
|--------------|------|------|------|------|
| Single bond  | 1.22 | 1.21 | 1.17 | 1.14 |
| Double bond  | 1.12 | 1.11 | 1.07 | —    |

|              | Sn   | Sb   | Te   | I    |
|--------------|------|------|------|------|
| Single bond  | 1.40 | 1.41 | 1.37 | 1.33 |
| Double bond  | 1.30 | 1.31 | 1.27 | —    |

(b)   Tetrahedral radii

| Be   | B    | C    | N    | O    | F    |
|------|------|------|------|------|------|
| 1.06 | 0.88 | 0.77 | 0.70 | 0.66 | 0.64 |

*(Contd.)*

|  | Mg | Al | Si | P | S | Cl |
|---|---|---|---|---|---|---|
|  | 1.40 | 1.26 | 1.17 | 1.10 | 1.04 | 0.99 |
| Cu | Zn | Ga | Ge | As | Se | Br |
| 1.35 | 1.31 | 1.26 | 1.22 | 1.18 | 1.14 | 1.11 |
| Ag | Cd | In | Sn | Sb | Te | I |
| 1.52 | 1.48 | 1.44 | 1.40 | 1.36 | 1.32 | 1.28 |
| Au | Hg | Tl | Pb | Bi |  |  |
| 1.50 | 1.47 | 1.47 | 1.46 | 1.46 |  |  |

(c)   Octahedral radii

$d^2sp^3$ hybrids

| $Fe^{II}$ | $Co^{II}$ | $Ni^{II}$ | $Ru^{II}$ |  | $Os^{II}$ |  |  |
|---|---|---|---|---|---|---|---|
| 1.23 | 1.32 | 1.39 | 1.33 |  | 1.33 |  |  |
|  | $Co^{III}$ | $Ni^{III}$ |  | $Rh^{III}$ |  | $Ir^{III}$ |  |
|  | 1.22 | 1.30 |  | 1.32 |  | 1.32 |  |
| $Fe^{IV}$ |  | $Ni^{IV}$ |  | $Pd^{IV}$ |  | $Pt^{IV}$ | $Au^{IV}$ |
| 1.20 |  | 1.21 |  | 1.31 |  | 1.31 | 1.40 |

$sp^3d^2$ hybrids

|  | $Ti^{IV}$ | $Zr^{IV}$ | $Sn^{IV}$ | $Te^{IV}$ | $Pb^{IV}$ |
|---|---|---|---|---|---|
|  | 1.36 | 1.48 | 1.45 | 1.52 | 1.50 |

(d)   Square radii

|  | $Ni^{II}$ | $Pd^{II}$ | $Pt^{II}$ | $Au^{III}$ |
|---|---|---|---|---|
|  | 1.39 | 1.31 | 1.31 | 1.40 |

(e)   Linear radii

|  | $Cu^{I}$ | $Ag^{I}$ | $Hg^{II}$ |
|---|---|---|---|
|  | 1.18 | 1.39 | 1.29 |

## 4.10   METALLIC RADII

To determine the metallic radii of metal elements is probably the simplest of all. Measurement of cell dimensions of the metallic crystals enables us to derive the characteristic atomic radii for given elements. In the case of metals with close packed structures, the atomic radius is clearly half the distance of closest approach. In structures of lower coordination, a similar definition of atomic radius is applicable, but the values so deduced are not immediately comparable with those derived from close packed structures. Study of polymorphous metals having several structures of different coordination, and alloy systems in which metal atoms often occur in a state of different coordination from that in the pure element shows that a small but systematic decrease of atomic radius takes place with decreasing coordination. Goldschmidt summarized the observations on a series of elements and alloy systems by expressing the radius in 8-, 6-, and 4-coordination corresponding to unity in a close packed structure (12-coordination) as follows:

| Coordination | 12 | 8 | 6 | 4 |
|---|---|---|---|---|
| Radius | 1.00 | 0.97 | 0.96 | 0.88 |

Problem is more difficult for B sub-group metals where the coordination is very irregular and so the concept of precise radius ceases to have a definite meaning. However, in these cases, we can define the radius as half the distance of closest approach, but the values so obtained will be of significance only in the structure of the element and will have no immediate influence on its behaviour in alloy systems. Values of the radii derived from study of alloys are therefore often of a more general utility than those deduced from the elements themselves. For this reason two radii are in general given for each element as in Table 4.9. One of these corresponds to the distance of closest approach in the structure of the element and the other, if necessary, is that appropriate to 12-coordination. For elements with close packed structures the two values are, of course, identical but in other cases they differ. For the B sub-group metals, in particular, the difference is often considerable.

Certain important features of Table 4.9 are described below:

**Table 4.9 The atomic radii of the metals**

Representative and Transition elements. All values are in Angstrom units.

| Metal | Atomic radius[1] | Atomic radius[2] | Metal | Atomic radius[1] | Atomic radius[2] |
|-------|------------------|------------------|-------|------------------|------------------|
| Li | 1.52 | 1.56 | Tc | 1.35 | 1.35 |
| Be | 1.12 | 1.12 | Ru | 1.33 | 1.33 |
| Na | 1.85 | 1.91 | Rh | 1.34 | 1.34 |
| Mg | 1.60 | 1.60 | Pd | 1.37 | 1.37 |
| Al | 1.42 | 1.42 | Ag | 1.44 | 1.44 |
| K | 2.31 | 2.38 | Cd | 1.48 | 1.52 |
| Ca | 1.96 | 1.96 | In | 1.62 | 1.67 |
| Sc | 1.60 | 1.60 | Sn | 1.40 | 1.58 |
| Ti | 1.46 | 1.46 | Sb | 1.45 | 1.61 |
| V | 1.31 | 1.35 | Te | 1.43 | — |
| Cr | 1.25 | 1.28 | Cs | 2.62 | 2.70 |
| Mn | 1.12 | 1.36 | Ba | 2.17 | 2.24 |
| Fe | 1.23 | 1.27 | La | 1.87 | 1.87 |
| Co | 1.25 | 1.25 | Hf | 1.58 | 1.58 |
| Ni | 1.24 | 1.24 | Ta | 1.43 | 1.47 |
| Cu | 1.28 | 1.28 | W | 1.37 | 1.41 |
| Zn | 1.33 | 1.37 | Re | 1.37 | 1.37 |
| Ga | 1.21 | 1.35 | Os | 1.35 | 1.35 |
| Ge | 1.22 | 1.39 | Ir | 1.35 | 1.35 |
| As | 1.25 | — | Pt | 1.38 | 1.38 |
| Se | 1.16 | — | Au | 1.44 | 1.44 |
| Rb | 2.46 | 2.53 | Hg | 1.50 | 1.55 |
| Sr | 2.15 | 2.15 | Tl | 1.71 | 1.71 |
| Y | 1.81 | 1.81 | Pb | 1.74 | 1.74 |
| Zr | 1.60 | 1.60 | Bi | 1.55 | 1.82 |
| Nb | 1.43 | 1.47 | Po | 1.68 | — |
| Mo | 1.36 | 1.40 | | | |

*(Contd.)*

| The Lanthanide elements | | | The actinide elements | | |
|---|---|---|---|---|---|
| **Metal** | **Atomic radius[1]** | **Atomic radius[2]** | **Metal** | **Atomic radius[1]** | **Atomic radius[2]** |
| Ce | 1.82 | 1.82 | Th | 1.80 | 1.80 |
| Pr | 1.82 | 1.82 | Pa | 1.60 | 1.63 |
| Nd | 1.81 | 1.81 | U | 1.38 | 1.54 |
| Pm | — | — | Np | 1.30 | 1.50 |
| Sm | — | — | Pu | 1.64 | 1.64 |
| Eu | 1.98 | 2.04 | Am | — | — |
| Gd | 1.78 | 1.78 | Cm | — | — |
| Tb | 1.77 | 1.77 | Bk | — | — |
| Dy | 1.75 | 1.75 | Cf | — | — |
| Ho | 1.76 | 1.76 | E | — | — |
| Er | 1.73 | 1.73 | Em | — | — |
| Tm | 1.74 | 1.74 | Mv | — | — |
| Yb | 1.93 | 1.93 | No | — | — |
| Lu | 1.73 | 1.73 | | | |

1. Half the distance of closest approach
2. Atomic radius corresponding to 12-coordination.

(i) The atomic radii are very much larger than the corresponding ionic radii (Table 4.3), owing to the greater number of electrons in the extranuclear structure, e.g.

| Atoms | Li | Cs | Be | Ba |
|---|---|---|---|---|
| Metallic radius | 1.56 | 2.70 | 1.12 | 2.24 |
| Ionic radius | 0.90 | 1.81 | 0.59 | 1.49 |

On the other hand, the atomic radii are not very different from the covalent radii (Table 4.8), and in a number of cases they are very nearly the same.

(ii) The extreme values of the radii of metal elements differ by a factor little greater than 2, even the elements of high atomic number with complex extranuclear structure does not show any marked increase in radius, because of the compensating influence of the greater nuclear charge. If the alkali and alkaline-earth metals are excluded, the radii of all other elements lie within the range 1.2 – 1.9Å.

(iii) In each period, the alkali metal has by far the largest radius. A marked decrease in the radius is observed with increasing valency in the A group elements. This decrease in the radius is arrested in the middle of each family of transition metals, so that all these elements whithin each period have roughly the same radius. In each of the families of B sub-group elements a pronounced increase in the radius takes place.

(iv) The systematic increase in radius of the transition elements which takes place in passing from the fourth to the fifth period is not observed in passing from the fifth to the sixth, so that the radii of corresponding elements in these last two periods are very nearly the same, e.g.

| Periods | Atomic radius (Å) | | | |
|---|---|---|---|---|
| | Cr | Fe | Ni | Cu |
| 4 | 1.28 | 1.27 | 1.24 | 1.28 |
| | Mo | Ru | Pd | Ag |
| 5 | 1.40 | 1.33 | 1.37 | 1.44 |
| | W | Os | Pt | Au |
| 6 | 1.41 | 1.35 | 1.38 | 1.44 |

This is another manifestation of lanthanide contraction already discussed in connection with ionic radii.

*Example:* The unit cell dimension of bcc iron is 2.81Å. Calculate the metallic radius of iron atom.

*Solution:* Given: Unit cell dimension of iron = 2.81Å, and the structure as bcc. Now, for a bcc structure we have

$$\sqrt{3}a = 4R$$

or

$$R = \frac{\sqrt{3}}{4}a = \frac{\sqrt{3}}{4} \times 2.81 = 1.22\text{Å}$$

*Example:* Metallic gold and platinum both have fcc structures with the unit cell dimension 4.08 and 3.91Å. Calculate the metallic radii of these atoms.

*Solution:* Given: Unit cell dimension of Au = 4.08Å, unit cell dimension of Pt = 3.19Å, both have fcc structures.

Now, for fcc structure we know that $\sqrt{2}a = 4R$. So that, the radius of gold atom

$$R = \frac{\sqrt{2}a}{4} = \frac{\sqrt{2} \times 4.08}{4} = 1.44\text{Å}$$

Similarly, the radius of the platinum atom

$$R = \frac{\sqrt{2} \times 3.91}{4} = 1.38\text{Å}$$

*Example:* Aluminium has an fcc structure. Its density is 2700 kg/m$^3$, at. number is 13 and the at. mass is 26.98. Calculate the unit cell dimension and atomic diameter.

*Solution:* Given: Atomic number of Al = 13, at. mass = 26.98, density = 2700 kg/m$^3$ and the crystal structure is fcc. Now, we know that the number of atoms in an fcc structure, $n = 4$. Thus using eq. 4 (Ch. 1), we have

$$n = \frac{V \times \rho \times N}{M}$$

where $V = a^3$ and $N = 6.023 \times 10^{26}$. Therefore, we can write

$$a^3 = V = \frac{n \times M}{\rho \times N} = \frac{4 \times 26.98}{2700 \times 6.023 \times 10^{26}} = 4.05 \times 10^{-10}\text{ m}$$

$$\Rightarrow \qquad\qquad a = 4.05 \text{ Å}$$

Now, for an fcc structure $\sqrt{2}a = 4R = 2D$ (diameter of the atom)

or
$$D = \frac{a}{\sqrt{2}} = 2.86\text{Å}$$

## 4.11 VAN DER WAALS RADII

In crystals composed of molecules or noble gas atoms, non bonded distances of closest-approach may be divided to get the values of van der Waals radii $r_w$, suitable for use in estimating various parameters of interest in crystal structure. A large number of research papers have been published by various investigators in regards to find the most accurate values. A qualitative interpretation of van der Waals radii due to Morrison (1955) and Bondi (1964) shows that

$$r_w = C\lambda_B \qquad\qquad (23)$$

where $\lambda_B = h\sqrt{M_c I_0}$, the de Broglie wavelength of the outermost valence electron ($M_c$ is the rest mass of the electron; $I_0$ is the first ionization potential and $C$ varies from 0.48 to 0.61 acccording to the group). Collecting constants we may write

$$r_w = K\sqrt{I_0} \qquad\qquad (24)$$

This is a simple, logical and satisfying relation which can be used to obtain van der Waals radii of less commonly studied atoms in molecular crystal. van der Waals radii of some atoms computed by Bondi is given in Table 4.10. These radii are used in computing the volumes of molecules and groups which help in determining the preferred orientation of bulky constituents, and in estimating modes of packing. These radii do not have the same degree of consistency as the ionic, covalent and the metallic radii, and variation of as much as 0.1Å may be found in different molelcular structures. These radii are also larger than the corresponding covalent radii of the same element (Table 4.8), emphasizing once again that in molecular structures the effective radius of an atom within a molecule is quite different from its radius towards other molecules.

**Table 4.10   Van der Waals radii (Å)**

|            |            |            | H          | He         |
|------------|------------|------------|------------|------------|
|            |            |            | 1.20       | 1.40       |
| C          | N          | O          | F          | Ne         |
| 1.70       | 1.55       | 1.52       | 1.47       | 1.54       |
| Si         | P          | S          | Cl         | Ar         |
| 2.10       | 1.80       | 1.80       | 1.75       | 1.88       |
|            | As         | Se         | Br         | Kr         |
|            | 1.85       | 1.90       | 1.85       | 2.02       |
|            |            | Te         | I          | Xe         |
|            |            | 2.06       | 1.98       | 2.16       |

## 4.12 SUMMARY

1. Shape of an atom remains spherical irrespective of addition or removal of electrons, however, its size changes.
2. Size of an atom depends on the coordination number, radius ratio and the type of forces existing between them.
3. Absolute value of the atomic size is only aproximately known.
4. In an ionic crystal, the radius of an ion is defined as

$$R_{ion} = \frac{C_n}{Z - S} = \frac{C_n}{Z_{eff}}$$

where $S$ is a screening constant, $C_n$ is a constant determined by the quantum number and $Z_{eff}$ is the effective nuclear charge.

5. Radius of multivalent ions could be determined by the equation

$$R_{multivalent} = R_{univalent} \times Z^{-2/(n-1)}$$

6. Ionic radii increase with atomic number, while decrease with increasing charge, atomic number and valency.
7. Covalent radii are simply additive and are equal to the half of the distance between the two bonded atoms (bond length), also called as atomic radii.
8. Metallic radii in metals with close packed structures, are half the distance of he closest approach.
9. metallic radii systemtically decrease with the decrease of coordination.
10. In crystals composed of molecules or noble gas atoms, non-bonded distance of closest approach may be divided to get the van der Waals radii.

## 4.13 DEFINITIONS

*Atom:* The smallest particle of an element that can take part in chemical reaction.

*Emission spectrum:* The spectrum of the radiation emitted from a substance as a result of change in energy level of its constituent atoms or molecules.

*Excited state:* The quantum state with energy higher than the ground state.

*Ground state:* The quantum state with lowest energy.

*Ionization potential:* The amount of energy required to remove an electron from an atom or molecule to infinity.

*Ionization Potential* (First): The amount of energy required to remove the least strongly bound electron (valence electron) from a neutral atom.

*Isoelectronic:* Ions having identical electronic structures.

*Monochromatic radiation:* Radiation restricted to a very narrow band of wavelengths; ideally one wavelength.

*Nucleus:* Central massive part of the atom consisting of protons and neutrons.

## REVIEW QUESTIONS AND PROBLEMS

1. Give an account of Rutherford's atomic model. What are the major shortcomings in Rutherford's nuclear model? How they are overcome by Bohr?
2. Derive the mathematical expression for energy of the electron in hydrogen atom. Give the interpretation of the negative sign.
3. Discuss Bohr's theory of hydrogen atom and derive an expression for the radius of the first Bohr orbit for the normal hydrogen atom.

4. Describe Bohr's atom model. Assuming that the nucleus is infinitely heavy and the electron mass $m$ and charge $e$, find out the energy of the electrons moving in the nth orbit.

5. Decribe Bohr's theory of hydrogen atom. How is it successful in explaining the spectrum of hydrogen atom?

6. Briefly discuss how covalent radii are formed.

7. Suggest possible reasons why fluorine is more electronegative than chlorine.

8. Suggest possible reasons why fluorine is more electronegative than oxygen.

9. Calculate for the hydrogen atom (i) velocity of the electron in the ground state (ii) radius of the orbit in the ground state (iii) time taken for the electron to traverse the first Bohr orbit.

   *Ans.* $2.187 \times 10^6$ ms$^{-1}$, 0.529 Å and $1.519 \times 10^{-16}$ s

10. At what speed the electron must revolve round the nucleus of the hydrogen in its ground state in order that it may not be pulled into the nucleus by electrostatic attraction (Given: the radius of the first Bohr orbit is 0.52Å).

11. Electrons of energies 10.2 eV and 12.09 eV can cause radiation to be emitted from hydrogen atoms. Calculate in each case, the principal quantum number of the orbit to which an electron in the hydrogen atom is raised and the wavelength of radiation if it drops back to the ground state.

    *Ans.* 2 and 3, 1216 Å and 1026 Å

12. The critical potential of hydrogen is 13.65 eV. Calculate the wavelength of the radiation emitted by hydrogen atom bombarded by an electron of corresponding energy.   *Ans.* 950 Å

13. How many revolutions does an electron in the $n = 2$ state of a hydrogen atom make before dropping to $n = 1$ state? (The average lifetime of an excited state is about $10^{-8}$ s).   *Ans.* $8.2 \times 10^6$

14. The lowest two excited states of hydrogen atom are 10.2 eV and 12 eV above the ground state, calculate the wavelength of radiation that could be produced by transition between these states and the ground state.

    *Ans.* 1215 Å, 1035 Å and 6902 Å

15. The energy of a Bohr orbit is given by $-B/n^2$, where $B = 2.179 \times 10^{-18}$ J. Calculate the frequency of radiation and also the wave number, when the electron jumps from the third orbit to the second.

    *Ans.* 6561 Å and $1.524 \times 10^6$ m$^{-1}$

16. How much energy is required to raise the hydrogen atom from the ground state $n = 1$ to the first excited state $n = 2$ ? What is the wavelength of the line emitted if the atom returned back to the ground stae.

    *Ans.* 10.2 eV, 1217 Å

17. Rubidium chloride assumes CsCl structure at high pressure. Calculate the RbCl distance in the CsCl structure from that for NaCl structure (from ionic radii).

18. Calculate the $M$-$X$ distances for Lif, BeO and BN as the sum of ionic radii and considering the charge effect.

19. Compare the radii of Na$^+$ and Mg$^{2+}$ and also of SO$^{2-}$ and Cl$^-$. Explain the cause of variations.

20. Determine the radius of a cation having CsCl structure, when all anions are in contact with the cation and touch each other. The critical radius of the anion is 1.90 Å.   *Ans.* 1.39 Å

# Chapter 5

# Crystal Imperfections

## 5.1 INTRODUCTION

Chapter 1 described the ideal crystals having perfectly periodic arrangements of atoms. This is true only for theoretical considerations, on the basis of which many structure-insensitive properties, such as density, electrical capacitivity, specific heat, and elastic properties, can be explained. This chapter considers the real crystals, which are not perfect. In general, any deviation from the perfect atomic arrangement in a crystal is said to contain certain imperfections (or defects). Imperfections affect the above mentioned properties only slightly but have strong influence upon many other properties of crystals, such as strength, electrical conductivity, and hysteresis loss of feromagnets. These are structure-sensitive properties of crystalline solids.

Imperfections in crystalline solids are normally classified according to their dimensions as follows:

   (i) Point imperfections (zero-dimensional defects),
  (ii) Line imperfections (one-dimensional defects),
 (iii) Surface imperfections (two-dimensional defects),
 (iv) Volume imperfections (three-dimensional defects).

We shall discuss only the first three in this chapter. Volume imperfections can be foreign-particle inclusions, large voids (or pores) or noncrystalline regions which have the dimensions of at least a few tens of angstrom.

## 5.2 POINT IMPERFECTIONS

Point imperfections are the simplest imperfections involving a single atom or two and therefore referred to as zero dimensional imperfections. The point imperfections commonly observed in metallic crystals are illustrated in Fig. 5.1, and those observed in ionic crystals are shown in Fig. 5.2. Broadly they are of two kinds.

### Interstitial atom

This is an extra atom positioned at the voids between the regular atomic sites. This may be an impurity atom (called interstitial impurity atom) or an atom of the host (called self-interstitial). Open structures can accommodate interstitials more readily than those having smaller interstitial spaces. As a result, the smaller atoms or ions can occupy interstitial sites more easily than the larger ones. A foreign atom that substitutes for or replaces a parent atom in the crystal is called a substitutional impurity atom (Fig. 5.1).

## Vacancy

In a monoatomic crystal, a vacancy refers to an atomic site from where the atom (electrically neutral) is missing (Fig. 5.1). Schottky imperfection is a type of vacancy in which an atom being free from regular site, migrates through successive steps and eventually settles at the crystal surface. In an ionic crystal, however, a vacancy on either a cation or anion site must be electrically balanced by some means (in the crystal as a whole). This may be achieved if there is an equal number of cation and anion vacancies, or if for every ionic vacancy a similar charged interstitial appears. The combination of anion and cation vacancies (in pairs) is called a Schottky imperfection while the combination of a vacancy and interstitial is called a Frenkel imperfection (Fig. 5.2).

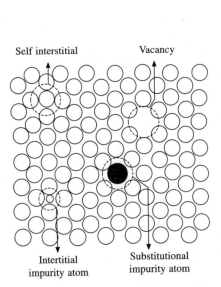

**Fig. 5.1** **A two-dimensional representation of a simple crystalline solid, illustrating some common point imerfections in metal crystals**

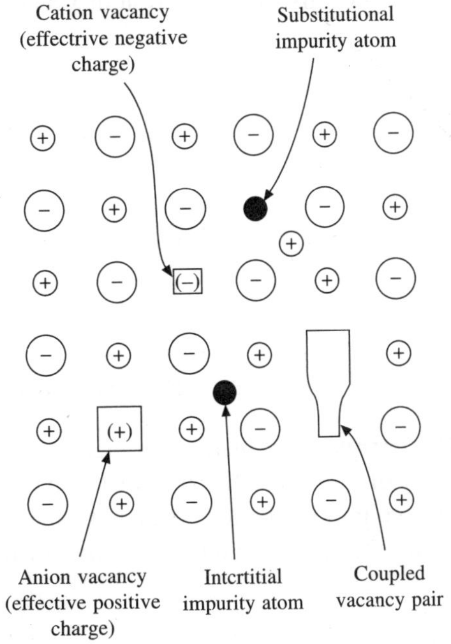

**Fig. 5.2** **Point imperfections in an ionic solid**

## 5.3 CONCENTRATION OF POINT IMPERFECTIONS

### Vacancy (Monoatomic Solid)

According to thermodynamics, the equilibrium state of a solid is the state of minimum free energy $F = E - TS$, where $E$ is the internal energy, $S$ is the entropy and $T$ is the temperature in the absolute scale. It is to be mentioned here that for condensed systems like the liquid and the solid state (at atmospheric pressure), the internal energy is equivalent to the enthalpy of the system (i.e. $E \cong H$) because $PV$ term is negligible in the expression $H = E + PV$. The free energy expression suggests the existence of a certain amount of disorder in the lattice at all temperatures $T > 0K$ (which otherwise seems to be a perfect crystal). It is to be noted that the defects under consideration are present as a result of thermodynamic conditions and do not include any accidental fault resulting from non-ideal growing conditions.

As pointed out above that a vacancy is a missing atom from a regular atomic site in the structure. A vacancy can be created deliberately by transferring an interior atom from its regular site to a site on the surface of a two-dimensional crystal as shown in Fig. 5.3. The change in the internal energy as a result of the introduction of defects into the crystal occurs due to (i) the energy needed to produce defects in the static lattice and (ii) the changed vibrational energy of the atoms coordinating the defects. A change in the entropy experienced by the crystal comes from two different sources. (i) Due to change of thermal entropy as a result of the change in the frequency of atomic oscillators, and (ii) due to configurational entropy associated with the number of ways of selecting which atomic sites will be vacant. In the following calculations, we shall consider first the formation of vacancy in a monoatomic crystal.

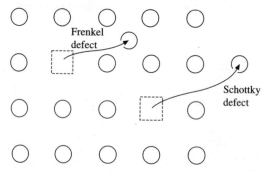

**Fig. 5.3   The formation of Schottky and Frankel imperfections**

The energy of formation of each imperfection $E_s$ taken in electron volts (also called the enthaply of formation $\Delta H_f$, usually taken in Joules per mole) is the energy, $E_H$, required to take an atom from interior to the crystal surface minus the lattice energy per atom $E_L$, i.e. $E_S = E_H - E_L$. Thus the change in the internal energy of the crystal is

$$nE_S = n(E_H - E_L) \tag{1}$$

and the internal energy of the imperfect crystal $E_1$ is

$$E_1 = E_P + nE_S \tag{2}$$

where $E_P$ is the internal energy of the perfect crystal.

In order to calculate the change in the thermal entropy of the crystal, we make use of the Einstein model of lattice vibration, according to which each atom in the crystal vibrates, independently with a frequency $v$. Neglecting the zero point vibrational energy and for $hv << kT$ the thermal entropy of the perfect crystal is approximately given by

$$S_P = 3Nk\left[1 + \ln\left(\frac{kT}{hv}\right)\right] \tag{3}$$

In the imperfect crystal, the atoms neighbouring a vacancy will have a frequency $v'$ (smaller than $v$ in perfect crystal) particularly along the line joining the atom to the vacancy, because the restoring forces are reduced. Therefore, it is assumed that in the imperfect crystal, each atom neighbouring a vacancy is equivalent to three independent harmonic oscillators of frequency $v'$ $< v$. Thus, if $x$ is the number of atoms surrounding a vacancy ($x$-fold coordination), then two possibilities arise: (i) For a coordination of 6-fold or below $nx$ atoms will oscillate with frequency $v'$ (axes parallel to the line joining the atom to the vacancy are affected) and $(3N - nx)$ with $v$. (ii) For a coordination greater than 6–fold (when all the three axes are affected) $3nx$ atoms will oscillate with frequency $v'$ and $(3N - 3nx)$ with $v$. The thermal entropy of the imperfect crystal is then obtained in analogy with eq. 3, for the case (ii) as

$$S_1 = 3nxk\left[1 + \ln\left(\frac{kT}{hv'}\right)\right] + (3N - 3nx)k\left[1 + \ln\left(\frac{kT}{hv}\right)\right] \tag{4}$$

Substracting eq. 3 from 4, we obtain the change in the thermal entropy as

$$\Delta S_{th} = (S_1 - S_P) = 3nxk\left[1 + \ln\left(\frac{kT}{hv'}\right)\right] + (3N - 3nx)k\left[1 + \ln\left(\frac{kT}{hv}\right)\right]$$

$$- 3Nk\left[1 + \ln\left(\frac{kT}{hv}\right)\right]$$

$$= 3nxk\left[1 + \ln\left(\frac{kT}{hv'}\right)\right] - 3nxk\left[1 + \ln\left(\frac{kT}{hv}\right)\right] = 3nxk \ln\left(\frac{v}{v'}\right) = nk \ln\left(\frac{v}{v'}\right)^{3x} \tag{5}$$

In a similar way, the thermal entropy of the imperfect crystal for the case (i) can be obtained as

$$\Delta S_{th} = nk \ln\left(\frac{v}{v'}\right)^{x} \tag{6}$$

As far as the configurational entropy of a crystal is concerned, it has nothing to do with the distribution of energy; it is solely determined by the number of different ways $W_{cf}$ in which the atoms may be arranged over the available number of lattice sites. For example, let us consider that there are $N$ lattice sites in the crystal and $n$ Schottky vacancies that are produced. Then the number of ways of arranging $n$ identical vacancies and $(N - n)$ identical atoms on $N$ sites is given by

$$W_{cf} = \frac{N!}{(N - n)!n!} \tag{7}$$

The configurational entropy associated with $W_{cf}$ is obtained from the Boltzmann equation

$$S_{cf} = k\ln W_{cf} = k\ln\left[\frac{N!}{(N - n)!n!}\right] \tag{8}$$

In the case of perfect crystal containing identical atoms, $W_{cf} = 1$ and $S_{cf} = 0$ because there is only one possible way of arranging the atoms. The total entropy occurring in the usual thermodynamic formulas is equal to the sum of the thermal and configurational entropies, i.e.

$$S = S_{th} + S_{cf} \tag{9}$$

Now using eq. 5 (i.e. taking into account the coordination of vacancy as 6-fold or greater) we may write the free energy of the imperfect crystal as

$$F = E_P + nE_S - nkT \ln \left(\frac{v}{v'}\right)^{3x} - kT \ln \left[\frac{N!}{(N-n)!n!}\right] \tag{10}$$

The equilibrium value of $n$ is obtained from this equation by setting $(\partial F/\partial n)_T = 0$ and making use of Stirling's approximation,

$$\ln x! \cong x \ln x - x \text{ for } x \gg 1$$

so that

$$\ln \left[\frac{N!}{(N-n)!n!}\right] = N \ln N - (N-n) \ln (N-n) - n \ln n$$

Consequently eq. 10 becomes

$$F = E_P + nE_S - nkT \ln \left(\frac{v}{v'}\right)^{3x} - kT \left[N \ln(N) - (N-n) \ln (N-n) - n \ln (n)\right]$$

Differentiating with respect to n partially, we get

$$\left(\frac{\partial F}{\partial n}\right)_T = E_S - kT \ln \left(\frac{v}{v'}\right)^{3x} - kT \ln \frac{(N-n)}{n} = 0$$

or

$$E_S - kT \ln \left(\frac{v}{v'}\right)^{3x} - kT \ln \frac{(N-n)}{n} = 0$$

or

$$kT \ln \frac{n}{N-n} = kT \ln \left(\frac{v}{v'}\right)^{3x} - E_S$$

or

$$\ln \frac{n}{N-n} = \ln \left(\frac{v}{v'}\right)^{3x} - \frac{E_S}{kT}$$

or

$$\frac{n}{N-n} = \left(\frac{v}{v'}\right)^{3x} \exp\left(-\frac{E_S}{kT}\right)$$

or

$$\frac{n}{N} = \left(\frac{v}{v'}\right)^{3x} \exp\left(-\frac{E_S}{kT}\right) \tag{11}$$

where $n \ll N$. Use of eq. 6 would result in

$$\frac{n}{N} = \left(\frac{v}{v'}\right)^{x} \exp\left(-\frac{E_S}{KT}\right) \tag{12}$$

For one mole of atoms, the internal energy $NkT = RT$, where $N$ is the Avogadro's number and $R$ is the gas constant. Therefore,

$$R = Nk = 6.023 \times 10^{23} \times 1.38 \times 10^{-23} = 8.314 \text{ Jmol}^{-1}\text{K}^{-1}$$

Making use of this, eq. 12 equivalently can be written as

$$\frac{n}{N} = \left(\frac{v}{v'}\right)^x \exp\left(-\frac{\Delta H_f}{RT}\right) \tag{12'}$$

where in eq. 12 the term $E_S$ is expressed in electron volts (eV) and in eq. 12' the $\Delta H_f$ is expressed in kJmol$^{-1}$, respectively. The energy required to form vacancies in some monoatomic crystals is listed in Table 5.1. Since $v > v'$, the change in thermal entropy favours the formation of vacancies as $v/v'$ is greater than 1. This factor may be large because $3x$ is rather a large number ( 24 for bcc and 36 for fcc).

**Table 5.1  Enthalpy of formation of vacancies in some crystals**

| Crystal | Kr | Cd | Pb | Zn | Mg | Al | Ag | Cu | Ni |
|---|---|---|---|---|---|---|---|---|---|
| $\Delta H_f$ kJ mol$^{-1}$ | 7.7 | 38 | 48 | 49 | 56 | 68 | 106 | 120 | 168 |
| eV/vacancy | 0.08 | 0.39 | 0.50 | 0.51 | 0.58 | 0.70 | 1.10 | 1.24 | 1.74 |

The results obtained above may be used to explain qualitatively the reason for the existence of lattice defects at any temperature $T > 0$. For example, suppose that in a perfect metallic crystal we produce certain number of vacancies by transferring the atoms from the interior of the crystal to the surface. This will require certain amount of energy so that the internal energy, $E$ of the crystal will increase. As a result of this, the free energy $F$ will also increase, which is unfavourable in the thermodynamic sense. On the other hand, creation of vacancies increases the disorder in the crystal which in turn increases the configurational entropy from zero to a certain value determined by the number of vacancies 'n' produced. Since the entropy appears in the free energy expression ($F = E - TS$) in the form $-TS$, an increase in the entropy reduces the free energy $F$, which is favourable in thermodynamic sense. As a result of the competition between internal energy and entropy, the stable state of a crystal will always contain a certain number of vacancies. A schematic representation of $F$ as a function of the fraction $n/N$ is shown in Fig. 5.4. For simplicity the thermal entropy has been assumed to be independent of $n/N$. The equilibrium corresponds to the minimum value of $F$ at temperature $T$.

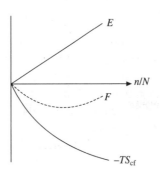

**Fig. 5.4  Schematic representation of the energy, configurational entropy and free energy term as a function of $n/N$**

### Frenkel Imperfection (Monoatomic Solid)

In this case, an atom is being transferred from a regular lattice site to an interstitial site (Fig. 5.3). A Frenkel defect thus consists of two components: a vacancy plus an interstitial atom. Let $E_F$ (or $\Delta H_f F_r$, the enthalpy of formation) be the energy required to form one Frenkel defect. Further, if there are $N$ lattice sites in the crystal, $N_i$ interstitial sites, and $n$ Frenkel imperfections being produced, then the number of ways of arranging $(N - n)$ identical atoms and $n$ identical vacancies on $N$ sites is

$$\frac{N!}{(N - n)!n!}$$

Also the number of ways of arranging $n$ identical vacancies and $(N_i - n)$ identical atoms on $N_i$ sites is

$$\frac{N_i!}{(N_i - n)!n!}$$

so that,
$$W_{cf} = \frac{N!}{(N - n)!n!} \times \frac{N_i!}{(N_i - n)!n!}$$

Following a similar procedure as in the preceding section, the expression for Frenkel defects can be obtained as

$$\frac{n}{(NN_i)^{1/2}} = \gamma \exp\left(-\frac{E_F}{2kT}\right) \qquad (13)$$

or equivalently as

$$\frac{n}{(NN_i)^{1/2}} = \gamma \exp\left(-\frac{\Delta H_f F_r}{2RT}\right) \qquad (13')$$

As above, the pre-exponential term $\gamma$ is related to the thermal entropy changes through the changes in the vibrational frequencies of those atoms neighbouring both the interstitial and the vacancy. That part of $\gamma$ related to the vacancy component of the Frenkel defect will be $(v/v')^{3x}$ as in eq. 11. If it is assumed that the interstitial site has $y$-fold coordination and that the frequencies of vibration of the interstitial and its immediate neighbours are $v_i$ and $v_i'$ respectively, then it can be easily shown that,

$$\gamma^2 = \left(\frac{v}{v'}\right)^{3x} \frac{\gamma^{y+1}}{v_i v_i'^{y}} \qquad (14)$$

This result has the following general implications: since $v > v'$ the change in thermal entropy favours the formation of Schottky vacancies. For example with $v = 2v'$ in a simple cubic structure ($x = 6$) we find that $\gamma = 64$. However, when Frenkel defects are formed $v_i$ and $v_i'$ are almost certainly greater than $v$, so that $\gamma$ may be less than unity. Consequently, the changes in the thermal entropy do not necessarily favour the formation of Frenkel defects. The factor 2 occurs in the exponential term in eq. 13 arises because the Frenkel defect has two components. This is a quite general result and can be applied to determine Schottky defects in alkali halide crystals, where a cation + anion vacancy is formed simultaneously to maintain thermal equilibrium.

### Schottky Imperfection (Ionic Solid)
Let us consider a perfect crystal composed of equal numbers of positively and negatively charged ions (i.e. an ionic crystal). In such crystals, it is energetically favourable to form equal

numbers of positive and negative ion vacancies (Fig. 5.2). The formation of such pair of vacancies keeps the crystal electrically neutral even on a local scale. Let us suppose that there are $n$ cation and $n$ anion vacancies with formation energies $E_C$ and $E_A$ respectively (or $\Delta H_f Sch$, the enthalpy of formation of one mole each of cation and anion vacancies). The energy of formation of pair of vacancies will therefore be given by

$$E = E_C + E_A \tag{15}$$

The internal energy of the imperfect crystal is therefore,

$$E_1 = E_P + nE \tag{16}$$

The free energy of the fictitious perfect crystal is given by

$$F_P = E_p - TS_P \tag{17}$$

where energy $E_P$ incorporates the binding energy as well as the vibrational energy. The entropy is only thermal, because for a perfect crystal, $W_{cf} = 1$ and $S_{cf} = 0$. The configurational entropy for the actual crystal having $n$ cation and anion vacancies each, is given as

$$S_{cf} = k \ln\left(\frac{N!}{(N-n)!n!}\right)^2 \tag{18}$$

where the square term represents the number of ways of arranging $n$ identical vacancies (cation or anion) and $(N - n)$ identical ions (cations or anions) on $N$ sites. The change in thermal entropy can be obtained in a similar way as discussed in the previous cases, by using Einstein model of lattice vibration. The imperfect (actual) crystal in this case will correspond to $6nx$ linear oscillators with frequency $v'$, and $(6N - 6nx)$ oscillators with frequency $v$, where $x$ (in general greater than 6) is the number of nearest neighbours surrounding a vacancy. The thermal entropies of the perfect and imperfect crystals, respectively, are then given by

$$S_P = 6Nk\left[1 + \ln\left(\frac{kT}{hv}\right)\right] \tag{19}$$

and

$$S_1 = 6Nxk\left[1 + \ln\left(\frac{kT}{hv'}\right)\right] + (6N - 6nx)k\left[1 + \ln\left(\frac{kT}{hv}\right)\right]$$

where we assumed $hv \ll kT$. Hence,

$$\Delta S = S_1 - S_P = 6nxh \ln\left(\frac{v}{v'}\right) \tag{20}$$

The free energy of the imperfect crystal is given as

$$F = E_P + nE - 6nxkT \ln\left(\frac{v}{v'}\right) - kT \ln\left(\frac{N!}{(N-n)!n!}\right)^2 \tag{21}$$

The equilibrium value of $n$ is obtained from this equation by setting $(\partial F/\partial n)_T = 0$ and using Stirling's approximation for solving factorial term, eq. 21 b

$$\left(\frac{\partial F}{\partial n}\right)_T = F - 6xkT \ln\left(\frac{v}{v'}\right) - 2kT \ln\left(\frac{N-n}{n}\right) = 0$$

or

$$E - 6xkT \ln\left(\frac{v}{v'}\right) + 2kT \ln\left(\frac{n}{N-n}\right) = 0$$

and consequently,

$$\frac{n}{N} = \left(\frac{v}{v'}\right)^{3x} \exp\left(-\frac{E}{2kT}\right)$$

or

$$\frac{n}{N} = \left(\frac{v}{v'}\right)^{3x} \exp\left(-\frac{E_C + E_A}{2kT}\right) \tag{22}$$

or equivalently as

$$\frac{n}{N} = \left(\frac{v}{v'}\right)^{3x} \exp\left(-\frac{\Delta H_f Sch}{2kT}\right) \tag{22'}$$

If thermal effect is neglected then the pre-exponential term $\gamma$ will disappear from equations 11, 12, 12′, 13, 13′, 22 and 22′. They will reduce to simple expressions consisting only configurational entropy term.

From above discussion, we find that the concentration of each point imperfection is different. It is because their energies of formation are different. Despite this, usually both kinds of imperfections are present in all solids, however, there is always a tendency for one type of imperfection to predominate. In metals, it appears that the energy favours the formation of vacancies, although Frenkel imperfections are also formed. On the basis of this, both experimental (measurements of ionic conductivity and density) and theoretical calculations, it has been established that the predominant imperfections in alkali halides are Schottky imperfections, whereas in pure silver halides the prevalent defects below 700K are Frenkel imperfections.

As a result of the formation of Schottky imperfections, volume of the crystal increases without any change in the mass and therefore, the density of the crystal decreases. On the other hand, the production of Frenkel imperfections does not change the volume of the crystal and hence the density of the crystal remains unchanged.

*Example*: Determine the fraction of atoms in a given solid with the energy equal to or greater than 1.5 eV at room temperature (300K) and at 1000K.

*Solution*: Given: $E = 1.5$ eV, temperatures $T_1 = 300$K and $T_2 = 1500$K.
Further, we know that the Boltzmann's constant in terms of electron volts is given as $k = 8.614 \times 10^{-5}$ eV.

Now, in order to find the required fraction of atoms, let us use simple form of eq. 12 containing only the configuration entropy term,

$$\frac{n}{N} = \exp\left(-\frac{E}{kT}\right)$$

Therefore at 300K, $\dfrac{n}{N} = \exp\left(-\dfrac{1.5}{8.614 \times 10^{-5} \times 300}\right) = \exp(-58.045) = 6.185 \times 10^{-26}$

Similarly, at 1500K, $\dfrac{n}{N} = \exp\left(-\dfrac{1.5}{8.614 \times 10^{-5} \times 1500}\right) = \exp(-11.609) = 9.084 \times 10^{-6}$

This implies that with a five-fold increase in temperature, the fraction of highly energetic atoms has increased by about twenty orders of magnitude.

*Example*: The energy of formation of a vacancy in copper is 1eV. Estimate the relative change in the density of copper due to vacancy formation at a temperature just below its melting point, 1356K.

*Solution*: Using the same equation as above, we find

$$\frac{n}{N} = \exp\left(-\frac{E}{kT}\right) = \exp\left(-\frac{1}{8.614 \times 10^{-5} \times 1356}\right) = \exp(-8.56) = 1.914 \times 10^{-4}$$

Therefore the number of vacancy per mole is

$$n = 6.023 \times 10^{23} \times 1.914 \times 10^{-4} = 1.1528 \times 10^{20}$$

Now the change in the density due to creation of vacancy is

$$n + N = 6.0241528 \times 10^{23}$$

Therefore the relative change in the density of copper due to vacancy formation is

$$\frac{n + N}{N} = 1.0001914 : 1$$

*Example*: The concentration of Schottky defects in an fcc crystal is 1 in $10^{10}$ at a temperature of 300 K. Estimate the average separation between the defects in terms of lattice spacing at 33 K and calculate the value of concentration to be expected at 1000 K.

*Solution*: Given: $n : N = 1 : 10^{10}$ at 300 K

Since $\quad \dfrac{n}{N} = \dfrac{1}{10^{10}} = 10^{-10}$, therefore, $n = 6.023 \times 10^{23} \times 10^{-10} \cong 10^{14}$

Let the interatomic spacing $\simeq 1 \ \text{Å} = 10^{-10}$ m
$\Rightarrow$ the volume of the unit cube =. $10^{-30}$ m$^3$
Since we know that in an fcc crystal the number of atoms per unit cell is 4, which occupies a volume of $10^{-30}$ m$^3$. Thus in one mole, $10^{23}$ atoms will occupy a volume of

$$10^{-30} \times 10^{+23} \simeq 10^{-7} \ \text{m}^3$$

Since $10^{14}$ defects are available within the same volume (i.e. within $10^{-7}$ m$^3$). Therefore volume per defect will be

$$V = a^3 \simeq \frac{10^{-7}}{10^{14}} = 10^{-21} \text{m}^3, \Rightarrow a \simeq 10^{-7} \text{m}$$

For the second part of the problem, let us again start with the given defect concentration, i.e.

$$\frac{n}{N} = \frac{1}{10^{10}} = 10^{-10} = \exp(-10 \times 2.303) = \exp(-23.03) = \exp\left(-\frac{E_v}{kT}\right)$$

$$\Rightarrow \qquad\qquad E_v = 23.03 \times 8.614 \times 10^{-5} \times 300 = 0.595 \text{ eV}$$

Therefore, the defect concentration at 1000 K is given as

$$\frac{n}{N} = \exp\left(-\frac{E_v}{kT}\right) = \exp\left(-\frac{0.595}{8.614 \times 10^{-5} \times 10^3}\right) = \exp(-6.909) = 9.987 \times 10^{-4} \simeq 10^{-3}$$

$$\Rightarrow \quad n : N = 1 : 10^3$$

*Example*: The energy required to remove a pair of ions, $Na^+$ and $Cl^-$, from NaCl is ~ 2 eV. Calculate the approximate number of Schottky imperfections present in the NaCl crystal at room temperature.

*Solution*: Given: Temperature $T$ = 300K and energy required to remove a pair of ions = 2 eV. Therefore, using the expression

$$\frac{n}{N} = \exp\left(-\frac{E_p}{2kT}\right) = \exp\left(-\frac{2}{2 \times 8.61 \times 10^{-5} \times 300}\right)$$

$$= \exp(-38.70) = 1.564 \times 10^{-17}$$

or $\qquad\qquad n = 6.023 \times 10^{23} \times 1.564 \times 10^{-17} = 9.42 \times 10^6$

Now, since the volume of one mole of the crystal = 26.83 cm$^3$,

Therefore, $\qquad\qquad n = \frac{9.42}{26.83} \times 10^6 = 0.35 \times 10^6 \text{ cm}^{-3}$

*Example*: The density of Schottky defects in a certain sample of sodium chloride is $5 \times 10^{11}$ m$^{-3}$ at 300K. If the interionic separation is 2.82Å, what is the average energy required to create one Schottky defect?

*Solution:* Given: Interionic separation = 2.82Å = $2.82 \times 10^{-10}$ m, the density of defects, $n = 5 \times 10^{11}$ m$^{-3}$, $T$ = 300K, $E_p$ = ?

Since the unit cell of sodium chloride (without defect) contains four ion-pairs, therefore its volume will be

$$V = (2 \times 2.82 \times 10^{-10})^3 = 1.794 \times 10^{-28} \text{ m}^3$$

Consequently, $1 m^3$ of an ideal crystal will contain,

$$\frac{4}{1.794 \times 10^{-28}} = 2.23 \times 10^{28} \text{ ion-pairs} = N$$

Now, using the equation $\frac{n}{N} = \exp\left(-\frac{E_p}{2kT}\right)$ and substituting various values, we obtain

$$E_P = 2kT \times \ln\left(\frac{2.23 \times 10^{28}}{5 \times 10^{11}}\right)$$

$$= 2 \times 8.614 \times 10^{-5} \times 300 \times \ln(4.46 \times 10^{16}) = 1.98 \text{ eV}$$

*Example*: The average energy required to create a Frenkel defect in an ionic crystal, $A^{2+}B^{2-}$, is 1.4 eV. Calculate the ratio of Frenkel defects at 300K and 600K in 1g of crystal.

*Solution:* Given: $E_F = 1.4$ eV, $T_1 = 300$ K, $T_2 = 600$ K, $(n_{300}/n_{600}) = ?$

Making use of the equation $n = (NN_i)^{1/2} \exp\left(-\dfrac{E_F}{2kT}\right)$, we obtain

$$n_{300} = (NN_i)^{1/2} \exp\left(-\frac{1.4}{600k}\right) \text{ and } n_{600} = (NN_i)^{1/2} \exp\left(-\frac{1.4}{1200k}\right)$$

so that

$$\frac{n_{300}}{n_{600}} = \exp\left(-\frac{1.4}{k}\right)\left(\frac{1}{600} - \frac{1}{1200}\right)$$

Simplifying this, we obtain $\dfrac{n_{300}}{n_{600}} = 1.316 \times 10^{-6}$

## 5.4 LINE IMPERFECTIONS

Any deviation from perfectly periodic arrangement of atoms along a line is called the line imperfection. In the geometrical sense, it is a one dimensional imperfection. In this case, the distortion is centered only along a line and therefore the imperfection can be considered as the boundary between two regions of a surface which are perfect themselves but are out of register with each other. The line imperfection acting as boundary between the slipped and unslipped regions, lies in the slip plane and is called a dislocation. Two extreme types of dislocations are distinguished as edge dislocation and the screw dislocation. Any particular dislocation is therefore a mixture of these two extreme dislocations. Let us discuss the edge and screw dislocations with the help of models based on simple cubic lattice.

### Edge Dislocation
The formation of an edge dislocation can be visualized in two different ways:

In first case, let us consider a block of crystal which is cut across the area ABEF such that the upper and lower parts are disconnected (Fig. 5.5). The plane ABEF acts as a slip plane. The upper half is now pushed side way such that it shifts by an amount $b$, the slip vector as indicated. As a result, the region to the left of *EF* is slipped while the region to the right of *EF* remains unslipped. The line *EF* within the crystal marks the boundary between the slipped and unslipped regions and so is the dislocation line. The upper half of the block will clearly be under compression while the lower half is under tension (Fig. 5.6). The atomic structure of the front face after the operation will look like the one as shown in Fig. 5.7. If there were $n$ vertical

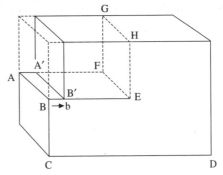

**Fig. 5.5** Formation of an edge dislocation by slip process, EF is the dislocation line

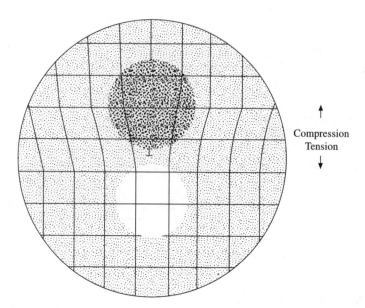

Compression
Tension

**Fig. 5.6**   **The region of tension (light) and compression (dark) around the edge dislocation in a simple cubic lattice**

atomic planes before the slip in both the upper and lower halves of the crystal, then, after the unit slip, $n$ atomic planes above the slip plane try to join $(n - 1)$ atomic planes below. Consequently, one vertical atomic plane in the upper half of the crystal has no counterpart in the lower half. It has to terminate on the slip plane. The dislocation lies at the edge of this extra half plane, and hence the name "edge dislocation". In this case, the dislocation line is normal to the slip vector.

The strain pattern (Fig. 5.7) suggests immediately an alternative way of forming an edge dislocation. Let us consider that the crystal block is cut along the plane EFGH and insert (in imagination) an extra half plane of atoms above the slip plane or remove an extra half plane from below the slip plane. Situations resulting from inserting an extra half plane either above or below the slip plane may be distinguished from one another as positive and negative edge dislocation (Fig. 5.8a) and are symbolically represented as ⊥ and ⊤, respectively.

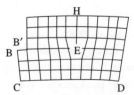

**Fig. 5.7**   **Front face of Fig. 5.5. Showing the strain pattern**

Just like the electrical charges, dislocations of the same sign repel, and those of opposite sign attract each other. Two edge dislocation $X$, $Y$ of opposite sign on the same slip plane attract and annihilate one another, leaving a perfect crystal with a consequent reduction in the elastic energy of the system (Fig. 5.8b).

## Screw Dislocation

The formation of screw dislocation may be illustrated by the crystal model shown in Fig. 5.9. The crystal is cut along ABEF as shown in Fig. 5.9a. The right half is then pushed down with respect to the left half by one atomic spacing. The result is shown in Fig. 5.9b. A step of height equal to the slip vector, $b$, is created on the surface of the crystal; it does not extend throughout

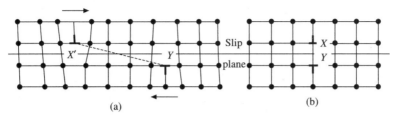

**Fig. 5.8** **Two edge dislocations of opposite sign on the same slip plane (a) attract and annihilate one another (b) leaving a perfect crystal**

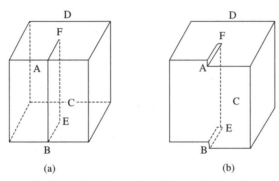

(a)         (b)

**Fig. 5.9** **The formation of screw dislocation**

the surface but is limited from the point *F* to the edge of the crystal. The line *EF* is the boundary between the slipped and unslipped regions of the crystal and hence is the dislocation line. Fig. 5.10 illustrates the formation of screw dislocation with the help of a simple cubic model. In this case, the dislocation line is parallel to the slip vector. Like edge dislocation, the screw dislocation may be either right handed or left handed; they are symbolically represented as ↻ or ↺ depending on whether the slip vector is parallel or antiparallel to the dislocation line.

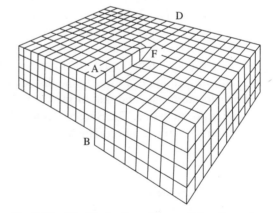

*Example*: A strip of iron of dimensions $1 \times 2 \times 15$ cm is bent into a radius of curvature of 12 cm. What is the dislocation density if [111] edge dislocations line up with their Burgers vector along the strip?

*Solution:* Given: The length of the strip $L = 15$ cm = 0.15 m, the thickness $t = 2$ cm = 0.02 m and the radius of curvature $r = 12$ cm = 0.12 m. Also, for iron $a = 2.81$Å.

**Fig. 5.10** **The illustration of screw dislocation using a simple cubic model**

Since iron has bcc structure, therefore the Burgers vector

$$b = \frac{\sqrt{3}a}{2} = \frac{\sqrt{3} \times 2.81}{2} = 2.43\text{Å} = 2.43 \times 10^{-10} \text{ m}$$

Now referring to Fig. 5.11, let us suppose that the whole strip contains $n$ positive edge dislocations, then we must have

$$nb = \frac{Lt}{r}$$

Since the density of the dislocation is simply given by the number of dislocation line piercing through a unit area of the plane of the paper, we obtain

$$\rho = \frac{n}{Lt} = \frac{1}{rb} = \frac{1}{0.12 \times 2.43 \times 10^{-10}}$$

$$= 3.42 \times 10^{10} , \text{m}^{-2}$$

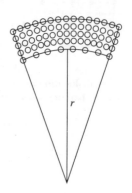

*Example:* An aluminum crystal is bent into a radius of curvature of 5 cm. What is the minimum dislocation density in the material (Burgers vector = 3Å)?

**Fig. 5.11   Edge dislocations on a curved surface**

*Solution:* Given: $b = 3\text{Å} = 3 \times 10^{-10}$ m and $r = 5$ cm $= 0.05$ m. Therefore, similar to the above, we obtain

$$\rho = \frac{n}{Lt} = \frac{1}{rb} = \frac{1}{0.05 \times 3 \times 10^{-10}} = 6.7 \times 10^{10}\,\text{m}^{-2}$$

## 5.5   BURGERS VECTOR AND BURGERS CIRCUIT

One property of a dislocation is its Burgers vector $b$, which describes both magnitude as well as direction of slip. The Burgers vector is usually defined from a Burgers circuit as shown in Fig. 5.12. A Burgers circuit is a sequence of lattice vectors, from one lattice point to the next such that it forms loop. This circuit around the dislocation fails to close the loop by the Burgers vector, whereas a similar circuit in a perfect lattice would complete the loop. The Burgers vector of a pure edge dislocation is normal to the dislocation line, that of pure screw dislocation is parallel to the dislocation line, and that of mixed dislocation makes an angle (lies between 0 and 90°) with the dislocation line. The Burgers vector of a dislocation is always the same and independent of position of the dislocation. The modulus of the Burgers vector is called dislocation strength.

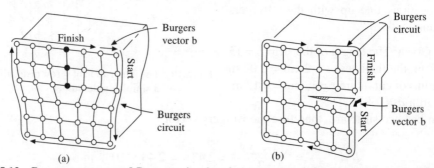

**Fig. 5.12   Burgers vectors and Burgers circuits of: (a) an edge dislocation; (b) screw dislocation**

The Burgers vector of an edge (or mixed) dislocation and the dislocation line define the slip plane. Under the normal circumstances such dislocations are forced to move on the slip plane. On the other hand, the Burgers vector and dislocation line of a pure screw dislocation, are parallel and do not define a unique plane. The screw dislocation is thus free to move on any of the several planes in which the Burgers vector lies. Both these processes take place without considerable activation energy.

*Example*: The Burgers vector of a mixed dislocation is 1/2 [110]. The dislocation line lies along the [112] direction. Find the slip plane on which this dislocation lies. Also, find the screw and the edge components of the Burgers vector.

*Solution:* From above discussion, we know that the Burgers vector of an edge or mixed dislocation and the dislocation line define the slip plane. This implies that they must lie within the slip plane. Now, referring to Fig. 5.13, we find that the required plane containing the Burgers vector and the dislocation line is ($\bar{1}$10).

Also referring to Fig. 5.35a and keeping in view the fact that in edge dislocation the Burgers vector is perpendicular to the dislocation line and in screw dislocation it is parallel, we can write the reaction.

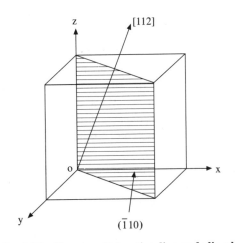

Fig. 5.13   **Showing dislocation line and slip plane**

$$\frac{1}{2}[110] = \frac{1}{6}[112] + \frac{1}{6}[22\bar{2}]$$

$$= \frac{1}{6}[112] + \frac{1}{3}[11\bar{1}]$$

Thus, the first and second term on the right side of the reaction respectively represent the screw and edge component of the Burgers vector.

## 5.6   PRESENCE OF DISLOCATION

The presence of dislocation in a real crystal can be well appreciated if we consider the deformation process in a perfect crystal under the influence of an external stress and the same is compared with the experimentally measured value in a real crystal. Deformation is of two types; Permanent or Temporary. If the deformation stays even after the removal of the applied stress, then it is called "permanent" or "plastic deformation". On the other hand, if the deformation disappears after the removal of the stress then it is called "elastic deformation". The observed stress-strain relationship is qualitatively represented in Fig. 5.14. It is to be noted that plastic deformation is inhomogeneous in the sense that relatively a small number of atoms (i.e. only those atoms which form layers on either side of a slip plane) actually take part in the slip process. Elastic deformation, on the other hand, affects all atoms in a crystal. Here we shall study the nature of the plastic deformation due to slip only and consequently obtain an expression for the critical resolved shear stress (CRSS) for such deformation to start.

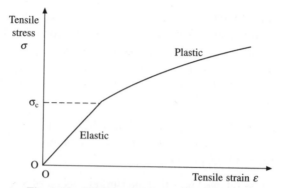

Fig. 5.14 **Elastic and plastic deformations**

Careful examinations of the surface of a deformed crystal under the microscope shows lines in the form of parallel ellipses running around the elongated crystal (Fig. 5.15). These are called slip lines. They indicate that the atomic planes within the crystal have sheared with respect to one another along the slip plane resulting in surface steps. It is generally found that the slip planes are the close packed planes and the direction along which the slip occurs are close packed directions.

Now, making use of simplified model suggested by Frenkel, let us estimate the stress required to cause slip in a perfect crystal. For the purpose, consider two neighbouring atomic planes separated by a distance $d$, and $a$ is the separation between two atoms in the same plane (Fig. 5.16). Further, suppose that $a$ stress $\tau$ is applied on the upper plane of atoms (called slip plane), so that it is displaced with respect to the lower plane of atoms by an amount $x$ relative to its original position. For small elastic strains, the stress $\tau$ is related to the displacement $x$ by the following equation

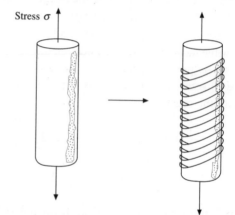

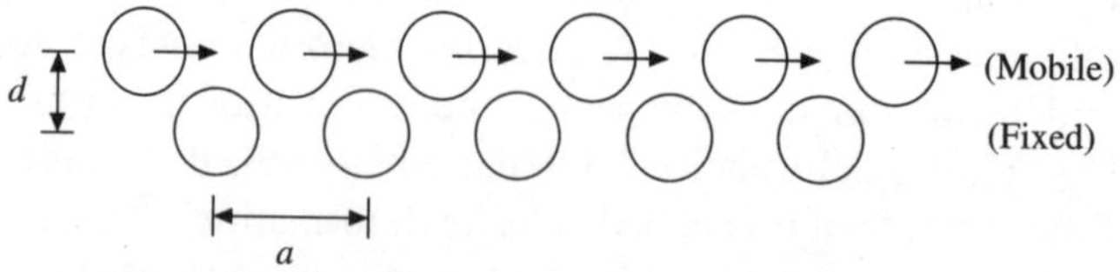

Fig. 5.15 **Formation of slip lines under tensile stress**

Fig. 5.16 **Representation of shear displacement**

$$\tau = \frac{\mu x}{d} \tag{23}$$

where $\mu$ is the shear modulus. But for large displacement, such as when the atoms progress by an interatomic distance $a$, we need another representation. We know that atoms in crystals are distributed in periodic manner and hence there exists a periodic potential (refer Chapter 11) inside the crystal. Consequently, as a first approximation we can represent the stress-displacement by a periodic function

$$\tau = K \sin\left(\frac{2\pi x}{a}\right) \qquad (24)$$

where $K$ is a constant and the estimation of its value requires that eq. 24 must reduce to eq. 23 for small displacements (i.e. $x \ll a$). Under such conditions

$$\tau = \frac{\mu x}{d} = K \frac{2\pi x}{a}$$

so that,

$$K = \frac{\mu a}{2\pi d} \qquad (25)$$

Substituting the value of $K$ in eq. 24, we have

$$\tau = \frac{\mu a}{2\pi d} \sin\left(\frac{2\pi x}{a}\right) \qquad (26)$$

The critical shear stress $\tau_c$, necessary for causing plastic deformation in a perfect crystal corresponds to the maximum amplitude of the sinusoidal wave (i.e. maximum value of $\tau$). Therefore,

$$\tau_c = \frac{\mu a}{2\pi d} \qquad (27)$$

Since this is rather a crude approach anyway, and no significant error will be introduced if we further assume that $a = d$ in eq. 27 to give

$$\tau_c = \frac{\mu}{2\pi} \qquad (28)$$

As an example, for aluminium we may take $\mu = 3 \times 10^{10}$ Nm$^{-2}$ so that the calculated value for $\tau_c$ is $\sim 5 \times 10^9$ Nm$^{-2}$. Now, in order to compare this value with the experimental one, it is necessary to resolve our tensile measurements into the appropriate shear component (Fig. 5.17). The stress at which slip starts in a crystal depends on the relative orientation of the stress axis with respect to the slip plane and the slip direction. Consider a single crystal of cross-sectional area $A$ under a tensile stress $\sigma$ (= $F/A$), where $F$ is the tensile force. Let $\phi$ be the angle between the slip plane normal and the tensile axis, and $\lambda$ be the angle between the slip direction and the tensile axis. The component of the applied force, acting along

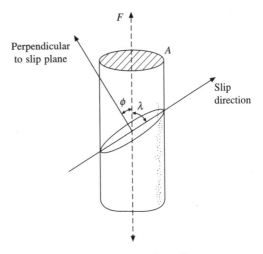

**Fig. 5.17  Resolution of tensile stress**

the slip direction is $F \cos \lambda$, and the area of the slip plane $A/\cos \phi$. The shear stress resolved along the slip direction is then

$$\tau = \frac{F \cos \lambda}{A/\cos \phi} = \left(\frac{F}{A}\right) \cos \phi \cos \lambda = \sigma \cos \phi \cos \lambda \qquad (29)$$

This resolved shear stress when reaches a critical value, is called the critical resolved shear stress (CRSS) for plastic deformation to start. This is given by

$$\tau_c = \sigma_c \cos \phi \cos \lambda \qquad (30)$$

For aluminum, from typical measured value of $\sigma_c$ we find that $\tau_c \sim 10^7$ Nm$^{-2}$. This gives us a difference of about three order of magnitude between the measured and calculated value of $\tau_c$. In other words, a real crystal deforms at a much lower stress than predicted by a model which is based on perfect crystal. This discrepancy can be explained on the basis of presence of dislocations in real crystals.

*Example*: What force does it take in the $[1\bar{1}0]$ direction to have a resolved force of 130 N in the [100] direction of a cubic crystal?

*Solution*: Given: $F_{[100]}$ = 130 N. Referring Fig. 5.18 and making use of the dot product for finding the angle between the directions [100] and $[1\bar{1}0]$ as discussed in section 1.9, we have

$$\frac{F_{[100]}}{F_{[1\bar{1}0]}} = \cos \text{ of angle between } [1\bar{1}0] \text{ and } [100]$$

$$= \cos [1\bar{1}0] \angle [100] = \frac{1 - 0 + 0}{\sqrt{2} \times \sqrt{1}} = \frac{1}{\sqrt{2}}$$

Therefore, $F_{[1\bar{1}0]} = 130 \times \sqrt{2} = 184$ N.

*Example*: A force of 660 N is applied along [111] direction of a cubic crystal. What is the resolved force in the [110] direction?

*Solution*: Given: $F_{[111]}$ = 660 N.
Referring Fig. 5.19 and making use of the dot product for finding the angle between the directions [110] and [111] as discussed above, we have

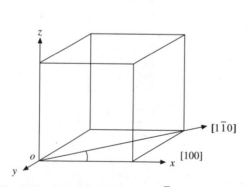

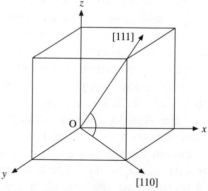

**Fig. 5.18** **Showing [100]] and $[1\bar{1}0]$ direction in a cubic crystal**

**Fig. 5.19** **Showing [110] and [111] directions in a cubic crystal**

$$\cos[110] \angle [111] = \frac{1+1+0}{\sqrt{2} \times \sqrt{3}}$$

so that,

$$\frac{F_{[110]}}{F_{[111]}} = \cos [110] \angle [111] = \frac{\sqrt{2}}{\sqrt{3}} = 0.816$$

or

$$F_{[110]} = 660 \times 0.816 = 639 \text{ N}$$

*Example*: The critical shear stress $\tau_c$ for the $<\bar{1}10>$ {111} slip system of copper is found to be 1 M Pa. (a) What stress must be applied along [001] direction to produce slip in the [101] direction on the $(\bar{1}11)$ plane? (b) In the [110] direction on the $(\bar{1}11)$ plane?

*Solution*: Given: $\tau_c$ = 1MPa for the slip system $<\bar{1}10>$ {111}.

(a) Now refer Fig. 5.20, for various directions and the plane $(\bar{1}11)$.

Using the dot product method, the angles between them can be found as:

$$\cos \phi = \cos [001] \angle [\bar{1}11] = \frac{1}{\sqrt{3}} = 0.577$$

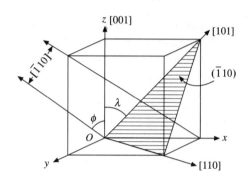

**Fig. 5.20** Showing [001], [101] and $[\bar{1}11]$ directions and $(\bar{1}11)$ plane in a cubic crystal

$$\cos \lambda = \cos [001] \angle [101] = \frac{1}{\sqrt{2}} = 0.707$$

Therefore,

$$\sigma = \frac{F}{A} = \frac{\tau}{\cos \phi \cos \lambda} = \frac{1 \text{ MPa}}{0.577 \times 0.707} = 2.45 \text{ MPa}$$

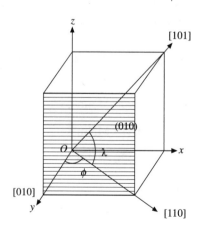

**Fig. 5.21** Showing [101], [110] and [010] directions and (010) plan in a cubic crystal

(b) In a similar way the angle between [001] and [110] is found to be 90°. Therefore, cos $\lambda$ = 0, and $\sigma = \infty$. This implies that slip cannot occur in [110] direction when the stress is applied along [001] direction.

*Example*: An axial stress of 123 MPa is applied in the [110] direction of bcc iron. What is the resolved shear stress in the [101] direction on the (010) plane?

*Solution*: Given: $\sigma$ = 123 M Pa along [110] in a bcc iron crystal.

Refer Fig. 5.21 for various directions and the plane (010). Again, using the dot product, the angles between them can be found as:

$$\cos \phi = \cos [010] \angle [110] = \frac{1}{\sqrt{2}} = 0.707, \text{ and } \cos \lambda = \cos [110] \angle [101] = \frac{1}{2} = 0.5$$

Therefore,

$$\tau = \sigma \cos \phi \cos \lambda = 123 \times 0.707 \times 0.5 = 43.5 \text{ MPa}$$

*Example*: An aluminum crystal slips on the (111) plane and in the $[1\bar{1}0]$ direction with a 3.5 MPa stress that was applied in the $[1\bar{1}1]$ direction. What is the critical resolved shear stress?

*Solution*: Given: Slip plane (111), slip direction $[1\bar{1}0]$ and the applied stress $\sigma = 3.5$ MPa along $[1\bar{1}1]$ direction. Further, we know that in a cubic system the normal to the slip plane (111) is [111]. Also referring Fig. 5.22, we have

$$\cos \phi = \cos [111] \angle [1\bar{1}1] = \frac{1}{\sqrt{3} \times \sqrt{3}} = \frac{1}{3}$$

and $\quad \cos \lambda = \cos [1\bar{1}0] \angle [1\bar{1}1]$

$$= \frac{2}{\sqrt{2} \times \sqrt{3}} = \frac{\sqrt{2}}{\sqrt{3}} = 0.816.$$

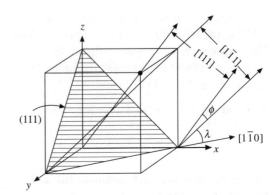

**Fig. 5.22  Showing $[1\bar{1}0]$, [111] and $[1\bar{1}1]$ directions and (111) plane in a cubic crystal**

Thus using eq. 30, the critical resolved shear stress is found to be

$$\tau_c = \sigma_c \cos \phi \cos \lambda = 3.5 \times \frac{1}{3} \times 0.816 = 0.95 \text{ MPa}$$

*Example*: A zinc crystal (hcp) is oriented with normal to the basal plane making an angle of 60° with the tensile axis and the three slip directions $x_1$, $x_2$, and $x_3$, lying on its plane making angles of 38°, 45° and 84° respectively with the tensile axis. If the plastic deformation is first observed at a stress of 2.3 $\text{MNm}^{-2}$, find which of the three slip directions has initiated slip and at what value of the resolved shear stress?

*Solution*: Given: $\sigma = 23$ $\text{MNm}^{-2}$, (refer Fig. 5.17) $\phi = 60°$ and $\lambda_1 = 38°$, $\lambda_2 = 45°$, $\lambda_3 = 84°$. Therefore, using eq. 29, we have

$$\tau_1 = \sigma \cos \phi \cos \lambda = 2.3 \times \cos 60 \times \cos 38 = 0.906 \text{ MNm}^{-2}$$

$$\tau_2 = \sigma \cos \phi \cos \lambda = 2.3 \times \cos 60 \times \cos 45 = 0.813 \text{ MNm}^{-2}$$

$$\tau_3 = \sigma \cos \phi \cos \lambda = 2.3 \times \cos 60 \times \cos 84 = 0.120 \text{ MNm}^{-2}$$

Since $\tau_1 > \tau_2 > \tau_3$, therefore slip will occur along the slip direction $x_1$ at $\tau_c = 0.906$ $\text{MNm}^{-2}$.

*Example*: An fcc crystal has a CRSS of 0.7 $\text{MNm}^{-2}$. What tensile stress must be applied along the [100] direction of the crystal to initiate plastic deformation?

*Solution*: Given $\tau_c = 0.7$ $\text{MNm}^{-2}$, direction of stress to be applied is [100]. Further, we know that for a cubic system the slip plane is (111) and the slip plane normal is [111].

Now, let $[1\bar{1}0]$ be the direction for the plastic deformation to start. Thus, making use of the dot product and also referring Fig. 5.23, we find

$$\cos \phi = \cos [100] \angle [111] = \frac{1}{\sqrt{3}}$$

and

$$\cos \lambda = \cos [100] \angle [1\bar{1}0] = \frac{1}{\sqrt{2}}$$

Therefore,

$$\sigma_c = \frac{\tau_c}{\cos \phi \times \cos \lambda} = 0.7 \times \sqrt{3} \times \sqrt{2}$$

$$= 1.7 \text{ MNm}^{-2}$$

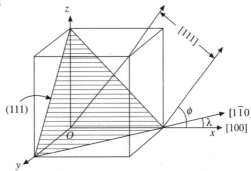

**Fig. 5.23  Showing [100], [1$\bar{1}$0] and [111] directions and (111) plane in a cubic crystal**

## 5.7  DISLOCATION MOTION

Let us consider the simplest possible case of dislocation motion, i.e. an edge dislocation moving to the right under the influence of shear stress $\tau$ (Fig. 5.24). The shear stress will have to do some work in pulling atom 1, just on the right to the dislocation center further away from its neighbour atom 2. The atom 3, however, simultaneously moves closer to its equilibrium distance from its neighbour atom 4, and releases almost the same amount of energy as has been spent in moving the atom 1.

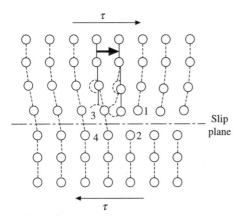

**Fig. 5.24  Atomic arrangements in the vicinity of an edge dislocation as it moves under stress**

As the nature of interatomic forces near the dislocation line is some-what different from the rest of the crystal, the atoms near and within the dislocation line almost completes the slip process when the next nearest neighbours are beginning to slip. Atoms away on either side of the dislocation line are not affected by the presence or motion of dislocation. To a first approximation, the increase in the attractive forces for the atoms on the left just equals the increase in the repulsive forces for the atom on the right, so that the forces on the dislocation line are balanced, and hence the dislocation should start moving under the influence of smallest shear stress.

Suppose a uniform shear shress $\tau$ is applied to the crystal along the direction of the Burgers vector $b$. Mott and Nabarro have shown that this leads to a force on the dislocation line such that the slipped area tends to grow. In order to find the amount of force acting on the dislocation as a result of applied stress $\tau$, let us consider an element $ds$ of the dislocation line which has slipped outwardly by an amount $dl$ along a direction perpendicular to $ds$. The area swept out by this line element is then $ds \times dl$. This corresponds to an average displacement of the upper part of the crystal relative to the lower part by an amount $(ds \times dl \times b)/A$, where $A$ is the area of the slip plane. Thus the work done by the shear stress is equal to the total shear force ($\tau A$) times the average shear displacement, i.e.

$$\tau \times A \times \frac{ds \times dl \times b}{A} = \tau \times b \times dl \times ds$$

Let the normal force on the element $ds$ of the dislocation line be $F. ds$, then the force per unit length on the dislocation due to the stress $\tau$ is

$$F = \tau b \qquad (31)$$

This force lies in the slip plane and is perpendicular to the dislocation line. If the force is large enough to make the dislocation to move in the direction of $F$, the slipped area will grow and the upper half of the crystal will displace over the lower half by an amount $b$ in the slip plane and thus creates a step (Fig. 5.25). Notice that the edge dislocation moves parallel to its Burgers vector while the screw dislocation moves perpendicular to its Burgers vector.

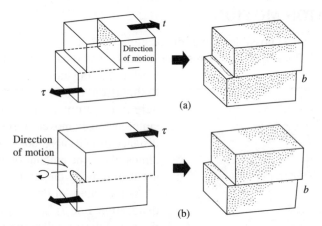

**Fig. 5.25** **Creation of a step by slip process by (a) An edge dislocation as it moves under stress (b) a screw dislocation**

Now let us visualize the motion of dislocation in the presence of some other imperfections and impurities. Suppose that in gliding along its slip plane an edge dislocation meets obstacles in the form of a pair of precipitate particles at $B$ and $C$ as shown in the Fig. 5.26. As compared to the matrix material, these are not easily sheared. The applied stress $\tau$ gives a normal force, $\tau b l$

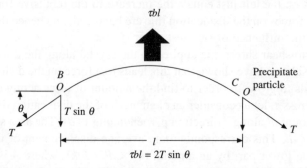

**Fig. 5.26** **Dislocation line tension when the dislocation encounters the obstacles B and C**

on the dislocation line, bowing it out between the points *B* and *C*. This force is balanced by the parallel component of the dislocation line tension *T*, so that

$$\tau b l = 2T \sin \theta \tag{32}$$

where *l* is the distance between *B* and *C*. The line tension, *T* is a vector and is given by the expression

$$T = Gb^2 \tag{33}$$

where *G* is the elastic shear modulus. From equations 32 and 33, we have

$$\tau = \frac{2Gb \sin \theta}{l} \tag{34}$$

This tells us that the maximum stress required to cause maximum bowing in the line segment is when it become semi-circular, i.e. at $\theta = 90°$, the stress assumes its maximum value:

$$\tau_{max} = \frac{2Gb}{l} \tag{35}$$

According to eq. 34, a dislocation which does not meet any obstacle (i.e. $\theta = 0$) should be capable of moving at a vanishingly small stress; a higher stress is required for smaller *l* when it does not meet any obstacle. Let us understand this further in a qualitative way by considering two edge dislocations as shown in Fig. 5.27. The dislocation in Fig. 2.27a is said to be stiff, i.e. no relaxing displacements have taken place in the adjacent planes around dislocation region. The bond lengths in this region are normal except below the incomplete plane, where they are virtually broken. On the other hand, the dislocation in Fig. 5.27b is said to be relaxed, i.e. relaxing displacements have taken place in the adjacent planes around dislocation region. In this case, the strains are distributed more evenly among the bonds to give rise to compression above and tension below the slip plane as shwon in Fig. 5.30.

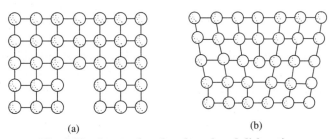

(a)                                          (b)

**Fig. 5.27   An unrelaxed and a relaxed dislocation**

The motion of a dislocation depends on its width. The width of a dislocation is defined as a measure of the distance on either side of the dislocation, upto which the stress-relaxing displacements are appreciable. Therefore, a dislocation is said to be wide if the displacements are distributed over an appreciable distance on either side from the core of dislocation. Accordingly, Fig. 5.27b is treated as having a wide dislocation. When such a dislocation moves, reallignment of a number of bonds takes place in the dislocation region, however, the change in any one bond length is very small. Contrary to this, Fig. 5.27a is treated as having a narrow dislocation, where the bonds are normal (except below the slip plane) and atoms remain undisplaced. In order to move this type of dislocation, the rows of atoms below the slip palne will have to be moved through full interatomic distance. Therefore the narrow dislocations are more difficult to move than the wide dislocations. Peierls and Nabarro calculated the stress necessary to move a dislocation in a crystal (in the absence of imperfections and impurities) in terms of its width $w$ and is given by

$$\tau_{PN} = \mu \exp\left(\frac{-2\pi w}{b}\right) \tag{36}$$

where $\mu$ is the shear modulus of the crystal and $b$ the magnitude of the Burgers vector of the dislocation. Strong dependence of $\tau_{PN}$ on width $w$ is illustrated in Table 5.2. For an accurate calculation of $\tau_{PN}$, a very precise measurement of the dislocation width is required. Since such measurements are inherently difficult, therefore our discussion has been only qualitative.

**Table 5.2  Dependence of $t_{PN}$ on width $w$**

| Width | 0 | b | 5b | 10b |
|---|---|---|---|---|
| $\tau_{PN}$ | $\mu$ | $\mu/400$ | $\mu/10^{14}$ | $\mu/10^{27}$ |

Dislocation motion can be assisted by thermal energy. The rate of plastic deformation, i.e. the strain rate $\dot{\varepsilon}$ is proportional to Boltzmann probability factor:

$$\dot{\varepsilon} \propto \exp\left(-\frac{Q}{kT}\right) \tag{37}$$

where $Q$ is the activation energy for dislocation motion. The strain rate during plastic deformation can also be expressed in terms of the velocity of dislocation $v_d$ as

$$\dot{\varepsilon} = \rho b v_d \tag{38}$$

where $\rho$ is the density of mobile dislocations and $b$ is their Burgers vector. Equation 37 indicates that thermal energy alone could move a dislocation from its initial position. However, such motions would be random, where a dislocation line will have equal probability of moving to the next minimum energy position on either side of the line. This kind of motion does not result in plastic deformation. Actually, a certain amount (threshold) stress is necessary to move the dislocation in a specified direction. Besides, the applied stress can lower the activation energy $Q$. Since eq. 36 does not have a $kT$ term, therefore let us suppose that $\tau_{PN}$ is the stress in the absence of thermal energy (i.e. at 0K). Thus, at absolute zero $\tau_{PN}$ is equal to $\tau_{app}$, which is necessary to move a dislocation, as no assistance from thermal energy is available. At higher temperatures, the required external stress ($\tau_{app}$) is lower than $\tau_{PN}$. These two stress terms multiplied by a volume term called the activation volume $V$ is related to $Q$ as:

$$Q = (\tau_{PN} - \tau_{app})V \tag{39}$$

From eqs. 37 and 39, we have

$$\dot{\varepsilon} \propto \exp\left(-\frac{(\tau_{PN} - \tau_{app})V}{kT}\right) \tag{40}$$

Equation 40 tells us that for a constant strain rate, the term within the exponential is constant. $\tau_{PN}$, as given by eq. 36 is constant for a particular crystal. If the activation volume $V$ is taken to be constant then it follows that, with increasing temperature, less and less external stress is required to cause plastic deformation at an increasing strain rate at constant temperature, the external stress should be increased. Equation 40 can be written as

$$\ln \dot{\varepsilon} = -\frac{(\tau_{PN} - \tau_{app})V}{kT} + A' = A + B\tau_{app} \tag{41}$$

where $A$, $A'$ and $B$ are constant at constant temperature.

Dislocation motion is analogous to a wormlike motion. A worm moves forward by displacing its segments one after the other rather than a simultaneous displacement of all the segments. In a similar way, dislocation moves in a sequential fashion, occupying successive positions during its motion.

When an edge dislocation moves in a direction perpendicular to its slip plane, the process is called climb. Such a motion must be accompanied by the generation or annihilation of vacancies or interstitials, depending upon the sense (positive or negative) of dislocation motion. Since the equilibrium concentration of vacancies (interstitials) depends on temperature, the dislocatin climb is temperature sensitive. Climb of an edge dislocation is illustrated in Fig. 5.28a. The change of slip plane by moving a screw dislocation is called cross slip and is illustrated in Fig. 5.28b.

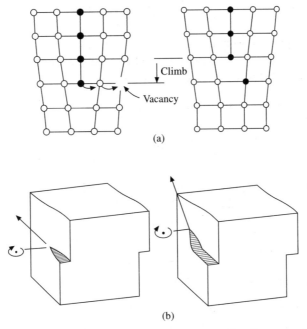

Fig. 5.28 (a) Climb of an edge dislocation (b) cross-slip of a screw dislocation

*Example*: Estimate the width of the dislocation in copper. The shear stress to initiate plastic deformation is $\mu/10^5$.

*Solution*: Given $\tau = \mu/10^5$. For Cu the lattice parameter $a = 3.61$ Å. Since copper is an fcc crystal, therefore the Burgers vector $b = a/\sqrt{2} = 2.55$ Å
Now using eq. 36, we have

$$\mu/10^5 = \mu \exp\left(\frac{-2\pi w}{2.55}\right)$$

or
$$10^{-5} = \exp(-2.46w)$$

Taking ln both sides and solving we find $w = 4.68$ Å.

*Example*: In a simple cubic crystal ($a = 3$Å), a positive edge dislocation 1 mm long climbs down by 1 $\mu$m. How many vacancies are lost or created?

*Solution*: Given: Dislocation length = 1 mm = $10^{-3}$ m, distance of dislocation climb 1 $\mu$m = $10^{-6}$m and $a = 3$ Å = $3 \times 10^{-10}$m.

Consider a case opposite to that shown in Fig. 5.28. When the dislocation climbs down vacancy will be created. Thus the affected area in this case is

$$10^{-3}\text{ m} \times 10^{-6}\text{ m} = 10^{-9}\text{m}^2$$

Since the area of the unit cell is $9 \times 10^{-20}$ m$^2$ and the number of atoms per unit cell in a simple cubic crystal is 1. Therefore the number of vacancies created within the affected area is

$$\frac{1 \times 10^{-9}}{9 \times 10^{-20}} = 1.1 \times 10^{10}$$

*Example*: A cube of copper of 10 mm × 10 mm × 10 mm is sheared at a rate of 10 mm per min. Estimate in order of magnitude the minimum number of dislocations in motion in this cube at a given instant. Assume a dislocation velocity of 1 kms$^{-1}$.

*Solution*: Given: $\dot{\varepsilon} = 10$ mm per min. = 0.166 mms$^{-1}$, $v_d = 1 \times 10^6$ mms$^{-1}$. Also volume of the crystal $V = 10^3$ mm$^3$.

Since copper is an fcc crystal, therefore the Burgers vector $b = a/\sqrt{2} = 2.55$ Å. Now using eq. 38, the density is

$$\rho = \frac{0.166}{2.55 \times 10^{-6} \times 10^6} = 0.065/\text{mm}^3$$

Therefore the number of dislocations in motion in the whole cube is

$$\rho \times V = 0.065 \times 10^3 = 65 \cong 10 \text{ (order of magnitude)}$$

## 5.8   ENERGY OF A DISLOCATION

Dislocations are thermodynamically unstable. Their presence always increase the free energy of the crystal. It is usually impossible to eliminate them completely and those which remain tend to assume certain metastable configuration.

In order to calculate the energy of a dislocation, let us consider a cylindrical crystal of length $l$ with a screw dislocation of Burgers vector $b$ along its axis. The elastic shear strain $\gamma$ in a thin annular section of radius $r$ and thickness $dr$ (Fig. 5.29) is

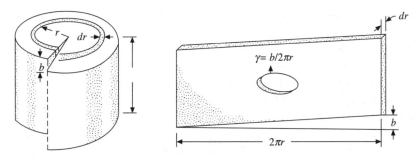

**Fig. 5.29** **Geometrical model for the calculation of shear strain around a screw dislocation**

$$\gamma = \frac{b}{2\pi r} \qquad (42)$$

where $b = |\,b\,|$.

The elastic energy per unit volume $dE/dV$, of this annular region is

$$\frac{dE}{dV} = \frac{1}{2}\tau\gamma = \frac{1}{2}G\gamma^2 = \frac{G}{2}\left(\frac{b}{2\pi r}\right)^2 \qquad (43)$$

where $G$ is the elastic shear modulus. The volume of the annular ring is

$$dV = 2\pi r l dr \qquad (44)$$

and thus the elastic energy per unit length of the shell is

$$dE = \frac{lGb^2}{4\pi} \cdot \frac{dr}{r} \qquad (45)$$

The strain energy due to the presence of this dislocation may be computed by integrating both sides of the eq. 45 within the limit $r_0$ to $R$. We therefore, have

$$E = \int_{r_0}^{R} \frac{lGb^2}{4\pi} \cdot \frac{dr}{r} = \frac{lGb^2}{4\pi}\ln\left(\frac{R}{r_0}\right) + E_0 \qquad (46)$$

If we choose the limits $r_0 = 0$ or $R = \infty$, in each case the integral becomes infinite, which is clearly unrealistic. The difficulty in choosing $r_0 = 0$ is that the Hooke's law is not valid for the high strain at the dislocation core. The value of $R = \infty$ is also unrealistic because at large values or $r$ the strain field of one dislocation is cancelled by those of other dislocations. It has been shown that if $r_0$ is taken as $b$, the real strain energy inside the core, $E_0$, is only a small fraction of the total energy and can be neglected. Since the energy is relatively insensitive to $R/r$, the ratio usually adopted is $\ln\left(\dfrac{R}{r_0}\right) = 4\pi$. Under the above approximations, the energy of a screw dislocation is given as

$$E \simeq lGb^2 \qquad (47)$$

Similarly, the energy of an edge dislocation is given approximately as

$$E = \frac{1}{1-v} \cdot \frac{lGb^2}{4\pi} \cdot \ln\left(\frac{R}{r_0}\right) + E_0 \simeq \frac{lGb^2}{1-v} \qquad (48)$$

where $\nu$ is Poisson's ratio. If $\nu = 1/3$, the energy of an edge dislocation is 3/2 times that of screw dislocation of the same length. Since the energy of a dislocation (edge or screw) is proportional to $b^2$, the most stable dislocations are those which have minimum Burgers vectors (i.e. those in close packed directions). Equations 47 and 48 also show that the energy of a dislocation is proportional to its length, i.e. the line energy is equivalent to line tension just as surface energy is equivalent to surface tension. Thus a curved dislocation will have a line tension $T$, a vector acting along the line so that

$$T = \frac{\partial E}{\partial l} \simeq Gb^2 \tag{49}$$

Fig. 5.30 illustrates the geometry of the stress field around edge and screw dislocations.

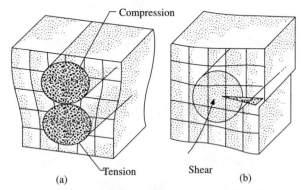

**Fig. 5.30** **Geometry of stress and strain fields surrounding (a) an edge dislocation (b) a screw dislocation**

*Example*: An aluminium crystal has a dislocation density of $10^{10}$ m$^{-2}$. The shear modulus of aluminium is 25.94 GNm$^{-2}$. Calculate the elastic energy of line imperfections stored in the crystal.

*Solution*: Given: $\rho = 10^{10}$ m$^{-2}$, $\mu = 25.94$ GN m$^{-2}$. For Al, $a = 4.05$Å $= 4.05 \times 10^{-10}$ m. Since Al is an fcc crystal, the Burgers vector

$$b = \frac{a}{\sqrt{2}} = 2.86 \text{ Å} = 2.86 \times 10^{-10} \text{ m}$$

Now, the elastic energy per unit length of the dislocation is

$$E = \frac{\mu b^2}{2} = \frac{25.94 \times 10^9 \times (2.86)^2 \times 10^{-20}}{2} = 10.63 \times 10^{-10} \text{ Jm}^{-1}$$

Therefore, the elastic energy stored in the crystal is

$$E \times \rho = 10.63 \times 10^{10} \times 10^{-10} \text{ Jm}^{-3} = 10.63 \text{ Jm}^{-3}$$

## 5.9 SLIP PLANES AND SLIP DIRECTIONS

Plastic deformation due to slip in a real crystal occurs as a result of dislocation motion. Therefore, those dislocations which require the lowest energy or stress will move most readily. Further, as the energy of a dislocation is proportional to the square of the Burgers vector, dislocations of the shortest Burgers vector, that is, those along the close packed directions, will require the least stress. The slip planes within which slip occurs are usually the most densely packed planes, which are also most widely separated (as discussed earlier in Sec. 1.11). The combination of a slip direction and the plane containing it, is defined as a slip system. For example, the combination of (111) and [$\bar{1}$10] forms a slip system but not (111) and [110], as the direction [110] does not lie on the (111) plane. The observed slip system in some fcc, bcc and hcp metals and fcc ionic crystals are listed in Table 5.3. The first listed plane in each case is the most commonly observed

**Table 5.3  Observed slip systems in Crystals**

| Structure | Slip plane | Slip direction | No. of slip systems | Pictorial view of slip system |
|---|---|---|---|---|
| FCC Cu, Al, Ni, Pb, Au, Ag, $\gamma$Fe, .... | {111} | < 1$\bar{1}$0 > | $4 \times 3 = 12$ | |
| BCC $\alpha$Fe, W, Mo, $\beta$Brass | {110} | < $\bar{1}$11 > | $6 \times 2 = 12$ | |
| $\alpha$Fe, Mo, W, Na | {211} | < $\bar{1}$11 > | $12 \times 1 = 12$ | |
| $\alpha$Fe, K | {321} | < $\bar{1}$11 > | $24 \times 1 = 24$ | |
| HCP Cd, Zn, Mg, Ti, Be,... | (0001) | < 11$\bar{2}$0 > | $1 \times 3 = 3$ | |
| Ti | {10$\bar{1}$0} | < 11$\bar{2}$0 > | $3 \times 1 = 3$ | |
| Ti. Mg | {10$\bar{1}$1} | < 11$\bar{2}$0 > | $6 \times 1 = 6$ | |
| NaCl, AgCl | {110} | < 1$\bar{1}$0 > | $6 \times 1 = 6$ | |

one. All members of an fcc metal slip system where each of the four planes of the family {111} has three slip directions < $\bar{1}$ 10 > which are listed below and are diagramatically shown in Fig. 5.31.

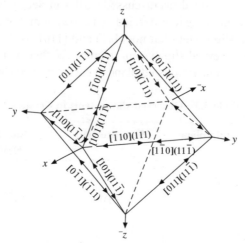

**Fig. 5.31   The 12 slip systems for fcc metals**

$[\bar{1}10] (111), [1\bar{1}0] (11\bar{1}), [110] (1\bar{1}1), [110] (\bar{1}11)$

$[10\bar{1}] (111), [101] (11\bar{1}), [10\bar{1}] (1\bar{1}1), [101] (\bar{1}11)$

$[0\bar{1}1](111), [011] (11\bar{1}), [011] (1\bar{1}1) [01\bar{1}] (\bar{1}11)$

In fcc metals, the predominating slip plane is the close packed plane (111), however, other planes may become active at elevated temperatures. In bcc and tetragonal metals, slip can occur on several planes, most of which are among those most densely packed and most widely spaced. Many metals change their slip planes when deformed at usually high or low temperatures. Although the slip planes that are active may vary with conditions, depending on which ones happen to have the lowest resistence to slip, the slip directions are not so fickle. Among the equivalent planes of given indices {*hkl*}, and the equivalent directions <*uvw*>, the ones that become active under a given applied stress are the one or two subjected to the highest resolved shear stress.

The ratio of the lattice parameters (the axial ratios) also plays an important role in determining whether some other slip systems are possible or not. For an ideal packing of spheres in hcp configuration, the *c/a* ratio is 1.632. However, this ratio is not found in any hcp metal. In Zn and Cd, *c/a* is considerably higher than the ideal: Zn (1.856) and Cd (1.886). In other hcp metals, *c/a* is lower than the ideal: Mg (1.624), Ti (1.587), Be (1.568), Zr (1.59), Hg (1.586), Re (1.617) and Co (1.624). When the *c/a* ratio is low, the (0001) plane loses the distinction of being the plane of highest atomic density. Thus Ti can show additional slip planes, and in Mg the {10$\bar{1}$1} planes are reported to contribute to deformation above 210°C. However, in all cases, the slip directions remain < 11$\bar{2}$0 >.

*Example:* Find all the slip systems that have the following slip planes: (a) (1$\bar{1}$1) in an fcc crystal and (b) (1$\bar{1}$0) in a bcc crystal.

*Solution: We* know that the combination of a slip direction and the plane containing it is defined as the slip system. Thus referring to Fig. 5.32 the plane $(1\overline{1}1)$ contains the directions [011], $[10\overline{1}]$, $[\overline{1}\,\overline{1}1]$ and their counter parts. Therefore, the required slip system are [011] $(1\overline{1}1)$, $[10\overline{1}]$ $(1\overline{1}1)$, $[\overline{1}\,\overline{1}0]$ $(1\overline{1}1)$ etc. Similarly slip system corresponding to the plane (110) are [111] (110), $[11\overline{1}]$ $(\overline{1}10)$ etc. (Fig. 5.33).

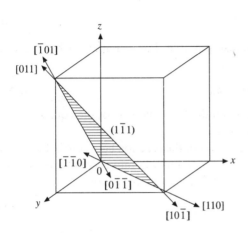

**Fig. 5.32  Slip systems corresponding to the plane $(1\overline{1}0)$ in an fcc crystal**

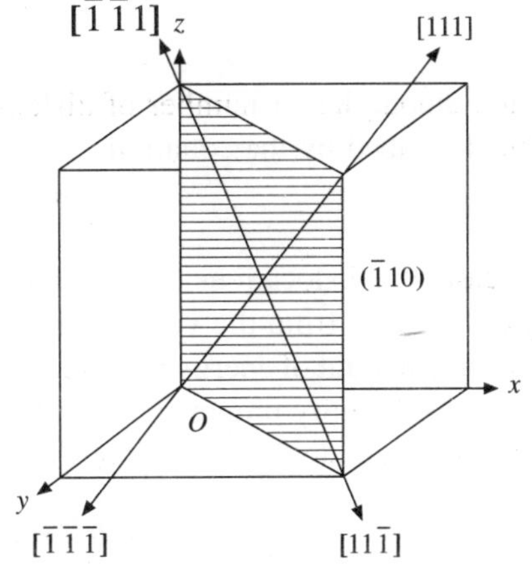

**Fig. 5.33  Slip systems corresponding to the plane $(1\overline{1}0)$ in a bcc crystal**

## 5.10  PERFECT AND IMPERFECT DISLOCATIONS

In general, the Burgers vectors of dislocations are associated with lattice translations. When the Burgers vector of a dislocation is an integral multiple of the lattice translation, the dislocation is called full or perfect dislocation. On the other hand, when the Burgers vector of the dislocation is a fraction of the lattice translation, the dislocation is called partial or imperfect dislocation. Formation of a perfect and an imperfect dislocations are shown in Fig. 5.34 for a simple cubic lattice.

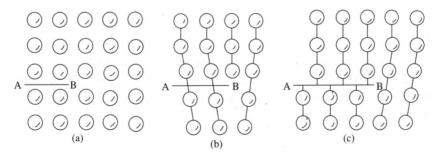

**Fig. 5.34 (a)  Crystal is cut and displaced along AB to form either, (b) perfect dislocation, or (c) an imperfect dislocation**

## 5.11 DISLOCATION REACTION

Various kinds of reactions can take place among the dislocations, producing new dislocations. However, since there exists only a finite number of possible Burgers vectors in a crystal, the number of directions of dislocation lines are therefore limited.

Two parallel dislocations of Burgers vectors $b_1$ and $b_2$ which are situated on the same slip plane, or on two intersecting slip planes, can react to form a third dislocation of Burgers vector $b_3$ and is given by the following equation

$$b_1 + b_2 = b_3 \tag{50}$$

Reaction among larger number of dislocations are also possible. For example, such a reaction may be described by the equation

$$b_1 + b_2 \Leftrightarrow b_3 + b_4 \tag{51}$$

In this case, the dislocations described by the vectors on the left hand side of the equation have energies different from the vectors on the right hand side.

A certain amount of energy is always liberated as a result of the reaction between dislocations. Let $Q$ be the quantity proportional to the energy liberated, and taking into account the fact that the energy of a dislocation is proportional to the Burgers vector, we may write

$$b_1^2 + b_2^2 = (b_1 + b_2)^2 + Q \tag{52}$$

where
$$Q = -2b_1 b_2 \tag{53}$$

Equation 53 can be accepted as a criterion for the stability of a dislocation. Two dislocations attract mutually if their Burgers vectors form an obtuse angle, or repel if the vectors form an acute angle. Equilibrium results, if the Burgers vector of both dislocations are perpendicular to each other.

Frank introduced the following criterion for the stability: that two parallel dislocations of Burgers vectors $b_1$ and $b_2$ may combine to form a third dislocation of Burgers vector $b_3$ only if the following relation is satisfied

$$b_1^2 + b_2^2 > b_3^2 \tag{54}$$

Similarly, a dislocation of Burgers vector $b_1$ may dissociate into two parallel dislocations $b_2$ and $b_3$, if

$$b_1^2 > b_2^2 + b_3^2 \tag{55}$$

It is easy to visualize that both the crystallographic direction and the magnitude of a Burgers vector are related to the distance between atomic sites. In Miller index notation $na[hkl]$ having components $nah$, $nak$, $nal$ along the three axes is used to describe a Burgers vector whose direction is $[hkl]$ and the magnitude is $na(h^2 + k^2 + l^2)^{1/2}$. Therefore,

$$b^2 = n^2 a^2 (h^2 + k^2 + l^2) \tag{56}$$

where $a$ is the length of the cell edge and $n$ is a number. In fcc crystals, slip occurs along <110> close packed directions and mostly on {111} close packed slip planes. A perfect or a unit dislocation in this case having a Burgers vector such as $(a/2)$ [110], of magnitude $a/\sqrt{2}$, connects a cube corner to a nearby face centre. In bcc crystals, the Burgers vector for a slip occuring from cube corner to cube centre along the close packed direction <111> is $(a/2)$ [111], with its magnitude equal to $a\sqrt{3}/2$. Close packed hexagonal crystals normally slip along direction having a Burgers vector (a/3) [11$\bar{2}$0] of magnitude $a$, where $a$ is the lattice translation in the (0001) plane.

Figure 5.35a shows a close packed plane of atoms in an fcc or hcp crystal. An atom sitting at $O$ on the next (upper) layer, can make a perfect displacement to $P$, $Q$, or $R$. Hence if this atom is moved from O $\rightarrow$ Q $\rightarrow$ P by two successive displacements with Burgers vectors $OQ$ and $OR$ (equivalent to $QP$), respectively, the effect is as if one dislocation with vector $OP$ has passed through. It is thus possible for three such dislocations, with these Burgers vectors to meet at a node, as shown in Fig. 5.35b. In Miller index notation this can be represented as,

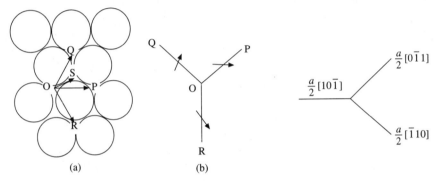

**Fig. 5.35** **Burgers vectors (a) On a close packed plane (b) meeting at a dislocation node**

$$\frac{a}{2}[10\bar{1}] + \frac{a}{2}[0\bar{1}1] + \frac{a}{2}[\bar{1}10] = 0$$

or
$$\frac{a}{2}[10\bar{1}] + \frac{a}{2}[0\bar{1}1] = \frac{a}{2}[1\bar{1}0] \qquad (57)$$

A billiard-ball model of close packed slip planes immediately shows that the atoms prefer to slide, not along perfect lattice vectors such as $OP$, but along zig-zag path such as O $\rightarrow$ S $\rightarrow$ P. The same effect appears in crystals, probably because the zig-zag slip, a perfect dislocation with Burgers vector $OP$ splits into two separate partial dislocations with Burgers vectors $OS$ and $SP$, respectively. For example, such a dislocation on (111) plane in an fcc crystal is

$$\frac{a}{2}[\bar{1}10] = \frac{a}{6}[\bar{1}2\bar{1}] + \frac{a}{6}[\bar{2}11] \qquad (58)$$

Using $a/6$ as the unit length, this reaction can be written in a more simplified form as

$$[\bar{3}30] = [\bar{1}2\bar{1}] + [\bar{2}11] \qquad (59)$$

The two dislocations [$\bar{1}2\bar{1}$] and [$\bar{2}11$] are partial dislocations, known as Shockley partials.

It is necessary in any proposed dislocation reaction to ensure that the sum of the components of the Burgers vector on both sides of the reaction is the same. Therefore, for the reaction (58), we can verify that

$$\frac{a}{2}[\bar{1}10] = \frac{a}{6}[\bar{1} + \bar{2}, 2 + 1, \bar{1} + 1] = \frac{a}{2}[110]$$

A simple and convenient way to represent all important dislocations and dislocation reactions in fcc crystals is possible with the help of Thompson's tetrahedron ABCD as shown in Fig. 5.36. The inner and outer faces of the tetrahedron represent the four possible {111} glide planes lie parallel to the four faces of the regular tetrahedron [eight if the plus-minus sense is distinguished, as for (111) and $(\bar{1}\,\bar{1}\,\bar{1})$]. The edges of the tetrahedron correspond to the six <110> glide directions of the fcc structure (12 with plus-minus sense). The atom at the origin is labelled $D$ and other corners of the tetrahedron are labelled $ABC$ in the clockwise order. The mid points of the faces opposite to the corners $A$, $B$, $C$ and $D$ are labelled $\alpha$, $\beta$, $\gamma$ and $\delta$, respectively, and the planes opposite to $A$, $B$, $C$ and $D$ outside the surface are denoted by $a$, $b$, $c$, and $d$, respectively. If the tetrahedron is opened up at $D$, it can be folded out into the planar arrangement as displayed in Fig. 5.37. The Burgers vector of dislocations are specified by their two end points on the tetrahedron. Accordingly, the Burgers vectors of the unit dislocations are defined both in magnitude and direction by the edges of the tetrahedron and will be $AB$, $BC$, etc. Similarly, Shockley partial dislocations can be represented by the line starting from the corner and ending at the centre of a face as $A\beta$, $A\gamma$ etc. The dislocation reaction described by the eq. 58 can be expressed alternatively by a reaction of the type:

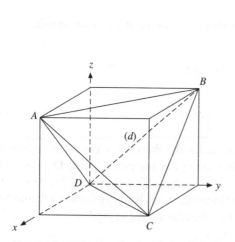

Fig. 5.36   Thompson's tetrahedron ABCD

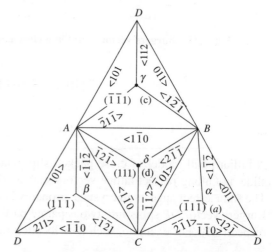

Fig. 5.37   Thomson's tetrahedron displaying planar arrangements. Notation [$\bar{1}$10> is used instead of the usual notation [$\bar{1}$10] to indicate the sense of direction

$$AB = A\delta + \delta B \qquad (60)$$

*Example*: Show that the reaction given by eq. 58 is energetically feasible.

*Solution:* From eq. 47, we know that the energy of a dislocation is given by $E \simeq lGb^2$. Now from Pythagoras theorem, we can calculate the (length)$^2$ of $[\bar{1}10]$ and of $[\bar{1}2\bar{1}]$ and $[\bar{2}11]$:

$$(\text{Length})^2{}_{[\bar{1}10]} = (-1)^2 + 1^2 + 0^2 = 2$$

$$(\text{Length})^2{}_{[\bar{1}2\bar{1}]} = (-1)^2 + 2^2 + (-1)^2 = 6$$

$$(\text{Length})^2{}_{[\bar{2}11]} = (-2)^2 + 1^2 + 1^2 = 6$$

Therefore the relative energies are

$$\frac{\text{Energy of one perfect dislocation}}{\text{Energy of two partial dislocations}} = \frac{lG(1/2)^2 \times 2}{lG[1/6)^2 \times 6 + (1/6)^2 \times 6]} = \frac{1/2}{1/3} = 1.5$$

From the above calculation, it is clear that the perfect dislocation has 50% more energy even though the two partial dislocations have a greater total length of Burgers vector. This is in accordance with the eq. 55 and hence the reaction in question is energetically feasible.

## 5.12 SURFACE IMPERFECTIONS

As the name indicates, the surface imperfections are two dimensional in geometrical sense. They refer to regions of distortions that lie about a surface having a thickness of a few atomic diameters. The surface imperfections include grain boundary, tilt and twist boundary, twin boundary and stacking faults.

### Grain Boundary

The most obvious manifestation of geometrical defects extending over whole surface is the appearance of grains and grain boundaries in polycrystalline materials. A typical polycrystalline solid consists of a number of interlocking crystals or grains, oriented randomly. The atoms along the boundary regions are being pulled by each of the two grains to join its own configuration. They can join neither grain due to the opposing forces and take up an equilibrium position. The boundary between the adjacent grains, therefore, must have a structure that somehow conform to the structures and orientations of both the grains and can be compared to a non crystalline material. Actually, the atoms along the boundary represent a transition between the two adjacent misoriented crystalline regions. The crystal orientation changes sharply at the grain boundary. The angles between the crystallite orientations of nearby grains are often large (greater than 10–15°), the boundary between the grains in such cases is known as high angle boundary (Fig. 5.38).

The average number of nearest neighbours for an atom near the boundary of a close packed crystal is 11, whereas in the interior of the crystal it is 12. On an average, one bond out of twelve bonds is broken at the boundary. The grain boundary between two crystals, which have different crystalline arrangements or differ in composition, is known as interphase boundary or simply an interface.

### Tilt and Twist Boundary

Tilt boundary may be defined as a boundary between two adjacent perfect regions in the same

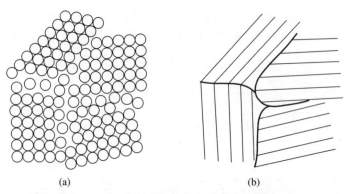

(a)                                      (b)

**Fig. 5.38  The atomic arrangements at grain boundaries**

crystal that are slightly tilted, with respect to one another. In other words, when the angle between the crystallite orientations of the two grains is small (less than 10°), the boundary is said to be a tilt boundary. They are also called as low angle boundaries (Fig. 5.39). The structure of such boundaries can be described by means of arrays of dislocations. It consists of a series of equally spaced edge dislocations of the same sign located one above the other.

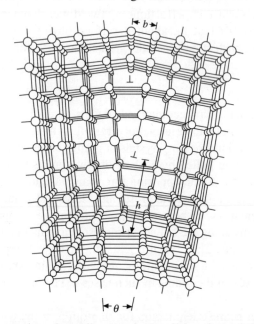

**Fig. 5.39  A tilt boundary consists of equally spaced edge dislocations of the same sign one above the other**

The angle of tilt $\theta$ is related to the Burgers vector $b$ of the edge dislocations by

$$\frac{b}{h} = \tan \theta \tag{61}$$

where $h$ is the vertical spacing between two neighbouring edge dislocations. For small angle of tilt,

$$\frac{b}{h} = \theta \tag{62}$$

If the two parts of the crystal are rotated through a small angle, about an axis which is perpendicular to the grain boundary (rather than about one that lies in the boundary as in the case of tilt boundary), a twist boundary is formed. Twist boundary consists of a set of screw dislocations, in contrast to the tilt boundary which consists of a set of edge dislocations.

If the misoriented single crystal sections are identical but are joined together in such a way that the boundary acts as a reflecting plane, the pair of crystals constitute a twin and the resulting boundary is said to be a twin boundary. In such cases, the atomic arrangement on one side of the boundary is a mirror reflection of the arrangement on the other side (Fig. 5.40).

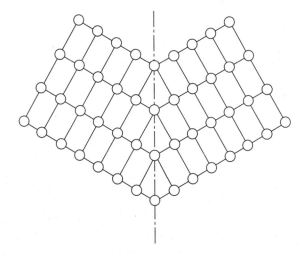

**Fig. 5.40  A twin plane**

There are several ways in which twinning can be produced. Growth twins are formed during the growth of a crystal. The transformation between high and low temperature modifications of a crystal may take place via twining. Twining produced during plastic deformation of a crystal is called deformation twinning. The simplest example of twinning in an fcc structure can be represented by the sequence

$$\downarrow$$
$$\ldots\ldots A\,B\,C\,A\,B\,C\,B\,A\,C\,B\,A\ldots\ldots$$

where the arrow indicates the twin plane and the centre of the fault. The occurrence of twinning is common especially in metals with bcc or hcp structure.

*Example*: Calculate the spacing between dislocations in a tilt boundary in fcc nickel, when the angle of tilt is 2°.

*Solution*: Given $\theta = 2°$. Crystal is fcc Nickel, so that $a = 3.52$Å and hence $h = a/\sqrt{2} = 2.489$Å. Now, using eq. 61, we have

$$h = \frac{b}{\tan \theta} = \frac{2.489}{\tan 2°} = 71.3\text{Å}$$

*Example*: A single crystal of copper contains a low angle tilt boundary on a (010) plane and the tilt axis parallel to the [001] direction. Calculate the tilt angle, if the spacing of the dislocations in the boundary is $1.5 \times 10^{-6}$m.

*Solution*: Given: $h = 1.5 \times 10^{-6}$ m $= 1.5 \times 10^4$ Å. Cu is an fcc crystal with $a = 3.61$Å and hence $b = a/\sqrt{2} = 2.55$ Å. Thus, using the eq. 61, we have

$$\tan \theta = \frac{b}{h} = \frac{2.55}{1.5 \times 10^4} = 1.7 \times 10^{-4} \text{ rad}$$

*Example*: A single crystal of copper contains low angle tilt boundary on (001) plane with a tilt axis parallel to [010]. Calculate the tilt angle if the spacing of the dislocation in the boundary is $3 \times 10^{-6}$ m and their Burgers vector is $0.4 \times 10^{-9}$ m.

*Solution*: Given: $h = 3 \times 10^{-6}$m $= 3 \times 10^4$ Å and $b = 0.4 \times 10^{-9}$ m $= 4$ Å
Therefore,

$$\tan \theta = \frac{b}{h} = \frac{4}{3 \times 10^4} = 1.33 \times 10^{-4} \text{ rad}$$

**Stacking Faults**

In Chapters 1 and 3, we studied about close packings. A close packed structure is generated by stacking close packed layers on top of one another with the restriction that no two adjacent layers are in the same orientation. Given a layer A, a close packing can be extended by placing the next layer such that its atoms occupy either B or C sites (Fig. 5.41). Here A, B and C refer to the three possible layer positions in a projection normal to the close packed layers. In the following, we shall discuss various ways of producing stacking faults in fcc and hcp crystals.

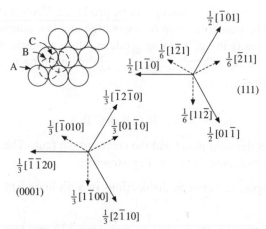

**Fig. 5.41**  **Projection normal to the (111) plane showing three types of stacking positions A, B and C. fcc and hcp notations are also presented**

## Stacking Faults in fcc Crystals

Stacking faults may be produced in fcc crystals in the following ways:

(a) *By removing a close packed plane:*

This can be achieved by diffusion of a sheet of vacancies into the plane and by collapsing together the adjoining planes to eliminate the layer of void between them. For example, removing a B layer, the cubic close packed sequence becomes

$$....A\,B\,C\,A\,|\,C\,A\,B\,C....$$

This is called an intrinsic fault. This can be regarded as a layer CACA of hcp or as two overlapping twin boundaries, CAC and ACA, across which next nearest layers are wrongly stacked. In such cases, the normal stacking sequence is maintained in the crystal on either side of the fault right upto the fault plane.

(b) *By inserting an extra plane*

This can be achieved by diffusion of interstitial atoms into the space between two close packed planes. If say, a B layer is introduced as in the sequence

$$.....A\,B\,C\,B\,A\,B\,C.....$$

This is called an extrinsic fault. This fault is equivalent to two neighbouring twin boundaries, BCB and BAB.

(c) *By slip on a close packed plane*

This can be produced by displacing all atoms above the reference plane by shearing operation on {111} planes. Let us consider an fcc crystal and suppose that the plane A as shown in Fig. 5.41 is a reference plane, and the next plane above it is a B plane. If the B plane and all other planes above it are displaced by the vector (1/6) [$\bar{2}$11], the B plane moves into C positions, and the planes above it transform in cyclic order, A → B → C → A, relative to the reference plane. The shear displacement is represented by the arrows in the reaction

$$.........A\,B\,C\,A\,B\,C\,A\,B\,C.......$$
$$\downarrow\downarrow\downarrow\downarrow\downarrow$$
$$C\,A\,B\,C\,A......$$

giving ....... A B C A C A B C A ...... The resultant fault is equivalent to an intrinsic fault as obtained in (a).

## Stacking Faults in hcp Crystals

In hcp crystals, close packed plane is the (0001) plane. This basal plane is also the most freuently observed glide plane in hcp crystals, but unlike fcc crystals, this does not correspond to twin plane. Referring again to the hard-ball model (Fig. 5.41), one can easily verify that there are two kinds of intrinsic faults and one extrinsic fault in hcp structures.

The mode of formation of these faults are as follows:

(a) *By removing a close packed plane and then shear*

Removal of a close packed plane in an hcp structure is done in the same way as was done in the cubic case. The resulting stacking becomes

$$.\,.\,.\,.\,A\,B\,A\,B\,A\,|\,A\,B\,A\,B\,.\,.\,.\,.$$

Here, either side of boundary has the same plane (i.e. A) which violates the rule of close packing. Moreover, this is unstable also. In order to acquire the stable configuration, the layer above the boundary must shear.

Therefore, shearing them by the vector $\frac{1}{3}[\bar{1}100]$, the A plane moves into C position, and the planes above it transform in anticyclic order, $A \rightarrow C \rightarrow B \rightarrow A$, relative to A plane, yielding the stacking sequence

$$.\,.\,.\,.\,A\,B\,A\,B\,A\,|\,C\,A\,C\,A\,.\,.\,.\,.\,.$$

This falt is equivalent to cubic layer BAC.

**(b)** *Simply by Shear*

Another intrinsic fault can be produced in the hcp structure by directly shearing all the planes above a reference plane by the vector $\frac{1}{3}[\bar{1}100]$, i.e. the sequence

$$.\,.\,.\,.\,.\,A\,B\,A\,B\,|\,A\,B\,A\,.\,.\,.\,.$$

after shearing yield a sequence

$$.\,.\,.\,.\,.\,A\,B\,A\,B\,|\,C\,A\,C\,A\,.\,.\,.\,.\,.$$

Similarly, this fault is equivalent two overlapping cubic layers, ABC and BCA.

**(c)** *By Inserting an Extra Plane*

This can be achievd by inserting a C plane in the normal hexagonal sequence A B A B . . . . such as

$$\downarrow$$
$$.\,.\,.\,.\,.\,A\,B\,A\,B\,C\,A\,B\,A\,B\,.\,.\,.\,.\,.$$

This is called an extrinsic fault and is equivalent to three overlapping cubic layers, i.e. ABC, BCA and CAB.

## 5.13   SUMMARY

1. Imperfections can be classified according to their geometry, such as point, line, plane and volume imperfections.
2. Point imperfections include vacancy, Schottky and Frenkel imperfections.
3. Line imperfections include edge and screw dislocations.
4. Surface imperfections include grain boundary, tilt and twist boundaries, twin boundary and stacking faults.
5. Measurements of critical resolved shear stress (CRSS) indicate the presence of dislocations in real crystals.
6. Dislocation motion is analogous to a wormlike motion. Movement of partial dislocation changed the layer orientation in the structure.
7. Dislocations are thermodynamically unstable and their presence always increase the free energy of the crystal.

8. The slip planes within which slip occurs are usually close packed planes.
9. The combination of a slip direction and the plane containing it, is defined as a slip system.
10. Since the energy of a dislocation is proportional to the square of the Burgers vector the dislocation of the shortest Burgers vector, that is, along the close packed directions require the least stress.
11. Two dislocations of Burgers vectors $b_1$ and $b_2$ can react to form a third dislocation of Burgers vector $b_3$ only if the condition $b_1^2 + b_2^2 > b_3^2$ is satisfied. Similarly $b_1$ may dissociate into $b_2$ and $b_3$ if $b_1^2 > b_2^2 + b_3^2$.

## 5.14 DEFINITIONS

*Burgers circuit:* A sequence of connected unit lattice translation vectors forming a circuit which would close in perfect lattice but fails to close when taken around a dislocation. The vector necessary to complete the circuit around a dislocation is the Burgers vector of that dislocation.

*Burgers vector:* The vector by which the lattice on one side of an internal surface is displaced relative to the lattice on the other side as a dislocation moves along the surface; it is a property of the dislocation.

*Climb:* The movement of a dislocation along any internal surface other than one of its slip planes.

*Critical resolved shear stress:* The resolved stress on an active slip system, at which the slip is initiated.

*Dislocation:* A line imperfection which can be visualized as the boundary between a region of an internal surface over which slip has occurred and another region over which no slip has occurred. The dislocation is called edge when the Burgers vector is perpendicular to the dislocation line; it is called screw when the Burgers vector is parallel to the dislocation line.

*Frenkel imperfection:* A point imperfection in which a cation vacancy is associated with an interstitial cation in an ionic crystal.

*Grain boundary:* A surface imperfection which separates crystal blocks of the crystal structure but different orientations in a polycrystalline aggregate.

*Interstitial impurity atom:* A point imperfection in which a foreign atom fits in an interstitial position on between the host atoms.

*Low-angle boundary:* A surface imperfection separating two misoriented regions of a crystal; the angle of misorientation is small (a few degree or less).

*Partial dislocation:* A dislocation having a Burgers vector not equal to the lattice translation.

*Schottky imperfection:* A point imperfection in which a cation vacancy is associated with an anion vacancy in an ionic crystal.

*Self-interstitial:* A point imperfection in which an atom of the same species as those of the host material is squeezed into an interstitial position between the host atoms.

*Slip:* The parallel movement of two adjacent crystal planes relative to one another.

*Slip plane:* Any crystallographic plane containing both the Burgers vector and the dislocation line.

*Slip system:* The combination of a plane and a direction lying in the same plane along which slip occurs.

*Stacking fault:* A surface imperfection which results from the stacking of one atomic plane on another out of sequence, so that the lattices on both sides of the fault have the same orientation but are translated by less than a lattice translation with respect to one another.

*Substitutional impurity atom:* A point imperfection in which a foreign atom occupies a site which would be occupied by a host atom if the crystal were prefect.

*Tilt boundary:* A low-angle boundary in which the misorientation is a rotation about an axis lying in the boundary.

*Twin boundary:* A surface imperfection separating two regions of a crystal which are mirror images of each other with respect to the plane of the boundary.

*Twist boundary:* A low-angled boundary in which the misorientation is a rotation about an axis normal to the boundary.

# REVIEW QUESTIONS AND PROBLEMS

1. The larger the coordination around an interstice, the larger is its size relative to the size of the coordinating atoms. Using this fact, explain why Frenkel imperfections are more likely in fluorite ($CaF_2$) than in lithium fluoride (NaCl crystal structure).

2. Show that the entropy of mixing equal number of two different kinds of atoms on one mole of fixed atomic sites is 5.76 J mol$^{-1}$K$^{-1}$.

3. Calculate the fraction of atoms with energies equal to or greater than 1 eV at 300 K and 1500 K
   *Ans.* $4.0 \times 10^{-34} : 1.9 \times 10^{-7}$

4. Calculate the ratio of the number of vacancies in equilibrium at 300 K in aluminium to that produced by rapid quenching from 800 K.
   *Ans.* $3.99 \times 10^{-8}$

5. Describe how the movement of atoms in a crystal might be accomplished by the motion of vacancies. Could the same result be achieved by the motion of self-interstitials?

6. Sketch how two edge dislocations of opposite sign on the same slip plane can anihilate each other. Can two screw dislocations of opposite sign also annihilate each other?

7. Show that vacancies must be either created or annihilated during the climb of a pure edge dislocation in a direction perpendicular to its slip plane.

8. What are the possible end results, if the two edge dislocations in question 6 are in the adjacent slip planes?

9. Make two neat sketches to show the climbing up and the climbing down of an edge dislocation. What happens to the vacancy concentration in the crystal during each process?

10. In a simple cubic crystal ($a = 3$Å), a positive edge dislocation of 1 mm long climbs up by 1 $\mu$m. How many vacancies are lost or created?
    *Ans.* $1.1 \times 10^{10}$ lost

11. Estimate approximately the atomic per cent of interstitial carbon required to fill all the core sites of edge dislocations in iron. Assume the edge dislocation density to be $10^{11}$ m$^{-2}$. Comment on the result that you obtain.
    *Ans.* $5 \times 10^{-9}$

12. Does the Burgers vector change with the size of the Burgers circuit? Explain.

13. Draw a Burgers circuit that encloses a positive and a negative edge dislocation each with one incomplete plane in a cubic crystal. What is the Burgers vector obtained? Comment on your result.

14. The Burgers vector of a mixed dislocation line is $1/2[\bar{1}10]$. The dislocation line lies along the $[\bar{1}12]$ direction. Find the slip plane on which this dislocation lies. Find also the screw and the edge components of the Burgers vector.
    *Ans.* $(\bar{1}10); 1/6[\bar{1}12]$ and $1/3[\bar{1}1\bar{1}]$

15. Sketch the arrangement given in Fig. 5.7, after the edge dislocation has reached to the right side of the face.

16. Distinguish among the direction of the dislocation line, the Burgers vector and the direction of motion for both edge and screw dislications, differentiating between positive and negative types.

17. A copper crystal has a dislocation density of $1.0 \times 10^{13}$ m$^{-2}$. The shear modulus of copper is 444 MN m$^{-2}$. Calculate the elastic energy of line imperfection stored in the crystal.
    *Ans.* 14.30 Jm$^{-3}$

18. Show both graphically and analytically that the first two dislocations add to give the third dislocation in the following reaction:
    $$1/6[21\bar{1}] + 1/6\,[121] \rightarrow 1/2\,[110]$$

19. Calculate the square of the Burgers vector of the above dislocations and determine whether the reaction from left to right is energetically favoured.

20. Would you expect a dislocation to dissociate on the close packed plane of hcp crystal? Why or why not?

21. Give three differences between dislocations in sc and fcc lattices. Compare both these with dislocations in a bcc lattice.

22. Sketch the distortion of the lattice around an edge dislocation and show the preferred regions for large substitutional atoms, small substitutional atoms and interstitial atoms.

23. The interfaces between three phases $\alpha$, $\beta$ and $\gamma$ meet along an edge. The angles subtended at the edge by the three phases are respectively 120°, 105° and 135°. If the surface energy of the $\alpha - \beta$ boundary is, 1.00 Jm$^{-2}$, find the surface energy of $\beta - \gamma$ and $\gamma - \alpha$ interfaces.

*Ans.* 1.225 and 1.366 Jm$^{-2}$

24. Calculate the spacing between dislocations in a tilt boundary in fcc copper crystal, when the angle of tilt is 10° (Burgers vector = 2.6Å).

*Ans.* 15Å

25. At a twin boundary, the orientation difference between adjacent parts of the crystal is as large as that at a grain boundary. Yet, the twin boundary energies are in the range of 0.01 to 0.05 Jm$^{-2}$ as compared to grain boundary energies in the range of 0.2 to 0.6 Jm$^{-2}$. What is the reason for this difference?

26. The Burgers vector of a mixed dislocation line is 1/2 [0$\overline{1}$1]. The dislocation line lies along the [2$\overline{1}$1] direction. Find the slip plane on which this dislocation lies. Find also the screw and edge components of the Burgers vector.

*Ans.* (111); 1/6 [2$\overline{1}$1] and 1/3 [$\overline{1}$ $\overline{1}$1]

27. Although MgO (NaCl crystal structure) is fcc, slip in it occurs primarily on {110} ⟨110⟩ rather than on {111} ⟨110⟩ as in fcc metal. Sketch a {110} plane and a ⟨110⟩ direction lying in it.

28. Cadmium slips on {0002} in ⟨11$\overline{2}$0⟩ direction; how many slip systems does it have? Titanium slips on {101$\overline{1}$} in ⟨11$\overline{2}$0⟩ directions; how many slip systems doe sit have?

*Ans.* 3, 3

29. Hexagonal crystal may twin on {10$\overline{1}$2} in a ⟨10$\overline{1}$1⟩ direction. Sketch a cross-section of such a twin in hexagonal Bravais lattice.

30. Grain boundaries and twin boundaries are sometimes called "high-angle boundaries". Can they be described in terms of dislocation arrays? Explain.

# Chapter 6

# Atomic Diffusion

## 6.1 INTRODUCTION

In general, it is believed that in a solid any given atom is fixed at a particular lattice site assigned to it and does not move from its position except due to thermal vibration. However, in reality the atoms do have more freedom and they move from one lattice site to another in discrete jumps. This kind of motion is called diffusion. therefore, diffusion is essentially an irreversible mass flow process by which atoms or molecules change their position relative to their neighbours and travel to a large distance. They do so under the influence of thermal energy or thermal gradient (other gradients like concentration, electric, magnetic field or stress gradients may also have similar effect). In other words, diffusion is the mechanism by which matter is transported through matter; on the atomic scale it is the net effect of random atomic motions.

*In fluids:* liquid and gases, the random molecular motion causes a relatively rapid disappearance of concentration difference. On the other hand, in solids, particularly in crystalline solids, where the atoms are more tightly bound, there still remains an element of uncertainty due to thermal vibrations that some atoms move at random through the lattice. A large number of such movements result in a significant transport of the material. This phenomenon is known as "solid state diffusion". Even in a pure substance, a particular atom does not remain at its equilibrium site indefinitely, but moves from place to place in the material. Such movements are known as "self diffusion". On the other hand, in a multicomponent substance, such as binary metallic alloy, the diffusion of one component through the lattice of the other is known as "interdiffusion".

## 6.2 FICK'S FIRST LAW

Let us consider a unidirectional flow of matter in a binary system of $A$ and $B$ atoms. In general, the two types of atoms will move in opposite directions under the influence of a concentration gradient. However, let us assume that only $B$ atoms move along the positive $x$-direction until an equilibrium is reached. Concentration -distance profile between two vertical planes of concentration $c_1$ and $c_2$ (where $c_1 > c_2$) for steady state diffusion is shown in Fig. 6.1. For this kind of a system, it would be reasonable to assume that the flux (i.e. the number of atoms flowing per unit cross-sectional area per unit time) across a given plane to be proportional to the concentration gradient across that plane. Therefore, if the $x$-axis is taken parallel to the concentration gradient, the flux $J$ of $B$ atoms along the gradient can be given by the equation

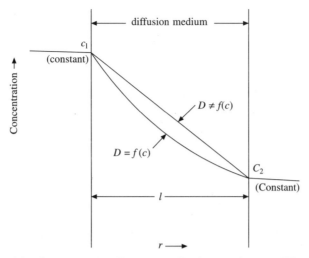

**Fig. 6.1   Concentration-distance profile for steady state diffusion**

$$J = \frac{1}{A} \cdot \frac{dn}{dt} = -D \left( \frac{dc}{dx} \right) \tag{1}$$

where $\frac{dn}{dt}$ is the number of moles of B atoms crossing per unit time through a cross-sectional plane of area $A$, $\frac{dc}{dx}$ the concentration gradient and $D$ is called diffusion coefficient (or diffusivity) and is a constant characteristic of the system. The value of $D$ depends on: (i) nature of diffusing species, (ii) the medium in which it is diffusing and (iii) the temperature. The negative sign indicates that the flow of matter occurs from regions of high concentration. The eq. 1 is known as Fick's first law under steady state condition and fits the empirical fact that the flux goes to zero as the specimen becomes homogeneous. It is analogous to Fourier's law for heat flow under a constant temperature gradient and Ohm's law for flow of current under a constant electric field gradient. Under steady state flow, the flux is independent of time and remains the same at all cross-section along the diffusion direction, i.e.

$$J \neq f(x, t) \tag{2}$$

Further, the concentration-distance profile in Fig. 6.1 is a straight line, when $D \neq f(c)$. On the other hand, for $D = f(c)$, the profile will be such that the product $D(dc/dx)$ is a constant. Thus in neither case, the profile changes with time under steady state flow.

*Example:* A steel tank contains nitrogen at a constant pressure of 10 atm., with a vacuum outside. The nitrogen concentration at the inner surface of the tank is equal to 10 kg m$^{-3}$. The diffusion coefficient of nitrogen in steel at room temperature is $10^{-19}$ m$^2$s$^{-1}$. Calculate the rate at which nitrogen escapes through the wall of the tank, which has a thickness of 10 mm.

*Solution:* As soon as steady state flow is established, a constant flux of nitrogen will escape through the tank wall, as the pressure drop inside the tank is negligible. There is a vacuum on the outside. So, the concentration of nitrogen on the outer surface of the wall is zero. From Fick's first law,

$$\text{Flux outward } J = 10^{-19} \times \frac{10}{10 \times 10^{-3}} = 1 \times 10^{-16} \text{ kgm}^{-2}\text{s}^{-1}$$

*Example:* In a pure thick aluminium sheet, there are 0.19 atomic percent of copper at a surface and 0.18 atomic percent at the depth of 1.2 mm from the surface. Calculate the flux of the copper atom from the surface at 550°C if the diffusion coefficient of copper in aluminium at this temperature is $5.25 \times 10^{-13}$ m²s⁻¹.

*Solution:* Given: $\quad c_2 = 0.18 = 0.0018$ per unit volume

$$c_1 = 0.19 = 0.0019 \text{ per unit volume}$$

$$dx = 1.2 \text{ mm} = 0.0012 \text{ m}$$

and $\qquad\qquad D = 5.25 \times 10^{-13}$ m²s⁻¹

Since aluminium is fcc crystal with lattice parameter $a = 4.05$ Å $= 4.05 \times 10^{-10}$ m. Therefore, the number of aluminium atoms per unit volume is

$$\frac{\text{Atoms}}{m^3} = \frac{4}{(4.05 \times 10^{-10})^3} = 6 \times 10^{28} \text{ m}^{-3}$$

Therefore,

$$\left(\frac{dc}{dx}\right)_{cu} = \frac{(0.0018 - 0.0019) \times 6 \times 10^{28}}{0.0012} = -5 \times 10^{27} \text{ Cu m}^{-4}$$

so that the flux

$$J = -D\left(\frac{dc}{dx}\right) = -(5.25 \times 10^{-13}) \times (-5 \times 10^{27})$$

$$= 26.25 \times 10^{14} \text{ Cu m}^{-2}\text{s}^{-1}$$

*Example:* At the surface of a steel bar there is one carbon atom per 20 unit cell of iron. At a depth of 1 mm from the surface there is one carbon atom per 30 unit cell. If the diffusion coefficient of carbon in iron at 1000°C is $3 \times 10^{-11}$ m²s⁻¹, find out the number of carbon atoms diffusing through each unit cell per minute? The structure of iron at 1000°C is fcc with $a = 3.65$ Å.

*Solution:* Given: $c_2 = \dfrac{1}{30 \times 3.65 \times 10^{-10}} = 0.68 \times 10^{27}$ m⁻³

and $\qquad\qquad c_1 = \dfrac{1}{20 \times 3.65 \times 10^{-10}} = 1.03 \times 10^{27}$ m⁻³

Therefore

$$J = -3 \times 10^{-10} \times \frac{(0.68 - 1.03) \times 10^{27}}{10^{-3}} = 1.05 \times 10^{19} \text{ m}^2\text{s}^{-1}$$

Now, since each unit cell has an area of $(3.65 \times 10^{-10})^2$, therefore

$$J_{u.c.} = 1.05 \times 10^{19} \times (3.65 \times 10^{-10})^2 \times 60 = 84 \text{ atoms m}^{-1}$$

## 6.3 FICK'S SECOND LAW

We now develop the diffusion equation in a more general form taking into account the non-steady flows in which the concentration at a point changes with time. Consequently, the concentration-distance profile, the gradient and the flux also change with time. Consider an elemental slab of thickness $\Delta x$ along the $x$-axis and unit cross-sectional area perpendicular to $x$. Under non-steady state conditions, the flux into the slab $J_1$ is not equal to the flux out of the slab $J_2$ (Fig. 6.2). If the thickness of the slab $\Delta x$ is very small, then $J_1$ and $J_2$ will be related by the expression

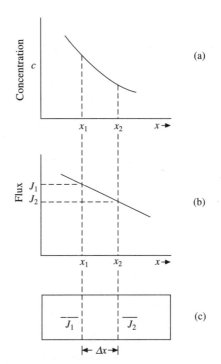

$$J_1 = J_2 - \Delta x \left( \frac{\partial J}{\partial x} \right) \qquad (3)$$

The volume of the elemental slab is $1.\Delta x$ (unit area times thinkness). The rate of change of concentration within this elemental volume $\Delta x$ is $(\partial c / \partial t)\Delta x$. This can be expressed as the difference of the fluxes in and out of the slab:

$$\left( \frac{\partial c}{\partial t} \right) \Delta x = J_1 - J_2 \qquad (4)$$

From eqs. 3 and 4, we have

$$\left( \frac{\partial c}{\partial t} \right) = - \left( \frac{\partial J}{\partial x} \right) \qquad (5)$$

**Fig. 6.2** **(a) An assumed plot, (b) $J(x)$ for this plot, (c) the element of volume with flux $J_1$ entering and $J_2$ leaving**

Equation 1 is still valid even if the concentration and concentration gradient at that point are changing with time. Therefore substituting the value of $J$ in eq. 5, we have

$$\left( \frac{\partial c}{\partial t} \right) = \frac{\partial}{\partial x} D \left( \frac{\partial c}{\partial x} \right) \qquad (6)$$

This is called Fick's second law of diffusion. Here concentration $c$ varies with distance $x$, time $t$ and diffusivity $D$. Partial derivatives are used to distinguish between the change of $c$ with $x$ at a given time $t$ and the change of $c$ with time at a given position $x$. If $D$ is a constant and independent of concentration, eq. 6 reduces to

$$\left( \frac{\partial c}{\partial t} \right) = D \left( \frac{\partial^2 c}{\partial x^2} \right) \qquad (7)$$

The generalisation of these equations to two or three dimensions is simple. In three dimensions eq. 6 becomes

$$\left( \frac{\partial c}{\partial t} \right) = \frac{\partial}{\partial x}\left( D_x \frac{\partial c}{\partial x} \right) + \frac{\partial}{\partial y}\left( D_y \frac{\partial c}{\partial y} \right) + \left( D_z \frac{\partial c}{\partial z} \right) \tag{8}$$

where $D_x$, $D_y$ and $D_z$ are the diffusion coefficients along the $x$, $y$ and $z$ axes, respectively. In an isotropic medium

$$D_x = D_y = D_z = D \tag{9}$$

These equations can also be transformed to suit particular geometries. If the concentration (or temperature) gradients have radial symmetry about a cylindrical axis, then eq. 7 for an isotropic material with a constant $D$ becomes

$$\left( \frac{\partial c}{\partial t} \right) = D\left( \frac{\partial^2 c}{\partial r^2} + \frac{1}{r} \cdot \frac{\partial c}{\partial r} \right) \tag{10}$$

where $r$ is the distance from the axis. Similarly, when the diffusion field has spherical symmetry about a point, i.e. $c$ varies only with radial distance $r$ from the point, then eq. 7 becomes

$$\left( \frac{\partial c}{\partial t} \right) = D\left( \frac{\partial^2 c}{\partial r^2} + \frac{2}{r} \cdot \frac{\partial c}{\partial r} \right) \tag{11}$$

## 6.4   SOLUTION TO FICK'S SECOND LAW (CONSTANT $D$)

**Steady State Solutions**

Steady state solution of the diffusion equations are important for analysing the conduction of heat through furnace walls, recuperator tubes, gas ducts, etc. Let us analyse the solutions of diffusion through plane, cylindrical and spherical surfaces:

**Diffusion through a Plane Surface**

Let us consider the case of one dimensional diffusion in a medium bounded by two parallel planes at $x = 0$ and $x = l$. These will apply in practice to diffusion into a plane sheet of material such as membrane so thin that effectively all the diffusion substance enters through the plane face and a negligible amount through the edges. Let the diffusion coefficient be $D$ and two surfaces are maintained at constant concentrations $c_1$ and $c_2$ respectively. After certain time, a steady state is reached in which the concentration remains constant at all points of the sheet and therefore, $\partial c/\partial t = 0$. Equation 7 then reduces to

$$\frac{d^2 c}{dx^2} = 0 \tag{12}$$

where $x$ is the distance into the sheet. Integrating twice, the solution of the equation can be obtained as

$$c = Ax + B \tag{13}$$

where $A$ and $B$ are constants and can be determined by applying the boundary conditions. At the two surfaces, the boundary concentrations are: $x = 0$, $c = c_1$ and $x = l$, $c = c_2$. Substituting these values and solving for $A$ and $B$, the solution becomes

$$\frac{c - c_1}{c_2 - c_1} = \frac{x}{l} \tag{14}$$

Both equations 13 and 14 show that the concentration changes linearly from $c_1$ to $c_2$ through the sheet as shown in Fig. 6.1. Also, the rate of transfer of diffusing substance is the same across all sectiomK–of the membrane and is given by

$$J = -D\frac{dc}{dx} = D\frac{c_1 - c_2}{l} \tag{15}$$

If the thickness $l$ and the surface concentrations $c_1$ and $c_2$ are known, $D$ can be determined from an observed value of $J$ by using eq. 15.

**Diffusion through a Cylinder**

We now consider a radially symmetrical diffusion through the walls of a hollow cylinder. Concentration is then a function of radius $r$ and time $t$, the diffusion eq. 10 can be written as

$$\left(\frac{d^2c}{dr^2} + \frac{1}{r} \cdot \frac{dc}{dr}\right) = 0 \tag{16}$$

The general solution of this equation is

$$c = A \ln r + B \tag{17}$$

Introducing the boundary conditions that $c = c_1$ and $c = c_2$, respectively at the two surfaces, $r = r_0$ and $r = r_1$, of the cylinder wall, and solving for $A$ and $B$, the solution becomes

$$\frac{c_1 \ln (r_1/r) + c_2 \ln (r/r_0)}{\ln (r_1/r_0)} \tag{18}$$

The flux through any shell of radius $r$ in a time $t$ is $-2\pi rtD(dc/dr)$, i.e.,

$$J = \frac{-2\pi Dt(c_2 - c_1)}{\ln (r_1/r_0)} \tag{19}$$

Since $J$ decreases only logarithmically with the increase in $r_1$, building up an excessively thick insulating lagging (i.e. $r_1 \gg 3r_0$) is a rather ineffective way of conserving heat in a cylindrical pipe; it is better to use a thinner coat of a more highly insulating material. Contrary to this, a plane surface can be insulated by a thick layer because $J$ varies directly as $l^{-1}$ in eq. 15.

*Example:* In a cylindrical crystal of radius $r = 12$ mm, calculate the ratio of cross-sectional area available for diffusion through the surface layers to the area available for mass transport through the cylinder.

*Solution:* The cross-sectional area for diffusion through the cylinder is

$$\pi r^2 = 452.39 \text{ mm}^2$$

Let us assume that the effective thickness of the surface is 4 Å ($\sim$ two atomic diameters), the cross-sectional area for diffusion along the surface will be

$$2\pi r \times 4 \times 10^{-7} = 301.59 \times 10^{-7} \text{ mm}^2$$

The ratio of the two cross-sectional areas will become

$$\frac{301.59 \times 10^{-7}}{452.39} = 6.66 \times 10^{-8}$$

## Diffusion through a sphere

In this case, we consider spherically symmetric diffusion through the wall of a hollow sphere. The diffusion eq. 11 becomes

$$\left( \frac{d^2c}{dr^2} + \frac{2}{r} \cdot \frac{dc}{dr} \right) = 0$$

or

$$\frac{d}{dr} \left( r^2 \frac{dc}{dr} \right) = 0 \tag{20}$$

The general solution of this equation is

$$c = \frac{A}{r} + B \tag{21}$$

Ingtroducing the boundary conditions $c = c_1$ and $c = c_2$, respectively, at the two surfaces, $r = r_0$ and $r = r_1$ of the sphere wall, and solving for $A$ and $B$, the solution becomes

$$c = \frac{r_0 c_1 (r_1 - r) + r_1 c_2 (r - r_0)}{r(r_1 - r_0)} \tag{22}$$

The flux through any spherical shell of radius $r$ in a time $t$ is given by

$$J = \frac{-4 \pi D t r_0 r_1 (c_2 - c_1)}{r_1 - r_0} \tag{23}$$

## Non-steady State Solutions

Non-steady state solutions of the diffusion equations are important in many problems of metallurgical reactions; i.e. heterogeneous reactions at interfaces between phases, dissolution, precipitation, etc. In the present case, we are interested in determining the concentration as a function of position and time, i.e. $c(x, t)$, for some simple cases. In general, the solutions of eq. 7 for constant $D$ fall into two forms: (i) when the diffusion distance is short relative to the dimension of initial inhomogeneity, $c(x, t)$ can be most simply expressed in terms of error functions, and (ii) when complete homogenization is approached, $c(x, t)$ can be represented by first few terms of an infinite trigonometric series (in the case of a cylinder, the trigonometric series is replaced by a series of bessel functions). We shall consider the former type for a simple problem of one dimensional diffusion from one lqDia to another across a common interface (Fig. 6.3). If the two mediums are sufficiently long such that the concentrations at their outer ends remain constant

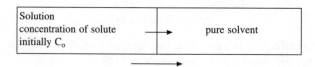

**Fig. 6.3    Diffusion across a common interface from one medium to another**

during the diffusion period, the general solution of eq. 7 in terms of error function is given as

$$c\,(x, t) = A - B\,\mathrm{erf}\left(\frac{x}{2\sqrt{Dt}}\right) \tag{24}$$

where $A$ and $B$ are constants to be determined from the initial boundary conditions of a particular problem, $x$ is the distance in either direction normal to the common interface and $t$ is the diffusion time. Let us consider some specific cases for illustration. Suppose that a gas $A$ which maintains a constant concentration $C_s$ on the surface diffuses into a solid $B$ (Fig. 6.4a), a process identical to the case of hardening of steel by gas carburizing. As the diffusion time increases, the concentration of the solute atom at any point in the $x$-direction also increases. Concentration-distance profiles of $A$ for times $t_1$ and $t_2$ are shown in Fig. 6.4b. It is also shown that the solid contains a uniform concentration of element $A$, called $C_0$, before the start of the diffusion. If the diffusion coefficient of the gas $A$ in the solid is independent of position, then the solution to the Fick's second law (eq. 7) will be given as

$$\frac{C_s - C_x}{C_s - C_0} = \mathrm{erf}\left(\frac{x}{2\sqrt{Dt}}\right) \tag{25}$$

where $C_s$ is the surface concentration of element in gas diffusing into the solid surface, $C_0 =$ initial uniform concentration of the element in solid and $C_x =$ concentration of element at a distance $x$ from the surface at a time $t$.

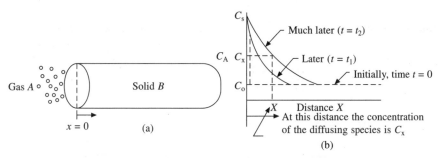

**Fig. 6.4** **Diffusion of a gas into a solid (a) Gas A diffuse into a solid B and (b) Concentration-distance profiles of element A for different times**

The error function, erf, can be found in standard tables in the same way as sines and cosines. Table 6.1 is an abbreviated table of the same.

Now, either applying the initial boundary conditions or just comparing equations 24 and 25, the constants $A$ and $B$ can be obtained as:

$C_x = C_0$ at $t = 0$, also $c\,(x, 0) = A - B$

$C_x = C_s$ at $x = 0$, also $c\,(0, t) = A$

so that $A = C_s$ and $B = C_s - C_0$

Thus, either eq. 24 or 25 could be used to represent the Fick's second law, depending upon the nature of the problem. In these equations, the error function erf, is a probability integral or Gaussian function and is defined as

$$\text{erf}\left(\frac{x}{2\sqrt{Dt}}\right) = \frac{2}{\sqrt{\pi}} \int_0^{x/2\sqrt{Dt}} \exp(-y^2)\,dy \tag{26}$$

where $2/\sqrt{\pi}$ is normalization factor. The value of Gaussian error function entirely depends on the upper limit of the intergral while the lower limit of the integral is always zero. Fig. 6.5 shows a curve between $\exp(-y^2)$ and $y$. The shaded area under the curve from $y = 0$ to $x/2\sqrt{Dt}$ is the value of the integral in eq. 26. On the other hand, the value of integral within the limit, 0 to $\infty$ and 0 to $-\infty$ comes out to be $\sqrt{\pi}/2$ and $-\sqrt{\pi}/2$, respectively. Therefore,

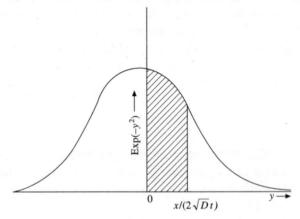

**Fig. 6.5   Illustration of the error function. Hatched area is equal to the value of the integral in eq. 26**

$$\text{erf}(\infty) = \frac{2}{\sqrt{\pi}} \times \frac{\sqrt{\pi}}{2} = 1$$

$$\text{erf}(-\infty) = \frac{2}{\sqrt{\pi}} \times -\frac{\sqrt{\pi}}{2} = -1$$

$$\text{erf}(0) = 0 \quad \text{and} \quad \text{erf}\left(-\frac{x}{2\sqrt{Dt}}\right) = -\text{erf}\left(\frac{x}{2\sqrt{Dt}}\right)$$

Now, let us suppose that it is desired to achieve some specific concentration (say $C_1$) of solute in an alloy, then the left hand side of the eq. 25 will become

$$\frac{C_s - C_1}{C_s - C_0} = \text{constant} \tag{27}$$

If this is the case, then the right hand side of the eq. 25 will also be a constant, and consequently

$$\frac{x}{2\sqrt{Dt}} = \text{constant}$$

Many other non-steady state solutions have been derived for various geometrical and physical conditions. They become increasingly complex as the conditions themselves become more complicated. In metallurgical reactions, where irregularly shaped lumps or drops of many phases may be reacting together under variable conditions, exact solutions of the diffusion equations are neither possible nor necessary. Fortunately, order of magnitude values can be obtained by a simple general argument. Diffusion as mentioned in the beginning is the overall result of random walks made by individual migrating particles. The theory of statistics suitably analyses such systems and shows that in a time $t$ a particle migrates on an average a distance of $\sqrt{Dt}$ from its starting point. This distance, is referred to as the "diffusion length", which is a rough but useful measure of the diffusion depth of diffusing species.

*Example:* The diffusion coefficient for Li in Ge at 500°C is of the order of $10^{-10}$ m²/s. What is its approximate distance of penetration in 1 hour?

*Solution:* Given: $D \simeq 10^{-10}$ m²/s, $t = 1$ hr, $T = 500°C = 773K$, $x = ?$ From above discussion, we know that the diffusion length is approximately given by

$$x = \sqrt{Dt}$$

Therefore, the distance of penetration corresponding to the given data is

$$x = \sqrt{10^{-10} \times 60 \times 60} = 0.6 \text{ mm} = 6 \times 10^{-4} \text{ m}$$

*Example:* The diffusion coefficient for Li in Ge at 500°C is of the order $10^{-10}$ m²/s. How much time it should take to penetrate a distance of 2 mm?

*Solution:* Given: $D \simeq 10^{-10}$ m²/s, $T = 500°C = 773K$, $x = 0.2$ mm $= 2 \times 10^{-4}$ m, $t = ?$ From the relation $x = \sqrt{Dt}$, we can obtain

$$t = \frac{x^2}{D} = \frac{(2 \times 10^{-4})^2}{10^{-10}} = 400 \text{ s}.$$

## 6.5 SOME APPLICATIONS OF DIFFUSION

### Measurement of Diffusion Coefficient (*D*)

The diffusion coefficient $D$ can be measured experimentally by placing two dissimilar and long bars in intimate contact so that they form a diffusion couple (Fig. 6.6) and then measure composition, distance, time and temperature. The temperature is kept such that there is a measurable amount of diffusion, after a reasonable length of time. Difffusion takes place across the common interface which is taken as the origin of the diffusion direction. The diffusion anneal is done at a constant temperature (to keep $D$ constant) for a known length of time. After the anneal, the slices of the couple normal to the diffusion direction $x$ are cut with the help of precision lathe. Composition can then be measured by fine scale X-ray analysis, hardness tests, chemical analysis or with some suitable radiation counting technique if the diffusing species is radioactive, to give the value of $c$ as a function of $x$.

Concentration-distance profile so obtained (Fig. 6.6) clearly indicates that the flux is changing as a function of $x$ at a given $t$, as well as with time $t$ at constant $x$, under the non-steady state conditions prevailing. When $D$ is independent of concentration, the concentration-distnce profiles are symmetrical about the junction as shown in Fig. 6.6. The concentration at the junction is

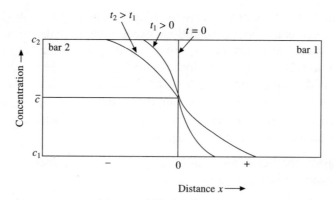

**Fig. 6.6   The diffusion couple for non steady state diffusion**

independent of time and is $\bar{c} = (c_1 + c_2)/2$, the average concentration. The constants $A$ and $B$ for above diffusion couple can be determined from initial conditions:

$$c\,(\text{x}, 0) = \begin{cases} c_1 & x > 0 \\ c_2 & x < 0 \end{cases} \tag{29}$$

Then substituting the values of erf $(+\infty)$ and erf $(-\infty)$ in eq. 25, the constants $A$ and $B$ can be found as

$$\left.\begin{aligned} A &= \frac{c_1 + c_2}{2} \\ B &= \frac{c_2 - c_1}{2} \end{aligned}\right\} \tag{30}$$

Now, since the annealing time $t$ is known $A$, $B$ and erf $(x/2\sqrt{Dt})$ can be determined from the initial conditions using eq. 24. The term $(x/2\sqrt{Dt})$ is then obtained from Table 6.1 directly or by suitable interpolation of the neighbouring data as the case may be. With $x$ and $t$ known, $D$ can be determined. If $D$ is a function of concentration, the above procedure can still be used, by choosing $c_1$ and $c_2$ within a narrow composition range for any one diffusion couple. The experiment can then be repeated with additional diffusion couples to cover the entire composition range.

Further, we know that the atomic diffusion is a result of the movement of atoms, therefore the rate of diffusion is expected to depend directly on temperature. In order to determine the value of $D$ as a function of temperature, the diffusion couple experiment can be repeated at different temperatures. The experimental results indicate that the diffusion coefficient $D$ of many systems obey Arrhenius type equation

$$D = D_0 \exp\left(-\frac{E}{kT}\right) \tag{31}$$

where $D_0$ is a pre-exponential constant independent of temperature in the range for which equation is valid, $E$ is the activation energy for diffusion (in Joules), $k$ is the Boltzmann constant and $T$ is the temperature in the absolute scale.

In terms of molar and calorie units (as discussed in section 5.2), eq. 31 can be written as

**Table 6.1** **The error function**

| $z$ | **erf** $(z)$ | $z$ | **erf** $(z)$ |
|-----|-----|-----|-----|
| 0.000 | 0.025 | 0.85 | 0.7707 |
| 0.025 | 0.0282 | 0.90 | 0.7970 |
| 0.05 | 0.0564 | 0.95 | 0.8209 |
| 0.10 | 0.1125 | 1.0 | 0.8427 |
| 0.15 | 0.1680 | 1.1 | 0.8802 |
| 0.20 | 0.2227 | 1.2 | 0.9103 |
| 0.25 | 0.2763 | 1.3 | 0.9340 |
| 0.30 | 0.3268 | 1.4 | 0.9523 |
| 0.35 | 0.3794 | 1.5 | 0.9661 |
| 0.40 | 0.4284 | 1.6 | 0.9763 |
| 0.45 | 0.4755 | 1.7 | 0.9838 |
| 0.50 | 0.5205 | 1.8 | 0.9891 |
| 0.55 | 0.5633 | 1.9 | 0.9928 |
| 0.60 | 0.6039 | 2.0 | 0.9953 |
| 0.65 | 0.6420 | 2.2 | 0.9981 |
| 0.70 | 0.6778 | 2.4 | 0.9993 |
| 0.75 | 0.7112 | 2.6 | 0.9998 |
| 0.80 | 0.7421 | 2.8 | 0.9999 |

$$D = D_0 \exp\left(-\frac{Q}{RT}\right) \tag{32}$$

The logarithm of the diffusion coefficient is related to the reciprocal of the temperature, $1/T$. Thus eq. 31 becomes

$$\ln D = \ln D_0 - \frac{E}{kT} \tag{33}$$

In terms of molar and calorie units eq. 32 can be written as

$$\ln D = \ln D_0 - \frac{Q}{RT} \tag{34}$$

or $\quad \log_{10} D = \log_{10} D_0 - \dfrac{Q}{2.303\,RT} \quad$ (35)

where $Q$ is the activation energy for diffusion (in cal/mol) and $R$ is the molar gas constant. The values of $D_0$ and $E$ (or $Q$) are determined from a plot of $\ln D$ vs $1/T$. This plot, according to eq. 33 or 34 is a straight line, whose intercept is $\ln D_0$ and slope $-E/k$ (or $-Q/R$) as shown in Fig. 6.7. In Table 6.2 we provide the experimentally determined values of $D_0$, $E$ and $Q$ for some important diffusion processes. It is interesting to see that the diffusion coefficient $D$ increases very rapidly with temperature. For

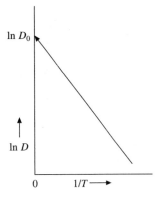

**Fig. 6.7** **Arrhenius plot of experimental data**

### Table 6.2   Constants for Diffusivity Calculations

| Solute | Solvent (host structure) | $D_0$ ($10^{-4} m^2 s^{-1}$) | $Q$ (cal mol$^{-1}$) | $E$ ($10^{-18}$ J/atom) |
|---|---|---|---|---|
| Carbon | fcc iron | 0.2 | 34,000 | 0.236 |
| Carbon | bcc iron | 2.2 | 29,300 | 0.204 |
| Iron | fcc iron | 0.22 | 64,000 | 0.445 |
| Iron | bcc iron | 2.0 | 57,500 | 0.400 |
| Nickel | fcc iron | 0.77 | 67,000 | 0.465 |
| Manganese | fcc iron | 0.35 | 67,500 | 0.469 |
| Zinc | Copper | 0.34 | 45,600 | 0.317 |
| Copper | Aluminium | 0.15 | 30,200 | 0.210 |
| Copper | Copper | 0.2 | 47,100 | 0.327 |
| Silver | Silver (crystal) | 0.4 | 44,100 | 0.306 |
| Silver | Silver (grain boundary) | 0.14 | 21,500 | 0.149 |
| Carbon | hcp titanium | 5.1 | 43,500 | 0.302 |

example: If $Q = 2$ eV, and $D_0 = 8 \times 10^{-5}$ m$^2$/s, then

(i) at $T = 300$ K, $D \simeq 8 \times 10^{-5} \times 10^{-34} \cong 10^{-38}$ m$^2$/s
(ii) at $T = 1500$ K, $D \simeq 8 \times 10^{-5} \times e^{-16} \simeq 8 \times 10^{-5} \times 10^{-7} \simeq 10^{-11}$ m$^2$/s

Thus, we observe that the value of $D$ increases by 27 orders of magnitude when the temperature is increased by a factor of 5 only.

*Example*: What is the diffusion coefficient of Cu in A1 at 550°C, assuming $Q = 121$ kJ mol$^{-1}$ and $D_0 = 0.25 \times 10^{-4}$ m$^2$s$^{-1}$? What is the approximate distance of penetration of Cu atoms in 1 hour?

*Solution:* Using eq. 32, we can write

$$D_{cu\ in\ A1} = D_0 \exp(-Q/RT)$$

$$= 0.25 \times 10^{-4} \times \exp\left(-\frac{121 \times 10^3}{8.314 \times 823}\right)$$

$$= 0.25 \times 10^{-4} \exp(-17.68) = 5.25 \times 10^{-13}\ m^2 s^{-1}$$

Therefore, the depth of penetration,

$$x = \sqrt{5.25 \times 10^{-13} \times 60 \times 60} = 0.434\ mm$$

*Example:* If the ratio of diffusion rate of silver in silicon at 1350°C and 1100°C is found to be 8 in a doping process, calculate the activation energy.

*Solution:* Given: Temperatures, say $T_1 = 1350 + 273 = 1623$ K and $T_2 = 1100 + 273 = 1373$ K and corresponding $D_1/D_2 = 8/1$.

Using eq. 32, we have

$$8 = D_0 \exp\left(-\frac{Q}{8.314 \times 1623}\right) = D_0 \exp(-Q \times 7.41 \times 10^{-5})$$

and similarly we can write

$$1 = D_0 \exp\left(-\frac{Q}{8.314 \times 1373}\right) = D_0 \exp\left(-Q \times 8.76 \times 10^{-5}\right)$$

Therefore, $D_1/D_2 = 8/1 = \exp(Q \times 1.35 \times 10^{-5})$
On simplifying this, we get

$$Q = \ln 8/(1.3 \times 10^{-5}) = 154 \text{ kJ mol}^{-1}$$

*Example:* The diffusivity of gallium in silicon is $8 \times 10^{-13}$ cm$^2$/s at 1100°C and $1 \times 10^{-10}$ cm$^2$/s at 1300°C. (1) Determine the values of diffusion constant $D_0$ and activation energy $Q$, assuming the Arrhenius rate law is obeyed for this diffusion system. (2) Calculate the diffusivity of the system at 1200°C.

*Solution:* Given: $D_{1100°C} = 8 \times 10^{-13}$ cm$^2$/s. $T_1 = 1373$ K, $D_{1300°C} = 1 \times 10^{-10}$ cm$^2$/s, $T_2 = 1573$ K, and $R = 1.987$ cal mol$^{-1}$ K$^{-1}$

$$D_0 = ?, \ Q = ? \quad \text{and} \quad D_{1200°C} = ?$$

(1) Using Arrhenius equation in the $\log_{10}$ form

$$\log_{10} D = \log_{10} D_0 - \frac{Q}{2.303 RT}$$

or
$$\log_{10} D = \log_{10} D_0 - \frac{Q \text{ cal/mol}}{2.303 \times 1.987 \times T(K)} \qquad (a)$$

Thus, at 1100°C,

$$\log_{10} 8 \times 10^{-13} = \log_{10} D_0 - \frac{Q}{4.576 \times 1373} \qquad (b)$$

And at 1300°C,

$$\log_{10} 1 \times 10^{-10} = \log_{10} D_0 - \frac{Q}{4.576 \times 1573} \qquad (c)$$

Subtracting eq. (c) from (b), we have

$$\log_{10} 8 \times 10^{-13} - \log_{10} 1 \times 10^{-10} = -Q \ (1.59 - 1.39) \times 10^{-4}$$
$$= -Q \times 0.20 \times 10^{-4}$$

or
$$0.9 - 13 + 10 = -Q \times 0.20 \times 10^{-4}$$

Therefore $Q = \dfrac{2.1 \times 10^4}{0.20} = 105000$ cal/mol $= 105$ kcal/mol

Now, substituting the value of $Q$ in eq. (c), we find

$$\log_{10} 10^{-10} = \log_{10} D_0 - \frac{105000}{4.576 \times 1573}$$

or
$$\log_{10} D_0 = -10 + 14.58 = 4.58$$

Therefore $$D_0 = 38645 \text{ cm}^2/\text{s}.$$

(2) Given: $T = 1200 + 273 + 1373$ K, $D_0 = 38645$ cm$^2$/s, and $Q = 105000$ cal/mol.

Now substituting these values in eq. (a), we have

$$\log_{10} D \times 10^{-10} = \log_{10} 38645 - \frac{105000}{4.576 \times 1473}$$

$$= 4.58 - 15.57 = -10.99$$

Therefore $$D = 1.02 \times 10^{-11} \text{ cm}^2/\text{s}.$$

*Example:* The diffusion rate of A in B was studied at 500°C and 850°C. It was found that, for the same diffusion time, the depth of penetration $x_1$ and $x_2$ in two experiments were in the ratio of 1 : 4. Calculate the activation energy for diffusion of A in B.

*Solution:* Given: Temperatures, say $T_1 = 500 + 273 = 773$ K

and $$T_2 = 850 + 273 = 1123 \text{ K}$$

The penetration depth $$x_1/x_2 = 1 : 4 \text{ and } t_1 = t_2 = t$$

From the problem, the quantity

$$\frac{x_1}{2\sqrt{D_1 t}} = \frac{x_2}{2\sqrt{D_2 t}}, \text{ or } x_1/x_2 = \sqrt{D_1/D_2}$$

or $$D_1/D_2 = (x_1/x_2)^2 = 1/16.$$

Now, let us suppose that $D_1$ corresponds to $T_1$ and $D_2$ corresponds to $T_2$ and finding their ratio as above, we get

$$D_1/D_2 = 1/16 = \exp(-0.485 \times 10^{-4} \times Q)$$

On simplifying this, we get

$$Q = \ln 16/(0.485 \times 10^{-4}) = 57.16 \text{ kJ mol}^{-1}$$

### Carburizing and Decarburizing Process in Steel

For many engineering components such as gears, shafts and valves it is an advantage to use steel with hard surface and a soft, tough interior. This could be achieved by surface hardening treatment in which the surface layer of the soft steel is enriched with hardening alloy element (usually carbon or nitrogen) by diffusion process. In carburizing process, the steel is heated for a few hours at about 900°C in a carbon-rich atmosphere provided by gaseous, liquid or solid carbonaceous substances. A carburized layer of about $10^{-3}$ m thick is produced. The surface is then hardened by quenching from about 750°C, a treatment that leaves the interior soft. In nitriding process, the metal containing about one percent aluminium is heated at 500–550°C, in ammonia for a few hours. Nitrogen atoms diffuse into the surface and form fine stable nitrid precipitates with the aluminium, so that the metal is precipitation hardened on its surface. No subsequent heat treatment is needed in this case. Surface hardening by carburizing, nitriding, surface hammering etc. are important for improving the fatigue strength of the material.

If the carbon content of the carburizing atmosphere remains constant (i.e. carbon concentration $C_s$) at the surface of the steel (Fig. 6.8a) as also the initial carbon content of the steel is $C_1$ (equivalent to $C_0$ in eq. 25), we can write

$$c\,(x, 0) = C_1 \qquad x > 0$$

$$c\,(0, t) = C_s$$

so that, from eq. 24 we have $A = C_s$ and $B = C_s - C_1$. Alternatively eq. 25 can be used directly. Thus, knowing the values of $D$, $C_s$ and $C_1$ the depth of carbon penetration as a function of time can be determined.

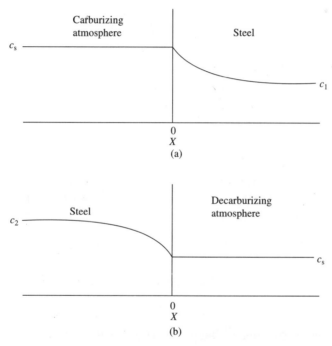

**Fig. 6.8   Concentration-distance profiles for (a) carburization, and (b) decarburization**

*Example*: Consider the gas carburizing of a gear of 1018 steel (0.18 wt.%) at 927°C. Calculate the time necessary to increase the carbon content to 0.30 wt.% at 0.60 mm below the surface of the gear. Assume the carbon content at the surface to be 1.00 wt% and that the nomimal carbon content of the steel gear before carburizing is 0.18 wt.%. $D$ ($C$ in $\gamma$ iron) at 927°C = $1.28 \times 10^{-11}$ m²/s.

*Solution:* Given: $C_0 = 0.18\%$, $C_x = 0.30\%$, $C_s = 1.0\%$

$$x = 0.60 \text{ mm} = 6 \times 10^{-4} \text{ m}, \ t = \ ?$$

Also $\qquad\qquad D_{927°C} = 1.28 \times 10^{-11}$ m²/s.

Now using eq. 25 and substituting the given values, we find

$$\frac{C_s - C_x}{C_s - C_0} = \text{erf}\left(\frac{x}{2\sqrt{Dt}}\right)$$

or
$$\frac{1.0 - 0.30}{1.0 - 0.18} = \mathrm{erf}\left(\frac{6 \times 10^{-4}}{2\sqrt{1.28 \times 10^{-11}(t)}}\right)$$

or
$$\mathrm{erf}\left(\frac{83.85}{\sqrt{t}}\right) = \frac{0.70}{0.82} = 0.8536.$$

Here, $Z = \dfrac{83.85}{\sqrt{t}}$ and erf $Z = 0.8536$. From Table 6.1 the value of $Z$ can be found by interpolation:

| erf $Z$ | $Z$ | |
|---------|-----|---|
| 0.8427 | 1.0 | $\dfrac{X - 1.0}{1.1 - 1.0} = \dfrac{0.8536 - 0.8427}{0.8802 - 0.8427} = \dfrac{0.0106}{0.0375}$ |
| 0.8536 | $X$ | |
| 0.8802 | 1.1 | $= 0.283$ |

$$\text{or } X = Z = 1.028.$$

Since, $Z = \dfrac{83.85}{\sqrt{t}} = 1.028$   or   $t = 6653 \text{ s} = 110 \text{ m}.$

*Example:* A gear made of 1020 steel (0.20 wt.% C) is to be gas carburized at 927°C. Calculate the carbon content at 0.060 inch below the surface of the gear after a 10h carburizing time. Assume the carbon content at the surface is 1.20 wt.%. $D$ ($C$ in $\gamma$ iron) at 927°C $= 1.28 \times 10^{-11}$ m²/s.

*Solution:* Given:   $C_0 = 0.20\%$, $C_s = 1.2\%$, $t = 10\text{h} = 36 \times 10^3\text{s}$

$$x = 0.060 \text{ inch} = 0.060 \times 25.4 = 1.524 \text{ mm}$$

Also        $D_{927°C} = 1.28 \times 10^{-11}$ m,²/s, $C_x = ?$

Again using eq. 25 and substituting different values, we find

$$\frac{1.20 - C_x}{1.20 - 0.20} = \mathrm{erf}\left(\frac{1.524 \times 10^3}{2\sqrt{1.28 \times 10^{-11} \times 36 \times 10^3}}\right)$$

or                $1.20 - C_x = \mathrm{erf}\,(1.1225).$

Here, $Z = 1.1225$. Let us find the erf of this value by interpolation:

| erf $Z$ | $Z$ | |
|---------|-----|---|
| 0.8802 | 1.1 | $\dfrac{X - 0.8802}{0.9103 - 0.8802} = \dfrac{1.1125 - 1.1}{1.2 - 1.1}$ |
| $X$ | 1.1125 | |
| 0.9103 | 1.2 | or $\dfrac{X - 0.8802}{0.0301} = \dfrac{0.0025}{0.10} = 0.025$ |

or   $X = 0.8809$

Therefore, $1.20 - C_x = $ erf $(1.1225) \times 0.8809$

or                $C_x = 1.20 - 0.8809 = 0.32\%$

The opposite of carburizing is the decarburizing process. In this case, carbon is lost in the form of CO or $CO_2$ from surface layers of the steel due to an oxidizing atmosphere. This makes the surface layer soft and ductile which in turn lowers the fatigue strength of the material. Therefore, during the carburizing process a protective atmosphere should be used. In case, the carburizing process is undertaken in a non-protective atmosphere (e.g. air), the extent (depth) of decarburization can be estimated from the diffusion equation so that the decarburized layers could be removed by proper machining.

Referring to Fig. 6.8b, the decarburizing atmosphere is equivalent to a lower carbon content at the steel surface, as compared to and initial carbon concentration $C_2$ ($\neq C_0$) of the steel.

Here,                $c\,(x, 0) = C_2$       $x < 0$

$$c\,(0, t) = C_s$$

Now from eq. 24, we have $A = C_s$ and $B = C_2 - C_s$. Alternatively an equation similar to the eq. 25 can used

$$\frac{C_s - C_x}{C_2 - C_s} = \text{erf}\left(\frac{x}{2\sqrt{Dt}}\right) \tag{36}$$

Thus, knowing the values of $D$, $C_s$ and $C_2$, the depth and the degree of decarburization as a function of heat treating time $t$ can be determined.

*Example*: At 927°C, a 1.2% carbon steel is getting decarburized for a duration of 5 hours in an atmosphere equivalent to 0% carbon at the surface of the steel. Determine the minimum depth upto which post machining is to be done, if the carbon content at the surface after machining should not be below 0.8%. $D$ ($C$ in $\gamma$ iron) at 927°C $= 1.28 \times 10^{-11}$ m²/s.

*Solution:* Given:   $C_2 = 1.2\%$, $C_x = 0.8\%$, $C_s = 0\%$

$$x = ?,\, t = 5h = 5 \times 3600 = 18000\text{s}.$$

Also        $D_{927°C} = 1.28 \times 10^{-11}$ m²/s.

Now, using eq. 36 and substituting the given values, we find

$$\frac{C_s - C_x}{C_2 - C_s} = \text{erf}\left(\frac{x}{2\sqrt{Dt}}\right)$$

or        $$\frac{0.0 - 0.80}{1.2 - 0.00} = \text{erf}\left(\frac{x}{2\sqrt{1.28 \times 10^{-11} \times 18 \times 10^3}}\right)$$

or        $$\text{erf}\left(\frac{x}{9.6 \times 10^{-4}}\right) = -\frac{0.80}{1.20} = -0.6666.$$

Here, $Z = \dfrac{x}{9.6 \times 10^{-4}}$ and erf $Z = 0.6666$. From Table 6.1, the value of $Z$ can be found by interpolation:

| ert $Z$ | $Z$ |
|---------|-----|
| 0.6420  | 0.65 |
| 0.6666  | $X$ |
| 0.6778  | 0.70 |

$$\frac{X - 0.65}{0.70 - 0.65} = \frac{0.6666 - 0.6420}{0.6778 - 0.6420}$$

or $\dfrac{X - 0.65}{0.65} = \dfrac{0.0246}{0.0358} = 0.687$

or $X = Z = 0.6843$.

Therefore, $Z = \dfrac{x}{9.6 \times 10^{-4}} = -0.6843$

or $\quad x = 6.57 \times 10^{-4}$ m.

Thus, the depth upto which machining is required is 0.66 mm.

### Preparation of Semiconductors

Semiconductor devices are prepared by first growing a pure semiconductor crystal by zone-refining process and then a known quantity of impurity atoms called dopants (e.g. As or Sb for *p*-type; In, Ga or Al for *n*-type) are allowed to diffuse into the crystal by a process known as "doping". The depth of penetration and the amount of dopant can be determined following the same procedure as above.

*Example:* If boron is diffused into a thick slice of silicon with no previous boron in it at a temperature of 1100°C for 2 hours. What is the depth below the surface at which the concentration is $10^{17}$ atoms/cm$^3$ if the surface concentration is $10^{18}$ atoms/cm$^3$? $D$ (boron into silicon) = $4 \times 10^{-13}$ cm$^2$/s at 1100°C.

*Solution:* Given: $C_0 = 0$, $C_x = 10^{17}$, $C_s = 10^{18}$, $T = 1373$K

$$t = 2\text{h} = 7200\text{s}, \ x = \ ?$$

Also $\qquad\qquad D_{1100°C} = 4 \times 10^{-13}$ cm$^2$/s.

Now, using eq. 25 and substituting the given values, we find

$$\frac{C_s - C_x}{C_s - C_0} = \text{erf}\left(\frac{x}{2\sqrt{Dt}}\right)$$

or

$$\frac{10^{18} - 10^{17}}{10^{18}} = \text{erf}\left(\frac{x}{2\sqrt{4 \times 10^{-13} \times 7200}}\right)$$

or

$$\text{erf}\left(\frac{x}{2\sqrt{10.73 \times 10^{-5}}}\right) = 0.9.$$

Here, $Z = \dfrac{x}{10.73 \times 10^{-5}}$ and erf $Z = 0.9$.

Now, making use of Table 6.1, let us find out the value of $Z$ by interpolation:

| erf $Z$ | $Z$ |
|---------|-----|
| 0.8802 | 1.1 |
| 0.9000 | $X$ |
| 0.9103 | 1.2 |

$$\frac{X - 1.1}{1.2 - 1.1} = \frac{0.9000 - 0.8802}{0.9103 - 0.8802}$$

or $X = Z = 1.658$.

Therefore, $\qquad 1.658 = \dfrac{x}{10.73 \times 10^{-5}}$

or $\qquad\qquad x = 1.24 \times 10^{-4}$ cm.

## 6.6  DIFFUSION MECHANISMS

Meterial may be transported by diffusive motion along surfaces, grain boundaries and through the volume of a solid. The fundamental mechanism by which atoms move through the crystals depends on crystal structure, atomic sizes, and the extent of defect in the crystals.

There are several mechanisms by which are diffusion of atoms in solids might occur. Fig. 6.9 shows some of the possiblities of volume (bulk) diffusion in a single crystal. Since these mechanisms are geometrically possible, they must all occur simultaneously to some extent. However, their relative importance will depend on the nature of the system as well as on the temperature. Detailed theoretical calculations of the energy required for tomic diffusion by above mechanisms show that the diffusion by vacancy motion is predominant in pure metal and substitutional alloys. However, for some alloys, it is the interstitial diffusion which predominates.

### Interstitial Diffusion

An interstitial atom, whether it is an impurity atom or a displaced atom of the host crystal, can jump into an adjacent interstitial site as shown in Fig. 6.9a. Successive jumps of this kind result in atomic motion over many atomic distances. Interstitial diffusion rates are often orders of magnitude greater than those for other bulk mechanisms, especially for small diffusing atoms and open lattices. Thus interstitial diffusion is strongly affected by size considerations. This not only limits the size of the interstitial atoms, but also the jump probability because of the hinderance caused by the atoms at the "neck" between interstitial sites.

### Dissociative Diffusion

A slight variation in interstitial diffusion mechanism, shown in Fig. 6.9b, is often called "dissociative diffusion". In this case, the foreign atoms present in normal substitutional lattice sites migrate via interstitial sites. Certain impurity systems, such as copper in germanium, show this behaviour; the copper can occupy both normal lattice sites and interstitial positions with an equilibrium governing the distribution between the two kinds of sites. Even if the concentration of interstitials present are less, they dominate the diffusion because of their much greater diffusion rates.

### Vacancy Diffusion

In thermal equilibrium, any crystal above absolute zero contains a certain number of vacant lattice sites. These vacancies provide an easy path for diffusion. An atom occupying a normal lattice site adjacent to a vacancy can jump into the vacant site and thus effectively interchanging positions with it. Successive jumps of this kind result in motion of the vacancy over large distances, and this will result in a net motion of the atoms in the direction opposite to the vacancy motion (Fig. 6.9c).

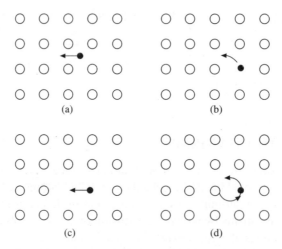

**Fig. 6.9 Atomic mechanism of diffusion in solids**

Both impurity and host atoms can diffuse by this mechanism. In the case of impurities, jumps are possible only when the vacancy is adjacent to the site of an impurity atom. The probability for jumps to occur may be different for the impurity and for the host atoms, because of the differences in their binding forces: hence their diffusivities will in general be different.

Diffusion rates for both interstitial and vacancy mechanisms depend directly on their concentrations. As we discussed in ch. 5 that a finite concentration of vacancy is always present in a real crystal at thermal equilibrium. However, excess concentrations can often be produced either by impurity additions or by sudden reduction of temperature of the growing crystal.

### Ring Diffusion

Diffusion mechanisms also include another broad class, involving atomic rotations (Fig. 6.9d). The cooperative motion of two (or more) atoms can result in a net diffusive motion, as the atoms simultaneously interchange their positions. No lattice defects are necessary or involved in this kind of motion. When the atoms are alike or reasonably simlar chemically, as in metals or alloys, a simple exchange (2 atom ring) is possible because the resulting structure is energetically as likely as the structure before the exchange. This is true for diffusion of either an impurity or host atom in these solids. In an ionic solid, however, there are clearly restrictions on such motions, as a cartion and an anion cannot exchange positions. This limitation greately reduces the possibilities of diffusion in ionic solods by this mechanism, since the only permissible rotation left is the cooperative motion of serveral ions.

In addition to the volume diffusion in single crystals, other diffusions along surfaces, grain boundaries, pores, cracks, dislocations etc. are also found to occur in solids. The concentration of surface atoms relative to the bulk is usually small enough so that only small quantities of material can generally be transported along the surface, although surface diffusivities may be high. In polycrystalline solids, grain boundary effects alomost certainly predominate in most diffusions. However, these are amenable neither to satisfactory theoretical treatment, nor to quantitative experimental study. Pores and cracks are even more difficult to deal with. Dislocations, normally present in most single crystals, may affect experimental diffusion studies by providing sinks or sources for vacancies. Fig. 6.10 gives a comparison of self diffusion in silver by various diffusion mechanisms.

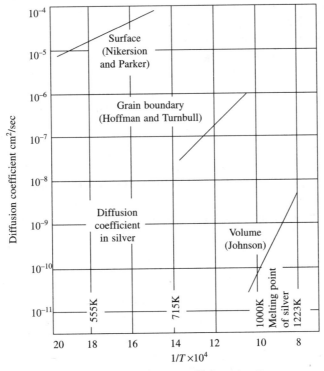

**Fig. 6.10  Diffusion coefficients in silver**

The interstitial and vacancy diffusion are more important than others in crystals and hence we shall consider them in some detail.

The unit jump in interstitial diffusion is the diffusion of an atom from one interstitial site to a neighbouring site. Interstitial diffusion and corresponding potential energy curve as a function of position in shown in Fig. 6.11. The points $a$ and $b$ represent the equilibrium interstitial sites and correspond to energy minima. While the point $c$ lying midway between the equilibrium sites represents energy maxima. The potential barrier $E_m$ (or $\Delta H_m$, called the enthalpy of motion) is mainly elastic strain energy arising when the interstitial atom squeezes through the narrow space between the host atoms. In order to diffuse, an atom must surmount the potential energy barrier presented by its neighbours. Let us consider the diffusion of impurity atoms through interstitial sites: identical results apply to the diffusion of vacacies. For many alloys, the potential barrier is about 1 eV, while the average thermal energy of an atom at reasonable temperatures is only about 0.1 eV. We know that an atom vibrates (oscillates) around its equilibrium position with a characteristic frequency, $v$, but usually its energy is far too small to allow it to jump through the potential barrier. However, during a fraction of time equal to the Boltzmann factor $\exp(-E_m/kT)$ [or $\exp(-\Delta H_m/RT)$], the atom has energy equal to the height of the potential barrier, when it is able to make necessary jump. Since $v$ is the frequency of oscillation, therefore the atom strikes the potential barrier $v$ times per second. The probability that sometime during one second the atom will have energy equal to the height of the potential barrier $E_m$ (or $\Delta H_m$) and crosses over it. Such a probaility is given by

$$p = v \exp\left(-\frac{E_m}{kT}\right) = v \exp\left(-\frac{\Delta H_m}{RT}\right) \quad (37)$$

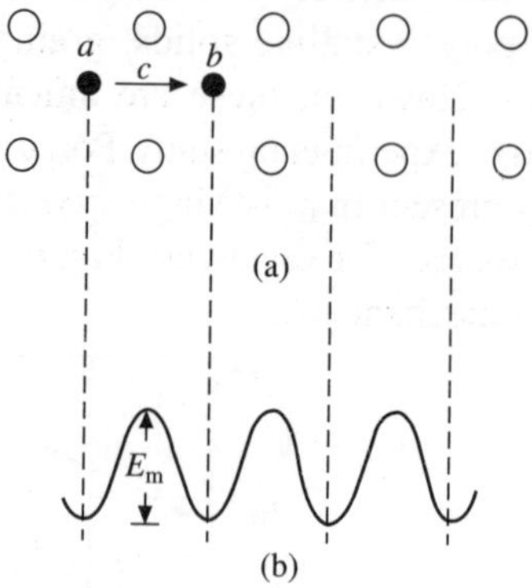

**Fig. 6.11   Interstitial diffusion and corresponding potential energy curve as a function of position**

On the other hand, the probability of escape on each trial is given by $\exp E_m/kT$ [or $\exp(-\Delta H_m/RT)$]. Thus, $p$ is the number of successful jumps per unit time, called the jump frequency and is related to the diffusion coefficient $D$. A simplified view of this relationship is as follows:

Let us consider a single jump of an atom to a vacant site. The jump distance in this case is $a$, the atomic diameter. Due to jump, the concentration changes (in a volume $a^3$) from unity to zero over the jump distance. Thus, the concentration gradient can be approximated as

$$\frac{dc}{dx} \simeq \frac{(-1/a^3)}{a} = -\frac{1}{4^4} \quad (38)$$

where concentration is expressed as number of atoms per unit volume. During an individual jump the flow is across a cross-sectional plane of area $a^2$ and therefore the flux $J$ is equal to $p/a^2$. From Fick's first law, the diffusion coefficient $D$ is given by

$$D = \frac{J}{(-dc/dx)} = \frac{P}{a^2} a^4 = p a^2 \quad (39)$$

Since the probability that a given site is vacant is given as $\exp(-E_v/kT)$ [or $\exp(-\Delta H_f/RT)$] it follows that the jump frequency of the diffusing atom is

$$p = v \exp\left(-\frac{E_v}{kT}\right) \cdot \exp\left(-\frac{E_m}{kT}\right)$$

$$= v \exp\left(-\frac{E_v + E_m}{kT}\right) = v \exp\left(-\frac{\Delta H_m + \Delta H_f}{RT}\right) \quad (40)$$

From eqs. 39 and 40, we obtain

$$D = v a^2 \exp\left(-\frac{E_v + E_m}{kT}\right) = v a^2 \exp\left(-\frac{\Delta H_m + \Delta H_f}{RT}\right) \quad (41)$$

Equations 32 and 41 have the same form with $D_0 = va^2$ and $Q = E_v + E_m = \Delta H_m + \Delta H_f$.

## 6.7 RANDOM WALK TREATMENT OF DIFFUSION

In the preceding section, we considered the possible diffusion mechanisms of atoms. Now, we shall relate the number of random jumps (i.e. the jumps may be forward, backward, up or down) made by an atom during diffusion to the effective distance travelled from the starting point. Since each jump is equal to the interatomic distance and the crystalline lattice is highly symmetrical, such a calculation should not be difficult. For simplicity, let us consider one dimensional motion only. The net distance travelled by the atom will be given by

$$X = d_1 + d_2 + d_3 + \ldots + d_n = \sum_{i=1}^{n} d_i$$

where $d_1, d_2, d_3, \ldots d_n$ are the first, second, third and $n$th jumps, respectively. Because the atomic jumps are completely random, the forward and backward jumps are equally probable and hence the average value of $X$ for a large number of such jumps is zero. However, it can be shown that the root mean square of the average has a non-zero value. Thus, we have

$$X^2 = (d_1 + d_2 + d_3 + \ldots + d_n) \cdot (d_1 + d_2 + d_3 + \ldots + d_n)$$

$$= d_1^2 + d_2^2 + d_3^2 + \ldots + d_n^2 + 2d_1d_2 + 2d_1d_3 + \ldots + 2d_1d_n + 2d_2d_3 + \ldots + 2d_{n-1}d_n$$

Now, each square term in the above equation is equal to $d^2$, since $|d_1| = |d_2| = \ldots = |d_n| = d$. Also, all the other terms like $2d_1d_2, 2d_2d_3, \ldots . 2d_{n-1}d_n$ are equal to zero, since each of the $d_1, d_2, \ldots d_n$ jumps are equally probable in both forward and backward directions.

Therefore,

$$X^2 = d_1^2 + d_2^2 + d_3^2 + \ldots + d_n^2$$

$$= nd^2$$

where $n$ is the number of jumps. If $v_0$ is the frequency of jumping and $t$ is the time for a jump, then $n = v_0 t$. If a one dimensional diffusion coefficient ($D$) is defined as

$$D = \frac{v_0 d^2}{2}$$

then

$$\sqrt{\overline{R^2}} = \sqrt{\overline{X^2}} = \sqrt{2Dt} = \sqrt{v_0 d^2 t}$$

In a crystal (e.g. for a cubic system), there are three mutually perpendicular directions available for jumping, therefore, the root mean square displacement will be given by

$$\sqrt{\overline{R^2}} = \sqrt{\overline{X^2} + \overline{Y^2} + \overline{Z^2}}$$

But for such a system,     $\overline{X^2} = \overline{Y^2} = \overline{Z^2}$

Therefore,     $\sqrt{\overline{X^2}} = \sqrt{\overline{R^2}/3} = \sqrt{v_0 d^2 t/3}$

Finally, the three dimensional diffusion coefficient will be

$$D = \frac{v_0 d^2}{6}$$

## 6.8   THE KIRKENDALL EFFECT

In binary substitutional alloys, the rates of diffusion of the two species of atoms are normally unequal (usually, the lower melting point species diffuse much faster than the other). This will not be possible if the atoms of the two species interdiffuse simply by exchanging places. Such interdiffusion can, however, be possible only through vacancy diffusion. Consider a two component alloy *A-B* in which vacancy diffusion occurs. It may well be understood that one species of atom (say *B* in the present case) changes place with a vacancy more easily than the other (because of a difference in energy barrier height), therefore the *B* atoms will diffuse more rapidly than the *A* atoms plus vacancy in the reverse direction, where vacancy flow is compensating for the slowness of the *A* flow.

The phenomenon of unequal diffusion in binary alloy was first observed by Kirkendall and hence is known as Kirkendall effect. This can be experimentally demonstrated by placing some inert (say Molybdenum) markers (of high melting point substance which is insoluble in diffusion matrix) at the interface of copper and brass (Cu-Zn) diffusion couple, prior to the diffusion anneal. As the copper and zinc interdiffuse across the interface during the anneal, these markers are found to shift in the direction of slower moving species as schematically shown in Fig. 6.12.

The displacement of the markers is larger than can be accounted for by the change in lattice parameters. More atoms have left the brass than have entered into it because the zinc atoms move faster than the copper. As a result, porosity or voids are left on the more rapidly diffusing component side (lower melting point side), indicating that the bulk flow does not fully compensate for the difference in diffusivities of the two species. For example in a system with 50/50 Au-Ag, the porosity is exceptionally large. The porosity zone moves as the diffusion proceeds, so as always to occur at a particular composition. It consists of larger or smaller holes, which are presumably formed by the condensation of excess vacancies.

Occurrence of Kirkendall effect, porosity, elastic and plastic strains etc. invalidates the applicability of the simple kinetic theory of chemical diffusion presented earlier in section 6.2. Also the thermodynamic treatment of section 6.1 breaks down, since no equilibrium exists with respect to the vacancy concentration. Measured diffusion curves in alloys rarely have the perfect symmetrical form as shown in Fig. 6.6. Thus, in a binary *A – B* alloy, we must give each component its own diffusion coefficients,

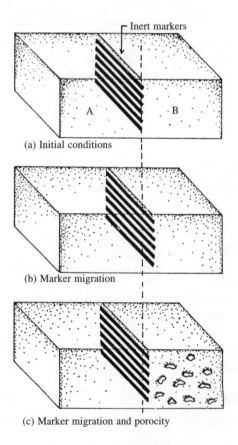

(a) Initial conditions

(b) Marker migration

(c) Marker migration and porocity

**Fig. 6.12   The Kirkendall effect**

e.g. $D_A$ and $D_B$. The Kirkendall effect occurs when $D_A \neq D_B$. If no porosity is generated by unequal migration, an overall chemical diffusion coefficient $D$ can be defined by the equation,

$$D = c_B D_A + c_A D_B \qquad (42)$$

as has been shown by Darken (1948), where $c_A$ and $c_B$ are the respective atomic concentrations.

## 6.9  DIFFUSION IN ALKALI HALIDES

We know that the diffusion of atoms (or ions) is impossible in a perfect crystal (because they do not have any vacant place to go) while it easily occurs in crystals containing imperfections. The presence of Schottky vacancies is a very common phenomenon in alkali halides particularly at high temperatures at which these imperfections are expected to be mobile. Thus, both the formation and mobility of crystal imperfections are important process in diffusive motion of atoms in crystalline solids.

Mapother, Crooks and Maurer made some measurements on diffusion in ionic crystals. They measured the self-diffusion of radioactive sodium in NaCl and NaBr crystals. For this purpose, they deposited a thin layer of about $5 \times 10^{-4}$ cm of radioactive salt containing $Na^{24}$ isotope on one face of a cubic crystal, approximately 1 cm on edge. The crystal was then held at a constant temperature for a certain length of time. After this diffusion anneal, the distribution of radioactive sodium was determined by means of a sectioning technique, employing a microtome. In a similar manner, Schamp investigated the diffusion of bromine in NaBr.

In order to understand the actual mechanism of diffusion in alkali halide crystals, let us consider a sodium chloride structure. For simplicity, assume the diffusion of radioactive sodium to be along the $x$-axis coinciding with one of the cube edges. Let there be a positive ion vacancy at the centre as indicated by square in Fig. 6.13. This vacancy may jump to any of the 12 surrounding positive ion sites lying at a distance $a\sqrt{2}$. Out of these possible jumps, four lie in the positive $x$-direction, four in the negative $x$-direction, and the remaining four in its own plane. If $p$ is the probability per second for the vacancy to make any jump, then $p/3$ will be the probability per second for a displacement $+a$, $-a$, and $0$, respectively, where $a$ is the shortest inter-ionic distance. In Fig. 6.13, let $N_R^*$ represents the number of radioactive +ve ions crossing 1 cm$^2$ of the plane

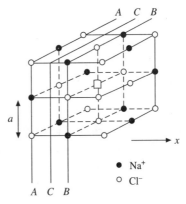

**Fig. 6.13**  **Positive ion vacancy in a NaCl structure. Planes $A$, $B$ and $C$ are perpendicular to the x-axis along which diffusion takes place**

$C$ by going from the plane $A$ to $B$ (moving towards right), while $N_L^*$ represents the same number crossing the plane $C$ from $B$ to $A$ (moving towards left). Further, if $N$ is the density of positive ions per cm$^3$, $n$ is the density of vacancies, and $n^*$ is the density of radioactive +ve ions, then we have

$$N_R^* = \frac{1}{2a^2} \frac{n}{N} \frac{p}{3} \frac{n^*}{N},$$

and

$$N_L^* = \frac{1}{2a^2} \frac{n}{N} \frac{p}{3} \frac{1}{N} \left( n^* + \frac{dn^*}{dx} a \right) \tag{43}$$

where $1/2a^2$ is the total number of positive lattice sites per cm$^2$ on plane $A$ or $B$, $n/N$ is the probability that such a site is vacant, and $n^*/N$ is the probability that a +ve ion in plane $A$ is radioactive. Consequently, the net number of radioactive +ve ions in passing through 1 cm$^2$ of plane $C$ per second from left to right is

$$J = N_R^* - N_L^* = -\frac{np}{6N^2 a} \cdot \frac{dn^*}{dx} \tag{44}$$

However, from Fick's first law, we known that the net flux is proportional to the concentration gradient, i.e.

$$J = -D \frac{dn^*}{dx} \tag{45}$$

Comparing equations 44 and 45 and taking into account that $N = 1/2a^3$, one can easily obtain the self-diffusion coefficient associated with the migration of single +ve ion vacancies,

$$D = \frac{1}{3} a^2 \frac{n}{N} p \tag{46}$$

As expected, the self-diffusion coefficient is proportional to the number of vacancies per unit volume $n$ and to the jump probability of a vacancy per second $p$. If we write eq. 40, in the form

$$p = v \exp \left( -\frac{\varepsilon_j}{kT} \right) \tag{47}$$

where $v$ is the frequency and $\varepsilon_j$ is the activation energy associated with a jump. Also recalling the expression of vacancy concentration $(n/N)$ as obtained in eq. 22 of ch. 5 for alkali halide crystals

$$\frac{n}{N} = C \exp \left( -\frac{\phi}{2kT} \right) \tag{48}$$

where $C = (v/v')^{3x}$ arises due to thermal entropy change associated with the production of vacancies. Now from eqs. 46, 47 and 48, we have

$$D = \frac{1}{3} Cva^2 \exp \left( -\frac{\phi}{2kT} \right) \cdot \exp \left( -\frac{\varepsilon_j}{kT} \right)$$

or

$$D = \frac{1}{3} Cva^2 \exp \left( -\frac{(\varepsilon_j + \phi/2)}{kT} \right) \tag{49}$$

A curve between $\ln D$ versus $1/T$ according to eq. 49, gives a straight line (Fig. 6.14), the slope of which is determined from the sum of energies $(\varepsilon_j + \phi/2)$, i.e. the energy required for the formation of vacancy plus the activation energy for its jumping. The diffusion measurements of radioactive sodium in NaCl show that the slope in the high temperature region $(\varepsilon_j + \phi/2)$ = 1.80 eV (41.6 kcal/mole).

A break in the ln$D$ versus $1/T$ curve (Fig. 6.14) may in principle be observed as a result of either or both of the following two reasons: (i) the presence of divalent positive impurities, (ii) the freezing in of vacancies. These can be understood as follows: Let us suppose that NaCl contains a small amount of divalent impurities such as Sr, Ba or Ca which occupy sites normally occupied by Na$^+$ ions. The condition of electrical neutrality then requires that for each divalent positive ion present, there must be a positive ion vacancy. Such crystals at low temperatures will contain more positive ion vacancy than is expected on the basis of thermal equilibrium alone. In fact below a critical temperature, the number of vacancies per unit volume remains constant and is approximately equal to the density of divalent metal ions (thermally produced vacancies is supposed to be negligible). Since the number of vacancies present in the low temperature region is independent of temperature and is determined only by impurity concentration, only the activation energy for diffusive jump $\varepsilon_j$ is to be included in the temperature dependence of diffusion coefficient (i.e. according to eqs. 46 and 47). Thus, if the presence of divalent metallic ions is accepted as the cause of the break in

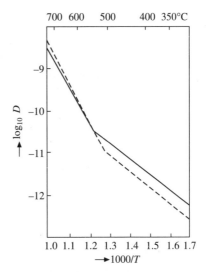

**Fig. 6.14** **Self-diffusion coefficient of Na in NaCl crystal as a function of temperature. Fully drawn and dashed curves represent the experimental and theoretical curves, respectively**

the ln$D$ versus $1/T$ curve, the activation energy for jumping $\varepsilon_j = 0.77$ eV (17.7 kcal/mole) in the low temperature region is to be considered. However, at high temperature, the number of thermally produced vacancies predominate over the number required by the presence of the divalent ions and the crystal will behave in a normal fashion. From the slope of the high temperature region of the curve $(\varepsilon_j + \phi/2) = 1.80$ eV (41.6 kcal/mole), while the experimental value of $\phi$ is found to be 2.06 eV (47.5 kcal/mole). Experimental value of 1.80 eV is in close agreement with the theoretical value of 1.86 eV given by Mott and Littleton.

The other hypothesis is based on the following reasonings: suppose a crystal contains a certain number of lattice defects in thermal equilibrium at high temperatures. If the temperature is suddenly lowered, it will take a certain amount of time to establish new equilibrium, because this requires migration of vacancies. At low temperatures, such time intervals may be very long and consequently, the crystal may contain many more defects than permitted by the equilibrium conditions. Because of the strong experimental evidence, the presence of divalent positive impurities is generally favoured over the freezing-in hypothesis.

Now comparing the theoretical and experimental values of pre-exponential factor appearing in eq. 49, we have

$$D_0 = \frac{1}{3} C v a^2 \simeq 1 \, \text{cm}^2 / \text{sec}$$

where $v \simeq 10^{13}$ per sec., $a \simeq 3 \times 10^{-8}$ cm and $C \simeq 100$, while the experimental value of $D_0$ according to Mapother, Crooks and Maurer is 3.1 cm²/sec. This discrepancy suggests that the diffusion of positive ions in NaCl does not necessarily take place as a result of migration of single positive ion vacancies only. Consequently, at least two other possible diffusion mechanisms must be considered in alkali halides: (i) Diffusion resulting from migration of pairs, and (ii) Diffusion resulting from migration of divalent positive impurities together with associated vacancies.

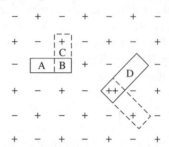

**Fig. 6.15  Possible diffusion mechanisms in alkali halide crystals**

These two mechanisms are illustrated in Fig. 6.15. A pair of vacancies may diffuse as a result of positive or negative ions jumping into the corresponding vacant site of the pair. The resulting diffusion expression is given by

$$D_{\text{pair}} = \text{Const. exp } (\phi - \varepsilon_p + \varepsilon_{jp}) \tag{50}$$

where $\phi$ is the energy required to produce ion pair vacancy, $\varepsilon_p$ is the binding energy of ion pair vacancy, and $\varepsilon_{jp}$ is the activation energy for the jumping of a pair. Theoretical values estimated by Dienes and by Mott and Gurney give $\varepsilon_p \simeq 1$ eV and $\varepsilon_{jp} \simeq 0.4$ eV for NaCl. On the basis of this, it is expected that the ion pair will diffuse much faster because their activation energy for jumping is about half the value for a single positive ion vacancy. That this must be so, may be seen qualitatively because the jumping ions are allowed more free space in former case.

The second mechanism may be understood as follows: As we know that for each divalent positive ion present, there must be a positive ion vacancy to satisfy the neutrality condition. Only a fraction of these vacancies are free and contribute to the diffusion as discussed above, most of these are being attracted by the divalent +ve ions as a result of Coulomb interaction. Thus, there will be a certain number of associated complexes, consisting of a divalent positive ion and a neighbouring vacant positive ion site. This unit may migrate through the crystal as a result of other positive ions jumping into the vacancy and as a result of possible jumps of the divalent ion into the vacancy.

Although we have limited our discussion to the diffusion in ionic crystal only, however, the same general idea may be applied to other cases. For further details refer the book of Jost.

## 6.10  IONIC CONDUCTIVITY IN ALKALI HALIDE CRYSTAL

Consider the presence of Schottky imperfection in an alkali halide crystal at high temperature, where both anion and cation vacancies are mobile. Since their motion is radom no current flows in the crystal. Whne an electric field is applied between two faces of an ionic crystal, the imperfections drift in a direction dictated by the applied field and the effective charge on the vacancies. As a result of this, an electric current may be detected. For alkali halide, these currents are too large to be explained in terms of free electrons only because the number of such electrons in the conduction band for the temperatures involved is usually much smaller. Thus, the current must be as a result of the migration of ions under the influence of the electric field, similar to the electrolytic conduction of aqueous solutions of salts. The nature of current is found to be ionic, which is indicated by the fact that decomposition occurs at the electrondes.

The problem reduces to determine the constituent which carries the current. Although the actual experiments are usually more involved, this question may be answered with the help of a simple experimental arrangement such as indicated in Fig. 6.16. Two slabs of salt $M^+X^-$ are pressed together between two electrodes of the metal M. For the polarity as indicated, the two following extreme possibilities exist:

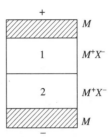

**Fig. 6.16  The simple experimental arrangement for measuring transport numbers**

(i)  Only positive ions move; in that case the cathode will grow at the expense of anode, the thickness of two salt slabs remaining the same.

(ii)  Only the negative ions move; the $X^-$ ions are then neutralized at the anode and form new layers of salts. Hence the anode decreases in thickness, the cathode increases. Further, slab 1 will grow at the expense of slab 2.

If both types of ions contribute to the current, the result will be intermediate between (i) and (ii). By knowing the relative contribution of the ionic current by the positive and negative ions, their amount can be determined.

The ionic conductivity of the isotropic crystal is defined by the scalar equation,

$$I = \sigma E \tag{51}$$

where $I$ is the current density, $E$ the electric field strength, and $\sigma$ the conductivity. If the conductivity of positive ions alone is $\sigma_+$, the transport number of these ions can be defined by

$$t_+ = \frac{\sigma_+}{\sigma} \tag{52}$$

Similarly,

$$t_- = \frac{\sigma_-}{\sigma} \tag{53}$$

so that,

$$t_+ + t_- = 1 \tag{54}$$

In alkali halides, the experimental observations show that the positive ions are much more mobile than the negative ions. For very pure KCl crystal, Kerkhoff found $t_+ = 0.88$ at 525°C and $t_+ = 0.70$ at 600°C.

Like diffusion in alkali halides, ionic conductivity is also explained in terms of migration of vacancy. The positive ion vacancies have an effective – ve charge and will therefore move towards the anode. Similarly, the negaive ion vacancies will move towards the cathode. Further, as mentioned above that the mobility of positive ion vacancies is much more than the negative ions and therefore let us assume that the conductivity is entirely due to the motion of positive ion vacancies. Now consider the sodium chloride structure (Fig. 6.13) and assume that the electric field is acting along the $x$-axis. Further, $N$ be the density of positive ions per $cm^3$ and $n$ the density of positive ion vacancies per cm$^3$. If the field in Fig. 6.13 is directed towards right (along + ve $x$-direction), a positive ion vacancy will jump with a higher probability to the left than to the right, because it has an effective –ve charge.

The potential energy along the line of motion may therefore be represented by the solid curve, which is the resultant of the dashed field free curve and the linear external field (Fig. 6.17). Then the probabilities per second for a jump to the left and to the right are, respectively,

$$p_L = \frac{1}{3} v \exp\left(-(\varepsilon_j - \frac{1}{2} aeE)/kT\right)$$

$$p_R = \frac{1}{3} v \exp\left(-(\varepsilon_j - \frac{1}{2} aeE)/kT\right) \quad (55)$$

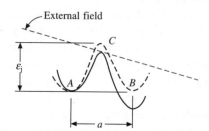

**Fig. 6.17  Field free potential energy curve, linear external field and the resultant potential energy curve. A, B, and C may be associated with positions of a positive ion in the planes A, B, C, of Fig. 6.13**

where $v$ and $\varepsilon_j$ have the same meaning as in the preceding section; $e$ is the effective charge due to missing ions and $E$ the effective field strength. The current density, ie. the net flux of charge passing per second through 1 cm$^3$ is then equal to

$$I = \frac{1}{2a^2} \frac{n}{N} (p_L - p_R)e \quad (56)$$

where $1/2a^2$ is the number of positive ion sites per cm$^2$ on plane $A$ or $B$ (perpendicular to $x$), and $n/N$ is the probability that such a site is vacant. Now, for nearly all practical cases, $aeE \ll kT$, so that the first approximation

$$I = \frac{n}{N} \frac{e^2 vE}{6\,akT} \exp\left(-\frac{\varepsilon_j}{kT}\right) = \sigma E \quad (57)$$

Substituting the value of $n/N$ from eq. 48, the conductivity becomes

$$\sigma = \frac{Ce^2 v}{6\,akT} \exp\left(-\frac{(\varepsilon_j + \phi/2)}{kT}\right) \quad (58)$$

It is to be noted that the current density is proportional to $E$ as long as $aeE \ll kT$, i.e. Ohms law is valid only under this particular condition. For very high electric field, $aeE$, is not small compared to $kT$ and the current increases exponentially with field strength.

## 6.11  DIFFUSION AND IONIC CONDUCTIVITY

According to eq. 50, the conductivity associated with the positive ion vacancies depends on two activation energies $\varepsilon_j$ and $\phi$, as does the coefficient of self-diffusion (eq. 49). In fact, the conductivity $\sigma$ is related to the diffusion coefficient in a simple manner, as was first pointed by Einstein. From eqs. 49 and 58 it follows that

$$\frac{\sigma}{D} = \frac{Ne^2}{kT} \quad (59)$$

It must be kept in mind that the Einstein relation is valid only if the conductivity and self-diffusion are due to the same mechanism. In order to derive this relation, it is assumed that both phenomena are a result of the migration of single positive ion vacancies. In Fig. 6.14 the dashed curve represents the diffusion coefficient calculated from the conductivity measurements by means of eq. 59. Actually the Einstein relation is not very accurate for the interpretation of the diffusion mechanism and therefore some discrepancy arises. This could be understood from the following. In the high temperaure region, theoretically calculated value of diffusion coefficient is slightly larger than the directly measured one. This may be explained as a result of the fact that a small fraction of ionic current is carried by the –ve ion vacancies; these, of course, do not contribute the self-diffusion of Na. In the low temperature region, the calculated diffusion coefficient is somewhat smaller than the directly measured one. This implies that besides the diffusion of positive ion vacancies, the diffusion of some neutral carriers also takes place. These may be either ion pair vacancies or positive divalent ion associated with vacancis. They contribute to the diffusion but not to the ionic conductivity.

## 6.12  SUMMARY

1. The process of diffusion is governed by Fick's first law and second law.
2. Steady state solutions of the diffusion equations are important for analysing the conduction of heat through furance wall, recuperator tubes, gas ducts, etc.
3. Non steady state solutions of the diffusion equations are important for hetrogenous reactions at interfaces between phases, dissolution, precipitation, etc.
4. The diffusion coefficient $D$ can be measured experimentally by placing two dissimilar long bars in intiamte contact to form a diffusion couple, and then measure composition, distance, time and temperature.
5. The diffusion coefficient $D$ of many mateials obeys Arrhenius equation.
6. Atomic diffusion may take place by interstitial diffusion, vacancy diffusion, dissociative diffusion and ring diffusion.
7. The phenomenon of unequal diffusion in binary alloy (i.e. $D_A \neq D_B$) was first observed by Kirkendall and hence is known as Kirkendall effect.
8. Diffusion in alkali halides are supposed to be due to the migration of divalent positive impurities together with associated vacancies.
9. Ionic conductivity in alkali halides, like diffusion is explained in terms of migration of positive ion vacancies.
10. If conductivity and self-diffusion are due to the same mechanism, then they are related through Einstein expression,

$$\frac{\sigma}{D} = \frac{Ne^2}{kT}$$

## 6.13  DEFINITIONS

*Activation energy*: The height of the energy barrier to a reaction which must be surmounted by thermal excitation.

*Arrhenius equation*: An empirically based equation describing the rate of a reaction as a function of temperature and any energy barriers to the reaction.

*Diffusion*: The motion of matter through matter.

*Diffusion coefficient*: The constant of proportionality in both of Fick's laws.
*Diffusion couple*: An assembly of two materials in close contact such that the atoms of one diffuse into another.
*Error function*: A mathematical function found in some solutions of Fick's second law.
*Fick's first law*: The rate of change of composition is proportional to the concentration gradient.
*Fick's second law*: The rate of change of composition is proportional to the second derivative (Laplacian) of the concentration.
*Grain boundary diffusion*: Atomic migration along the grain boundaries.
*Self-diffusion*: The migration of atoms in pure materials.
*Surface diffusion*: Atomic migration along the surface of a plane: for instance, along a solid vapour interface.
*Volume diffusion:* Atomic migration through the bulk of the material.

## REVIEW QUESTIONS AND PROBLEMS

1. Derive Fick's second law (eq. 6) by recognizing that the time rate of composition change in the unit area slab of Fig. 6.2 is equal to the difference between the flux into the slab, $J(x)$, and the flux out of the slab $J(x + \Delta x)$; also that $J(x + \Delta x)$ equals $J(x) + \left(\dfrac{\partial J}{\partial x}\right)\Delta x$.

2. Derive the Fick's second law under the following boundary conditions. If the solid extends to infinity from $x = 0$, the appropriate boundary conditions will be $c = c_1$ at $x = 0$ and all values of time, $c = c_0$ at $t = 0$ for all values of $x$. Also at all values of time, $c = c_0$ at $x = \infty$.

3. Prove that the net flux across a symmetry plane is zero in a three-dimensional medium where $D$ is a constant. [Hint: A symmetry plane is said to exist on the plane $x = 0$ if $c(x, y, z) = c(-x, y, z)$.]

4. Discuss the condition under which a metastable phase could be found in a binary diffusion couple.

5. Determine the ratio of diffusion rate of silver in silicon at 1350°C to that 1100°C in a doping process. The activation energy $Q$ for silver diffusion in silicon is 154 kJ mol$^{-1}$.

    *Ans.* 8.

6. The diffusion rate of $A$ in $B$ was studied at 500°C and 850°C for the same diffusion time. If the activation energy $Q$ for diffusion of $A$ in $B$ is 57.16 kJ mol$^{-1}$. Determine the ratio of depth of penetration $x_1$ and $x_2$ in the two experiments.

    *Ans.* 1 : 4.

7. Amorphous selenium used as a semiconductor material exhibits unusual diffusion characteristics. The following is the set of experimental data for self-diffusion in amorphous selenium. Calculate $D_0$ and $Q$ and comment on your results.

    | $T$, °C | $D$, m$^2$s$^{-1}$ |
    |---|---|
    | 35 | $7.7 \times 10^{-16}$ |
    | 40 | $2.4 \times 10^{-15}$ |
    | 46 | $3.2 \times 10^{-14}$ |
    | 56 | $3.2 \times 10^{-13}$ |

    *Ans.* $D_0 = 10^{27}$ m$^2$s$^{-1}$; $Q = 248$ kJ mol$^{-1}$

8. A diffusion couple of 95% Cu – 5% Zn and pure copper is annealed at 900°C for 50 hr. The Zn concentration at a depth of 2 mm inside the copper bar was found to be 0.3% after the anneal. Determine the diffusion coefficient of zinc in copper.

    *Ans.* $5.0 \times 10^{-12}$ m$^2$s$^{-1}$

9. Compare the diffusivities of hydrogen, nitrogen, and nickel in iron at 300K and explain the difference among the values.

10. Calculate the rate at which a vacancy jumps in copper at 20°C. The activation barrier for the jumps is 100 kJ mol$^{-1}$.

    *Ans.* $1.5 \times 10^{-5}$ s$^{-1}$.

11. How will the diffusivity of NaCl change, when it is doped with KCl, and CaCl$_2$? Explain.

12. At what relative temperatures do surface, grain boundary, and volume diffusion predominate? How do these compare with the temperature at which the respective diffusivities are equal?

13. What is the driving force for self-diffusion?
14. How do you expect inert gases to diffuse through metals?
15. In a short essay with figures describe the use of radioactive tracers in diffusion experiments.
16. Find the grain size of a polycrystalline solid for the same amount of material to be transported through (i) the grain and (ii) the grain boundary at 500°C. Assume that the grains are cube shaped and gain boundaries are 5Å thick.

For lattice diffusion: $D_0 = 0.7 \times 10^{-4}$ m$^2$s$^{-1}$

$Q = 188$ kJ mol$^{-1}$

For grain boundary diffusion: $D_0 = 0.09 \times 10^{-4}$ m$^2$s$^{-1}$

$Q = 90$ kJ mol$^{-1}$                                    *Ans*: 0.54 mm.

17. Make a plot of the activation energy $Q$ for diffusion of different species as a function of the melting point of the species. Comment on your result.
18. Two markers are placed in a couple formed of two semi-infinite regions of $A$ and $B$, one at the initial weld and the other at a short distance away. Show qualitatively how the position of each marker varies with time if $D_A > D_B$. Derive these curves by plotting $N(x)$ and $\delta N/\delta x$ versus $x$ and using the equation

$$U = (D_A - D_B) \, \delta N_A / \delta x.$$

# Chapter 7

# Lattice (Atomic) Vibrations

## 7.1 INTRODUCTION

In chapter 6, we have seen that the atoms in a real crystal are not at rest indefinitely, but they move from one lattice site to another in a discrete jump under the influence of a suitable field gradient. In this chapter, we shall discuss the elastic vibrations of the atoms in a solid under the influence of thermal energy or thermal gradient. We know that the internal energy of a solid increases by heat energy. This is manifested mainly as: (i) the increase in the vibration of atoms (usually called the lattice vibrations) about their mean positions (actual lattice site) and (ii) the increase in the kinetic energy of free electrons.

The thermal energy present as lattice vibrations is looked upon theoretically as a series of superimposed sound waves or strain waves or lattice waves with a frequency spectrum determined by the elastic properties of the crystal. The quantum of energy of an elastic wave is called phonon, in analogy with the photon (which is the quantum of energy of an electromagnetic wave). Almost all concepts such as the wave particle duality, which apply to photons apply equally well to phonons. Like photons, phonons are bosons and are not conserved; they can be either created or destroyed during collisions.

Based on the above discussion, sound wave or elastic wave in crystals are said to be composed of phonons. Therefore, thermal vibrations in crystals are thermally excited phonons, analogous to thermally excited phonons of black-body radiation in an enclosure. The energy of each phonon (photon) is

$$\varepsilon = h\nu \tag{1}$$

where $h$ is the Planck's constant ($=6.626 \times 10^{-34}$ J-s). In eq. 1, the zero point term is omitted as it has no direct effect on the matters we are going to discuss.

We know that the photoelectric effect provides strong evidence for the quantization of an electromagnetic wave (light). So far, no direct analogue of the photoelectric experiment has been carried out with phonons. However, some indirect evidence in support of the phonons (the quantized elastic wave) are:

1. The lattice contribution to the specific heat of solids (sec. 9.3) always approaches zero as the temperature approaches zero; this can be explained only if the lattice vibrations are quantized, implying the existence of phonons.

2. *X*-rays and neutrons are scattered inelastically by crystals, with energy and momentum changes corresponding to the creation or absorption of one or more phonons. By measuring the recoil of the scattered *X*-ray or neutron, it is possible to determine the properties of individual phonons. Such experiments provide the best way of determining the dispersion relations (a relation between frequency and wave vector for phonons) which consequently provide the strongest evidence for the existence of phonons.

## 7.2 DYNAMICS OF THE CHAIN OF IDENTICAL ATOMS

A convenient way to visualise lattice vibrations is to consider a system of identical atoms elastically coupled to each other by springs as shown in Fig. 7.1. Let us suppose that the system has a simple cubic arrangement of masses *M* joined by springs of force constants *K* (some cross-bracing is necessary for structure rigidity, but this does not matter for the present purpose), the interatomic spacing is *a*. These elastic couplings provide restoring forces on the atoms when they are displaced from their equilibrium positions. If each atom is imagined to be vibrating about its equilibrium position, a fairly accurate picture of lattice vibrations emerges. However, this is not practically the case.

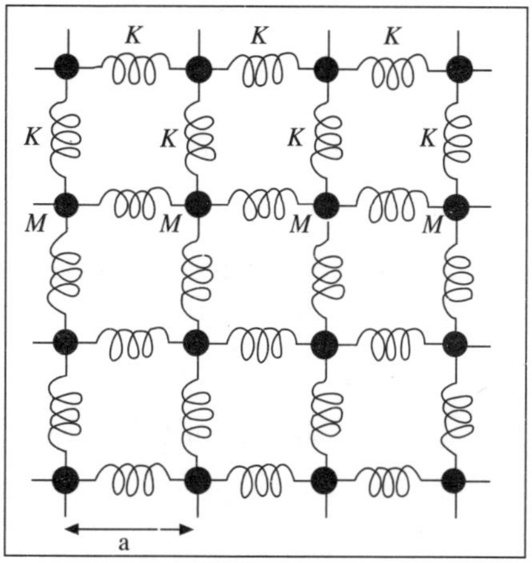

In order to make the treatment more simple, let us consider a model in which the longitudinal waves are parallel to the cube edge, i.e. along [100] direction. In other words, consider the case of a one dimensional chain of atoms. Fig. 7.2 shows one such system of atoms in the equilibrium position as well as in the displaced one due to the passage of longitudinal waves. One dimensional approximation is considered because of the fact that for a longitudinal motion the transverse springs in Fig. 7.1 have no effect.

**Fig. 7.1 Elastic coupling of vibrating atoms in a simple cubic lattice**

Further, let us suppose that the chain consists of a large number of atoms, say *N*, and that the last atom is connected with the first so as to form a ring. This assumption is simply to make the chain endless so that all atoms have identical environment. Now, allow the system to vibrate. If one atom starts vibrating, it does not continue to vibrate with a constant amplitude because each atom in the ring interacts (since a solid can be characterized by short range forces therefore only nearest neighbour interactions are considered) with its neighbours. In such a system, the transfer of energy from one atom

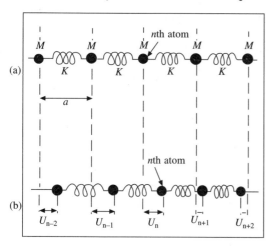

**Fig. 7.2 Equilibrium and displaced positions of vibrating atoms for a one dimensional chain of atoms**

to another takes place in a complicated way. Here, we consider the motion of entire chain of atoms. If $u_n$ is the displacement of the $n$th atom, then within the elastic limit (i.e. when the force is proportional to the displacement), the force on the $n$th atom due to $(n-1)$th and $(n+1)$th atoms will be:

(i) $K(u_n - u_{n-1})$ to the left, from the springs on its left
(ii) $K(u_{n+1} - u_n)$ to the right, from the springs on its right.

Since these forces are acting in opposite directions, the net force on the $n$th atom is

$$F_n = K[(u_{n+1} - u_n) - (u_n - u_{n-1})]$$

or

$$M\frac{d^2u_n}{dt^2} = K(u_{n+1} - 2u_n + u_{n-1}) \tag{2}$$

Let the solution of this equation is

$$u_n = A \exp i\,(nka - \omega t) \tag{3}$$

Equation 3 represents a travelling wave, in which all atoms oscillate with the same frequency $\omega$ and have the same amplitude $A$. Substituting this in eq. 2, we have

$$-\omega^2 M u_n = K(e^{ika} - 2 + e^{-ika})u_n$$

or

$$-\omega^2 M = K(e^{ika} - 2 + e^{-ika}) = 2K(\cos ka - 1)$$

(where, $2\cos ka = e^{ika} + e^{-ika}$)

$$\Rightarrow \qquad \omega^2 M = 4K \sin^2 \frac{ka}{2}$$

or

$$\omega = \left(\frac{4K}{M}\right)^{1/2} \left| \sin \frac{ka}{2} \right| \tag{4}$$

From eq. 4, the maximum (natural cutoff) frequency is obtained as

$$\omega_m = \left(\frac{4K}{M}\right)^{1/2} \tag{5}$$

so that eq. 4 can be written as

$$\omega = \omega_m \left| \sin \frac{ka}{2} \right| \tag{6}$$

Equation 6 is a dispersion relation between the angular frequency $\omega$ and the wave vector $k$ for a one dimensional periodic lattice. A corresponding plot shown in Fig. 7.3 is a dispersion curve which is sinusoidal with a period $2\pi/a$ in $k$-space. The dispersion relation (eq. 6) has several important properties which are applicable to all the three kinds of lattices (i.e. linear, plane and space lattice).

**Symmetry in $k$-space (the First Brillouin Zone)**
There exist two types of symmetry elements (i.e. the translational symmetry and the mirror

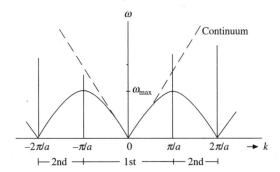

**Fig. 7.3 Dispersion curve *w* versus *k* for a one dimensional monoatomic lattice with nearest neighbour interactions**

symmetry) in the above dispersion curve (Fig. 7.3). The one dimensional chain of atoms has a translational periodicity "*a*". Because of this, the frequency $\omega$ is a periodic function of $k$ with a period $2\pi/a$, giving several values of $k$ for each $\omega$ below $\omega_m$. To each of these $k$'s, there is a corresponding wavelength, because

$$k = \frac{2\pi}{\lambda} \tag{7}$$

In order to make a unique representation, one must therefore choose a certain interval in $k$-space whose length is equal to the period, $2\pi/a$. In principle, the choice is entirely arbitrary; however, the most convenient one to specify unique $k$ and hence a unique $\lambda$ is to take $k$ in the range

$$-\pi/a < k < \pi/a \tag{8}$$

The region of $k$-space defined by eq. 8 is called the first Brillouin zone (*BZ*) for a one dimensional periodic lattice. The extreme values of $k$ in this region are

$$k_{max} = \pm\ \pi/a \tag{8'}$$

In addition to the translational symmetry, the dispersion curve also has a mirror symmetry (about the origin $k = 0$) in $k$-space; That is

$$\omega(-k) = \omega(k) \tag{9}$$

where mode $k$ (with $k > 0$) represents *a* wave travelling through the lattice in the positive $x$-direction and mode $-k$ represents a wave of the same wavelength but travelling in the opposite direction. Since the lattice is symmetric in the two directions, it responds to the two waves in the same fashion and hence the corresponding frequencies must be identical, as indicated in eq. 9.

**Number of Modes in the First Zone**
The assumption that the last atom of the one dimensional periodic lattice joins the first to make the chain of atoms endless and have identical environment, provides the basis to apply a periodic boundary condition. Therefore,

$$u_n(x = 0) = u_{N+n}\ (x = L) \tag{10}$$

where $L = Na$ is the length of the ring of atoms. Substituting eq. 3 into 10, we find that

$$\exp\, ikL = 1 \tag{11}$$

This equation imposes a restriction on the permissible values of $k$; only those values which satisfy eq. 11 are allowed. For any integer $n$, eq. 11 will satisfy only if $kL = 2n\pi$, or

$$k = n\,\frac{2\pi}{\lambda} \tag{12}$$

where $n = 0, \pm 1, \pm 2$, etc. When these values are plotted along a $k$-axis, they form a one dimensional mesh of regularly spaced points with the spacing $2\pi/L$ between them, as shown in Fig. 7.4. When $L$ is large (as would be the case for any lattice of macroscopic size encountered in actual practice), the allowed points come close together to form a quasi continuous mesh along the $k$-axis. Thus the total number of points inside the first zone will be given by

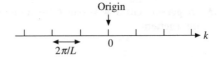

**Fig. 7.4   allowed values of $k$**

$$\frac{2\pi/a}{2\pi/L} = \frac{L}{a} = N$$

where $N$ is the total number of atoms or unit cells in the lattice and is equal to the number of allowed values of $k$ inside the first Brillouin zone. This is expected because the values of $k$ inside the zone uniquely describe all the vibrational modes of the lattice. Therefore, the number of modes must be equal to the number of degrees of freedom in the lattice, which is $N$. This is an important conclusion and holds good in general.

**Long Wavelength Limit**

We have seen that the dispersion curve is periodic and symmetric about the origin (Fig. 7.3). In order to know the behaviour of the lattice during the wave propagation through it, let us consider $0 < k < \pi/a$ part of the curve within which the frequency of the wave varies in the range $0 < \omega < \omega_m$ (where $\omega_m$ is the natural cutoff frequency). This implies that the one dimensional crystal lattice allows the propagation of frequencies lying between 0 and $\omega_m$ only while strongly attenuates all other frequencies and hence behaves as a low pass mechanical filter. In the long wavelength limit ($k \to 0$), the eq. 6 may be approximated as

$$\omega = \left(\frac{\omega_m a}{2}\right)k \tag{13}$$

This shows a linear relationship between $\omega$ and $k$, an expected result, because in this limit the lattice behaves as an elastic continuum. The quantity within the parenthesis is equal to the velocity of sound in a solid medium and hence

$$v_s = \frac{\omega_m a}{2} = \sqrt{(Y/\rho)} \tag{14}$$

where $Y$ is the Young's modulus and $\rho$ is the density of the solid material. Substituting $\omega_m$ from eq. 5 and $\rho = M/a^3$ in eq. 14, we obtain

$$K = aY \qquad (15)$$

a useful relation for estimating force constant $K$.

The linear relationship between $\omega$ and $k$ ceases to exist when the value of $K$ increases slowly. The dispersion curve begins to deviate from the straight path and eventually saturates at $k = \pi/a$ with a maximum frequency given by eq. 5.

**Phase and Group Velocities**

From eq. 6, the phase velocity ($v_p = \omega/k$) and the group velocity ($v_g = d\omega/dk$) are obtained as

$$v_p = v\,\frac{\sin(ka/2)}{ka/2} \qquad (16)$$

and

$$v_g = v \cos(ka/2) \qquad (17)$$

where $v = a(K/M)^{1/2}$ is the ordinary speed of sound in a solid, $v_p$ the velocity of propagation for a pure wave of an exactly specified $\omega$ and $k$ and $v_g$ is the velocity of a wave packet whose average frequency and wave vector are specified by $\omega$ and $k$. Since energy and momentum are practically transmitted via pulse rather than by the waves, group velocity is physically more significant.

Thus, considering the case when $k \to 0$,

$$\left(\frac{\sin(ka/2)}{ka/2}\right) \to 1 \text{ and } \cos(ka/2) \to 1$$

$$\Rightarrow v_p \equiv v_g \equiv v$$

This is expected as the waves of the long wavelength are not sensitive to the discreteness of the crystal structure. That is, in the above limit the lattice behaves as a continuum and no dispersion takes place. But, as $k$ increases (Fig. 7.3), $v_g$ being slope ($d\omega/dk$) of the dispersion curve, decreases steadily and becomes zero at $k = \pi/a$ (also from eq. 17).

At the zone boundary, $k = \pm\pi/a$, $v_p = 2v/\pi$ (from eq. 16) and $\lambda = 2a$. This indicates that the nearest neighbour atoms are moving in antiphase. Further, at $k = \pm \pi/a$, $v_g = 0$ means no energy is being propagated; the wave is a standing wave. The situation is equivalent to Bragg reflection in X-ray diffraction.

## 7.3 DYNAMICS OF A DIATOMIC LINEAR CHAIN

In this section, we shall consider slightly more complicated case, viz. the lattice dynamics of a diatomic chain having masses $M$ and $m$ (where $M > m$) alternately such that the nearest neighbour distance is a. This is a one dimensional analogue of the three dimensional NaCl structure. For convenience, the atoms are numbered in such a way that the even numbers correspond to the masses $M$ and the odd ones to $m$. Fig. 7.5 shows the equilibrium and displaced positions of such a system. The equations of motion in this case may be written in the same way as eq. 2, so that we have:

For masses $M$

$$M\frac{d^2 u_{2n}}{dt^2} = K\,(u_{2n+1} - 2u_{2n} + u_{2n-1}) \qquad (18)$$

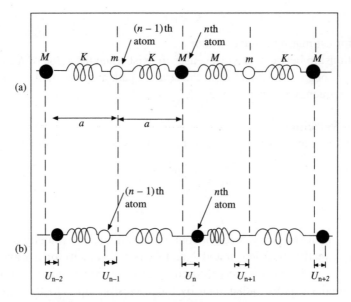

**Fig. 7.5 Equilibrium and displaced positions of vibrating diatomic system**

and for masses $m$

$$M\frac{d^2u_{2n-1}}{dt^2} = K\,(u_{2n} - 2u_{2n-1} + u_{2n-2}) \tag{19}$$

These equations can be solved as before by assuming a solution of the form

$$u_{2n} = A \exp i\,[2nka - \omega t] \tag{20}$$

and

$$u_{2n-1} = B \exp i\,[(2n - 1)\,ka - \omega t] \tag{21}$$

On substitution of eqs. 20 and 21 in eqs. 18 and 19 respectively, we obtain

$$(2K - \omega^2 M)\,A - (2K \cos ka)\,B = 0 \tag{22}$$

and

$$(-2K \cos ka)\,A + (2K - \omega^2 m)\,B = 0 \tag{23}$$

These are a set of homogeneous simultaneous equations in the unknowns $A$ and $B$. A nontrivial solution exists only if the determinant of their coefficient is zero.
This leads to the secular equation,

$$\begin{vmatrix} 2K - \omega^2 M & -2K \cos ka \\ -2K \cos ka & 2k - \omega^2 m \end{vmatrix} = 0 \tag{24}$$

i.e.

$$4K^2 - 2K\omega^2\,(M + m) + Mm\omega^4 - 4K^2 \cos^2 ka = 0 \tag{25}$$

This is a quadratic equation in $\omega^2$ and its roots are

$$\omega^2 = K\left(\frac{1}{M} + \frac{1}{m}\right) \pm K\left[\left(\frac{1}{M} + \frac{1}{m}\right)^2 - \frac{4 \sin^2 ka}{Mm}\right]^{1/2} \tag{26}$$

Equation 26 is the required dispersion relation between $\omega$ and $k$ for one-dimensional lattice. Because of the positive and negaive terms on the right hand side of the equation, each $k$ corresponds to two values of $\omega$. Graphs shown in Fig. 7.6 represent the corresponding dispersion curves in reduced zone scheme. These are referred to as branches. The lower branch of the curve corresponding the minus sign in eq. 26 is the acoustic branch, while the upper curve due to the positive sign is the optical branch. The former name is due to the fact that near $k = 0$ the lower branch represents long wavelength elastic waves with a frequency independent velocity ($\omega \propto k$), and longitudinal elastic waves are identical with the sound waves. The latter is due to the fact that near $k = 0$, the frequency of upper branch lies near infrared region of the spectrum, the corresponding wavelength is a typical wavelength for infrared absorption due to molecular vibration.

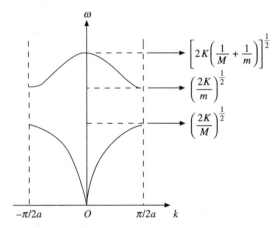

**Fig. 7.6  The dispersion curve, $\omega$ versus $k$ for a one dimensional diatomic lattice ($M > m$) in reduced zone scheme**

The frequency range between the top of the acoustic branch and the bottom of the optical branch is forbidden, and the lattice cannot transmit such a wave. Therefore, waves in this region are strongly attenuated by the diatomic lattice which behaves as a band-pass mechanical filter.

### The Acoustic Branch

Dispersion relation corresponding to the acoustic branch is given by

$$\omega_-^2 = K\left(\frac{1}{M} + \frac{1}{m}\right) - K\left[\left(\frac{1}{M} + \frac{1}{m}\right)^2 - \frac{4\sin^2 ka}{Mm}\right]^{1/2} \tag{27}$$

Since the acoustic branch begins at $k = 0$, this is mathematically defined as

$$\lim_{k \to 0}(\omega_-) \to 0 \tag{28}$$

Under this limit, eq. 27 becomes

$$\lim_{k \to 0}\omega_-^2 = K\left(\frac{1}{M} + \frac{1}{m}\right) - K\left[\left(\frac{1}{M} + \frac{1}{m}\right)^2 - \frac{4k^2a^2}{Mm}\right]^{1/2}$$

$$= K \left( \frac{1}{M} + \frac{1}{m} \right) \left[ 1 - \left( 1 - \frac{2\,k^2 a^2 Mm}{(M+m)^2} \right) \right]$$

$$= K \left( \frac{m+M}{Mm} \right) \frac{2\,k^2 a^2 Mm}{(M+m)^2}$$

so that
$$\omega_- = ka \left( \frac{2K}{m+M} \right)^{1/2} \tag{29}$$

With the help of this, the phase velocity and the group velocity can be obtained as

$$\lim_{k\to 0} (v_p) = \lim_{k\to 0} \left( \frac{\omega_-}{k} \right) = a \left( \frac{2K}{m+M} \right)^{1/2} = v \tag{30}$$

and
$$\lim_{k\to 0} (v_g) = \lim_{k\to 0} \left( \frac{d\omega_-}{dk} \right) = a \left( \frac{2K}{m+M} \right)^{1/2} = v \tag{31}$$

Now, as the value of $k$ increases, acoustic branch of the curve rises linearly first and then slowly decreases and eventually saturates at $k = \pi/2a$. Thus, the maximum allowed frequency for this mode is obtained by putting $ka = \pm\pi/2$ in eq. 27, i.e.

$$(\omega_-)_{max} = \left( \frac{2K}{M} \right)^{1/2} \tag{32}$$

This is independent of the lighter atoms in the chain. This physical distinction between the acoustical and optical modes of lattice vibration can be appreciated by looking at the ratio of the wave amplitudes $A/B$ and the phases of the solutions for each branch of the dispersion relation. From eq. 22, the ratio $A/B$ is

$$\frac{A}{B} = \frac{2K \cos ka}{2K - M\omega_-^2} \tag{33}$$

Making use of the limit $(k \to 0)$ given in eq. 28, the above ratio reduces to

$$\frac{A}{B} = 1 \tag{34}$$

Thus, at $k = 0$, for the acoustical branch, the two atoms in the cell have the same amplitude and are also in phase as shown in Fig. 7.7. Again from eq. 23, we have

$$\frac{B}{A} = \frac{2K \cos ka}{2K - m\omega_-^2} \tag{35}$$

At first zone boundary, $ka = \pm \pi/2$, so that $B = 0$ implying that the smaller atoms are stationary in the acoustic branch. Consequently, $A/B \to \infty$. These two observations are shown in Fig. 7.7.

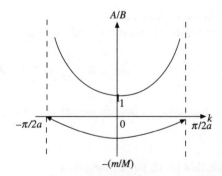

**Fig. 7.7 Ratio $(A/B)$ of the amplitudes of the two branches of dispersion relation for a diatomic linear chain**

**The Optical Branch**

The upper branch of the curve corresponding to the positive sign in eq. 26, is the optical branch and is given by

$$\omega_+^2 = K\left(\frac{1}{M} + \frac{1}{m}\right) + K\left[\left(\frac{1}{M} + \frac{1}{m}\right)^2 - \frac{4\sin^2 ka}{Mm}\right]^{1/2} \tag{36}$$

On simplifying eq. 36 at $k = \pm \pi/2a$, the minimum allowed frequency corresponding to the optical branch is found to be

$$(\omega_+)_{min} = \left(\frac{2K}{m}\right)^{1/2} \tag{37}$$

at $k = 0$, the maximum frequency is

$$(\omega_+)_{max} = \left[2K\left(\frac{1}{M} + \frac{1}{m}\right)\right]^{1/2} \tag{38}$$

Substituting the value of $\omega$ from eq. 37 into eq. 23, we find

$$MA + mB = 0 \tag{39}$$

From eq. 39, ratio of two amplitudes

$$\frac{A}{B} = -\left(\frac{m}{M}\right) \tag{40}$$

Again putting $ka = \pm \pi/2$ in eq. 22, we have

$$\frac{A}{B} = 0 \quad \text{or} \quad A = 0 \tag{41}$$

This corresponds to the optical branch of the curve.

From the above discussion, it may be concluded that for $k = 0$ in the acoustical branch, the two types of atoms may be considered as vibrating in phase (together with their centers of mass) as one would expect in an ordinary elastic wave propagation, whereas in the optical branch they vibrate out of phase, keeping their centers of mass fixed (as one might expect in a system of alternating charges under the action of an electric field parallel to the linear chain). Similarly, at the boundary ($k = \pi/2a$), in the acoustical branch only the heavy atoms ($M$) move, $\pi$ out of phase and in the optical branch the light atoms ($m$) move, also $\pi$ out of phase. They have been shown in fig. 7.8.

**Symmetry in *k*-space and Number of Modes in First Zone**

Like monoatomic system, the diatomic chain also satisfies symmetry properties in $k$-space. For example, it has a reflection symmetry about $k = 0$, however the periodicity of the dispersion curve in this case is $\pi/2a$ and not $\pi/a$ (unlike monoatomic case). Consequently, the first Brillouin zone lies in the range $-\pi/2a < k < \pi/2a$ since the period of the real lattice is $2a$ and not $a$. These can be easily verified by considering either eq. 26 or Fig. 7.6. Further, using the periodic

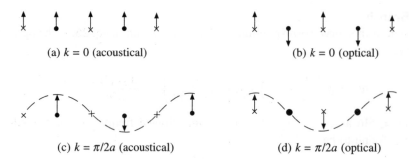

(a) $k = 0$ (acoustical)
(b) $k = 0$ (optical)

(c) $k = \pi/2a$ (acoustical)
(d) $k = \pi/2a$ (optical)

**Fig. 7.8  Motion of atoms in the acoustic and optical modes for a diatomic linear chain**

boundary conditions, that the number of allowed $k$-values inside the first zone is $N$ and hence the total number of modes inside this zone is $2N$ (because of the presence of two modes—acoustic and optical—for each $k$), which is equal to the number of degrees of freedom in the lattice, as must be the case.

**Frequency Gap**

Inspection of Fig. 7.6 further reveals that no solution exists for the frequencies lying between 0 < $\omega$ < $(\omega_+)_{max}$ at the origin ($k = 0$) and $(\omega_+)_{min}$ < $\omega$ < $(\omega_-)_{max}$ at the first zone boundary ($k = \pm\pi/2a$). Separation between acoustic and optical branches is maximum at the origin and minimum at the boundary. The gap between the two branches at the zone boundary is known as frequency gap and is a characteristic feature of a diatomic lattice. It is, however, possible to obtain solutions in this region by introducing an impurity atom (e.g., by replacing one of the atoms of mass $m$ by one of mass $M$), such solutions are called gap mode. Another possibility of looking solutions in the gap with real $\omega$ will have complex $k$, so that the wave is damped in space.

*Example*: If the velocity of sound in a solid is taken to be $3 \times 10^3$ m/s and the interatomic distance as $3 \times 10^{-10}$ m, calculate the value of cutoff frequency assuming a linear lattice.

*Solution*: Given: $v = 3 \times 10^3$ m/s, $a = 3 \times 10^{-10}$m, critical frequency, $v = ?$ As we know that the cutoff frequency occurs at $k = \pi/a$ (i.e. $\lambda \simeq 2a$). Further, the velocity and the frequency are related by the equation

$$v = v\lambda = 2va$$

or
$$v = \frac{v}{2a} = \frac{3 \times 10^3}{2 \times 3 \times 10^{-10}} = 5 \times 10^{12} \text{ Hz}$$

*Example*: If the velocity of sound in a solid is of the order $10^3$ m/s, compare the frequency of the sound wave $\lambda = 10$Å for (a) a monoatomic system, and (b) acoustic waves and optical waves in a diatomic system containing two identical atoms ($M = m$) per unit cell of interatomic spacing 2.5Å.

*Solution*: Given: Velocity of sound $v_0 = 10^3$ m/s.
(a) In case of a monoatomic lattice, the frequency is given by

$$\omega = v_0 k = \dot{v}_0 \frac{2\pi}{\lambda}$$

$$= \frac{10^3 \times 2\pi}{10 \times 10^{-10}} = 6.28 \times 10^{12} \text{ rad/sec}.$$

(b) For acoustic waves in a diatomic (identical $M = m$) lattice, the frequency varies from

$$\omega = 0 \text{ at } k = 0 \text{ to } \omega = \left(\frac{2K}{m}\right)^{1/2} \text{ at } k = \pi/2a$$

Also, the velocity expression is given by

$$v_0 = a \times \left(\frac{2K}{m}\right)^{1/2}$$

or

$$\omega = \frac{v_0}{a} = \left(\frac{2K}{m}\right)^{1/2} = \frac{10^3}{2.5 \times 10^{-10}} = 4 \times 10^{12} \text{ rad/sec}.$$

For optical waves, the frequency varies from

$$\omega = \left(\frac{4K}{m}\right)^{1/2} \text{ at } k = 0 \text{ to } \omega = \left(\frac{2K}{m}\right)^{1/2} \text{ at } k = \pi/2a$$

Therefore,

$$\omega = \sqrt{2} \times \frac{v_0}{a} = 4\sqrt{2} \times 10^{12} \text{ rad/sec}. \text{ (at } k = 0)$$

and

$$\omega = \frac{v_0}{a} = 4 \times 10^{12} \text{ rad/sec}. \text{ (at } k = \pi/2a)$$

*Example*: The unit cell parameter of NaCl crystal is 5.6Å and the modulus of elasticity along [100] direction is $5 \times 10^{10}$ N/m$^2$. Estimate the wavelength at which an electromagnetic radiation is strongly reflected by the crystal. At. wt. of Na = 23 and of Cl = 37.

*Solution*: Given: $a = 5.6$Å, $Y = 5 \times 10^{10}$ N/m$^2$, At. wts. Na = 23, Cl = 37, 1 amu = $1.67 \times 10^{-27}$ kg. The maximum frequency of radiation (in optical range) strongly reflected by the NaCl crystal will be given by

$$(\omega_+)_{max} = \left[2K\left(\frac{1}{M} + \frac{1}{m}\right)\right]^{1/2}$$

Let us assume that an extension along [100] direction will have negligible effect on vertical springs. Therefore, we can write

$$K = aY$$

The frequency expression becomes

$$(\omega_+)_{max} = \left[2aY\left(\frac{1}{M} + \frac{1}{m}\right)\right]^{1/2}$$

$$= \left[\frac{2 \times 5.6 \times 10^{-10} \times 5 \times 10^{10}}{1.67 \times 10^{-27}}\left(\frac{1}{37} + \frac{1}{23}\right)\right]^{1/2}$$

$$= 4.86 \times 10^{13} \text{ rad/sec.}$$

Hence, the wavelength at which this radiation is strongly reflected is

$$\lambda = \frac{c}{v} = \frac{2\pi c}{\omega} = \frac{2\pi \times 10^8}{4.86 \times 10^{13}} = 3.88 \times 10^{-5} \text{ m}$$

## 7.4   DYNAMICS OF IDENTICAL ATOMS IN THREE DIMENSIONS

In the foregoing sections, we discussed the dynamics of one dimensional chain of atoms (monoatomic and diatomic cases). It was pointed out that the properties of dispersion relations corresponding to one dimensional cases are also applicable to two and three dimensional systems. However, the only additional feature of considerable importance that emerges in two and three dimensional system (a crystal) is the polarization of lattice waves. But the basic difficulty in developing the lattice dynamics of a two dimensional plane lattice or a three dimensional space lattice containing one or more atoms per unit cell is that they involve very complex mathematics. Thus, to avoid mathematical details we shall present here only a qualitative discussion of the subject.

Let us consider a system of monoatomic Bravais lattice (e.g. a simple cubic lattice) consisting of one atom per unit cell. The equation of motion of each atom can be written in a manner similar to that of eq. 2. The normal mode solution may therefore be written as

$$u_n = A \exp i(k. \, r - \omega t) \tag{42}$$

where the wave vector $k$ specifies both the wavelength and direction of propagation, $A$ represents the amplitude as well as the direction of vibrations of the atoms and $r$ is the position vector. Thus, the polarization of lattice wave is observed when the wave is longitudinal ($A$ parallel to $k$) or transverse ($A \perp k$). However, in general the wave in a lattice is neither purely longitudinal nor purely transverse, but a mixture of both.

On substitution of eq. 42 into the equations of motion, three simultaneous equations involving $A_x$, $A_y$, $A_z$ (components of $A$) are obtained. These equations are coupled together and are equivalent to a $3 \times 3$ matrix and so is the secular equation. This gives three dispersion relations as its roots and hence three dispersion curves as shown in the Fig. 7.9a. However, for a nonprimitive lattice containing two atoms in the unit cell will look like as shown in Fig. 7.9b. Six dispersion curves are because of the fact that for $r$ atoms per unit cell there are $3r$ dispersion curves as discussed earlier. Out of these, three branches are acoustic (because it can be shown that three of the roots always vanish at $k = 0$), and the remaining $(3r - 3)$ are optical. Acoustic branches may be classified at $T_1$, $T_2$ and L according to their polarization. Similarly optical branches may be classified as LO and TO when $k$ lies along high symmetry directions, such as [100] or [110]. Dispersion curves along three symmetry directions in aluminium crystal are shown in Fig. 7.10.

## 7.5   EXPERIMENTAL MEASUREMENTS OF DISPERSION RELATION

From the discussion of lattice specific heat of solid (refer chapter 9), we observe that even the Debye model is unable to provide completely satisfactory explanation to the experimental data

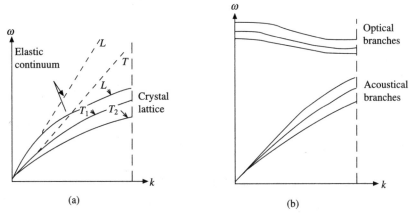

**Fig. 7.9** **Schemetic dispersion relation for a: (a) primitive lattice (b) lattice with a basis of two atoms per unit cell.**

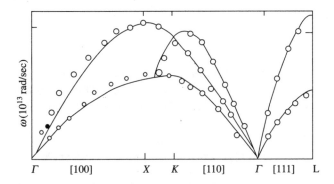

**Fig. 7.10** **Dispersion curves along three symmetry directions in aluminium crystal**

in the intermediate temperature range for want of correct dispersion relation. In the present section, we shall study the same from experimental point of view.

At present, inelastic scattering of thermal neutrons is the most powerful tool for experimental observation of lattice waves. it is well known from nuclear physics that neutrons are produced by fission of heavy nuclei, such as uranium ($U_{235}$). Such neutrons are fast and have an average energy of about 2 MeV. However, they can be slowed down by passing the beam through enough matter untill the beam is in thermal equilibrium with the molecular motions of the material: such neutrons are called slow or thermal neutrons. The energies of these neutrons are about 0.025 eV, which is of the order of $kT$ at room temperature ($T \sim 300$ K). The wavelength of such neutrons is of the order of 1 Å, suitable for diffraction experiments.

A triple axis (neutron) spectrometer (TAS) is used to measure the magnitude and direction of the scattered beam as shown in Fig. 7.11. The wave vector $k_i$ of the incoming neutron beam is known from the reactor characteristics. On the other hand, the final neutron wave vector $k_f$ is known by measuring the angle $\phi$ between $k_i$ and $k_f$ and the angle $\psi$ between $k_i$ (or $k_f$) and the crystal. In this case, the diffraction pattern obeys the Bragg's law in the form

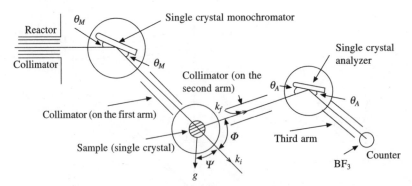

**Fig. 7.11   Geometry of a triple axis neutron spectrometer**

$$k_i - k_f = q \qquad (43)$$

Similarly, the energy of the inelastically scattered thermal neutron also obeys the energy-conservation equation

$$\frac{h^2}{2m_n} (k_i^2 - k_f^2) = h\omega_q \qquad (44)$$

when $k_i$ and $k_f$ are initial and final neutron wave vectors, respectively; $m_n$ is the mass of a neutron; $\omega_q$ is the frequency of a lattice wave of wave vector $q$. Thus, from accurate measurements of $k_i$, $k_f$ and the energy loss of the neutron beam, the dispersion relation $\omega$ versus $q$, for the lattice wave can be determined experimentally.

## 7.6   ANHARMONICITY AND THERMAL EXPANSION

In the above discussion of thermal vibrations and the development of the theory of lattice specific heat of solids, we restricted ourselves to harmonic approximation according to which the elastic force acting on a particle displaced from its equilibrium position is proportional to the displacement and is directed towards the equilibrium position, i.e.

$$f = -\beta x \qquad (45)$$

and the corresponding potential energy is

$$U(x) = -\beta \frac{x^2}{2} \qquad (46)$$

   This is represented by a parabola as shown in Fig. 7.12, indicating that the amplitude of the atomic lattice vibration increases with the increase of temperature and becomes as high as 12% of the interatomic spacing, at the melting point. However, the increase in temperature does not affect the mean position of oscillations and hence the average interatomic spacing remains unchanged. Under such a condition, heating a body would not bring about its expansion. But, it is an experimental fact that most of the solids expand on heating, implying thereby that the vibrations of the particles in a solid are not truly harmonic, i.e. it is actually anharmonic. This is supported by the fact that the potential energy curve expressed as the sum of attractive and repulsive terms as shown in Fig. 2.1 is assymmetric in nature. A similar potential energy curve

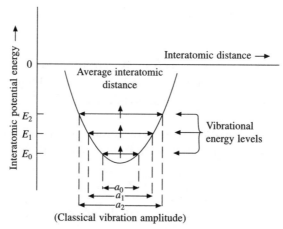

**Fig. 7.12 Parabolic potential corresponding to harmonic oscillator**

is presented in Fig. 7.13. To account for the assymmetry, eqs. 45 and 46 must be modified to include the assymmetry term. Hence they assume the following form:

$$U(x) = \beta \frac{x^2}{2} - g \frac{x^3}{3} \tag{47}$$

and

$$f(x) = -\frac{\partial U}{\partial x} = -\beta x + g x^2 \tag{48}$$

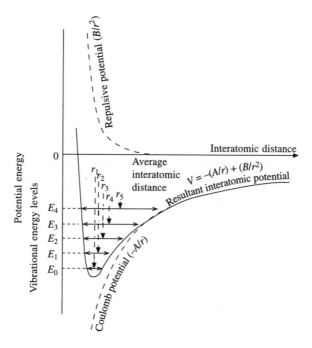

**Fig. 7.13 Potential energy as a function of distance between two atoms**

where $g$ is a proportionality factor. When a particle is displaced to the right ($x > 0$), the cubic term is subtracted from the quadratic term and hence the right side of the curve flattens. On the other hand, when the particle is displaced to the left ($x < 0$), the cubic term is added to quadratic term and hence the left side of the curve steepens. As a result, the central position of the particle no longer coincides with the equilibrium position but is displaced to the right (Fig. 7.13). This corresponds to an increase in the average interatomic spacing $\bar{x}$. Hence on heating a material body, it should expand.

Now, let us estimate the value of the thermal expansion coefficient. The average value of the force caused by the displacement of the particle from its equilibrium position is

$$\bar{f} = -\beta\bar{x} + g\,\bar{x}^2$$

However, when the particle vibrates freely, $\bar{f} = 0$, therefore,

$$g\,\bar{x}^2 = \beta\bar{x}$$

so that

$$\bar{x} = g\,\frac{\bar{x}^2}{\beta} \tag{49}$$

The expression for the average potential energy of a vibrating particle could be written from eq. 46 as

$$\overline{U(x)} \sim \beta\,\frac{\bar{x}^2}{2}$$

or

$$\bar{x}^2 \simeq 2\,\frac{\overline{U(x)}}{\beta}$$

substituting this into eq. 49, we obtain

$$\bar{x} = 2g\,\frac{\overline{U(x)}}{\beta^2} \tag{50}$$

However, in addition to the potential energy, a vibrating particle has kinetic energy $E_k$, such that $\overline{U(x)} = \bar{E}_k$. So that the total average energy of the particle is $\bar{E} = \bar{E}_k + \overline{U(x)} = 2\overline{U(x)}$. Making use of this, eq. 50 can be written as

$$\bar{x} = g\,\frac{\bar{E}}{\beta^2} \tag{51}$$

The relative linear expansion, i.e. the ratio of the average interatomic spacing, $\bar{x}$, and the equilibrium interatomic spacing, $r_0$, is equal to

$$\frac{\bar{x}}{r_0} = \frac{g}{\beta^2 r_0}\,\bar{E}$$

and the coefficient of linear thermal expansion is

$$\alpha = \frac{1}{r_0}\frac{d\bar{x}}{dT} = \frac{g}{\beta^2 r_0}\frac{d\bar{E}}{dT} = \chi C_v \tag{52}$$

where $\chi = g/\beta^2 r_0$ and $C_v$ is the specific heat of the solid per particle.

From eq. 52, it is clear that the coefficient of thermal expansion and the specific heat of the solid is interrelated. Fig. 7.14 shows the temperature dependence of $C_v$ and $\alpha$.

In the high temperature range, the energy of a particle engaged in linear vibrations is $kT$ and its specific heat $C_v = k$. Therefore, the coefficient of thermal expansion of a linear atomic chain will be

$$\alpha = \chi C_v = g\frac{k}{\beta^2 r_0} \tag{53}$$

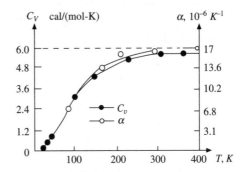

**Fig. 7.14 Temperature dependents of coefficient of linear expansion a and specific heat $C_v$ of copper**

Substituting the values for $g$, $k$, $\beta$ and $r_0$ for various solids, $\alpha$ is found to be of the order of $10^{-4} - 10^{-5}$, which is in fair agreement with the experiment. Experiments also support the conclusion that in the high temperature range $\alpha$ is practically independent of temperature (Fig. 7.14). In the low temperature range, $\alpha$ behaves similar to that of $C_v$.

Using the Debye model, Gruneisen has derived an expression for coefficient of linear expansion $(\alpha_L)$ in terms of the molar specific heat $C_v$ and the compressibility $K$

$$\alpha_L = \frac{\gamma C_v K}{3V} \tag{54}$$

where $\gamma$ is the Gruneisen's constant (or parameter) and $V$ is the molar volume. Gruneisen's parameter $(\gamma)$ is defined by the equation

$$\gamma = -\frac{\ln v}{\ln V_a} \tag{55}$$

where $v$ is the frequency of atomic vibration and $V_a$ is the atomic volume. Gruneisen's parameter for different metals varies from 1.5 to 3.0 and is not strictly constant, although the variation is very small.

## 7.7  SUMMARY

1. The concept of quantized lattice vibrations (i.e. the existence of phonons) helps to explain a number of properties of solids including the specific heat near absolute zero.
2. The dispersion relation between $\omega$ and $k$ for a one dimensional lattice with nearest neighbour interaction is given by

$$\omega = \omega_m \left|\sin\frac{ka}{2}\right|$$

3. The natural cutoff frequency $\omega_m$ is given by

$$\omega_m = \left( \frac{4K}{M} \right)^{1/2}$$

where $K$ and $M$ are the force constant and the atomic mass, respectively.

4. The dispersion curve near $k = 0$ (i.e. in the long wavelength limit) is linear, periodic and symmetric. This curve saturates at large values of $k$. Under the low wavelength limit, the lattice acts as a low pass filter, i.e. only the frequencies lying in the range $0 < \omega < \omega_m$ are transmitted while higher frequencies get attenuated.

5. Near $k = 0$, both the phase velocity and the group velocity are equal to the velocity of sound. On the other hand, at $k = \pm\pi/a$ i.e. at $\lambda = 2a$, $v_g = 0$ and $v_p = 2v/\pi$, indicating that the nearest neighbout atoms are out of phase by $\pi$. Under this limit, no energy is being propagated; the wave is a standing wave. The situation is the same as the Bragg condition.

6. The dispersion curves for a one dimensional diatomic linear chain of atoms consist of two branches: the lower one is acoustic branch and the upper one is optical branch.

7. The acoustic branch is similar to the monoatomic case, whereas the optical branch is almost flat throughout the $k$-space. There exists a frequency gap between the two branches and the lattice acts as band pass filter.

8. The dispersion relation in a three-dimensional lattice is an extension of the one-dimensional case. The wave vector $k$ is now a three-dimensional vector, and the frequency is a function of both the magnitude and direction of $k$.

9. Inelastic scattering of thermal neutrons using a triple axis neutron spectrometer is a powerful tool for experimental measurement of lattice waves.

10. Thermal expansion of most of solids is anharmonic. According to Gruneisen, the coefficient of linear expansion in terms of molar specific heat $C_v^-$ and compressibility $K$ is given by

$$\alpha_L = \frac{\gamma C_v K}{3V}$$

## 7.8  DEFINITIONS

*Anharmonic Motion*: The motion of a particle subjected to a restoring force that is not directly proportional to the displacement from a fixed point in the line of motion.

*Black body radiation*: Thermal radiation from a black body (full radiator) at a given temperature. It, generally, covers the entire wavelength range, the exact spectral distribution depends on the temperature of the body.

*Brillouin zones*: The volumes contained within the drawn surface which indicate the forbidden values of $k$, in $k$-space.

*Degree of freedom*: It is the number of independent variables needed to specify the state of a mechanical system.

*Group velocity*: It is the velocity with which a group of waves travel. It is equal to the phase velocity, if the phase velocity does not depend on wavelength.

*Gruneisen Parameter* ($\gamma$): The negative rate of change of atomic vibration frequency with respect to atomic volume change; or where it is assumed that $\gamma$ is the same for all vibrational states within the solid.

$$\gamma = -\frac{\ln v}{\ln V_a}$$

*Hooke's law*: For a certain range of stresses, the strain produced in a body is proportional to the applied stress.

*Longitudinal wave*: A wave in which the direction of the displacement of the particle is the same as the direction of wave propagation.

*Phase velocity:* The velocity with which the wave crests and troughs travel through a medium.

*Phonon:* The quantum of elastic or strain energy.

*Photon:* The quantum of electromagnetic energy.

*Transverse wave:* A wave in which the direction of the displacement of the particle is perpendicular to the direction of wave propagation.

## REVIEW QUESTIONS AND PROBLEMS

1. Suppose that longitudinal vibrations in a linear chain of $N$ identical atoms obey periodic boundary conditions, so that the motion of the first and last atom of the chain is identical. Find the number of normal modes of vibration for this system.

2. Find the dispersion relation for a one-dimensional crystal with two types of atoms and discuss the nature of the optical and acoustic modes.

3. Analyse the vibrational motion of a diatomic periodic linear chain and obtain expression for the vibration frequencies $\omega$ as a function of the wave number $k$. Show that $d\omega/dk$ must vanish at the zone boundary.

4. Discuss the energy and momentum conservation law for neutrons inelastically scattered by phonons.

5. Show that for a diatomic linear chain with two types of atoms of mass $m$ and $M$, the density of phonon modes per unit frequency interval diverges at the maximum frequency on either side of the gap: while it tends to acquire a constant value as $\omega \to 0$. Assuming the nearest neighbour interaction described by a single force constant $K$, for all interacting pair.

6. Discuss the vibrations of diatomic lattice and describe its optical and acoustic modes.

7. Describe with necessary theory the method of neutron diffraction for the study of phonons in crystals. Mention the advantages and limitations of this method.

8. Derive the vibrational modes of a diatomic linear chain of atoms. What is the difference between the two branches and why are they named so?

9. Obtain the dispersion relation for elastic waves in a linear monoatomic chain with nearest neighbour interaction and show that the group velocity vanishes at the zone boundaries. Find the density of the vibrational states as a function of the angular frequency and sketch the dispersion curve.

10. Derive equation of state for solid and Gruneisen relation.

11. The unit cell of NaCl is a cube of side 5.6Å and the Young's modulus in a [100] direction is $5 \times 10^{10}$ Nm$^{-2}$. Etimate the wavelength at which the electromagnetic radiation is strongly reflected by the crystal. Assuming that for extension along [110], the crystal may be considered as a set of linear chain in which the parallel and the lateral forces are ignored. (At. wts. Na = 23, Cl = 37).

    *Ans.* $38.8 \times 10^{-6}$ m.

12. Prove that in a one dimensional diatomic lattice, both acoustic and optical branches in dispersion curve meet the zone boundary normally.

13. Prove that the gradient of optical branch of the dispersion curve at the maximum frequency is zero.

14. Prove that in a one dimensional diatomic lattice, the optical branch is given by

$$\lim_{k \to 0}(\omega_-) \to ka \left( \frac{2K}{m + M} \right)^{1/2}$$

15. Prove that in a one dimensional diatomic lattice, the two kinds of atoms oscillate with amplitudes related to each other by

$$B = A \left( 1 - \frac{M\omega^2}{2K} \right) \sec ka$$

16. In a linear chain, all atoms are identical but connected alternately by springs of force constants $K_1$ and $K_2$. Show that the frequency-wavevector spectrum is

$$\omega^2 = \left( \frac{K_1 + K_2}{M} \right) \pm \frac{1}{M} [(K_1 + K_2)^2 - 4K_1 K_2 \sin^2 ka]^{1/2}$$

17. If in a one dimensional lattice, $x = M/m \ll 1$, prove that the square of the widths of the optical and acoustic branches are in the ratio $x : 4$.

18. A more accurate description of lattice vibration is obtained if higher neighbour interactions are also included. Prove that the inclusion of nth neighbours modifies the dispersion relation of a one dimensional monoatomic system to

$$M\omega^2 = 2 \sum_{s=1}^{N} K_s [1 - \cos(ska)]$$

# Chapter 8

# Diffraction of Waves and Particles by Crystals

## 8.1  INTRODUCTION

Earlier chapters describe in detail the geometry and symmetry of the arrangement of atoms (or molecules) in ideal crystals and their difference from the real crystals containing imperfections, from theoretical point of view. This chapter, studies them from experimental point of view. Experimental study of crystalline materials became possible only after the discovery of X-rays by Roentgen in 1895. In 1912, Max Von Laue recognised that the wavelengths of these rays were of the order of interatomic spacing in crystals, i.e. about 1 Å. He therefore proposed that the crystals could be used as a three-dimensional diffraction grating to study the nature of newly discovered X-rays. This is because of the fact that the spacing between the adjacent lines on a diffraction grating must be of the order of the wavelength of the light used and that the gratings with such a minute spacing (~ Å) as required by the X-rays cannot be ruled on any glass plate. Therefore, now X-rays and beam of electrons and neutrons are used to study the structure of materials.

Electromagnetic radiation such as X-rays are regarded as waves because under certain conditions they exihibit interference, diffraction and polarization. Similarly, electrons and neutrons are regarded as particles because they possess mass and follow the laws of particle mechanics. However, we know that every moving object (particle) is associated with a wave. In a particular event, X-rays may behave either as waves or particles, but simultaneously not both. Same X-rays that are diffracted by a crystal can cause the emission of photoelectrons from a suitable surface, but these processes occur independently.

## 8.2  X-RAYS AND THEIR GENERATION

X-rays like visible light are a form of electromagnetic radiation having shorter wavelengths, typically of the order of 1 Å, i.e. they represent a relatively high-energy form of radiation. In the electromagnetic spectrum they lie between ultraviolet and $\gamma$-rays. X-rays are produced when a stream of high energy charged particles, e.g. a beam of electrons are allowed to strike a metal target. In the process, electrons loose certain amount of their energy which is converted into electromagnetic radiations, i.e. $\Delta E = h\nu$. Such processes give "white radiations" or continuous X-rays. Fig. 8.1 shows continuous X-rays spectra corresponding to a tungsten target at several different accelerating potentials, which tails off gradually at higher wavelength side, but terminate abruptly at shorter wavelength limit $\lambda_{swl}$ (or $\lambda_{min}$). As the accelerating potential increases, both the maxima in the intensity distribution and the $\lambda_{min}$ shift towards the shorter wavelength side. At particular $V$, the $\lambda_{min}$ is fixed and is related to each other as

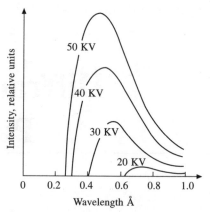

**Fig. 8.1 X-ray spectra of tungsten at various accelerating potentials**

$$\lambda_{min} = \frac{1.24 \times 10^{-6}}{V} \text{ V-m} \qquad (1)$$

$\lambda_{min}$ in eq. 1 means a maximum frequency which consequently means a maximum photon energy, $h\nu_{max}$. The maximum energy that X-rays photon can have cannot exceed the maximum energy of the electron beam, which in turn is determined by the voltage applied to the X-ray tube. Thus

$$\Delta E_{max} = eV_{max} = h\nu_{max} = \frac{hc}{\lambda_{min}}$$

or 
$$\frac{hc}{\lambda_{min}} = eV_{max} \quad \text{or} \quad \lambda_{min} = \frac{hc}{eV_{max}} \qquad (2)$$

Substituting the values of constants, we obtain

$$\lambda_{min} = \frac{6.63 \times 10^{-34} \, Js \times 3 \times 10^8 \, ms^{-1}}{1.6 \times 10^{-19} \times C \times V} = \frac{1.24 \times 10^{-6}}{V} \text{ V-m} \qquad (3)$$

which is just the same as the experimental relation given by eq. 1.

*Example*: Find the shortest wavelength that is present in the X-rays produced at an accelerating potential of 50 KV. Calculate the corresponding frequency also.

*Solution*: Given: Accelerating potential, $V = 50$ KV $= 5 \times 10^4$ V. Now using eq. 3, we have

$$\lambda_{min} = \frac{1.24 \times 10^{-6}}{5 \times 10^4 \, V} \text{ V-m} = 2.5 \times 10^{11} \text{ m} = 0.25 \text{Å}$$

Corresponding frequency is given by

$$\nu_{max} = \frac{c}{\lambda_{min}} = \frac{3 \times 10^8 \, ms^{-1}}{2.5 \times 10^{-11} \, m} = 1.2 \times 10^{19} \text{ Hz}$$

The characteristic (or monochromatic) X-rays result in the form of excess of energy $E_{K\alpha}$ when the incident electron beam ejects some of the most energetic $K$-electrons from the atoms of a metal target by absorbing an energy equal to $W_K$ and the resulting vacancies in the $K$-shell are replaced by less energetic electrons $W_L$ from the $L$-shell. Such X-rays are called $K_\alpha$ radiations (Fig. 8.2). If the vacancies in the $K$-shell are replaced by electrons from M-shell, the resulting X-rays are called $K_\beta$ radiations, however this is less probable transition. Fig. 8.3 shows the energy level diagram and possible transitions. They are:

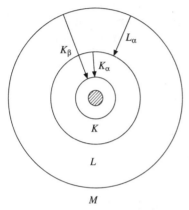

**Fig. 8.2  Electron orbits in an atom, showing transitions associated with the production of characteristic X-rays**

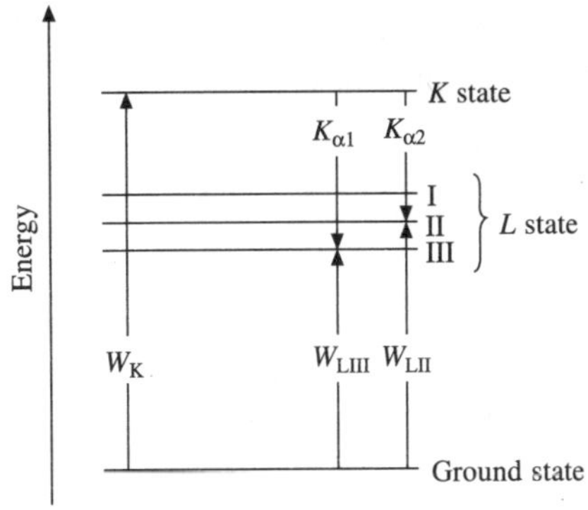

**Fig. 8.3  Energy level diagram showing the allowed transitions**

$$E_{K\alpha1} = W_K - W_{LIII} \text{ due to } K \rightarrow L_{III} \text{ transition}$$

and

$$E_{K\alpha2} = W_K - W_{LII} \text{ due to } K \rightarrow L_{II} \text{ transition}$$

where $K_{\alpha1}$ = 1.54051 Å and $K_{\alpha2}$ = 1.54433 Å respectively for copper target.

Complete X-ray spectrum ($I$ versus $\lambda$ curve) emitted by copper target is shown by solid line in Fig. 8.4. The $K$-radiations from elements of intermediate atomic weights have wavelengths comparable to interatomic dimensions and these are suuitable for crystal differaction experiments.

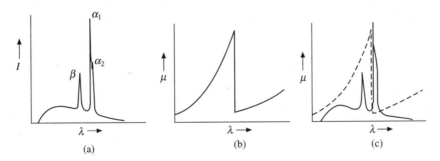

**Fig. 8.4  Complete X-ray spectrum, I versus $\lambda$ curve: solid line shows the characteristic lines superimposed on a background of while radiation. Dotted line shows $K$ absorption edge suitable for use as a $\beta$-filter**

The essential parts of an X-ray tube are shown in Fig. 8.5. A heated tungsten filament (acting as cathode) provides the electron beam, which under a large negative potential (~50 KV) is accelerated towards the target (acting as anode) to give reasonable amount of *K*-radiations. In order to prevent the electrons from losing their energy by colliding with gas molecules before they reach the target, the intervening space is evaluated. The negatively charged screen surrounding the filament serves to focus the electron beam into the target. The X-rays produced in this process leave the X-ray tube through windows usually made of beryllium, which when not in use are covered by shutters made of lead. Beryllium and lead are chosen because they have respectively low and high absorption coefficients for X-rays. In general, absorption increases with the increase of atomic number of element.

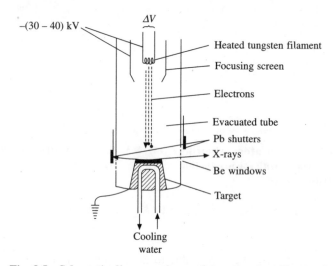

**Fig. 8.5 Schemetic diagram of essential parts of an X-ray tube**

The choice of target material depends on several factors. From the engineering point of view, it should be a good conductor of heat so that it can be effectively cooled (a huge amount of heat is generated on the target for being at a large electrode potential) and of electricity (because it has to function as an anode). These requirements suggest the target material to be a metal having reasonably high melting point. Further, from the crystallographer's point of view, it should emit X-rays having wavelengths of the order of 1 Å. The above mentioned requirements limit the choice to the first and second-row transition metals. The most widely used target material is copper which fulfils the above conditions well. Besides, there are some other metals used as target element for the generation of X-rays of desired specifications. A list of commonly used target elements along with the wavelengths of their characteristic $K_\alpha$ lines is provided in Table 8.1.

X-ray tubes may be permanently sealed after evacuation, or may be demountable in which vacuum is maintained by continuous pumping. A sealed tube has neither rotating anode facility nor it is possible to replace any of its component if goes wrong, the whole tube has to be replaced. Also, a different tube is needed for each type of radiation. On the other hand, despite having certain advantages, demountable tubes require an extra maintenance facility and not

**Table 8.1   Target elements, corresponding X-ray wavelengths and filter elements**

| Elements | with at. no. | X-ray | wavelengths | Density | Optimum |
|----------|--------------|-------|-------------|---------|---------|
| Target | Filter | $K_{\alpha 1}$ | $K_{\alpha 2}$ | | thickness |
| Cr  (24) | V  (23) | 2.2896 | 2.2935 | 0.009 | 0.016 |
| Fe  (26) | Mn  (25) | 1.9360 | 1.9399 | 0.012 | 0.016 |
| Cu  (29) | Ni  (28) | 1.5405 | 1.5443 | 0.019 | 0.021 |
| Mo  (42) | Nb  (41) | 0.7093 | 0.7135 | 0.069 | 0.108 |
| Au  (47) | Pd  (46) | 0.5594 | 0.5638 | 0.030 | 0.030 |

readily available for use. This may be one of the reasons that most crystallographers use permanently sealed tubes for their X-ray diffraction work.

*Example*: If the potential difference across an X-ray tube is 6000 volt and the current through it is 2.5 mA, calculate the number of electrons striking the target per second and the speed at which they strike. Also calculate the shortest wavelength of X-rays produced.

*Solution*: Given: $I = 2.5$ mA $= 2.5 \times 10^{-3}$ A, $n = ?$, and $\lambda_{min} = ?$

We know that
$$n = \frac{Q}{e} = \frac{I \times t}{e} = \frac{2.5 \times 10^{-3}}{1.6 \times 10^{-19}} = 1.56 \times 10^{16}$$

Further, we have $eV = (1/2)\, mv^2$,

or
$$v^2 = \frac{2eV}{m} = \frac{2 \times 1.6 \times 10^{-19} \times 6 \times 10^3}{9.1 \times 10^{-31}} = 21.078 \times 10^{14}$$

or
$$v = 4.59 \times 10^7 \text{ m/s}$$

Also,
$$\lambda_{min} = \frac{1.24 \times 10^{-6}}{V} \text{ V-m} = \frac{1.24 \times 10^{-6}}{6000} = 2.06 \text{ Å}$$

*Example*: If $K$, $L$ and $M$ energy levels of platinum lie roughly at 78, 12 and 3 k eV, respectively, calculate the approximate wavelength of the $K_\alpha$ and $K_\beta$ lines.

*Solution*: Draw the energy level diagram as shown in Fig. 8.6, we can obtain

$$(h\nu)_{K\alpha} = E_L - E_K = -12 + 78 = 66 \text{ k eV}$$

and

$$(h\nu)_{K\beta} = E_M - E_K = -3 + 78 = 75 \text{ k eV}$$

The first equation can be written as

$$\frac{hc}{\lambda_{K\alpha}} = 66 \text{ keV} \quad \text{or} \quad \lambda_{K\alpha} = \frac{hc}{66\,\text{keV}}$$

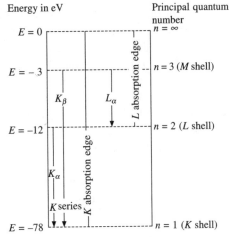

**Fig. 8.6   K, L and M energy levels for platinum**

or
$$\lambda_{K\alpha} = \frac{6.626 \times 10^{-34} \times 3 \times 10^8}{66 \times 1.6 \times 10^{-19} \times 10^3} = 0.19 \text{Å}$$

Similarly, from second equation, we can obtain $\lambda_{K\beta} = 0.17$ Å.

## 8.3 MOSELEY'S LAW

During 1913-14, Moseley carried out a systematic study of the characteristic X-ray spectra emitted by various elements that were used as targets in X-ray tubes. He used Bragg's spectrometer for the purpose and found that the spectra of different elements are similar to the extent that they all contain K, L, M and N-series. However, he found them to differ from one another in one respect, i.e. in terms of frequency. The characteristic frequency emitted by an element (in every series) was found to depend on its atomic number according to the equation

$$\sqrt{v} \propto a(Z - b)$$

or
$$v = [a\,(Z - b)]^2 \tag{4}$$

where $a$ and $b$ are constants for a particular series (their values are different for different series). The constant $a$ is related to Rydberg constant, $b$ is a small number called the nuclear screening constant and $(Z - b)$ is the effective mass number of the element. For $K$ spectrum; $b = 1$, and hence the eq. 4 reduces to

$$v = [a\,(Z - 1)]^2 \tag{5}$$

Moseley plotted a graph between the atomic weight of the elements and the square root of the frequencies of characteristic X-rays and also between the square root of the frequencies and the atomic number of elements emitting them. He found that in the first case, the points lie on or near the straight line, while in the second case, they lie exactly on the straight line (Fig. 8.7). With the help of such a plot missing elements like promethium (Pm) and technetium (Tc) were predicted. Further, Moseley's results made it possible to determine the exact atomic number of many elements which were not known correctly at that time. For example he found that the atomic number of Argon (Ar) should be less than Potasium (K) and hence to be put first in the serial order. Earlier, they were wrongly placed in the order of increasing atomic

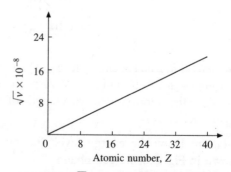

**Fig. 8.7** $\sqrt{v}$ **versus atomic number**

weights. Moseley, thus came to an important conclusion that it is the Atomic number rather than the atomic weight which determines the chemical and X-ray emitting properties of an atom. He identified the atomic number with the positive charge on the nucleus.

Moseley's law can be deduced theoretically from Bohr's atomic model, according to which the energy of an electron moving in an orbit of principal quantum number $n_1$ (as derived in section 4.2), is given by

$$E_1 = -\frac{me^4 Z^2}{8\varepsilon_0^2 n_1^2 h^2} \tag{6}$$

and for an electron moving in an orbit of principal quantum number $n_2$ is given by

$$E_2 = -\frac{me^4 Z^2}{8\varepsilon_0^2 n_2^2 h^2} \tag{7}$$

However, taking into account the screening effect of the nucleus, the effective atomic number of an element changes from $Z$ to $(Z - b)$. Thus, the above expression can be written as

$$E_1 = -\frac{me^4 (Z - b_1)^2}{8\varepsilon_0^2 n_1^2 h^2}$$

and

$$E_2 = -\frac{me^4 (Z - b_1)^2}{8\varepsilon_0^2 n_2^2 h^2}$$

so that, $\qquad \Delta E = E_1 - E_2 = \dfrac{me^4}{8\varepsilon_0^2 h^2} \left( \dfrac{(Z - b_2)^2}{n_2^2} - \dfrac{(Z - b_1)^2}{n_1^2} \right)$

For high $Z$ values, $b_1 \simeq b_2 \simeq b$, therefore

$$\Delta E = \frac{me^4 (Z - b)^2}{8\varepsilon_0^2 h^2} \left( \frac{1}{n_2^2} - \frac{1}{n_1^2} \right)$$

But, $\Delta E = h\nu$, the therefore

$$h\nu = \frac{me^4 (Z - b)^2}{8\varepsilon_0^2 h^2} \left( \frac{1}{n_2^2} - \frac{1}{n_1^2} \right)$$

or $\qquad\qquad\qquad \nu = \dfrac{me^4 (Z - b)^2}{8\varepsilon_0^2 h^3} \left( \dfrac{1}{n_2^2} - \dfrac{1}{n_1^2} \right) \tag{8}$

The eq. 8 can also be written as $\nu \propto (Z - b)^2$, which is the required Moseley's law

*Example*: The wavelength of $L_\alpha$ X-ray line of platinum (at. number 78) is 1.321Å. An unknown element emits $L_\alpha$ X-rays of wavelength 4.174Å. Calculate the atomic number of unknown element where $b$ for $L_\alpha$ is 7.4.

*Solution*: Given: $\lambda_{L\alpha}(\text{Pt}) = 1.321$Å, At. No. (Pt) = 78, $b = 7.4$, $\lambda_{L\alpha}$ of unknown element say, $x = 4.174$Å, At. No. $(x) = ?$
Making use of eq. 4, we have

$$\nu = [a(Z - b)]^2$$

Therefore, $\qquad\qquad \nu_{\text{Pt}} = \dfrac{c}{\lambda_{\text{Pt}}} = [a(78 - 7.4)]^2$

Similarly,
$$v_x = \frac{c}{\lambda_x} = [a(x - 7.4)]^2$$

Dividing one from the other and solving for $x$, we have

$$x = 7.4 + \left(\frac{\lambda_{pt}}{\lambda_x}\right)^{1/2} \times 70.6 = 7.4 + 70.6 \times \left(\frac{1321}{4174}\right)^{1/2} = 47.1$$

*Example*: The wavelength of $K_\alpha$ (X-ray line) for tungsten is 210 Å. Calculate its value for copper, if the atomic number of tungsten is 74 and that of copper is 29.

*Solution*: Given $\lambda_{K\alpha}(W) = 210$ Å $= 210 \times 10^{-10}$ m, At. No. (W) = 74, At. No.(Cu) = 29, for K-series $b = 1$, $\lambda_{K\alpha}$ (Cu) = ?
Again, making use of eq. 4, we obtain

$$v_w = \frac{c}{\lambda_w} = (a \times 73)^2$$

Similarly, for Cu
$$v_{Cu} = \frac{c}{\lambda_{Cu}} = (a \times 28)^2$$

From these two equations, we can obtain

$$\lambda_{Cu} = \left(\frac{73}{28}\right)^2 \times 210 = 1427 \text{ Å}$$

*Example*: What element has a $K_\alpha$ X-ray line of wavelength 0.7185 Å?

*Solution*: Given: $\lambda_{K\alpha} = 0.7185$ Å $= 0.7185 \times 10^{-10}$m. Now, let us make use of the equation

$$v = \frac{c}{\lambda} = \frac{me^4(Z - b)^2}{8\varepsilon_0^2 h^3}\left(\frac{1}{n_2^2} - \frac{1}{n_1^2}\right)$$

Since, the $K_\alpha$ transition takes place from $n = 2$ to $n = 1$ and $b = 1$. Therefore, substituting $n_1 = 1$ and $n_2 = 2$ and $b = 1$ in the above equation, we obtain

$$\lambda_{K\alpha} = \frac{4}{3}\left(\frac{8\varepsilon_0^2 ch^3}{me^4(Z - 1)^2}\right)$$

or
$$(Z - 1)^2 = \frac{32 \times \varepsilon_0^2 \times c \times h^3}{3m \times e^4 \times \lambda_{K\alpha}}$$

$$= \frac{32 \times (8.85 \times 10^{-12})^2 \times 3 \times 10^8 \times (6.626 \times 10^{-34})^3}{3 \times 9.1 \times 10^{-31} \times (1.6 \times 10^{-19})^4 \times 0.7185 \times 10^{-10}} = 1701.54$$

or
$$Z = 1 + 41.25 \simeq 42$$

This implies that the element is molybdenum.

*Example*: The wavelengths of $K_\alpha$ lines for iron and platinum are 1.93 Å and 0.19 Å, respectively. Determine the $K_\alpha$ lines for tin and barium.

*Solution*: Given: $\lambda_{Fe} = 1.93$ Å, $\lambda_{Pt} = 0.19$Å, $\lambda_{Sn} = ?$ and $\lambda_{Ba} = ?$
We know that $Z_{Fe} = 26$, $Z_{Pt} = 78$, $Z_{Sn} = 50$ and $Z_{Ba} = 56$, also for $K_\alpha$ line, $b = 1$.
Now, for $K_\alpha$ lines, the Moseley's law is given by

$$v \propto (Z - 1)^2 \text{ or } \frac{c}{\lambda} \propto (Z - 1)^2$$

or

$$\lambda \propto \frac{1}{(Z - 1)^2}$$

so that

$$\lambda_{Fe} \propto \frac{1}{(25)^2} \text{ and } \lambda_{Sn} \propto \frac{1}{(49)^2}$$

and

$$\frac{\lambda_{Sn}}{\lambda_{Fe}} = \frac{(25)^2}{(49)^2}$$

or

$$\lambda_{Sn} = \frac{(25)^2}{(49)^2} \times \lambda_{Fe} = \frac{(25)^2}{(49)^2} \times 1.93 = 0.5 \text{ Å}$$

Making a similar calculation, we can obtain

$$\lambda_{Ba} = 0.37 \text{ Å}$$

## 8.4 ABSORPTION OF X-RAYS (CLASSICAL THEORY)

When X-rays are pased through a material, the intensity of the transmitted beam is less than that of the incident beam It is due to the scattering of the X-rays in all directions by the electrons present in the material. In order to estimate the amount of loss, suppose the material contains $n$ electrons per gram of mass. For convenience, let us suppose that the material has a unit cross sectional area perpendicular to the beam and a thickness $x$ parallel to it (Fig. 8.8). Next, consider a slice of thickness $dx$ whose volume is

$$dV = 1 \times 1 \times dx \text{ cm}^3$$

If the density of the material is $\rho$, then the total number of electrons in the slice is $n\rho dV$. Therefore, the total scattered radiation going out in all directions from the slice of volume $dV$ is

$$dp = I\sigma_e n\rho dV \tag{9}$$

where $\sigma_e$ is the classical scattering cross-section or the scattering coefficent of an electron.
Now, the decrease in the intensity of the transmitted beam due to scattering by the electrons of the slice is

$$dI = -dp = -I\sigma_e n\rho(1) \, dx \tag{10}$$

where the minus sign indicates the decrease in the intensity. Writing like terms of eq. 10 seperately and integrating both sides, we obtain

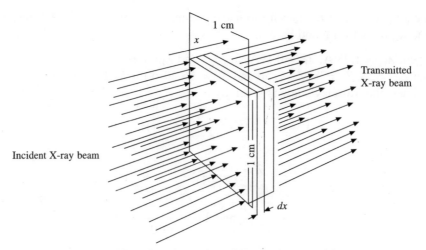

**Fig. 8.8    Absorption of X-rays by material**

$$\int \frac{dI}{I} = -\int \sigma_e n\rho dx$$

or $$\qquad\qquad \ln I = -\sigma_e n\rho x + \text{constant} \qquad\qquad (11)$$

Applying the boundary condition that $I = I_0$ when $x = 0$, the value of the constant in eq. 11 is equal to $\ln I_0$, which on substitution gives

$$\frac{I}{I_0} = \exp(-\sigma_e)n\rho x$$

or $$\qquad\qquad I = I_0 \exp(-\sigma_e)n\rho x \qquad\qquad (12)$$

Now, writing eq. 12 in terms of mass scattering coefficient which is equal to $n\sigma_e$, we have

$$I = I_0 \exp(-\sigma_m)\rho x \qquad\qquad (13)$$

Again, writing $\sigma_m \rho = \mu$, where $\mu$ is the linear attenuation coefficient, then eq. 13 becomes

$$I = I_0 \exp(-\mu)x \qquad\qquad (14)$$

A curve between $I$ versus $x$ (Fig. 8.9) indicates that the intensity of X-ray beam decreases

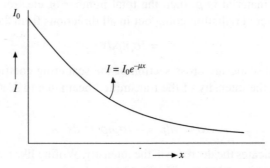

**Fig. 8.9    Intensity as a function of thickness of the absorbing material**

exponentially with the thickness of the absorbing material. In deriving eq. 14, we have considered only coherent scattering responsible for the attenuation in the intensity of the X-ray beam passing through a material. Actually, in addition to this there are some other processes (viz. Compton scattering, fluorescence and pair production) which are also responsible for the attentuation of the transmitted beam.

In terms of the linear attenuation coefficient, eq. 14, may be rewritten as

$$\mu = -\frac{dI/I}{dx} \tag{15}$$

where $\mu$ is defined as the fractional fall in the intensity of the X-rays per unit thickness of the absorber. However, the actual value of $\mu$ depends on the wavelength of the X-rays and on the absorbing material. The value of $\mu$ can be determined by finding the thickness of the absorbing material which reduces the intensity of the X-ray beam to half of its initial value. Such a thickness of absorbing material is known as half-value layer, $x_H$, Thus, eq. 14 can be written as

$$\frac{I}{I_0} = \frac{1}{2} = \exp(-\mu x_H)$$

or $$\exp(\mu x_H) = 2$$

or $$\mu x_H = 2.303 \times \log_{10}2 = 0.693$$

or $$\mu = \frac{0.693}{x_H} \tag{16}$$

*Example*: The linear attenuation coefficient for aluminium is 139 m$^{-1}$ for $K_\alpha$ line emitted by a tungsten target in an X-ray tube. Calculate what percentage of the intensity of this line will pass through 0.005 m thick sheet of aluminium.

*Solution*: $\mu = 139$ m$^{-1}$, $x = 0.005$ m, Percentage of transmitted intensity = ?
Let X% of the intensity is being transmitted through the aluminium sheet, then we have

$$X\% = \frac{I}{I_0}$$

or $$\frac{X}{100} = \exp(-\mu x)$$

or $$X = 100 \times \exp(-\mu x) = 100 \times \exp(-139 \times 0.005) = 50\%$$

*Example*: A beam of X-rays consists of equal intensities of wavelengths 0.064Å and 0.098 Å. When they pass through a piece of lead, their attenuated beam intensity are in the ratio 3:1. The mass absorption coefficients are 0.164 m$^2$/kg for the harder component and 0.35 m$^2$/kg for the softer component. If the density of the lead is 11340 kg/m$^3$, calculate the thickness of the lead piece.

*Solution*: Given: $\lambda_1 = 0.064$ Å, $\lambda_2 = 0.098$ Å, $\mu_{m1} = 0.164$ m$^2$/kg for $\lambda_1$, $\mu_{m2} = 0.35$ m$^2$/kg for $\lambda_2$, $I(\lambda_1) = I(\lambda_2)$ and $\rho = 11340$ kg/m$^3$, also according to question, $I_1 : I_2 = 3 : 1$, $x = ?$

Here, $$\mu_1 = \mu_{m1} \times \rho = 0.164 \times 11340 = 1859.76 \text{ m}^{-1}$$

$$\mu_2 = \mu_{m2} \times \rho = 0.35 \times 11340 = 3969.00 \text{ m}^{-1}$$

Now, making use of eq. 14, we have

$$3 = \frac{\exp(-1859.76)x}{\exp(-3969.00)x} = \exp(2109.24)x$$

or $\qquad\qquad$ $2104.24\ x = \ln 3$ and $x = 5.22 \times 10^{-4}$m

## 8.5  ABSORPTION EDGE

From Section 8.2 we know that the spectrum emitted by a conventional X-ray tube operating under normal conditions consists of characteristic lines (of the target material) superimposed on a continuous background of "white" radiation (Fig. 8.4a). Since most X-ray diffraction experiments require a monochromatic beam therefore it is necessary to separate the characteristic $K_\alpha$ radiation by filtering out $K_\beta$ and the continuous background radiations. This can be achieved if we use a suitable filter element whose absorption edge (it is the vertical portion of the curve shown in Fig. 8.4b and corresponds to the energy required to eject $K$-electrons from the filter element) lies between $K_\alpha$ and $K_\beta$ wavelengths of the radiation to be filtered. This condition is found to satisfy when the atomic number of the filter element is one or two less than the corresponding target element. The dotted line in Fig. 8.4c represents the absorption curve (atomic absorption coefficient $\mu$ versus $\lambda$) of nickel filter (whose atomic number is one less than that of copper) used for Cu target.

A convenient practical rule is to select a filter that reduces the intensity of the $\beta$ component relative to that of $\alpha$ component in the ratio 1 : 600, and the resulting beam, while not strictly monochromatic, is quite suitable for many diffraction experiments. The data regarding suitable filter elements (for given target materials), their densities and optimum thickness are provided in Table 8.1.

## 8.6  X-RAY DIFFRACTION

X-rays, like other electromagnetic waves, interact with the electron cloud of the atoms. Because of their shorter wavelengths, X-rays are scattered by adjacent atoms in crystals which can interfere and give rise to diffraction effects. When X-rays enter into a crystal, each atom acts as a diffraction centre and crystal as a whole acts like a three dimensional diffraction grating. The diffraction pattern so produced can tell us much about the internal arrangement of atoms in crystals. In order to visualise this, let us consider a crystal made up of equidistant parallel planes of atoms with the interplanar spacing as $d$. Further, consider a monochromatic X-ray beam of wavelength $\lambda$ having a common wave front, falls at an angle $\theta$ on these planes (Fig. 8.10). Each atom scatters the X-rays more or less uniformly in all directions, but because of the periodic arrangement of atoms, the scattered radiation from all atoms in a set of planes is in phase (i.e. in certain directions only) where they interfere constructively. In all other directions, there is destructive interference.

Consider two of the incoming X-rays $OE$ and $O'A$ inclined at an angle $\theta$ with the top most plane of the crystal and are scatterred in the directions $AP$ and $EP'$, also at an angle $\theta$ with that plane. Since the path length of the rays $OEP'$ and $O'AP$ are the same, they arrive at $P$ and $P'$,

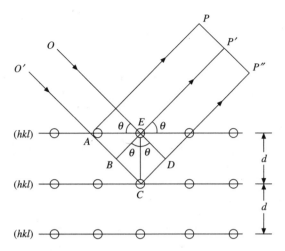

**Fig. 8.10 Diffraction of X-rays by crystal planes**

respectively in phase with each other and again form a common wave front. This is the condition for scattering in phase by one (top) plane of the crystal. In order to see the effect of an adjacent plane, let us consider the incoming beam $O'C$ and scattered ray $CP''$. If $EB$ and $ED$ are parallel to the incident and scattered wave front respectively then the total path $O'CP''$ is longer than the path $OEP'$ (or $O'AP$) by an amount

$$\Delta = BCD = 2BC$$

by construction. And, from right angle triangle $EBC$, we have $BC = d \sin \theta$ so that the path difference

$$\Delta = 2BC = 2d \sin \theta$$

If the two consecutive planes scatter in phase with each other, then we know that the path difference $\Delta$ must be equal to an integral multiple of wavelength, i.e. $\Delta = n\lambda$, where $n = 0, 1, 2\ldots$ gives the order of reflection. Thus the condition for in-phase scattering by a set of equidistant parallel planes in a crystal is given by

$$2d \sin \theta = n\lambda \qquad (17)$$

Equation 17 is the well known Bragg's law, after W.L. Bragg who first derived it. The diffracted beams thus fulfil the geometry of a reflection but arise only for certain discrete values of $\theta$ for which the Bragg's law is fulfilled.

We know that $(\sin \theta)_{max} = 1$. Using this in eq. 17, we obtain

$$\frac{n\lambda}{2d} \leq 1$$

This indicates that $\lambda$ must not be greater than twice the interplanar spacing, otherwise no diffraction will occur.

*Example*: Determine the angle through which an X-ray of wavelength 0.440Å be reflected from the cube face of a rocksalt crystal ($d = 2.814$ Å).

*Solution*: Given: $\lambda = 0.440\text{Å}$, $d = 2.814\text{Å}$. Using eq. 17, angles for various orders of reflections (i.e. $\theta_1$ for $n = 1$, $\theta_2$ for $n = 2$, etc.) can be determined.
We know that

$$\sin \theta = \frac{n\lambda}{2d} \text{ or } \theta = \sin^{-1}\left(\frac{n\lambda}{2d}\right)$$

Therefore,

$$\theta_1 = \sin^{-1}\left(\frac{1\lambda}{2d}\right) = \sin^{-1}\left(\frac{0.440}{5.628}\right) = 0.0782 = 4° \ 29'$$

Similarly,

$$\theta_2 = \sin^{-1}(2 \times 0.0782) = 8° \ 59'$$

$$\theta_3 = \sin^{-1}(3 \times 0.0782) = 13° \ 34'$$

$$\theta_4 = \sin^{-1}(4 \times 0.0782) = 18° \ 13'$$

$$\theta_5 = \sin^{-1}(5 \times 0.0782) = 23°$$

Hence, the reflected beam will be observed at the following angles, i.e. $4° \ 29'$, $8° \ 59'$, $13° \ 34'$, $18° \ 13'$ and $23°$, etc.

*Example*: Determine the wavelength of the diffracted beam, when a beam of X-rays having wavelengths in the range 0.2 Å to 1 Å incident at an angle of 9° with the cube face of a rocksalt crystal ($d = 2.814$ Å).

*Solution*: Given: $d = 2.814$ Å, Bragg's angle $\theta = 9°$. Again using the Bragg's equation, $2d \sin \theta = n\lambda$, we have

| | |
|---|---|
| $1\lambda_1 = 5.628 \sin 9°$ | or $\lambda_1 = 0.8804$ Å |
| $2\lambda_2 = 0.8804$ Å | or $\lambda_2 = 0.4402$ Å |
| $3\lambda_3 = 0.8804$ Å | or $\lambda_3 = 0.2935$ Å |
| $4\lambda_4 = 0.8804$ Å | or $\lambda_4 = 0.2201$ Å |
| and $5\lambda_5 = 0.8804$ Å | or $\lambda_5 = 0.1760$ Å |

The last one is less than 0.2 Å and hence the diffracted beam contains the first four wavelengths, i.e. 0.8804 Å, 0.4402 Å, 0.2935 Å and 0.2201 Å in the ratio $1 : \frac{1}{2} : \frac{1}{3} : \frac{1}{4}$.

## 8.7   THE LAUE EQUATIONS

Although the Bragg's equation is a result of the fundamental periodic arrangement of crystal planes, but in true sense it does not refer to the actual arrangement of the atoms associated with them. On the other hand, the Laue equations are more general and are derived from a simple static atomic model of a crystal. The Bragg's equation can be shown to be quivalent and also a consequence of the Laue equations.

We know that when a beam of X-rays of wavelength $\lambda$ strikes a row of equally spaced atoms, each atom becomes a source of scattering of waves in all directions which reinforce in certain directions to produce various orders of differaction spots. The condition of reinforcement is that the path difference between the rays diffracted by two adjacent atoms in the row must be an integral multiple of the wavelength.

For simplicity, let us consider a one dimensional row of atoms with interatomic distance $a$ (Fig. 8.11). Suppose that $AB$ is the incident plane wave front making an angle $\alpha_0$ with a row of atoms, and $CD$ is the diffracted plane wave front leaving at an angle $\alpha$ with the same row of atoms. Then the path difference between the two consecutive rays is

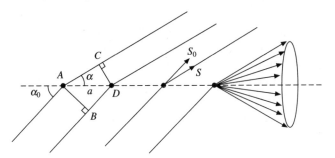

**Fig. 8.11   Diffraction of X-rays by one row of atoms**

$$\Delta = (AC - BD) = a\,(\cos\alpha - \cos\alpha_0)$$

and a diffracted beam is observed only if

$$a\,(\cos\alpha - \cos\alpha_0) = e\lambda \tag{18}$$

where $e = 0, 1, 2, \ldots$, is any integer giving the order of diffraction.

This equation will be satisfied by all the diffracted beams lying on the concentric cone with respect to the line of atoms and has the semiapex angle $\alpha$ (Fig. 8.11). Thus, for any given angle of incidence there will be a series of concentric cones surrounding the row of atoms, where each cone represents various orders of diffraction. The direction of the primary beam is indicated by the downward arrow, while the higher orders of diffraction are indicated by the numbers (Fig. 8.12).

If we assume $S_0$ and $S$ as the unit vectors, respectively in the directions of the incident and diffracted beam and "$a$" is the translation vector along the $x$-axis, then in vector notation the eq. 18 can be written as

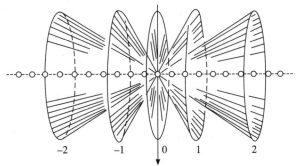

$$\begin{array}{ccccc} -2 & -1 & 0 & 1 & 2 \end{array}$$

**Fig. 8.12   Diffraction cones around a row of atoms. Direction of primary beam is indicated by the arrow. Numbers indicate the order of differaction**

$$a \cdot (S - S_0) = e\lambda \qquad (18')$$

In a two dimensional plane lattice with an interatomic spacing "$a$" in one direction and "$b$" in another, for intense diffracted beams to occur the two equations of the type 18 or 18′ must be satisfied simultaneously

$$\left.\begin{array}{l} a(\cos \alpha - \cos \alpha_0) = a \cdot (S - S_0) = e\lambda \\ b(\cos \beta - \cos \beta_0) = b \cdot (S - S_0) = f\lambda \end{array}\right\} \qquad (19)$$

where $\beta_0$, $\beta$ and $f$ respectively have the same meaning for the $b$-rows of atoms as $\alpha_0$, $\alpha$ and $e$ for the $a$-rows of atoms. The inclusion of the second row of atoms strongly limits the number of possible diffracted beams. Further, the two equations correspond to two sets of cones, one set each around $a$-and $b$-rows of atoms and the most intense diffracted beam will be directed along the intersection of the two sets of cones, as shown in Fig. 8.13. The stereographic projection of the diffracted beams for a two dimensional square lattice ($a = b$, $\phi = 90°$) is illustrated in Fig. 8.14.

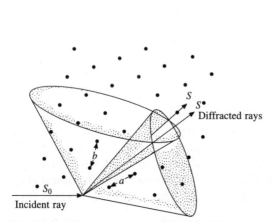

**Fig. 8.13** **Intersection of two diffraction cones, one each for a- and b-rows of atoms**

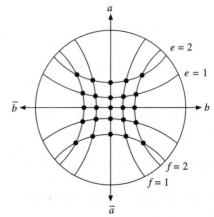

**Fig. 8.14** **Steriographic projection of diffracted beams from a two dimensional square lattice. Cones are concentric with a and b axes. Intersections give the direction of most intense diffracted beams**

Finally, as we know that a crystal is a three dimensional periodic arrangement of atoms. Thus the diffraction to occur from a simple space lattice with a unit cell defined by the primitive translations $a$, $b$ and $c$, the following three equations must be satisfied simultaneously;

$$a(\cos \alpha - \cos \alpha_0) = a \cdot (S - S_0) = e\lambda$$

$$b(\cos \beta - \cos \beta_0) = b \cdot (S - S_0) = f\lambda \qquad (20)$$

$$c(\cos \gamma - \cos \gamma_0) = c \cdot (S - S_0) = g\lambda$$

where $\gamma_0$, $\gamma$ and $g$ respectively have the same meaning for the $c$-rows of atoms as ($\alpha_0$, $\alpha$, $e$) and

($\beta_0$, $\beta$, $f$) for $a$- or $b$-rows of atoms. These three equations together are called Laue equations. Like the first two, the third equation corresponds to a set of concentric cones around $c$-rows of atoms. Thus for a crystal, there are three sets of cones, one each around $a$, $b$ and $c$-rows of atoms and the most intense diffracted beam will be directed along the intersection of three sets of cones. The inclusion of the third row of atoms further limits the number of possible diffracted beams.

It is to be noted that for a fixed $\lambda$ (i.e. a monochromatic beam) and an arbitrary direction of incidence (i.e. fixed $S_0$) it is not possible to find a direction $S$ which satisfies the Laue equations simultaneously and hence in general no diffraction should be observed. This actually means that the diffraction will occur only for particular angle of incidence.

## 8.8   EQUIVALENCE OF BRAGG AND LAUE EQUATIONS

To prove the Bragg equation to be equivalent to Laue equations, let us consider the case of a simple cubic lattice with $a = b = c$ and assume the angle between incident and diffracted beam to be equal to $2\theta$. Then squaring and adding the three Laue equations we can write

$$a^2[\cos^2\alpha + \cos^2\beta + \cos^2\gamma + \cos^2\alpha_0 + \cos^2\beta_0 + \cos^2\gamma_0 - 2$$

$$(\cos\alpha\cos\alpha_0 + \cos\beta\cos\beta_0 + \cos\gamma\cos\gamma_0)] = \lambda^2[e^2 + f^2 + g^2] \tag{21}$$

From solid geometry we know that the law of direction cosines states that

$$\cos^2\alpha + \cos^2\beta + \cos^2\gamma = \cos^2\alpha_0 + \cos^2\beta_0 + \cos^2\gamma_0 = 1$$

and $\qquad\qquad \cos\alpha\cos\alpha_0 + \cos\beta\cos\beta_0 + \cos\gamma\cos\gamma_0 = \cos 2\theta$

Making use of these results, eq. 21 reduces to

$$2(1 - \cos 2\theta) = \frac{\lambda^2}{a^2}(e^2 + f^2 + g^2)$$

or $\qquad\qquad\qquad\qquad \sin^2\theta = \frac{\lambda^2}{4a^2}(e^2 + f^2 + g^2) \tag{22}$

Similarly, squaring the Bragg's equation, we have

$$\sin^2\theta = \frac{n^2\lambda^2}{4a^2}(h^2 + k^2 + l^2) \tag{23}$$

where $d = \dfrac{a}{(h^2 + k^2 + l^2)^{1/2}}$ for a cubic system (section 1.11).

Now, comparing eqs. 22 and 23, we find that

$$e = nh, f = nk \text{ and } g = nl$$

This means that a diffracted beam defined in the Laue's treatment by the integers $e$, $f$, $g$ may be interpreted as the $n^{th}$ order diffraction from a set of ($hkl$) planes in the Bragg's treatment. The order of diffraction $n$ is simply equal to the largest common factor of the numbers $e$, $f$, $g$. This proves the equivalence of Bragg and Laue equations and suggests that the Bragg equation is a consequence of more general Laue equations.

## 8.9 INTERPRETATION OF BRAGG'S EQUATION

Bragg's diffraction condition given by eq. 17 has been obtained from the assumption that a crystal is made up of a large number of equidistant parallel planes. The integer $n$ in the expression gives the order of diffraction. It is conventional to incorporate the order of integer $n$ with the interplanar spacing $d$. Then the eq. 17 becomes

$$\lambda = 2\frac{d}{n}\sin\theta \tag{24}$$

Here $d/n$ has a simple meaning in crystallography because it is possible to assign the indices ($nh$, $nk$, $nl$) to some imaginary planes whose spacing is $d_{hkl}/n$. In practice, $n$ is omitted from the equation and hence the modified form of Bragg's law can be written as

$$\lambda = 2d_{hkl}\sin\theta_{hkl} \tag{25}$$

which indicates the diffraction by the specific planes ($hkl$) or at a particular angle $\theta_{hkl}$ (often called the Bragg angle) corresponding to a particular plane ($hkl$). Equation 25 can be written as,

$$\sin\theta_{hkl} = \frac{\lambda/2}{d_{hkl}} = \frac{1/d_{hkl}}{2/\lambda} \tag{26}$$

Now from the knowledge of simple geometry, we know that a triangle inscribed inside a circle is a right-angled triangle when the diameter of the circle is taken as the hypotenuse of the triangle. Let us draw a circle whose diameter is $2/\lambda$ and inscribe a triangle satisfying eq. 26. The perpendicular component is $1/d_{hkl}$ and the opposite angle is $\theta_{hkl}$ as shown in Fig. 8.15a. This is simply a graphical representation of the Bragg's law.

To understand the physical meaning of geometrical representation, assume that the horizontal diameter AO is the direction of incident X-ray beam. Since the line AP makes an angle $\theta$ with respect to the incident beam, it has the slope of a crystal plane (as shown at the centre of the circle). Since OP is the normal to the crystal plane as also to AP and has the length $1/d_{hkl} = \sigma_{hkl}$ = $G$ called as reciprocal lattice vector. Further, $\angle OCP = 2 \angle OAP = 2\theta$ so that CP is the direction of diffracted beam. Thus, Fig. 8.15b is a graphical interpretation of Bragg's law in terms of reciprocal lattice vector $\sigma_{hkl}$. The whole process can be stated briefly as:

1. Imagine the crystal to be at the centre $C$ of a circle (sphere in three dimension) of radius $1/\lambda$.

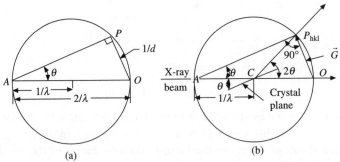

(a)　　　　　　　　　(b)

**Fig. 8.15 (a) Geometric representation of Bragg's law. (b) Graphical interpretation of Bragg's law**

2. Point $O$ where direct X-ray beam leaves the circle (after passing through the crystal) is the origin of the reciprocal lattice net.

3. Whenever a reciprocal lattice vector intersect the circle (sphere in three dimension), the Bragg's condition (eq. 26) is satisfied, then a diffracted beam passes through the point of intersection and hence the X-ray diffraction becomes possible.

4. The locus of a point where the diffracted beam and reciprocal lattice point intersect a circle (or a sphere in 3-dimension) of radius $1/\lambda$ is called Ewald sphere or sphere of reflection.

## 8.10 EWALD CONSTRUCTION

From above discussion, it is clear that the relationship between the space lattice (in real space) and the corresponding reciprocal lattice is completely symmetrical, i.e. the planes in one system can be represented as perpendicular to the rows of points in the other system. However, to make the quantities in reciprocal space numerically as well as dimensionally same as the quantities in real space, a factor of $2\pi$ (which a crystallographer prefers to omit) is introduced. As a result, for example the reciprocal lattice vector will now be equal to $2\pi$ times the reciprocal of the spacing of the $(hkl)$ planes of the crystal lattice. Thus, multiplying all the vectors appearing in Fig. 8.15b by the factor $2\pi$ the resulting Ewald construction will become as shown in Fig. 8.16.

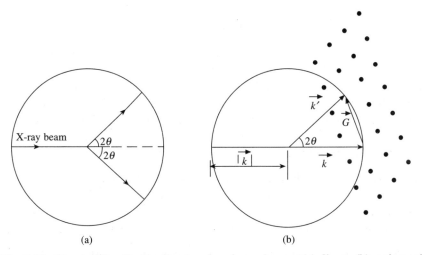

**Fig. 8.16 X-ray diffraction in direct and reciprocal space (a) direct, (b) reciprocal**

Here, two possibilities may arise:

1. If the circle (sphere in three dimension) does not pass through any reciprocal lattice point, it will indicate that the particular wavelength in question will not be diffracted by the crystal in that orientation and a reorientation of the crystal has to be made. Further, if the magnitude of the vector $|\ OA\ | < 1/2a$ (where $a$ is the lattice parameter), the circle will not pass through any reciprocal lattice point, indicating that the X-ray diffraction will not occur if $\lambda > 2a$. On the other hand, it may be seen from the figure that the longer the vector $OC$ the shorter the wavelength, greater is the possibility of circle's intersecting a reciprocal lattice point and hence the occurrence of diffraction is more probable.

2. If the circle passes through a reciprocal lattice point $P$, then $OP$ is a recirocal lattice vector normal to some set of lattice planes, e.g. AP. Hence, $OP = |\sigma| = |G| = 1/d$. Let $k = OC$ and $k' = CP$ be the incident and reflected wave vector, respectively. Then disposition of the vector requires that

$$k' = k + G \tag{27}$$

Equation 27 shows that: (i) the scattering changes only the direction of $k$, and (ii) the scattered wave differ from the incident wave by a reciprocal lattice vector $G$.

Since for elastic scattering, there will be no change in the magnitude of the vector, i.e.

$$|k| = |k'| = \frac{2\pi}{\lambda} \tag{28}$$

Now, squaring eq. 27, we obtain

$$k'^2 = (k + G)^2 = k^2 + G^2 + 2k \cdot G$$

Making use of eq. 28, we have

$$G^2 + 2k \cdot G = 0 \tag{29}$$

This is the Bragg's law in vector form.

## 8.11   THE RECIPROCAL LATTICE

According to section 1.9, a crystal lattice may be considered as an assembly of various different sets of equidistant parallel planes. Instead, it is conceptually more easy to visualize them in terms of their normals as one dimensional lines. Such a description has been the basis of a number of crystallographic projections, viz. gnomonic, stereographic etc. However, these projections display only the orientation of the planes with respect to the crystallographic axes and not the interplanar spacings. We shall now discuss about a projection which displays both.

Consider any given space lattice (or a real crystal lattice) and apply the following:

1. From a common origin draw a normal to each crystal plane.
2. Set the length of each normal equal to or $2\pi$ times the reciprocal of the interplanar spacing $d_{hkl}$.
3. Mark a point at the end of each normal which represents the crystal plane.

A collection of points obtained in this way corresponding to various crystal planes form a lattice array and is known as reciprrocal lattice. The reciprocal lattice points preserve all characteristics of the planes they represent. The direction from the origin preserves the orientation of the plane, and the distance of the point from the origin preserves the interplanar spacing of the planes it represents. The concept of the reciprocal lattice plays a very important role in the field of X-ray crystallography, lattice vibrations, electronic band structure, and in fact, all of the solid state physics. This concept was first given by P.P. Ewald (1921) and application was made by J.D. Bernal (1972).

The development of mathematical expressions (using vector algebra) showing relationships between direct and reciprocal lattices is comparatively compact and easy to understand. For simplicity, let us consider the two dimensional case first. To simplify further, let us take the case of a rectangular lattice with primitive translation vectors $a \neq b$ and $\phi = 90°$. Now, following the above stated procedure, draw the primitive reciprocal lattice vectors. They are shown in Fig. 8.17a and are related as:

$$a* \cdot a = 2\pi, \; b* \; \vdots \; b = 2\pi$$

and
$$a* \cdot b = b* \cdot a = 0$$

Similar to the translation vector in the direct lattice, the reciprocal lattice vector (connecting any point of the reciprocal lattice from the origin) may be defined as

$$G = n_1 \cdot a* + n_2 \cdot b*$$

where the magnitude of the primitive translation vectors of the reciprocal lattice are given by

$$a* = \frac{2\pi}{a} \text{ and } b* = \frac{2\pi}{b}$$

For a general lattice ($a \neq b$ and $\phi \neq 90°$), the relationship between the direct and the reciprocal lattice is not as straightforward as in the above case. Here, if the angle between $a$ and $b$ is $\theta$ then the angle between $a*$ and $b*$ will be $180 - \theta$ as shown in Fig. 8.17b. In this case, the magnitude of the reciprocal lattice vectors are

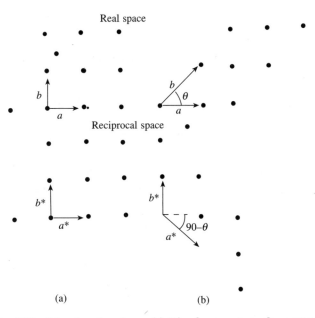

(a)                  (b)

**Fig. 8.17 Direct and reciprocal lattice for a rectangular system**

$$a* = \frac{2\pi}{a \cos(90 - \theta)} = \frac{2\pi}{a \sin \theta} \text{ and } b* = \frac{2\pi}{b \sin \theta}$$

In a three dimensional case, consider a direct crystal lattice whose unit cell is defined by the vectors $a$, $b$ and $c$ (Fig. 8.18). If the area of $bc$- plane is $A$, then the volume of the unit cell $V$ is given by

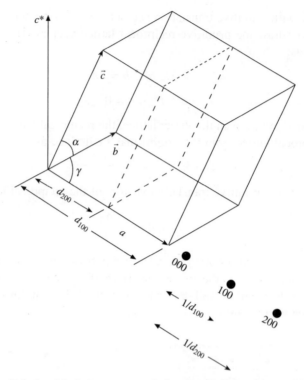

**Fig. 8.18** **Relationship between crystal planes and their reciprocal lattice points**

$$V = \text{Area of } bc\text{-plane} \times \text{height} = A \times d_{100}$$

so that

$$a^* = \frac{2\pi}{d_{100}} = \frac{2\pi A}{V} \tag{30}$$

Now, from vector algebra we know that the area of the $bc$-plane $A = bc \sin \alpha = b \times c$, and the volume of a primitive unit cell (section 1.3) $V = a \cdot b \times c$. Therefore,

$$a^* = \frac{2\pi}{s_{100}} = 2\pi \frac{b \times c}{a \cdot b \times c} \tag{31}$$

Similarly,

$$b^* = \frac{2\pi}{d_{010}} = 2\pi \frac{c \times a}{a \cdot b \times c} \tag{32}$$

and

$$c^* = \frac{2\pi}{d_{001}} = 2\pi \frac{a \times b}{a \cdot b \times c} \tag{33}$$

The exact relationships between the direct and the reciprocal lattice parameters, interaxial angles for orthorombic and monoclinic systems are diagramatically shown in Fig. 8.19 while their values have been tabulated in Tables 8.2 and 8.3, respectively.

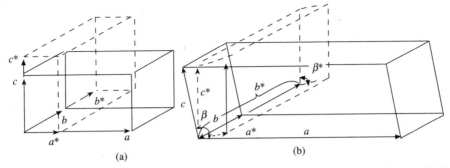

**Fig. 8.19  Relationship between direct and reciprocal lattice for orthorhombic and monoclinic systems**

**Table 8.2  Direct/reciprocal relationships in orthorhombic system**

| | | |
|---|---|---|
| $a^* = \dfrac{2\pi}{a}$ | $a = \dfrac{2\pi}{a^*}$ | $\alpha = \beta = \gamma = \alpha^* = \beta^* = \gamma^* = 90°$ |
| $b^* = \dfrac{2\pi}{b}$ | $b = \dfrac{2\pi}{b^*}$ | $V = \dfrac{(2\pi)^3}{V^*} = abc$ |
| $c^* = \dfrac{2\pi}{c}$ | $c = \dfrac{2\pi}{c^*}$ | $V^* = \dfrac{(2\pi)^3}{V} = a^*b^*c^*$ |

**Table 8.3  Direct/reciprocal relationships in monoclinic system**

| | | |
|---|---|---|
| $a^* = \dfrac{2\pi}{a \sin \beta}$ | $a = \dfrac{2\pi}{a^* \sin \beta^*}$ | $\alpha = \gamma = \alpha^* = \gamma^* = 90°$ |
| | $\beta^* = 180° - \beta$ | |
| $b^* = \dfrac{2\pi}{b}$ | $b = \dfrac{2\pi}{b^*}$ | $V = \dfrac{(2\pi)^3}{V^*} = abc \sin \beta$ |
| $c^* = \dfrac{2\pi}{c \sin \beta}$ | $c = \dfrac{2\pi}{c^* \sin \beta^*}$ | $V^* = \dfrac{(2\pi)^3}{V} = a^*b^*c^* \sin \beta^*$ |

where $\sin \beta^* = \sin \beta$ and $\cos \beta^* = -\cos \beta$

With the help of above equations, several useful information can be obtained. First, see the result of the dot product of these reciprocal lattice vectors with their respective counterparts,

$$a^* \cdot a = 2\pi \frac{b \times c}{a \cdot b \times c} \cdot a = 2\pi \tag{34}$$

Similarly, we can obtain $b^* \cdot b = 2\pi$ and $c^* \cdot c = 2\pi$. On the other hand, taking the dot product of these vectors with the other vectors of the real lattice, we find

$$a^* \cdot b = 2\pi \frac{b \times c}{a \cdot b \times c} \cdot b \text{ and } a^* \cdot c = 2\pi \frac{b \times c}{a \cdot b \times c} \cdot c$$

Since $b \times c$ is a vector which is perpendicular to both $b$ and $c$, therefore, $b \times c \cdot b = 0$ and $b \times c \cdot c = 0$. This gives

$$a* \cdot b = 0, \, a* \cdot c = 0 \qquad (35)$$

Similarly, we can verify that

$$b* \cdot c = 0, \, b* \cdot a = 0$$

and

$$c* \cdot a = 0, \, c* \cdot b = 0$$

These important results tell us the following:

$a*$ is normal to $b$ and $c$

$b*$ is normal to $c$ and $a$

$c*$ is normal to $a$ and $b$

Now using the reciprocal lattice vectors $a*$, $b*$ and $c*$, a reciprocal lattice can be constructed. With the help of eqs. 31–33, the reciprocal lattice vector in general can be written as

$$G = \sigma_{hkl} = h \, a* + k \, b* + l \, c* \qquad (36)$$

That is to reach any reciprocal lattice point *hkl*, one has to move *h* units along $a*$, *k* units along $b*$ and *l* units along $c*$.

## 8.12   RECIPROCAL LATTICE TO SC, BCC AND FCC LATTICES

### Reciprocal Lattice to sc Lattice

The primitive translation vectors of a simple cubic lattice may be written as:

$$a = a\hat{i}, \, b = b\hat{j}, \, c = c\hat{k}$$

where the volume of the unit cell is $(a \cdot b \times c) = a^3$. The primitive translation vectors of the reciprocal lattice of the simple cubic lattice will be

$$a* = 2\pi \frac{b \times c}{a \cdot b \times c} = \frac{2\pi}{a} \hat{i} \qquad b* = 2\pi \frac{c \times a}{a \cdot b \times c} = \frac{2\pi}{a} \hat{j} \qquad c* = 2\pi \frac{a \times b}{a \cdot b \times c} = \frac{2\pi}{a} \hat{k}$$

From these equations, it is evident that the reciprocal lattice to sc lattice is itself a simple cubic lattice with a lattice constnat $2\pi/a$.

The boundaries of the resulting primitive unit cell are the planes normal to the six reciprocal lattice vectors $\pm a*$, $\pm b*$, $\pm c*$ at their midpoints, i.e.

$$\pm \frac{a*}{2} = \pm \frac{\pi}{a} \hat{i} \qquad \pm \frac{b*}{2} = \pm \frac{\pi}{b} \hat{j} \qquad \pm \frac{c*}{2} = \pm \frac{\pi}{c} \hat{k}$$

The space bounded by these six planes is a cube of side $2\pi/a$ and volume $(2\pi/a)^3$. This cube is known as the first Brillouin zone of the simple cubic lattice as shown in Fig. 8.20.

### Reciprocal Lattice to bcc Lattice

The primitive translation vectors of the bcc lattice shown in Fig. 8.21 ae given by:

$$a' = \frac{a}{2} (\hat{i} + \hat{j} - \hat{k}) \qquad b' = \frac{a}{2} (-\hat{i} + \hat{j} + \hat{k}) \qquad c' = \frac{a}{2} (\hat{i} - \hat{j} + \hat{k})$$

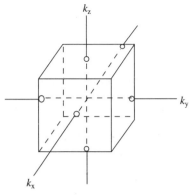

**Fig. 8.20 The first BZ of a simple cubic lattice**

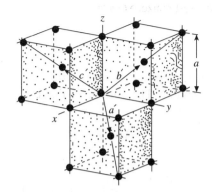

**Fig. 8.21 Primitive translation vectors of the bcc lattice**

where $a$ is the side of the conventional unit cube and $\hat{i}, \hat{j}, \hat{k}$ are orthogonal unit vectors parallel to the cube edges. The volume of the primitive unit cell is

$$V = |a' \cdot b' \times c'| = \frac{a^3}{2}$$

The primitive translation vectors $a^*$, $b^*$, $c^*$ of the reciprocal lattice are defined by eqs. 31 to 33. Thus

$$a^* = 2\pi \frac{b' \times c'}{a' \cdot b' \times c'} = 2\pi \frac{a/2(-\hat{i} + \hat{j} + \hat{k}) \times a/2(\hat{i} - \hat{j} + \hat{k})}{a^3/2}$$

$$= \frac{\pi}{a} [\hat{i} \times \hat{j} - \hat{i} \times \hat{k} + \hat{j} \times \hat{i} + \hat{j} \times \hat{k} + \hat{k} \times \hat{i} - \hat{k} \times \hat{j}]$$

$$= \frac{\pi}{a} [\hat{i} \times \hat{j} + \hat{k} \times \hat{i} - \hat{i} \times \hat{j} + \hat{j} \times \hat{k} + \hat{k} \times \hat{i} + \hat{j} \times \hat{k}]$$

$$= \frac{\pi}{a} [\hat{k} + \hat{j} - \hat{k} + \hat{i} + \hat{j} + \hat{i}] = \frac{2\pi}{a} [\hat{i} + \hat{j}]$$

where $\hat{i} \times \hat{i} = \hat{j} \times \hat{j} = \hat{k} \times \hat{k} = 0$ and $\hat{i} \times \hat{j} = \hat{k}, \hat{j} \times \hat{k} = i$ and $\hat{k} \times \hat{i} = \hat{j}$.

Similarly,
$$b^* = \frac{2\pi}{a} [\hat{j} + \hat{k}] \text{ and } c^* = \frac{2\pi}{a} [\hat{k} + \hat{i}]$$

On comparison with Fig. 8.23, we observe that these reciprocal lattice vectors are just the primitive vectors of the fcc lattice. Thus, the fcc lattice is the reciprocal lattice of the bcc latttice.

If $h$, $k$, $l$ are integers, the general form of reciprocal lattice can be written as

$$G = ha^* + kb^* + lc^* = \frac{2\pi}{a} [h(\hat{i} + \hat{j}) + k(\hat{j} + \hat{k}) + l(\hat{i} + \hat{k})]$$

$$= \frac{2\pi}{a} [(h + l)\hat{i} + (h + k)\hat{j} + (k + l)\hat{k}]$$

The shortest nonzero $G$'s are the following twelve vectors, where all choices of sign are independent:

$$\frac{2\pi}{a}(\pm\hat{i}\pm\hat{j}); \quad \frac{2\pi}{a}(\pm\hat{j}\pm\hat{k}); \quad \frac{2\pi}{a}(\pm\hat{i}\pm\hat{k}) \tag{37}$$

The resulting primitive cell of the reciprocal lattice is a parallelepiped described by the vectors $a^*$, $b^*$, and $c^*$. The volume of this cell is given by

$$V = |a^* \cdot b^* \times c^*| = \left(\frac{2\pi}{a}\right)^3 (\hat{i}+\hat{j})\cdot[(\hat{j}+\hat{k})\times(\hat{k}+\hat{i})]$$

$$= \left(\frac{2\pi}{a}\right)^3 [(\hat{i}+\hat{j})\cdot(\hat{i}+\hat{j}-\hat{k})] = 2\left(\frac{2\pi}{a}\right)^3$$

Being a primitive cell, it contains only one reciprocal lattice point. This cell is bounded by planes normal to the twelve vectors given by eq. 37 at their midpoints. This is also known as first Brillouin zone of a bcc lattice. This is a twelve faced solid, a rhombic dodecahedron as shown in Fig. 8.22. The vectors from the origin to the centre of each face are half of the vectors in eq. 37, or

$$\frac{\pi}{a}(\pm\hat{i}\pm\hat{j}); \frac{\pi}{a}(\pm\hat{j}\pm\hat{k}); \frac{\pi}{a}(\pm\hat{i}\pm\hat{k}) \tag{38}$$

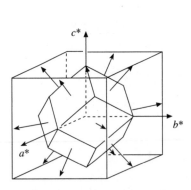

**Fig. 8.22  First BZ of a bcc lattice**

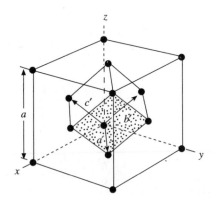

**Fig. 8.23  Primitive translation vectors of the fcc lattice**

## Reciprocal Lattice to fcc Lattice

The primitive translation vectors of the fcc lattice (Fig. 8.23) are

$$a' = \frac{1}{2}a(\hat{i}+\hat{j}) \quad b' = \frac{1}{2}a(\hat{j}+\hat{k}) \quad c' = \frac{1}{2}a(\hat{k}+\hat{i})$$

where $a$ is the side of the conventional unit cube and $\hat{i},\hat{j},\hat{k}$ are orthogonal unit vectors parallel to the cube edges. The volume of the primitive cell is

$$V = |a' \cdot b' \times c'| = \frac{a^3}{4}$$

The primitive translation vectors $a^*$, $b^*$, $c^*$ of the reciprocal lattice are defined by eqs. 31 to 33. Making similar calculations as above, we obtain

$$a^* = \frac{2\pi}{a}(\hat{i} + \hat{j} - \hat{k}) \quad b^* = \frac{2\pi}{a}(-\hat{i} + \hat{j} + \hat{k}) \quad c^* = \frac{2\pi}{a}(\hat{i} - \hat{j} + \hat{k})$$

These vectors turn out to be the translation vectors of a bcc lattice, so that the bcc lattice is the reciprocal lattice of the fcc lattice. The volume of the resulting primitive cell is

$$V = |a^* \cdot b^* \times c^*| = 4\left(\frac{2\pi}{a}\right)^3$$

If $h$, $k$, $l$ are integers, the $G$ type reciprocal lattice vector is

$$G = \frac{2\pi}{a}[h(\hat{i} + \hat{j} - \hat{k}) + k(-\hat{i} + \hat{j} + \hat{k}) + l(\hat{i} - \hat{j} + \hat{k})]$$

$$= \frac{2\pi}{a}[(h - k + l)\hat{i} + (h + k - l)\hat{j} + (-h + k + l)\hat{k}] \tag{39}$$

In this case, the shortest nonzero $G$'s are eight vectors, which are passing through the corners of the fcc lattice. They are given by

$$\frac{2\pi}{a}(\pm\hat{i} \pm \hat{j} \pm \hat{k}) \tag{40}$$

Other six vectors corresponding to the next nearest neighbour atoms and lying at the face centres of the neighbouring fcc lattice are given by

$$\frac{2\pi}{a}(\pm 2\hat{i}), \frac{2\pi}{a}(\pm 2\hat{j}), \frac{2\pi}{a}(\pm 2\hat{k}) \tag{41}$$

Like bcc case, the primitive cell obtained in this case is bounded by planes normal to the fourteen vectors given by eqs. 40 and 41 at their midpoints. This is a fourteen faced solid, a truncated octahedron as shown in Fig. 8.24.

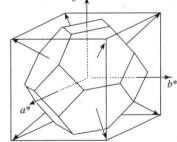

**Fig. 8.24   The first BZ of an fcc lattice**

## 8.13   SOME IMPORTANT PROPERTIES OF THE RECIPROCAL LATTICE

1. Every reciprocal lattice vector $G$ is normal to the plane of the crystal lattice $(hkl)$.

*Proof*: This can be proved if we can show that the scalar product of the reciprocal lattice vector $G$ and a vector lying in the $(hkl)$ plane vanishes. The plane is shown in Fig. 8.25, intercepts the axes $a$ at $a/h$, $b$ at $b/k$ and $c$ at $c/l$, respectively. Now, let us consider a vector $C = (a/h) - (b/k)$ which lies in the $(hkl)$ plane. Taking the scalar product of this with $G$, we obtain

$$C \cdot G = \left(\frac{a}{h} - \frac{b}{k}\right) \cdot (ha^* + kb^* + lc^*)$$

$$= \frac{a}{h} \cdot (ha^* + kb^* + lc^*) - \frac{b}{k} \cdot (ha^* + kb^* + lc^*)$$

$$= \left(\frac{h}{h} + 0 + 0\right) - \left(0 + \frac{k}{k} + 0\right) \text{ using eqs. 34 and 35}$$

$$= 0$$

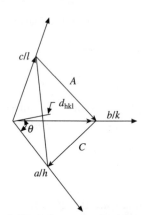

Fig. 8.25 **Intercepts of a plane on three crystallographic axes and the interplanar spacing**

Similarly, it can be shown that $A \cdot G = 0$. Accordingly, the reciprocal lattice vector, $G$ is normal to both $C$ and $A$, where the vectors $C$ and $A$ are lying within the $(hkl)$ plane and hence it is normal to the plane containing $C$ and $A$, i.e. the plane $(hkl)$ itself.

2. The interplanar spacing $d_{hkl}$ in a real crystal lattice is equal to $1/|G|$.

*Proof:* Let us suppose that $n$ is a unit vector normal to the plane $(hkl)$ or is parallel to $G$ (from above proof), then eq. 36 can be written as

$$|G| \cdot n = (ha^* + kb^* + lc^*) \text{ or } n = \frac{ha^* + kb^* + lc^*}{|G|}$$

In Fig. 8.25, the length of the interplanar spacing $d_{hkl}$ is

$$d_{hkl} = \frac{a}{h} \cos \theta = \frac{a}{h} \cdot n = \frac{a}{h} \cdot \frac{ha^* + kb^* + lc^*}{|G|}$$

Making use of the eqs. 34 and 35, we find

$$d_{hkl} = \frac{1}{|G|}$$

3. The reciprocal of the reciprocal lattice is a direct lattice.

*Proof:* From eq. 31, we have

$$a^* = 2\pi \frac{b \times c}{a \cdot b \times c}$$

Taking reciprocal of this, we can write

$$(a^*)^* = 4\pi^2 \frac{b^* \times c^*}{a^* \cdot b^* \times c^*}$$

Since $a \cdot a^* = 2\pi$ (eq. 34), therefore, the above equation becomes

$$(a^*)^* = 2\pi a \cdot a^* \frac{b^* \times c^*}{a^* \cdot b^* \times c^*} = 2\pi a \cdot \frac{a^* \cdot b^* \times c^*}{a^* \cdot b^* \times c^*} = 2\pi a$$

Similarly, $(b*)* = 2\pi b$ and $(c*)* = 2\pi c$. Consequently, we have

$$(a*)* = 4\pi^2 \frac{b* \times c*}{a* \cdot b* \times c*} = 2\pi a \qquad (b*)* = 4\pi^2 \frac{c* \times a*}{a* \cdot b* \times c*} = 2\pi b$$

$$(c*)* = 4\pi^2 \frac{a* \times b*}{a* \cdot b* \times c*} = 2\pi c$$

4. Volume of the unit cell of the reciprocal lattice is inversely proportional to that of corresponding direct lattice.

*Proof*: We know that the volume of the primitive cell of a direct lattice is $a \cdot b \times c$. Therefore, the volume of the reciprocal unit cell is $a* \cdot b* \times c*$. Writing this in terms of direct lattice, we have

$$a* \cdot b* \times c* = \left[ \frac{b \times c}{a \cdot b \times c} \right] \cdot \left[ \frac{c \times a}{a \cdot b \times c} \right] \times \left[ \frac{a \times b}{a \cdot b \times c} \right]$$

$$= \frac{1}{(a \cdot b \times c)^3} [(b \times c) \cdot \{(c \times a) \times (a \times b)\}]$$

$$= \frac{1}{(a \cdot b \times c)^3} (b \times c) \cdot [\{(c \cdot (a \times b) a - \{a \cdot (a \times b)\}c]$$

$$= \frac{1}{(a \cdot b \times c)^3} [(c \cdot (a \times b)\{a \cdot b \times c\} - 0)]$$

$$= \frac{1}{(a \cdot b \times c)^3} (a \cdot b \times c)^2 = \frac{1}{a \cdot b \times c}$$

*Example*: A two dimensional direct lattice is formed from a repetion of points ABCD (Fig. 8.26) in which AB = CD = 3 Å, AD = BC = 5Å and the angle BAD = 60°. Draw a small area (about four unit cells) of the direct lattice. Calculate the basis vector and draw the corresponding cells of reciprocal lattice.

*Solution*: From Fig. 8.26, we suppose that $a$ and $b$ are the lattice vectors representing $AB$ and $AD$ in the direct lattice, respectively. Similarly, $a*$ and $b*$ are the lattice vectors for the corresponding reciprocal lattice. Then

$$a* \cdot a = 2\pi \text{ and } a* \cdot b = 0$$

This indicates that $a*$ is perpendicular to $b$ and is given by

$$a* = \frac{2\pi}{3 \cos 30°} = \frac{4\pi}{3\sqrt{3}} \text{ Å}^{-1}$$

Similarly, $b*$ is perpendicular to $a$ and is given by

$$b* = \frac{2\pi}{5 \cos 30°} = \frac{4\pi}{3\sqrt{3}} \text{ Å}^{-1}$$

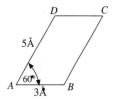

**Fig. 8.26  Showing lattice vectors in the direct lattice**

The angle between $a*$ and $b*$ will be 120°. The direct cells and the corresponding reciprocal cells are drawn in Fig. 8.27.

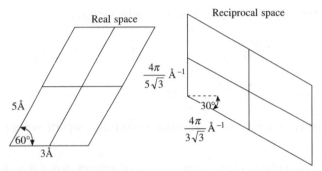

**Fig. 8.27 Showing direct cells and corresponding reciprocal cells**

## 8.14   DIFFRACTION INTENSITY

The different directions of the diffracted beam obtained according to Bragg's law or Laue equations are governed entirely by the geometry and the size of the unit cell, and therefore, these directions are not affected by the arrangement of atoms associated with each lattice point. However, the complexity of the atomic structure within the unit cell does affect the intensity of the diffracted beams. The intensity of the diffracted beams primarily depends on the atomic scattering factor, and the position of each atom in the unit cell. Since, the electrons are the only components of the atom that scatter X-rays significantly, the X-rays scattered from one part of an atom interfere with those scattered from the other part at all angles of scattering (at $2\theta = 0°$, all atoms scatter in planes). Since, the electrons are distributed throughout the atomic volume, the diffracted beams are obtained as a result of combination of the scattered waves from the electrons of all atoms in the unit cell. This process involves two distinct contributions:

1. Scattering from electrons in the same atom (the atomic scattering factor or atomic form factor $f$).
2. The summation of this scattering from all atoms in the unit cell (the geometrical structure factor $F$).

The atomic scattering factor is a measure of the efficiency of an atom in scattering X-rays. It is defined as the ratio of the amplitude scattered by the actual electron distribution in an atom to that scattered by one electron localized at a point. Therefore, if the atoms are assumed to be points only, then the atomic scattering factor is just equal to the number of electrons present (i.e. the atomic number of neutral atoms, $Z$). The atomic scattering factor of an atom falls off with increasing scattering angle or, more precisely with increasing value of ($\sin \theta/\lambda$) as shown in Fig. 8.28. On the other hand, neutrons are scattered by atomic nuclei rather than by electrons around a nucleus. Since, the nucleus is very small as compared to the size of the

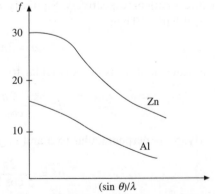

**Fig. 8.28   Variation of atomic scattering factor with ($\sin \theta/\lambda$)**

atom (it can be treated as a point atom), the scattering for a non-vibrating nucleus is almost independent of scattering angle.

In order to know the intensity of the X-ray beam scattered by one unit cell in a articular direction where there is diffraction maximum, it is necessary to sum the waves that arise from all the atoms in the unit cell. Mathematically, this involves adding the waves of the same wavelength but with different amplitudes and phases. The intensity of the scattered beam is then obtained by squaring the resultant amplitude.

If the position of the atoms in the unit cell are denoted by $x$, $y$ and $z$, the resultant amplitude for a given ($hkl$) reflection can be expressed as

$$F(hkl) = \sum_{i=1}^{N} f_i \exp\{2\pi j(hx_i + ky_i + lz_i)\} \tag{42}$$

or

$$F(hkl) = \sum_{i=1}^{N} f_i \cos 2\pi(hx_i + ky_i + lz_i)\} + j\sum_{i=1}^{N} f_i \sin 2\pi(hx_i + ky_i + lz_i)\} \tag{43}$$

where the coordinates $x$, $y$, $z$ are expressed as fraction of the unit cell parameters. As mentioned above, the intensity of the diffracted beam is given by the square of the amplitude, i.e.

$$I \propto |F(hkl)|^2 \tag{44}$$

where,

$$|F(hkl)|^2 = \left(\sum_{i=1}^{N} f_i \cos 2\pi(hx_i + ky_i + lz_i)\}\right)^2 + \left(\sum_{i=1}^{N} f_i \sin 2\pi\{(hx_i + ky_i + lz_i)\}\right)^2 \tag{45}$$

Let us take a practical example for better understanding. For simplicity, let us consider a bcc structure consisting of identical atoms in the unit cell. Position of the atoms in the unit cell are: (000) and (1/2 1/2 1/2). Here, for one atom $x_1 = y_1 = z_1 = 0$ and for the other atom $x_2 = y_2 = z_2 = 1/2$. Then eq. 45 becomes

$$|F|^2 = f_i^2\left(\cos 2\pi \cdot 0 + \cos 2\pi\left(\frac{h}{2} + \frac{k}{2} + \frac{l}{2}\right)\right)^2 + f_i^2\left(\sin 2\pi \cdot 0 + \sin 2\pi\left(\frac{h}{2} + \frac{k}{2} + \frac{l}{2}\right)\right)^2$$

or $$|F|^2 = f_i^2\{1 + \cos \pi(h + k + l)\}^2 + \sin^2\pi(h + k + l) \tag{46}$$

From eq. 46, one can verify that

$$F = 2f \text{ and } I = 4f^2 \text{ when } h + k + l = \text{even integer}$$

$$F = 0 \text{ and } I = 0 \quad \text{when} \quad h + k + l = \text{odd integer}$$

Metallic sodium has bcc structure. The diffraction spectrum for Na does not show (100), (300), (111) or (221) lines, while (200), (110) and (222) lines are present. The absence of (100) and other lines could be understood from the fact that in a bcc structure, there exists a parallel plane at midway between the two (100) planes. The diffracted beam from these middle planes are out of phase by $\pi$ with respect to the first plane. As the effective number of the body centred atom is equal to the effective number of corner atom in a bcc structure, the intensity of the diffracted beam from atoms at these two locations will be exactly equal and cancel each other.

Let us apply the above derived formula to CsCl crystal, in which there is a cesium ion at (000) and the chlorine ion at (1/2 1/2 1/2), a different result is obtained, although the structure resembles a bcc structure. In this case, $f$ values of the two ions are not the same and the lattice is not body centred. The structure factor in this case, yield

$$F^2 = \{f_{Cs} + f_{Cl} \cos \pi (h + k + l)\}^2 + \{f_{Cl} \sin \pi (h + k + l)\}^2$$

or $F^2 = (f_{Cs} + f_{Cl})^2$ when $(h + k + l)$ is even

$$F^2 = (f_{Cs} - f_{Cl})^2 \text{ when } (h + k + l) \text{ is odd}$$

A similar analysis in the case of a simple fcc structure with atoms at positions (000), (1/2 1/2 0), (1/2 0 1/2) and (0 1/2 1/2), reveals that the intensity is zero for all reflections in which the indices (*hkl*) are partly even or partly odd (i.e. reflections are allowed when *hkl* are all odd or all even).

Because of the systematic absence of particular reflections, the observed series of (*hkl*) values obtained from the measured values of $\sin^2\theta$ enable us to determine the basic structure.

## 8.15  THE X-RAY DIFFRACTION EXPERIMENT

When reduced to the basic essentials, the X-ray diffraction experiment requires an X-ray source, the sample under investigation and a photographic film or a detector to record the diffraction beam as shown in Fig. 8.29. Within this broad framework, there are three variables which govern the different X-ray diffraction techniques.

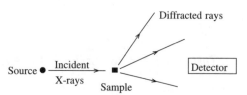

**Fig. 8.29   The X-ray differaction experiment**

They are:

 (i)  radiation—monochromatic or of variable $\lambda$.

 (ii)  sample—single crystal, polycrystal (powder) or a solid-piece (amorphous).

(iii)  detector—photographic film or radiation counter.

These are summarised for the most important experimental techniques in Fig. 8.30. With the exception of the Laue method, monochromatic radiation is almost always used.

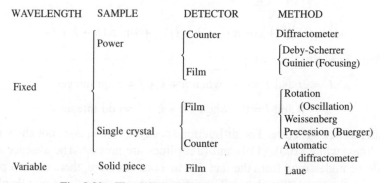

**Fig. 8.30   The different X-ray diffraction techniques**

## 8.16 THE POWDER METHOD

The powder method is the most convenient and quickest method for obtaining diffraction data and is readily applicable to all crystalline materials. Since the diffraction data are unique for a particular substance, this method can be used for identification of materials (just as finger prints of a person is unique and is used to identify a human being).

A schematic diagram of a powder camera (also known as Debye Scherrer camera) is shown in Fig. 8.31. There is a specimen holder at the centre of the cylindrical camera. A powder sample of fine grained polycrystalline substance filled in a thin walled capillary tube or a thin wire prepared from finely powdered specimen mixed with a little adhesive material is placed on the sample holder and set it correctly on its axis with the help of plunger. Then the camera along with the specimen is taken to the dark room where a thin strip of X-ray film is loaded in the cylindrical casette in such a way that the two ends of the film meet midway between the entry and exit points of X-ray beam. This particular film placement was first suggested by Straumanis and Ievins and has two special features: (i) It allows to record a complete diffraction pattern ranging from $\theta = 0$ to $\theta = 90°$ on the same film, and (ii) the presence of pair of arcs around $\theta = 0$ and $\theta = 90°$ enable us to locate the low and high angle positions on the film accurately. Before the camera is loaded, the film is punched to make two holes to fit the collimater and the direct beam catcher containing a fluorescent screen. The film is suitably wrapped in a black paper to protect it from stray light and unwanted X-rays. Replace the cover and place the camera in front of the X- ray source for exposure.

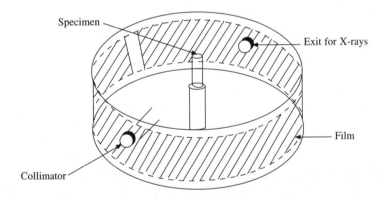

**Fig. 8.31 Schematic representation of the powder method**

A monochromatic X-ray beam is allowed to fall on the powder sample. Since the sample prepared in the manner discused above contains a large number of tiny crystallites randomly arranged in all possible orientations. For each set of planes, there exist some crystallites which are oriented in a direction to satisfy the Bragg condition and give rise the diffraction effect. The locus of the diffracted beam will lie on a cone with half-apex angle $2\theta$ (Fig. 8.32). In a similar way, other sets of lattice planes give their diffraction cones on the X-ray film (each cone consists of a large number of closely spaced diffracted beams). These cones are recorded in the form of pair arcs on the X-rays film. When the Bragg angle is 45°, the corresponding cone opens out into a circle whose intersection with the Ewald sphere gives rise a straight line and is recorded at the

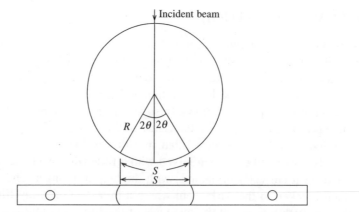

**Fig. 8.32   Relation between the Bragg angle and the linear distance between pair of arcs**

midpoint of the film situated between the incident and exit point. When the Bragg angle is greater than 45°, back reflection are obtained. This way, the Bragg angle from zero upto the maximum value of 90° can be obtained using a cylindrical film. After completion of exposure, the film is processed (developed and fixed) in the dark room and dried for indexing. A typical schematic powder pattern is shown in Fig. 8.33.

**Fig. 8.33   Schematic powder pattern**

### Interpretation of Powder Lines

*The Measurement of Interplanar Spacings (d Values)*
Before we start any measurement on the film, it is necessary to ensure $\theta = 0$ and $\theta = 90°$ positions, i.e. to distinguish the low and high angle diffraction lines. This can be done by simply observing the following two characteristic features on the film: (i) The background intensity on the film is maximum near $\theta = 0$. This arises mainly due to the scattering of radiation from the air molecules present inside the camera. Thus, one expects more blackening of the film near the low angle side, i.e. around the exit hole whose centre corresponds to $\theta = 0$. (ii) splitting of diffraction lines at higher angle side: we know that the CuK$\alpha$ radiation which is usually employed for Powder diffraction contains a doublet, i.e., CuK$\alpha_1$ ($\lambda = 1.5405$ Å) and CuK$\alpha_2$ ($\lambda = 1.5443$ Å) hence in general every diffraction line should be a doublet. However, the two components get resolved only in the higher angle side, where the separation is clearly visible. For the usual camera diameter (57.3 mm), the doublet appears to be a pair of closely spaced lines merging with each other to form a thick line.

After ensuring the low and high angle positions, the film is placed over the film reader in such a way that it is truly parallel to the scale of the measuring device. Cross hair of the telescope is adjusted vertically at the centre of each arc to record the linear distance with respect to any given reference to determine the arc length (Fig. 8.34). Put all the readings in a tabulated data sheet as shown in Fig. 8.35. Knowing the linear distances between the pair of arcs, various diffraction

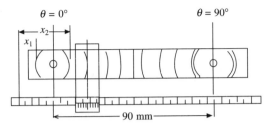

**Fig. 8.34 Measurement of linear distances of arc on a schematic powder pattern**

| Line No. | $x_2$ | $x_1$ | Check $x_2 + x_1$ | Arc length $S = x_2 - x_1$ | Correction $\frac{p}{100} \times S$ | Corrected arc length $S'$ | $\theta = \frac{S'}{4}$ | $\sin \theta$ | $d = \frac{\lambda}{2\sin\theta}$ | $Q = \frac{1}{d^2}$ | hkl |
|---|---|---|---|---|---|---|---|---|---|---|---|
| | | | | | | | | | | | |
| | | | | | | | | | | | |

**Fig. 8.35 Data sheet in tabulated form**

angles $\theta$'s can be calculated for a known camera radius $R$. They are related to each other according to (Fig. 8.32).

$$4\theta = \frac{S}{R} \quad \text{or} \quad \theta = \left(\frac{1}{4R}\right) S \text{ radians}$$

$$\text{or } \theta = \left(\frac{180}{\pi} \cdot \frac{1}{4R}\right) S \text{ degrees} \tag{47}$$

It is interesting to note that $180/\pi = 57.3$. Thus for a camera diameter $2R = 57.3$ mm, $\theta = S/2$, so that $1°$ in $\theta$ corresponds to 2 mm in $S$. In view of this simple conversion factor, camera diameter is usually taken as 57.3 mm or a multiple of it such as $2 \times 57.3$ mm = 114.6 mm. In this case, 4 mm in $S$ will correspond to $1°$ in $\theta$.

Although the conversion factor of $S$ into $\theta$ is straight forward. However, in actual practice the film is processed, washed and dried. As a result, some shrinkage in the film occurs, which should be taken into account for correct results. The shrinkage factor (SF) is defined as the ratio of the actual hole to hole distance after shrinkage to 90 mm, i.e.

$$SF = \frac{\text{Actual hole to hole distance after shrinkage}}{90 \text{ mm}} \tag{48}$$

Let the actual distance differ from 90 mm by p%, then a corresponding correction of $\frac{p}{100} \times S$ must be added to each value of $S$ to obtain the corrected arc length $S'$. Therefore,

$$S' = S + \frac{p}{100} \times S \tag{49}$$

Now substituting the values of camera radius $R = 180/\pi \, (=57.3 \text{ mm})$ and the corrected arc length $S'$ for $S$ in eq. 47, we obtain

$$\theta = \left( \frac{180}{\pi} \cdot \frac{1}{4} \cdot \frac{\pi}{180} \right) S'$$

or
$$\theta = \frac{S'}{4} \tag{50}$$

After knowing the Bragg angles $\theta$ for different arcs (diffraction lines), it is easy to determine the various interplanar spacings ($d$ values) using Bragg's equation. This helps in determining $hkl$ values for various diffraction lines. Let us consider the case of a simple cubic crystal for the purpose.

Squaring and arranging the Bragg's equation $2d \sin \theta = \lambda$, we have

$$\sin^2 \theta = \frac{\lambda^2}{4d^2}$$

where $d = \dfrac{a}{(h^2 + k^2 + l^2)^{1/2}}$ for a simple cubic crystal. Therefore,

$$\sin^2 \theta = \frac{\lambda^2}{4a^2} (h^2 + k^2 + l^2) \tag{51}$$

Now, for a monochromatic X-ray beam, $\lambda$ is fixed and for a given sample, the lattice parameter "$a$" is fixed. Thus for fixed $\lambda$ and given crystal system, $\lambda^2/4a^2$ is a constant quantity. This implies that $\sin^2\theta$ (or $\theta$) is proportional to $(h^2 + k^2 + l^2)$. Therefore, for a simple cubic crystal, it is possible to list all combinations of $h$, $k$ and $l$ and arrange $(h^2 + k^2 + l^2)$ in increasing order. However, for other cubic systems such as bcc and fcc some of the diffraction lines are absent and hence all $hkl$ values are not present. For example, in a bcc crystal (100) reflection is absent because the reflections from the corner atoms and the body centre atoms have the same intensity but have a phase difference of $\lambda/2$, resulting in a zero reflected intensity. The systematic absences give rise extinction values following which, all possible $hkl$ values for different cubic systems can be obtained. The extinction rules for various crystal systems are summarized in Table 8.4. From these rules, it is possible to derive the ratio of $(h^2 + k^2 + l^2)$ values for allowed reflections in the various cubic systems and are given as

SC-------    $1 : 2 : 3 : 4 : 5 : 6 : 8 : 9 : 10$

BCC----    $1 : 2 : 3 : 4 : 5 : 6 : 7 : 8 : 9$

FCC----    $3 : 4 : 8 : 11 : 12 : 16 : 19 : 20$

DC------    $3 : 8 : 11 : 16 : 19$

**Table 8.4   Extinction rules for cubic crystals**

| Crystals | Allowed reflections |
|---|---|
| SC | for all values of $(h^2 + k^2 + l^2)$ |
| BCC | for even values of $h + k + l$ |
| FCC | when $h$, $k$ and $l$ are all odd or all even, |
| DC | when $h$, $k$, and $l$ are all odd or all even, $(h + k + l)$ should be divisible by four |

*Example*: Find the Bragg angles and the indices of diffraction for the three lowest angle lines on the powder photograph of an fcc crystal whose lattice parameter $a$ is 6 Å and the wavelength used is 1.54 Å.

*Solution*: Given: $a = 6$ Å, $\lambda = 1.54$ Å, crystal is fcc, $hkl$ for three lowest powder lines = ?, $\theta$'s = ?

In the case of an fcc crystal, the ratio of $(h^2 + k^2 + l^2)$ for allowed reflections are:

$$3 : 4 : 8 : 11 : 12 \ldots$$

Now, for $N = 3$, we have $hkl \equiv 111$, so that

$$d_{111} = \frac{a}{\sqrt{3}} = \frac{6}{\sqrt{3}} \text{ and } \sin \theta_{111} = \frac{\lambda}{2d}$$

or

$$\theta_{111} = \sin^{-1}\left(\frac{\lambda}{2d}\right) = \sin^{-1}\left(\frac{1.54 \times \sqrt{3}}{2 \times 6}\right) = 12° \, 50'$$

Similarly, for $N = 4$, $hkl \equiv 200$, so that $d_{200} = 3$, and

$$\theta_{200} = \sin^{-1}\left(\frac{\lambda}{2d}\right) = \sin^{-1}\left(\frac{1.54}{2 \times 3}\right) = 14° \, 52'$$

and for $N = 8$, $hkl \equiv 220$, so that $d_{220} = \frac{6}{\sqrt{8}}$, and

$$\theta_{220} = \sin^{-1}\left(\frac{\lambda}{2d}\right) = \sin^{-1}\left(\frac{1.54 \times \sqrt{8}}{2 \times 6}\right) = 21° \, 17'$$

## 8.17 POWDER DIFFRACTOMETER

The photographic methods of recording diffraction patterns are now supplemented in almost every X-ray laboratory by the X-ray diffractometer. The advantages of this method are considerable, e.g. the intensities can be measured directly. Also, the work and time required are very less, especially if only a certain part of the intensity chart is required.

Apart from the X-ray generator and the X-ray tube, the diffractometer includes an X-ray diffraction goniometer, several amplifiers and the detector. Details of the construction and operation of the commercially available instruments may be found particularly in manufacturers' literature and vary for different makes. However, here we are concerned only with the fundamental principles common to all.

A typical X-ray diffraction system is illustrated in Fig. 8.36. where the plane of the sample lies at the centre of the diffractometer circle. Also, the source, the sample and the detector all lie on the circumference of the focusing circle (Fig. 8.37a). The size of the diffractometer circle remains constant while that of the focusing circle vary inversely with the Bragg angle $\theta$ (Fig. 8.37b). In order to preserve the focusing action with changing $2\theta$, the surface of the sample must remain tangential to the focusing circle. This is achieved by coupling the sample and the detector

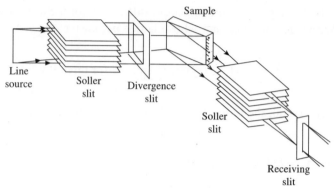

**Fig. 8.36    A typical X-ray diffraction system**

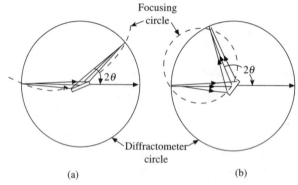

**Fig. 8.37    Alignment of the sample and detector with respect to the source. (a) All lie on the circumference of the circle , (b) relationship between diffractometer circle and focusing circle**

such that the plane of the sample rotates (in the same direction) at half the angular speed of the detector, i.e. retaining *a* $\theta/2\theta$ relationship with each other.

The ideal powder sample should be homogeneous, with a grain size of about 1 to 25 microns. There should be no preferred orientation, or any micro/macro crystalline strain.

In order to interpret the diffractogram (it is a plot of intensity of diffracted radiation versus diffraction angle), the first step is to determine the interplanar spacing *d*. Earlier in the photographic method, it was found with the help of Bragg equation. However, for the interpretation of the diffractogram, prepared Table of $2\theta$ angle versus *d* spacing are available in A.S.T.M data file for all common wavelengths. The spacing in angstrom can be read directly if $2\theta$ angle is known. Record these values immediately over the appropriate peaks on the diffractogram. Secondly, the relative intensities of the peaks are estimated and compared with peak intensities in the Table for identification of the given material.

## 8.18    THE LAUE METHOD

As it has been pointed out in the beginning that in 1912 it was Max Von Laue who first of all suggested the use of a crystal as three dimensional diffraction grating to study the nature of X-rays. That way the Laue method is the oldest X-ray diffraction method. This is one of the most convenient and accurate methods of determining the orientation of a crystal or of individual grains in an aggregate and hence is widely used to orient crystals for solid state experiments. It quickly determines the crystal symmetry. However, since white radiation is used to get the Laue photograph (where different orders of reflection may superpose on a single spot), this method is hardly used for crystal structure determination.

A suitable crystal (as perfect as possible) is selected by examining the same under polarizing microscope. It is mounted on a glass fibre parallel to the principal axis using some adhesive (like shellac, glue, or even quick fix) material. The fibre alongwith the crystal is then mounted on a goniometer head with the help of modelling clay as shown in Fig. 8.38. The crystal is then aligned properly on the goniometer head with the help of four arcs (two mutually perpendicular

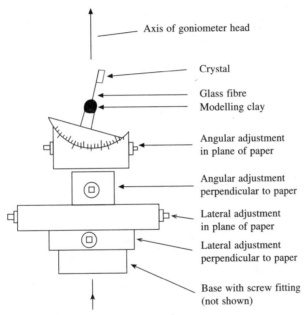

Axis of goniometer head

Crystal

Glass fibre
Modelling clay

Angular adjustment
in plane of paper

Angular adjustment
perpendicular to paper

Lateral adjustment
in plane of paper

Lateral adjustment
perpendicular to paper

Base with screw fitting
(not shown)

**Fig. 8.38  Basic parts of goniometer head. A key is provided to fit the square pins for moving the arcs**

arcs are for angular adjustment and the other two arcs are for linear adjustment). The goniometer head alongwith the aligned crystal is then placed on a single crystal X-ray diffraction camera. The goniometer head is held fixed such that the incident X-ray beam (continuous radiation) is normal to one face of the crystal and a flat plate film cassette is placed either in between the source and the crystal for recording the back reflections on the X-ray film or behind the crystal to record the transmission Laue spots. A schematic representation of the Laue technique is shown in Fig. 8.39. The crystal to film distance in both the cases is normally kept small and is fixed between 3-5 cm. This increases the number

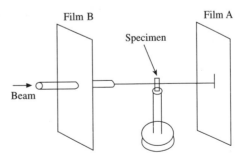

**Fig. 8.39  Schematic representation of the Laue technique**

of reflections intercepted by the film and reduces the exposure time. The two arrangements differ from one another in one respect. To intercept the direct incident beam a small lead cup is fixed at the centre of the cassette for recording the transmission Laue photograph, whereas in the back reflection a hole is made at the same point of the cassette to fit the collimator for the X-ray beam to pass.

### Interpretation of Laue Photographs

Because of a close relationship between gnomonic projection and reciprocal lattice, the former is found to be extremely useful in the interpretation of Laue photographs. A relationship among the reflecting plane of a crystal, its normal, and the direction of the reflected beam is shown in Fig. 8.40. Here, it is assumed that the photographic film and the plane of projection are coincident and represent the vertical line PR. If the crystal-to-film distance is taken to be unity, then the distance $r$, the point of intersection of the reflected beam with the vertical line from the centre of the photographic plate (through which the direct beam passes), is

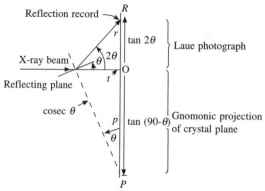

**Fig. 8.40    Relationship among the reflecting plane, its normal and the direction of the diffracted beam**

$$r = \tan 2\theta \tag{52}$$

or

$$2\theta = \tan^{-1} r \tag{53}$$

Similarly, the distance $p$, the point of intersection of normal to the reflecting plane ($hkl$) with the vertical line from the centre of the photographic plate, is

$$p = \tan (90 - \theta) = \cot \theta \tag{54}$$

The above two eqs. 52 and 54 show that the distances $p$ and $r$ are related inversely. Combining eqs. 53 and 54, we obtain

$$p = \cot \frac{1}{2} \tan^{-1} r \tag{55}$$

This equation is derived by assuming the crystal-to-film distance to be unity. However, it is often more convenient to place the film at some other distance, say $D$ and yet measure $p$ in a plane at a unit distance from the crystal. In this case, the eq. 55 is replaced by

$$p = \cot \frac{1}{2} \tan^{-1}\left(\frac{r}{D}\right) \tag{56}$$

With the help of this equation, it is easy to transform the location of each spot of the Laue photograh to the gnomonic projection of the plane whose reflectin produces it.

*Example*: In a Laue photograph of an fcc crystal whose lattice parameter is 4.5Å. Determine the minimum distance from the centre of the pattern at which reflections can occur from the planes of maximum spacing, if the potential difference across the X-ray tube is 50 kV and the crystal to film distance is 5.0 cm.

*Solution*: Given: Crystal is *fcc*, $a = 4.5$Å, $V = 50$ kV, crystal to film distance, $D = 5$ cm $= 0.05$ m, $x = ?$

In an fcc crystal we know that the planes of maximum spacing is (111).

Now, we know that in case of X-rays, the minimum wavelength is given by

$$\lambda_{min} = \frac{1.24 \times 10^{-6}}{V} = \frac{1.24 \times 10^{-6}}{5 \times 10^{-4}} = 0.25 \text{Å}$$

Similarly, for an fcc crystal, $d_{111} = \dfrac{4.5}{\sqrt{3}}$, so that

$$\theta_{111} = \sin^{-1}\left(\frac{\lambda}{2d}\right) = \sin^{-1}\left(\frac{0.25 \times \sqrt{3}}{2 \times 4.5}\right) = 2.76°$$

Now, from Fig. 8.41, we can obtain $\tan 2\theta = \dfrac{x}{5}$

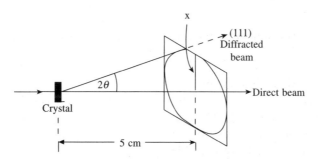

**Fig. 8.41 Schematic Laue pattern**

or $\qquad\qquad x = 5 \times \tan 2\theta = 5 \times \tan 5.52 = 0.48$ cm

## 8.19 THE ROTATION/OSCILLATION METHOD

Although the powder method is widely used for identification of materials, it is not suitable for complete structure determination particularly when a single crystal is available. Also, structure determination requires the intensity data of a large number of reflections. This is possible in the case of single crystals only. Thus, if a single crystal is available, rotation/osicillation method is generally employed for its study.

The crystal alignment is done exactly as in the case of Laue method. However, in this case instead of keeping the crystal stationary it is either rotated or oscillated (usual oscillation range is 15°) by coupling the goniometer head with a motor having suitable gear arrangement (Fig. 8.42). A monochromatic beam of X-ray is allowed to fall on the crystal through a collimator of about 1 mm internal diameter. The X-ray reflections are recorded on an X-ray film loaded in a cylindrical camera (usually of 3 cm radius) whose axis is coincident with the axis of rotation (or oscillation). A direct beam stopper is kept at the exit point of the X-ray beam. A schematic view of rotating crystal technique is shown in Fig. 8.42. A typical rotation photograph after unrolling and developing the film looks like as shown in Fig. 8.43. Interpretation of rotation photographs only is presented below.

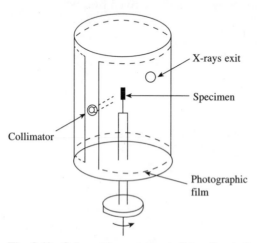

**Fig. 8.42  Schematic representation of rotating crystal technique**

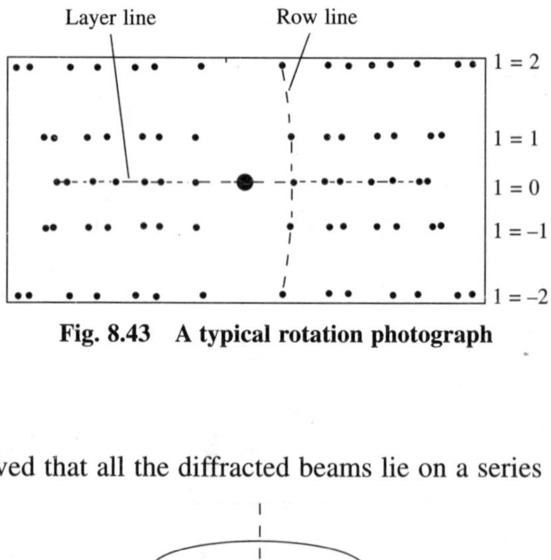

**Fig. 8.43  A typical rotation photograph**

### Interpretation of Rotation Photographs

In deriving Laue equations (sec. 8.7), we observed that all the diffracted beams lie on a series of concentric cones (representing different orders of diffractions) surrounding the row of atoms. These cones are actually responsible for the formation of layer lines in a rotation photograph (Fig. 8.44). All the reflections on the zero layer line come from the planes which are parallel to the axis of rotation and hence the corresponding Miller index is zero. The position of various reflections on this layer line depends on the $d$-spacings of planes in question (i.e. on the other Miller indices). The planes that have the larger $d$-spacing diffract X-rays at low Bragg angles and the corresponding reflections are nearer to the centre of the film (exit point of the direct X-

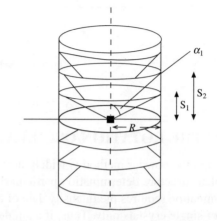

**Fig. 8.44  Formation of layer lines from cones of the diffracted rays**

ray beam corresponds to the zero Bragg angle). Other layer lines are separated by $S_1$, $S_2$, $S_3$, . . . etc. from zero layer line.

If a crystal is assumed to be rotated about $a$-axis and the incident X-ray beam is perpendicular to the axis of rotation, then eq. 18 reduces to

$$a \cos \alpha = n\lambda \qquad (57)$$

where $e$ is replaced by $n$ and is equal to zero for (zero), $\pm 1$ for (first), $\pm 2$ for (second) layer lines, etc. Similar equations hold for rotation of the crystal about other axes. If $S_n$ is the separation of $n$th layer line from zero layer line, and $R$ is the radius of the camera used then from Fig. 8.44, we have

$$\cot \alpha_n = \frac{S_n}{R} \qquad (58)$$

With the help of eqs. 57 and 58, we obtain

$$S_n = \frac{(n\lambda/a)}{\sqrt{1 - (n\lambda/a)^2}} R \qquad (59)$$

so that

$$a = \frac{n\lambda}{S_n} (R^2 + S_n^2)^{1/2} \qquad (60)$$

Similarly, by taking $b$-axis and $c$-axis rotation photographs, their unit cell parameters can be easily determined.

*Example*: In a rotation photograph, six layer lines are observed both above and below the zero layer line. If the heights of these layer lines above (or below) the zero layer are 0.29, 0.59, 0.91, 1.25, 1.65 and 2.12 cm, obtain the cell height of the crystal along the axis of rotation. The radius of the camera is 3 cm and the wavelength of the X-rays is 1.54 Å.

*Solution*: Given: $S_1 = 0.29$ cm, $S_2 = 0.59$ cm, $S_3 = 0.91$ cm, $S_4 = 1.25$ cm, $S_5 = 1.65$ cm and $S_6 = 2.12$ cm, $R = 3$ cm $\lambda = 1.54$ Å $= 1.54 \times 10^{-8}$ cm, unit cell height along the axis of rotation = ?

Let us suppose that the photograph is an $a$-axis photograph, then from eq. 60, we have

$$a = \frac{n\lambda}{S_n} (R^2 + S_n^2)^{1/2}$$

For
$$n = 1, a = \frac{1 \times 1.54 \times 10^{-8}}{0.29} (3^2 + (0.29)^2)^{1/2} = 16\text{Å}$$

Making a similar calculation by substituting different values of $n$ and corresponding $S$ values, we can see that in each case we obtain the same value of $a$. This implies that the unit cell height of the crystal

$$a = 16 \text{ Å}$$

## 8.20 OTHER DIFFRACTION METHODS

In addition to the X-ray diffraction, there are two other important diffraction methods which are widely used for characterization of materials. They are neutron and electron diffraction methods. They are often complementary and supplementary to X-ray diffraction. Unlike X-rays which are electromagnetic waves, neutrons and electrons are particles. However, according to de Broglie's hypothesis we know that every moving particle (object) has a wave associated with it, whose length is given by the de Broglie equation

$$\lambda = \frac{h}{mv} \tag{61}$$

where $h$ is Planck's constant, $m$ is the mass of the particle ($m_n$ for neutron and $m_e$ for electron) and $v$ is its velocity. Equation 61 connects the momentum (which is characteristic of particles) with the wavelength (which is characteristic of waves). From this equation, it follows that:

1. Lighter is the particle, greater is the de Broglie wavelength.
2. The faster the particle moves, smaller is its associated wavelength.
3. The de Broglie wavelength of a particle is independent of the charge (or nature) of the particle.

The wavelength of the associated wave therefore depends on the velocity of the particle, which in turn depends on its kinetic energy $E$ where $E = mv^2/2$. Substituting $v = \sqrt{(2E/m)}$, the eq. 61 becomes

$$\lambda = \frac{h}{m\sqrt{(2E/m)}} = \frac{h}{\sqrt{2mE}} \tag{62}$$

**Neutron Diffraction**

Substituting the appropriate mass value for neutron $m_n = 1.675 \times 10^{-27}$ kg, the above equation reduces to

$$\lambda = \frac{0.28}{E^{1/2}} \tag{63}$$

where $\lambda$ is in angstroms and $E$ is in electron volts. As we know that the wavelength suitable for diffraction experiment must be of the order of interatomic spacings (~1Å) of crystalline solids. Therefore, the wavelength $\lambda = 1$ Å in eq. 63 yields an energy of about 0.08 eV. This energy is of the same order as the energy of the thermal neutrons, 0.025 eV (which is of the order of kT at room temperature, T ~ 300K). Fig 8.45a shows a typical wavelength distribution for the neutron beam from the pile of a reactor. Unlike the spectral distribution of X-rays from an X-ray tube (Fig. 8.45b), there are no sharp characteristic peaks in the reactor spectrum. The most common method for obtaining a more or less monochromatic beam of neutron is to use a crystal monochromator as shown in Fig. 7.11. The "white" neutron beam from the reactor face is allowed to fall, through a collimator on to a large single crystal of lead, beryllium or germanium, etc. oriented suitably so that the Bragg condition (eq. 17) is satisfied for chosen wavelength. The reflection angle $\theta$ is adjusted so that the fraction of neutrons having energies close to kT is selected. The extent of angular range over which the neutrons are to be collected is a compromise

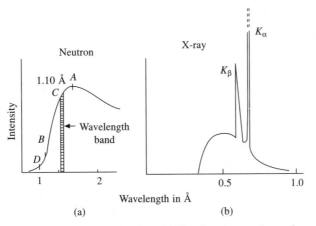

**Fig. 8.45** **Intensity versus wavelength distribution. (a) For the neutron beam from the pile of the reactor (b) from an X-ray tube**

between the two cases: (i) if the range is small, the beam will be highly monochromatic but very weak and (ii) if the range is large, the beam will be stronger but less monochromatic. In any case, the beam is not very strong. A typical monochromatised neutron beam has an intensity of the order of $10^6$ neutrons/cm$^2$/sec., which is about four orders of magnitude smaller than that obtained with X-rays. Thus for neutron diffraction, the single crystal to be studied must be much larger (at least 1 mm$^2$ or more) than those required for X-ray diffraction. However, for crystals of very large molecules, there is an additional difficulty, i.e. the low intensity problem cannot be solved simply by using bigger crystals or by increasing the counting times. Actually, the unit cells of these crystals are very large and the corresponding diffraction maxima are therefore very closely spaced, their resolution is a great problem.

The diffracted beams of neutron cannot be recorded on film like X-rays. This must be measured with the help of a counter. Therefore, the whole apparatus must be heavily shielded, making it very massive as compared to X-ray diffraction equipment. Besides, the facility of neutron beam is relatively rare. These are some of the reasons because of which the neutron diffraction is much less widely used than X-ray diffraction.

Neutron diffraction fundamentally differs from X-ray diffraction in the sense that the X-rays are scattered by the electron clouds associated with the atoms, while with certain exceptions (e.g. the atoms that have magnetic moments, whose electron clouds do interact with neutrons), neutrons are scattered by the nuclei of the atoms. This property makes it a useful tool to locate the position of light atoms (particularly the hydrogen atom) even in the presence of heavy ones, which may be difficult or impossible from X-ray data. Usually the non-hydrogen part of the structure is solved from the X-ray diffraction data in the normal way, and this partial structure is coupled with the neutron diffraction data for the determination of the position of the hydrogen atoms. Since neutron diffraction locates the nuclei of atoms and X-ray diffraction gives a picture of their electron clouds, a combination of the two techniques should provide complete information in regards to the distribution of electron clouds about the nucleus.

Because the nucleus of an atom, unlike the associated electron cloud, is negligibly small as compared to the wavelength of the scattered radiation. Consequently, the neutron waves diffracted from opposite sides of the atom do not interfere destructively. As a result of this, neutron scattering factors remain nearly constant unlike X-ray curves, which decrease rapidly with increasing Bragg angle $\theta$. Also, unlike X-rays, neutron scattering factors are not proportional to atomic numbers.

*Example*: A beam of thermal neutrons emitted from the opening of a reactor is diffracted by the (111) planes of nickel crystal at an angle of 28° 30′. Calculate the effective temperature of the neutrons. Nickel has fcc structure and its lattice parameter is 3.52 Å.

*Solution*: Given: $\theta = 28°\ 30′ = 28.5°$, structure is fcc, $a = 3.52$ Å $= 3.52 \times 10^{-10}$ m, $m_n = 1.67 \times 10^{-27}$ kg, $T = ?$
The interplanar spacing $d$ is given by

$$d = \frac{a}{\sqrt{3}} = \frac{3.52 \times 10^{-10}}{\sqrt{3}} = 2.03 \times 10^{-10}\,\text{m}$$

Now, from Bragg's equation (for $n = 1$), we can have

$$\lambda = 2d \sin \theta = 2 \times 2.03 \times 10^{-10} \times \sin 28.5° = 1.94 \times 10^{-10} \text{ m}$$

In order to find the temperature of neutrons, let us make use of the kinetic energy expression, i.e.

$$(1/2)\ mv^2 = (3/2)\ kT$$

Substituting the value of $v$ in eq. 61, we obtain

$$\lambda^2 = \frac{h^2}{3mkT}$$

or $\quad T = \dfrac{h^2}{3mk\lambda^2} = \dfrac{(6.626 \times 10^{-34})^2}{3 \times 1.67 \times 10^{-27} \times 1.38 \times 10^{-23} \times (1.94 \times 10^{-10})^2} = 169 \text{ K}$

### Electron Diffraction
A beam of electrons can be employed to characterize materials in a way similar to the X-rays and neutrons as discussed above. The stream of electrons emitted from a hot wire (as in thermionic emission) is accelerated through vacuum under a very large electrode potential and is passed through a collimating system before it gets diffracted by the specimen to be studied. A schematic view of the electron diffraction system is shown in Fig. 8.46.

The energy $E$ acquired by these electrons depends on the accelerating voltage $V$, approximately as

$$E = eV \qquad (64)$$

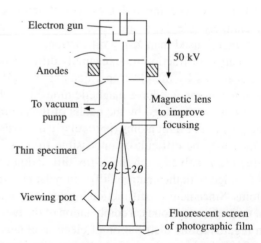

**Fig. 8.46 Schematic view of the electron diffraction technique**

where $e$ is the charge on the electron. The eq. 64 is only an approximate because at the higher voltages (usual in electron diffraction) the electron velocity begins to approach the velocity of light, so that they gain mass due to effect of relativity. However, if we ignore the relativity correction, the wavelength associated with the moving electrons can be written as

$$\lambda = \frac{h}{\sqrt{2mE}} = \frac{h}{\sqrt{2meV}} \tag{65}$$

where $m = 9.11 \times 10^{-31}$ kg, the mass of an electron. Substituting the appropriate mass value for an electron, the eq. 65 reduces to

$$\lambda(\text{Å}) = \left(\frac{150}{V}\right)^{1/2} = \frac{12.24}{(V)^{1/2}} \tag{66}$$

From the above equations, it is clear that the wavelength is roughly inversely proportional to the square root of the accelerating voltage and hence can be easily varied to get the desired wavelength electron beam. Monochromatic beam is obtained simply by applying stabilized voltages to accelerate the electrons. Calculations show that the scattering of electrons from an atom is about four orders of magnitude greater than the scattering of X-rays from the same atom. This suggests that the electron beam has a short stopping distance of about 500 Å or so and hence the specimen to be studied must be thin.

*Example*: Calculate the Bragg angle at which electrons accelerated from rest through a potential difference of 80 $V$ will be diffracted from the (111) planes of an fcc crystal of lattice parameter 3.5 Å.

*Solution*: Given: $V = 80V$, Diffracting planes (111), crystal is fcc, $a = 3.5$ Å $= 3.5 \times 10^{-10}$ m, $\theta = ?$

We know that the wavelength associated with the moving electron is given by

$$\lambda = \frac{h}{\sqrt{2mE}} = \frac{h}{\sqrt{2meV}}$$

Substituting the values of the constants, we can obtain

$$\lambda = \frac{h}{\sqrt{2meV}} \cong \left(\frac{150}{V}\right)^{1/2} \times 10^{-10} \, \text{m}$$

$$= \left(\frac{150}{80}\right)^{1/2} \times 10^{-10} = 1.37 \times 10^{-10} \, \text{m}$$

and

$$d_{111} = \frac{3.5 \times 10^{-10}}{\sqrt{3}} = 2.02 \times 10^{-10} \, \text{m}$$

Now from Bragg's equation for $n = 1$, we can have

$$\theta_{111} = \sin^{-1}\left(\frac{\lambda}{2d}\right) = \sin^{-1}\left(\frac{1.37 \times 10^{-10}}{4.04 \times 10^{-10}}\right) = 19° \, 40'$$

## 8.21  SUMMARY

1. X-rays like visible light, are a form of electromagnetic radiation having wavelengths of the order of 1 Å. X-rays are produced when a beam of fast moving electron strikes a metal target. For a given electrode potential, the wavelength of the resulting X-ray is

$$\lambda(\text{Å}) = \frac{1.24 \times 10^{-6}}{V} V - m$$

2. X-rays may be either monochromatic (containing single wavelength also called characteristic X-ray) or continuous (containing all wavelengths also called white radiation).

3. The target material should be:
   (i)   Good conductor of heat so that it can be efficiently cooled.
   (ii)  Good conductor of electricity because it has to function as an anode.
   (iii) Metal which could emit X-rays of wavelengths of the order of 1 Å suitable for the study of crystalline materials.

4. Intensity of an X-ray beam passing through a given material decreases exponentially as

$$I = I_0 e^{-\mu x}$$

5. Each atom in a crystal acts as a diffraction centre and the crystal as a whole acts like a three dimensional diffraction grating. The condition for diffraction is given by well known Bragg's law

$$2d \sin \theta = n\lambda$$

6. Laue equations are derived on the basis of a simple static atomic model. They are given by:

$$a \left(\cos\ \alpha - \cos \alpha_0\right) = e\lambda$$
$$b \left(\cos \beta - \cos \beta_0\right)\ = f\lambda$$
$$c \left(\cos \gamma - \cos \gamma_0\right)\ \ = g\lambda$$

   All the three equations must satisfy simultaneously to get the most intense beam.

7. Bragg equation is a consequence of more general Laue equations. The order of diffraction $n$ in the Bragg's equation is simply equal to the largest common factor of the numbers $e$, $f$, $g$ appearing in the Laue equations.

8. Graphical interpretation of Bragg's law help understand the reciprocal lattice concept. The reciprocal lattice vector is given by

$$G = \frac{K}{d_{\text{hkl}}}$$

9. X-ray diffraction experiment essentially requires an X-ray source, sample under investigation and a photographic film or a detector.

10. The Powder method is the most conveninet and quickest method for obtaining diffraction data. The Bragg angle $\theta$ and the distance between a pair of arcs are related through

$$\theta = \frac{S}{4}$$

11. Laue method is one of the most convenient and accurate methods for determining the orientation and symmetry of a single crystal. Gnomonic projection is extremely useful in the interpretation of the Laue photographs.

12. Rotation/Oscillation method is normally used to determine the lattice parameters of single crystals. For an $a$-axis rotation photograph, the separation of $n$th layer line (with respect to zero layer) and the lattice parameter $a$ are given by

$$S_n = \frac{(n\lambda/a)}{\sqrt{1 - (n\lambda/a)^2}} \cdot R$$

and

$$a = \frac{n\lambda}{S_n}(R_n^2 + S_n^2)^{1/2}$$

13. Depending upon the energy of neutron from the pile of a reactor, the wavelength of the neutron beam is given by

$$\lambda(\text{Å}) = \frac{0.28}{E^{1/2}}$$

14. Ignoring the relativistic correction, the wavelength associated with the moving electron beam is given by

$$\lambda(\text{Å}) = \frac{12}{[E(eV)]^{1/2}}$$

## 8.22 DEFINITIONS

*Absorption Edge*: An abrupt discontinuity in the intensity of an X-ray absorption spectrum at a particular wavelength.

*Compton Scattering*: It is the elastic scattering of phonons by electrons.

*De Broglie Hypothesis*: With every moving particle (such as electron or proton) a wave is associated whose wavelength is inversely proportional to the momentum of the particle.

*Ewald Sphere*: It is the sphere of radius $1/\lambda$ within which the diffracted beam and reciprocal lattice point intersect each other. It is also called sphere of reflection.

*Fluorescence*: It is the process that certain substances absorb radiation of a particular wavelength and emit light (i.e. exhibit luminescence) of longer wavelength. The emission of light stops the moment the incident radiation is cutoff.

*Linear Attenuation Coefficient*: It is a measure of the fractional fall in the intensity of X-rays per unit thickness of absorbing medium.

*Mass Absorption Coefficient*: It is the fractional decrease in the intensity of a beam of unit cross-section in travelling unit mass of the absorbing medium.

*Monochromatic radiation*: It is the radiation restricted to a very narrow band of wavelength; ideally one wavelength.

*Pair Production*: Simultaneous production of an electron and a positron from high energy (> 1.022 MeV) photon.

*Reciprocal Lattice*: A theoretical lattice associated with a crystal lattice. The reciprocal lattice points are obtained by drawing normals to each crystal plane from a common origin and lying at a distance equal to the reciprocal of interplanar spacing.

*X-rays*: Electromagnetic radiation of very short wavelength (~1 Å) lying between ultraviolet and $\gamma$-rays in the spectrum.

# REVIEW QUESTIONS AND PROBLEMS

1. Show that the reciprocal lattice for a simple cubic structure is also simple cubic.
2. Show that the reciprocal lattice for a body centred cubic is a face centred cubic.
3. Show that the reciprocal lattice for a face centred cubic is a body centred cubic.
4. Explain the concept of reciprocal lattice. Derive the Bragg's condition in terms of the reciprocal lattice vectors.
5. Derive Bragg's law in X-ray diffraction. Give an account of powder method of crystal structure analysis.
6. What are Laue equations for diffraction of X-rays by a crystalline solid? Show that the Bragg's equation is a special case of the Laue equations.
7. Describe briefly the methods for crystal structure determination by X-ray diffraction. Explain the importance of geometrical structure factor taking the example of cubic crystals.
8. Find the geometrical structure factor for fcc structure in which all atoms are identical. Hence show that for fcc lattice no reflections can occur for which the indices are partly even and partly odd.
9. (a)   What is the minimum wavelength in white radiation of X-ray if the applied voltage on the tube is 30 kV?
   (b)   What is the wavelength associated with an electron of kinetic energy of 10 keV?
   (c)   What is the wavelength associated with a neutron at 300 K (K.E = 1/2 kT)?
   
   *Ans.* 0.40 Å, 3.85 Å, 2.52 Å
10. Calculate the geometrical structure factor for a bcc lattice. Name some important planes which will be missing from the X-ray diffraction spectrum.
11. The $K_\alpha$ line from molybdenum has a wavelength 0.71 Å. Calculate the wavelength of $K_\alpha$ line of copper. The atomic number of molybdenum is 42 and that of copper is 29.
    
    *Ans.* 1.52 Å
12. What element has a $K_\alpha$ X-ray line of wavelength 0.71 Å?
    
    *Ans.* Z = 42 (molybdenum).
13. Electrons bombarding the anode of a coolidge tube produce X-rays of wavelength 1 Å. Find the energy of each electron at the moment of impact.
    
    *Ans.* $1.24 \times 10^4$ eV
14. The wavelength of the $L_\alpha$ (X-ray) line of platinum (atomic number 78) is 1.32 Å. An unknown substance emits $L_\alpha$ (X-ray) of wavelength 4.17 Å. Calculate the atomic number of the unknown substance. Given $b = 7.4$ for $L_\alpha$.
    
    *Ans.* Z = 47 (silver)
15. The diamond structure is formed by the combination of two interpenetrating fcc sub-lattices; the basis being (000) and (1/4 1/4 1/4). Find the structure factor of the basis and prove that if all indices are even the structure factor of the basis vanishes unless $h + k + l = 4n$, where $n$ is an integer.
    
    $$Ans.\ 1 + \exp\left(-\frac{i\pi}{2}(h + k + l)\right)$$
16. What is the attenuation of an X-ray beam after passing through a thickness of a material equal to four-half value thickness?
    
    *Ans.* 93.7%.
17. The mass absorption coefficient of aluminium for X-rays of a certain energy is 0.027 m²/kg. Calculate the half-value thickness of aluminium for these X-rays. What thickness of aluminium would attenuate the X-rays by 80% ? Density of aluminium is 2700 kg/m³.
    
    *Ans.* 0.022 m
18. A beam of neutron with energies ranging from zero to several electron volts is directed at a crystal with interplanar spacing 3.03 Å. Determine the angle between the incident beam and the crystal so that the reflected neutrons will have a kinetic energy of 0.1 eV.
    
    *Ans.* 8° 36′
19. Calculate the glancing angle on the plane (110) of a cube rock salt ($a = 2.81$ Å) corresponding to second order diffraction maximum for the X-rays of wavelength 0.71 Å.
    
    *Ans.* 20.9°
20. A beam of X-rays incident on a sodium chloride crystal ($a = 2.81$ Å). The first order reflection is

observed at a glancing angle 8° 35′. What is the wavelength of the X-rays ? At what angle should the second order Bragg's reflection occur? *Ans.* 0.842 Å, 17.4°

21. Sylvine (KCI) crystallizes in the form of simple cubic structure. Determine the interatomic spacing $d$ and the glancing angle at which an X-ray of wavelength of 1.1787 Å is reflected in the third order. The density of KCI is 1990 kg/m$^3$ and the molecular weight is 74.6. *Ans.* 3.96 Å, 42.6°.

22. A bcc crystal is used to measure the wavelength of some X-rays. The Bragg angle for reflection from (110) plane is 20.2°. What is the wavelength? The lattice parameter of the crystal is 3.15 Å.
*Ans.* 1.54 Å

23. X-rays with a wavelength of 1.54 Å are used to calculate the spacing of (200) plane in platinum. The Bragg angle for this reflection is 22.4°. What is the side of the unit cell of the aluminium crystal ?
*Ans.* 4.05 Å

24. Using a diffractometer and a radiation of wavelength 1.54 Å, only one reflection from an fcc crystal is observed when $2\theta$ is 121°. What are the indices of reflection? What is the interplanar spacing?
*Ans.* {111}, 0.885 Å

25. The first three lines from the powder pattern of a cubic crystal have the following $S$ values: 24.95, 40.9 and 48.05 mm. The camera radius is 57.3 mm. Molybdenum $K_\alpha$ radiation of wavelength 0.71 Å is used. Determine the structure and the lattice parameter of the material. *Ans.* DC, 5.66 Å

26. The Bragg angle corresponding to a reflection for which $(h^2 + k^2 + l^2) = 8$ is found to be 14.35°. Determine the lattice parameter of the crystal. X-rays or wavelength 0.71 Å are used. If there are two other reflections with smaller Bragg angles, what is the crystal structure? *Ans.* 4.05 Å, fcc.

27. Aluminium (fcc) has a lattice parameter of 4.05 Å. When a monochromatic radiation of 1.79 Å is used in a powder camera, what would be the first four $S$ values? The camera diameter is 114.6 mm.
*Ans.* 90.1, 105.0, 154.7, and 188.7 mm.

28. The first reflection using copper $K_\alpha$ radiation from a sample of copper powder (fcc) has $S$ value of 86.7 mm. Compute the camera radius.
*Ans.* 57.3 mm.

# Chapter 9

# Thermal Properties of Materials

## 9.1 INTRODUCTION

In chapter 7, we discussed about lattice vibrations and some related aspects, the knowledge of which is very useful in understanding various thermal properties of solid materials, such as specific heat, thermal conductivity, etc. In this chapter, we shall discuss in detail the analysis of these properties. In regards to the specific heat of solids, we shall discuss various proposed models under different temperature range.

## 9.2 THE SPECIFIC HEAT OF SOLID

From elementary knowledge, we know that the specific heat is the amount of heat energy that must be supplied to a mole of solid to raise its temperature by one degree. So, when some heat energy is supplied to a solid, its temperature rises and its internal energy is increased. The increase in the internal energy is manifested mainly as (i) an increase in the vibration of atoms about their mean position and (ii) an increase in the kinetic energy of free electrons. The corresponding specific heats are known as the lattice specific heat and the electronic specific heat, respectively. In order to measure the specific heat, either the volume or the pressure must be kept constant. In general, it is measured at constant volume, i.e.

$$C_v = \left( \frac{dE}{dT} \right)_v \tag{1}$$

where $E$ is the internal energy and $T$ is the temperature of the system.

## 9.3 THE CLASSICAL MODEL

From the kinetic theory of gases, we know that the kinetic energy of an atom of a monoatomic gas at temperature $T$ is $(3/2)\,kT$, where $k$ is the Boltzmann constant. Since an atom has three degrees of (translational) freedom, therefore the energy $(1/2)\,kT$, is associated with each degree of freedom of the atom. Also, to each translational degree of freedom, there are associated two additional degrees of freedom, because energy can appear as kinetic or potential. If there are $N$ atoms ($=N_A$, Avogadro's number for a monoatomic solid) in a mole of the solid, the total internal energy is

$$3 \times 2 \times N \times \frac{1}{2} \, kT = 3NkT = 3RT \qquad (2)$$

where $kT = R$, the universal gas constant. Therefore, the specific heat at constant volume is

$$C_v = \left( \frac{dE}{dT} \right)_v = 3R = 5.96 \text{ cal.mol}^{-1} \text{ K}^{-1}$$

This is known as Dulong and Petit's law and is found to be generally correct at room temperature and above, for elements of atomic weight greater than 40. However, the following experimental facts suggest that the above law fails under other conditions, viz.

1. At low temperatures, the specific heat of all elemental solids is found to approach zero (Fig. 9.1) as $T^3$ in insulators and as $T$ in metals. In superconductors, the drop is even faster.

2. In magnetic solids, there is a large contribution to the specific heat near the temperature at which the magnetic moments become ordered.

3. A number of low atomic number and high melting point elements (e.g. B, Be, C, and Si) show lower specific heats than predicted by Dulong Petit's law.

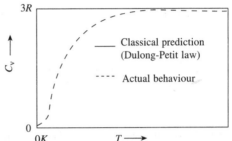

**Fig. 9.1  Specific heat of a solid at low temperatures**

4. A number of electropositive metals (e.g. Na, Cs, Ca, and Mg) show an increase of specific heat above the maximum value $3R$ with an increase of temperature.

## 9.4  THE EINSTEIN MODEL

Einstein was the first person to resolve the problem of specific heat of solids by the application of Planck's quantum theory. He assumed that a crystalline solid made up of $N$ atoms (per mole) could be regarded as an array of atomic oscillators vibrating in three independent directions (as assumed for the classical calculations) with a constant frequency $v$ and that the allowed energy states of oscillators are integral multiples of $hv$.

It may be shown that a crystal containing $N$ atoms which interact according to Hooke's law is mechanically equivalent to a set of $3N$ independent oscillators. Thus, the total internal energy of the crystal is equal to the sum of the mean energies of the individual oscillators. Accordingly, each of the $3N$ harmonic oscillators will have quantised energies

$$\varepsilon_n = n\hbar\omega = nhv \qquad (4)$$

when the quantum number $n = 0, 1, 2, 3...$, $\hbar = h/2\pi$ and $\omega = 2\pi v$. Here the 'zero point energy' $(hv)/2$ is neglected as it will not affect the result.

The number of oscillators $N_n$ of each energy state is determined from the Boltzmann function as

$$N_n = N_0 \exp\left( -\frac{\varepsilon_n}{kT} \right) = N_0 \exp\left( -\frac{nhv}{kT} \right) \qquad (5)$$

where $N_0$ is the number of oscillators in the zero energy state. Further, the average vibrational energy of an oscillator is given by

$$\bar{\varepsilon} = \frac{\varepsilon}{N} = \frac{\sum\limits_n N_n \varepsilon_n}{\sum\limits_n N_n} = \frac{hv}{\exp\left(\dfrac{hv}{kT}\right) - 1} \tag{6}$$

Taking into account the three independent harmonic oscillators ($N$ atoms and 3 independent directions), the total internal energy is given by

$$E_{\text{mol}} = \frac{3Nhv}{\exp\left(\dfrac{hv}{kT}\right) - 1} \tag{7}$$

and the specific heat

$$C_v = \left(\frac{dE}{dT}\right)_v = 3Nk\left(\frac{hv}{kT}\right)^2 \cdot \frac{\exp\left(\dfrac{hv}{kT}\right)}{\left[\exp\left(\dfrac{hv}{kT}\right) - 1\right]^2} \tag{8}$$

The Einstein specific heat curve is fairly close to the experimental curve except at low temperatures (Fig. 9.2). In this region, the Einstein specific heat approaches zero more rapidly than the observed values. However, at high temperatures, it approaches the classical value. Let us consider the two temperature ranges separately.

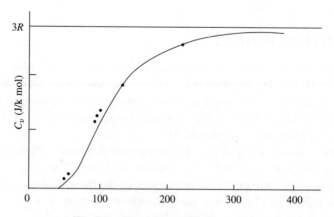

**Fig. 9.2   Einstein specific heat curve**

### High Temperature Range

Let us define a quantity $x = hv/kT$. In this temperature range, $hv \ll kT$ and therefore, the eq. 6 can be written as

$$\bar{\varepsilon} = \frac{hv}{e^x - 1}$$

where $e^x = 1 + x + \dfrac{x^2}{2!} + \dfrac{x^3}{3!} + \ldots \cong 1 + x$. Hence, at high temperature,

$$\bar{\varepsilon} = \frac{hv}{x} = \frac{hv}{hv}\, kT = kT$$

So that
$$E_{mol} = 3N\bar{\varepsilon} = 3NkT$$

and
$$C_v = \left(\frac{dE}{dT}\right)_v = 3Nk = 3R$$

This is same as the classical result.

**Low Temperature Range**

At low temperatures, $hv >> kT$ and hence $e^x >> 1$. Therefore,

$$\bar{\varepsilon} = \frac{hv}{\exp\left(\dfrac{hv}{kT}\right)}$$

so that
$$E_{mol} = 3N\bar{\varepsilon} = 3Nhv\, \exp\left(-\frac{hv}{kT}\right)$$

and
$$C_v = \left(\frac{dE}{dT}\right)_v = 3Nhv\left[-\exp\left(-\frac{hv}{kT}\right) \cdot \frac{hv}{kT^2}\right]$$

$$= 3Nk\left(\frac{hv}{kT}\right)^2 \exp\left(-\frac{hv}{kT}\right) \tag{9}$$

Equation 9 indicates that the exponential term is more important than the term $(hv/kT)^2$ in determining the variation of $C_v$ with temperature. Thus with decreasing temperature, $C_v$ drops exponentially.

*Example*: While silver metal obeys the Dulong-Petit law at room temperature, the diamond does not, explain.

*Solution*: According to the Einstein's theory of specific heat, if $hv << kT$, $C_v \rightarrow 3R$. For silver, $v = 4 \times 10^{12}$ cycles/sec., so that

$$hv = 6626 \times 10^{-34} \times 4 \times 10^{12} = 2.65 \times 10^{-21}\ \text{J}$$

For diamond, $v = 2.4 \times 10^{13}$ cycles/sec., so that

$$hv = 6.626 \times 10^{-34} \times 2.4 \times 10^{13} = 15.9 \times 10^{-21}\ \text{J}$$

Now, at room temperature, the value of $kT$ is found to be

$$kT = 1.38 \times 10^{-23} \times 300 = 4.14 \times 10^{-21}\ \text{J}$$

Comparing these values, we find that for silver the energy $hv$ is less than $kT$ while for the diamond it is high. The high value of energy (or frequency) is due to strong covalent bonding between the adjacent carbon atoms. As a result, much higher temperature is required for the Dulong-Petit law to be obeyed in this case.

## 9.5 THE DENSITY OF STATES

One of the important problems of the theory of lattice vibrations is to find out the frequency distribution of normal modes. For the purpose we consider a one dimensional chain of atoms (string) of length $L$ with fixed ends (Fig. 9.3) and that only longitudinal displacement occurs in it. Suppose $u(x, t)$ represents the displacement of string at any point $x$ at a time $t$. The one dimensional wave equation describing the displacement is

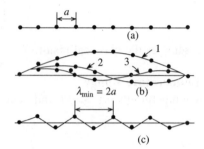

$$\frac{\partial^2 u}{\partial x^2} = \frac{1}{v^2} \frac{\partial^2 u}{\partial t^2} \tag{10}$$

**Fig. 9.3** **Normal modes of a linear chain of identical atoms (a) linear chain (b) normal modes of the chain (c) normal modes of the chain corresponding to shortest wavelength (to highest frequency)**

where $v$ is the velocity of the wave in the string. Solving for above boundary conditions (i.e. $u = 0$ at $x = 0$ and $x = L$), the normal mode solutions of eq. 10 are obtained in the form of standing waves as

$$u(x, t) = A \sin\left(\frac{n\pi x}{L}\right) \cos 2\pi v_n t \tag{11}$$

where $n$ is any positive integer $\geq 1$ and $A$ is a constant. In such cases, there should be an integral number of half wavelengths in the chain, i.e.

$$L = n\frac{\lambda}{2}$$

Differentiating eq. 11 with respect to $x$ and $t$ twice, we get

$$\frac{\partial^2 u}{\partial x^2} = -\frac{un^2\pi^2}{L^2} \text{ and } \frac{\partial^2 u}{\partial t^2} = -u4\pi^2 v^2 \tag{12}$$

Substituting these values in eq. 10, the frequency can be obtained as

$$v^2 = \frac{n^2 v^2}{4L^2} \tag{13}$$

The wavelengths and frequencies of the possible vibrations represented by eq. 11, are given by

$$\lambda_n = \frac{2L}{n} \text{ and } v_n = \frac{v}{\lambda_n} = n\left(\frac{v}{2L}\right) \tag{14}$$

The frequency spectrum is discrete, one frequency corresponds to each integer value $n$. Therefore, the number of possible modes of vibrations $g(v)$ in a frequency interval $dv$ is, on the average

$$g(v) = dn = \frac{2L}{v} \, dv \tag{15}$$

According to eq. 15, the frequency spectrum corresponds to an infinite number of equidistant lines, as shown in Fig. 9.4a.

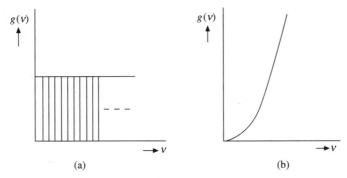

(a)                                    (b)

**Fig. 9.4 (a)** **Frequency spectrum for a finite continuous string according to eq. 15. (b) frequency spectrum for a three-dimensional continuum according to eq. 28**

In a three dimensional case, the situation is different. In this case, we have two distinguishable velocities of propagation, $v_1$ for longitudinal wave (a non-degenerate mode) along the direction of propagation and $v_t$ for the transverse waves (doubly degenerate modes) perpendicular to the direction of propagation. Consequently, we have two different equations involving $v_1$ and $v_t$, each analogous to eq. 10, i.e.,

$$\frac{\partial^2 u_1}{\partial x^2} + \frac{\partial^2 u_1}{\partial y^2} + \frac{\partial^2 u_1}{\partial z^2} = \frac{l}{v_1^2} \frac{\partial^2 u_1}{\partial t^2} \tag{16}$$

and

$$\frac{\partial^2 u_t}{\partial x^2} + \frac{\partial^2 u_t}{\partial y^2} + \frac{\partial^2 u_t}{\partial z^2} = \frac{l}{v_t^2} \frac{\partial^2 u_t}{\partial t^2} \tag{17}$$

Choosing again the simplest boundary conditions that the surface planes of the cube are rigidly held, we obtain the following standing wave solutions

$$u_1(x, y, z) = A_1 \sin\left(\frac{n_x \pi x}{L}\right) \sin\left(\frac{n_y \pi y}{L}\right) \sin\left(\frac{n_z \pi z}{L}\right) \cos 2\pi v_1 t \tag{18}$$

and

$$u_t(x, y, z) = A_t \sin\left(\frac{n_x \pi x}{L}\right) \sin\left(\frac{n_y \pi y}{L}\right) \sin\left(\frac{n_z \pi z}{L}\right) \cos 2\pi v_t t \tag{19}$$

where $n_x$, $n_y$ and $n_z$ are positive integers $\geq 1$ and $A_1$ and $A_t$ are constants as pointed out earlier.

Differentiating eqs. 18 and 19 with respect to $x$, $y$, $z$, twice and substituting the resulting values in eqs. 16 and 17, we obtain the following expressions for the possible modes of vibration,

$$v_l^2 = \frac{v_l^2}{4L^2} (n_x^2 + n_y^2 + n_z^2) \tag{20}$$

and

$$v_t^2 = \frac{v_t^2}{4L^2} (n_x^2 + n_y^2 + n_z^2) \tag{21}$$

Thus, for any chosen set of integers $n_x$, $n_y$ and $n_z$, there are three independent modes of vibrations (one longitudinal and two transverse). Now, employing the relation $k = \dfrac{2\pi}{\lambda} = \dfrac{2\pi v}{v}$, the components of the wave vector $k$ from eq. 20 can be written as

$$k_x = \frac{\pi n_x}{L}, k_y = \frac{\pi n_y}{L}, k_z = \frac{\pi n_z}{L} \tag{22}$$

Further, if we suppose that $k^2 = k_x^2 + k_y^2 + k_z^2$, then from eqs. 20 and 21, it follows that

$$v_l = \frac{v_l k}{2\pi} \text{ and } v_t = \frac{v_t k}{2\pi} \tag{23}$$

The standing waves 18 and 19 may be viewed as eq. 42 (chapter 7), where $k$ may now be identified as the wave vector with the components $k_x$, $k_y$, and $k_z$ and $r$ as the position vector. A plot of the allowed values of $k$ in reciprocal space or $k$-space is shown in Fig. 9.5. Points defined in eq. 22 are distributed as lattice points in the positive octant. The volume of the octant of radius $k$ is

$$\frac{1}{8} \times \frac{4}{3} \pi k^3 = \frac{1}{6} \pi k^3$$

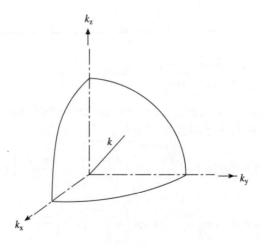

**Fig. 9.5 Representation of wave vectors in $k$-space**

and the volume occupied by each point is $(\pi/L)^3$. Therefore, the total number of lattice points in the octant is

$$\frac{Vk^3}{6\pi^2}$$

where $V (= L^3)$ is the volume of the crystal. For a particular frequency $v$, the eq. 23 will give rise to two wave numbers $k_1$ and $k_t$ as

$$k_1 = \frac{2\pi v}{v_1} \text{ and } k_t = \frac{2\pi v}{v_t} \tag{24}$$

Thus, the total number of lattice points in the octant with the radii $k_1$ and $k_t$, respectively are

$$\frac{V}{6\pi^2} \left( \frac{2\pi v}{v_1} \right) \text{ and } \frac{V}{6\pi^2} \left( \frac{2\pi v}{v_t} \right)^3$$

However, since with every lattice point, we may associate one longitudinal mode and two transverse modes, the number of modes $g(v)$ of frequency less than $v_D$ is given by

$$g(v) = \frac{8\pi^3 V}{6\pi^2} \left( \frac{1}{v_1^3} + \frac{2}{v_t^3} \right) v^3 \tag{25}$$

where a mean velocity $v$ may be defined by the equation

$$\frac{3}{v^3} = \frac{1}{v_1^3} + \frac{2}{v_t^3} \tag{26}$$

so that eq. 25 becomes, $\qquad g(v) = \frac{4\pi V v^3}{v^3} \tag{27}$

Differentiating this expression, we obtain the required frequency distribution function

$$g(v) \, dv = \frac{12\pi V}{v^3} v^2 \, dv \tag{28}$$

or similarly from eq. 25, we obtain

$$g(v) \, dv = 4\pi V \left( \frac{1}{v_1^3} + \frac{2}{v_t^3} \right) v^2 \, dv \tag{29}$$

This is the number of modes whose frequencies lie between the interval $v$ and $v + dv$. A curve between the density of states $g(v)$ and $v$ (Fig. 9.4b) shows that $g(v)$ increases as $v^2$. The function $g(v)$ is also known as spectral distribution function of normal modes.

Since the number of normal vibrations in a three dimensional crystal lattice is $3N$, the function $g(v)$ should satisfy the following normalization condition

$$\int_0^{v_D} g(v) \, dv = 3N \tag{30}$$

where $v_D$ is the maximum frequency limiting the spectrum of normal modes from above and is known as Debye frequency. Substituting eq. 29 into eq. 30 and integrating, we obtain

$$4\pi V \left( \frac{1}{v_l^3} + \frac{2}{v_t^3} \right) \int_0^{v_D} v^2 dv = 3N$$

or

$$v_D^3 = \frac{9N}{4\pi V} \left( \frac{1}{v_l^3} + \frac{2}{v_t^3} \right)^{-1} \qquad (31)$$

Substituting eq. 31 back into eq. 29, we obtain the distribution function

$$f(v) = \sum_{l,t} g(v) = \frac{9N}{v_D^3} v^2$$

which gives

$$f(v) = Kv^2 \qquad \text{(for } v \leq v_D) $$
$$= 0 \qquad \text{(for } v \leq v_D) \qquad (32)$$

where $K = \dfrac{9N}{v_D^3}$ is a constant (independent of $v$). This function is compared with the Einstein's function in Fig. 9.6.

## 9.6 THE DEBYE MODEL

In 1912, Debye pointed out that the source of error lies in the assumption (that all atomic oscillators vibrate independently at a constant frequency) made by Einstein. According to him, the assumption is not justifiable since all atoms are elastically coupled to its neighbours, as shown in Fig. 7.1. Debye therefore, simplified the problem by considering a solid as a continuously vibrating medium (as an elastic continuum), which gives rise to a spectrum of

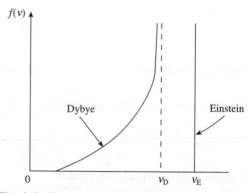

Fig. 9.6   Frequency spectrum according to Debye model and Einstein model

frequencies instead of a single frequency as assumed in the Einstein's model. Once, the frequency distribution is known, it is a simple matter to calculate the total internal energy and hence the specific heat of the solids. Taking into account the density of states as obtained in the preceding section, we can write the internal energy of the Debye solid as

$$E = \int_{\substack{\text{all allowed} \\ \text{frequencies}}} \bar{\varepsilon}(v)\, g(v)\, dv \qquad (33)$$

Using eqs. 6 and 29, we get

$$E = 4\pi V \left( \frac{1}{v_l^3} + \frac{2}{v_t^3} \right) \int_0^{v_D} \frac{hvv^2 dv}{\exp\left( \dfrac{hv}{kT} \right) - 1}$$

which in terms of eq. 31 can be written as

$$E = \frac{9N}{v_D^3} \int_0^{v_D} \frac{hvv^2 dv}{\exp\left( \dfrac{hv}{kT} \right) - 1} \tag{34}$$

To simplify eq. 34, let us suppose that $x = hv/kT$, so that $dv = (kT\, dx)/h$. Further, if we suppose that $x_D = (hv_D)/kT$, eq. 34 becomes

$$E = 9N \left( \frac{kT}{hv_D} \right)^3 kT \int_0^{x_D} \frac{x^3}{e^x - 1} dx \tag{35}$$

Now, we can define the Debye temperature as $\theta_D$ according to the equation, $hv_D = k\theta_D$, then

$$\theta_D = \frac{hv_D}{k} \quad \text{and} \quad x_D = \frac{\theta_D}{T}$$

so that, eq. 35 becomes

$$E = 9NkT \left( \frac{T}{\theta_D} \right)^3 \int_0^{x_D} \frac{x^3}{e^x - 1} dx \tag{36}$$

which does not depend explicitly on the volume and looks similar to the expression obtained for Einstien's model. However, let us examine the dependence of the integral (eq. 36) on temperature. For simplicity, we shall consider the following three temperature ranges.

**High Temperature Range**
We assumed earlier that $x = hv/kT$. In this temperature range, $T \gg \theta_D$ and hence $kT \gg hv$ even when $v = v_D$, implying that $x$ will be small over the whole range of integration. So that

$$\int_0^{x_D} \frac{x^3}{e^x - 1} dx \rightarrow \int_0^{x_D} \frac{x^3}{x} dx = \frac{x_D^3}{3} = \frac{1}{3} \left( \frac{\theta_D}{T} \right)^3$$

Therefore,

$$E = 9NkT \times \frac{1}{3} = 3NkT \tag{37}$$

which is the classical result. This implies that in the high temperature range, the specific heat of solids is the same as measured in Dulong and Petit's experiment. This can be understood from the following arguments: when $T \gg \theta_D$, every mode of oscillation is completely excited, and has an average energy equal to the classical value i.e. $\bar{\varepsilon} = kT$. Substituting this in eq. 33 and also making use of the eq. 30, we obtain, $E = 3\,NkT$, which is same as eq. 37.

**Low Temperature Range**

In the low temperature range, $T \ll \theta_D$, so that $kT \ll h\nu_D$. In this case, the upper limit of the integration can be replaced by infinity (i.e. $x_D \to \infty$) and hence the above integral becomes

$$\int_0^{x_D} \frac{x^3}{e^x - 1}\, dx \to \int_0^{\infty} \frac{x^3}{e^x - 1}\, dx \to \frac{\pi^4}{15}$$

Therefore,

$$E = 9NkT \left(\frac{T}{\theta_D}\right)^3 \times \frac{\pi^4}{15} = \frac{3}{5}\pi^4 NkT \left(\frac{T}{\theta_D}\right)^3$$

and

$$C_v = \frac{12}{5}\pi^4 Nk \left(\frac{T}{\theta_D}\right)^3 \tag{38}$$

This is a famous expression known as Debye $T^3$ law for specific heat at low temperature. Fig. 9.7 shows a typical Debye plot alongwith the measured data, Einstein plot and the classical value.

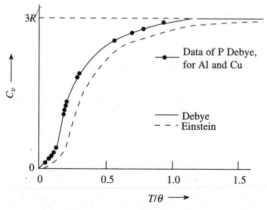

**Fig. 9.7   Various specific heat curves of a solid**

The $T^3$ dependence can be understood from the following arguments: when $T \ll \theta_D$, only low frequency normal modes having energy $h\nu < kT$ are excited to an appreciable degree. The average energy of these modes may be obtained from eq. 6 by expanding the denominator of the expression.

$$\bar{\varepsilon}_{n,m} = \frac{h\nu}{\exp\left(\dfrac{h\nu}{kT} - 1\right)} \cong h\nu \left(1 + \frac{h\nu}{kT} + \dots - 1\right)^{-1} \cong kT \tag{39}$$

This shows that the average energy of every normal mode is proportional to the absolute temperature $T$ (i.e. energy varies linearly with $T$). In addition to this, the rise in temperature in the low temperature range causes new higher frequency ($v \cong kT/h$) normal modes to be excited. The number of there modes may be calculated using eq. 29 and is found to be proportional to $v^3 \sim T^3$. Thus in the low temperature range, we observe that the energy of a solid rises with the rise in temperature by means of two mechanisms:

(i) the increase in the average energy of every normal mode, $\bar{\varepsilon}_{n,m}$, proportional to $T$ due to the rise in the probability of its excitation, and

(ii) the increase in number of normal modes of the lattice, proportional to $T^3$. Therefore, the total energy of excitation is proportional to $T^4$ and hence a rise in the specific heat is proportional to $T^3$, which is in agreement with eq. 38.

**Intermediate Temperature Range**

Debye model is found to agree very well with the experiment at the two extremes of temperatures i.e. in the range $T \le \theta_D/50$ and $T \ge 0.2\theta_D$. However, at the intermediate temperatures $\theta_D/50 \le T \le 0.2\theta_D$, where a gradual transition of Debye $T^3$ law to the Dulong and Petit law takes place, the agreement is not so good.

This is expected because a solid cannot be represented by a continuum at frequencies near $v_D$ as has been assumed in Debye model. Actually, this frequency corresponds to a wavelength of the order of the atomic spacing. Frequency spectrum according to Debye model is found to be different from the one expected from a real crystal as shown in Fig. 9.8. However, it is interesting that area under the two curves are same. In order to improve upon the Debye model, we must use the correct dispersion relation and the corresponding density of states.

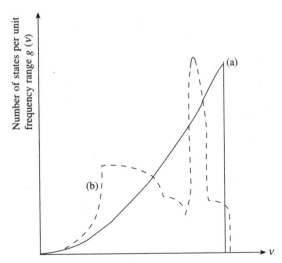

**Fig. 9.8 Frequency spectrum (a) according to the Debye model, (b) behaviour expected from a real crystal**

*Example*: Copper has an atomic weight 63.5, the density $8.9 \times 10^3$ kg/m$^3$, $v_t = 2.32 \times 10^3$ m/s and $v_1 = 4.76 \times 10^3$ m/s. Estimate the specific heat at 30K.

*Solution*: Given: at. wt. of Cu = 63.5, $\rho = 8.9 \times 10^3$ kg/m$^3$, $v_t = 2.32 \times 10^3$ m/s, $v_1 = 4.76 \times 10^3$ m/s and $T = 30$K, $C_v = ?$.

Substituting the value of Debye frequency from eq. 31 into the equation $h\nu_D = K\theta_D$, the Debye temperature can be obtained as

$$\theta_D = \frac{h}{k} \cdot \left( \frac{9N}{4\pi V[(1/v_1^3) + (2/v_t^3)]} \right)^{1/3}$$

where $h = 6.626 \times 10^{-34}$ Js and $k = 1.38 \times 10^{-23}$ JK$^{-1}$. Now, substituting the above values and simplifying, we get

$$\theta_D = 340\text{K}$$

Further, substituting the values of $\theta_D$ and the given temperature ($T = 30$K) in eq. 38 (where $R = Nk$), the specific heat can be obtained as

$$C_v = \frac{12}{5} \pi^4 R \left( \frac{T}{\theta_D} \right)^3 = \frac{12 \times \pi^4 \, 8.31 \times 10^3}{5} \left( \frac{30}{340} \right)^3 = 1.33\text{kJ mol}^{-1}\text{K}^{-1}$$

*Example*: The Debye temperature for diamond is 2230K. Calculate the highest possible vibrational frequency and the molar heat capacity of diamond at 10K.

*Solution*: Given: $\theta_D = 2230$K, $T = 10$K, $\nu_D = ?$

Making use of the expression $h\nu_D = k\theta_D$ and substituting the required values, the Debye frequency can be obtained as

$$\nu_D = \frac{k\theta_D}{h} = \frac{1.38 \times 10^{-23} \times 2230}{6.626 \times 10^{-34}} = 4.64 \times 10^{13} \text{ s}^{-1}$$

Further, similar to the above calculation, the Debye molar specific heat can be obtained as

$$C_v = \frac{12}{5} \pi^4 R \left( \frac{T}{\theta_D} \right)^3 = \frac{12 \times \pi^4 \, 8.31 \times 10^3}{5} \left( \frac{10}{2230} \right)^3 = 0.175\text{J kmol}^{-1}\text{K}^{-1}$$

*Example*: For copper, the lattice specific heat at low temperature has the behaviour of $[C_v]_1 \cong 4.6 \times 10^{-2} \times T^3$ J kmol$^{-1}$ K$^{-1}$. Estimate the Debye temperature for copper.

*Solution*: Given: $[C_v]_1 \cong 4.6 \times 10^{-2} \times T^3$ J kmol$^{-1}$ $K^{-1}$, $\theta_D = ?$

We know that the actual low temperature Debye equation is given by

$$C_v = \frac{12}{5} \pi^4 R \left( \frac{T}{\theta_D} \right)^3$$

Comparing the two specific heat equations, we obtain

$$\frac{12 \times \pi^4 R}{5\theta_D^3} = 4.6 \times 10^{-2}$$

or $\qquad \theta_D^3 = \dfrac{12 \times \pi^4 R}{5 \times 4.6 \times 10^{-2}} = \dfrac{12 \times \pi^4 \times 8.31 \times 10^3}{5 \times 4.6 \times 10^{-2}} = 42233194 \ (K)^3$

or $\qquad \theta_D = 348K$

*Example*: Estimate the Debye temperature of gold if its atomic weight is 197, the density is 1.9 $\times 10^4$ kg/m$^3$ and the velocity of sound in it is 2100 m/s.

*Solution*: Given: At. wt. of Au = 197, $\rho = 1.9 \times 10^4$ kg/m$^3$, $v_S = 2100$ m/s, $\theta_D$ = ?

We know that the volume $V = \dfrac{M}{\rho} = \dfrac{194}{1.9 \times 10^{-4}} = 103.68 \times 10^{-4} \text{m}^3$

Now making use of the eq. 31 in terms of the mean velocity and also taking into account the expression $h v_D = k \theta_D$, the Debye temperature can be written as

$$\theta_D = \frac{hv}{k} \cdot \left( \frac{9N}{12\pi V} \right)^{1/3}$$

Substituting different values, we get

$$\theta_D = \frac{6.626 \times 10^{-34} \times 2100}{1.38 \times 10^{-23}} \cdot \left( \frac{9 \times 6.02 \times 10^{26}}{12\pi \times 103.68 \times 10^{-4}} \right)^{1/3}$$

$$= 240 \ K$$

*Example:* At low temperatures, the specific heat of rock salt varies with the temperature according to the Debye $T^3$ law:

$$[C_v]_l = A \left( \frac{T}{\theta_D} \right)^3$$

where $A$ = 464 cal gmol$^{-1}$ K$^{-1}$ an $\theta_D$ = 281K. How much heat is required to raise the temperature of 2 gmol of rock salt from 10 to 50K?

*Solution*: Given: $[C_v]_1 = A(T/\theta_D)^3$, $A$ = 464 cal gmol$^{-1}$ K$^{-1}$ and $\theta_D$ = 281K, Q = ?
Since, the specific heat varies as $T^3$, the calculation must be made by taking into account the different ranges of temperatures. Let the ranges of temperatures in °K be

$$10–20, \ 20–30, \ 30–40, \text{ and } 40–50$$

The rise of temperature in each case is 10K. The mean temperatures are: 15, 25, 35 and 45K. Therefore, the quantity of heat required to raise the temperature of 2 gmol of salt through 10K is given by,

$$Q = 2 \times 10\{[C_v] \text{ at } 15K + [C_v] \text{ at } 25K + [C_v] \text{ at } 35K + [C_v] \text{ at } 45K\}$$

$$= \frac{20 \times 464}{(281)^3} \{(15)^3 + (25)^3 + (35)^3 + (45)^3\}$$

$$= 4.182 \times 10^{-4} \times 153000$$

$$= 63.99 \text{ cal}$$

## 9.7 THERMAL CONDUCTIVITY OF SOLIDS

Thermal conductivity is a process in which heat is transferred from one part of the body to another as a result of temperature gradient. If the gradient is uniform, then the amount of the thermal energy crossing a unit area in unit time is directly proportional to the temperature gradient, i.e.

$$Q \propto \frac{dT}{dx}$$

or

$$Q = K \left( \frac{dT}{dx} \right) \qquad\qquad 40$$

where the proportionality constant $K$ is called the thermal conductivity. In metallic conductors, heat is carried by free electrons, while in insulators, it is mainly carried by phonons. Therefore, in general the transfer of heat can take place both by electrons and phonons and hence the total thermal conductivity can be written as

$$K_{\text{total}} = K_{\text{electron}} + K_{\text{phonon}} \qquad\qquad (41)$$

In order to determine the value of $K$ in eq. 40, let us consider a conductor in the form of rod of uniform cross-section (say 1 sq.m) with the assumption that there exists a uniform temperature gradient. Let us draw three parallel planes at $A$, $B$ and $C$ normal to the direction of heat flow which are separated by one mean free path $\lambda$ as shown in Fig. 9.9.

According to the kinetic theory, the number of electrons flowing in a given direction through unit area in unit time is $\frac{1}{6}(nv)$, where $n$ is the density of electrons moving with an average velocity $v$. Further, the excess of energy carried by an electron from plane $A$ to plane $B$ is $(dE/dx)\lambda$. Thus the excess energy flowing through the plane $B$ to the right is

$$Q_{\text{right}} = \frac{1}{6} nv\lambda \left( \frac{dE}{dx} \right) \qquad (42)$$

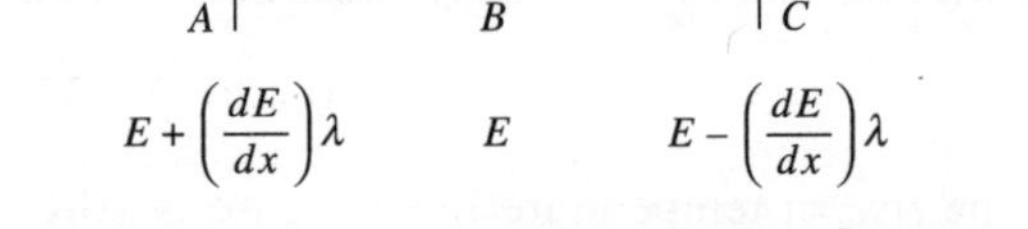

Similarly, the energy flowing through the plane $B$ to the left is

**Fig. 9.9   Flow of heat through a conductor**

$$Q_{\text{left}} = -\frac{1}{6} nv\lambda \left( \frac{dE}{dx} \right) \qquad\qquad (43)$$

Therefore, the net amount of energy flowing through the plane $B$ is

$$Q = Q_{\text{right}} - Q_{\text{left}} = \frac{1}{6} nv\lambda \left( \frac{dE}{dx} \right) - \left[ -\frac{1}{6} nv\lambda \left( \frac{dE}{dx} \right) \right] = \frac{nv\lambda}{3} \left( \frac{dE}{dx} \right) \qquad\qquad (44)$$

But
$$n \left( \frac{dE}{dx} \right) = n \left( \frac{dE}{dT} \right) \cdot \left( \frac{dT}{dx} \right) = nC_v \left( \frac{dT}{dx} \right)$$

where $C_v$ is the specific heat of solid at constant volume. Therefore, eq. 44 becomes

$$Q = \frac{nC_v v \lambda}{3} \left( \frac{dT}{dx} \right) \tag{45}$$

Now, comparing eqs. 40 and 45, we obtain

$$K = \frac{1}{3} v \lambda C_v \tag{46}$$

## 9.8  THERMAL CONDUCTIVITY DUE TO ELECTRONS

In order to derive an expression for thermal conductivity of metals where the heat is predominantly carried by the electrons, we make the following assumptions:

  (i) The metal consists of fixed positive ions in a sea of electrons. In general, there will be one or two electrons per ion.
 (ii) The electrons behave as a perfect gas and they transport thermal energy from the hotter to the colder region.
(iii) Each electron travels a distance $\lambda$ in a mean free time $\tau$ before colliding with a positive ion where it gives up all its thermal energy.
 (iv) Only those electrons that lie within the range $kT$ of the Fermi level are active in the transport process. The velocity of such electrons is calculated from the formula

$$\frac{1}{2} m v_F^2 = E_F \tag{47}$$

Substituting the value of electronic specific heat from eq. 44 (chapter 10) and $\lambda = v_F \tau$ in eq. 46 and making use of the eq. 47, we obtain the electronic contribution of thermal conductivity as

$$K_e = \left( \frac{2 \tau E_F}{3m} \right) \left( \frac{\pi^2 N k^2}{2 E_F} \right) T = \left( \frac{\pi^2 N k^2 \tau}{3m} \right) T \tag{48}$$

Since, the mean free time $\tau$ varies as $T^{-1}$ above the Debye temperature, the electronic contribution of thermal conductivity is nearly temperature independent. This is consistent with the experimental facts. However, at low temperatures, the behaviour is more complicated as illustrated in Fig. 9.10 for copper.

## 9.9  THERMAL CONDUCTIVITY DUE TO PHONONS

As we know that in insulators, there are no mobile electrons and hence phonons carry most of the heat energy. Thus, for insulators in eq. 46, $v$ is the velocity of sound, $\lambda$ is the phonon mean free path and $C_v$ is the lattice specific heat per unit volume given by the Debye $T^3$ law:

$$C_v = \begin{cases} \alpha T^3 & (T < \theta_D) \\ 3Nk & (T > \theta_D) \end{cases} \tag{49}$$

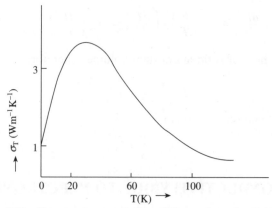

**Fig. 9.10 Temperature variation of thermal conductivity for copper**

Consequently, the thermal conductivity of an insulator is proportional to $T^3$ at low temperatures, as shown in Fig. 9.11. At high temperatures $(T \gg \theta_D)$, the lattice specific heat is constant (i.e. equal to $3Nk$, the Dulong-Petit's value) and any temperature dependence of $K$ arises predominantly from the variation of the mean free path $\lambda$ due to phonon-phonon interaction (i.e. due to anharmonicity). However, a small contribution may also arise from collisions of phonons with crystal boundaries and impurities. Therefore, for all practical purposes only phonon-phonon contribution is considered. The lattice dynamics of anharmonic crystals which takes into account the phonon-phonon collision is very complicated, but leads to a simple final result, viz. the phonon mean free path is inversely proportional to the absolute temperature, i.e. $\lambda = T^{-1}$, so that,

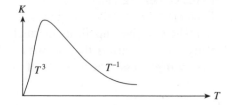

**Fig. 9.11 Typical variation of phonon thermal conductivity with temperature**

$$K = T^{-1} \tag{50}$$

Thus, the thermal conductivity of an insulator is proportional to $T^{-1}$ at high temperatures

## 9.10 THERMAL RESISTANCE OF SOLIDS

For a given solid, thermal resistance may arise as a result of the following scattering mechanisms:

1. The phonon-phonon interaction (Umklapp process), $K_u$
2. Scattering of phonons by boundaries of the specimen or grains, $K_b$
3. Scattering by impurities and lattice imperfections, $K_i$

Each of the above mechanisms will have an associated mean free path such as $\lambda_u$, $\lambda_b$ and $\lambda_i$ and corresponding thermal resistance such as $R_u$, $R_b$ and $R_i$. These resistances form a series combination to give the effective resistance $R$, i.e.

$$R = R_u + R_b + R_i$$

and hence the overall thermal conductivity is

$$\frac{1}{K} = \frac{1}{K_u} + \frac{1}{K_b} + \frac{1}{K_i}$$ (51)

If all the interactions are equally strong and coexistent, the situation would be very complicated. Let us discuss these scattering mechanisms separately.

## I. Phonon-Phonon Interaction

In a linear material medium, the propagation of waves follows the principle of superposition and are said to be harmonic. The resultant displacement of the medium at any point can be obtained by adding separate amplitude of the individual wave at that point and the energy is taken simply as the square of the resultant amplitude. However, for a non-linear medium, the principle of superposition breaks and the waves are said to be anharmonic. For example, if two waves of angular frequencies $\omega_1$ and $\omega_2$ are propagated through such a medium, then the resultant wave will contain the waves of frequencies $\omega_1 + \omega_2$, $\omega_1$, $- \omega_2$ and possibly others.

A medium can normally be treated as linear if the amplitude of the waves is small, so that any higher order (anharmonic) term may be neglected. For phonons in a crystal, this is the case at very low temperatures where the interaction between phonons is negligible. However, at higher temperatures, when the atomic displacements are large, the anharmonic terms become appreciable. In this region, the corresponding mean free path is inversely proportional to the temperature. This is reasonable, since the larger the $T$ is, the greater the number of phonons participating in the collision process.

### Normal Process

Let us analyse a three-phonon process in which either two phonons of frequencies $\omega_1$, $\omega_2$ and the momenta $k_1$, $k_2$ combine to form one phonon of frequency $\omega_3$ and momenta $k_3$, or one phonon splits into two. For the first case, the law of conservation of energy and momentum are respectively

$$\hbar\omega_1 + \hbar\omega_2 = \hbar\omega_3 \quad \text{or} \quad \omega_1 + \omega_2 = \omega_3$$ (52)

and $\qquad\qquad \hbar k_1 + \hbar k_2 = \hbar k_3 \quad \text{or} \quad k_1 + k_2 = k_3$ (53)

Any process satisfying the above two equations simultaneously is called a normal process or $N$-process. This is illustrated in Fig. 9.12 for a two dimensional square lattice, where $\pm\pi/a$ indicates the boundaries of the first Brillouin zone. The $k$ vectors pointing towards the centre of the zone represent phonons which are absorbed in the collision process, while the $k$ vectors pointing away from the centre of the zone represent phonons which are emitted in the collision process. In a normal process, since the direction of the energy flow remains the same after collision therefore it makes no contribution towards the thermal resistance. Consequently, an exclusive $N$-process will provide an infinite thermal conductivity in a perfect crystal. This leads us to conclude that the presence of other interactions in crystals are responsible for limiting the conductivity to a finite value.

### Umklapp Process

When either of the incident phonons or both have fairly large wave vectors such as $k_1$ and $k_2$, the

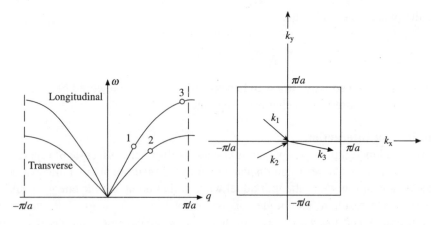

**Fig. 9.12 (a)   A normal process, (b) wave vector conservation in *N*-process**

resultant wave vector $k_3$ in eq. 53 may be so large (i.e. $k_3 > \pi/a$) that the corresponding wavelength is shorter than twice the interatomic spacing. For a periodic structure, the equivalent wave can be shown to have a wave vector equal to $k_3' = k_3 - 2\pi/a$. Under the condition $(2\pi/a) > |k_3| > \pi/a$, the resultant wave vector $k_3$ will be negative so that the phonon velocity is reversed. Such processes are called umklapp processes or *U*-processes (which in German means flip over). It is to be noted that *U*-processes cannot occur in continuous medium.

Fig. 9.13 shows how a collision of two phonons $k_1$, $k_2$ (both having positive $k_x$) can by umklapp give a phonon of negative $k_x$ after collision. The vector sum of $k_1$ and $k_2$ must extend beyond the boundaries of the first Brillouin zone for a *U*-process to occur. *P* and *P'* are equivalent points in neighbouring Brillouin zones.

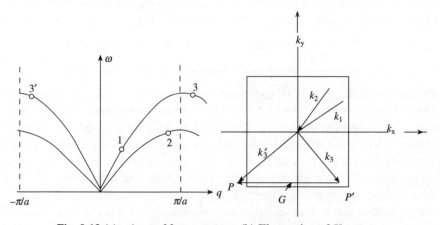

**Fig. 9.13 (a)   An umklapp process. (b) Illustration of *U*-process**

According to Peierls, the three-phonon processes for thermal resistivity are given by not eq. 53 but by

$$k_1 + k_2 = k_3 + G \tag{54}$$

where $G$ is a reciprocal lattice vector (Fig. 9.13b). Therefore, in eq. 54, $G = 0$ represents the *N*-process, while *U*-processes are characterized by $G \neq 0$.

## II.  Scattering of Phonons by Boundaries or Grains

In a chemically pure and structurally perfect crystal, the thermal resistance is determined by *U*-processes for most of the temperature range except at low temperatures where the mean free path $\lambda$ becomes comparable to the size of the specimen and hence the thermal conductivity is a function of the dimension of the crystal. In the low temperature region, the mean free path $\lambda$ becomes constant and is of the order of the diameter of the specimen, so that

$$K_b \sim CvD \tag{55}$$

where the only temperature dependent term on the right hand side is $C$ (the heat capacity) which varies as $T^3$. This implies that $K$ should also vary as $T^3$ at low temperatures (Fig. 9.14a).

In a polycrystalline sample, the value of $D$ will be restricted by the size of the crystallite blocks (or grains) and not by the specimen diameter.

## III.  Scattering by Impurities and Imperfections

As we know that the scattering of phonons by an obstacle depends on its size, the smaller the obstacle the less is the scattering. This is true for samples containing point imperfections, isotopes of different masses, chemical impurities and amorphous structures (all are of atomic dimensions). For such systems, theory of Rayleigh scattering is applicable, according to which the mean free path $\lambda$ varies as $T^{-4}$, at low temperatures. Hence the conductivity $K_i$ in the low temperature region varies as $T^{-1}$ (Fig. 9.14b). However, at higher temperatures where the mean free path $\lambda$ is comparable to the atomic dimensions and the specific heat is constant, the conductivity $K_i$ becomes independent of temperature.

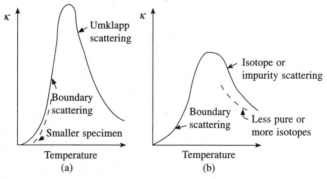

**Fig. 9.14**  **General behaviour of the phonon thermal conductivity in insulator at low temperatures, (a) A pure specimen in which *U*-Process dominates over the rise in conductivity, and (b) in an impure specimen in which phonon scattering by impurities is dominant**

Large amount of impurity will reduce the conductivity. From chapter 5, we know that the stress field is always associated with dislocations. This gives rise to a thermal resistance, which is proportional to the dislocation density, i.e. the conductivity is inversely proportional to the dislocation density. The presence of dislocations is more effective at low temperatures, while the effect of impurities is more important at higher temperatures.

In amorphous substances like glass and plastics, phonon scattering is large. The mean free path $\lambda$ is very small and is temperature independent. The thermal conductivity in these materials is low at room temperature and decreases fast (according to $T^3$) as the temperature is reduced. Consequently, these materials are good thermal insulators.

## 9.11   SUMMARY

1. According to the classical model, the molar specific heat is given by

$$C_v = \left( \frac{dE}{dT} \right)_v = 3R$$

This is known as Dulong-Petit law and is found to be valid only at higher temperatures. However, experimentally $C_v$ is found to decrease with the decrease of temperature and vanishes at $T = 0K$.

2. Einstein's quantum theory assumes that the crystal is made up of $N$ atoms vibrating in three independent directions with a constant frequency $v$. According to him, the specific heat is given by

$$C_v = \left( \frac{dE}{dT} \right)_v = 3Nk \left( \frac{hv}{kT} \right)^2 \cdot \frac{\exp\left( \dfrac{hv}{kT} \right)}{\left[ \exp\left( \dfrac{hv}{kT} \right) - 1 \right]^2}$$

The Einstein specific heat curve is fairly close to the experimental curve except at low temperatures. In this region, the Einstein specific heat approaches zero more rapidly than the observed values. However, at high temperatures, it approaches the classical result.

3. The number of vibrational modes per unit volume (where longitudinal wave has one state of polarization and transverse wave has two states of polarization) is given by

$$g(v)\, dv = 4\pi V \left( \frac{1}{v_l^3} + \frac{2}{v_t^3} \right) v^2\, dv$$

where a mean velocity $v$ may be defined by the equation

$$\frac{3}{v^3} = \frac{1}{v_l^3} + \frac{2}{v_t^3}$$

4. Debye explained the discrepancy existing in the Einstein relation by considering a solid as an elastic continuum where all the atoms are elastically coupled to its neighbours and vibrate collectively with a spectrum of frequencies. He found that the molar specific heat at low temperature is given by

$$C_v = \frac{12}{5} \pi^4 Nk \left( \frac{T}{\theta_D} \right)^3$$

This is a famous Debye $T^3$ law. The Debye specific heat curve is more close to the experimental curve.

5. In general, the transfer of heat can take place both by electrons (as in metals) and phonons (as in insulators). Making use of the kinetic theory, the expression for thermal conductivity is obtained as

$$K = \frac{1}{3} v \lambda C_v$$

where $v$ is the average velocity of the electrons or phonons, $\lambda$ is the mean free path and $C_v$ is the specific heat per unit volume for electrons or phonons.

6. For a given solid, thermal resistance may arise as a result of various scattering mechanisms and is given by

$$R = R_u + R_b + R_i$$

and hence the overall thermal conductivity is given by

$$\frac{1}{K} = \frac{1}{K_u} + \frac{1}{K_b} + \frac{1}{K_i}$$

7. A three phonon process is called a normal or *N*-process when it satisfies the following conservation laws simultaneously

$$\omega_1 + \omega_2 = \omega_3$$

and

$$k_1 + k_2 = k_3$$

Similarly, it is called an Umklapp or *U*-process, when it satisfies the conservation law

$$k_1 + k_2 = k_3 + G$$

## 9.12 DEFINITIONS

*Dulog-Petit Law:* All elemental solids approach a specific heat $C_v = 3R$ cal. mol$^{-1}$ K$^{-1}$ at sufficiently high temperatures.

*Debye Temperature ($\theta_D = h v_D/k$):* A parameter in the Debye's formula for the lattice specific heat, proportional to the maximum phonon frequency $v_D$. In practice, $\theta_D$ may be found by fitting the Debye formula into the specific heat data.

*Heat Capacity:* The amount of heat necessary to raise the temperature of a system through one degree.

*Internal Energy:* If $E$ is the internal energy of the solid, $dE/dT$ is the rate of change of internal energy with temperature. Then $(dE/dT)_v$ is the rate of change of internal energy at constant volume.

*kgmol:* a kgmol (kmol) of any substance is that mass of the substance that contains a specified number of molecules ($6.023 \times 10^{26}$) called Avogadro's number.

*Lattice Specific Heat:* The contribution to the total specific heat due to transitions of the vibrating atoms in the crystal lattice to vibrational states of higher energy.

*Specific Heat:* The heat capacity per unit mass. Sometimes used to refer to the heat capacity per unit mole.

## REVIEW QUESTIONS AND PROBLEMS

1. State Dulong and Petit's law and show how the departure from the law at lower temperatures has been explained by Einstein's theory.

2. Show that the Einstein's relation for the specific heat per kmol of a solid reduces to the classical value $3Nk$ when $kT > hv$.

3. Derive an expression for the specific heat of solids following the Einstein model. How does the specific heat depends on temperature and on to what extent does this model agrees with the experimental results?

4. Derive an expression for the specific heat of solids on the basis of Debye model. How does the Debye model differs from the Einstein model? Discuss the variation of Debye specific heat with temperature.

5. Give an account of the various theories of specific heat of solid. Discuss any of them in detail.

6. Show that because of the changes induced by harmonicity in a solid the specific heat at high temperatures might be expected to vary not as

$$C_v = Nk \text{ but as } C_v = 2Nk(1 + \alpha kT)$$

where $\alpha$ is constant.

7. Derive an expression for the thermal conductivity of a crystal. Discuss its variation with temperature and size of the crystal.

8. What are Normal and Umklapp processes? Discuss briefly the importance of Umklapp process in explaining the thermal conductivity in non-metallic solids.

9. The Debye temperature of carbon (diamond) is 1850 K. Calculate the specific heat per kmol for diamond at 20 K. Also compute the highest lattice frequency involved in the Debye theory.

   *Ans.* 2.45 J kmol$^{-1}$ $K^{-1}$, 3.856 $\times$ 10$^{13}$ Hz.

10. If the classical theory is valid, what would be the thermal energy of one kmol of copper at the Debye temperature? The Debye temperature of copper is 340 K. *Ans.* 8.47 $\times$ 10$^3$ kJ.

11. Calculate the Debye specific heat of copper at (i) 10 K and (ii) 300 K, given that the Debye characteristic frequency is 6.55 $\times$ 10$^{12}$Hz.

   *Ans.* 62.67 J/kmol-K, 1.6 $\times$ 10$^3$ kJ/kmol-K.

12. In aluminium, $v_1 = 6.32 \times 10^3$ m/s and $v_t = 3.1 \times 10^3$ m/s. The density of aluminium is 2.7 $\times$ 10$^3$ kg/m$^3$ and its atomic weight is 26.97.

    (a) Calculate the Debye cut off frequency for aluminium.

    (b) The Debye temperature for aluminium, as obtained from specific heat measurement, is 375 K. Find the cut off frequency and compare it with result obtained in (a).

   *Ans.* 8.44 $\times$ 10$^{12}$ Hz, 7.8 $\times$ 10$^{12}$ Hz. They are comparable.

13. Lead has an fcc structure with a lattice constant of 4.94 Å. Young's modulus of lead is 1.6 $\times$ 10$^{10}$ N/m$^3$. If lead melts when the average amplitude of its atomic vibrations is 15.8 per cent of the interatomic spacing, calculate the melting point of lead. *Ans.* 616.6 K.

14. For copper the specific heat at low temperature has the behaviour of $C_v \cong 4.6 \times 10^{-2} \ T^3$ J/kmol-K. Estimate the Debye temperature for copper.

   *Ans.* 348 K.

15. At very low temperatures, the specific heat of rock salt varies with temperature according to the Debye $T^3$ law

$$C_v = \frac{12}{5} \pi^4 Nk \left( \frac{T}{\theta_D} \right)^3$$

where $\theta_D$ for rock salt is 281 K. How much heat is required to raise the temperature of 2 kmol of rock salt from 10 to 50 K?

   *Ans.* 2.68 $\times$ 10$^4$J.

16. Diamond (atomic weight of carbon = 12) has Young's modulus of 10$^{12}$ Nm$^{-2}$ and a density of 3500kg/ m$^3$. Compute the Debye temperature for diamond.

   *Ans.* 2780 K.

17. Copper has an atomic weight of 63.5, a density of 8.9 $\times$ 10$^3$ kg/m$^3$, and $v_1 = 4.76 \times 10^3$ m/s and $v_t = 2.32 \times 10^3$ m/s. Estimate the specific heat of copper at 30 K.

   *Ans.* 1.328 kJ/kmol-K.

# Chapter 10

# Free Electrons in Crystals

## 10.1  INTRODUCTION

In the first five chapters while dealing with the structural aspect we ignored the effects arising due to electrons in the crystals. We assumed that the electrons surrounding the nucleus of an atom are tightly bound. This is valid for insulators, but not for semiconductors and metals. In order to understand the properties of semiconductors and particularly of metals, it is essential to take into account the behaviour of electrons in them. In this chapter, we shall concentrate mainly on the nature of existence and the role of electrons in deciding the properties of metals.

The outstanding properties of metals are their high electrical and thermal conductivities. Thus, soon after the discovery of electron, a number of investigators, particularly Drude and Lorentz attempted to explain these properties on the basis of free electron model. For the purpose, they made certain basic assumptions, which are as follows:

1. That a metal crystal consists of positive metal ions whose valence electrons are free to move between the ions as if they constitute an electron gas.
2. The crystal is then held together by electrostatic forces of attraction between the positively charged ions and the negatively charged electron gas.
3. The mutual repulsion between the electrons is ignored.
4. The potential field due to positive ions is completely uniform, so that electrons can move from place to place in the crystal without any change in their energy.
5. They collide occasionally with the atoms, and at any given temperature, their velocities could be determined according to Maxwell-Boltzmann distribution law.

The free electron model was successful in explaining the properties such as electrical and thermal conductivities, thermionic emission, thermoelectric and galvanomagnetic effects, etc. However, this model failed to explain the properties of solids which are determined by their internal structure. It was unable to explain even the observed facts that why some solids are conductors and some insulators.

The first success was achieved in 1927 when Pauli applied quantum statistics to explain the weak paramagnetism of alkali metals. The very next year Sommerfeld published a modified free electron theory by replacing classical statistics of Maxwell-Boltzmann by Fermi-Dirac statistics. The Sommerfeld free electron theory of metals could be better described as the statistical thermodynamical behaviour of a gas obeying Fermi-Dirac statistics.

## 10.2 ELECTRONS MOVING IN A ONE-DIMENSIONAL POTENTIAL WELL

Before we proceed further to discuss the modified free electron theory proposed by Sommerfeld and how it conforms with the quantum mechanical model of electrons, let us first determine the restrictions imposed by the laws of quantum mechanics on the energies of an electron inside a crystal. For the sake of mathematical simplicity, let us consider the case when an electron is limited to remain within a one-dimensional crystal of length $a$. Also, assume that the potential energy everywhere within this crystal is constant and equal to zero. However, at the two ends of the crystal the electron is prevented from leaving the crystal by a very high potential energy barrier ($V_0 \rightarrow \infty$) as shown in Fig. 10.1, i..e

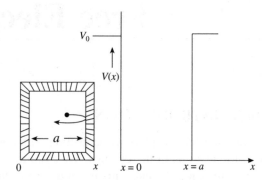

$$V(x) = \begin{cases} V_0 & \text{for } x \le 0 \text{ and } x \ge a \\ 0 & \text{for } 0 < x < a \end{cases} \qquad (1)$$

**Fig. 10.1  A one dimensional potential box**

Therefore, inside the crystal, the Schrodinger wave equation becomes

$$\frac{d^2\psi(x)}{dx^2} + \frac{8\pi^2 m}{h^2} E\psi(x) = 0 \qquad (2)$$

Any periodic function will satisfy this equation, and for the sake of simplicity let us suppose that the general solution of eq. 2 is of the type

$$\psi(x) = A \sin kx + B \cos kx \qquad (3)$$

where $A$ and $B$ are arbitrary constants to be determined by applying boundary conditions. Since the electron is bound inside the crystal of length $a$, the electron wave function has to satisfy the following boundary conditions simultaneously, i.e.

(i)  $\psi = 0$ at $x = 0$. This gives us $B = 0$ and hence $\psi = A \sin kx$.
(ii)  $\psi = 0$ at $x = a$. This gives us $A \sin (ka) = 0$. Since $A$ is not zero, therefore $\sin (ka) = 0$. Consequently,

$$k = \frac{n\pi}{a} \qquad (4)$$

where $n = 1, 2, 3 \ldots$ represents the order of the state, $n = 0$ is not allowed because this will mean $k = 0$ and hence $\psi = 0$ everywhere in the box. Therefore, the solution to the Schrodinger wave eq. 2 in the region $0 < x < a$ becomes

$$\psi_n = A \sin \frac{n\pi x}{a} \qquad (5)$$

For each value of "$n$" there is a corresponding quantum state $\psi_n$ whose energy $E_n$ can be obtained from eqs. 2 and 5 as

$$E_n = \frac{h^2 k^2}{8\pi^2 m} = \frac{h^2 n^2}{8 m a^2} \qquad (6)$$

Equation 6 shows that:

(i) The bound electrons can have only discrete energy values corresponding to $n = 1, 2, 3,$ ... and not any arbitrary value of energy.

(ii) The lowest energy of the particle is obtained from this equation by putting $n = 1$. It is given by

$$E_1 = \frac{h^2}{8 m a^2}$$

$\Rightarrow \qquad\qquad\qquad E_n = n^2 E_1$

(iii) The spacing between the two consecutive levels increases as

$$(n + 1)^2 E_1 - n^2 E_1 = (2n + 1) E_1$$

Fig. 10.2 shows the energy level diagram for the particle. The value of the constant $A$ could be determined by normalizing the wave function, according to which the total probability that the particle is somewhere in the box must be unity, i.e.

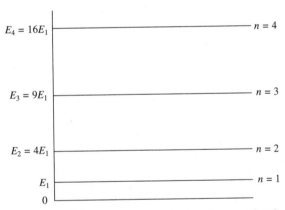

**Fig. 10.2  Schematic representation of energy levels**

$$\int_0^a P(x)\,dx = \int_0^a |\psi_n|^2\,dx = 1$$

or

$$\int_0^a A^2 \sin^2 \frac{n\pi x}{a}\,dx = 1$$

or

$$A^2 \int_0^a \frac{1}{2}\left(1 - \cos\frac{2n\pi x}{a}\right)dx = 1$$

or
$$\frac{A^2}{2}\left[x - \frac{a}{2\pi n}\sin\frac{2n\pi x}{a}\right]_0^a = 1$$

Since the second term of the integrated expression becomes zero for both $x = 0$ and $x = a$, therefore this gives us

$$\frac{A^2 a}{2} = 1 \quad \text{or} \quad A = \left(\frac{2}{a}\right)^{1/2}$$

Thus the normalized wave function is

$$\psi_n = \left(\frac{2}{a}\right)^{1/2}\sin\frac{n\pi x}{a}$$

It can be shown that the wave function $\psi_1$ has two nodes at $x = 0$ and $x = a$, $\psi_2$ has three nodes at $x = 0$, $x = a/2$ and $x = a$ and $\psi_3$ has four nodes at $x = 0$, $x = a/3$, $x = 2a/3$ and $x = a$. Consequently, the wave function $\psi_n$ will have $(n + 1)$ nodes. The wave function for the first three values of $n$ are shown in Fig. 10.3.

To determine the probability distribution of particles within the potential well, let us start with the expression $P(x)\,dx = |\psi_n|^2\,dx$ over a small distance $dx$ at $x$, i.e.

$$P(x)\,dx = \frac{2}{a}\sin^2\frac{n\pi x}{a}\,dx$$

Thus the probability density for one dimensional system is

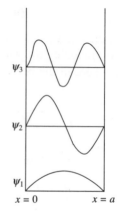

**Fig. 10.3   The wave function for $n = 1$, 2, and 3**

$$P(x) = \frac{2}{a}\sin^2\frac{n\pi x}{a} \qquad (8)$$

where $P(x)$ is maximum when $n\pi x/a$ is an odd multiple of $\pi/2$, i.e.

$$\frac{n\pi x}{a} = \frac{(2n-1)\pi}{2}$$

or
$$\frac{n\pi x}{a} = \frac{\pi}{2}, \frac{3\pi}{2}, \frac{5\pi}{2}$$

or
$$x = \frac{a}{2n}, \frac{3a}{2n}, \frac{5a}{2n}$$

Thus, the most probable positions corresponding to different quantum states of the particle can be obtained as

For $n = 1$, $$x = \frac{a}{2}$$

For $n = 2$, $$x = \frac{a}{4}, \frac{3a}{4}$$

For $n = 3$, $$x = \frac{a}{6}, \frac{3a}{6} = \frac{a}{2} \text{ and } \frac{5a}{6}$$

The probability density for the first three values of $n$ are shown in Fig. 10.4. According to the classical mechanics, the probability for finding the particle within a small distance $dx$ anywhere in the box is the same and is equal to $dx/a$. The probability density is simply $1/a$ throughout the box, which is contrary to the quantum mechanical result. Similarly, according to the classical prediction, there is a continuous range of possible energies. This is contrary to the quantum mechanical result, according to which the energy is quantized and so, it cannot vary continuously. Consequently, the quantum mechanical energy levels are discrete. However, if the particle becomes heavier and the length of the crystal is large (the electrons will be free within this length), the energy levels will be spaced very closely together and eventually may become continuous. For example, if $a = 1$ cm, then

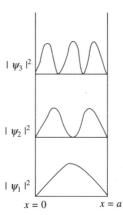

**Fig. 10.4  The probability density for $n = 1, 2,$ and 3**

$$E_n - E_{n\pm1} \sim 3.5 \times 10^{-19} \text{ eV}$$

The energy spectrum for such cases seems practically continuous. Thus the wave equation predicts that the bound particles (electrons) are associated with a discrete energy spectrum and free particles with a continuous spectrum.

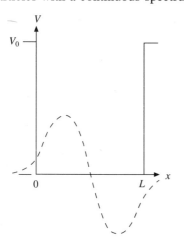

**Fig. 10.5  The wave function for $n = 2$ when the potential barrier is not infinite**

In the interior of a real crystal the potential barriers for confining electrons are not infinitely high and are determined in a complex way by the surface energies of the crystal. If the potential barrier at the surface of a crystal is high but not infinite, the wave function for $n = 2$ will have the form as shown in Fig. 10.5. Note that the wave function is sinusoidal in the region $0 \leq x \leq a$ and exponential outside this region. It is expected that the extention of the wave function beyond the potential barrier is inversely proportional to the height of the barrier. Further, if the barrier is narrow, it is possible that the wave function can extend beyond it. In this case, there is a little but finite probability ($\sim |\psi|^2$) of finding the electrons on the other side of the barrier. The ability of electrons to penetrate a potential barrier is called the "tunneling effect" and is a direct consequence of quantum mechanics to this problem.

*Example*: If a dust particle of one $\mu$gm requires 100 s to cross a distance of 1 mm which is the separation between two rigid walls of the potential, determine the quantum number described by this motion.

*Solution*: Given: Separation between the walls, $d = 1$ mm $= 10^{-3}$ m, the mass of the dust particle, $m = 1$ $\mu$gm $= 10^{-9}$ kg, $t = 100$ s, the quantum number, $n = ?$

Since in 100 s, the dust particle moves $10^{-3}$ m. So that in 1s, it will move $10^{-5}$ m. This is the velocity of the particle. The energy of the dust particle is then given by

$$E = \frac{1}{2} mv^2 = \frac{1}{2} \times 10^{-9} \times (10^{-5})^2 = 5 \times 10^{-20} \text{ J}$$

We also know that for a one-dimensional potential the energy eigen value is given by

$$E_n = \frac{h^2 n^2}{8 ma^2}$$

or

$$n^2 = \frac{8 ma^2 E}{h^2} = \frac{8 \times 10^{-9} \times (10^{-3})^2 \times 5 \times 10^{-20}}{(6.626 \times 10^{-34})^2} = 9.11 \times 10^{32}$$

or

$$n = 3 \times 10^{16}$$

## 10.3  THREE DIMENSIONAL POTENTIAL WELL

For simplicity, let us now consider a situation when the electrons are moving inside a three dimensional potential box of side "$a$" as shown in Fig. 10.6. Like one dimensional case, the potential energy inside the cube is taken as zero and very high (tending to infinity) outside it. Under this assumption, the Schrodinger wave equation becomes

$$\frac{d^2 \psi(x, y, z)}{dx^2} + \frac{d^2 \psi(x, y, z)}{dy^2} + \frac{d^2 \psi(x, y, z)}{dz^2}$$

$$+ \frac{8 \pi^2 m}{h^2} E\psi(x, y, z) = 0$$

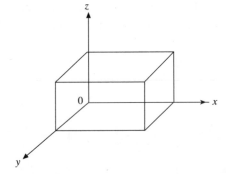

**Fig. 10.6  A three dimensional potential box**

for which straightforward solution of the standing wave type may be assumed, i.e.

$$\psi(x, y, z) = A_x \sin(k_x x) \, A_y \sin(k_y y) \, A_z \sin(k_z z) \qquad (10)$$

where

$$k_x = \frac{n_x \pi}{a}, \, k_y = \frac{n_y \pi}{a}, \, k_z = \frac{n_z \pi}{a}.$$

Like one dimensional case, the value of the constants $A_x$, $A_y$ and $A_z$ can be determined by applying the suitable boundary conditions, i.e. $x = 0$ and $x = a$, $y = 0$ and $y = a$ and $z = 0$ and $z = a$, we have

$$A_x = \left(\frac{2}{a}\right)^{1/2}, A_y = \left(\frac{2}{a}\right)^{1/2} \quad \text{and} \quad A_z = \left(\frac{2}{a}\right)^{1/2}$$

Therefore, the normalized wave function for a cubical box becomes

$$\psi_n = \left(\frac{2}{a}\right)^{3/2} \sin \frac{n_x \pi x}{a} \cdot \sin \frac{n_y \pi y}{a} \cdot \sin \frac{n_z \pi z}{a} \tag{11}$$

The corresponding form of energy is given by

$$E_n = \frac{h^2}{8ma^2}(n_x^2 + n_y^2 + n_z^2) \tag{12}$$

or

$$E_n = \frac{h^2 n^2}{8ma^2}, \quad \text{where} \quad n^2 = n_x^2 + n_y^2 + n_z^2 \tag{13}$$

Thus, in three-dimensions, we have three quantum numbers $n_x$, $n_y$ and $n_z$ which can take only positive integer values.

*Example*: Find the lowest energy of an electron confined to move in a three dimensional potential box of length 0.5 Å

*Solution*: Given: $a = 0.5\text{Å} = 0.5 \times 10^{-10}$ m, $E$ (lowest) = ?
The possible energies of a particle in a cubical box of side $a$ are given by

$$E_n = \frac{h^2}{8ma^2}(n_x^2 + n_y^2 + n_z^2)$$

For lowest energy $n_x = n_y = n_z = 1$. Therefore

$$E_{111} = \frac{3h^2}{8ma^2} = \frac{3 \times (6.26 \times 10^{-34})^2}{8 \times 9.1 \times 10^{-31} \times (0.5 \times 10^{-10})^2}$$

$$= 7.24 \times 10^{-17} \text{ J} = \frac{7.24 \times 10^{-17}}{1.6 \times 10^{-19}} = 452 \text{ eV}$$

*Example:* Calculate the energy of an electron in the energy state immediately above the lowest energy level in a cubic box of side 1Å. Also find the temperature at which the average energy of the molecules of a perfect gas would be equal to the energy of the electron in the upper level.

*Solution*: Given: $a = 1$ Å $= 1 \times 10^{-10}$ m, $E$ (next to the lowest) = ? $T = ?$

$$E \text{ (next to the lowest)} = 3/2 \,(k/T),$$

The lowest energy level is $E_{111}$ and the next to the lowest level is $E_{112}$. Therefore,

$$E_{112} = \frac{6h^2}{8ma^2} = \frac{6 \times (6.26 \times 10^{-34})^2}{8 \times 9.1 \times 10^{-31} \times (1.0 \times 10^{-10})^2}$$

$$= 3.62 \times 10^{-17} \text{ J} = \frac{3.62 \times 10^{-17}}{1.6 \times 10^{-19}} = 226 \text{ eV}$$

Further, according to the question

$$\frac{3}{2} kT = 226 \text{ eV} = 3.62 \times 10^{-17} \text{ J}$$

or

$$T = \frac{2 \times 3.62 \times 10^{-17}}{3 \times 1.38 \times 10^{-23}} = 1.75 \times 10^6 \text{ K}$$

## 10.4   QUANTUM STATE AND DEGENERACY

The most important consequence of the three quantum numbers appearing in eq. 12 is that several combinations can yield the same value of energy. Each combination of the quantum numbers is called a quantum state and several states having the same energy are said to be degenerate. To make this more clear, let us take an example and suppose that one of the quantum numbers is equal to 2 and the others as unity. This gives three possible combinations of quantum numbers which are as follows:

(i)   $n_x = 1, n_y = 1, n_z = 2$
(ii)   $n_x = 1, n_y = 2, n_z = 1$
(iii)   $n_x = 2, n_y = 1, n_z = 1$

Substituting these values in eq. 11, the corresponding wave functions become

$$\psi_{112} = \left(\frac{2}{a}\right)^{3/2} \sin\frac{\pi x}{a} \sin\frac{\pi y}{a} \sin\frac{2\pi z}{a}$$

$$\psi_{121} = \left(\frac{2}{a}\right)^{3/2} \sin\frac{\pi x}{a} \sin\frac{2\pi y}{a} \sin\frac{\pi z}{a}$$

and

$$\psi_{211} = \left(\frac{2}{a}\right)^{3/2} \sin\frac{2\pi x}{a} \sin\frac{\pi y}{a} \sin\frac{\pi z}{a}$$

From eq. 12, the corresponding energies are found to be

$$E_{112} = E_{121} = E_{211} = \frac{6h^2}{8ma^2} \tag{14}$$

In the above example, since three wave functions are associated with the same energy, the corresponding energy level is said to be three-fold degenerate. On the basis of this model, the level in which all the quantum numbers have the same value (e.g. $n_x = n_y = n_z = 1$ or 2, etc.) would be non-degenerate. Fig. 10.7 shows the energy level diagram for a particle in a three dimensional cubic box for the ground state and some excited states, together with the degree of degeneracy and quantum numbers.

It can be shown that the degeneracy breaks when a small modification is introduced to the system. For the purpose, let us consider the above discussed triply degenerate level which has

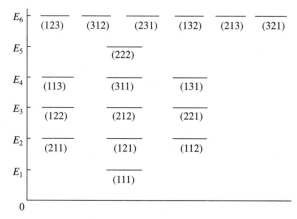

**Fig. 10.7** **Six lowest energy levels for an electron in a three dimensional potential box**

three independent energy states with quantum numbers (2, 1, 1), (1, 2, 1) and (1, 1, 2). The energy associated with the state having quantum number (2, 1, 1) is given by

$$\frac{4h^2}{8ma^2}$$

On the other hand, the energy associated with each of the other two states is given by

$$\frac{h^2}{8ma^2}$$

Now, let the length of the cubical box be increased by a small amount $da$, along the $x$-axis while keeping the other dimensions unchanged. The corresponding change in the energy of the state (2, 1, 1) is

$$\frac{4h^2}{8m(a + da)^2}$$

Hence, the decrease in the energy is, say

$$E_2 = \frac{4h^2}{8ma^2} - \frac{4h^2}{8m(a + da)^2} = \frac{4h^2}{8m}\left(\frac{1}{a^2} - \frac{1}{(a + da)^2}\right)$$

$$= \frac{4h^2}{8m}\left(\frac{a^2 + 2a(da) + (da)^2 - a^2}{a^4}\right)$$

$$= \frac{4h^2}{8m}\left(\frac{2\,da}{a^3}\right) = \frac{h^2}{8ma^2}\left(\frac{8da}{a}\right) \tag{15}$$

But for the remaining two states (1, 2, 1) and (1, 1, 2), the energy decrease is given by

$$E_1 = \frac{h^2}{8ma^2} - \frac{h^2}{8m(a+da)^2} = \frac{h^2}{8m}\left(\frac{1}{a^2} - \frac{1}{(a+da)^2}\right)$$

$$= \frac{h^2}{8m}\left(\frac{a^2 + 2a(da) + (da)^2 - a^2}{a^4}\right)$$

$$= \frac{h^2}{8m}\left(\frac{2\,da}{a^3}\right) = \frac{h^2}{8ma^2}\left(\frac{2\,da}{a}\right) \qquad (16)$$

Thus, $\Delta E = E_2 - E_1 = \dfrac{h^2}{8ma^2}\left(\dfrac{8\,da}{a} - \dfrac{2\,da}{a}\right) = \dfrac{h^2}{8ma^2}\left(\dfrac{6\,da}{a}\right)$

This breakdown in the degeneracy is shown in Fig. 10.8. This aspect is relevant in explaining the fact such as the splitting of spectral lines in a magnetic or electric field. Under the action of the field, the degenerate level breaks up into separate levels.

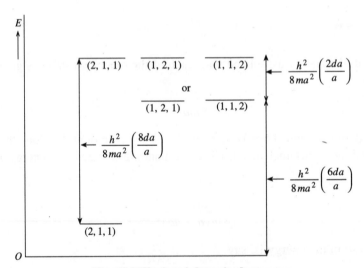

**Fig. 10.8 The breakdown in degeneracy**

*Example:* Determine the degree of degeneracy of the energy level $38h^2/8ma^2$ of a particle in a cubical box of side $a$.

*Solution:* Given: $(n_x^2 + n_y^2 + n_z^2) = 38$. By trial and error method, we can find that there exist two sets of values. They are:

$$n_x = 1,\ n_y = 1,\ n_z = 6$$

and

$$n_x = 2,\ n_y = 3,\ n_z = 5$$

Again, by simple manipulations, it is easy to determine the different members of the degenerate levels. They are:

116, 161, 611 three-fold degenerate

532, 325, 253, 352, 523, 235 six-fold degenerate

Thus, the given energy level is nine-fold degenerate.

## 10.5 THE DENSITY OF STATES

In ordre to determine the actual number of electrons in a given energy state, it is necessary to know the number of states in the system which have the energy under consideration multiplied by the probability distribution function. Therefore, if $g(E)dE$ is the number of available quantum states in the energy range $E$ and $E + dE$ and $F(E)$ is the probability function of the electrons occupying a particular energy state $E$, then the actual number of electrons $N(E)dE$ present in the so called free state in the above energy range at any temperature is given by

$$N(E)dE = F(E)\ g(E)dE \qquad (17)$$

Now, in order to calculate the density of states of electrons in the energy range $E$ and $E + dE$, let us draw two spheres having radii $n$ and $n + dn$ in the $n$-space as shown in Fig. 10.9. Any point $(n_x, n_y, n_z)$ with integer values of coordinates represents an energy state. Thus, all the points on the surface of the sphere of radius $n$ (where $n^2 = n_x^2 + n_y^2 + n_z^2$) will have the same energy. Since, $n_x$, $n_y$, $n_z$ can have positive integral non-zero values; therefore the number of states of energy less than $E$ will be given by the positive octant of the sphere, i.e.

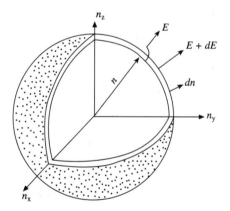

**Fig. 10.9  Spheres representing density of states in $n$-space**

$$g(E) = \frac{1}{8} \cdot \frac{4\pi n^3}{3} \qquad (18)$$

Substituting the value of $n$ from eq. 13, eq. 18 becomes

$$g(E) = \frac{1}{8} \cdot \frac{4\pi}{3} \left( \frac{8ma^2E}{h^2} \right)^{3/2} = \frac{4\pi V}{3h^3} (2m)^{3/2} E^{3/2} \qquad (19)$$

where $V = a^3$. Now, differentiating both sides of the eq. 19 with respect to $E$, we obtain the density of states in the energy interval $dE$ as

$$g(E)\,dE = \frac{2\pi V}{h^3}(2m)^{3/2}\,E^{1/2}\,dE$$

Since, the Pauli's exclusion principle allows two electrons in each state, so that the actual density of states in a volume $V$ is given by

$$g(E)\,dE = \frac{4\pi V}{h^3}(2m)^{3/2}\,E^{1/2}\,dE \qquad (20)$$

Hence, the density of states per unit volume in an energy interval $dE$ is given by

$$g'(E)\,dE = \frac{4\pi}{h^3}(2m)^{3/2}\,E^{1/2}\,dE \qquad (21)$$

The eq. 21 is diagramatically illustrated in Fig. 10.10. Now substituting the value of density of states and the probability distribution function (which is nothing but the Fermi-Dirac distribution function) in eq. 17, the density of states within the energy interval $dE$ is given by

$N(E)\,dE = F(E)\,g(E)\,dE$

$$= \frac{4\pi V}{h^3}(2m)^{3/2}\,E^{1/2}\,\frac{dE}{\exp\left(\dfrac{E-E_F}{kT}\right)+1} \qquad (22)$$

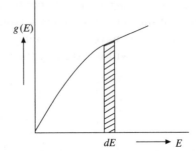

**Fig. 10.10   Density of states as a function of electron energy**

This distribution is diagramatically shown in Fig. 10.11. The calculation of $N(E)$ is illustrated in Fig. 10.12 which shows that the free electrons do not have zero energy at an absolute zero of temperature as one would have expected if the electrons were to obey classical statistics. Actually, the electron energy vary from zero to $E_F$ and also the number of electrons increases with the increase of energy which becomes maximum at $E_F$. Since at absolute zero, $F(E) = 1$, therefore the total number of electrons is

$$\int N(E)\,dE = \frac{4\pi V}{h^3}(2m)^{3/2}\int_0^{E_F} E^{1/2}\,dE$$

or
$$N = \frac{2}{3}\times\frac{4\pi V}{h^3}(2m)^{3/2}\,E_F^{3/2} \qquad (23)$$

The number of electrons $n$ per unit volume (called the density of electrons) is

$$n = \frac{N}{V} = \frac{8\pi}{3h^3}(2m)^{3/2}\,E_F^{3/2} \qquad (24)$$

Hence, the Fermi energy at absolute zero is given by

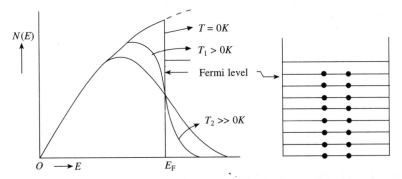

Fig. 10.11 Density of states as a function of electron energy at different temperature

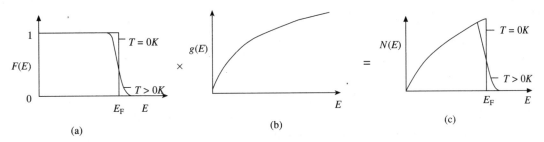

Fig. 10.12 The calculation of the density of occupied electron states $N(E)$ **(a)** Fermi-Dirac function, **(b)** Density of states, and **(c)** $N(E) = F(E) \times g(E)$

$$E_F = \frac{h^2}{2m} \left(\frac{3n}{8\pi}\right)^{2/3} = 3.65 \times 10^{-19} \, n^{2/3} \, eV \qquad (25)$$

Further, at absolute zero, the average energy of an electron is given by

$$\overline{E} = \frac{1}{N} \int_0^{E_F} EN(E)\,dE = \frac{4\pi V}{Nh^3} (2m)^{3/2} \int_0^{E_F} E^{3/2}\,dE = \frac{2}{5} \times \frac{4\pi V}{Nh^3} (2m)^{3/2} E_F^{5/2} \qquad (26)$$

Substituting the value of $N$ from eq. 23, we obtain

$$\overline{E} = \frac{3}{5} E_F \qquad (27)$$

*Example:* The density of *Zn* is $7.13 \times 10^3$ kg/m$^3$ and its atomic weight is 65.4. Calculate the Fermi energy in zinc. Also calculate the mean energy at 0K. The effective mass of the electron in zinc is $0.85 \, m_e$.

*Solution:* Given: $\rho = 7.13 \times 10^3$ kg/m$^3$, $M = 65.4$, $m_{\text{eff}} = 0.85 \, m_e$, $E_F = ?$ $\overline{E}_0 = ?$

Since zinc is a divalent metal, the number of electrons per unit volume will be

$$n = \frac{2\rho N}{M} = \frac{2 \times 7.13 \times 10^3 \times 6.023 \times 26^{26}}{65.4} = 13.13 \times 10^{28}$$

Now, according to eq. 25, the Fermi energy is

$$E_F = \frac{h^2}{2m} \left(\frac{3n}{8\pi}\right)^{2/3} = 3.65 \times 10^{-19} \, n^{2/3} eV$$

$$= 3.65 \times 10^{-19} \times (13.13 \times 10^{28})^{2/3} = 11.1 \text{ eV}$$

and

$$\overline{E}_0 = \frac{3}{5} E_F = \frac{3}{5} \times 11.1 = 6.66 \text{ eV}$$

## 10.6 FERMI-DIRAC STATISTICS

Since, the electrons are Fermions and also obey the Pauli's exclusion principle, therefore, their energy distribution at any temperature $T$ can be expressed by Fermi-Dirac distribution function as

$$F(E) = \frac{1}{\exp\left(\dfrac{E - E_F}{kT}\right) + 1} \qquad (28)$$

where $E$ is the energy of an allowed state and $E_F$ the Fermi energy. At absolute zero, the distibution function has the following properties:

$$F(E) = 1 \text{ for all values of } E < E_F$$

$$F(E) = 0 \text{ for all values of } E > E_F$$

That is the levels below $E_F$ are completely filled, and all those above $E_F$ are completely empty. Hence, $E_F$ is the maximum energy of the filled state. However, for any temperatue greater than zero, $F(E) = 1/2$ at $E = E_F$. Therefore, the Fermi level in a metal is that energy level for which the probability of occupation is half. Further, at very high temperatures, as $T$ tends to infnity, $kT \gg E_F$. The electrons lose their quantum mechanical character and Fermi-Dirac distribution function reduces to classical Boltzmann distribution, exp $(-E/kT)$. Fig. 10.13 gives a plot of the Fermi function versus allowed energy $E$ at different temperatures.

*Example:* At what temperature we can expect a 10% probability that electrons in silver have an energy which is 1% above, the Fermi energy? The Fermi energy of silver is 5.5 eV.

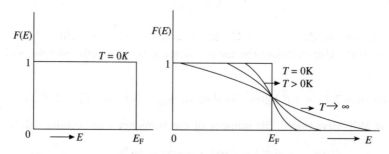

**Fig. 10.13   The Fermi distribution function at different temperatures**

*Solution:* Given: $F(E) = 10\%$, $E = E_F + 1\%$ of $E_F$, $E_F = 5.5$ eV, $T = ?$ Here,

$$E = 5.5 + \frac{5.5}{100} = 5.5 + 0.055 = 5.555 \quad \text{or} \quad E - E_F = 0.055$$

Now, substituting the value of $E - F_F$ in eq. 28, we have

$$0.1 = \frac{1}{\exp\left(\dfrac{0.055 \times 1.6 \times 10^{-19}}{1.38 \times 10^{-23} \times T}\right) + 1} = \frac{1}{\exp\left(\dfrac{637.7}{T}\right) + 1}$$

or $\quad \exp\left(\dfrac{637.7}{T}\right) = 9 \quad$ or $\quad \dfrac{637.7}{T} = \ln 9 \quad$ or $\quad T = \dfrac{637.7}{\ln 9} = 290\,\text{K}$

## 10.7 EFFECT OF TEMPERATURE ON FERMI DISTRIBUTION FUNCTION

As we increase the temperature, the electrons lying just below the Fermi level gain energy and get excited. They occupy the energy level which were vacant at absolute zero. The number of free electrons lying in the energy interval $dE$ at any temperature greater than absolute zero is given by

$$N = \int_0^\infty N(E)\,dE = \int_0^\infty g(E)\,dE \cdot F(E) = \int_0^\infty \frac{g(E)\,dE}{\exp\left(\dfrac{E - E_F}{kT}\right) + 1}$$

$$= \frac{4\pi V}{h^3}(2m)^{2/3} \int_0^\infty \frac{E^{1/2}\,dE}{\exp\left(\dfrac{E - E_F}{kT}\right) + 1} \tag{29}$$

Now, let us evaluate the integral in eq. 29 using the method of integration by parts, i.e. using the formula

$$\int u\,dv = uv - \int v\,du$$

we have

$$I = \int_0^\infty \frac{E^{1/2}\,dE}{\exp\left(\dfrac{E - E_F}{kT}\right) + 1}$$

$$= \left|\frac{2E^{3/2}}{3} \times \frac{dE}{\exp\left(\dfrac{E - E_F}{kT}\right) + 1}\right|_0^\infty + \frac{2}{3}\int_0^\infty \frac{E^{3/2}\exp\left(\dfrac{E - E_F}{kT}\right)dE}{\left[\exp\left(\dfrac{E - E_F}{kT}\right) + 1\right]^2 \cdot kT} \tag{30}$$

The first term on the right side of eq. 30 is zero for both the limits, because the probability of finding an electron for both (zero energy and infinite energy) is zero. The second term can be evaluated by making use of the Taylor's series, according to which any function $g(E)$ in the neighbourhood of $E = E_F$ can be expanded in powers of $(E - E_F)$ as

$$g(E) = g(E_F) + (E - E_F)\, g'(E_F) + \frac{(E - E_F)^2}{2!}\, g''(E_F) + \dots \tag{31}$$

This will give us

$$E^{3/2} = E_F^{3/2} + (E - E_F)\, \frac{3}{2}\, E_F^{1/2} + \frac{(E - E_F)^2}{2}\, \frac{3}{4}\, E_F^{-1/2} + \dots \tag{32}$$

Substituting eq. 32 into 30, the integral I becomes

$$\frac{2}{3kT} \int_0^\infty \frac{\exp\left(\dfrac{E - E_F}{kT}\right)}{\left[\exp\left(\dfrac{E - E_F}{kT}\right) + 1\right]^2} \left[E_F^{3/2} + \frac{3}{2}(E - E_F)\, E_F^{1/2} + \frac{3}{8}(E - E_F)^2\, E_F^{-1/2} + \dots\right] dE \tag{33}$$

In order to simplify the above integral, let us put

$$\frac{E - E_F}{kT} = x, \text{ so that } dE = kT\, dx$$

Further, taking into account the fact that at low temperatures such as $kT \ll E_F$, the derivative $F'(E)$ is large only at energies near $E = E_F$ as shown in Fig. 10.14.

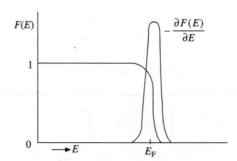

**Fig. 10.14** The Fermi distribution function and its derivative at $E = E_F$

where
$$F(E) = \frac{1}{\exp\left(\dfrac{E - E_F}{kT}\right) + 1} = \left[\exp\left(\frac{E - E_F}{kT}\right) + 1\right]^{-1}$$

and
$$F'(E) = \frac{dF(E)}{dE} = -\frac{\left[\exp\left(\dfrac{E - E_F}{kT}\right) + 1\right]^{-2}}{kT} \cdot \exp\left(\frac{E - E_F}{kT}\right)$$

$$= -\left(\frac{1}{kT}\right)\frac{\exp\left(\dfrac{E - E_F}{kT}\right)}{\left[\exp\left(\dfrac{E - E_F}{kT}\right) + 1\right]^2}$$

For other values of $E$ (particularly for negative values of $E$), $F'(E)$ is negligible. Therefore, the lower limit in the integral may be taken as $-\infty$ instead of $(-E_F/kT)$. The above integral becomes

$$I = \frac{2}{3kT}\int_{-\infty}^{\infty}\frac{e^x}{(e^x + 1)^2}\left[E_F^{3/2} + \frac{3}{2}kTxE_F^{1/2} + \frac{3}{8}(kT)^2 x^2 E_F^{-1/2} + \ldots\right]kTdx$$

$$= \frac{2}{3}\left[E_F^{3/2}\int_{-\infty}^{\infty}\frac{e^x dx}{(e^x + 1)^2} + \frac{3}{2}kTE_F^{1/2}\int_{-\infty}^{\infty}\frac{xe^x dx}{(e^x + 1)^2} + \frac{3}{8}(kT)^2 E_F^{-1/2}\int_{-\infty}^{\infty}\frac{x^2 e^x dx}{(e^x + 1)^2} + \ldots\right] \quad (34)$$

Now, making use of the standard integrals such as

$$\int_{-\infty}^{\infty}\frac{e^x dx}{(e^x + 1)^2} = 1, \int_{-\infty}^{\infty}\frac{xe^x dx}{(e^x + 1)^2} = 0 \text{ and } \int_{-\infty}^{\infty}\frac{x^2 e^x dx}{(e^x + 1)^2} = \frac{\pi^2}{3}$$

eq. 34 becomes

$$I = \frac{2}{3}\left[E_F^{3/2} 2 \cdot \frac{1}{2} + 0 + \frac{3}{8}(kT)^2 2 \cdot \frac{\pi^2}{6} E_F^{-1/2} + \ldots\right] = \frac{2}{3}E_F^{3/2}\left[1 + \frac{\pi^2}{8}\left(\frac{kT}{E_F}\right)^2 + \ldots\right] \quad (35)$$

Taking into account only upto the second term and substituting the value of this integral (eq. 35) into eq. 29, we obtain

$$N = \frac{4\pi V}{h^3}(2m)^{3/2} \times \frac{2}{3}E_F^{3/2}\left[1 + \frac{\pi^2}{8}\left(\frac{kT}{E_F}\right)^2\right] \quad (36)$$

At absolute zero, $E_F = E_{F0}$. Therefore, eq. 36 reduces to

$$N = \frac{4\pi V}{h^3}(2m)^{3/2} \times \frac{2}{3}E_{F0}^{3/2} \quad (37)$$

This is same as eq. 23, except subscript 0 in eq. 37, Now, substituting eq. 37 into 36, we obtain

$$E_{F0}^{3/2} = E_F^{3/2}\left[1 + \frac{\pi^2}{8}\left(\frac{kT}{E_F}\right)^2\right] \quad \text{or} \quad E_F = E_{F0}\left[1 - \frac{\pi^2}{12}\left(\frac{kT}{E_{F0}}\right)^2\right] \quad (38)$$

Equation 38 indicates that the Fermi energy is not constant but decreases slightly as the temperature is increased. However, the value of the factor $(kT/E_{F0})^2$ is very small at room temperature and the Fermi energy is considered to be a constant. Hence, subscript 0 is dropped from eq. 37.

## 10.8 THE ELECTRONIC SPECIFIC HEAT

According to Drude and Lorentz, the conduction electrons are treated as free particles as if they are electron gas molecules which obey the classical laws of mechanics and statistical mechanics (sec. 10.1). Further, from classical statistical mechanics (lke kinetic theory of gases), the average energy of a free electron is $(3/2)kT$. Thus if a metal contains $N$ free electrons per mole then the average energy of the electrons per mole should be

$$\langle \overline{E} \rangle = \frac{3}{2} NkT = \frac{3}{2} RT \tag{39}$$

where $N$ is the Avogadro's number and $R = Nk$. Therefore, the electronic specific heat is given by

$$C_e = \frac{\partial(\overline{E})}{\partial T} = \frac{3}{2} R \cong 3 \text{ cal/mol. } °K \tag{40}$$

However, the experimental measurements show that the electronic specific heat is smaller than the classical value (eq. 40) by a factor of about $10^{-2}$. This discrepancy was removed by the introduction of quantum statistics developed by E. Fermi and P.A.M. Dirac and is known as Fermi-Dirac statistics (eq. 28).

As the temperature increases, the electrons whose energy is close to the Fermi energy ($E_F$), gain thermal energy of the order of $kT$, and go to the higher energy state above the Fermi level. That is the electrons having the energies between $E_F$ and $(E_F - kT)$ alone are likely to be raised above $E_F$ and the electrons below $(E_F - kT)$ remain unaffected. An electron at the Fermi level may increase its energy from $E_F$ to $(E_F + kT)$ at the most, so that a fraction $kT/E_F$ of the electrons is affected. Therefore, the number of electron excited per mole is approximately given by $NkT/E_F$. And since on an average each electron absorbs an energy of the order of $3kT/2$, it follows that the thermal energy per mole is approximately given by

$$\overline{E} = \frac{NkT}{E_F} \times \frac{3kT}{2} = \frac{3Nk^2}{2E_F} \cdot T^2 \tag{41}$$

and hence the specific heat

$$C_e = \frac{\partial \overline{E}}{\partial T} = 3Nk \left( \frac{kT}{E_F} \right) = 3R \left( \frac{kT}{E_F} \right) \tag{42}$$

The approximate value of the electronic specific heat (eq. 42) obtained after the introduction of quantum statistics is in agreement with the experimental value. For a better agreement between the theoretically estimated value and the experimental result, it is necessary to know the average energy possessed by a free electron at any temperature $T$ greater than absolute zero. It is given by

$$\overline{E} = \frac{1}{N} \int_0^\infty EN(E)\,dE = \frac{4\pi V}{Nh^3} (2m)^{3/2} \int_0^\infty \frac{E^{3/2}\,dE}{\exp\left( \dfrac{E - E_F}{kT} \right) + 1} \tag{43}$$

From a calculation similar to the above, the average energy of an electron at any temperature $T$ is obtained as

$$\overline{E}_T = \overline{E}_0 \left[ 1 + \frac{5\pi^2}{12} \left( \frac{kT}{E_{F_0}} \right)^2 \right] \tag{44}$$

Equation 44 indicates that the average energy is not constant and increases slightly as the temperature is increased. Now, the electronic specific heat at constant volume per electron can be obtained as

$$C_e = \frac{\partial(\overline{E}_T)}{\partial T} \cong \frac{5\pi^2 k^2 T}{6 E_{F_0}^2} (\overline{E}_0) \tag{45}$$

Making use of the eq. 27 after putting the subscript 0 for absolute zero, eq. 45 becomes

$$C_e = \frac{\pi^2 k^2 T}{2 E_{F_0}} \tag{46}$$

If we define the Fermi temperature by $T_F = E_F/k$, then eq. 46 becomes

$$C_e = \frac{\pi^2}{2} \times \frac{kT}{T_F} \tag{47}$$

This result is in fair agreement with the experimental values. It is interesting to note that the electronic specific heat varies linearly with the temperature whereas the lattice specific heat varies as cube of the absolute temperature at low temperatures (eq. 36 of chapter 9) and so that the total specific heat of a metal at low temperature may be written as

$$C_v = C_e + C_1$$

or
$$C_v = AT + BT^3 \tag{48}$$

Fig. 10.15a shows the variation of the two specific heats with temperature, indicating that the electronic contribution dominates in the helium region and only after certain temperature the lattice contribution becomes predominant. On the other hand, a plot between $C_v/T$ versus $T^2$ shows a straight line having the intercept $A$ and the slope $B$ (Fig. 10.15b).

*Example:* Estimate the electronic contribution of specific heat kmol of copper at 4 K and 300 K. The Fermi energy of copper is 7.05 eV and is assumed to be temperature independent.

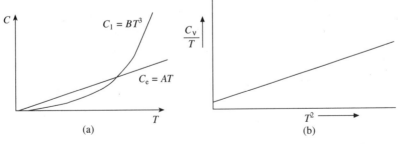

**Fig. 10.15 (a)** **The variation of two specific heats of metal at low temperatures, (b) A plot between $C_v/T$ versus $T^2$**

*Solution:* Given: $E_F = 7.05$ eV $= 7.05 \times 1.6 \times 10^{-19}$ J, $T_1 = 4$ K, $T_2 = 300$ K, $C_e = ?$

Making use of eq. 46, and substituting various values, we obtain at 4 K,

$$C_e = \frac{\pi^2 k^2 T}{2 E_{F_0}} \times N = \frac{\pi^2 \times (1.38 \times 10^{-23})^2 \times 4 \times 6.023 \times 10^{26}}{2 \times 7.05 \times 1.6 \times 10^{-19}}$$

$$= 2.00 \text{ J kmol}^{-1} \text{ K}^{-1}$$

At 300 K,

$$C_e = 150 \text{ J kmol}^{-1} \text{ K}^{-1}$$

## 10.9   THE ELECTRICAL CONDUCTIVITY OF METALS

### Electron Drift in an Electrical Field

According to the free electron theory, electrons move freely in a conductor. In the absence of an electric field, the electron gas is in an equilibrium state described by equilibrium distribution functions, viz, the Fermi-Dirac distribution function for a degenerate electron gas and the Maxwell-Boltzmann distribution function for non-degenerate electron gas (Fig. 10.16). Because of the fact that in a conductor the number of electrons moving in opposite directions is always the same, their average velocity in any direction is zero and consequently the distribution functions are symmetric about the axis of ordinates. This explains the fact that in the absence of an external electric field there is no electric current in a conductor, no matter how many free electrons it contains.

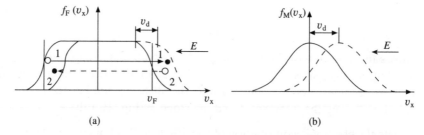

(a)                                              (b)

**Fig. 10.16 (a)   Fermi-Dirac and (b) Boltzmann distribution function**

When an electric field $E$ is applied to a conductor, the random motion of the electrons gets modified in such a way that they drift slowly, in a direction opposite to that of the field, with an average drift velocity $v_d$. As a result, the distribution functions experience a change as shown by dotted lines in Fig. 10.16. In order to calculate the drift velocity, let us consider a free electron in an electric field $E$. It will experience a force $eE$, which accelerates the electron according to Newton's second law of motion

$$a = \frac{eE}{m} \tag{49}$$

where $e$ is the electronic charge and $m$ is the electronic mass, respectively. Prima facie, it appears that the electrons should be accelerated indefinitely and their velocity should grow continuously as a result of the electric field. However, this is not correct. In fact, during their motion the electrons collide with the phonons, impurities and lattice imperfections. As a result, they regularly lose their kinetic energy and hence the velocity they gained in the field. In other words, the electrons have to surmount a reaction force $F_r$ during their motion through the lattice. The reaction force is proportional to the drift velocity $v_d$ and is directed against it.

$$F_r = -\frac{1}{\tau} m v_d \tag{50}$$

where $\tau$ is called the relaxation time. Taking into account the eqs. 49 and 50, the equation of directional motion of the electron in the lattice may be written as

$$m \frac{dv_d(t)}{dt} = eE - \frac{mv_d}{\tau} \tag{51}$$

Equation 51 tells us that the velocity of the directional motion of the electrons will rise and they will be accelerated until the two forces on the right hand side become equal when the resultant force acting on the electron, and accordingly the acceleration will become zero. Consequently,

$$v_d = \frac{eE\tau}{m} \tag{52}$$

Since an electron has a negative charge, it drifts in a direction opposite to that of the field.

In a chemically pure and structurally perfect crystal where the resistance force approaches zero, even a small field is enough to accelerate the electron indefinitely so that its velocity grows continuously which could become infinitely high. Actually, in a perfect lattice, electron wave propagation in an optically transparent medium.

## 10.10  RELAXATION TIME AND MEAN FREE PATH

Let us suppose that as soon as the velocity of the directional motion of the electrons attains a constant value $v_d$, the field is turned off. This velocity starts diminishing as a result of collisions of the electrons with the phonons, impurities and lattice imperfections, and the electron gas ultimately return to an equilibrium state. Such a process leading to the establishment of equilibrium in a system is termed as relaxation process. Thus for $E = 0$, the eq. 51 becomes

$$\frac{dv_d(t)}{dt} = -\frac{v_d(t)}{\tau}$$

so that
$$v_d(t) = v_d \exp\left[-\frac{t}{\tau}\right] \tag{53}$$

where $v_d(t)$ is the velocity of the directional motion of the electrons and $t$ is the time after the field is turned off. In eq. 53, $\tau$ characterizes the rate at which the equilibrium state of a system is reached; smaller is the $t$ sooner the system reaches to equilibrium state. For $t = \tau$, the velocity of the directional motion decreases by $1/e$ of its initial value. For pure metals, $\tau \approx 10^{-14}$ s.

The motion of an electron in a crystal may be conveniently described in terms of mean free path. By analogy with the kinetic theory of gases one may presume that an electron in a crystal moves along a straight line until it collides with the lattice imperfection and gets scattered. The average distance $\lambda$ that the electron travels between two successive collisions is taken as the mean free path of the electrons by an applied electric field is much smaller than the average thermal velocity, the time $\tau$ taken by the electrons is travelling the distance $\lambda$ will thus be decided not by the drift velocity due to the field but by the average velocity $\bar{v}$, due to random thermal motion. Therefore,

$$\tau = n\frac{\lambda}{\bar{v}} \tag{54}$$

where $n$ is the number of collisions that are required to nullify the directional velocity completely.

## 10.11  ELECTRICAL CONDUCTIVITY AND OHM'S LAW

Ohm's law is the most established experimental law relating to the conduction in metals and can be used to test the validity of the theory of electrical conductivity.

Knowing the drift velocity of the electrons, it is easy to calculate the current density and hence the conductivity of a metal. For the purpose, let us consider a cylindrical conductor of length $v_d$ and area of cross-section of unity as shown in Fig. 10.17. Suppose it contains $N$ electrons per unit volume. Imagine any section of the conductor and count the number of charges passing through this section per second. Obviously, it will be equal to all the electrons inside this cylinder of volume 1. $v_d$. Therefore, a current flowing through the conductor with a density

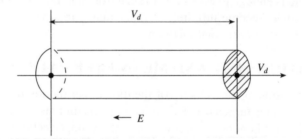

**Fig. 10.17    Calculation of current density**

$$I = N\,(1.v_d)\,e = Ne\left(\frac{eE\tau}{m}\right) \quad \text{(from eq. 52)}$$

$$= \left(\frac{Ne^2\tau}{m}\right)E \tag{55}$$

This is at once recognizable as Ohm's law ($I = \sigma E$) where the conductivity $\sigma$ is given by

$$\sigma = \left(\frac{Ne^2\tau}{m}\right) = Ne\mu \tag{56}$$

where $\mu = e\tau/m$ is called the carrier mobility and is defined as the average drift velocity per unit electric field, i.e.

$$\mu = \frac{v_d}{E} = \frac{e\tau}{m}$$

and the resistivity $\rho$ is given by

$$\rho = \frac{m}{Ne^2\tau} \qquad (57)$$

Equation 56 can be easily understood as follows: we expect the charge transported in the medium to be proportional to the charge density ($n = Ne$), the factor ($e/m$) enters because the acceleration in a given electric field is proportional to $e$ and inversely proportional to $m$ (eq. 49) and the time $\tau$ describes the time during which the field acts on the carrier. This equation is of fundamental importance. The electrical conductivity $\sigma$ depends on two factors, the number $n$ of carriers per unit volume and their mobility $\mu$. The dependence of these quantities particularly on temperature provides the basic understanding of the electrical properties of materials. For example, in metals, $n$ is constant and $\mu$ varies relatively slowly with temperature. In semiconductors, the exponential dependence of $n$ is of primary importance while in some insulators, it is the exponential dependence of $\mu$ on temperature that is significant while $n$ is constant. An understanding of the relative contributions of $n$ and $\mu$ to $\sigma$ enables us to explain the whole spectrum of values of $\sigma$.

*Example:* Sodium metal with a bcc structure has two atoms per unit cell. The radius of the sodium atom is 1.85 Å. Calculate its electrical resistivity at 0°C if the classical value of the mean free time at this temperature is $3 \times 10^{-14}$ s.

*Solution:* Given: $\tau = 3 \times 10^{-14}$ s, Na has bcc structure with $n = 2$, $R_{Na} = 1.85$ Å $= 1.85 \times 10^{-10}$ m, $\rho = ?$
For a bcc structure, we know that

$$\sqrt{3}a = 4R,$$

or
$$a = \frac{4}{\sqrt{3}}R = \frac{4}{\sqrt{3}} \times 1.85 \times 10^{-10} = 4.27 \times 10^{-10} \text{ m}$$

Further, the number of electrons per unit volume in sodium atom is given by

$$n' = \frac{\rho N}{M} = \frac{n}{a^3} = \frac{2}{(4.27 \times 10^{-10})^3} = 2.57 \times 10^{28}/\text{m}^3$$

Making use of eq. 57 and substituting different values, we can obtain

$$\rho = \frac{m}{n'e^2\tau}$$

$$= \frac{9.1 \times 10^{-31}}{2.57 \times 10^{28} \times (1.6 \times 10^{-19})^2 \times 3.1 \times 10^{-14}} = 4.46 \times 10^{-8} \ \Omega\text{m}$$

*Example:* A uniform copper wire whose diameter is 0.16 cm carries a steady current of 10 amp. Its density and atomic weight are respectively, 8920 kg/m$^3$ and 63.5. Calculate the currnt density and the drift velocity of the electrons in copper.

*Solution:* Given: Density, $\rho = 8920$ kg/m$^3$, At. wt. = 63.5, $I = 10$ A, Diameter, $d = 0.16$ cm = 16 $\times 10^{-4}$ m, and hence $r = 8 \times 10^{-4}$ m, $J = ?$ $v_d = ?$ The number of electrons per unit volume in copper is given by

$$n = \frac{\rho N}{M} = \frac{8920 \times 6.023 \times 10^{26}}{63.5} = 8.46 \times 10^{28} / m^3$$

Now, the current density

$$J = \frac{I}{a} = \frac{10}{\pi r^2} = \frac{10}{\pi (8 \times 10^{-4})^2} = \frac{10^9}{64 \pi} = 4.97 \times 10^6 \text{ A/m}^2$$

The drift velocity can be obtained by using the relation

$$v_d = \frac{J}{ne} = \frac{4.97 \times 10^6}{8.46 \times 10^{28} \times 1.6 \times 10^{-19}} = 3.67 \times 10^{-4} \text{ m/s}$$

*Example:* A uniform silver wire has a resistivity of $1.54 \times 10^{-8}$ $\Omega$m at room temperature. For an electric field along the wire of 1 Volt/cm, compute the average drift velocity of the electrons, assuming that there are $5.8 \times 10^{28}$ conduction electrons/m$^3$. Also calculate the mobility and the relaxation time of the electron.

*Solution:* Given: $\rho = 1.54 \times 10^{-8}$ $\Omega$m, $E = 1$ V/cm = 100 V/m, $n = 5.8 \times 10^{28}$/m$^3$, $v_d = ?$

From eq. 56, the mobility is found to be

$$\mu = \frac{\sigma}{ne} = \frac{1}{\rho ne} = \frac{1}{1.54 \times 10^{-8} \times 5.8 \times 10^{28} \times 1.6 \times 10^{-19}}$$

$$= 6.99 \times 10^{-3} \text{ m}^2/\text{Vs}$$

Further, the drift velocity is given by

$$v_d = \mu E = 100 \times 6.99 \times 10^{-3} = 0.69 \text{ m/s}$$

Also, the relaxation time $\tau$ is given by

$$\tau = \frac{\mu m}{e} = \frac{6.99 \times 10^{-3} \times 9.1 \times 10^{-31}}{1.6 \times 10^{-19}} = 3.97 \times 10^{-14} \text{ s}$$

## 10.12   WIEDEMANN-FRANZ-LORENTZ LAW

From earlier discussions, we have come to know that the electrons are not only the agencies of electrical conduction in an electric field but also responsible for the transport of the thermal energy in a solid. For this reason, it would be natural to expect a relationship between the two conductivities, i.e.

$$\frac{K_e}{\sigma} = \left( \frac{\pi^2 Nk^2 T\tau}{3m} \right) \cdot \left( \frac{m}{Ne^2\tau} \right) = \left( \frac{\pi^2 k^2}{3e^2} \right) T \tag{58}$$

This relationship was first experimentally established by G. Wiedemann and P. Franz and then theoretically explained by L. Lorentz for metals. Wiedemann and Franz observed that the ratio $K_e/\sigma$ remans constant for all metals at a fixed temperature. However, this was modified by Lorentz, who observed that it is $K_e/\sigma(T)$ which remains constant. Accordingly, eq. 58 reduces to

$$\frac{K_e}{\sigma(T)} = \frac{\pi^2}{3}\left(\frac{k^2}{e^2}\right) = L \qquad (59)$$

where $L = \dfrac{\pi^2}{3}\left(\dfrac{k^2}{e^2}\right) = 2.45 \times 10^{-8}$ Watt ohm deg$^{-2}$, and is known as Lorentz number. Table 10.1 shows the experimental values of $L$ for some metals at 0°C and 100°C, respectively. They are found to agree with the theoretical value (eq. 59). At low temperatures ($T \ll \theta_D$), Lorentz number tends to decrease because the collision time involved in the two conductivities is not identical.

**Table 10.1   Experimental Lorentz numbers for some metals**

| Metals | Lorentz numbers 0°C | ($L \times 10^{-8}$ Watt-ohm/dey$^2$) 100°C |
|---|---|---|
| Aq | 2.31 | 2.37 |
| Au | 2.35 | 2.40 |
| Cd | 2.42 | 2.43 |
| Cu | 2.23 | 2.33 |
| Ir | 2.49 | 2.49 |
| Mo | 2.61 | 2.79 |
| Pb | 2.47 | 2.56 |
| Pt | 2.51 | 2.60 |
| Sn | 2.52 | 2.49 |
| W | 3.04 | 3.20 |
| Zn | 2.31 | 2.33 |

*Example:* A uniform copper wire of length 0.5 m and dimeter 0.3 mm has a resistance of 0.12 $\Omega$ at 293 K. If the thermal conductivity of the specimen at the same temperature is 390 Wm$^{-1}$ K$^{-1}$, calculate the Lorentz number. Compare this value with the theoretical value.

*Solution:* Given: $1 = 0.5$ m, $d = 0.3$ mm $= 0.3 \times 10^{-3}$ m, so that $r = 0.15 \times 10^{-3}$ m, $R = 0.12$ W, the Lorentz number = ?

We know that the resistance of a wire in terms of its length and its radius is given by

$$R = \rho\frac{1}{\pi r^2} = \frac{1}{\sigma \pi r^2}$$

or

$$\sigma = \frac{1}{R\pi r^2} = \frac{0.5}{0.12 \times \pi\,(0.15 \times 10^{-3})^2} = 5.89 \times 10^7\ \Omega^{-1}\mathrm{m}^{-1}$$

Hence, using eq. 59, we can obtain the Lorentz number as

$$L = \frac{K_e}{\sigma(T)} = \frac{'\,390}{5.89 \times 10^7 \times 293} = 2.26 \times 10^{-8}\ \mathrm{W\Omega K}^{-2}$$

On the other hand, the theoretical value of the Lorentz number can be obtained by using the expression

$$L = \frac{\pi^2}{3}\left(\frac{k^2}{e^2}\right) = \frac{\pi^2}{3}\left(\frac{1.38 \times 10^{-23}}{1.6 \times 10^{-19}}\right)^2 = 2.84 \times 10^{-8} \text{ W}\Omega\text{K}^{-2}$$

Comparing the above two values of Lorentz numbers, we observe that the theoretical value is about 1.26 times higher than the experimental one.

## 10.13   THE ELECTRICAL RESISTIVITY OF METALS

At room temperature (~300 K) the electrical resistivity of most metals is dominated by the collisions of conduction electrons with the phonons of the lattice (arising due to any perturbation in the normal positions of the atoms). On the other hand, at liquid helium temperature (or around absolute zero) it is due to the collisions of electrons with the impurity atoms or other imperfections (such as vacancies, dislocations, grain boundaries, etc.) that are present in a real crystal (Fig. 10.18). Thus in general, the resistivity of a metal containing imperfections is given by

$$\rho = \rho_1 + \rho_i \tag{60}$$

where $\rho_1$ is the resistivity caused by the thermal vibrations of the lattice, $\rho_i$ (also called the residual resistivity) is the resistivity caused by the scattering of electrons by impurity atoms. For small impurity content, $\rho_1$ is often independent of the number of defects $N_i$, and $\rho_i$ is proportional to the $N_i$ but independent of temperature. Equation 60 is known as Matthiessen's rule. This becomes less accurate at high temperatures or at high impurity content.

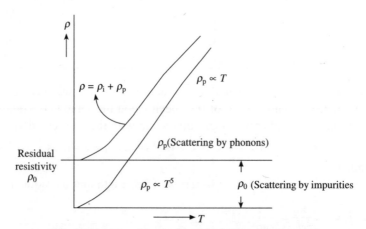

**Fig. 10.18   The electrical resistivity in a real crystal**

At very low temperatures, the scattering by phonon is negligible because of negligibly small amplitude of vibration. Therefore, as $T$ approaches zero, $\tau_1$ tends to infinity so that $\rho_1$ approaches zero and hence $\rho = \rho_i$ from eq. 60. This is in agreement with the experimental results. Measurements on sodium show that $\rho_i(0)$ may vary from specimen to specimen, whereas $\rho_1(T) = \rho - \rho_i(0)$ is independent of the specimen. As the temperature increases, the scattering by phonons becomes more effective and $\rho_1(T)$ increases linearly with temperature. This again, is in agreement with the experimental results.

A simple method to estimate the overall impurity and perfection of a metal (conductor) is to measure the ratio of the resistivities at room temperature and at helium temperature, i.e.

$$\frac{\rho(300 \text{ K})}{\rho(4.2 \text{ K})}$$

Since, at 4.2 K, $\rho = \rho_i$, the resistivity ratio is approximately given by

$$\frac{\rho_1(300 \text{ K}) + \rho_i}{\rho_i}$$

For chemically pure and structurally perfect metals, the resistivity ratio may be as high as $10^6$. On the other hand, for commercial purity materials, this ratio is of the order of $10^2$, while for some alloys, it is as low as 1.

Matthiessen's rule is not always valid. Calculation of resistivity due to lattice vibration $\rho_1$, have been quite successful in some metals. Empirically, one finds that $\rho_1$ is rather well represented by a universal function,

$$\rho_1 \propto \left(\frac{T}{M\theta_R^2}\right) \cdot f\left(\frac{T}{\theta_R}\right) \tag{61}$$

where the function $f$ goes to unity at high temperatures. However, at low temperatures, $f \propto (T/\theta_R)^4$. The resistive characteristic temperature $\theta_R$ is close to the Debye temperature for metals.

*Example:* Calculate the percentage increase in the resistivity of nichrome when it is heated from 300 K to 1000 K. The temperature coefficient of resistance of nichrome is 0.0001.

*Solution:* Given: $T_1 = 300$ K, $T_2 = 1000$ K, $\alpha = 0.0001$, $(\rho_{1000} - \rho_{300}) = ?$ According to Matthiessen's rule, we know that the resistivity of a metal containing impurity can be written as

$$\rho = \rho_i + \rho_1(T) = \rho_i + \alpha T$$

Therefore, $\qquad \rho_{300} = \rho_i + \alpha T_1$ and $\rho_{1000} = \rho_i + \alpha T_2$

or $\qquad \rho_{1000} - \rho_{300} = \alpha(T_2 - T_1) = 700\alpha = 700 \times 0.0001 = 0.07$

Therefore the percentage increase in the resistivity is

$$0.07 \times 100 = 7\%$$

## 10.14 THERMIONIC EMISSION

When a metal is heated, electrons are emitted from its surface, a phenomenon called thermionic emission. In sections 10.2 and 10.3, we considered that the height of the potential barrier is infinitely large. However, this is not actually the case in real crystals. At absolute zero:

(i)  the height of the potential energy barrier can be taken equal to $E_F + e\phi$ as shown in Fig. 10.19, where $E_F$ is the Fermi energy and $e\phi$ is the work function.

(ii)  all the levels upto the Fermi level are filled, and all the levels above the Fermi level are empty.

(iii)  no electrons can escape from the metals.

The work function $e\phi$ is the minimum energy required to remove an electron from the Fermi surface to the vacuum outside the metal, where $\phi$ is expressed in volts and $e\phi$ in electron volts (eV). The voltage $\phi$ is required to overcome the attraction due to positive ions at the surface of the metal. Fig. 10.20 shows an ideal potential (periodic in nature) encountered by electrons along a row of atoms near the surface and the potential energy barrier at the surface of the metal. In our day to day life, we do not observe any electron emission from metal surface even at room temperature. However, as the temperature is increased further, the electrons lying near the Fermi level get exited and begin to fill the levels above $E_F$. Thus, when a metal is heated, (i.e. when an energy greater than $E_F + e\phi$ is supplied), electrons are observed to be emitted from its surface. This phenomenon is known as thermionic emission.

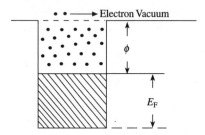

**Fig. 10.19  Thermionic emission**

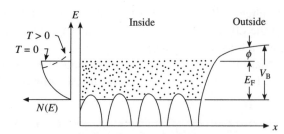

**Fig. 10.20  Idealized potential energy of an electron along a row of atoms near the surface, and the potential energy barrier at the surface of the metal. The shaded area represents electron energy as given by the Fermi distribution shown on the left**

In order to evaluate the current density for the emitted electrons, let us consider a metal surface held normal to the x-direction. Then, for an electron to escape from the metal surface, we must have

$$\frac{1}{2} m v_x^2 \geq (E_F + e\phi) \tag{62}$$

where $v_y$ and $v_z$ can have any values including $+\infty$ and $-\infty$.

Now, let us write the density of occupied states (eq. 19) per unit volume in terms of velocity of electrons by substituting $E = 1/2(m/v^2)$, so that $dE = mv\,dv$. The modified equation becomes

$$N(v)dv = F(v)g(v)dv = \frac{8\pi m^3}{h^3} \cdot \frac{v^2 dv}{\exp\left(\dfrac{E - E_F}{kT}\right) + 1} \tag{63}$$

Then the current density $J_x$ will be $eV_x$ times the density of occupied states per unit volume. To simplify the problem, let us integrate the resulting equation over all electon velocities using cartesian coordinate system instead of spherical coordinate system. Thus replacing the quantity $\int 4\pi v^2 dv$ by $\int dv_x dv_y dv_z$, the current density $J_x$ can be written as

$$J_x = \frac{2\,em^3}{h^3} \int\limits_{v_x=\sqrt{\frac{2(E_F+e\phi)}{m}}}^{\infty} \int\limits_{V_y=-\infty}^{\infty} \int\limits_{V_z=-\infty}^{\infty} \frac{v_x\,dv_x\,dv_y\,dv_z}{\exp\left(\dfrac{E-E_F}{kT}\right)+1} \tag{64}$$

In general, $(E - F_F) \gg kT$, therefore the exponential term in the above equation is also very very large than unity. Thus neglecting the digit 1 which is appearing in the denominator, the eq. 64 reduces to

$$J_x = \frac{2\,em^3}{h^3} \int\limits_{v_x=\sqrt{\frac{2(E_F+e\phi)}{m}}}^{\infty} \int\limits_{V_y=-\infty}^{\infty} \int\limits_{V_z=-\infty}^{\infty} \exp\left[-\frac{1}{kT}\left(\frac{mv_x^2}{2}+\frac{mv_y^2}{2}+\frac{mv_z^2}{2}-E_F\right)\right] \tag{65}$$

Now, making use of the standard form of the integral, i.e.

$$\int\limits_{-\infty}^{\infty} \exp(-\alpha x^2) = \left(\frac{\pi}{\alpha}\right)^{1/2}$$

the above integrals separately can be given by

$$\int\limits_{-\infty}^{\infty} \exp\left(-\frac{mv_z^2}{2kT}\right)dv_z = \int\limits_{-\infty}^{\infty} \exp\left(-\frac{mv_y^2}{2kT}\right)dv_y = \left(\frac{2\pi kT}{m}\right)^{1/2} \tag{66}$$

and

$$\int\limits_{v_x=\sqrt{\frac{2(E_F+e\phi)}{m}}}^{\infty} v_x \cdot \exp\left(-\frac{mv_x^2}{2kT}\right)dv_x = \frac{kT}{m} \cdot \exp\left(-\frac{E+e\phi}{kT}\right) \tag{67}$$

Hence, the current density is given by

$$J_x = \frac{4\,\pi emk^2}{h^3} T^2 \cdot \exp\left(-\frac{e\phi}{kT}\right) = AT^2 \cdot \exp\left(-\frac{e\phi}{kT}\right) \tag{68}$$

where $A = (4\pi em\,k^2/h^3) = 1.20 \times 10^6$ Am$^{-2}$K$^{-2}$. Equation 68 is commonly known as Richardson-Dushman equation. This is in agreement with the experimental results. The eq. 68 can further be written as

$$\frac{J_x}{T^2} = A \exp\left(-\frac{e\phi}{kT}\right)$$

or

$$\ln\frac{J_x}{T^2} = \ln A - \left(\frac{e\phi}{k}\right)\frac{1}{T} \tag{69}$$

If we plot a curve between $\ln (J_x/T^2)$ versus $1/T$, we obtain a straight line which has a slope of $(e\phi/k)$ and the intercept equal to $\ln A$ as shown in Fig. 10.21.

*Example:* The work function of tungsten is 4.5 eV. Calculate the thermionic emission of a filament 0.05 m long and $10^{-4}$ m diameter at 2400 K.

*Solution:* Given: $\phi = 4.5$ eV, $2r = D = 10^{-4}$ m, $1 = 0.05$m, $T = 2400$K, $A = 1.20 \times 10^6$ Am$^{-2}$ K$^{-2}$, $I = ?$

The surface area of the filament, $a = 2\pi r 1 = \pi \times 10^{-4} \times 0.05 = 5\pi \times 10^{-6}$ m$^2$. Now, making use of the eq. 68 and substituting different values, the value of the current can be obtained as

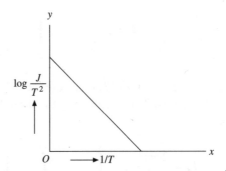

**Fig. 10.21   A plot between $1/T$ and log $J/T^2$**

$$I = a \times J = a \times AT^2 \cdot \exp\left(-\frac{e\phi}{kT}\right)$$

$$= 5\pi \times 10^{-6} \times 1.20 \times 10^6 \, (2400)^2 \times \exp\left(-\frac{4.5 \times 1.6 \times 10^{-19}}{1.38 \times 10^{-23} \times 2400}\right)$$

$$= 5\pi \times 10^{-6} \times 1.20 \times 10^6 \, (2400)^2 \times \exp(-21.739)$$

$$= 5\pi \times 10^{-6} \times 1.20 \times 10^6 \, (2400)^2 \times 3.62 \times 10^{-10} = 393 \times 10^{-4} \text{ amp}$$

## 10.15   THE HALL EFFECT

Let us consider a rectangular metal slab carrying a current density $J_x$ in the positive $x$-direction and placed in a uniform magnetic field of induction $B$ acting perpendicular to both the conductor and the current as shown in Fig. 10.22. Under such an experimental arrangement, in 1879 G. Hall found that a voltage (called the Hall voltage) is developed at right angles to both the current and the magnetic field.

In the absence of the magnetic field, the conduction electrons drift with a velocity $v_x$ in the negative $x$-direction. However, when the field is applied, a force (called the Lorent force) causes the electron path to deflect towards the front face of the rectangular block. As a result, an excess of electrons accumulate on the front face of the slab. Simultaneously, equal number of positive charge appears (due to the deficiency

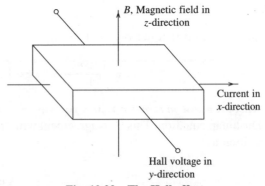

**Fig. 10.22   The Hall effect**

of electrons) on the opposite face of the slab. The appearance of the opposite charges on the opposite faces creates an electric field (called the Hall field) directed towards the positive $y$-axis.

The Lorentz force $F_L$ acting on an electron which is moving from right to left with a velocity $v$ is

$$F_L = -ev_x \times B_z = -ev_zB_z \text{ (since } v_x \text{ is } \perp B) \tag{70}$$

Further, the accumulated charges on the oppositive faces produce a force (called Hall force) opposite to the Lorentz force. Hence, the accumulation process continues unit to the Hall force completely cancels the Lorentz force. In equilibrium, $F_H = F_L$, i.e.

$$eE_H = -ev_xB_z \quad \text{or} \quad E_H = -v_xB_z \tag{71}$$

Further, the current density, $J_x$ is given by the equation

$$J_x = nev_x \quad \text{or} \quad E_H = -\left(\frac{1}{ne}\right)B_zJ_x \tag{72}$$

This shows that the Hall field is proportional to both the magnetic field and the current density. The constant of proportionality in eq. 72 is known as Hall constant and is defined by

$$R_H = -\frac{1}{ne} \tag{73}$$

which is inversely proportional to the density of charge carrier, $n$. The sign of the Hall constant indicates the nature of the charge carrier that predominate in the conduction process. If $R_H$ is negative, the predominant charge is electron and vice-versa. The measurement of Hall voltage helps us to know the following:

1. The sign of the predominant charge carrier.
2. The charge density.
3. The mobility of the charge carriers.

*Example:* Calculate the Hall coefficient of sodium based on free electron model. Sodium has bcc structure and the side of the cube is 4.28Å.

*Solution:* Given: $a = 4.28$ Å $= 4.28 \times 10^{-10}$m, crystal has a bcc structure indicating it contains 2 atoms per unit cell, Hall coefficients = ?
The number of electrons per unit volume for the sodium crystal is given by

$$n = \frac{2}{a^3} = \frac{2}{(4.28)^3 \times 10^{-30}} = 2.55 \times 10^{28} / \text{m}^3$$

Now, making use of eq. 73, the Hall coefficient can be obtained as

$$R_H = -\frac{1}{ne} = \frac{1}{2.55 \times 10^{28} \times 1.6 \times 10^{-19}} = 2.45 \times 10^{-9} \text{ m}^3\text{C}^{-1}$$

## 10.16  SUMMARY

1. The free electron model successfully explains some of the properties of solids, such as electrical and thermal conductivities, thermionic emission, etc. However, it fails to explain many other important properties such as behaviour of solids as conductors, semiconductors or insulators, etc.
2. Free electrons are associated with a continuous energy spectrum and bound electrons with a discrete energy spectrum. The energy corresponding to the electrons moving in box of side $a$ is given by

$$E_n = \frac{h^2}{8ma^2}(n_x^2 + n_y^2 + n_z^2)$$

where $n_x$, $n_y$ and $n_z$ are quantum numbers and can take only positive integer values.

3. Each combination of these quantum numbers is called a quantum state while several states having the same energy are said to be degenerate.
4. At absolute zero, the density of electrons (the number of electrons per unit volume) below the Fermi level is given by

$$n = \frac{8\pi}{3h^3}(2m)^{3/2} E_F^{3/2}$$

5. As the temperature is increased (particularly above room temperature) the Fermi energy is found to decrease according to the relation.

$$E_F = E_{F_0}\left[1 - \frac{\pi^2}{12}\left(\frac{kT}{E_{F_0}}\right)^2\right]$$

6. At low temperatures, the electronic specific heat of solids is found to be predominant and varies linearly with $T$. The electronic specific heat per mole is given by

$$C_e = \frac{\pi^2}{2} \times \frac{kT}{T_F}$$

7. The electrical conductivity of conduction electrons, treated as free particles with a collision time $\tau$ is given by

$$\sigma = \frac{Ne^2\tau}{m}$$

8. Wiedemann-Franz-Lorentz law connects the thermal and electrical conductivities according to the relation

$$\frac{K_e}{\sigma} = \frac{\pi^2}{3}\left(\frac{k^2}{e^2}\right)$$

9. Taking into account the lattice vibrations and static impurities, the electrical resistivity of a solid is governed by Matthiessen's rule

$$\rho = \rho_1 + \rho_i$$

10. When a metal is heated, some electrons which are lying just below the Fermi level acquire sufficient energy and escape from the surface of the metal. The thermionic current density is given by

$$J_x = AT^2 \cdot \exp\left(-\frac{e\phi}{kT}\right)$$

where $A$ is constant and $\phi$ is the work function of the metal.

11. Hall effect helps use to determine the following:

(i)    The sign of the current carrying charges.
(ii)   The charge density.
(iii)  The mobility of the charge carriers

## 10.17   DEFINITIONS

*Current Density:* The electric current per unit area, amperes per square meter.
*Electrical conductivity:* The proportionality constant in Ohm's law as stated below.
*Electric Current:* The time rate of passage of charge through a conductor. In SI units, coulomb per second, called amperes.
*Electrical Resistivity:* The inverse of the electrical conductivity, so that the Ohm's law is also $E = \rho J$.
*Electronic Specific Heat:* The contribution to the total specific heat due to transitions of electrons to states of higher energy.
*Fermi Level:* In a partially filled energy band at 0K, the Fermi level is the energy of the highest filled state. At higher temperatures, one half of the states at the Fermi level are full.
*Mantlhiessen's Rule:* The total resistivity of a conductor is the sum of lattice contribution as a result of lattice vibrations and the impurity contribution as a result of presence of imperfections.
*Residual Resistivity:* The temperatue independent part of the resistivity of a conductor. This is due to imperfections.
*Resistivity Ratio:* Usually, it is defined as $\rho(300K)/\rho(4.2K)$, although the lower temperature may vary. In order to estimate the value of residual resistivity $\{\rho_1(300K) + \rho_i\})/\rho_i$ is approximately taken as $\rho_1(300K)/\rho_i$.

## REVIEW QUESTIONS AND PROBLEMS

1.  A particle moving in a one dimensional potential, is given by

    $$V(x) = 0 \quad \text{for} \quad x < 0$$

    $$\text{and } V(x) = V_0 \quad \text{for} \quad x \geq 0$$

    Write down the Schrodinger wave equation for the particle and solve it.
2.  What is an infinite potential well? Obtain Schrodinger's time independent wave equation. Solve it for a particle in a cubical box of side "*a*" and hence obtain expressions for the allowed wave functions and discrete energy values of the particle.
3.  Obtain the eigen values and normalized wave functions for a particle in a one dimensional infinite potential box of side "*a*".
4.  A particle of mass *m* is confined in a field free region between impenetrable walls at $x = 0$ and $x = a$. Show that the stationary energy levels of the particle is given by

    $$E_n = \frac{h^2 n^2}{8 m a^2}$$

    Discuss the physical significance of the wave function $\psi$.
5.  Define Fermi energy. Write down the expression for Fermi-Dirac distribution function. Derive an expression for Fermi energy of a system of free electrons.
6.  Based the Fermi-Dirac statistics, state the nature of the Fermi distribution function. How does it vary with temperature?
7.  What are the density of states in metals? Derive an expression for the density of energy states and hence obtain the Fermi energy of a metal.
8.  What is meant by the Fermi level in metals? How does it vary with temperature in metals?
9.  Show that the wavelength associated with an electron having an energy equal to the Fermi energy is given by

    $$2\left(\frac{\pi}{3n}\right)^{1/2}$$

Calculate the molar specific heat of metals on the basis of Fermi-Dirac statistics and compare it with the classical predicted value.

10. The Fermi energy expression at room temperature is given by

$$E_F = E_{F_0} \left[ 1 - \frac{\pi^2}{12} \left( \frac{kT}{E_{F_0}} \right)^2 \right]$$

where $E_{F_0}$ is the Fermi energy at 0K.

Using the above equation, obtain the expression for the mean energy of the electron at room temperature. Also obtain the expression for the molar specific heat of metals on the basis of this distribution.

11. What do you understand by "degenerate" and "non degenerate" states? Taking the example of a particle in a cubical box of side "$a$", obtain first few states and present them graphically.

12. Derive an expression for the electrical conductivity of a free electron gas using the collision time concept. Does this result explain the experimental value of resistivity of a normal metal like sodium.

13. On the basis of free electron theory derive an expression for the electrical and thermal conductivity of metal and hence establish Wiedemann-Franz-Lorentz law.

14. What are the main sources of electrical resistance in metals? Discuss the effect of impurity, temperature and alloying on the electrical conductivity of metals.

15. Explain the variation of electrical conductivity with temperature both at low and high temperature regions. Hence explain Matthiessen's rule.

16. Discuss electron-scattering mechanisms in metals and show that the mean free path is inversely proportional to absolute temperature for $T \gg \theta_D$.

17. Obtain the expression of Lorentz number on the basis of quantum theory. Compare it with the one predicted on the basis of classical theory.

18. Discuss the Hall effect. Explain how the measurement of Hall coefficient helps one to determine the mobility of electrons in metals.

19. Show that the Hall coefficient is independent of the applied magnetic field and is inversely proportional to the current density and electronic charge. Mention the important applications of Hall effect.

20. Discuss the phenomenon of thermionic emission in metals. Obtain Richardson Dushman equation for the emission of current density.

21. The thermal conductivity of aluminum at 20°C is 210 $Wm^{-1}K^{-1}$. Calculate the electrical resistivity of aluminum at this temperature. The Lorentz number for aluminium is $2.02 \times 10^{-8} W\Omega K^{-2}$.

*Ans.* $2.82 \times 10^{-8} \Omega m$

22. A copper wire of cross sectional area $5 \times 10^{-2}$ sq. cm. carries a steady current of 50 ampere. Assume one electron per atom, calculate the density of free electrons, the average drift velocity and the relaxation time. Given: the resistivity of copper = $1.7 \times 10^{-8} \Omega m$.

*Ans.* $8.4 \times 10^{28}/m^3$, $7.4 \times 10^{-4}$ m/s and $2.46 \times 10^{-4}$ s.

23. (a) Find the lowest energy of an electron confined in a box of side 1 Å.

(b) Find the temperature at which the average energy of the molecule of a perfect gas would be equal to the lowest energy of the electron.

*Ans.* 112.9 eV, $8.72 \times 10^5$ K.

24. The electrons in a cubical box of a metal are subject to the influence of a magnetic field such that the length increases by $da$ while the width and thickness remain the same. Show that the energy difference between the states (311) and (131) is $(h^2/8ma^2)$ $(16da/a)$ in the new position.

25. Evaluate the temperature at which there is 1% probability that a state with an energy 0.5 eV above the Fermi energy will be occupied by an electron.

*Ans.* 1264 K.

26. Calculate the number of states lying in an energy interval of 0.02 eV above the Fermi energy of sodium crystal of unit volume. For sodium, $E_F = 3.22$ eV. *Ans.* $2.47 \times 10^{26}$

27. Use the Fermi distribution function to obtain the value of $F(E)$ for $E - E_F = 0.01$ eV at 200 K.

*Ans.* 0.36

28. Show that the probability that a state $\Delta E$ above the Fermi level $E_F$ is filled equals the probability that a state $\Delta E$ below is empty.

29. Assuming the electrons to be free, calculate the total number of states below $E = 5$ eV in a cubical box of volume of $10^{-5}$ m$^3$. *Ans.* $5.1 \times 10^{23}$.

30. The Fermi energy of silver is 5.5 eV. Calculate the fraction of free electrons at room temperature located upto a width of $kT$ on either side of $E_F$. *Ans.* 0.01.

31. Calculate the heat capacity of electron gas at room temperature in copper assuming one free electron per atom. Compare this with the lattice specific heat value of $2.4 \times 10^4$ J kmol$^{-1}$ K$^{-1}$. The Fermi energy of copper is 7 eV.

*Ans.* $146 \times 10^2$ J kmol$^{-1}$ K$^{-1}$, 0.608%.

32. An alloy of a metal is found to have a resistivity of $10^{-6}$ $\Omega$m at 0°C. When it is heated to a temperature of 700°C, the resistivity increases by 8%. Using Matthiessen's rule, find the resistivity of the alloy.

*Ans.* $0.969 \times 10^{-6}$ $\Omega$m.

33. The electrical and thermal conductivities of silver at 20°C are $6.22 \times 10^7$ $\Omega^{-1}$ m$^{-1}$ and 423 Wm$^{-1}$K$^{-1}$, respectively. Calculate the Lorentz number on the basis of quantum free election theory.

*Ans.* $2.32 \times 10^{-8}$ W$\Omega$K$^{-2}$.

# Chapter 11

# Band Theory

## 11.1 BLOCH THEOREM

In the case of free electron theory we assumed that the electrons move in a region of constant potential inside a one or three dimensional potential well. Although the free electron theory is able to explain the phenomena such as electrical conductivity, thermionic emission etc., it fails to explain why some materials are good electrical conductors while some are good electrical insulators and still some others are semiconductors?

In order to understand the difference between the conductors and insulators, it is necessary to incorporate the variation of potential inside the crystal due to the presence of positive ion cores in the free electron model (Fig. 11.1a). It appears more realistic to assume the potential inside a metallic crystal to be periodic with the periodicity of the lattice, somewhat as shown in Fig. 11.1b. The potential is minimum at the positive ion sites and maximum between the two ions. The corresponding one dimensional Schrodinger equation can be written as:

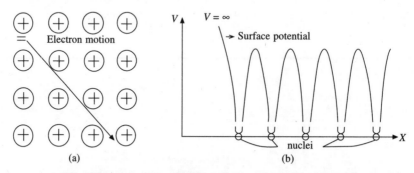

Fig. 11.1   One dimensional periodic potential in a crystal

$$\frac{d^2\psi}{dx^2} + \frac{8\pi^2 m}{h^2}\,[E - V(x)]\,\psi = 0 \tag{1}$$

where the periodic potential $V(x)$ may be defined by means of the lattice constant "$a$" as

$$V(x) = V(x + a) \tag{2}$$

Employing the periodic potential, Bloch has shown that the one dimensional solution of the Schrodinger equation takes the form

$$\psi(x) = \exp{(ikx)}\, u_k(x) \tag{3}$$

In three dimensions it is given by

$$\psi_k(r) = \exp{(ik.r)}\, u_k(r) \tag{4}$$

The equation 3 (or 4) is known as Bloch function in one and three dimensions, respectively. They represent the free electron wave modulated by the periodic function $u_k(x)$ or $u_k(r)$, where $u_k(x)$ or $u_k(r)$ is periodic with the periodicity of the lattice in one and three dimensions, respectively. Therefore, considering only the one dimensional case and suppose if we have $N(N$ even) number of atoms in a linear chain of atoms of length $L$, then we can write

$$u_k(x) = u_k(x + Na) \tag{5}$$

and depends on the exact nature of the potential field. From eqs. 3 and 5, we have

$$\psi_k(x + Na) = u_k(x + Na)\exp{[ik(x + Na)]}$$

$$= \exp{(ikNa)}\, u_k(x)\exp{(ikx)} = \psi_k(x)\exp{(ikNa)} \tag{6}$$

This is frequently referred to as the Bloch condition. Similarly, the complex conjugate of eq. 6 can be written as

$$\psi_k^*(x + Na) = \exp(-ikNa)\,\psi_k^*(x) \tag{7}$$

The eqs. 6 and 7 give us

$$\psi_k(x + Na)\,\psi_k^*(x + Na) = \psi_k(x)\,\psi_k^*(x) \tag{8}$$

This indicates that the probability of finding the electron is same everywhere in the whole chain of atoms, i.e. it is not localized around any particular atom but is shared by all atoms in the chain (the whole crystal in three dimensions). Thus, eq. 6, gives us

$$\exp{(ikNa)} = 1$$

This will be true only if

$$kNa = 2\pi \times \text{integer} = 2\pi n$$

or

$$k = \frac{2\pi n}{Na} = \frac{2\pi n}{L} \tag{9}$$

where $n = 0, \pm 1, \pm 2, \ldots$ and $L$ is the length of chain of atoms. When $n = N/2$, we have $k = \pi/a$, which is the edge of the first Brillouin zone. When $L$ is large (i.e. $N$ is large), the allowed values of $k$ would come close together and their distribution along $k$-axis becomes quasi-continuous. The total number of allowed $k$-values in the first zone is

$$\frac{\text{Length of the first zone}}{\text{Length of the unit spacing}} = \frac{2\pi/a}{2\pi/L} = \frac{L}{a} = N \tag{10}$$

This is equal to the total number of atoms in the chain of atoms (or in the unit cell in three dimensions).

## 11.2 THE KRONIG-PENNEY MODEL

In the preceding section, we qualitatively discussed the behaviour of an electron in an undefined periodic potential. However, in order to know the exact *E-k* relationship it is necessary to consider a well defined one dimensional periodic potential. For the purpose, we shall consider Kronig-Penney model. They suggested a simpler potential in the form of an array of square wells as shown in Fig. 11.2.

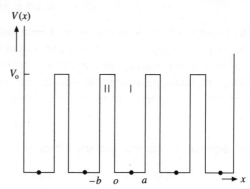

The corresponding Schrodinger equations for the two regions I and II are of the form

$$\frac{d^2\psi}{dx^2} + \frac{8\pi^2 m}{h^2} E\psi = 0 \quad \text{for} \quad 0 < x < a$$

**Fig. 11.2   Ideal periodic square well potential suggested by Kronig and Penney**

or
$$\frac{d^2\psi}{dx^2} + \alpha^2\psi = 0 \qquad (11)$$

where
$$\alpha^2 = \frac{8\pi^2 mE}{h^2} \qquad (12)$$

and
$$\frac{d^2\psi}{dx^2} + \frac{8\pi^2 m}{h^2}(E - V_0)\psi = 0 \quad \text{for} - b < x < 0$$

or
$$\frac{d^2\psi}{dx^2} - \beta^2\psi = 0 \qquad (13)$$

where
$$\beta^2 = \frac{8\pi^2 m}{h^2}(V_0 - E) \qquad (14)$$

Since the expected solutions of the above Schrodinger equations should have the form of Bloch function (eq. 3), this requires both $\psi$ and $(d\psi/dx)$ to be continuous throughout the crystal. Therefore, let us suppose that the general solution of the eqs. 11 and 13 are of the form

$$\psi_1(x) = A \exp(i\alpha x) + B \exp(-i\alpha x) \qquad (15)$$

and
$$\psi_2(x) = C \exp(\beta x) + D \exp(-\beta x) \quad \text{for} \quad E < V_0 \qquad (16)$$

where *A*, *B* and *C*, *D* are constants in the region I and II, respectively. Their values can be obtained by applying the following boundary conditions,

$$|\psi_1(x)|_{x=0} = |\psi_2(x)|_{x=0} \qquad (17)$$

$$\left[\frac{d\psi_1}{dx}\right]_{x=0} = \left[\frac{d\psi_2}{dx}\right]_{x=0} \qquad (18)$$

$$|\psi_1(x)|_{x=0} = |\psi_2(x)|_{x=-b} \tag{19}$$

and
$$\left[\frac{d\psi_1}{dx}\right]_{x=a} = \left[\frac{d\psi_2}{dx}\right]_{x=-b} \tag{20}$$

Since, for a periodic lattice with $V(x + a) = V(x)$, it is expected that the wavefunction will also exhibit the same periodicity. Therefore, the expected solutions of the above Schrodinger equation must have the same form as that of the Bloch function (i.e. like eq. 3). Making use of eq. 6, we can write

$$\psi_k(x + a + b) = \psi_k(x) \exp[ik(a + b)]$$

or
$$\psi_k(x) = \psi_k(x + a + b) \exp[-ik(a + b)]$$

Incorporating this requirement at $x = -b$ and $x = a$, the eqs. 19 and 20 become

$$\psi_2(-b) = \psi_1(a) \exp[-ik(a + b)] \tag{21}$$

and
$$\left[\frac{d\psi_2}{dx}\right]_{x=-b} = \left[\frac{d\psi_1}{dx}\right]_{x=a} \exp[-ik(a + b)] \tag{22}$$

Now, applying the boundary conditions in equation 17, 18, 21 and 22, we obtain the following modified equations

$$A + B = C + D \tag{23}$$

$$i\alpha(A - B) = \beta(C - D) \tag{24}$$

$$Ce^{-\beta b} + De^{\beta b} = e^{-ik(a+b)} [Ae^{i\alpha a} + Be^{-i\alpha a}] \tag{25}$$

$$\beta Ce^{-\beta b} + \beta De^{\beta b} = i\alpha e^{-ik(a+b)} [Ae^{i\alpha a} - Be^{-i\alpha a}] \tag{26}$$

The equations 23, 24, 25 and 26 will have non-vanishing solutions if and only if the determinant of the coefficients A, B, C and D vanishes, i.e.

$$\begin{vmatrix} 1 & 1 & -1 & -1 \\ i\alpha & -i\alpha & -\beta & \beta \\ -e^{-ik(a+b)+i\alpha a} & -e^{-ik(a+b)-i\alpha a} & e^{-\beta b} & e^{\beta b} \\ -i\alpha e^{ik(a+b)+i\alpha a} & i\alpha e^{-ik(a+b)-i\alpha a} & \beta e^{-\beta b} & -\beta e^{\beta b} \end{vmatrix} = 0$$

On simplifying this determinant, we obtain

$$\cos k(a + b) = \left(\frac{\beta^2 - \alpha^2}{2\alpha\beta}\right) \sin \alpha a \sinh \beta b + \cos \alpha a \cosh \beta b \tag{27}$$

In order to simplify eq. 27 further, Kronig and Penney assumed that the potential energy is zero at lattice sites and equals $V_0$ in between them. They further assumed that as the height of the potential barrier $V$ tends to infinity and the width of the barrier $b$ approaches zero in such a way that the product $V_0 b$ remains finite. This assumption is equivalent to a Dirac $\delta$-function type potential energies $V_0$ separated by a distance $a$, the potential energy being zero in between the $\delta$-function spikes. Under these assumptions,

$$\sinh \beta b \to \beta b \text{ and } \cosh \beta b \to 1 \text{ as } b \to 0$$

Hence, eq. 27 becomes

$$\cos ka = \frac{\beta^2 - \alpha^2}{2\alpha\beta} \beta b \sin \alpha a + \cos \alpha a \tag{28}$$

where

$$\beta^2 - \alpha^2 = \frac{8\pi^2 m}{h^2}(V_0 - E) - \frac{8\pi^2 mE}{h^2} = \frac{8\pi^2 m}{h^2}(V_0 - 2E)$$

Since, $V_0 \gg E$, so that

$$\beta^2 - \alpha^2 = \frac{8\pi^2 m}{h^2}V_0$$

Substituting this in eq. 28, we obtain

$$\cos ka = \frac{8\pi^2 m}{2\alpha\beta h^2}V_0\beta b \sin \alpha a + \cos \alpha a$$

$$= \frac{4\pi^2 ma}{h^2}V_0 b \frac{\sin \alpha a}{\alpha a} + \cos \alpha a$$

$$= \frac{P \sin \alpha a}{\alpha a} + \cos \alpha a \tag{29}$$

where

$$P = \frac{4\pi^2 ma}{h^2}V_0 b \tag{30}$$

Equation 29 is schematically represented in Fig. 11.3. The quantity on its right hand side is plotted as a function of $\alpha a$. The cosine term on the left hand side of the equation can only have

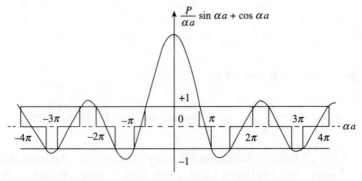

**Fig. 11.3**   Plot of $\dfrac{P \sin \alpha a}{\alpha a} + \cos \alpha a$ vs $\alpha a$

values between −1 and +1 as indicated by horizontal lines in the figure. A consequence of this limitation is that only certain values of $\alpha$ (and hence $E$) are allowed. Further, from the left side of eq. 29, it is clear that for a specific value of energy $E$ (as in eq. 12), cos $ka$ can have only one value. Moreover, since cos $ka$ is an even periodic function, it will have the same value whether $ka$ is positive, negative or it is increased by integral multiple of $2\pi$. Accordingly, the total energy $E$ of the electron is an even periodic function of $k$ with a period of $2\pi/a$. Fig. 11.4 shows a plot of energy as a function of $k$. If $k$ is to be real, the magnitude of cos $ka$ should be less than 1 (i.e. |cos $ka$ | <1) which corresponds to the allowed energy band. On the other hand, those value of energy $E$ for which | cos $ka$ | >1, only the imaginary values of $k$ are possible which correspond to the forbidden bands. The allowed and the forbidden energy bands are schematically shown in Fig. 11.4.

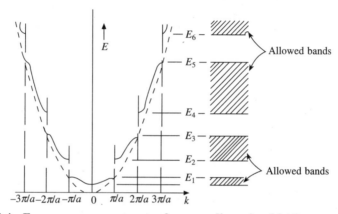

**Fig. 11.4   Energy versus wave vector for a one dimensional lattice**

The analysis of eq. 29 leads us to the following inferences:

1.  Allowed range of $\alpha a$ permits a wave mechanical solution to exist as shown in Fig. 11.5. Thus, the motion of electrons in a periodic lattice is characterized by the bands of allowed energy separated by forbidden regions.

2.  As the value of $\alpha a$ increases, the width of the allowed band also increases while the width of the forbidden band decreases. This is because of the fact that the first term on the right side of eq. 29 on an average decreases with increasing $\alpha a$.

3.  For further understanding, let us look at the influence of $P$ on the energy spectrum. The quantity $P$ is known to be a measure of the potential barrier strength. If $P$ is large, means the potential barrier $V_0 b$ is large (eq. 30), the function described by the right hand side of eq.

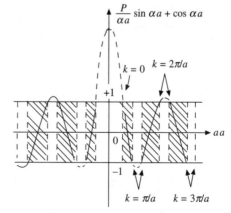

**Fig. 11.5   A plot of** $\dfrac{P \sin \alpha a}{\alpha a} + \cos \alpha a = \cos ka$
**with** $P = 3\pi/2$

29 crosses +1 and –1 region at a steeper angle as shown in Fig. 11.6. Thus, the allowed bands are narrower and the forbidden bands are wider. Hence, the ratio of the width of the forbidden band to that of the allowed band increases. let us take the case when the potential barrier strength is very large, i.e. $P$ tends to infinity. However, as the right side of the eq. 29 has to stay within the limit ±1, it follows from eq. 29 that

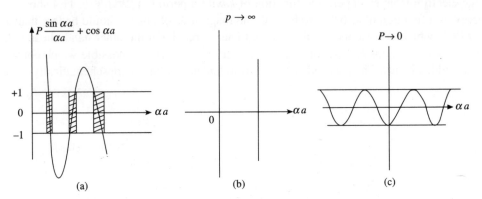

**Fig. 11.6 (a) Right side of eq. 29 for $P = 6\pi$ as a function of $\alpha a$ (b) $P \to \infty$ (c) $P \to 0$**

$$\frac{\sin \alpha a}{\alpha a} \to 0, \quad \text{i.e.} \quad \sin \alpha a \to 0$$

$$\Rightarrow \qquad \alpha a = \pm\, n\pi \text{ and } \alpha^2 = \frac{n^2 \pi^2}{a^2}$$

However, from eq. 12, we have

$$\alpha^2 = \frac{n^2 \pi^2}{a^2} = \frac{8\pi^2 mE}{h^2} \text{ or } E = \frac{n^2 h^2}{8ma^2} \tag{31}$$

This is equivalent to the case of discrete energy spectrum of a particle in a constant potential box of atomic dimensions. This is expected because for large $P$ tunnelling through the barrier becomes almost improbable.

If on the other hand, $P$ is made equal to zero, then the eq. 29 leads to

$$\cos \alpha a = \cos k\alpha \text{ or } \alpha = k$$

$$\Rightarrow \qquad \alpha^2 = k^2 = \frac{8\pi^2 mE}{h^2}$$

or

$$E = \frac{h^2}{8\pi^2 m} k^2 \tag{32}$$

Substituting $k = \frac{2\pi}{\lambda}$, eq. 32 becomes

$$E = \frac{h^2}{8\pi^2 m} k^2 = \frac{h^2}{8\pi^2 m} \left(\frac{2\pi}{\lambda}\right)^2$$

$$= \frac{h^2}{2m} \cdot \frac{1}{\lambda^2} = \frac{h^2}{2m} \cdot \frac{p^2}{h^2} = \frac{p^2}{2m} = \frac{1}{2} m v^2$$

where $\lambda = h/p$ and $p = mv$.

This is equivalent to the case of a free particle. Hence, no energy level exists; allowed.

*Example*: Prove that for the Kronig-Penney potential with $P \ll 1$, the energy of the lowest energy band at $k = 0$ is

$$E = \frac{h^2 P}{4\pi^2 m a^2}$$

*Solution*: For $k = 0$, the eq. 29 reduces to

$$\frac{P \sin \alpha a}{\alpha a} + \cos \alpha a = 1$$

or

$$\frac{P}{\alpha a} = \frac{1 - \cos \alpha a}{\sin \alpha a}$$

where

$$\cos \alpha a = 1 - \frac{(\alpha a)^2}{2!} + \ldots \cong 1 - \frac{\alpha^2 a^2}{2}$$

and

$$\sin \alpha a = \alpha a - \frac{(\alpha a)^3}{3!} + \ldots \cong \alpha a$$

Thus

$$\frac{P}{\alpha a} = \frac{(\alpha a)^2}{2 \alpha a} \quad \text{or} \quad P = \frac{\alpha^2 a^2}{2}$$

But

$$\alpha^2 = \frac{8\pi^2 m E}{h^2}$$

Therefore,

$$P = \frac{8\pi^2 m E}{h^2} \times \frac{a^2}{2} \quad \text{or} \quad E = \frac{h^2 P}{4\pi^2 m a^2}$$

## 11.3   CONSTRUCTION OF BRILLOUIN ZONES

The Brillouin zone is a representation of permissive values of k of the electrons in one, two or three dimensions. The concept of Brillouin zone provides a way to understand the origin of allowed and forbidden bands in solids. Let us follow an intuitive approach to discuss the construction of BZ in one, two and three dimensional lattices.

### In One-dimension

Let us consider the motion of an electron along a one dimensional periodic latice. A direct consequence of the periodicity is that the energy spectrum consists of allowed and forbidden regions as shown in Fig. 11.4. Let us now consider the values of k at which the discontiuities in E occur. They occur whenever the left side of the eq. 29 reaches its maximum value, i.e. when

$$\cos ka = \pm 1$$

or
$$k = \pm n \ \frac{\pi}{a}, \text{ where } n = 1, 2, 3, \ldots \tag{33}$$

At these values of $k$, a small increase in electron momentum (or equivalently in electron wave vector $k$) will increase the energy of the electron so that it can jump discontinuously from the top of one allowed band to the bottom of the next. The region between the first and the second values of $k$ for which discontinuities occur is called the second Brillouin zone and so on. Fig. 11.7 shows two Brillouin zones for one dimensional lattice.

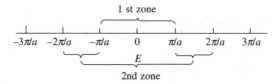

**Fig. 11.7   The first two Brillouin zones for a one dimensional lattice**

## In Two Dimensions

Let us consider the motion of an electron in the field of a two dimensional square lattice, keeping the treatment just qualilative. We know that the de Broglie wavelength of a free electron of momentum $p$ and energy $E$ is given by

$$\lambda = \frac{h}{p} = \frac{h}{\sqrt{2mE}} \tag{34}$$

Low energy electrons will have long wavelengths as compared to the interatomic spacing (i.e. $\lambda \gg a$) and can travel freely through a crystal without being diffracted. However, more energetic electrons (i.e. the electrons near the Fermi level with $E \simeq E_F$), have comparable wavelength with the interatomic spacing (i.e. $\lambda \simeq a$). Such electrons will be diffracted in the same way as X-rays or electrons (neutrons) in a beam according to Bragg diffraction law.

$$n\lambda = 2a \sin \theta, \quad \text{where } n = 1, 2, 3 \tag{35}$$

where $\theta$ is the angle of incidence of the beam of electrons (X-rays or neutrons).

Since it is useful to describe the motion of the electron in a crystal in terms of wave number, therefore let us replace $\lambda$ in eq. 35 by $k$. It is a vector quantity and its magnitude is related to the wavelength by the equation

$$|k| = \frac{2\pi}{\lambda} \tag{36}$$

The direction of k is the same as the direction of propagation of the wave train. From eqs. 35 and 36, we obtain

$$|k| = \frac{n\pi}{a \sin \theta} \equiv k \tag{37}$$

In eq. 37, the critical value of k depends on the angle of incidence $\theta$. Considering a two-dimensional square lattice (Fig. 11.8), we can express the Bragg condition (eq. 37) by saying that the reflection from vertical rows of ions occurs when the component of the vector k in the x-direction is

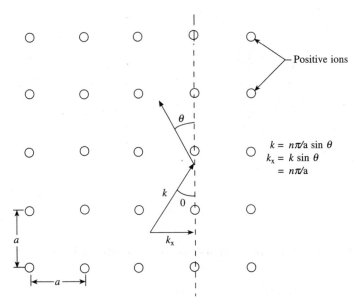

$$k = n\pi/a \sin \theta$$
$$k_x = k \sin \theta$$
$$= n\pi/a$$

**Fig. 11.8  Bragg reflection from the vertical rows of ions occur when $k_x = n\pi/a$**

$$k_x = k \sin \theta = \frac{n\pi}{a}$$

Similarly, reflection from horizontal rows occurs when

$$k_y = \frac{n\pi}{a}$$

for first zone, n = ±1, therefore,

$$k_x = \pm\frac{n\pi}{a} \quad \text{and} \quad k_y = \pm\frac{n\pi}{a}$$

Thus, the first zone is bounded along the x and y axes by the points A, B, C and D as shown in Fig. 11.9. The rest of the boundary may be evaluated according to the following procedure.

Consider a square lattice whose primitive translation vectors are given as:

$$a = ai \quad \text{and} \quad b = bj$$

where a is the side of the square and i, j are the unit vectors along the x, y axes, respectively. The corresponding primitive reciprocal lattice translation vectors can be written as:

$$a^* = \frac{2\pi}{a}i \quad \text{and} \quad b^* = \frac{2\pi}{a}j$$

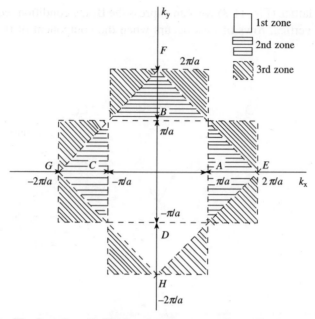

**Fig. 11.9** **The first three Brillouin zones for a two-dimensional square lattice**

so that the reciprocal lattice vector $G$ can be written as

$$G = n_1 a^* + n_2 b^* = \frac{2\pi}{a} [n_1 i + n_2 j] \tag{39}$$

Further, the wave vector $k$ in terms of its component vectors $k_x$ and $k_y$ can be written as

$$k = k_x i + k_y j \tag{40}$$

Substituting eqs. 39 and 40 in the Bragg's condition $2k. G + G^2 = 0$, we obtain

$$2(k_x i + k_y j) \cdot \frac{2\pi}{a} (n_1 i + n_2 j) + \frac{4\pi^2}{a^2} (n_1 i + n_2 j)^2 = 0$$

or

$$\frac{4\pi}{a} (n_1 k_x + n_2 k_y) + \frac{4\pi^2}{a^2} (n_1^2 + n_2^2) = 0$$

where $i \cdot i = j \cdot j = 1$, and $i \cdot j = 0$. Further simplifying this, we obtain

$$n_1 k_x + n_2 k_y = \frac{\pi}{a} (n_1^2 + n_2^2) \tag{41}$$

where $n_1$ and $n_2$ are integers for diffraction by the vertical and horizontal rows of ions. For the first zone, one integer is $\pm 1$, and the other is zero. Therefore, the equations for the first zone boundaries are:

$$n_1 = \pm 1, n_2 = 0 \text{ giving } k_x = \pm \frac{\pi}{a}$$

and
$$n_1 = 0,\ n_2 = \pm1 \text{ giving } k_y = \pm\frac{\pi}{a}$$

This is illustrated in Fig. 11.9.

Thus the region in k-space that the electrons can occupy without being diffracted is called the first Brillouin zone. When $k < \pi/a$, the electrons can move freely in any direction inside the square without being diffracted. However, when $k = \pi/a$, they are prevented from moving in the x or y directions due to diffraction. The more k exeeds $\pi/a$, the more limited the possible direction of motion, until when $k = \pi/a \sin 45° = \sqrt{2}\pi/a$, the electrons are diffracted even when they move diagonally (at 45° with $k_x$ and $k_y$ axes) inside the square. It is here the first zone ends and the second zone begins.

For the second zone, both the integers ($n_1$ and $n_2$) in eq. 41 are equal to ±1. Therefore the equations for the second zone boundaries are:

$$n_1 = +1,\ n_2 = +1 \text{ giving } k_x + k_y = \frac{2\pi}{a}$$

$$n_1 = -1,\ n_2 = +1 \text{ giving } -k_x + k_y = \frac{2\pi}{a}$$

$$n_1 = +1,\ n_2 = -1 \text{ giving } k_x - k_y = \frac{2\pi}{a}$$

$$n_1 = -1,\ n_2 = -1 \text{ giving } -k_x - k_y = \frac{2\pi}{a}$$

The above four equations describe a set of four lines at 45° to the $k_x$ and $k_y$ axes passing through E, F, G and H as shown in Fig. 11.9. Similarly, the third zone is defined by giving $n_1$ and $n_2$ the values such as 0, ±1, and ±2.

The second Brillouin zone contains electrons with k values from $\pi/a$ (that do not fit into the first zone) to $2\pi/a$, or the region between the square ABCD and EFGH as shown in Fig. 11.9.

### In Three Dimensions

Similar to the two dimensional case, the form of the Brillouin zones in three dimensions can be easily evaluated using the equation

$$n_1 k_x + n_2 k_y + n_3 k_z = \frac{\pi}{a}(n_1^2 + n_2^2 + n_3^2) \tag{42}$$

It follows from this equation that the first zone for a simple cubic lattice is a cube whose walls intersect the $k_x$, $k_y$ and $k_z$ axes at the points $\pm\pi/a$ as shown in Fig. 11.10a. The second zone is obtained by adding a pyramid (like a triangle in two dimensions in Fig. 11.9) to each face of the first zone as shown in the first figure of second row of Fig. 11.10.

In a similar but more complicated manner, the first and the second Brillouin zones for bcc; fcc and hcp can be determined by using eq. 42. They are also shown in the second row of Fig. 11.10. The equations which define the boundaries of these zones are all based on the Bragg equation for the reflection of waves by a periodic lattice. Thus, the Brillouin zones in metals, for example, are polyhedra whose plane surfaces are parallel to the reflecting planes which are responsible for X-ray diffraction.

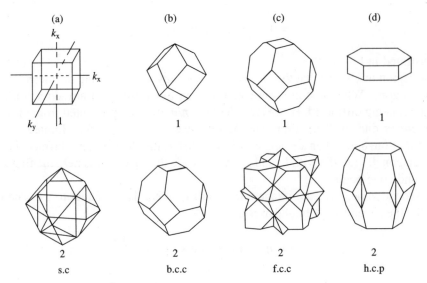

**Fig. 11.10    The first and second Brilliouin zones for some simple lattices**

*Example*: Find the ratio between the kinetic energies of an electron in a two dimensional square lattice (a) when $k_x = k_y = \pi/a$ and (b) when $k_x = \pi/a$ and $k_y = 0$.

*Solution*: Given: Case I: $k_x = k_y = \pi/a$ and case II: $k_x = \pi/a$ and $k_y = 0$. We know that the energy of an electron inside a BZ is given by

$$E = \frac{h^2}{8\pi^2 m} k^2$$

For case I, the energy becomes

$$E_1 = \frac{h^2}{8\pi^2 m} (k_x^2 + k_y^2) = \frac{h^2}{8\pi^2 m} \times \frac{2\pi^2}{a^2} = \frac{h^2}{4a^2 m}$$

Similarly, for case II

$$E_2 = \frac{h^2}{8\pi^2 m} \frac{\pi^2}{a^2} = \frac{h^2}{8a^2 m}$$

This gives

$$\frac{E_1}{E_2} = 2$$

## 11.4   SYMMETRY PROPERTIES OF THE ENERGY FUNCTION

Based on the earlier discussions and from chapter 12 it can be shown that each energy band $E_n(k)$ satisfies the following symmetry properties:

### (i) Translational Symmetry: $E_n(k + G) = E_n(k)$
This indicates that $E_n(k)$ is periodic, with a period equal to the reciprocal lattice vector $(G = 2\pi/a)$.

In other words, any two points in k-space related to each other by a displacement equal to a reciprocal lattice vector, have the same energy. let us take the case of $E$ versus $k$ for a square lattice as shown in Fig. 11.11a. The points $P_1$, $P_2$ and $P_3$ will have the same energy, because $P_2$ is related to $P_1$ by a translation equal to $-G_2$ and $P_3$ is related to $P_1$ by a translation $-G_1$, where $-G_1$ and $-G_2$ are reciprocal lattice vectors.

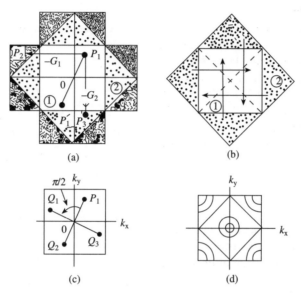

Fig. 11.11 (a) **The translational symmetry of the energy $E(k)$ in $k$-space for a square lattice. (b) Mapping of the second zone into the first zone. (c) The rotational symmetry of the energy $E(k)$ in $k$-space for a square lattice**

Making use of this translational symmetry, if we translate four pieces of the second zone in backward directions by the respective lattice vectors, it can be shown that the pieces just fit into the first zone as illustrated in Fig. 11.11b. This means that the first and the second zones are equivalent. The same is valid for higher-order zones. Hence, the first zone contains all necessary information of higher zones.

**(ii)   Inversion Symmetry: $E_n (-k) = E_n(k)$**
This shows that the band is symmetric with respect to the inversion around the origin $k = 0$. Accordingly, in Fig. 11.11a, energy at the point $P_1'$ is equal to that at $P_1$.

**(iii)   Rotational Symmetry**
The energy band $E_n(k)$ has the same rotational symmetry as that of a real lattice. Thus, for a square lattice a rotation of $\pi/2$ will give rise to four equivalent energy positions. Accordingly, the value of energy at points $Q_1$, $Q_2$ and $Q_3$ should be the same as that of $P_1$ as shown in Fig. 11.11c.

## 11.5   EXTENDED, REDUCED AND PERIODIC ZONE SCHEME

The wave vector representation of a plane wave eigenstate is simple and unambiguous while the representation of Bloch states are not so because the Bloch function is not a simple plane wave but a modulated plane wave. To represent such states, three different schemes are commonly used. They are called the extended zone scheme (or the Brillouin zone scheme), the reduced zone scheme and the periodic zone scheme (or the repeated zone scheme). All the three schemes represent the identical physical behaviour and any of these can be used for convenience.

### Extended Zone Scheme

Let us consider a one dimensional lattice in which the energy of an electron is being slowly increased so that the value of $k$ is also increased. When the value of $k$ becomes large enough, the wavelength becomes small enough as $k = 2\pi/\lambda$, the electron will suffer a Bragg reflection following the Bragg's condition $2d \sin\theta = n\lambda$. For a one dimensional lattice, $d = a$ (the spacing between the atoms), so that the Bragg reflections will occur at

$$k = \frac{n\pi}{a}, \text{ where } n = \pm 1, \pm 2, \ldots$$

As a result of these reflections, energy gaps are developed in the free electron parabola as shown in Fig. 11.12. This representation of energy as a function of $k$ is known as extended zone scheme. Physically, this scheme is very close to the free electron scheme and differ only at the zone boundaries. However, like free electon case, the $k$-space is infinite in the extended zone scheme but is dissected by the planes of energy discountinuity into segments called Brillouin zones. The first BZ is that part of the $k$-space which is located in the neighbourhood of the origin and is bounded by the first set of planes. Similarly, the $n$th zone is reached after crossing $(n-1)$ such planes and is bounded by the $n$th planes, where the $n$th zone is represented by composite segments of $k$-space between $(n-1)$th planes and the $n$th planes. The extended zone scheme represents various Brillouin zones in $k$-space.

### Reduced Zone Scheme

In eq. 3, it is observed that the wave vector $k$ is not uniquely defined since we may write the same as

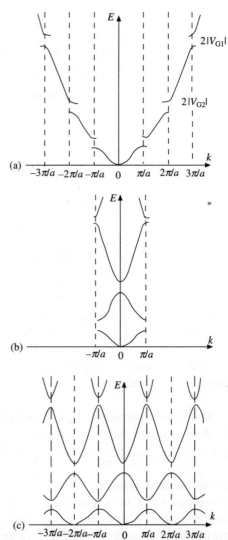

**Fig. 11.12  Energy as a function of wave vector for a one dimensional lattice in (a) extended, (b) reduced, (c) periodic zone scheme**

$$u_k(x) \exp(ikx) = \exp\left[i\left(k + \frac{2\pi n}{a}\right)x\right] \exp\left(-\frac{2\pi inx}{a}\right)u_k(x) \tag{43}$$

where $n$ is an integer. The second exponential on the right hand side of eq. 43, $\exp(-2\pi inx/a) = \exp(ingx)$ contains the necessary lattice periodicity. It is therefore possible to restrict the value of $k$ to an interval of length $2\pi/a$ without loss of information.

For simplicity, let us start with a free electron case. We know that an ordinary free electron wave is given by

$$\psi_k(x) = \exp(ikx) \tag{44}$$

and the corresponding energy expression is

$$E(k) = \frac{h^2 k^2}{8\pi^2 m} \tag{45}$$

A plot between $E$ versus $k$ gives a famous free electron parabola as shown in Fig. 11.13a. Let us now write eq. 44 as

$$\psi_k(x) = \exp(ikx) = \expi(k + g) \exp(-igx)$$

$$= \exp(ik'x) \exp(-igx) \tag{46}$$

where $k'$ $(= k + g)$ is the reduced value of the original wave vector $k$. Since, the second term on the right hand side of eq. 46 is periodic function in the lattice, this has the form of eq. 3. But it is extremely artificial representation of a plane wave. Actually, it is the limiting case of a vanishingly small periodic potential. Under this assumpsion, one must take into account the symmetry requirement of the periodicity. The general demand of the pereodicity implies that the possible electron states are not restricted to a single parabola in $k$-space, but can be found equally well on parabolas shifted by a vector $g = 2\pi/a$ (Fig. 11.13b). The energy expression in the reduced zone scheme becomes

$$E(k') = E(k + g) = \frac{h^2}{8\pi^2 m}\left(k + \frac{2\pi n}{a}\right)^2 \tag{47}$$

where $n = 0, \pm1, \pm2, ....$

Since, the behaviour of $E(k)$ is periodic in $k$-space and hence follows the symmetry properties, it is sufficient to represent this in the first zone only. In order to achieve this, let us displace the part of the parabola of interest linearly by the appropriate multiple of $g = 2n\pi/a$ as shown by arrows in Fig. 11.13b. The $E$ versus $k$ curves for several values of $n$ reduced into the first zone for a simple cubic lattice with vanishing potential are shown in Fig. 11.13c. Each value of $n$ defines a Brillouin zone in the reduced zone scheme representation.

Let us consider the Bloch function give by eq. 3 and try to choose $k$ such that $u_k(x)$ is as constant as possible and the electron wave function for a given $k$ look as much as possible like a free electron wave. Therefore, writing eq. 43 in vector notation, we have

$$\psi_k(x) = u_k(x) \exp(ikx) = \exp i (k + g)x [\exp(-igx) u_k(x)] = \exp(ik'x)u'_k(x) \tag{48}$$

where $k' = k + g$, and $g$ is some geometrical reciprocal lattice vector. The new function $u'_k(x)$

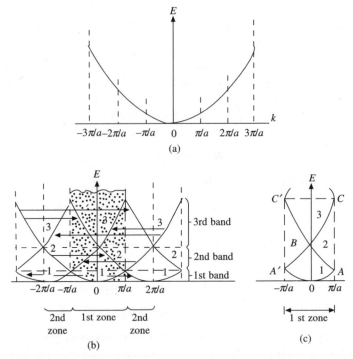

**Fig. 11.13 (a)**  Energy as a function of wave vector for a free electron (b) Dispersion curve with the translational symmetry and the various bands (c) The same disperson curve in the first zone only

has the same periodicity as $u_k(x)$, so that $k'$ is as good a wave vector as the original vector k. Although every electron state is characterized by a wave vector, but it is not unique. They differ from one another by a reciprocal lattice vector. This nonuniqueness allows us to bring all wave vectors into the first Brillouin zone following above discussed procedure. Thus, the Fig. 11.13b showing the dispersion curve in the extended zone scheme is transferred into the reduced zone using suitable translational symmetry. This is shown in Fig. 11.13c.

**Periodic Zone Scheme**

In the preceding section, we obtained the E versus k plot in reduced zone scheme by translating the desired portion of the neighbouring parabolas into the first zone as the energies obey translational symmetry. A reverse process is equally probable. Accordingly, we can translate the desired portion of the first zone to any or every other zone, we can obtain a periodically repeated zone as shown in Fig. 11.12c. This construction is known as periodic or repeated zone scheme. This representation leads us to a very important result that the electrons in a crystal behave like free electrons for most of the k values except when k approaches $n\pi/a$.

## 11.6   EFFECTIVE MASS OF AN ELECTRON

As we know that the free electron energy in terms of $k$ is given by

$$E = \frac{h^2 k^2}{8\pi^2 m}$$

where $m$ is the mass of the electron. Differentiating this expression, we get

$$\frac{dE}{dk} = \frac{h^2 k}{4\pi^2 m} \quad \text{and} \quad \frac{d^2 E}{dk^2} = \frac{h^2}{4\pi^2 m} \tag{49}$$

so that

$$m = \frac{h^2}{4\pi^2} \left( \frac{d^2 E}{dk^2} \right)^{-1} \tag{50}$$

For a free electron model, where $E$ versus $k$ has a parabolic relationship. As the mass of the electron is considered to be constant therefore $d^2E/dk^2$ can also be taken as constant (eq. 49). However, when the electrons move in a periodic potential of the crystal lattice the parabolic relationship between $E$ and $k$ no longer exists. There is a breakup in the curve at various zone boundaries leading to the origin of allowed and forbidden bands. Near the forbidden band, the curvature of $E$ versus $k$ curve changes, and can become negative (since as $k$ approaches the zone boundary $d^2E/dk^2$ first reduces to zero and then becomes negative). Therefore, $d^2E/dk^2$ is no longer a constant as also the mass of the electron, actually both of them are a function of $k$. Thus, under periodic potential, the mass of the electron given by eq. 50 is known as effective mass and is represented by the symbol $m^*$. So that

$$m^* = \frac{h^2}{4\pi^2} \left( \frac{d^2 E}{dk^2} \right)^{-1} \tag{51}$$

The effective mass is a new concept and arises because of the interaction of the electron wave packet with the periodic lattice. If the interaction between them is very large or in other words if there is a strong binding force between the electron and the lattice, it will be difficult for the electrons to move, meaning thereby that the electron has acquired a large (or even infinite) effective mass. To explain a negative effective mass, let us suppose that there is an electron with $k$ value just less than $\pi/a$ at the boundary. It will manage to move through the crystal. But then suppose that a field is applied which should accelerate it and increase $k$. As the electron responds to the field, it will meet the condition for Bragg reflection and will be scattered back in the opposite direction. In this way, it will behave like a particle with a negative charge and negative mass(strictly speaking the situation in a real crystal is more complicated than this). A force applied in one direction may cause acceleration in other not necessarily just the opposite direction. The effective mass of an electron may be positive or negative and is shown in Fig. 11.14 by plotting a curve between

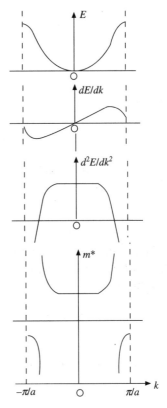

**Fig. 11.14** **The effective mass, energy and the first and the second derivatives of energy as a function of $k$**

$m^*$ and $k$ in the first Brillouin zone for one-dimensional lattice. It is clear that the effective mass is positive in the lower part of the band (lower $k$ value) and negative close to the zone boundary (near $k \sim \pi/a$). The figure also shows the curves $E$ versus $k$, $dE/dk$ versus $k$ and $d^2E/dk^2$ versus $k$ in qualitative form.

The effective mass $m^*$ may be equal to $m(m^* = m)$ only when the energy is not near the edge of a band and $E$ versus $k$ curve is parabolic (i.e. only under the free electron approximation). In most conductors, $m^* = m$ as the band is only partially filled. In semiconductors, insulators, and certain conductors (e.g. bismuth) where full or almost full valence bands are involved, the effective mass differs from $m$.

## 11.7  THE NEARLY FREE ELECTRON MODEL

In this model, the crystal potential is assumed to be very weak as compared to the electron kinetic energy so that the electrons behave essentially like free particles. The weak periodic potential introduces only a small amount of perturbing effect on the free electrons in the solid. Therefore, this model demands the application of very elementary perturbation theory. For simplicity, only the one dimensional case is discussed. It is convenient to choose the zero of energy so that the mean value of the potential function is zero, i.e.

$$\int_0^a V(x)dx = 0 \tag{52}$$

where $a$ is the periodicity of the lattice. The unperturbed wave functions corresponding to $V = 0$ are the plane waves

$$\phi_k(x) = \frac{1}{\sqrt{Na}} \exp(ikx) \tag{53}$$

where the wave functions are normalized over a microcrystal containing $N$ atoms. The unperturbed electron energies are

$$E^0(k) = \frac{h^2 k^2}{8\pi^2 m} \tag{54}$$

This is free electron case where $k$ can take any value. Now suppose, we take into account the periodicity of the lattice keeping $V = 0$ and restricting $k$ to lie in the first Brillouin zone only. Then, we have

$$\psi_k(x) = \frac{1}{\sqrt{Na}} \exp(ik'x)$$

where $k' = k + g = k + n\dfrac{2\pi}{a}$, and

$$E^0(k') = \frac{h^2}{8\pi^2 m}\left(k + n\frac{2\pi}{a}\right)^2 \tag{55}$$

where $k \le \dfrac{\pi}{a}$ and $n = 0, \pm 1, \pm 2, \ldots$.

As we introduce the periodic potential, the real wave function becomes

$$\psi_k(x) = \phi_k(x) + \sum_{k' \neq k} A_{k'}(k) \phi_{k'} \tag{56}$$

where $A_{k'}(k)$ are constants and are found to be small from perturbation theory. Their values corrected to first order are given by

$$A_{k'}(k) = \frac{<k'|V|k>}{E^0(k) - E^0(k')} \tag{57}$$

where

$$< k'|V| k > = \int \phi_k^* V \phi_k dx \tag{58}$$

The perturbed energy, corrected to second order is

$$E(k) = E^0(k) + \sum_{k'} \frac{|<k'|V|k>|^2}{E^0(k) - E^0(k')} \tag{59}$$

Because of eq. 52, the first order term is zero.

Now, let us take into account the real periodic potential which may have the same periodicity as that of the lattice. In terms of the Fourier series, it can be expressed as

$$V(x) = \sum_{n \neq 0} V_n \exp(-igx) \text{ and } V_n^* = V_{-n}$$

Then the integral 58 becomes

$$< k' |V| k > = V_n \quad \text{if } k - k' = n\frac{2\pi}{a}$$

$$= 0 \text{ otherwise} \tag{60}$$

Consequently, the wave function becomes

$$\psi_k(x) = \exp(ikx) \left( \frac{1}{\sqrt{Na}} \sum_{n=0} A_n(k) \exp(-igx) \right) \tag{61}$$

with $A_0 = 1$ and $A_n = \dfrac{V_n}{E^0(k) - E^0\left(k - n\dfrac{2\pi}{a}\right)}$ where $n \neq 0$

The perturbed energy is

$$E(k) = E^0(k) + \sum_{n \neq 0} \frac{|V_n|^2}{E^0(k) - E^0\left(k - n\dfrac{2\pi}{a}\right)} \tag{62}$$

The energy is either decreased or increased slightly with respect to $E^0(k)$ depending on the difference $E^0(k) - E^0(k')$, which is given by

$$E^0(k) - E^0(k') = \frac{h^2}{8\pi^2 m} [k^2 - (k + g)^2]$$

$$= \frac{h^2}{8\pi^2 m} \left[ k^2 - \left( k + n\frac{2\pi}{a} \right)^2 \right] = \frac{h^2}{8\pi^2 m} \left( k + \frac{n\pi}{a} \right) \left( -\frac{2n\pi}{a} \right)$$

$$= -\frac{h^2 n}{2\pi m a} \left( k + \frac{n\pi}{a} \right) \tag{63}$$

At or near the zone boundary

$$k = -\frac{n\pi}{a} = -k' = -\frac{g}{2}$$

where $n$ is an integer. The perturbation theory therefore breaks down whenever the wave vector is an integral multiple of $\pm n\pi/a$ and the wave is reflected ($k = -k'$). Near a zone boundary, it is necessary to write

$$\psi_k(x) = A_0 \exp(ikx) + A_n \exp i(k + g)x \tag{64}$$

where $A_0$ and $A_n$ are constants. The eq. 64 means that one Fourier coefficient $V_n$ will be large near the boundary $k = \pm \pi/a$. Substituting eq. 64 in eq. 1, we obtain

$$[E^0(k) - E(k) + V_n(x)]A_0 \exp(ikx) + [E^0(k + g) - E(k) + V(x)]A_n \exp i (k + g)x = 0 \tag{65}$$

If we multiply eq. 65 either by $\exp(ikx)$ or by $\exp[-i(k + g)x]$ and integrate, we obtain the following simultaneous equations, i.e.

$$[E^0(k) - E(k)]A_0 + V_n A_n = 0$$

$$V_n^* A_0 + [E^0(k + g) - E(k)]A_n = 0 \tag{66}$$

For a non-trivial solution, the determinant of coefficients must vanish. The resulting quadratic equation has two solutions

$$2E(k) = [E^0(k + g)] \pm [\{E^0(k) - E^0(k + g)\}^2 + 4|V_n|^2]^{1/2} \tag{67}$$

At the zone boundary, $k = \pm n\pi/a$ and $E^0(k) = E^0(k + g)$. Therefore, the two energies are

$$E^+ \left( \frac{n\pi}{a} \right) = E^0 \left( \frac{n\pi}{a} \right) + |V_n|$$

$$E^- \left( \frac{n\pi}{a} \right) = E^0 \left( \frac{n\pi}{a} \right) - |V_n|$$

Thus, the energy gap at the first zone boundary ($n = 1$) is

$$\Delta E = E^+ - E^- = 2V$$

Fig. 11.15 shows the energy gap at the first and the second zone boundaries in extended and reduced zone schemes. Also, in this case, $|A_n/A_0| = 1$, so that at $k = \pm \pi/a$ the wave function is a

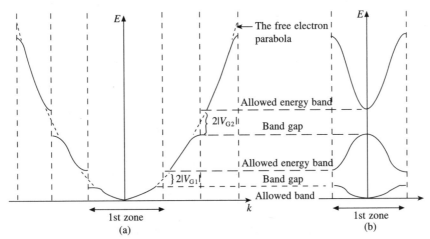

**Fig. 11.15** **Energy band in the NFE model, (a) the extended zone scheme, (b) the reduced zone scheme**

superposition of two plane waves traveling in opposite directions and thus represents a standing wave.

Near $k = 0$, the difference in the unperturbed energies is so large that the perturbation effect is negligible and hence there is no effect on the curve in this region.

When $E^0(k) - E^0(k + g) >> V_n$, then $E(k) \cong E^0(k)$ or $E^0(k + g)$, i.e. away from Bragg reflection, the energy values are practically plane waves, the same as that of the free electrons.

## 11.8 TIGHT BINDING APPROXIMATION

It is another extreme view point to see the electrons in a periodic potential. In the NFE case, we observed that the electron wave functions outside the ion core look very nearly as plane waves. However, near the ion cores they look like atomic orbitals. This suggests an entirely different scheme for the construction of wave functions. In 1928 , Bloch suggested that the crystal wave function with the correct symmetry could be constructed from the linear combination of atomic orbitals (LCAO).

Let us start from an electron in a free atom and then suppose that a number of such atoms are brought together to form a crystal. For simplicity, a two dimensional arrangement of atoms on a square lattice is shown in Fig. 11.16. Let $r$ and $R_n$ be the position vector of the electron (at $p$) and $n$th atom in the crystal. The potential of an electron in a free atoms is $V(r - R_n)$ and that in a crystal is $V(r)$. In Fig. 11.17, they are represented by dashed and the solid curves, respectively. In tight binding approximation, it is assumed that the electron wave function is influenced by the nearest atom and is unaffected by other atoms of the lattice. The wave function of an electron for a free atom is then

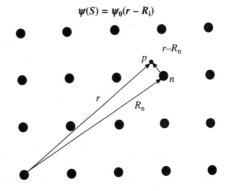

**Fig. 11.16** **An atom in the tight binding approach**

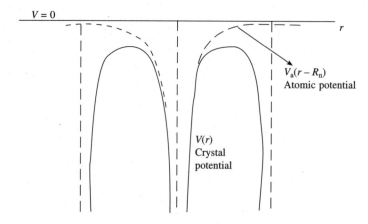

**Fig. 11.17   Atomic and crystal potentials**

approximated as $\psi\,(r - R_n)$, so that, in general, the crystal wave function may be written as a linear combination of the form

$$\psi_k(r) = \sum_n \exp(ik\cdot R_n)\psi_0\,(r - R_n) \tag{68}$$

The summation in eq. 68 is over all atoms of the crystal, which for simiplicity we assume is infinite. Since, we have considered that the electrons are in a periodic potential, $\psi_k(r)$ must be a Bloch function because it can be shown that

$$\psi_k(r + R_m) = \sum_n \exp(ik\cdot R_n)\psi_0\,(r - R_n + R_m)$$

$$= \exp(ik\cdot R_m) \sum_n \exp[ik\cdot(R_n - R_m)]\psi_0\,[r - (R_n - R_m)]$$

$$= \exp(ik\cdot R_m)\,\psi_k(r) \tag{69}$$

This shows that the Bloch condition (eq. 3) is satisfied. $\psi_k(r)$ given by eq. 68 is a solution of the Schrodinger equation for the whole crystal:

$$H\psi_k(r) = E\psi_k(r) \tag{70}$$

The crystal Hamiltonian $H$ may be written as the sum of the Hamiltonian for a free atom

$$H = H_0 + H_1 \tag{71}$$

with

$$H_0 = -\frac{h^2}{8\pi^2 m}\,\nabla^2 + V_0\,(r - R_n) \tag{72}$$

and

$$H_1 = V(r) - V_0(r - R_n) \tag{73}$$

where $V_0(r - R_n)$ is the potential due to $n$th ground state atom on the electron at $r$. The energy of the electron in the crystal $E(k)$ can be found by evaluating

$$E(k) = \frac{\int \psi_k^*(r)[H_0 + H_1]\psi_k(r)dr}{\int \psi_k^*(r)\psi_k(r)dr} \tag{74}$$

where the denominator

$$\int \psi_k^*(r)\psi_k(r)dr = \sum_m \sum_n \exp[ik\cdot(R_n - R_m)]\int \psi_k^*(r - R_m)\psi_0(r - R_n)$$

Neglecting the overlap of electron wave functions between the neighbouring atoms such that

$$\int \psi_0^*(r - R_m)\psi_0(r - R_n)dr = \delta_{nm} \tag{75}$$

and

$$\int \psi_k^*(r)\psi_k(r)dr = N \tag{76}$$

where $N$ is the total number of electrons (atoms) in the crystal. Therefore, eq. 74 becomes

$$E(k) = \frac{1}{N}\int \psi_k^*(r)[H_0 + H_1]\psi_k(r)dr$$

$$= \frac{1}{N}\int \psi_k^*(r)\left(-\frac{h^2}{8\pi^2 m}\nabla^2 + V_0(r - R_n)\right)\psi_k(r)dr$$

$$+ \frac{1}{N}\int \psi_k^*(r)[V(r) - V_0(r - R_n)]\psi_k(r)dr$$

$$= \frac{E_0}{N}\int \psi_k^*(r)\psi_k(r)dr + \frac{1}{N}\sum_m \sum_n \exp[ik\cdot(R_n - R_m)]\int \psi_k^*(r - R_m) \times$$

$$[V(r) - V_0(r - R_n)]\,\psi_0(r - R_n)]\,dr$$

$$= E_0 + \frac{1}{N}\sum_m \sum_n \exp[ik\cdot(R_n - R_m)]\int \psi_k^*(r - R_m) \times$$

$$[V(r) - V_0(r - R_n)]\,\psi_0(r - R_n)]\,dr \tag{77}$$

Here, we expect that every term in the summation from $n = 0$ to $n = N - 1$ to contain $N$ identical terms, which may be evaluated most easily by substituting $n = 0$. Hence, eq. 77 reduces to

$$E(k) = E_0 + \sum_m \exp(-ik\cdot R_m)\int \psi_0^*(r - R_m)\,[V(r) - V_0(r)]\,\psi_0(r)\,dr \tag{78}$$

Further, if we make an approximation that $\psi_0$ is spherically symmetric (i.e. to consider alkali metals for which the ground electronic state is an $s$-state) so that the contributions due to all nearest neighbours may be assumed to be identical. For $m = 0$, the integral in eq. 78 gives

$$\int \psi_0^*(r) \, [V(r) - V_0(r)] \, \psi_0(r) \, dr = -\alpha \tag{79}$$

and for the nearest neighbour atoms

$$\int \psi_0^*(r) \, [V(r) - V_0(r)] \, \psi_0(r) \, dr = -\beta \tag{80}$$

where $\alpha$ and $\beta$ are constants and are known as overlap integrals. Since $V(r) - V_0(r)$ is negative therefore $\alpha$ and $\beta$ are positive. Consequently, the eq. 78 can be written in a simplified form as

$$E(k) = E_0 - \alpha - \beta \sum_m \exp(-ik \cdot R_m) \tag{81}$$

where the summation is to be carried out over the nearest neighbours only. It is observed that the eq. 81 consists of a constant term $E_0 - \alpha$ together with the term dependent on $k$. It is the latter term which transforms the discrete atomic levels into the energy bands in the solid.

In order to demonstrate the application of the above method, let us take the case of a simple cubic crystal and consider only the nearest neighbout interaction. For an atom which is taken as the origin, there are six nearest neighbours whose lattice vectors are:

$$R_m = (\pm a, 0, 0), \, (0, \pm a, 0), \, (0, 0, \pm a) \tag{82}$$

Substituting this in eq. 81, we obtain

$$E(k) = E_0 - \alpha - 2\beta \, (\cos k_x \, a + \cos k_y \, a + \cos k_z \, a) \tag{83}$$

For small value of $k$, we may expand the cosines and retaining upto the second term, eq. 83 becomes

$$E(k) = E_0 - \alpha - 2\beta \left[ \left( 1 - \frac{k_x^2 a^2}{2} \right) + \left( 1 - \frac{k_y^2 a^2}{2} \right) + \left( 1 - \frac{k_z^2 a^2}{2} \right) \right]$$

$$= E_0 - \alpha - 6\beta + \beta a^2 \left( k_x^2 + k_y^2 + k_z^2 \right) \tag{84}$$

Since, the last term on the right hand side of eq. 83 is periodic and hence $E(k)$ is also periodic with the periodicity $2\pi/a$. Thus, the first Brillouin zone is defined as $-\pi/a \le k \le \pi/a$. The resulting Brillouin zone is a cube. Further, along a cube axis, the energy is minimum at $k_x = k_y = k_z = 0$. Thus, the bottom of the band is given by

$$E(k)_{min} = E(k)_{bottom} = E_0 - \alpha - 6\beta. \tag{85}$$

Similarly, the energy is maximum at $k_x = k_y = k_z = \pm\pi/a$, and hence the top of the energy band will be given by

$$E(k)_{max} = E(k)_{top} = E_0 - \alpha + 6\beta \tag{86}$$

The constant energy surfaces near the bottom and top of the band for simple cubic are shown in Fig. 11.18. The width of the energy band is

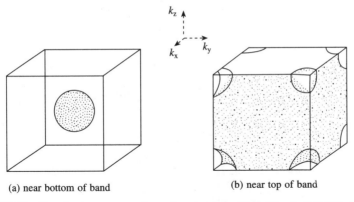

(a) near bottom of band          (b) near top of band

**Fig. 11.18   Constant energy surfaces for simple cubic lattice in tight binding model**

$$E(k)_{\text{top}} - E(k)_{\text{bottom}} = 12\beta \qquad (87)$$

The two dimensional view of the energy contours for simple cubic case for tight binding and free electron model are shown in Fig. 11.19. In tight binding model, the Brillouin zone of a simple

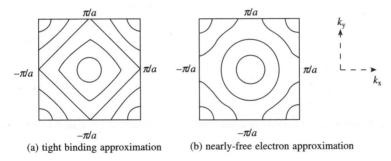

(a) tight binding approximation          (b) nearly-free electron approximation

**Fig. 11.19 Electron energy contours for simple cubic lattice**

cubic lattice and the $E$ versus $k$ curve along a cube axis are shown in Fig. 11.20. Further, from eq. 80, it follows that the energy width of the band becomes greater as the overlap of the wave functions on the neighbouring atoms increases. Thus, the inner electronic levels of the free atoms give rise to narrow bands in the solids and increase as we proceed to the outer levels.

## 11.9   ORTHOGONALIZED PLANE WAVE (OPW) METHOD

After noticing some inadequacies in the NFE and the tight binding models, in 1940 Herring introduced the orthogonalized plane wave (OPW) method for energy band calculation.

In the OPW method, it is necessary to make a clear cut distinction between the core state and the valence state. For example, in aluminium the core states are associated with $1s^2\ 2s^2\ 2p^6$ atomic shells, while valence states are associated with $3s^2\ 3p$ shells. Further, the core wave functions rapidly oscillate and are highly localized about the lattice sites. On the other hand, the

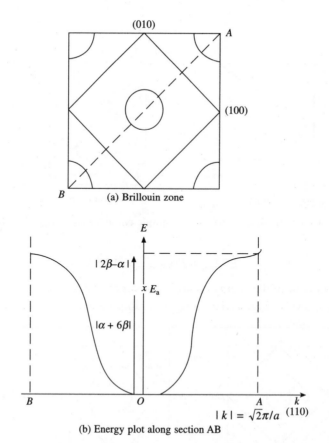

(a) Brillouin zone

(b) Energy plot along section AB

**Fig. 11.20 (a)    Brillouin zone (b) Energy as a function of $k$ along the cube diagonal of a simple cubic lattice**

valence wave functions are approximated as small number of plane waves in the interstitial regions as shown in Fig. 11.21. However, this approximation fails to produce the rapid oscillatory behaviour required in the core region. In order to overcome this problem, Herring used those plane waves which have been made orthogonal to the core states, instead of using simple plane waves. Accordingly, he defined the orthogonalized plane wave (OPW) $\phi_k$ by

$$\phi_k = \exp(ik \cdot r) + \sum_c B_c \psi_k^c(r) \tag{88}$$

where the summation is over all core states with Bloch wave vector $k$. A logical relation of the same is given by

$$\text{OPW} = \text{plane wave} - \text{core function.}$$

The constant $B_c$ in eq. 88 can be determined from orthogonality condition,

$$\int \psi_k^{c*}(r)\ \phi_k(r)\ dr = 0 \tag{89}$$

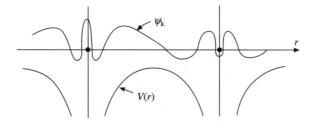

**Fig. 11.21** **The Bloch wave function oscillates rapidly near the atomic sites where the lattice potential is deep and attractive**

which implies that
$$B_c = - \int \psi_k^{c*}(r) \exp(ik \cdot r) \, dr \tag{90}$$

Since both the plane wave $\exp(ik \cdot r)$ and the core wave function $\psi_k^c(r)$ separately satisfy the Bloch condition with wave vector $k$, therefore the OPW $\phi_k$ will also satisfy it. We may therefore expand the Bloch function(i.e. the actual eigenstate of the Schrodinger wave equation) in terms of OPW's as a Fourier series:

$$\psi_k(r) = \sum_g a_g \, \phi_{k+g}(r)$$

or
$$|\psi_k\rangle = \sum_g a_g \, |\phi_{k+g}\rangle \tag{91}$$

Substituting eq. 91 into the Schrodinger equation

$$H\psi_k(r) \equiv (T + V) \, \psi_k(r) \equiv E \, \psi_k(r) \tag{92}$$

we obtain a secular equation

$$\sum_g a_g(T + V - E) \, |k + g\rangle - (T + V - E) \sum_{cl} |\psi_{cl}\rangle \langle \psi_{cl} \,|\, k + g\rangle = 0 \tag{93}$$

This is simplified further by taking into account that

$$(T + V) \, |\psi_{cl}\rangle = E_c| \, \psi_{cl}\rangle \tag{94}$$

where $E_c$ is an atomic energy eigenvalue of the appropriate core level and $\psi_{cl}$ is the core function centred at the lattice site $l$. Now, operating from the left of eq. 93 with $\langle \phi_{k+g}|$ and rearranging the terms, we obtain

$$\sum_g a_g\left[\left(\frac{h^2}{8\pi^2 m}(k + g)^2 - E\right)\langle\phi_{k+g'} |\, \phi_{k+g}\rangle + \langle k + g'|V_{eff}(r)|k + g\rangle\right] = 0 \tag{95}$$

where
$$\langle k + g'|V_{eff}(r)| \, k + g\rangle \equiv \langle k + g'|V| \, k + g\rangle + \sum_{cl} (E - E_c) \, \langle k + g'|\psi_{cl}\rangle\langle\psi_{cl}| \, k + g\rangle \tag{96}$$

defines a new effective weak potential, known as OPW pseudopotential. OPW method is one of the most widely used methods to describe electron in metals. Apart from visual physically, this method is relatively convenient. The OPW method is also the basis of pseudopotential method.

## 11.10   THE PSEUDOPOTENTIAL METHOD

The pseudopotential method is just an extension of the OPW method. Philips and Kleinman in 1959 noticed that the effective potential $V_{eff}(r)$ defined by eq. 95 is weaker than the true potential $V$ and called it the pseudopotential. They observed that the contribution from the first term on the right side of eq. 95 is negative, while the contribution from the second term is positive. Consequently, the two terms cancel each other and lead to a weak effective potential, $V_{eff}(r)$.

Physically, the cancellation between the true attractive potential and the repulsive orthogonalization term may be viewed as an elimination of rapid oscillations so that the valence electron appears to see only the weak pseudopotential. The true crystal potential, the true wave function, and their corresponding pseudo counterparts are as shown in Fig. 11.22. On the other hand, mathematically, the above cancellation may be viewed as a transformation of the true wave equation to a pseudo wave equation. Accordingly, let us write the true wave function for a valence state as a linear combination of OPW's as in eq. 91. Further, suppose that $\phi_k^v$ be the plane wave part of this expansion. Then, eq. 88 can be rewritten as:

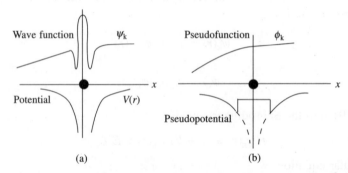

**Fig. 11.22   The pseudopotential concept (a) the actual potential and the corresponding wave function, as seen by electrons, (b) the corresponding pseudopotential and pseudofunction**

$$\phi_k^v (r) = \sum_g a_g \exp i(k + g)\cdot r$$

or
$$|\phi_k^v\rangle = \sum_g a_g |k + g\rangle \tag{97}$$

This defines the pseudo wave function as a linear combination of ordinary plane waves. Further, eq. 91 can be rewritten as

$$|\psi_k\rangle = (1 - P) |\phi_k^v\rangle \tag{98}$$

where $P = \sum_{cl} |k_{cl}\rangle\langle\psi_{cl}|$ and is known as projection operator. Substituting eq. 98 into 91, we obtain

$$(T + V)|\phi_k^v\rangle - (T + V)P|\phi_k^v\rangle + EP|\phi_k^v\rangle = E|\phi_k^v\rangle$$

or
$$\{T + V_{eff}(r)\} |\phi_k^v\rangle = E|\phi_k^v\rangle \tag{99}$$

Further, similar to eq. 94, we may define

$$(T + V)P = E_c P \tag{100}$$

With the help of these equations, we may define the pseudopotential according to the relation:

$$V_{eff}(r) = V(r) + \sum_{cl} (E - E_c) |\psi_{cl}\rangle\langle\psi_{cl}| \tag{101}$$

The cancellation between the two contributions in real space is now clear from the fact that the valence level E is generally higher than the core level $E_c$. Thus, the second term in eq. 101 is positive and the first term is negative. The smallness of the pseudopotential explains why the electrons in metals can (in many cases) be regarded as quasi-free particles. Because of the same reason, it is possible to use the perturbation theory to find out the energy eigen states. Free electron wave function may be used as a zero approximation.

## 11.11   CONDUCTORS, SEMICONDUCTORS AND INSULATORS

In sections 11.2 and 11.3, we discussed the origin of allowed and forbidden bands in solids, a result of electrons in periodic potential. Each allowed energy band was found to contain a limited number of energy levels. Further, in compliance with the Pauli's Exclusion Principle each energy level must be occupied by no more than two electrons. However, with a limited number of electrons in the atoms of a solid, it is expected that only the lower energy bands will be filled. The outermost energy band that is completely or partially filled is called the valence band in solids. the band that is above the valence band and that is empty at 0K, is called the conduction band. Hence, according to the nature of band occupation by electrons, all solids can be classified broadly into two groups.

The first group includes solids in which there is a partially filled band immediately above the uppermost filled (valence) band. This is possible in two ways. In the first case, the valence band is only partially filled as shown in Fig. 11.23a. In the second case, a completely filled valence band overlaps the partially filled conduction band as shown in Fig. 11.23b.

The second group includes solids with empty bands lying above completely filled bands. The solids of this group are conveniently subdivided into insulators (dielectrics) and semiconductors depending on the width of the forbidden band. Fig. 11.24 shows the difference between them in terms of the magnitude of the energy gap.

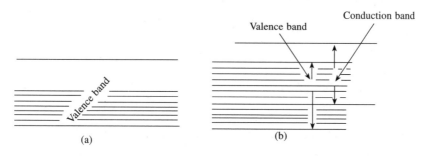

**Fig. 11.23   Metals have partially filled or overlapping bands**

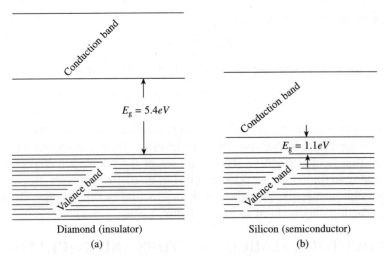

Diamond (insulator)
(a)

Silicon (semiconductor)
(b)

**Fig. 11.24    The difference between an insulator and a semiconductor in terms of energy gap**

Insulators include solids with relatively wide forbidden bands. For typical insulators the band gap $E_g > 3$ eV. Diamond with $E_g = 5.4$ eV, boron nitride with $E_g = 4.6$ eV, $Al_2O_3$ with $E_g = 7$ eV etc. are some typical examples of insulators.

On the other hand, semiconductors include solids with relatively narrow forbidden bands. For typical semiconductors $E_g \leq 1$ eV. Germanium with $E_g = 0.7$ eV, silicon with $E_g = 1$ eV, indium antimonide with $E_g = 0.17$ eV, gallium arsenide with $E_g = 1.43$ eV, etc. are some typical examples of semiconductors.

Monovalent metals such as Cu, Ag and Au have one electron in the outermost shell and hence the corresponding energy band is only half filled in these metals. On the other hand, the divalent metals such as Be, Mg, Ca, etc. have overlapping valence and conduction bands. The band structure of trivalent metals such as Al, Ga, etc. is similar to that of monovalent metals (the outermost band is only half filled in trivalent metals also). The tetravalent metals such as carbon (diamond), Si, etc. have even number (4 electrons in each case) of electrons in the outer shell like divalent metals. The corresponding valence band is full but unlike the divalent metals there is no overlapping of valence band with the conduction band in this case. However, as we go down the column from carbon to lead in this group of the periodic Table, the energy gap at room temperature (300 K) decreases in the order

| | |
|---|---|
| C (diamond) | 5.5 eV |
| Si | 1.12 eV |
| Ge | 0.67 eV |
| Sn (grey) | 0.1 eV |
| Pb | 0.0 eV |

As a result, diamond behaves like an insulator at usual temperature, metallic (grey) tin and lead as conductors and silicon and germanium as semiconductors.

# 11.12 SUMMARY

1. The wave function of an electron moving in a periodic potential, as in the case of a crystal, may be written in the Bloch form,

$$\psi_k(r) = \exp(ik \cdot r) \, u_k(r)$$

where the function $u_k(r)$ has the periodicity of the lattice.

2. Making use of the Bloch theorem and Kronig-Penney model, the energy spectrum of the electron is found to comprise a set of continuous bands, separated by the regions of forbidden energies which are called energy gaps.

3. Motion of electrons in a periodic potential such as Kronig-Penney type gives rise to an energy spectrum which consists of allowed and forbidden bands. This can be understood from the construction of Brillouin zones. The first BZ is defined as the region in $k$-space lying in the range

$$-\pi/a < k < \pi/a$$

4. The energy bands $E_n(k)$ satisfy the following symmetry properties:
   (i) Translational symmetry: $E_n(k + G) = E_n(k)$
   (ii) Inversion symmetry: $E_n(-k) = E_n(k)$
   (iii) Rotational symmetry: The energy band $E_n(k)$ has the same rotational symmetry as the real lattice.

5. The effective mass of a Bloch electron is a function of $k$ and is given by

$$m^* = \frac{h^2}{4\pi^2} \left( \frac{d^2 E}{dk^2} \right)^{-1}$$

The mass is positive near the bottom of the band, (for low $k$ values), where the curvature is positive. On the other hand, the mass is negative close to the zone boundary (near $k \sim \pi/a$), where the curvature is negative.

6. In the NFE model, the crystal potential is taken to be very weak. The solution of Schrodinger equation shows that the electron behaves essentially as a free particle except when $k$ is very close to or at $\pi/a$. At the zone boundary, the potential leads to the creation of energy gaps. The energy gap at the first zone boundary ($n = 1$) is

$$\Delta E = E^+ - E^- = 2V$$

7. In TB model, the crystal potential is taken to be strong. This also leads to the same general conclusions as the NFE model, i.e. the energy spectrum is composed of a set of continuous bands. The TB model shows that the width of the band increases and the mobility of the electron becomes greater as the overlap between the neighbouring atomic functions increases.

8. In OPW method, the wave function of an electron in the crystal lattice is regarded as a linear combination of a plane wave in the interstitial region and a rapidly oscillating wave in the ion core region. The logical relation is

$$\text{OPW} = \text{Plane wave} - \text{Core function}$$

9. The OPW method is the basis of pseudopotential method, which makes it possible to describe the motion of valence electrons in a metal. The smallness of the pseudopotential explains why the electrons in metal can in many cases be regarded as quasi-free particles.

10. Depending on the nature of band occupation by electrons and the forbidden gaps between them, solids are classified into conductors, semiconductors and insulators. Further, semiconductors are classified as intrinsic or extrinsic.

## 11.13  DEFINITIONS

*Conductor:* A substance or a body that offers a relatively small resistance to the passage of the current.

*Effective Mass:* The effective mass of conduction electron is determined by its response to an applied field. Due to quantum mechanical effect, the effective mass may be large, small, positive or negative.

*Insulator:* A material whose conductivity is very low at room temperature, usually less than $10^{-6}$ mho/m.

## REVIEW QUESTIONS AND PROBLEMS

1. (a) Prove the Bloch theorem and explain the reduced zone scheme.
   (b) Explain the significance of the effective mass of the electron.

2. Discuss the Kronig-Penney model for a linear lattice. How does it lead to the formation of energy bands in solids? What happens to the width of the allowed and forbidden bands with the change in the strength of the periodic potential.

3. Discuss the Kronig-Penney model for the motion of electrons in a periodic potential. Show from $(E - k)$ graph that the materials can be classified into coductors, insulators and semiconductors.

4. What are Brillouin zones? How are they related to the energy levels of an electron in a metal? Draw the Brillouin zones for a two-dimensional square lattice of side "$a$".

5. How does the zone theory explains the conducting or insulating behaviour of a metal? Discuss the problem of an electron moving in a periodic potential. Explain the occurrence of energy gap in a semiconductor.

6. How does the band theory of solids lead to the classification of solids into conductors, semiconductors and insulators?

7. Distinguish between reduced zone, extended zone, and periodic zone scheme of representing energy bands. Derive an expression for the effective mass of the electron in a crystal and explain the physical basis of it.

8. Describe the nearly free electron model for determining the electron energy bands in metal and show that the model leads to finite discontinuities in energy at the zone boundaries.

9. Using the tight binding approximation, show the formation of energy bands in a simple cubic crystal. Show from the calculations that for small values of $k$ electron will behave like a free particle.

10. Describe tight binding approximation, show the formation of energy states of an electron in a solid. How can this method be compared with the nearly free electron model in the case of a metal.

11. Describe orthogonalized plane wave (OPW) method for studying the band structure of solids. Show how this method justifies the success of nearly free electron model for metals.

12. Show that for a simple square lattice, the kinetic energy of a free electron at a corner of the first zone is higher than that of an electron at mid point of a side face of zone by a factor of 2.

13. If electrons are treated as distinguishable particles, at what temperature would they have an average energy of 5.5 eV (i.e. the Fermi energy of silver).

   *Ans.* $4.25 \times 10^4$ K.

14. The Fermi energy of copper is 7 eV. Calculate (a) The Fermi momentum of electron in copper, (b) the de Brogile wavelength of the electron and (c) the Fermi velocity.

   *Ans.* $14.28 \times 10^{-25}$ kg m, $4.64 \times 10^{-10}$ m, $2.00 \times 10^{-10}$ m/s

15. The fcc lattice has 12 neighbours at $a$ $(0, \pm 1, \pm 1)$, $a$ $(\pm 1, 0, \pm 1)$, $a$ $(\pm 1, \pm 1, 0)$. Use the tight binding method to show that the energy band constructed from an atomic $s$-state, upto nearest neighbours, is given by

$$E(k) = E_0 - \alpha - 4\beta(\cos k_y a \cos k_z a + \cos k_z a \cos k_x a + \cos k_x a \cos k_y a)$$

where $E_0$ is the free atom energy.

16. The bcc lattice has 8 nearest neighbours $(\pm a, \pm a, \pm a)$. Use the LCAO method to show that the energy band constructed from an atomic $s$-state, upto nearest neighbours, is given by

$$E(k) = E_0 - \alpha - 8\beta \cos k_x a \cos k_y a \cos k_z a$$

# Chapter 12

# The Fermi Surface

## 12.1 INTRODUCTION

The Fermi surface (FS) is defined as the surface of constant energy $E_F$ in $k$-space inside which all the states are occupied by the valence electrons, while all the states lying outside it are empty. Alternatively, it can be defined as the boundary between the filled and empty states (in $k$-space) in the ground state of the crystal. This definition is strictly valid only at absolute zero. However, as observed in section 10.7, the effect of temperature on the FS is very slight and the surface remains sharp even at room temperature or higher. The shape of the FS is determined by the geometry of the energy contours in a zone. For a free electron, the FS is a sphere of radius $k_F$ when it lies well within the first BZ. However, non-spherical and complicated shapes are observed when the FS and BZ are close to or touch one another under the effect of pseudopotential $V_{eff}(r)$. Hence, a study of the shape of the FS and its proximity ot the BZ is necessary for a better understanding of the intricate details of various properties of solids, such as heat capacity, Pauli's paramagnetism, electrical conductivity, etc.

## 12.2 FERMI SURFACE AND BRILLOUIN ZONES

In the preceding chapter, we discussed the method of constructing the Brillouin zones in one, two and three dimensions. In the present section, our aim is to construct the energy spectrum of electrons in $k$-space in the Brillouin zones and observe if any change is taking place in the shape of the FS near the zone boundary. As far as the electrons in the metals are concerned, it is immaterial whether they are Fermi gas or Fermi liquid, since both of them obey the Ferimi-Dirac statistics and each electron occupies a definite volume in $k$-space.

In order to demonstrate the effect of increasing the number of valence electrons on the shape of the FS in the Brillouin zones, let us gradually fill with the electrons the Brillouin zones obtained from a plane square lattice with a lattice parameter $a$. Figure 12.1 shows the evolution of the shape of constant energy curve (i.e. FS) as the number of electrons are gradually increased. The kinetic energy of a free electron in $k$-space is given by the parabolic equation

$$E(k) = \frac{\hbar^2 k^2}{2m} \tag{1}$$

The centre of the first BZ (where $k = 0$) is a minimum energy position, $E = 0$. This implies that for $k = 0$ all the states are empty inside the BZ. For small number of (valence) electrons, only the states lying near the bottom of the band (i.e. the centre of the first BZ) are filled and the occupied volume is a sphere (circles in two dimensions) of radius $k_F$ given by eq. 1. As the number of valence electrons are increased, more and more states are occupied and so the Fermi volume gradually expands. The FS begins to deform and loses its spherical shape near the zone boundary. The degree of distortion depends on (i) how near is the FS to the zone boundaries, and (ii) the magnitude of the effective pseudopotential.

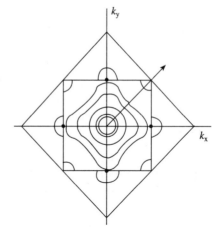

**Fig. 12.1** **The evolution of the shape of the FS as the concentration of valence electron increases**

## 12.3 HARRISON'S METHOD OF CONSTRUCTING FERMI SURFACES

### 1. Extended Zone Scheme

Harrison's method is based on a weak pseudopotential $V_{eff}(r)$. The effect of this potential is to introduce a small perturbation into the motion of free electrons in the whole $k$-space except the region near the zone boundaries. It is this potential which causes the energy discontinuities $\Delta E$ as well as distortions in the FS at the zone boundaries. Therefore, if $V_{eff}(r)$ is made arbitrarily low, the energy discontinuities and the distortions in the FS can be removed.

We shall begin with the assumption that $V_{eff}(r)$ is made arbitrarily low so that we can describe the Fermi sphere (circle in two dimensions) of any radius $k_F$ from the centre of the first Brillouin zone (i.e. a Fermi sphere consisting of any number of electrons) which will cross a whole number of zone boundaries without distortion. This representation is an example of extended zone scheme. Thus, using Harrison's method, let us construct Fermi surfaces for some simple lattices in two and three dimensions.

*Fermi Surfaces in Two Dimensions*—For simplicity, we consider a square lattice of lattice periodicity "$a$" to illustrate the construction of Fermi surfaces. The Brillouin Zones are constructed by following the procedure discussed in section 11.3. In order to know the size of the Harrison's (Fermi) circle, let us consider the following cases of increasing electron concentration.

*Monovalent Metal*—From section 11.3, we know that the area of a BZ corresponding to a square lattice of periodicity $a$ is given by

$$A = \frac{4\pi^2}{a^2} \tag{2}$$

Since, for a monovalent case only half the area of the BZ is occupied, therefore,

or
$$\pi k_F^2 = \frac{1}{2}\frac{4\pi^2}{a^2} \text{ or } k_F = \sqrt{\frac{2}{\pi}}\left(\frac{\pi}{a}\right) = 0.798\frac{\pi}{a} \tag{3}$$

where $\pi/a$ is the distance of the zone boundary from the centre of the zone, since the value of $k_F$ lies between $0 < k_F < \pi/a$. This indicates that the Fermi circle lies well within the first BZ as shown in Fig. 12.2. Hence, the FS remains undistorted.

*Divalent Metal*  For a divalent metal with the same type of the crystalline lattice as above, the area of the Fermi circle is

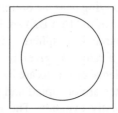

**Fig. 12.2   Free electron FS within the first BZ**

$$\pi k_F^2 = \frac{2}{2}\frac{4\pi^2}{a^2}$$

or
$$k_F = \frac{2}{\sqrt{\pi}}\left(\frac{\pi}{a}\right) = 1.228\frac{\pi}{a} \tag{4}$$

Further, the distance of a corner of the first zone from the centre is

$$\sqrt{2}\frac{\pi}{a} = 1.414\frac{\pi}{a} \tag{5}$$

From eqs. 4 and 5, we have

$$\frac{\pi}{a} < k_F < 1.414\frac{\pi}{a}$$

This implies that a circle of radius $k_F$ will go beyond the first zone boundary but will remain inside the corner of the first BZ as shown in Fig. 12.3a. In other words, it can be said that the

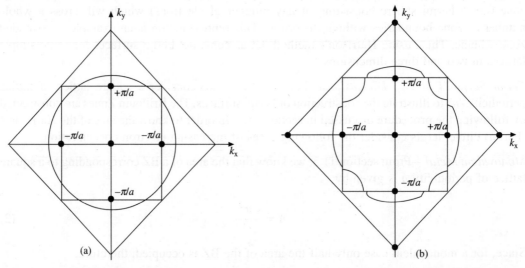

**Fig. 12.3   (a) FS partially on first and second brillouin zones. (b) Separate pieces of Hamison's circle at zone boundaries**

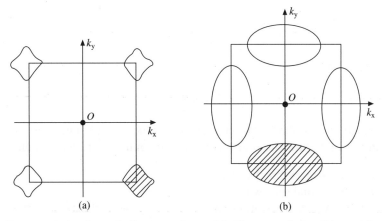

**Fig. 12.4** **Representation in periodic zone scheme (a) First zone holes, (b) second zone electrons**

first zone of the "metal" is not completely filled with electrons while the second zone is partially filled. Since the above Fermi circles are drawn with the assumption that $V_{eff}(r) = 0$. However, if we assume that $V_{eff}(r) \neq 0$ but small (i.e. a weak pseudopotential), then it will have the following effects:

 (i) energy discontinuities will appear at the zone boundaries
 (ii) constant energy curves will be a periodic function (in $k$-space) with a period $2\pi/a$ along the $k_x$ and $k_y$ axes.

As a result of energy discontinuities, Fermi circle breaks up into a number of separate "pieces" of constant energy curves at the zone boundaries as shown in Fig. 12.3b. If we translate these pieces through a distance of $2\pi/a$ along the $k_x$ and $k_y$ axes we can construct closed curves around the corners and the boundaries of the zone as shown in Fig. 12.4 in a periodic zone scheme. In the first case, the constnat energy curves (surfaces in three dimensions) surround empty areas (spaces in three dimensions) and are known as first zone holes while in the second case these curves which surround the areas filled with electrons are known as second zone electrons. For a trivalent metal, the radius of the Fermi circle is found to be

$$k_F = \sqrt{\frac{6}{\pi}} \left( \frac{\pi}{a} \right) = 1.38 \frac{\pi}{a} \tag{6}$$

Further, from eqs. 5 and 6, we have

$$\frac{\pi}{a} < k_F < 1.414 \frac{\pi}{a}$$

This indicates that the radius of the Fermi circle is still smaller than the distance of the corner of the first zone from the centre. Hence, the nature of the Fermi surface will be similar to the divalent case. However, the size of the first zone holes will be smaller and the second zone electrons will be larger for trivalent case.

*Tetravalent Metals*—For a tetravalent metal with the same type of crystalline lattice as monovalent case, the area of the Fermi circle will be given by

$$\pi k_F^2 = \frac{4}{2} \frac{4\pi^2}{a^2} \quad \text{or} \quad k_F = \sqrt{\frac{8}{\pi}} \left( \frac{\pi}{a} \right) = 1.596 \frac{\pi}{a} \tag{7}$$

Now comparing eqs. 5 and 7, we have

$$\frac{\pi}{a} < 1.414 \frac{\pi}{a} < k_F$$

This indicates that the Fermi circle for tetravalent case completely encloses the first BZ and passes through the second, third and fourth zones as shown in Fig. 12.5a. As considered before,

a weak pseudopotential causes breaks in the Fermi circle at the zone boundaries which are shown in Fig. 12.5b. Again translating the separate pieces of Fermi circle belonging to the same zone through a distance of $2\pi/a$, we can construct closed constant energy curves in various zones. Since the first BZ is completely filled, there are no constant energy curves in it (Fig. 12.6a). The constant energy curves in the second, third and fourth zones are shown in Fig. 12.6b, *c* and *d*, respectively. Here the second zone is represented in a reduced zone scheme while the third and fourth zones are represented in a periodic zone scheme. In a reduced zone scheme only one closed energy curve will correspond to each zone. Classifying as before, we have the second zone holes and third and fourth zone electrons.

Instead of translating the separate pieces of the FS as discussed above, we may also translate the various triangular parts of the second, third etc. zones (Fig. 12.7) into the first BZ by $2\pi/a$ in suitable directions to represent them in a reduced zone scheme, we observe that they completely fill the first BZ. The result of such translation for the first three Brillouin zones is shown in Fig. 12.8. This indicates that the first BZ is multivalued containing all possible straight lines (planes in three dimensions) on which energy goes discontinuous.

## II. Periodic Zone Scheme

Let us consider a plane in $k$-space which is completely filled with the first Brillouin zones (obtained from a square lattice of periodicity

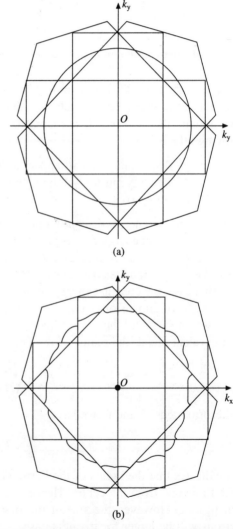

(a)

(b)

**Fig. 12.5** Extended zone scheme of a square lattice with Harrison's sphere for 4 electrons per unit cell

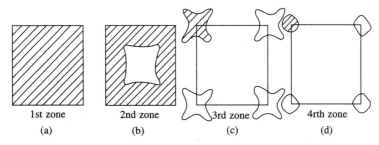

**Fig. 12.6** **Mapping of the 1st, 2nd, 3rd and 4rth Brillouin zones in the reduced zone scheme**

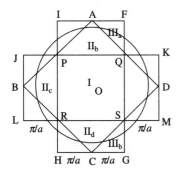

**Fig. 12.7** **Brillouin zones of a square lattice in two dimensions**

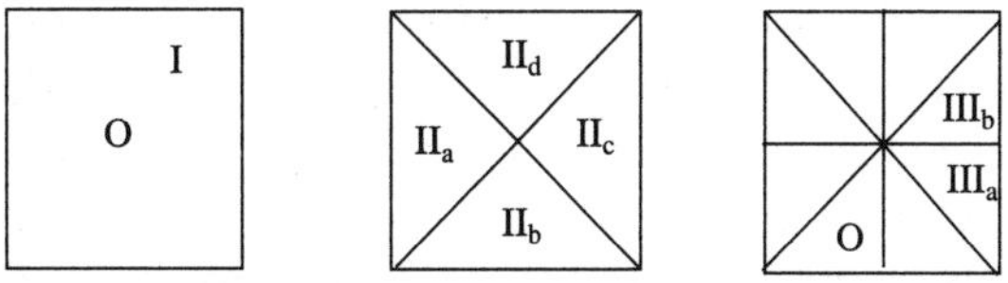

**Fig. 12.8** **Mapping of the 1st, 2nd, and 3rd Brillouin zones in the reduced zone scheme**

"$a$") represented in a periodic zone scheme. For example, let us take the case of a tetravalent metal and draw corresponding Fermi circles from the centres of each zone. They intersect each other and form closed constant energy curves which belong to second, third and fourth zones and marked as 2, 3, and 4, respectively as shown in Fig. 12.9. This construction gives us the similar pictures as constructed earlier in the extended zone scheme. An analysis of Fig. 12.9 reveals the following guidelines:

1. The regions bounded by concave lines (i.e. the lines of the negative curvature relative to the inner areas) and belonging simultaneously to $n$ or more circles, represent the zone holes in $(n + 1)$th energy zone.

2. The regions bounded by convex lines (i.e. the lines of positive curvature relative to inner areas) and belonging simultaneously to $n$ or more circles, represent the zone electrons in the $n$th energy zone.

Let us illustrate the use of these rules for various constant energy curves shown by numbers 2, 3 and 4 in Fig. 12.9. As evident

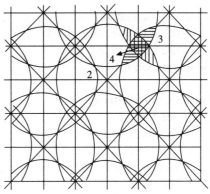

**Fig. 12.9** **Periodic zones of a square lattice with Harrison's spheres for 4 electrons per unit cells**

from the figure, the region 2 is bounded by concave lines and belongs only to one circle drawn from the centre of the first zone. Thus, according to rule 1, it represents second zone holes. The regions 3 and 4 together belong simultaneously to three circles and are called "rosettes". They are bounded by convex lines and according to rule 2 belong to third zone electrons. Finally, the region 4 which is the central portion of the rosette simultaneously belongs to four circles. It is bounded by convex lines and hence according to rule 2, is a fourth zone electron.

It can be easily seen from Fig. 12.9 that energy is multivalued function of $k$. As we know that the central portion of the "rosette" belongs to the fourth energy band as well as included in the third energy band, it can be seen that it also belongs to the second and first energy bands. Thus, for each value of $k$ in the region 4, there corresponds the values of energy of electrons from the first, second, third and fourth bands. Similarly, for each value of $k$ in the region 3, the energy is triply degenerate and so on.

## 12.4 FERMI SURFACES IN METALS

In the last section, we discussed the construction of FS in two dimensions using extended zone scheme and periodic zone scheme following Harrison's method. Oridinarily, one can simply generalize the above discussed two dimensional case to a three dimensional one. But the determination of a constant energy surfaces in real metals is not that easy, since it requires the construction of a number of Brillouin zones, identification of the pieces of Fermi sphere in these zones and finally to bring them into a single zone. However, based on the two dimensional discussion, it is possible to formulate a simple procedure which is very helpful in the construction of Fermi surfaces of metals. The procedure consists of the following steps:

1. For a given metal lattice, construct the corresponding reciprocal lattice.
2. Near each reciprocal lattice point, construct a unit cell (known as BZ) by the Wigner-Seitz method.
3. For the given parameters of the BZ and valence of the metal, determine the radius of the Fermi sphere $k_F$. A sphere of this radius is drawn from the centres of the periodically repeating zones (or from the centre of the extended zone).
4. The constant energy surfaces (the FS) formed by the intersection of the Fermi spheres are classified by the rules given in the preceding section.

Making use of the above procedure, let us construct Fermi surfaces for some simple crystal lattices of common metals.

### 1. Simple Cubic Lattice

This is the simplest case to be treated in three dimension. In the whole periodic Table only polonium belongs to this system which is a non-metal. Therefore, the study of FS in simple cubic case is only of theoretical interests.

Let us consider a simple cubic unit cell whose lattice parameter is "$a$". Determine the reciprocal lattice points and construct the first BZ which is again a cube of side $2\pi/a$ as shown in Fig. 12.10. The radius of the Fermi sphere can be

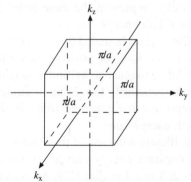

**Fig. 12.10 First BZ for simple cubic lattice**

determined by using the eq. 25 (chapter 10). Accordingly,

$$k_F = \left(3\pi^2 \frac{N}{a^3}\right)^{1/3} = \left(\frac{3\pi^2}{a^3}\right)^{1/3} = \left(\frac{3}{\pi}\right)^{1/3} \frac{\pi}{a} = 0.985 \frac{\pi}{a} \tag{8}$$

where $N = 1$. Equation 8 shows that the $k_F$ will lie between

$$0 < k_F < \frac{\pi}{a}$$

where $\pi/a$ is the distance from centre of the zone boundaries. Further, eq. 8 indicates that $k_F$ is very close to the zone boundaries. If we describe such spheres in a periodic zone scheme whose planar section (in $k_x - k_y$ plane) will look like Fig. 12.11. Finally, taking into account the effect

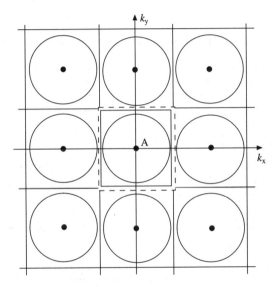

**Fig. 12.11** **Planar section of Brillouin zones for SC and Harrison's sphere for one electron per unit cell in the periodic zone scheme**

of a weak pseudopotential $V_{eff}(r)$, the Fermi spheres will stick to one another across the zone boundaries and will take the shape as shown in Fig. 12.12. A surface of this type is called "monster" in literature.

## Body Centred Cubic Lattice

The simplest family of metals belonging to this crystal system is alkali metals (Table 12.1). In section 11.3, we constructed the first BZ for a body centred cubic lattice, which has the form of rhombic dodecahedron (Fig. 12.13). It has twelve identical faces and are located at the same distance $\sqrt{2}\pi/a$ from the centre of the zone, where "$a$" is the periodicity of the lattice. For a bcc structure, as we know that there are two atoms per unit cell, therefore,

$$k_F = \left(3\pi^2 \cdot \frac{2}{a^3}\right)^{1/3} = \left(\frac{6}{\pi}\right)^{1/3} \frac{\pi}{a} = 1.24 \frac{\pi}{a} \tag{9}$$

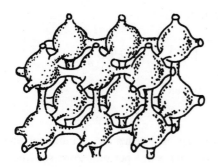

Fig. 12.12   First zone monster for sc in periodic zone scheme

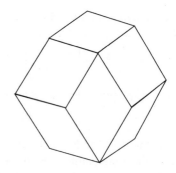

Fig. 12.13   First BZ for bcc lattice

Table 12.1   The monovalent metals and their structures.

| Alkali metals (bcc-structure) | Noble metals (fcc-structure) |
|---|---|
| Li: $1s^2 2s^1$ | ————— |
| Na: [Ne] $3s^1$ | ————— |
| K: [Ar] $4s^1$ | Cu: [Ar] $3d^{10}4s^1$ |
| Rb: [Kr] $5s^1$ | Aq: [Kr] $4d^{10}5s^1$ |
| Cs: [Xe] $6s^1$ | Au: [Xe] $4f^{14}5d^{10}6s^1$ |

Further, the shortest distance of a zone face from the centre of the zone is

$$d = \frac{2\pi}{a}\sqrt{(1/2)^2 + (1/2)^2 + (0)^2} = \sqrt{2}\left(\frac{\pi}{a}\right) = 1.414\left(\frac{\pi}{a}\right) \tag{10}$$

From eqs. 9 and 10, we have

$$0 < k_F < d.$$

Further, we have

$$\frac{k_F}{d} = 0.88 \text{ and } d - k_F = 0.174\frac{\pi}{a}$$

These imply that: (i) the Fermi sphere is entirely contained within the first BZ, (ii) it covers 88 per cent of the shortest distance from the centre of the zone and (iii) it is separated by a distance of 0.174 ($\pi/a$) from the zone boundaries. Under low pseudopotential, the separation 0.174 ($\pi/a$) between the FS and the faces of BZ seems to be relatively large to have any effect on the

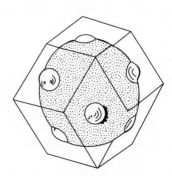

Fig. 12.14   The FS in the first zone for alkali metals

FS. However, still some noticeable distortions do appear on the FS at twelve different positions which are closest to the zone boundaries as shown in Fig. 12.14. They are located along <110> directions from the centre of the zone to its twelve identical faces.

**Face Centred Cubic Lattice**

The noble metals are the simplest members of metals belonging to the face centred cubic system. The first BZ of an fcc structure is cubooctahedron, which has fourteen faces including eight hexagonal and six square. We know that there are four atoms in an fcc unit cell, therefore the radius of the Fermi sphere is given by

$$k_F = \left(3\pi^2 \cdot \frac{4}{a^3}\right)^{1/3} = \left(\frac{12}{\pi}\right)^{1/3} \frac{\pi}{a} = 1.563\left(\frac{\pi}{a}\right) \tag{11}$$

Further, the shortest distance of a square face from the centre of the zone is

$$d_s = \frac{2\pi}{a}\sqrt{1^2 + 0^2 + 0^2} = \frac{2\pi}{a} \tag{12}$$

Similarly, the shortest distance of the hexagonal face from the centre is

$$d_h = \frac{2\pi}{a}\sqrt{(1/2)^2 + (1/2)^2 + (1/2)^2} = \sqrt{3}\left(\frac{\pi}{a}\right) = 1.732\left(\frac{\pi}{a}\right) \tag{13}$$

Equations 11 and 13 give us

$$0 < k_F < d_h, \frac{k_F}{d_h} = 0.90 \text{ and } d_h - k_F = 0.169\frac{\pi}{a}$$

These imply that:

   (i) The Fermi sphere is entirely contained within the first BZ.
   (ii) It covers 90 per cent of the distance (of the hexagonal face) from the centre of the zone.
   (iii) It is separated by a distance of 0.169 $(\pi/a)$ from the zone boundaries.

In this case, we observe that the FS is slightly more closer to the zone boundaries than in the alkali metals. In addition, the effective potential is greater in this case due to more complex shape of the ionic structure. These two together suggest that the FS near the centres of the hexagonal faces must be substantially distorted. Experimental results show that the FS near these points opens and sticks to the zone boundaries as shown in Fig. 12.15a. This is in agreement with the qualitative discussion in section 12.2. A (110) section of the FS parallel to the $k_z$ axis and bisecting the angle between $k_x$ and $k_y$ axes in the first BZ is shown in Fig. 12.15b. In a periodic zone scheme, the same is represented as shown in Fig. 12.16. The connecting portions near the zone boundaries have been described as "necks" and the nearly spherical portion as "belly" in the literature. The diameter of the neck strongly depends on the pseudopotential. This is in agreement with the experimental results in the case of Cu, Ag and Au, where we observe the increasing neck diameter due to increasing atomic number and hence an increasing effective potential.

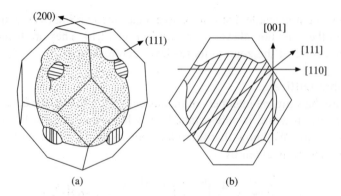

(a)                    (b)

**Fig. 12.15    The FS in the first zone for noble metals**

In order to see the nature of the FS in higher energy zones, let us take the case of trivalent metals having the same crystal structure as above (i.e. the fcc). Among the trivalent, let us discuss the case of aluminium in particular (it is being the simplest). The radius of the Fermi sphere for aluminium is

$$k_F = (3)^{1/3} \times 1.563 \left( \frac{\pi}{a} \right) = 2.225 \left( \frac{\pi}{a} \right) \tag{14}$$

Further, from eqs. 12, 13 and 14, we have

$$d_h < k_F < \frac{3\pi}{a}, d_s < k_F < \frac{3\pi}{a}, \frac{k_F}{d_h} = 1.30 \quad \text{and} \quad \frac{k_F}{d_s} = 1.128$$

These imply that the Fermi sphere completely encloses the first BZ (indicating that the first BZ is completely filled with electrons) and passes through the second, third and fourth zones. In order to construct the constant energy surfaces in these zones, let us consider the first BZ in periodic zone scheme (Fig. 12.17). We observe that the two zones share the faces, three share the

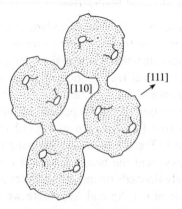

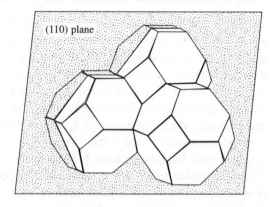

**Fig. 12.16    The FS for noble metal in periodic zone scheme showing various orbits**

**Fig. 12.17    Periodic zones of an fcc lattice sectioned by (110) plane**

edges and four share the corners. Accordingly, two Fermi spheres (which completely enclose the first BZ) overlap near zone faces, three near zone edges and four near zone corners. Next, consider the system of BZ and the coresponding Fermi sphere in a periodic zone scheme and draw two vertical sections of the system, one along the coordinate plane and the other along the diagonal plane as shown in Fig. 12.18. The empty space left inside the Fermi sphere (Fig. 12.18a) resembles a cubo-octahedron with concave faces and edges and hence according to the rule 1 (as pointed out earlier), it belongs to the second zone holes as shown in Fig. 12.19a in a

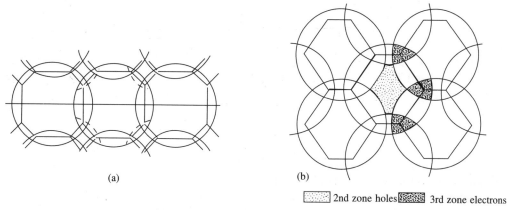

(a)        (b)

☐ 2nd zone holes ▨ 3rd zone electrons

**Fig. 12.18  (a) (111) and (b) (110) sections of an fcc lattice in periodic zone scheme**

reduced zone scheme. On the other hand, in Fig. 12.18b, the shaded volumes which belong simultaneously to three spheres and bounded by convex surfaces belong to third zone electrons as shown in Fig. 12.19b. In the absence of effective potential, they have triangular shaped "tubes" of variable cross-sections, i.e., wider at the middle and narrower towards the end of the edges. They give rise to the third zone "monsters". In the fourth zone, only small electron pockets exist. However, when $V_{eff}(r)$  0 these electron pockets vanish.

For tetravalent solids such as lead with an fcc structure, the size of the second zone hole decreases, while the cross-section of third zone monster and fourth zone electron pockets increases because of greater size of Fermi sphere. The fourth zone electron pockets are shown in Fig. 12.20.

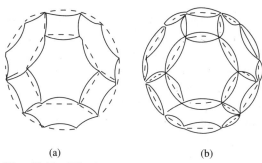

(a)        (b)

**Fig. 12.19  FS of (a) second zone hole (b) third zone monster**

**Fig. 12.20  Fourth zone electron pockets in reduced zone scheme**

## 12.5 CHARACTERISTICS OF FERMI SURFACES

From the preceding discussions, we find that the FS has the following characteristic features:

1. The FS represents the dynamic and inertial properties of conduction electron in $k$-space.
2. The volume of the FS represents the number of conduction electrons.
3. The FS has spherical shape within the first BZ and non-spherical in higher zones.
4. The FS always meets the zone boundary at right angles along the line of intersection.
5. For a spherical FS (i.e. for free electron case), the velocity of an electron is

$$v = \frac{\hbar k}{m_0} \tag{15}$$

where $v$ is proportional to and parallel to the wave vector $k$ as shown in Fig. 12.21a. On the other hand, for non-spherical Fermi surfaces (i.e. for electrons under periodic potential), the velocity is a non-linear function of $k$, which is given by

$$v = \frac{1}{\hbar} \nabla_k E(k) \tag{16}$$

where the velocity is proportional to the gradient of the energy in $k$-space. Since the gradient vector is perpendicular to the contour lines (i.e. the constant energy curves), a well known fact from vector analysis, it follows that the velocity $v$ at every point in $k$-space is normal to the energy curve passing through that point and hence the velocity may or may not be parallel to $k$. This is shown in Fig. 12.21b.

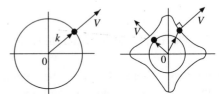

**Fig. 12.21 The velocity of (a) a free electron, and (b) a Bloch electron**

6. Study of FS provides us to know many important properties of solids, such as heat capacity, Pauli's paramagnetism, electrical conductivity, etc.

## 12.6 EFFECT OF ELECTRIC FIELD ON FS

Let us consider the case when free electron FS is wholly contained in the first BZ (i.e. BZ is only partly filled) as shown in Fig. 12.22a. In the absence of an electric field, each electron within the FS moves with a velocity determined by its energy and follow symmetry property. Accordingly, for each electron with an energy $E(k)$ moving in a particular direction there is a symmetrically located electron with energy $E(-k)$ moving in opposite direction and hence no net electron movement occurs. When an external electrical field is applied, the equation of motion in the absence of electron collision with imperfection, phonons or any other impurities, is given by

$$\frac{d(\hbar k)}{dt} = -eE \quad \text{or} \quad \hbar \frac{dk}{dt} = -eE \tag{17}$$

where the negative sign indicates the charge is due to eectrons. The quantity $dk/dt$ is the velocity of electrons in $k$-space. Equation 17 indicates that for a constant electric field, the velocity of each electron is constant, consequently, the entire FS moves through $\Delta k$ in $k$-space opposite to the field direction. It is because of the movement of electrons from near the FS into the adjacent quantum states within the same zone as shown by the dashed circle in Fig. 12.22b. The great majority of electron velocities still cancel each other pairwise (due to symmetry). However, some electrons remain uncompensated, resulting in a net current.

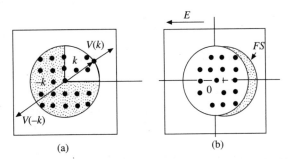

(a)  (b)

**Fig. 12.22** **The Fermi sphere in the first BZ (a) in the absence of an electric field (b) in the presence of electric field**

In the energy band model where the electrons are under the influence of a periodic crystal potential, we observe a similar result except that the FS has a non-spherical shape. For example, consider the FS of Cu, a section of which is shown in Fig. 12.23. When an external field is applied, the FS gets displaced in a direction opposite to the field direction as shown in Fig. 12.24. In the process, some of the electrons lying close to the zone boundary move out of the first zone. They can be brought back into the first zone by translating them through a reciprocal lattice vector $G$. In other words, these electrons did not leave the first zone and Bragg reflected

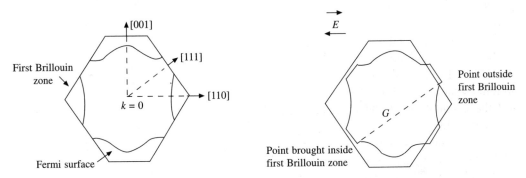

**Fig. 12.23** **Cross section of the FS of copper**

**Fig. 12.24** **Displacement of the FS of copper in an electric field**

into the same zone by the zone boundary. The resulting FS is shown in Fig. 12.25. Such a displacement of the FS leaves some of the electrons uncompensated. These are shown by shaded regions in Fig. 12.26. The amount of electric current depends on the number of these uncompensated electrons. This, in turn, depends on the displacement, shape and area of the FS. Since the area

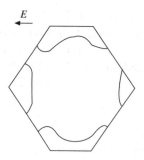

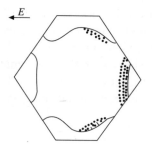

**Fig. 12.25   Displaced FS of copper in the first BZ**     **Fig. 12.26   Uncompensated electrons in copper**

of the FS for Cu and Al is nearly same and hence the number of uncompensated electrons in Al is about the same as in Cu. This explains why the electrical conductivity of Al is also about the same as that of Cu, although Al has three times as many conduction electrons as Cu.

## 12.7   EFFECT OF MAGNETIC FIELD ON FS

In the absence of collisions as considered above, the equation of motion of an electron in a magnetic field is given by

$$\hbar\frac{dk}{dt} = e(v \times B) \tag{18}$$

where $e(v \times B)$ is the Lorentz force experienced by the electrons moving with a velocity $v$ in a magnetic field $B$. In metals, sicne $v$ is perpendicular to FS in $k$-space, the force is parallel to the FS and perpendicular to both $v$ and $B$. The component of $k$ parallel to $B$ is therefore constnat, so that electron orbit in $k$-space is obtained by taking the intersection of the FS with a plane normal to $B$ as shown in Fig. 12.27. In fact, the shape of the electron orbit in $k$-space depends on the shape of the FS and the orientation of the external applied magnetic field.

Let us consider two closely spaced electron orbits in $k$-space with energies $E$ and $E + dE$ as shown in Fig. 12.28a. The shape of the electron orbit in $r$-space can be obtained by integrating eq. 18, i.e.

$$k = \frac{e}{\hbar}(r \times B) \tag{19}$$

**Fig. 12.27   "Orbit" of an electron in a magnetic field**

This shows that the electron orbit in $r$-space is similar in shape with the $k$-space orbit but differs by a scale factor of $\hbar/eB$ and rotation of $\pi/2$. This is shown in Fig. 12.28b.

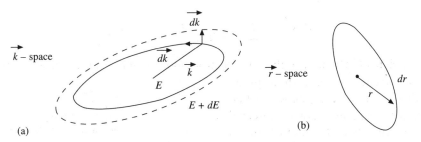

**Fig. 12.28 Orbits of an electron in *k*-and *r*- space**

The period of an electron orbit in a magnetic field is obtained as

$$T = \oint dt = \oint \frac{dr}{v} \tag{20}$$

Further, from eq. 16, we know that the velocity of an electron in a band of energy $E$ in k-space is given by

$$v = \frac{dr}{dt} = \frac{1}{\hbar} \cdot \frac{dE(k)}{dk} = \frac{1}{\hbar} \cdot \frac{dE}{dk_{\perp}} \tag{21}$$

where $dk_{\perp}$ is the normal distance in $k$-space (Fig. 12.28), projected on a plane perpendicular to $B$, between constant energy surfaces of energy $E$ and $E + dE$. Equations 19,20 and 21 yield

$$T = \hbar \oint \frac{dr \cdot dk_{\perp}}{dE} = \frac{\hbar^2}{eB} \oint \frac{|dk \times dk_{\perp}|}{dE} = \frac{\hbar^2}{eB} \cdot \frac{dA_k}{dE} \tag{22}$$

where $A$ is the area of the orbit in $k$-space. Therefore, cyclotron frequency is

$$\omega_c = \frac{2\pi}{T} = \frac{2\pi eB}{\hbar^2} \cdot \frac{dE}{dA_k} \tag{23}$$

The cyclotron frequency is also given by

$$\omega_c = \frac{v}{r} = \frac{eB}{m_c} \tag{24}$$

where $m_c$ is the cyclotron effective mass and can be determined by comparing eqs. 23 and 24,

$$m_c = \frac{\hbar^2}{2\pi} \cdot \frac{dA_k}{dE} \tag{2.5}$$

This is quite different from the effective mass of an electron discussed earlier.

## 12.8 QUANTIZATION OF ELECTRON ORBITS

Based on classical statistics we know that the energy $E$ of a free electron is a continuous quantity and can be expressed in $k$-space as

$$E(k_x, k_y, k_z) = \frac{\hbar^2}{2m_0} (k_x^2 + k_y^2 + k_z^2) \qquad (26)$$

Under the action of magnetic field, the electrons do not move in a straight path but start rotating in circular orbits in a plane perpendicular to the field as shown in Fig. 12.29. Let the magnetic field be directed along the z-axis, then the motion of an electron can be resolved into two components: (i) the longitudinal component (i.e. the motion along the field *B*), and (ii) the transverse component (i.e. the motion in a plane perpendicular to *B*). The magnetic field does not change the longitudinal component and hence the energy related to this is

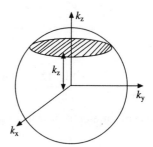

**Fig. 12.29  Motion of an electron in a magnetic field**

$$E_{||} = \frac{\hbar^2 k_z^2}{2m_0} \qquad (27)$$

The transverse motion is similar to the motion of linear harmonic oscillator which oscillates about an equilibrium position with the cyclotron frequency given by eq. 24. Such an oscillatory motion is quantized and hence the corresponding energy spectrum consists of discrete energy levels

$$E_\perp = \left(n + \frac{1}{2}\right)\hbar\omega_c \qquad (28)$$

where $n = 0, 1, 2, \ldots$ From eqs. 27 and 28, the energy of electron states can be expressed as the sum of a translational energy along the magnetic field, together with the quantized energy in a plane perpendicular to the field. Thus the net energy of the electron states in the magnetic field without taking into account its spin is

$$E(n, k_z) = \left(n + \frac{1}{2}\right)\hbar\omega_c + \frac{\hbar^2 k_z^2}{2m_0} \qquad (29)$$

For a classical motion, any values of $E_\perp$ are allowable, i.e.

$$E_\perp(cl) = \frac{1}{2} m_0 v_\perp^2 = \frac{m_0 \omega_c^2 r^2}{2} \qquad (30)$$

On the other hand, for a quantum motion, only discrete values of $E_\perp$ (eq. 28) are allowable, i.e.

$$E_\perp(qua) = \left(n + \frac{1}{2}\right)\hbar\omega_c \qquad (31)$$

The radii of different orbits can be found by correspondence principle (used in quantum mechanics to establish the relation between classical and quantum quantities), according to which we have

$$\frac{m_0 \omega_c^2 r^2}{2} = \left(n + \frac{1}{2}\right) \hbar \omega_c$$

Hence the radius of the $n$th orbit is given by

$$r_n = \left[\frac{2\hbar}{m_0 \omega_c}\left(n + \frac{1}{2}\right)\right]^{1/2} \tag{32}$$

Fig. 12.30 shows $E$ versus $k$ curves (according to the eq. 29) for different radii of curvatures. These are known as Landau levels.

In order to see the nature of distribution of electron states in $k$-space under the action of magnetic field, let us consider the case of a one zone metal with spherical FS without spin. When $B = 0$ the allowed states are distributed uniformly inside the Fermi sphere. Fig. 12.31a shows the section of the Fermi sphere along $k_x - k_y$ plane passing through the centre (i.e. $k_z = 0$). Allowed states fill the circle of maximum radius $k_F = \sqrt{2mE_F}$ in that plane. For any other parallel section $k_z = $ constant and the radius of the circle is

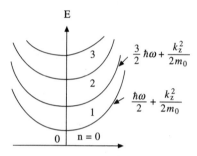

**Fig. 12.30    Landau levels**

$$\sqrt{k_F^2 - k_z^2}$$

As $k_z$ increases from zero to $k_F$, this radius decreases and becomes zero when $k_z = k_F$.

A uniform filling of the Fermi sphere by the points depicting the allowed states corresponds to quasi-continuous energy spectrum $E = E(k_x, k_y, k_z)$, where $k_x$, $k_y$, $k_z$ run through quasi-continuous sets of values from 0 to $k_F$.

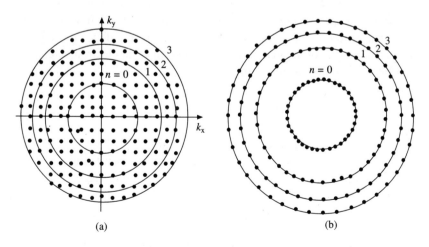

(a)                                    (b)

**Fig. 12.31    Quantization schemes for free electrons (a) without magnetic field (b) in a magnetic field**

Application of a magnetic field does not change the total number of electrons in the metal, but causes their redistribution between the bands. As an example, consider only the first band which is partly filled, whereas the other bands are empty. When the magnetic field is applied (say along $z$-axis), the discrete energy levels given by eq. 31 determine the allowed electron orbits in the planes $k_z$ = constant in $k$-space. The radius $k_n$ of the orbit relating to a level with quantum number $n$ is found by the correspondence principle as pointed out earlier, i.e.

$$\frac{\hbar^2 k_n^2}{2m} = \left(n + \frac{1}{2}\right)\hbar\omega \quad \text{or} \quad k_n = \left[\frac{2m\omega}{\hbar}\left(n + \frac{1}{2}\right)\right]^{1/2} \tag{33}$$

This shows that under the effect of magnetic field, the states lying between the orbits of radii $k_n$ (where $n = 0, 1, 2, \ldots$) are forbidden. Hence, all the allowed states in the plane $k_2$ = constant are drawn onto the nearest orbit as shown in Fig. 12.31b. When a three dimensional analogue is considered, this means that in the magnetic field all allowed states within the FS are condensed on the surface of coaxial cylinders parallel to $k_z$ axis. Fig. 12.32 shows the occupied regions of $k$-space without a magnetic field, whereas Fig. 12.33 shows the occupied regions of $k$-space with a magnetic field. The lower graph in Fig. 12.33 shows the dependence of the energy (represented by eq. 31) of states on each cylinder in the plane $k_z = 0$, on the radius of the cylinder. The right hand curve represents the relationship between $k_z$ and the energy of state on each cylinder.

**Fig. 12.32   Occupied region of $k$-space without a magnetic field**

In the above discussion, we considered a simple case of one zone metal with free electron spherical Fermi surface. Now, let us consider a more general case of a crystal where electrons are in a periodic potential and the corresponding FS may have any arbitrary shape. For this case, quasi-classical quantization given by Bohr-Sommerfeld correspondence principle can be used. According to this, an integral of the generalized momentum of an electron taken over the closed contour of its orbit of periodic motion is given by

$$\oint p \cdot dr = (n + \gamma)2\pi\hbar \tag{34}$$

where $n$ is an integer, and $\gamma$ is a phase correction (typically $\gamma = 1/2$ and $p$ and $r$ are conjugate variables representing momentum and position of the particles as it traces out its orbit.

The generalized momentum of a free electron in the presence of a magnetic field cannonically conjugate to $r$ is given by

$$p = \hbar k + eA \tag{35}$$

where $A$ is a vector potential (Curl $A = B$). Substituting the value of $k$ from eq. 19 into 35 and then $p$ in eq. 34, we have

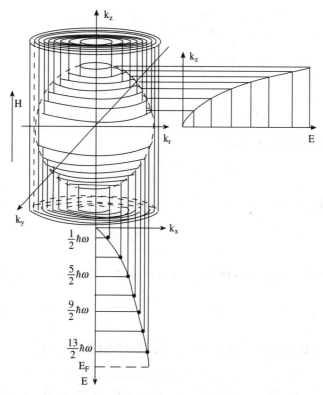

**Fig. 12.33   Occupied region of *k*-space with a magnetic field**

$$\oint \hbar \frac{e}{\hbar}(r \times B) \cdot dr + \oint eA \cdot dr = 2\pi\hbar\left(n + \frac{1}{2}\right)$$

or
$$-e\oint B \cdot (r \times dr) + e\oint A \cdot dr = 2\pi\hbar\left(n + \frac{1}{2}\right)$$

or
$$-2e\Phi + e\Phi = 2\pi\hbar\left(n + \frac{1}{2}\right)$$

or
$$-e\Phi = 2\pi\hbar\left(n + \frac{1}{2}\right) \tag{36}$$

where $\Phi$ is the magnetic flux through the orbit in $r$–space and $\oint r \times dr$ is twice the area of the orbit. Equations 34 and 36 give us

$$\oint p \cdot dr = -e\Phi = 2\pi\hbar\left(n + \frac{1}{2}\right) \tag{37}$$

Equation 37 indicates that the flux through an electron orbit in $r$-space is quantized in uunits of $2\pi\,(\hbar/e)$. However, we know that in real space the flux is given by $\Phi = BA_r$, where $A_r$ is the area of the orbit in that space. This can be related to FS in $k$-space through eq. 19, which says that the orbit in $k$-space is $eB/\hbar$ times larger than the orbit in the real space. Therefore,

$$\pi k^2 = \left(\frac{eB}{\hbar}\right)^2 \pi r^2 \quad \text{or} \quad A_k = \left(\frac{eB}{\hbar}\right)^2 A_r$$

so that

$$\Phi = BA_r = B\left(\frac{\hbar}{eB}\right)^2 A_k = \frac{\hbar^2}{e^2 B} A_k \tag{38}$$

Substituting this into eq. 36, we have

$$A_k = \frac{2\pi eB}{\hbar}\left(n + \frac{1}{2}\right) \tag{39}$$

This is known as Onsager-Lifshitz quantization condition. The change in the area $A_k$ for a unit chagne of quantum number is given by

$$A_{k+1} - A_k = \frac{2\pi eB}{\hbar} \tag{40}$$

Substituting this in eq. 23, we obtain the corresponding change in the energy at the FS

$$dE = \hbar \omega_c \tag{41}$$

This is just expected.

## 12.9 EXPERIMENTAL STUDY OF FERMI SURFACES

In the preceding sections, we discussed the construction of FS in two and three dimensions for different metals and the effect of electric and magnetic fields on it. In this section, we shall describe some of the important experimental techniques commonly used to study the Fermi surfaces for a better understanding of the physics of electrons. They are discussed as under:

### 1. Anomalous Skin Effect

Pippard was the first person to employ this technique to determine the FS of copper under the action of an electromagnetic field. The electromagnetic field interacts with the electrons of the metal which absorbs a part of its energy. The nature of interaction depends essentially on the ratio of skin depth (it is defined as the distance in which the amplitude of the wave falls to $1/e$ of its original value) and the mean free path of the electrons (i.e. $\delta/\lambda$).

When $\lambda \ll \delta$, all Fermi electrons lying within the skin layer interact with the electromagnetic field with an equal effectiveness. The values $\lambda \ll \delta$ correspond to the region of normal skin effect. In order to calculate the classical skin depth, let us suppose that $E_x$ and $H_x$ be the strength of the electric and magnetic fields acting on the surface of a metal. They are time dependent and are proportional to the Boltzmann factor $\exp(-i\omega t)$, where $\omega$ is the frequency of the electromagnetic field. For calculating the classical skin depth, we proceed by considering the following Maxwell's equations:

$$\nabla \times H = \frac{4\pi}{c} J + \frac{1}{c}\frac{\partial D}{\partial t}, \nabla \times E = -\frac{1}{c}\frac{\partial H}{\partial t} \tag{41}$$

where the current density, $J = \sigma E$. Now, let us make the following assumptions:

1. The frequency of the magnetic field is low enough ($\omega \ll \sigma$) so that the ordinary displacement current, $\dfrac{\partial D}{\partial t}$ can be droped form the Maxwell equation.

2. The metal is non-magnetic, so that $B \simeq H$.

If we consider that the surface of the metal is normal to the $z$-axis as shown in Fig. 12.34, the Maxwell's equations give us,

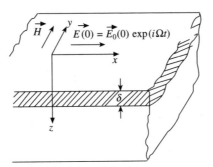

**Fig. 12.34   Azbel-Kaner geometry**

$$\nabla^2 E = \frac{4\pi\sigma}{c^2} \cdot \frac{\partial E}{\partial t} \tag{42}$$

Let the solution of this equation is

$$E = E_x (0) \exp (-i\omega t) \cdot \exp (\lambda z) \tag{43}$$

then eq. 42 yields $\lambda^2 = \dfrac{4\pi i\omega\sigma}{c^2}$

or

$$\lambda = \alpha + i\beta = (1 + i)\left[\frac{2\pi\omega\sigma}{c^2}\right]^{1/2} \tag{44}$$

where the root $\sqrt{i} = (1 + i)/\sqrt{2}$. In eq. 44, the real part, $\sigma$ is the attenuation factor and the imaginary part, $\beta$ is the phase factor. In order to obtain a quantitative measure of the classical skin depth, let us write the expression for spatial variation of electric field inside the metal. For $\sigma$ real, it is expressed as

$$E \propto \exp\left(-\frac{z}{\delta}\right) \exp\left(\frac{iz}{\delta}\right) \tag{45}$$

where

$$\delta \equiv \left(\frac{2\pi\omega\sigma}{c^2}\right)^{-1/2} \tag{46}$$

If $\sigma$ is not real in the frequency region of interest, we define $\delta$ as the reciprocal of the imaginary part of $\lambda$ in eq. 44. In eq. 45, at $z = 0$, $E_x = E_x (0)$, this is the amplitude of the field at the surface. At $z = \delta$, the amplitude of the field is

$$|E_x| = E_x (0) \, e^{-1} \tag{47}$$

Thus the amplitude decreases to $1/e$ of the initial value, while the field penetrates to a distance of $\delta$. Hence $\delta$ is called the penetration depth.

The normal skin effect is oberved in metals around room temperature. For example, let us take the case of a good conductor at room temperature: $\sigma \sim 5 \times 10^5$ ohm$^{-1}$ cm$^{-1}$ $\approx 5 \times 10^{17}$ sec$^{-1}$ and $\omega \sim 3 \times 10^{10}$ sec$^{-1}$. According to eq. 46, $\delta \sim 10^{-4}$ cm. However, under the same conditions, $\lambda \sim 10^{-7} - 10^{-8}$ cm. This gives that $\delta$ is several orders of magnitude greater than $\lambda$. Hence, normal skin effect is observed at and above room temperatures.

When the temperature is reduced, the mean free path increases and may become greater than the skin depth. The values $\lambda > \delta$ correspond to the region of anomalous skin effect. In this region, the effectiveness of interaction between the electrons within the skin layer and the electromagnetic field depends on the direction of their motion.

According to Pippard, only the electrons moving within an angle of the order of $(\delta/\lambda)$ with respect to the surface of the metal can interact effectively with the electromagnetic field. Accordingly, the electrons travelling almost parallel to the surface of the metal remain in the field for a longer time and absorb sufficient amount of energy from it, while the electrons moving at large angles to the surface leave the skin layer quickly and penetrate into the metal (Fig. 12.35). The concentration of effective electrons in the extreme anomalous limit ($\lambda \gg \delta$) is given by

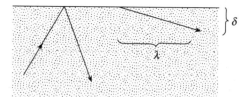

**Fig. 12.35 Effective electrons in the skin depth**

$$n_{\text{eff}} \approx \frac{n \cdot \delta_{\text{eff}}}{\lambda} \tag{48}$$

where $n$ is the total concentration of electrons in the metal and $\delta_{\text{eff}}$ is the effective skin depth in the extreme anomalous region. The corresponding effective conductivity is given by

$$\sigma_{\text{eff}} \approx \frac{\sigma \delta_{\text{eff}}}{\lambda} = \frac{ne^2 \tau \delta_{\text{eff}}}{m\lambda} = \frac{ne^2 \delta_{\text{eff}}}{m v_F} \tag{49}$$

where $\lambda = v_F \tau$ and $v_F$ is the velocity of electron at the FS. The effective skin depth in the extreme anomalous region can be obtained after substituting $\sigma_{\text{eff}}$ for $\sigma$ in eq. 46. Therefore,

$$\delta_{\text{eff}} \approx \left( \frac{c^2}{2\pi\omega\sigma_{\text{eff}}} \right)^{1/2} \approx \left( \frac{c^2 m v_F}{2\pi\omega ne^2 \delta_{\text{eff}}} \right)^{1/2}$$

or

$$\delta_{\text{eff}} = \left( \frac{c^2 m v_F}{2\pi\omega ne^2} \right)^{1/3} \tag{50}$$

The eq. 50 is independent of $\lambda$. Thus, the determination of skin depth in the anomalous region enables us to measure the electron velocity at the FS. The anomalous skin effect is observed at low temperature, where the simple picture of decaying field over a distance $\delta$ breaks down completely.

## 2. Cyclotron Resonance

The phenomenon of cyclotron resonance in metals was first predicted by Azbel-Kaner in 1956 and its experimental verification was made on tin by Fawcett in the same year. The most suitable experimental arrangement employed to observe cyclotron resonance is known as Azbel-Kaner geometry where the applied alternating electric field may be parallel or perpendicular to the static magnetic field $B$, but both $E$ and $B$, must be parallel to the surface of the specimen as shown in Fig. 12.36. Azbel-Kaner showed that the cyclotron resonance could be observed under the following conditions:

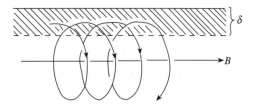

**Fig. 12.36   Azbel-Kaner resonance**

$$\lambda > r_B, \quad \text{and} \quad r_B \gg \delta \tag{51}$$

i.e. the cyclotron resonance is observed in the extreme anomalous region. The first inequlity in eq. 51 is a well known condition of cyclic motion according to which the electrons must complete more than one rotation around a closed orbit before being scattered. Further, since under the above experimental geometry, the electrons can either describe closed orbits in planes perpendicular to the surface or move along helices whose axes are parallel to the direction of the magnetic field (Fig. 12.36). The second inequality in eq. 51 implies that the electrons can interact with the electric field within the skin layer only during a small fraction of the period of their motion. They absorb a little energy each time when they pass through the skin layer. The resonant absorption of energy can occur only if the electrons experience an electric field of the same phase each time when they enter the skin layer. This is possible when the frequency of the oscillating electric field is an integral multiple of the cyclotron frequency, i.e.

$$\omega = n\omega_c \tag{52}$$

This is called Azbel-Kaner resonance, Substituting the value of cyclotron frequency $\omega_c$ from eq. 24 into eq. 52, we obtain,

$$\omega = n\frac{eB}{m_c} \quad \text{or} \quad \frac{1}{B} = \frac{ne}{\omega m_c} \tag{53}$$

Next, substituting the value of cyclotron effective mass from eq. 25 into eq. 53, we obtain the reciprocal value of magnetic field when $n$th harmonic is observed as

$$\frac{1}{B(n)} = \frac{2\pi ne}{\omega \hbar^2}\frac{dE}{dA_k} \tag{54}$$

In practice, one keeps the frequency $\omega$ constant and varies the magnetic field, then the expected periodicity with which the successive resonant peaks appear can be given by the interval of reciprocal magnetic fields between two consecutive resonances [e.g. the $n$th and $(n + 1)$th] as,

$$\delta\left(\frac{1}{B}\right) = \frac{1}{B(n + 1)} - \frac{1}{B(n)} = \frac{2\pi e}{\omega \hbar^2}\frac{dE}{dA_k} \tag{55}$$

An experimental measurement of a quantity which is proportional to the derivative of the real component of the impedance ($Z = R + iX$) over the magnetic field, $dR/dB$ for copper at 24 GHz is depicted in Fig. 12.37.

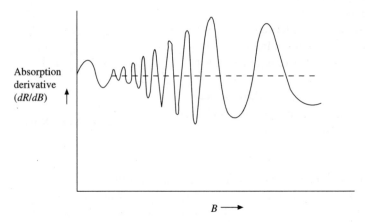

Absorption derivative ($dR/dB$)

$B \longrightarrow$

**Fig. 12.37   Field derivative of the surface impedance ($dR/dB$) of copper as a function of the field**

This cyclotron resonance curve makes it possible to determine very accurately the magnitude of the cyclotron mass and the relaxation time $\tau$ of the corresponding group of carriers. However, the observation of cyclotron resonance requires a complicated experimental technique, a highly pure and perfect single crystal and accuracy in the orientation of the crystal surface relative to the electric and magnetic field vectors.

### 3   de Hass-van Alphen Effect

We know that when a metal is placed in a magnetic field, the electrons do not move in straight path but rotate in quantized orbits around the FS in a plane perpendicular to the field. Based on this concept, de Haas and van Alphen in 1931 discovered that at low temperatures the diamegnetic susceptibility of pure bismuth as a function of magnetic field in high fields exhibits periodic oscillations (Fig. 12.38a). This was later termed as de Haas-van Alphen ($dHvA$) effect. The

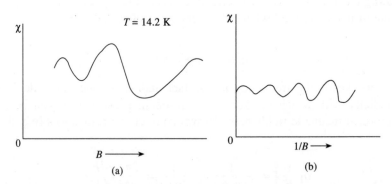

**Fig. 12.38   de Hass-van Alphen oscillations in (a) Bismuth and (b) copper**

oscillations display a remarkable periodicity when the magnetic susceptibility is plotted against the inverse of the field (Fig. 12.38b).

Similar oscillatory behaviour has also been observed in the experimental measurement of many other quantities such as electrical conductivity (known as Shubnikov-de Hass effect), heat capacity, entropy, thermal conductivity and so on. Actual usefulness of the *dHvA* effect was made possible due to Onsager's theoretical development in 1952. According to him, the change in the inverse field $1/B$ through a single period of oscillation, $\delta(1/B)$ could be determined by

$$\delta\left(\frac{1}{B}\right) = \frac{2\pi e}{\hbar} \frac{1}{Ae} \tag{56}$$

where $Ae$ is any extremal (maximal or minimal) cross-sectional area of the FS in a plane perpendicular to the magnetic field as illustrated in Fig. 12.39. If the magnetic field is taken along the *z*-axis, the cross-sectional area of the FS at a height $k_z$ is $A(k_z)$, and the extremal areas $Ae$ are the values of $A(k_z)$ at the $k_z$, where $dA/dk_z = 0$. Thus for $B$ along $k_z$-axis, (1) and (2) are maximal (extremal) orbits and (3) is a minimal (extremal) orbit. When the field is along $k_x$ -axis, only one extremal orbit (4) is present.

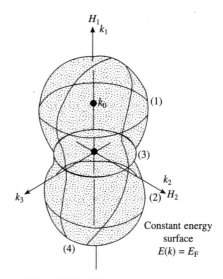

Measurements of the period of oscillation $\delta(1/B)$ can be made for different orientations of the magnetic field relative to the axes of a single crystal to be studied. Further, eq. 56 makes it possible to determine the extremal areas of the FS normal to the direction of the field directly. This information can be used to correct the initial model of the FS constructed by the Harrison's method. Practically all known Fermi Surfaces of simple metals have been constructed by this method.

**Fig. 12.39 Various extremal orbits**

## 12.10 SUMMARY

1. Radius of the Fermi sphere in *k*-space is given by

$$k_F = \left(\frac{3\pi^2 n}{a^3}\right)^{1/3}$$

where *n* is the number of atoms in the unit cell and *a* is the lattice parameter.

2. FS has many characteristic features. For example, it has spherical shape when it lies well within the first BZ and non-spherical when it lies near the first zone boundary, at the first zone boundary and in the higher zones.

3. The velocity of a free electron is given by

$$v = \frac{\hbar k}{m_0}$$

where $V$ is proportional to and parallel to the wave vector $k$. On the other hand, the velocity of a Bloch electron (electron in periodic potential) is given by

$$v = \frac{1}{\hbar} \nabla_k E(k)$$

where the velocity is proportional to the gradient of the energy in $k$-space. However, in both cases, the velocity $v$ is directed normal to the FS.

4. The motion of a free electron in an electric field in $k$-space is given by

$$\hbar \frac{dk}{dt} = -eE$$

5. The motion of a Bloch electron in a magnetic field in $k$-space is given by

$$\hbar \frac{dk}{dt} = e(v \times B)$$

The electron moves along an energy contour in a trajectory perpendicular to the field $B$. This motion is referred to as cyclotron motion.

6. The cyclotron frequency is found to be

$$\omega_c = \frac{2\pi e B}{\hbar^2} \cdot \frac{dE}{dA_k}$$

Its measurement gives us the information about the shape of the contours, and hence about the shape of the band.

7. In a constant magnetic field, the electron orbits are quantized in such a way that the flux through the orbit in $r$-space is

$$\Phi = \frac{2\pi \hbar}{e}(n + \gamma)$$

where $n$ is an integer and $\gamma$ is a phase correction. Typically by $\gamma = 0.5$.

8. The FS can be determined by various experimental methods. Some of them are: (i) Anomalous skin effect, (ii) Cyclotron resonance, and (iii) de Haas-van Alphen effect. They help us to understand the physics of electrons in metals.

9. At radio frequencies, the flow of current in a good conductor is confined to a thin layer whose thickness is determined by the skin depth

$$\delta = \left( \frac{2\pi \omega \sigma}{c^2} \right)^{-1/2}$$

10. The high temperature skin effect is called normal, while the low temperature skin effect is called anomalous.

11. The *dHvA* (de Haas-van Alphen) effect is the periodic oscillation of diamagnetic susceptibility $\chi$ of a metal at low temperatures when plotted against the applied magnetic field. The change in $1/B$ through a single period of oscillation is determined by the equation

$$\delta\left(\frac{1}{B}\right) = \frac{2\pi e}{\hbar}\frac{1}{Ae}$$

where $Ae$ is any extremal (maximal or minimal) cross-sectional area of the FS in a plane perpendicular to the magnetic field.

## 12.11 DEFINITIONS

*Anomalous Skin Effect*: At low temperatures, the mean free path of electrons increases and becomes greater than the skin depth, i.e. $\lambda > \delta$. Application of fields shows some unusual behaviour in this region.

*Brillouin Zone*: The volumes contained in surfaces which indicate the forbidden values of $k$, in $k$-space.

*Extremal Orbits*: The maximal or minimal electron orbits as a result of the application of magnetic field which is directed perpendicular to the orbits.

*Fermi Surface*: The surface in $k$-space corresponding to $E_F$, the Fermi level.

*Fermi Level* ($E_F$): The energy of the highest filled state in the highest energy band which contains electrons, in metal, at 0K.

*Skin Depth*: It is the depth of penetration of the field where amplitude of the field reduces to $1/e$ of its initial value.

## REVIEW QUESTIONS AND PROBLEMS

1. Consider a two dimensional square lattice. Take a value of electron concentration such that the Fermi surface extends to the fourth zone. Describe through Harrison construction or otherwise how can we draw Fermi surface in the reduced zone scheme in the first, second and the third zone. Assume that the electron behaves as free electron.

2. Explain the terms Fermi surface and Brillouin zone. What inference you draw from a spherical and elliptical Fermi surface? Discuss one experimental method for determining the Fermi surface of metal.

3. Distinguish between Fermi surface and Brillouin zone. How is the Fermi surface of metal experimentally determined?

4. Enumerate various experimental methods for the determination of Fermi surface. Explain in detail how cyclotron resonance studies help us to determine Fermi surfaces.

5. Describe the principle of cyclotron resonance method for determining the Fermi surface of a metal like copper. Why does the consideration of extremal orbits become important in this method?

6. Give an account of a de Hass-van Alphen effect. Explain why it is considered to be the most powerful method for the study of Fermi surface.

7. Sodium has a density of 971 kg/m$^3$ and an atomic weight of 22.99. Calculate its Fermi energy.

   *Ans.* 3.15 eV.

8. Assuming that silver is a monovalent metal with a spherical Fermi surface, calculate the following: Fermi energy, Fermi temperature, radius of the Fermi sphere, Fermi velocity and cyclotron frequency in a field of 5000 oersted.

   *Ans.* 5.5 eV, 63800 K, $1.2 \times 10^{10}$m$^{-1}$, $1.39 \times 10^6$ m/s, $1.4 \times 10^{10}$ Hz.

9. If an electric field equal to 1.0 V/m is applied to a specimen of sodium metal, find the drift velocity of the conduction electrons and the displacement $\Delta k$ of the Fermi surface.

   *Ans.* $5.90 \times 10^{-3}$ m/s, 51.0 m$^{-1}$.

10. Prove that the electron density at which the free electron spherical Fermi surface first touches the zone boundary in a bcc metal is $2\sqrt{2}\,(\pi/a^3)/3$.

11. The Fermi energy of Al is 12 eV and its electrical conductivity is $3 \times 10^{-8}$ $\Omega$m. Calculate the mean free path of the conduction electrons and their mean drift velocity in a field of 1000 Vm$^{-1}$. For Al, the atomic weight = 27, and density = 2700 kg m$^{-3.}$

    *Ans.* 216 Å, 1.85 m$^{-1}$.

12. In a cyclotron resonance experiment in potassium at 68 GHz, three consecutive resonances were observed at magnetic fields of 0.74 T, 0.59 T, 0.49 T. Calculate the cyclotron effective mass of electrons in potassium.

*Ans.* $1.08 \times 10^{-30}$kg.

13. The de Haas-van Alphen effect is studied in Cu at a field of 10 T. What is the order of maximum temperature which can be tolerated while still getting a good effect. *Ans.* 1.3 K.

14. In observing a de Haas-van Alphen effect, it is necessary that collision broadening should be comparatively small. If the impurity density $n$ and electron collision time $\tau$ are related by $n\tau = 10^{14}$ m$^{-3}$s, upto what density of impurities can the effect still be readily observed ? *Ans.* $n < 10^{25}$ m$^{-3}$.

# Chapter 13

# Semiconducting Properties of Materials

## 13.1 SEMICONDUCTORS

In section 11.11, we observed, that the magnitude of the band gap of semiconductors lies between that of insulators and metals. Further, like the band gap the resistivity of semiconductors has been found to lie in the intermediate range as evident from Table 13.1. Also, over a certain range of temperature, contrary to metal conductors, the resistance of semiconducting crystals decreases with the increase of temperature. In other words, semiconducting crystals have negative temperature coefficient of resistance. Broadly speaking we can have two types of semiconductors, i.e. instrinsic semiconductors and extrinsic semiconductors.

**Table 13.1 Resistivity of some common materials at room temperature**

| Material | Resistivity ($\Omega$m) |
|---|---|
| Quartz | $10^{13}$ |
| Glass | $10^{12}$ |
| Diamond | $10^{11}$ |
| Pure silicon | $10^{3}$ |
| Pure germanium | $10^{-1}$ |
| Lead, Iron | $10^{-7}$ |
| Copper, Silver | $10^{-8}$ |

**Intrinsic Semiconductors**

Intrinsic semiconductors are those materials having an energy gap of the order of 1 eV (which is comparable to thermal energies). Hence the conduction process in these materials is achieved as a result of thermal excitation of electrons across the energy gap. Pure chemical substances such as silicon and germanium (elements of group IV of the periodic Table), GaAs, InSb (III-V compounds), SiC (a IV-IV compound) and PbS (a IV-VI compound) are some examples of intrinsic semiconductors. At absolute zero, the valence band of an intrinsic semiconductor is completely filled and the conduction band which is separated by a distance $E_g$ (the band gap) from the valence band is empty. For this reason, at absolute zero, an intrinsic semiconductor behaves as an insulator and has zero conductivity. Fig. 13. 1a shows a simplified schematic diagram of an intrinsic semiconductor.

However, as the temperature is gradually increased, the electrons of the valence band get excited. For some electrons, the thermal energy $kT$ available at the room temperature is sufficient to surmount the forbidden energy gap and move into the conduction band (Fig. 13. 1b). The excitation of electrons from the valence band to the conduction band leaves an equal number of vacancies (called holes) in the valence band. Both, electrons in the conduction band and holes in the valence band serve as charge carriers and contribute to the electrical conductivity.

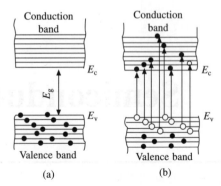

(a)                    (b)

**Fig. 13.1    Intrinsic semiconductor: (a) at absolute zero the valence band is completely filled by electrons and the conduction band is completely empty; (b) at temperature above absolute zero some of the electrons from the valence band are excited to the conduction band; holes appear in the valence band and free electrons in the conduction band**

### Extrinsic Semiconductors

A real semiconducting crystal grown in a laboratory (no matter how pure) always contains some impurity atoms (in addition to other imperfections), which create their own energy levels termed as impurity levels. These levels may occupy positions anywhere in the allowed and forbidden bands of the semiconductors. However, frequently some known impurities (in terms of both qualities and quantities) are introduced intentionally to impart specific properties to the host material. The resulting semiconducting material is known as extrinsic semiconductor, whose properties depend on the type of the impurity introduced into the host material. For this purpose, normally a few parts per million of suitable impurity material is added to the melt during the growth of semiconductor crystal. For silicon (and germanium) two types of impurities are used. These are from group III and V of the periodic Table, i.e. trivalent elements such as born and indium and pentavalent elements such arsenic and phosphorus.

When intrinsic silicon is doped (it is a process of homogeneous mixing of a small quantity of known impurity into the host material) with one of the group V elements, e.g. arsenic, then each arsenic atom is found to occupy an atomic site normally occupied by a silicon atom as shown in Fig. 13.2a. Since the host silicon atoms are tetravalent, only four of the five valence electrons of the impurity are used in forming the covalent bond, leaving one electron weakly bound to its parent atom. This electron can be easily excited into the conduction band by supplying an energy equal to $E_d \simeq 0.013$ eV. This electron leaves the atom and is free to move in the germanium lattice (Fig. 13.2b). Such an electron behaves as conduction electron.

In terms of the band theory, this process may be understood as follows:

The energy levels of the fifth electron of the impurity atoms occupy positions between the valence band and the conduction band as shown in Fig. 13.2c. These levels are at a distance of $E_d$ (~0.013 eV) below the conduction band. At absolute zero, all these levels are occupied but even at moderately low temperatures most of the electrons from them get excited into the conduction band (Fig. 13.2d) because of the small $E_d$. The remaining positive charge (a hole) is localized on the immobile arsenic atom and does not take part in the electrical conductivity.

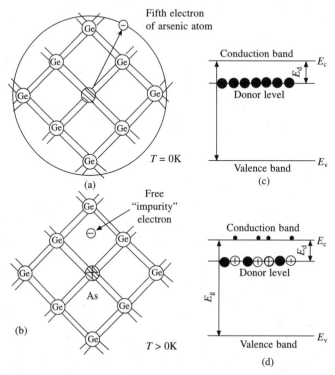

**Fig. 13.2 Charge carrier excitation in an *n*-type semiconductor.**

(a) at $T = 0K$, the atoms of pentavelent arsenic in the germanium lattice are in a non-ionized state
(b) at $T > 0K$, ionization of arsenic atoms and generation of conductin electrons
(c) energy levels of one of the five electrons of every arsenic atom are donor levels
(d) electron transition from a donor level to the conduction band at $T > 0K$.

The impurities which supply electrons without simultaneously creating holes are termed as donors and the corresponding energy levels as donor levels. The semiconductors doped with donor impurities are known as *n*-type semiconductors. Since the conduction in this case is peredominantly due to electrons in the conduction band, they are called majority carriers and the holes in the valence band become minority carriers.

Now, suppose that silicon is doped with a trivalent impurity such as indium. Again, it is found that the impurity atoms occupy sites normally occupied by germanium atoms as shown in Fig. 13.3a. The indium atom is short of one electron to establish saturated bonds with all the four nearest neighbours. However, it can borrow the required electron from a germanium atom, if an energy equal to $E_a \simeq 0.01$ eV is supplied to the system. The transfer of an electron from the germanium atom leaves a hole in the valence band which causes a break in one of the neighbouring germanium bonds as shown in Fig. 13.3b.

The energy level of the impurity atoms occupy positions between the valence and the conduction band (Fig. 13.3c). These levels are at a distance of $E_a$ (~0.011 eV) above the valence band. At absolute zero, all these levels are vacant but at any temperature above this electrons from neighbouring atoms can fill the vacancy and thereby leaving holes in the valence band (Fig. 13.3d). They establish bonds with the indium atoms and lose their ability to move in the germanium lattice and hence do not take part in the electrical conductivity.

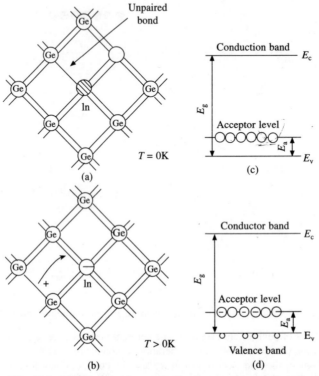

**Fig. 13.3   Charge carrier excitation in a *p*-type semiconductor:**

(a)  at $T = 0K$, the atoms of trivalent indium in the germanium lattice (the fourth bond of the indium atom is unpaired)
(b)  at $T > 0K$, the electron can go over to the unpaired bonds of impurity atoms creating an indium ion and a vacant level (hole) in the valence band of germanium,
(c)  energy levels of unpaired bonds of indium atoms are acceptor levels
(d)  electron transition from the valence band to an acceptor level at $T > 0K$ results in the generation of holes in this band

The impurities which trap electrons and add holes in the valence band without simultaneosly adding conduction electrons are termed as acceptors and the corresponding energy levels as acceptor levels. The semiconductors doped with acceptor impurities are known as *p*-type semiconductors. In this case, the holes are majority carriers in the valence band and the electrons in the conduction band (if any) are the minority carriers.

The electronic properties of extrinsic semiconductors can be suitably described in terms of their energy band configurations plus certain intraband energy levels introduced by the impurities which are rather sparingly distributed throughout the host material. It is often more convenient, however, to consider the position of Fermi level when discussing the electrical and other related properties of solids.

## 13.2   FREE CARRIER CONCENTRATION IN SEMICONDUCTORS

### Intrinsic Semiconductors

As we know that in semiconductors the magnitude of the energy gap, $E_g$ is very small, therefore some of the electrons lying on the top of the valence band gain sufficient thermal energy (which is the most usual source, other energy sources may be electrical or radiant) even at moderate temperatures and get excited into the conduction band leaving behind equal number of holes in the valence band (in a pure semiconductor under thermal equilibrium the number of electrons and holes are equal since they are produced as electron-hole pairs). These holes attract electrons, in the process one of the neighbouring electrons will jump to fill the vacancy. This process will continue and is identical to the vacancy diffusion as discussed in section 6.6.

When an electric field is applied, the electrons drift towards the positive electrode and constitute a current. Similarly, the holes move towards the negative electrode and constitute a current. However, since the electrons and holes have opposite charges, the current due to both is in the same direction. Their drift velocities under the action of an applied electric field $E$ are

$$v_e = \mu_e E$$

and
$$v_h = \mu_h E \tag{1}$$

where the subscripts $e$ and $h$ refer to electrons and holes, respectively. The proportionality factor $\mu$ is known as the mobility (the freedom of charge movement) and is a function of thermal vibration of the atoms and the crystal structure.

Under equilibrium conditions, in intrinsic semiconductors, the rate of generation of electron-hole pair $g(T)$ depends on the nature of material and the temperature. To maintain a constant concentration of pairs, the rate of recombination $r(T)$ (which depends on the properties of material and is proportional to the concentrations of two charges) must be equal to $g(T)$. Then

$$g(T) = r(T) = K n_i \, p_i \tag{2}$$

where $n_i$ and $p_i$, refer to intrinsic electron and hole densities, respectively. The proportionality constant $K$ takes into account the charge densities and properties of the semiconductor material.

Now for pair generation, $n_i = p_i$. So that,

$$g(T) = r(T) = K n_i \, p_i = K \, n_i^2 \tag{3}$$

and
$$n_i \, p_i = n_i^2 \tag{4}$$

Since the densities $n_i$ and $p_i$ are inherent property of a semiconductor at a given temperature, then the product $n_i^2$ or the square of the intrinsic charge density, also has a fixed value at a given temperature and depends only on the nature of material. This result is analogous to the constant solubility product in chemistry.

In an intrinsic semiconductor, such as germanium having an energy gap of 0.75eV, the intrinsic electron density at 300K is $2.4 \times 10^{19}$ electrons per m$^3$. Since germanium has $4.4 \times 10^{28}$ atoms per m$^3$, it is clear that only about 5 atoms out of every $10^{10}$ atoms of germanium will have broken valence bonds and can contribute to the intrinsic conduction at usual ambient temperature but increases rapidly with the temperature. In contrast, metallic copper has about $10^{28}$ electrons per m$^3$ available for conduction.

Since $n_i$ or $p_i$ strongly depends on temperature, it is necessary to limit the operating temperature of germanium devices to about 85°C to 100°C and of silicon devices to 190°C to 200°C. The higher permissible temperature of silicon is because of its larger energy gap.

### Extrinsic Semiconductors

In the preceding section, we observed that when a small quantity of suitable impurity element from group V of the periodic Table is added to pure material, *n*-type semiconductor results, where electrons act as majority charge carriers. Similarly, the addition of suitable group III element produces *p*-type semiconductor, where holes are majority charge carriers.

In both *n* and *p* type semiconductors, the electrons which create the ions (donor impurity atoms become positively ionized after donating electrons and acceptor atoms become negatively ionized) receive relatively higher energy than needed to create electron-hole pairs. Therefore, it is possible to establish conditions for conduction by holes in *p*-type semiconductors, and conduction by electrons in *n*-type semiconductors, at temperatures much below than the temperature at which intrinsic conduction by holes and electrons occur. Since no charge is added or removed during the above processes, the crystal as a whole is assumed to be electrically neutral.

Because of the ease with which the electrons from the donor impurity can be excited to the conductin band, it is reasonable to assume that these (donor impurity) atoms are totally ionized at usual ambient temperatures. Hence, the density of conduction electrons, $N_D$ can be assumed equal to the density of donor impurity atoms. Likewise, the acceptor states may assumed to be filled completely in a *p*-type semiconductor at usual temperatures, and so the density of holes in the valence band, $N_A$ is taken as equal to the density of acceptor atoms.

As a matter of fact, the concentration of impurity atoms is very low (usually one atom per $10^6 - 10^{10}$ host atoms) as compared to the parent semiconductor atom and therefore impurity doping does not appreciably affect the thermal generation and recombination process. Making use of the argument that the recombination is proportional to concentrations of two charges, for *p*-type material, the eq. 4 becomes

$$n_p p_p = n_i^2 \tag{5}$$

It is to be noted that when the concentration of majority charges is increased over its intrinsic value by doping, the concentration of minority charges is found to decrease to maintain the concentration product, $n_i^2$, constant. Based on above considerations, the amount of reduction in the minority charges can be determined by the use of an equation expressing the overall charge neutrality of the material as

$$p + N_D = n + N_A \tag{6}$$

Now, making use of the equality $np = n_i^2$, we have

$$n = \frac{n_i^2}{p}, \text{ and } p = \frac{n_i^2}{n} \tag{7}$$

So that from eq. 6, we have

$$p = N_A - N_D + n = N_A - N_D + \frac{n_i^2}{p}$$

or

$$p^2 - p(N_A - N_D) + n_i^2 = 0$$

This is a quadratic equation of the type $ax^2 + bx + c = 0$. Therefore, the roots of the above equation are

$$p = \frac{N_A - N_D}{2} \pm \left( \frac{(N_A - N_D)^2}{4} + n_i^2 \right)^{1/2} \tag{8}$$

Similarly,

$$n = \frac{N_D - N_A}{2} \pm \left( \frac{(N_D - N_A)^2}{4} + n_i^2 \right)^{1/2} \tag{9}$$

For an intrinsic semiconductor, where $N_A = N_D = 0$, from eqs. 8 and 9, we obtain $n = p = n_i$, as they should be. These are general equations for charge densities and let us see how they change under special cases:

Case I: *n-type Semiconductors*
In this case, $N_D \gg n_i$ and $N_A \cong 0$, then the hole density is

$$p_n = \frac{-N_D + N_D \sqrt{1 + (4n_i^2 / N_D^2)}}{2} \tag{10}$$

The second term under the radical is less than unity and may be expanded as a power series. Neglecting the higher power terms, the approximate hole density can be found as

$$p_n \cong -\frac{N_D}{2} + \frac{N_D}{2}\left(1 + \frac{2n_i^2}{N_D^2}\right) = \frac{n_i^2}{N_D} \tag{11}$$

Similarly, eq. 9 provides the electron density in *n*-type material as

$$n_n \cong \frac{N_D}{2} + \frac{N_D}{2}\left(1 + \frac{2n_i^2}{N_D^2}\right) = N_D + \frac{n_i^2}{N_D} \cong N_D \tag{12}$$

*Case II: p-type Semiconductors*
In this case, $N_A \gg n_i$ and $N_D \cong 0$, then the charge densities can be found as

$$n_p \cong \frac{n_i^2}{N_A} \tag{13}$$

and
$$p_P \cong N_A + \frac{n_i^2}{N_A} \cong N_A \tag{14}$$

The density of majority carriers is thus approximately equal to the density of impurity atom (as in eqs. 12 and 14) at usual ambient temperatures. On the other hand, because of recombination process the density of minority carriers remains significantly below the intrinsic $n_i$ or $p_i$ level. The following examples will be helpful in understanding this aspect more clearly.

*Example*: An intrinsic germanium semiconductor has a charge density of $2.4 \times 10^{19}$ charges per $m^3$ at 300 K. The material is made extrinsic with an indium $p$ impurity at the rate of one indium atom per $4 \times 10^8$ germanium atoms. If there are $4.4 \times 10^{28}$ germanium atoms per $m^3$, determine the concentration of minority charge carrier and discuss the result.

*Solution*: Given $n_i \cong 2.4 \times 10^{19}$ charges per $m^3$, one impurity atom per $4 \times 10^8$ germanium atoms, density of germanium is $4.4 \times 10^{28}$ atoms per $m^3$. Now for $p$ - type semiconductor, we know that $N_D \cong 0$. Further, the density of the acceptor atom is given by

$$N_A = \frac{4.4 \times 10^{28}}{4 \times 10^8} = 1.10 \times 10^{20} \ \text{per } m^3$$

and
$$n_i^2 = 5.76 \times 10^{38}$$

Now using eq. 14, we have

$$p_p \cong N_A + \frac{n_i^2}{N_A} = 1.10 \times 10^{20} + \frac{5.76 \times 10^{38}}{1.10 \times 10^{20}}$$

$$= 1.15 \times 10^{20} \ \text{per } m^3 \cong N_A$$

and from eq. 13, we have

$$n_p \cong \frac{n_i^2}{N_A} = \frac{5.76 \times 10^{38}}{1.10 \times 10^{20}} = 5.24 \times 10^{18} \ \text{per } m^3$$

so that
$$\frac{n_i}{n_p} = \frac{2.4 \times 10^{19}}{5.24 \times 10^{18}} \cong 5$$

$\Rightarrow n_p$ is one-fifth of $n_i$. In other words, the concentration of minority carriers reduces to about one-fifth of the intrinsic value.

*Example*: A specimen of germanium is doped with 0.1 atomic percent of arsenic. Assuming that at room temperature all the arsenic atoms are ionised, find the electron and hole densities in germanium. The arsenic carrier density at room temperature in germanium is $2.37 \times 10^{19}/m^3$. The density of germanium atom is $4.41 \times 10^{28}/m^3$.

*Solution*: Given: Crystal-Ge impurity = 0.1% arsenic, $n_i \cong 2.37 \times 10^{19}/m^3$, the density of germanium atom = $4.41 \times 10^{28}/m^3$, electron and hole densities = ?

Now for $n$-type semiconductor, we know that $N_A \cong 0$. Further, the electron density (which is equal to the density of the donor atom) is given by

$$N_D = \frac{0.1 \times 4.41 \times 10^{28}}{100} = 4.41 \times 10^{25}/m^3$$

and $$n_i^2 = 5.62 \times 10^{38}$$

Now, using eq. 11, we have the hole density as

$$p_n = \frac{n_i^2}{N_D} = \frac{5.62 \times 10^{38}}{4.41 \times 10^{20}} = 1.27 \times 10^{13}/m^3$$

## 13.3 FERMI LEVEL AND CARRIER CONCENTRATION IN SEMICONDUCTORS

We know that the Fermi-Dirac distribution function is given by

$$F(E) = \frac{1}{\exp\left(\dfrac{E - E_F}{kT}\right) + 1} \tag{15}$$

In section 10.6, we discussed this aspect for metals, where we observed that the Fermi energy, $E_F$ is the highest filled electronic energy at 0K. However, the meaning of $E_F$ may not be immediately obvious for semiconductors. In general, of course, we may say that $E_F$ corresponds to that level which has a probability of occupancy 1/2. This immediately follows from eq. 15.

For semiconductors, we know that at $T = 0K$, the valence band is completely filled, so that $E_F$ must be greater than $E_V$, the energy corresponding to valence band (i.e. the Fermi level must lie somewhere above the valence band). Similarly the conduction band is completely empty and hence $E_F$ must be less than $E_c$, the energy corresponding to conduction band (i.e. the Fermi level must lie somewhere below the conduction band). Thus, it follows that in a semiconductor the Fermi level must lie somewhere between the valence band and the conduction band (i.e. somewhere within the forbidden gap). Its exact position will depend upon temperature.

Now, the probability that the states at the bottom of the conduction band is occupied by electrons can be determined if we substitute $E = E_c$ in eq. 15. Similarly the probability that the states at the top of the valence band is unoccupied by electrons (or occupied by holes) can be determined if we replace $E$ by $E_V$. Also, from section 10.5 we know that the number of electrons occupying energy states between $E$ and $E + dE$ in a unit volume is given by

$$n(E)\, dE = F(E)\, g(E)\, dE \tag{16}$$

where $$g(E) = CE^{1/2} \text{ and } C = 4\pi(2m_e^*)^{3/2} h^{-3}$$

Here, $m_e^*$ represents the effective mass of an electron in the semiconductor. Now let us discuss the following three cases separately.

### Intrinsic Semiconductor

In an intrinsic semiconductor at a temperature well above 0K there are thermal electrons in the conduction band and an equal number of holes in valence band. Shockley has shown that the number of energy states in the conduction band varies as

$$g(E) = C \, (E - E_c)^{1/2} \tag{17}$$

at the energy levels near the bottom of conduction band. Now, to obtain the density of electrons in the conduction band at any temperature $T$, we integrate eq. 16 over the energy values corresponding to the conduction band, i.e. from $E_c$ to $E_{top}$. Therefore,

$$n = C \int_{E_e}^{E_{top}} \frac{(E - E_c)^{1/2} \, dE}{\exp\left(\dfrac{E - E_F}{kT}\right) + 1} \tag{18}$$

For simplicity, we shall assume that $(E_c - E_F) \gtrsim 4kT$, so that the term unity in the denominator may be neglected to a good approximation. As a result, the eq. 18 becomes

$$n = C \int_{E_c}^{E_{top}} (E - E_c)^{1/2} \, \exp\left(-\frac{E - E_F}{kT}\right) dE \tag{19}$$

Since the function $\exp(-E/kT)$ decreases very rapidly as $E$ growns; therefore it is possible to substitute infinity for $E_{top}$ in the above integral, Further, let us assume that the quantity $(E - E_c)/kT \equiv x$. Above expression reduces to

$$n = C (kT)^{3/2} \, \exp\left(-\frac{E_c - E_F}{kT}\right) \int_0^\infty x^{1/2} e^{-x} dx \tag{20}$$

Simplifying the above integral, we obtain

$$\int_0^\infty x^{1/2} e^{-x} \, dx = \frac{\pi^{1/2}}{2}$$

and hence

$$n = N_c \, \exp\left(-\frac{E_c - E_F}{kT}\right) \tag{21}$$

where,

$$N_c = 2 \left(\frac{2\pi m_e^* kT}{h^2}\right)^{3/2} \tag{22}$$

For germanium, $N_c = 5 \times 10^{25}$ m$^{-3}$ at 300 K. This is the density of occupied states of energy $E_c$ in the conduction band. For an intrinsic semiconductor, we know that $E_c - E_F = E_g/2$. Therefore, eq. 21, equivalently can be written as

$$n = N_c \, \exp\left(-\frac{E_g}{2kT}\right) \tag{23}$$

The results obtained in eqs. 21 and 23 state that the density of electrons in the conduction band is a function of temperature.

In order to find the Fermi energy ($E_F$), we make use of the fact that $N_c$ must be equal to the number of holes in the valence band. To calculate the latter, we note that $[1 - F(E)]$ represents the probability for a state of energy $E$ to be unoccupied [since $F(E)$ represents the fraction of states to be occupied]. The density of holes or unoccupied states near the top of the valence band may thus be written as

$$p = \int_0^{E_V} g(E)[1 - F(E)dE] \tag{24}$$

where the zero limit refers to the energy at the bottom of the valence band. Since the holes are created by the most energetic electrons, factor $[1 - F(E)]$ is found to decrease rapidly as one goes down below the top of the valence band. Therefore, it is reasonable to assume that the holes lie near the top of the valence band, and Shockley has shown that the number of energy states there is given by

$$g(E) = C(E_v - E)^{1/2} \tag{25}$$

If we again assume that $E_F$ lies in the forbidden gap about $4kT$ above $E_v$, then we may use the approximation

$$1 - F(E) \simeq \exp\left(\frac{E - E_F}{kT}\right) \tag{26}$$

The density of holes in the valence band can then be written as

$$p = C \int_0^{E_V} (E_v - E)^{1/2} \exp\left(\frac{E - E_F}{kT}\right) dE \tag{27}$$

By a method similar to that used for the conduction band, it is possible to estimate the holes in the valence band, as

$$p = N_v \exp\left(-\frac{E_F - E_v}{kT}\right) \tag{28}$$

where,

$$N_v = 2\left(\frac{2\pi m_h^* kT}{h^2}\right)^{3/2} \tag{29}$$

Here $m_h^*$ is the effective mass of a hole. The value of $N_v$ from eq. 29 is approximately equal to the value of $N_c$ (eq. 22). However, $N_v$ is the density of unoccupied states of energy $E_v$ in the valence band.

Now, for an intrinsic semiconductor we know that

$$n_i = p_i = n = p$$

It follows from eqs. 21 and 28 that

$$E_F = \frac{E_c + E_v}{2} + \frac{kT}{2} \ln\frac{N_v}{N_c} = \frac{E_c + E_v}{2} + \frac{3kT}{4} \ln\frac{m_h^*}{m_e^*} \tag{30}$$

In case $m_e^* = m_h^*$, then the Fermi level lies exactly halfway between the top of the valence band and the bottom of the conduction band (i.e. at the middle of the forbidden gap). However, in general $m_h^*, > m_e^*$, the Fermi level is raised slightly as $T$ increases. The location of Fermi level in an intrinsic semiconductor is shown in Fig. 13.4.

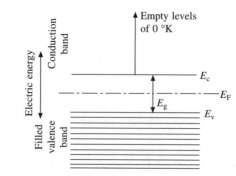

**Fig. 13.4   The location of Fermi level at 0 K in an intrinsic semiconductor**

Further, from eqs. 22 and 29 the product

$$N_c N_v = 4 \left( \frac{2\pi k}{h^2} \right)^3 \cdot (m_e^* \cdot m_h^*)^{3/2} T^3$$

Similarly, the product of eqs. 21 and 28 is

$$np = n_i^2 = N_c N_v \exp\left( -\frac{E_c - E_v}{kT} \right) = 4 \left( \frac{2\pi kT}{h^2} \right)^3 \cdot (m_e^* \cdot m_h^*)^{3/2} \exp\left( -\frac{E_c - E_v}{kT} \right)$$

This gives us

$$n_i = 2 \left( \frac{2\pi kT}{h^2} \right)^{3/2} (m_e^* \cdot m_h^*)^{3/4} \exp\left( -\frac{E_c - E_v}{2kT} \right)$$

or

$$n_i = 2 \left( \frac{2\pi kT}{h^2} \right)^{3/2} (m_e^* \cdot m_h^*)^{3/4} \exp\left( -\frac{E_g}{2kT} \right) \tag{31}$$

where $E_c - E_v = E_g$. This is in agreement with the earlier development which showed that $n_i^2$ is a constant for a given material and temperature. The eq. 31 is independent of the Fermi level. Assuming that the energy gap, $E_g = 0.75$ eV for germanium, and with $N_c \simeq N_v = 5 \times 10^{25}$, the intrinsic carrier density in germanium at 300 K is

$$n_i = p_i = 2.4 \times 10^{19} \text{ m}^{-3}$$

*Example*: Calculate the intrinsic concentration of charge carriers at 300 K. Given that $m_e^* = 0.12 \, m_0$, $m_h^* = 0.28 \, m_0$ and the energy gap for the germanium is 0.67 eV.

*Solution*: Given: $m_e^* = 0.12 m_0$, $m_h^* = 0.28 m_0$, $m_0 = 9.1 \times 10^{-31}$ kg, $T = 300$ K and $E_g = 0.67$ eV. $n_i = ?$

Making use of eq. 31 and substituting various values, we obtain

$$n_i = 2\left(\frac{2\pi kT}{h^2}\right)^{3/2} (m_e^* \cdot m_h^*)^{3/4} \exp\left(-\frac{E_g}{2kT}\right)$$

$$= 2\left(\frac{2\pi \times 1.38 \times 10^{-23} \times 300}{(6.626)^2 \times 10^{-68}}\right)^{3/2} (0.12 \times 0.28)^{3/4} (9.1 \times 10^{-31})^{3/2}$$

$$\times \exp\left(-\frac{0.67 \times 1.6 \times 10^{-19}}{2 \times 1.38 \times 10^{-23} \times 300}\right)$$

$$= 2 \times 14.42 \times 10^{69} \times 0.068 \times 10^{-45} \times 2.4 \times 10^{-6} = 4.7 \times 10^{18}/m^3$$

*Example:* An intrinsic semiconductor material $A$ has an energy gap 0.36 eV while material $B$ has an energy gap 0.72 eV. Compare the intrinsic carrier densities in these two materials at 300 K. Assume that the effective masses of all the electrons and holes are equal to the free electron mass.

*Solution:* Given: $m_e^* = m_h^* = m$, $T = 300$ K, $E_g(A) = 0.36$ eV and $E_g(B) = 0.67$ eV, also $2kT = 0.052$ eV, $\dfrac{n_i(A)}{n_i(B)} = ?$

The ratio of the carrier densities can be written as

$$\frac{n_i(A)}{n_i(B)} = \frac{\exp(-0.36/2kT)}{\exp(-0.72/2kT)} = \exp\left(\frac{0.72 - 0.36}{2kT}\right) = \exp\left(\frac{0.36}{0.052}\right) = 1015$$

### *n and p type Semiconductors*

In section 13.1 we have seen how the donor and acceptor levels (Figs. 13.2, 13.3) are being created when suitable impurity atoms are added to an intrinsic semiconductor material. In the following, we shall study the effect of impurity levels and temperature on Fermi level. For the purpose, let us consider three temperature ranges separately.

### 1.  Low Temperature Range

At low temperatures, the average energy of the lattice ($\approx kT$) due to thermal vibrations is about two orders of magnitude less than the width of the forbidden gap, $E_g$ and is insufficient to excite the electrons of the valence band to the conduction band. However, this energy is sufficient enough to excite the electrons from donor impurity levels $E_i$ to the conduction band and holes from the acceptor impurity levels $E_i$ to the valence band. Therefore, at low temperatures practically only the "impurity" charge carriers (electrons in $n$-type and holes in $p$-type semiconductors) are excited.

Calculations similar to the intrinsic case show that the position of the Fermi level in the low temperature range is

$$E_{Fn} = \frac{E_d + E_c}{2} + \frac{kT}{2} \ln \frac{N_D}{N_c} \tag{32}$$

for the $n$-type semiconductors, and

$$E_{\text{Fp}} = \frac{E_{\text{a}} + E_{\text{v}}}{2} + \frac{kT}{2} \ln \frac{N_{\text{A}}}{N_{\text{v}}} \tag{33}$$

for $p$-type semiconductors, where $N_{\text{D}}$ and $N_{\text{A}}$ being the density of donors and acceptors, respectively.

From eqs. 32 and 33, it follows that at $T = 0\text{K}$, the Fermi level will lie halfway between $E_{\text{c}}$ and $E_{\text{d}}$ in $n$-type and between $E_{\text{a}}$ and $E_{\text{v}}$ in $p$-type semiconductors, respectively (Fig. 13.5).

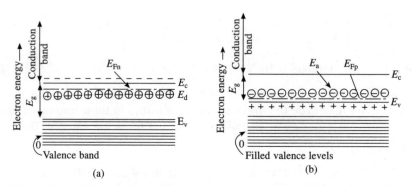

**Fig. 13.5** **The location of Fermi levels in $n$-type and $p$-type semiconductors**

Substituting $E_{\text{Fn}}$ and $E_{\text{Fp}}$ from eqs. 32 and 33 into 21 and 28, respectively, we can obtain the following expressions for the concentrations: (i) electron concentration in $n$-type semiconductors,

$$n = \sqrt{2N_{\text{D}}} \left( \frac{2\pi m_{\text{e}}^{*} kT}{h^2} \right)^{3/2} \exp\left( -\frac{E_{\text{d}}}{2kT} \right) \tag{34}$$

(ii) hole concentration in $p$-type semiconductors,

$$p = \sqrt{2N_{\text{A}}} \left( \frac{2\pi m_{\text{h}}^{*} kT}{h^2} \right)^{3/2} \exp\left( -\frac{E_{\text{a}}}{2kT} \right) \tag{35}$$

where $E_{\text{c}} - E_{\text{i}} = E_{\text{d}}$ and $E_{\text{i}} - E_{\text{v}} = E_{\text{a}}$.

## 2. Impurity Exhaustion Range (Extrinsic Range)

As the temperature is increased, the electron concentration in the conduction band increases and that on the donor levels decreases. At a particular temperature, the donor levels get exhausted. The behaviour of acceptor levels in $p$-type semiconductors is similar. Under the complete exhaustion of donor and acceptor levels, the electron concentration in the conduction band of an $n$-type semiconductor becomes practically equal to the concentration of donor impurity, $N_{\text{D}}$, i.e.

$$n = N_{\text{D}} \tag{36}$$

and the hole concentration in a $p$-type semiconductor, to that of the acceptor impurity, $N_{\text{A}}$, i.e.

$$p = N_{\text{A}} \tag{37}$$

The exhaustion (or saturation) temperature of the impurity levels, $T_{\text{s}}$ is proportional to the activation energy, $E_d$ (or $E_a$) of the impurity and its concentration. As an example, for germanium with $N_d = 10^{22}$ m$^{-3}$ and $E_d = 0.01$ eV, the saturation temperature is about 30 K.

## 3. High Temperature Range

As the temperature is increased further, the excitation of intrinsic carriers become more intense and the given semiconductor (including its Fermi level) is rapidly approaching the state which corresponds to an intrinsic semiconductor. The resultant concentration practically remains constant

$$n = n_i + N_D \cong N_D \text{ (if } n_i \ll N_D) \tag{38}$$

and

$$n = n_i + N_D \cong n_i \quad \text{(if } n_i \gg N_D) \tag{39}$$

for relatively low and high temperatures, respectively. The temperature ($T_i$) at which $n \cong n_i$, marks the transition to intrinsic conductivity. $T_i$ is higher for large forbidden gap and the impurity concentration. For germanium with $N_D = 10^{22}$ m$^{-3}$, $T_i = 450$ K. Fig. 13.6 shows schematically the dependence of the natural logarithm of the electron concentration in the conduction band of an *n*-type semiconductor on the reciprocal temperature. Three sections may be marked on the curve: (i) corresponding to impurity conduction, (ii) corresponding to impurity exhaustion range; and (iii) corresponding to intrinsic conductivity.

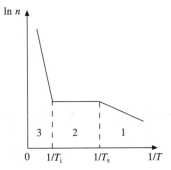

**Fig. 13.6   Temperature dependence of electron concentration** *in n*-type semiconductors

As the temperature goes up, the Fermi level in an *n*-type semiconductor falls steadily in the energy gap, and the Fermi level in a *p*-type semi-conductor rises in same proportion. Above $T_i$, the Fermi levels of these semiconductors coincide with that of intrinsic semiconductor which itself varies slightly with temperature. Also their carrier concentrations become identical to that of intrinsic semiconductor. Variation of the Fermi level in impurity materials as a function of temeprature is illustrated in Fig. 13.7.

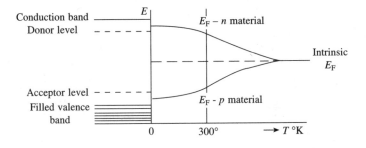

**Fig. 13.7   Temperature dependence of Fermi level in *n* and *p* materials. Electron and hole masses are assumed to be equal**

*Example*: In a *p*-type semiconductor, the Fermi level lies 0.4 eV above the valence band. If the concentration of the acceptor atom is tripled, find the new position of the Fermi level.

*Solution:* Given: *p*-type semiconductor, $E_F - E_v = 0.4$ eV, $N_A' = 3N_A$, also $kT = 0.03$ eV $E_F' = ?$
For a *p*-type semiconductor, the hole density is given by

$$p = N_A = N_v \exp\left(-\frac{E_F - E_v}{kT}\right)$$

similarly
$$P' = N_A' = 3N_A = N_v \exp\left(-\frac{E_F' - E_v}{kT}\right)$$

Comparing these two equations and removing exponential term, we have

$$(E_F' - E_V) = (E_F - E_V) - kT \ln 3$$

$$= 0.4 - 0.03 \times 1.098$$

$$= 0.4 - 0.03294$$

$$= 0.367 \text{ eV}$$

## 13.4 MOBILITY OF CHARGE CARRIERS

The mobility of a charge carrier is defined as the average drift velocity per unit electric field, i.e.

$$\mu = \frac{v}{E} \tag{40}$$

Therefore, from eq. 1, the mobilities of electrons and holes in a semiconductor can be written as

$$\mu_e = \frac{v_e}{E} \text{ and } \mu_h = \frac{v_h}{E} \tag{41}$$

In a metal, where only conduction electrons flow when an electric field is applied to it, the electrical conductivity is expressed as

$$\sigma_e = \frac{J}{E} = \frac{nev}{E} = ne\mu_e \tag{42}$$

On the other hand, in a semiconductor where both electrons and holes carry current and the mechanism of their motion is different, it is expected that their average drift velocities and hence their mobilities must also be different. Fig. 13.8 shows schematically the migration of a free electron and a hole under the influence of an electric field. A free electron moves in a random path between the atoms in a direction opposite to the direction of the field (Fig. 13.8a), whereas the hole moves along the direction of the field as a result of discrete electron jumps as indicated in Fig. 13.8b. Thus, in a semiconductor, where both electrons and holes carry current, the electrical conductivity may be defined as

$$\sigma_e = \frac{J_e}{E} = \frac{nev_e}{E} = ne\mu_e \tag{43}$$

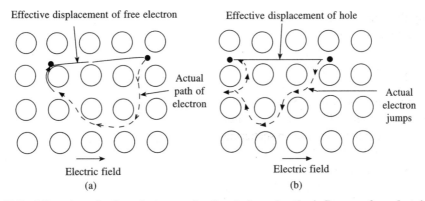

Fig. 13.8  **Migration of a free electron and a free hole under the influence of an electric field**

and
$$\sigma_h = \frac{J_h}{E} = \frac{ne\,v_h}{E} = ne\mu_h \tag{44}$$

Since the electrons and holes have opposite charges, the current due to both is in the same direction and hence the conductivities are additive. Therefore,

$$\sigma = \sigma_e + \sigma_h = ne\mu_e + pe\mu_h = e(n\mu_e + p\mu_h) \tag{45}$$

## 13.5  EFFECT OF TEMPERATURE ON MOBILITY

The mobility of electrons or holes is influenced by scattering. The two important sources of scattering in a semiconductor are due to phonons (due to lattice vibrations) and ionized impurity atoms (donors and acceptors). Other imperfections such as dislocations also contribute but to a lesser degree in most useful materials. The phonon mobility $\mu_L$ and the ion mobility $\mu_I$ are theoretically found to be

$$\mu_L = AT^{-3/2} \tag{46}$$

and
$$\mu_I = BT^{3/2} \tag{47}$$

where $A$ and $B$ are constants for given materials. If the carrier densities are known, we can calculate the total resistivity and consequently the resultant mobility analogous to the Matthiessen's rule for conductors (section 10.13) by adding the phonon and ion resistivities

$$\rho = \frac{1}{\sigma} = \rho_L + \rho_I \quad \text{or} \quad \frac{1}{\sigma} = \frac{1}{\sigma_L} + \frac{1}{\sigma_I}$$

Now, making use of eq. 42, the above equation can be written as

$$\frac{1}{ne\mu} = \frac{1}{ne\mu_L} + \frac{1}{ne\mu_I}$$

or
$$\frac{1}{\mu} = \frac{1}{\mu_L} + \frac{1}{\mu_I} \tag{48}$$

Substituting the values of $\mu_L$ and $\mu_I$ from eqs. 46 and 47 into eq. 48, we

$$\frac{1}{\mu} = \frac{T^{3/2}}{A} + \frac{T^{-3/2}}{B} \qquad (49)$$

At low temperatures, the ion scattering dominates, so that $\mu \propto T^{3/2}$. On the other hand, at high temperatures the phonon scattering prevails and hence $\mu \propto T^{-3/2}$. Further, for very pure samples ( e.g., intrinsic semiconductor or nearly so) the ion scattering is absent and only eq. 46 is applicable over a large temperature range. Fig. 13.9 shows the temperature variation of mobility for pure and impure samples of typical semi-conductors.

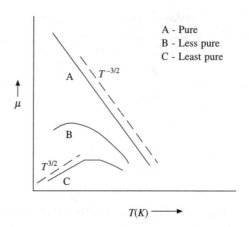

**Fig. 13.9   Temperature variation of mobility for pure and impure semiconductors**

## 13.6   ELECTRICAL CONDUCTIVITY OF SEMICONDUCTORS

**Intrinsic Semiconductors**

The electrical conductivity of a pure and perfect semiconductor crystal at any temperature (not very low) is due to intrinsic charge carriers, i.e. electrons and holes. Such conductivity is termed as intrinsic. For an intrinsic semiconductor, $n = p = n_i$ and therefore from eq. 45, the intrinsic conductivity becomes

$$\sigma_i = n_i e(\mu_e + \mu_h) \qquad (50)$$

Substituting the value of $n_i$ from eq. 31 into eq. 50, we obtain

$$\sigma_i = 2e\left(\frac{2\pi kT}{h^2}\right)^{3/2} (m_e^* \cdot m_h^*)^{3/4} \exp\left(-\frac{E_g}{2kT}\right)(\mu_e + \mu_h) \qquad (51)$$

At higher temperatures, when the material is intrinsic ($n_i \gg N_D$), the scattering is dominated by phonons. The mobility in this case is proportional to $T^{-3/2}$. Taking this into account, eq. 51 can be written as

$$\sigma_i = \sigma_i(0) \exp\left(-\frac{E_g}{2kT}\right) \qquad (52)$$

where $$\sigma_i(0) = 2e\left(\frac{2\pi kT}{h^2}\right)^{3/2} (m_e^* \cdot m_h^*)^{3/4} (\mu_e + \mu_h)$$

This is pre-exponential constant and is practically independent of temperature. From eq. 52, it follows that $\sigma_i \to \sigma_i(0)$ as $T \to \infty$. Taking the logarithm of eq. 52, we obtain

$$\ln \sigma_i = \ln \sigma_i(0) - \frac{E_g}{2kT} \qquad (53)$$

A plot of ln $\sigma_i$ versus $1/T$ will be a straight line with a slope $E_g/2k$. Thus, knowing the slope of the line, the band gap, $E_g$ can be easily determined. In Fig. 13.10, the first part of the curve indicates the intrinsic range.

*Example*: The intrinsic carrier density at room temperature in germanium is $2.37 \times 10^{19}/m^3$. If the electron and hole mobilities are 0.38 and 0.18 $m^2V^{-1}s^{-1}$, respectively, calculate the resistivity of the intrinsic germanium.

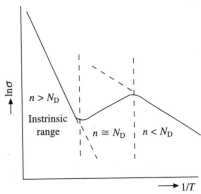

**Fig. 13.10  A plot of ln $\sigma_i$ as a function of $1/T$ for an *n*-type semiconductor**

*Solution:* Given: $n_i = 2.37 \times 10^{19}/m^3$, $\mu_e = 0.38$ $m^2V^{-1}s^{-1}$, $\mu_h = 0.18$ $m^2V^{-1}s^{-1}$, $T = 300$ K, $\rho_i = $ ?

From eq. 50, the intrinsic conductivity in terms of the electron and hole mobilities is given by

$$\sigma_i = n_i e(\mu_e + \mu_h)$$

$$= 2.73 \times 10^{19} \times 1.6 \times 10^{-19} \times 0.56 = 2.12352 \ \Omega^{-1}m^{-1}$$

Since, the resistivity is simply reciprocal of the conductivity, therefore

$$\rho_i = \frac{1}{\sigma_i} = \frac{1}{2.12352} = 0.47 \ \Omega m$$

*Example*: The intrinsic carrier density at 300 K in silicon is $1.5 \times 10^{16}/m^3$. If the electron and hole mobilities are 0.13 and 0.05 $m^2V^{-1}s^{-1}$, respectively. Calculate the conductivity of (a) intrinsic silicon and (b) silicon containing 1 donor impurity atom per $10^8$ silicon atoms.

*Solution:* Given $n_i = 1.5 \times 10^{16}/m^3$, $\mu_e = 0.13$ $m^2V^{-1}s^{-1}$, $\mu_h = 0.05 m^2V^{-1}s^{-1}$, $T = 300$ K, 1 impurity atom/$10^8$ silicon atoms. $\sigma_i = $ ? and $\sigma_{ext} = $ ?

From eq. 50, the intrinsic conductivity in terms of the electron and hole mobilities is given by

$$\sigma_i = n_i e (\mu_e + \mu_h)$$

$$= 1.5 \times 10^{16} \times 1.6 \times 10^{-19} \times 0.18$$

$$= 0.432 \times 10^{-3} \ \Omega^{-1}m^{-1}$$

Further, $\dfrac{28.09}{2.33 \times 10^3}$ $m^3$ contains $6.023 \times 10^{26}$ Si atoms

Therefore, No. of Si atoms/$m^3$ $= \dfrac{6.023 \times 10^{26} \times 2.23 \times 10^3}{28.09} = 5 \times 10^{28}/m^3$

Now, the density of the donor impurity will be given by

$$N_D = \frac{5 \times 10^{28}}{10^8} = 5 \times 10^{20}/m^3$$

Therefore, $\qquad \sigma_{ext} = N_D \, e\mu_e = 5 \times 10^{20} \times 1.6 \times 10^{-19} \times 0.13 = 10.4 \ \Omega^{-1}m^{-1}$

*Example*: Find the resistance of an intrinsic germanium rod which is 1 cm long, 1 mm wide and 1 mm thick at 300 K. The intrinsic carrier density at 300 K is $2.5 \times 10^{19}/m^3$ and the mobilities of electron and hole are 0.39 and 0.19 $m^2V^{-1}s^{-1}$, respectively.

*Solution*: Given: Crystal-Ge, $T = 300$ K, $l = 1$ cm $= 10^{-2}$ m, $b = 1$ mm $= 10^{-3}$ m, $t = 1$ mm $= 10^{-3}$ m, $n_i = 2.5 \times 10^{19}/m^3$, $\mu_e = 0.39$ $m^2V^{-1}s^{-1}$, $\mu_h = 0.19$ $m^2V^{-1}s^{-1}$, $R = ?$

From eq. 50, the intrinsic conductivity in terms of the electron and hole mobilities is given by

$$\sigma_i = n_i e(\mu_e + \mu_h) = 2.5 \times 10^{19} \times 1.6 \times 10^{-19} \times 0.58 = 2.32 \ \Omega^{-1}m^{-1}$$

Now, the surface area of the rod is

$$A = b \times l = 1 \text{ mm} \times 1 \text{ mm} = 10^{-6} \text{ m}^2$$

Further, the resistance of the rod is given by

$$R = \rho \frac{l}{A} = \frac{1}{\sigma} \cdot \frac{l}{A} = \frac{10^{-3}}{2.32 \times 10^{-6}} = 4.3 \times 10^3 \ \Omega$$

## Extrinsic Semiconductor

In an extrinsic semiconductor, either *n*- or *p*- type impurity is present. Let us consider, *n*-type semiconductor first, the carrier concentration for which is expressed by eq. 34. Substituting this in eq. 42, we obtain

$$\sigma_e = \sigma_e(0) \exp\left(-\frac{E_d}{2kT}\right) \tag{54}$$

where

$$\sigma_e(0) = \sqrt{2N_D} \ e \left(\frac{2\pi m_e^* kT}{h^2}\right)^{3/2} \mu_e$$

This is again a pre-exponential constant and is very weakly dependent on temperature as compared with the exponential term. Here, the mobility for *n*-type material ($n \ll N_D$) at low temperatures is due to ionized impurity atoms and is proportional to $T^{3/2}$. Taking the logarithm of eq. 54, we obtain

$$\ln \sigma_e = \ln \sigma_e(0) - \frac{E_d}{2kT} \tag{55}$$

Like intrinsic case, a plot of $\ln \sigma_e$ versus $1/T$ will be a straight line with a slope $E_d/2k$. In Fig. 13.10, the third part of the curve indicates the extrinsic range. The slope of this line gives the impurity ionization energy $E_d$.

In most of the semiconductors, both the phonon scattering and the impurity ionization scattering takes place. The former dominates at higher temperatures and latter at low temperatures. However, in the intermediate temperature range, neither mechanism is strong. This is the saturation region and corresponds to $n \simeq N_D$. This is depicted in the second part of the curve as shown in Fig. 13.10.

## 13.7 HALL EFFECT IN SEMICONDUCTORS

In section 10.15, we discussed the Hall effect for metals containing electrons as charge carrier. The same treatment is valid for extrinsic (*n*- or *p*-type) semiconductors, where the majority charge carrier is either electrons or holes. In the following, we shall consider the case of an intrinsic semiconductor, where simultaneously both electrons and holes are present. Since, their charges are different and they move in the opposite directions in an electric field, the Lorentz force ($F_L = qv \times B$) deflects them in the same direction (i.e. towards the front face of the slab) as shown in Fig. 13.11. However, the Hall field developed by the deflection of electrons is in the opposite direction to the Hall field developed by the deflection of holes. The two charge carriers flow in the *x*-direction under the electric field $E_x$ and according to eqs. 43 and 44, the current due to them is given by

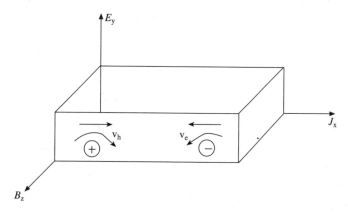

**Fig. 13.11  Deflection of electrons and holes moving in a semiconductor subjected to a transverses magnetic field**

$$J_x = J_x(e) + J_x(h) = eE_x \, (n\mu_e + p\mu_h) \tag{56}$$

Along *y*-direction, the two charges experience more than one fields. These are: Lorentz field $E_L(e)$ experienced by electrons, $E_L(h)$ by holes and Hall field $E_H$ by both. Under the action of these fields, the current along the *y*-direction is given by

$$J_y = J_y(e) + J_y(h) = ne\mu_e(E_y - v_{ex}B_z) + pe\mu_h(E_y - v_{hx}B_z) \tag{57}$$

where
$$v_{ex} = -\mu_e E_x \text{ and } v_{hx} = \mu_h E_x \tag{58}$$

Since, the charges are not allowed to flow along the *y*-direction, the current $J_y$ vanishes. Therefore, setting $J_y = 0$ in eq. 57 and substituting the values of $v_{ex}$ and $v_{hx}$ from eq. 58, we obtain

$$E_y = B_z E_x \cdot \frac{p\mu_h^2 - n\mu_e^2}{n\mu_e + p\mu_h} \tag{59}$$

Further, substituting the value of $E_x$ from eq. 56 into eq. 59, we have

$$E_y = \frac{J_x B_z}{e} \cdot \frac{p\mu_h^2 - n\mu_e^2}{(n\mu_e + p\mu_h)^2} \tag{60}$$

Therefore,
$$R_H = \frac{E_y}{J_x B_z} = \frac{1}{e} \cdot \frac{p\mu_h^2 - n\mu_e^2}{(n\mu_e + p\mu_h)^2} \tag{61}$$

For *n*- and *p*-type semiconductors, the eq. 61 reduces to

$$R_H = -\frac{1}{ne} \text{ for } n\text{-type}$$

and
$$R_H = -\frac{1}{pe} \text{ for } p\text{-type}$$

From eq. 61, we can determine the two-carrier Hall mobility as

$$\mu_H = \sigma R_H = \frac{p\mu_h^2 - n\mu_e^2}{n\mu_e + p\mu_h} \tag{62}$$

For an intrinsic semiconductor, where $n = p = n_i$, eq. 62 reduces to

$$\mu_H = \mu_h - \mu_e \tag{63}$$

Since, usually $\mu_e > \mu_h$, hence $\mu_H$ is negative for an intrinsic semiconductor. Further, from eq. 61, it follows that in an intrinsic range the sign of the Hall coefficient is determined by the carriers with greater mobility. Since, $\mu_e > \mu_h$, therefore when an intrinsic *p*-type goes over to extrinsic range, the sign of the Hall coefficient changes.

*Example:* The Hall coefficient of a certain silicon specimen was found to be $-7.35 \times 10^{-5}$ m$^3$C$^{-1}$ from 100 to 400 K. Determine the nature of the semiconductor. Further, the electrical conductivity was found to be 200 $\Omega^{-1}$m$^{-1}$. Calculate the density and mobility of charge carriers.

*Solution:* Given: $R_H = -7.35 \times 10^{-5}$ m$^3$C$^{-1}$, $\sigma = 200$ $\Omega^{-1}$m$^{-1}$, $T = 300$ K, $\mu = ?$ and $n = ?$
The negative sign of the Hall coefficient indicates that the nature of the semiconductor is *n*-type. Hence, the electron density can be obtained from the equation

$$n = -\frac{1}{eR_H} = \frac{1}{1.6 \times 10^{-19} \times 7.35 \times 10^{-5}} = 8.5 \times 10^{22} \text{ m}^3$$

and the mobility

$$\mu_e = \frac{\sigma}{ne} = \frac{200}{8.5 \times 10^{22} \times 1.6 \times 10^{-19}} = 14.7 \times 10^{-3} \text{ m}^3\text{V}^{-1}\text{s}^{-1}$$

## 13.8 JUNCTION PROPERTIES

### 1 Metal-Metal Junction

Let us consider first the simplest kind of junction between two dissimilar metals 1 and 2. Let the workfunctions of these metals be $\phi_1$ and $\phi_2$ with $\phi_2 > \phi_1$. When they are brought into contact, the electrons lying near the Fermi level in metal 1 flow into metal 2 until the Fermi energies in both metals are equal. In the process, the surface of metal 2 becomes negatively charged while the surface of the metal 1 becomes positively charged, thus giving rise to an electric double layer. Fig. 13.12 shows the energy levels before and after the contact, at absolute zero. At equilibrium, a contact potential is developed between the metal surfaces which is given by

$$eV = \phi_2 - \phi_1 \qquad (64)$$

Since, metals are good conductors of electricity, the electrical double layer is confined to the junction region only (i.e. the surface of contact between the two metals).

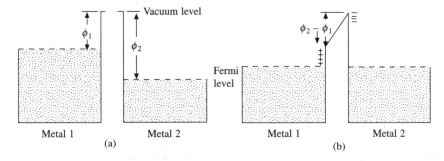

**Fig. 13.12   Energy levels for two metals before and after contact at $T = 0K$**

According to the Joule's law (of heating effect of current), we know that when a current is passed through a conductor of resistance $R$, then a heat equal to $I^2Rt$ or $V$ it is dissipated to the surroundings. However, when a potential is applied across the metal-metal junction, an additional heat is generated or absorbed at the junction. The additional heat (generated or absorbed per second) is proportional to current such that,

$$|Q| = I^2R + \pi_{12}I \qquad (65)$$

where $\pi_{12}$ is called the Peltier coefficient and the phenomenon is called the Peltier effect. If the current flows from the metal 1 to metal 2, heat is generated and the corresponding Peltier coefficient is said to be positive. When the current is reversed, the Peltier coefficient changes its sign and the heat is being absorbed. This effect is employed in electronic refrigerators.

It is possible to make use of this effect in still another way. Suppose, if the two sides of the junction are maintained at different temperatures $T_1$ and $T_2$, respectively, then the electrons in the hot metal gain thermal energy and flow to the colder side. This produces a thermoelectric emf at the junction. This phenomenon is called Seebeck effect. Thermocouples consist of metal-metal junctions are widely used in temperature measurements.

## 2.   Metal-Semiconductor Junction

It is interesting to note that metal-semiconductor contact may be either Ohmic or non-Ohmic (rectifying) depending on the type of the metal used, but both are equally important. Ohmic contacts exist whenever (a) the workfunction of an $n$-type semiconductor is greater than that of the metal and/or (b) the workfunction of a $p$-type semiconductor is smaller than that of the metal.

Similarly, non-Ohmic contacts exist whenever (a) the workfunction of an n-type semiconductor is smaller than that of the metal and/or (b) the workfunction of a p-type semiconductor is greater than that of the metal.

*Rectifying Contacts*

Let $\phi_M$ and $\phi_S$ be the workfunctions of a metal and an n-type semiconductor, respectively, when $\phi_M > \phi_S$. Let us assume here that the donor levels in the semiconductor are completely ionized at room temperature. The workfunction, $\phi_S$ for the semiconductor can be regarded as the sum of the workfunctions, i.e. $\phi_S = \phi_I + \phi_E$, where $\phi_I$ is the internal workfunction (which is the energy difference between the Fermi level and the bottom of the conduction band) and $\phi_E$ is the external workfunction (which is the energy required to remove a conduction electron) as shown in Fig. 13.13a. When the metal-semiconductor contact is made, the conduction electrons begin to flow from the semiconductor into the metal until the Fermi energies on both sides of the junction are equal. In the process, the surface of the metal becomes negatively charged and the surface of the semiconductor (which is now depleted of electrons) becomes positively charged. As a result, a potential barrier is formed at the metal-semiconductor junction. Since, the Fermi energy on both sides have the same value, the energy levels in the bulk of the semiconductor are lowered by an amount $\phi_M - \phi_S$ as shown in Fig. 13.13b. If the system is viewed from the semiconductor side, the height of the potential barrier between the semiconductor and the metal (in volts) is given by

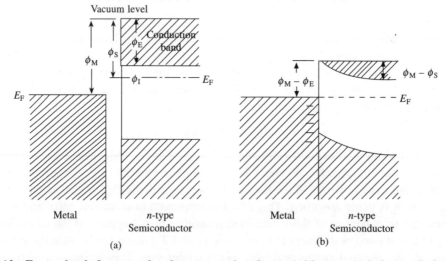

**Fig. 13.13**  **Energy levels for a metal and *n*-type semiconductor (with $\phi_M > \phi_S$) before and after contact**

$$eV_{SM} = \phi_M - \phi_S \qquad (66)$$

On the other hand, if viewed from the metal side, the barrier height in volts is

$$eV_{MS} = \phi_M - \phi_E \qquad (67)$$

Although the barrier heights given by eqs. 66 and 67 are different, but in equilibrium the number of electrons diffusing in both directions must be identical. It is due to the fact that the metal contains more free electrons but have to climb a higher potential barrier than the electrons in the semiconductor whose conduction band contains less free electrons. Thus, in equilibrium no net current flows across the metal-semiconductor junction.

Now, after the equilibrium is reached, a voltage $v$ is applied to the system so as to make the semiconductor side positive with respect to the metal side, then the height of the barrier from the semiconductor side increases from $eV_{SM}$ to $e(V_{SM} + V)$ while the barrier height from the metal side remains the same as shown in Fig. 13.14a. This increased barrier height impedes the flow of electrons from the semiconductor into the metal while the flow of electrons from the metal into the semiconductor remains as before. Thus, there is a net flow of current from the metal to the semiconductor and the semiconductor is said to have been applied a reverse bias. The net current flowing from the metal into the semiconductor is

$$I_{MS} = ACT^2 \exp\left[-\left(\frac{\phi_M - \phi_E}{kT}\right)\right] \tag{68}$$

Conversely, if the voltage applied in a reverse direction so as to make the semiconductor side negative with respect to the metal side, then the barrier height is reduced from $eV_{SM}$ to $e(V_{SM} - V)$. In this case, there is net flow of current from the semiconductor into the metal and the semiconductor is said to have been applied a forward bias. This is shown in Fig. 13.14b. The net current flowing from the semiconductor into the metal is given by

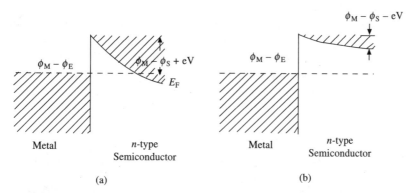

**Fig. 13.14**  **Energy levels for a metal and *n*-type semiconductor contact with $\phi_M > \phi_S$ (a) when a positive voltage *v* is applied to the semiconductor, i.e. reverse bias (b) when a positive voltage *v* is applied to the metal, i.e. forward bias**

$$I_{SM} = ACT^2 \exp\left[-\left(\frac{\phi_M - \phi_E - eV}{kT}\right)\right] \tag{69}$$

For very low temperatures, one can approximate $\phi_S \sim \phi_E$. Thus, the net current during the forward bias is given by

$$I_{net} = I_{SM} - I_{MS} = I_S\left[\exp\left(\frac{eV}{kT}\right) - 1\right] \tag{70}$$

where $I_S$ is called the saturation current and is given by

$$I_S = ACT^2 \exp\left[-\left(\frac{\phi_M - \phi_S}{kT}\right)\right] \tag{71}$$

If the sign of $V$ is taken to be the polarity of the metal, then according to eq. 70, for forward bias (positive $V$) the net current increases exponentially with voltage. On the other hand, for reverse bias (negative $V$), the current is essentially constant and is equal to $-I_S$. The metal-semiconductor contact acts like a rectifier and hence it is called rectifying contact. The voltage-current characteristic of a rectifier is shown in Fig. 13.15.

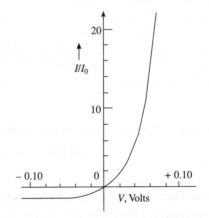

**Fig. 13.15   I-V characteristics of a non-ohmic metal-semiconductor junction**

*Ohmic Contacts*

When the workfunction of the metal is less than that of the *n*-type semiconductor (i.e. $\phi_M < \phi_S$), the contact between such metals and semiconductors is said to be ohmic. Fig. 13.16 shows the energy level diagrams before and after the contact is made. Since, initially, the Fermi level in the semiconductor is lower than the Fermi level in the metal by an amount $\phi_S - \phi_M$, therefore the electrons flow from the metal into the semiconductor, making the metal surface positive and the semiconductor surface negative. At equilibrium, the negative surface charge on semiconductor depresses the bottom of the conduction band at the contact.

Similar to the above, when potential is applied, the energy levels in the bulk of the semiconductor

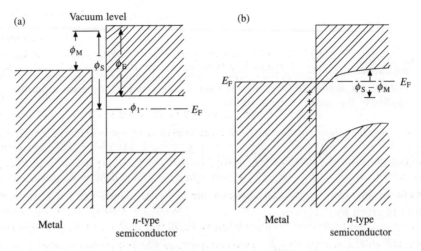

**Fig. 13.16   Energy bands for a metal and *n*-type semiconductor (with $\phi_M < \phi_S$), before and after contact**

are shifted. When the semiconductor is made positive with respect to the metal, the corresponding shifts in the energy levels are shown in Fig. 13.17a. The current is carried by the electrons from semiconductor to the metal flows "downhill" without encountering an appreciable barrier. On the other hand, when the semiconductor is made negative with respect to the metal as shown in Fig. 13.17b, the current is carried by electrons flowing from the metal to the semiconductor again "downhill". In both the cases, the magnitude of the current is directly proportional to the applied voltage in accordance with the Ohm's law. Accordingly, such a contact is called ohmic contact. A similar situation exists for a contact between a metal and a *p*-type semiconductor when $\phi_M > \phi_S$.

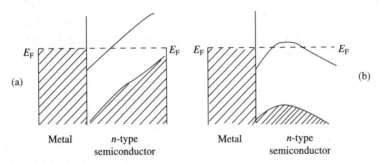

**Fig. 13.17  Energy bands for a metal and *n*-type semiconductor (with $\phi_M < \phi_S$) in contact. (a) when a positive voltage *V* is applied to the semiconductor, (b) when a positive voltage *V* is applied to the metal**

### 3.  Semiconductor-Semiconductor (p-n) Junction

Here, we shall discuss the simplest type of semiconductor-semiconductor junction, i.e. a junction between an *n*-type semiconductor and a *p*-type (which is chemically same as *n*-type) semiconductor (or *p–n* junction). There are several methods of preparing a *p – n* junction. One such method is to grow a single crystal of germanium or silicon from melt by slowly withdrawing the solidified crystal from the melt while adding suitable acceptor impurity in the initial part, and the donor impurity in the latter part of the growth. The density of electrons being greater in the *n*-region, they diffuse into the *p*-region and combine with the free holes there. As a result, the *p*-region becomes negatively charged with respect to the *n*-region and a barrier is formed which stops further diffusion. The region over which the barrier is formed contains space charge and is usually called as the space charge region or the transition region. At equilibrium, the Fermi energy has the same value throughout the crystal and the energy levels of the *p-n* junction looks like Fig. 13.18.

Now let us consider first, the conduction of electrons only. Although the density of conduction electrons in the *p*-region is smaller, they can flow "downhill" while those in the *n*-region have to surmount the potential energy barrier at the junction. A thermally generated electron current, $I_g$ is proportional to the thermally excited electrons in the *p*-region according to the relation

$$n_p = \exp\left(-\frac{E_c^p - E_F}{kT}\right) \qquad (72)$$

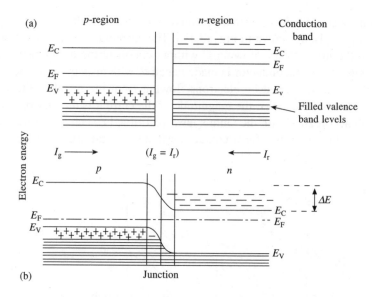

**Fig. 13.18** **Energy levels for *p* and *n*-type semiconductors before and after junction formation**

At the same time, the number of electrons in the conduction band of *n*-region is given by

$$n_n = \exp\left(-\frac{E_c^n - E_F}{kT}\right) \tag{73}$$

However, all these electrons (given by eq. 73) cannot surmount the potential barrier and cross over into the *p*-region. The fraction of electrons able to do so is given by

$$\exp\left(-\frac{\Delta E}{kT}\right)$$

where $\Delta E = E_c^P - E_c^n$. If $n_n'$ is the effective density of conduction electrons capable to cross over into the *p*-region, then

$$n_n' = \exp\left[-\left(\frac{\Delta E + (E_c^n - E_F)}{kT}\right)\right] = \exp\left[-\left(\frac{E_c^P - E_c^n + E_c^n - E_F}{kT}\right)\right] = \exp\left(-\frac{E_c^P - E_F}{kT}\right) \tag{74}$$

These electrons can combine with the holes in the *p*-region and thus constitute a current called the recombination current $I_r$. Further, a comparison of eqs. 72 and 74 gives us $n_p = n_n'$. Consequently, $I_g = I_r$, they are shown by arrows on the top of the figure. Hence, at equilibrium, the net current is zero. The same is true for the holes in the valence band.

Now, let us suppose that an external voltage *v* is applied to the junction so that the *p*-region is made positive with respect to the *n*-region (i.e. when a forward bias is applied) as shown in Fig. 13.19a. This decreases the height of the energy barrier by an amount eV as shown in

Fig. 13.19b. Further, the recombination current $I_r$ is increased above its equilibrium value by a factor $\exp(eV/kT)$ while thermally generated electron current $I_g$ remains as before. Thus, the increased current in the forward direction is given by

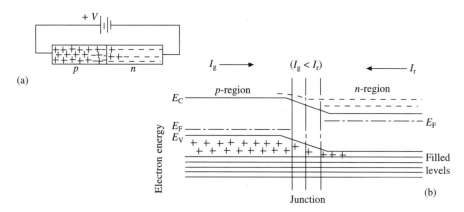

**Fig. 13.19** **(a) Junction under forward bias, (b) energy levels with forward bias**

$$I_r = I_g \exp\left(\frac{eV}{kT}\right) \tag{75}$$

The net forward current $I_v$ due to the external voltage $V$ is given by

$$I_v = I_r - I_g = I_g\left[\exp\left(\frac{eV}{kT}\right) - 1\right] \tag{76}$$

The same is true for the hole current in the valence band. The combined current (due to holes and electrons) represented by the so called dark current $I_0$, then eq. 76 can be modified to a more familiar form

$$I_v = I_0\left[\exp\left(\frac{eV}{kT}\right) - 1\right] \tag{77}$$

If an external voltage $V$ is applied to the junction so that $n$-region is made more positive with respect to the $p$-region (i.e. when a reverse bias is applied) as shown in Fig. 13.20a. There is an increase in the barrier height by $eV$ and a consequent decrease in the value of $I_r$, while $I_g$ remains unaffected (Fig. 13.20b). Proceeding as above, the combined current for reverse bias can be easily obtained as

$$I_v = I_0\left[\exp\left(-\frac{eV}{kT}\right) - 1\right] = -I_0 \text{ (constant)} \tag{78}$$

whereas the value of the potential $V$ is increased, the exponential term $\exp\left(-\frac{eV}{kT}\right) \ll 1$ for $eV \geq 4kT$. The forward bias current increases exponentially, whereas the reverse bias current approaches a saturation value $I_0$. They are shown in Fig. 13.21.

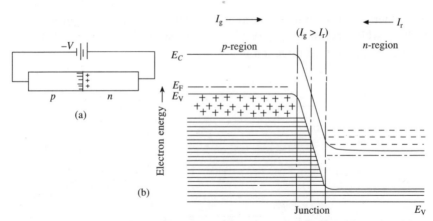

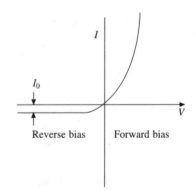

**Fig. 13.20   (a) Junction under reverse bias, (b) energy levels with reverse bias**

*Example*: A potential difference of 0.35 volts is applied across a germanium diode at 300 K. Calculate the forward current in terms of the reverse saturation current.

*Solution:* Given: Potential difference = 0.335 volt, $T = 300$ K, $I_v = ?$
Making use of eq. 77 and substituting various values, the forward current is obtained as

$$I_v = I_0\left[\exp\left(\frac{eV}{kT}\right) - 1\right] \sim I_0\,\exp\left(\frac{eV}{kT}\right)$$

$$= \exp\left(\frac{1.6 \times 10^{-19} \times 0.35}{1.38 \times 10 \times 300}\right) I_0$$

$$= \exp(13.53)\,I_0 = 7.52 \times 10^5\,I_0$$

**Fig. 13.21   I-V characteristics of a biased *p–n* junction at some temperature T**

*Example*: For what voltage will the reverse current in a $p - n$ junction germanium diode attain a value of 90% of its saturation value at room temperature?

*Solution:* Given: $I_v = 90\%$ of $I_0$, $T = 300$ K, $V = ?$
The general form of the rectifier equation is

$$I_v = I_0\left[\exp\left(\frac{eV}{kT}\right) - 1\right]$$

or $\qquad\qquad \dfrac{9}{10} = \exp\left(\dfrac{eV}{kT}\right) - 1$

or $\qquad\qquad 1.9 = \exp\left(\dfrac{eV}{kT}\right)$

or $\qquad \dfrac{eV}{kT} = \ln 1.9$

or $\qquad V = \dfrac{\ln 1.9 \times kT}{e} = \dfrac{\ln 1.9 \times 1.38 \times 10^{-23} \times 300}{1.6 \times 10^{-19}} = 0.0166 \text{ volt}$

## 13.9  SUMMARY

1. At an ambient temperature, the free intrinsic carrier concentration $n_i$ (in intrinsic semiconductor) is very small and increases rapidly with the temperature. On the other hand, the density of majority charge carrier in $n$-type semiconductor $n_n \simeq N_D$ and in $p$-type semiconductor $p_p \simeq N_A$, the density of impurity donor or acceptor atoms, respectively.

2. In general, the Fermi level lies somewhere within the forbidden band in a semiconductor. For $m_e^* = m_h^*$, the Fermi level lies exactly halfway between the valence and the conduction bands in an intrinsic semiconductor.

3. In extrinsic $n$- and $p$ -type semiconductors, the Fermi level lies halfway between $E_c$ and $E_d$ and between $E_a$ and $E_v$, respectively at low temperatures. On the other hand, at high temperatures, the Fermi levels of extrinsic semiconductors coincide with that of intrinsic one.

4. Since the electrons and holes have opposite charges, the current due to both is in the same direction and hence the conductivities are additive. Therefore,

$$\sigma = \sigma_e + \sigma_h = e \, (n\mu_e + p\mu_h)$$

where $\mu_e$ and $\mu_h$ are the mobilities of electrons and holes, respectively.

5. The mobility of a given semiconductor varies with temperature according to the relation

$$\frac{1}{\mu} = \frac{1}{\mu_L} + \frac{1}{\mu_I} = \frac{T^{3/2}}{A} + \frac{T^{-3/2}}{B}$$

where $A$ and $B$ are constants for the given semiconductor. At low temperatures, the ion scattering dominates, so that $\mu \propto T^{3/2}$. On the other hand, at high temperatures, the phonon scattering prevails and hence $\mu \propto T^{-3/2}$.

6. When both electrons and holes are present as charge carriers (as in a pure semiconductor), both contribute towards the Hall constant. The resulting expression is given by

$$R_H = \frac{1}{e} \cdot \frac{p\mu_h^2 - n\mu_e^2}{(n\mu_e + p\mu_h)^2}$$

For $n$-and $p$-type semiconductors, this reduces to

$$R_H = -\frac{1}{ne} \text{ for } n\text{-type}$$

and $\qquad\qquad\qquad R_H = \dfrac{1}{pe} \text{ for } p\text{-type}$

7. When two dissimilar metals are brought into contact, electrons from the metal with lower workfunction flow into other until the Fermi energies in both the metals are equal. At equilibrium, the contact potential developed between the metal surfaces is given by

$$eV = \phi_2 - \phi_1$$

where $\phi_2 > \phi_1$.

8. When a potential is applied across metal-metal junction, an additional heat is generated or absorbed at the junction. This is proportional to the current such that

$$|Q| = I^2 R + \pi_{12} I$$

where $\pi_{12}$ is called the Peltier coefficint.

9. If the two sides of the junction are maintained at different temperatures, the electrons in the hot metal gain thermal energy and flow to the colder side. This produces thermoelectric emf at the junction. This is called Seebeck effect. Thermocouples consist of metal-metal junctions.

10. Metal-semiconductor junction may be either Ohmic or rectifying depending on the type of the metal used. Ohmic contacts exist whenever the workfunction of an *n*-type semiconductor is greater (or the workfunction of a *p*-type semiconductor is smaller) than that of metal. Inverse is the case for non-ohmic contacts.

11. The simplest type of semiconductor-semiconductor junction is a *p–n* junction. A *p – n* junction can perform various functions depending on the geometry, the bias conditions and the doping level in each semiconductor region. Under forward bias condition (i.e. when the *p*-region is made positive with respect to the *n*-region), a net current flows in the internal circuit, which is given by

$$I_v = I_0 \left[ \exp\left( -\frac{eV}{kT} \right) - 1 \right]$$

where *V* is the external applied voltage and $I_0$ is called the dark current. On the other hand, under reverse bias condition

$$I = -I_0 \text{ (constant)}$$

This current is small and is independent of the voltage.

## 13.10   DEFINITIONS

*Acceptor Levels:* Local energy levels which lie near the valence band.

*Conduction Band:* The lowest energy band which is not completely filled with electrons. In a conductor, the electrons in the conduction band are generally free to move if they are close enough to the Fermi level.

*Donor Levels:* Local energy levels near the conduction band which bind the electron to the vicinity of the donor atom.

*Intrinsic Semiconductor:* A material whose conductivity lies between those of insulators and conductors; its valence band is full, and is separated from the conduction band by an energy gap small enough to be surmounted by thermal excitation; current carriers are electrons in the conduction band and holes in the valence band in equal amounts.

*Minority Carriers:* In an *n*-type semiconductor, the holes are called minority carriers, while in *p*-type semiconductor, the electrons are called minority carriers.

*Majority Carriers:* The type of charge carrier which is most prevalent; holes in a *p*-type and conduction electrons in an *n*-type semiconductor.

*Mobility ($\mu$):* It is defined by the relation $v_d = \mu E$, i.e. the proportionality constant between the drift velocity and the applied field.

*n-type semiconductor:* A semiconductor containing donor impurities which can donate electrons to the conduction band by thermal excitation; the majority carriers are electrons.

*p-type semiconductor:* A semiconductor containing acceptor impurities which can accommodate electrons that have been thermally excited from the full valence band in local levels; the resulting holes in the valence band are the majority carriers.

*Rcombination:* The process by which excess carriers produced by radiation or other means in a semiconductor crystal return to their equilibrium state when the radiation is removed. This usually occurs by sequential quantum jumps called recombination transitions.

*Valence Band:* The band containing the valence electrons. In a conductor, the valence band is also called the conduction band.

# REVIEW QUESTIONS AND PROBLEMS

1. What is intrinsic semiconductor? Obtain an expression for the intrinsic carrier concentration in an intrinsic semiconductor. Under what condition will the Fermi level be in the middle of the forbidden gap?

2. What are intrinsic and extrinsic semiconductors? Discuss the location of the Fermi levels under suitable limiting conditions and give the necessary theory.

3. Derive an expression relating the shift in the Fermi level and the carrier density in an intrinsic semiconductor.

4. Why does the conductivity of a semiconductor change with impurity content? Compare this with the behaviour of metallic conductor.

5. Explain the Hall effect. Derive an expression for the Hall coefficient of semiconductor on two band model carriers.

6. Find the fraction of electrons excited into conduction band in germanium at 100 K, 300 K and 1200 K.
   *Ans.* $2.3 \times 10^{-18}$, $1.3 \times 10^{-6}$, and $3.4 \times 10^{-2}$.

7. In an intrinsic semiconductor, the effective mass of the electron is 0.07 $m_0$ and that of hole is 0.4 $m_0$, where $m_0$ is the rest mass of the electron. Calculate the intrinsic concentration of charge carriers at 300 K. Given: the energy gap = 0.7 eV.
   *Ans.* $2.4 \times 10^{18}$/m$^3$.

8. A sample of germanium whose intrinsic carrier concentration is $2.5 \times 10^{19}$/ m$^3$ at 300 K, is made *p*-type material by adding acceptor atoms at a rate of one atom per $4 \times 10^8$ germanium atoms. The density of germanium atom is $4.4 \times 10^{28}$/m$^3$. Compare the density of electrons with intrinsic charge carriers. Assume that all the acceptor atoms are ionized at 300 K.    *Ans.* 0.22.

9. The intrinsic carrier concentration of a germanium sample is $2.4 \times 10^{19}$/m$^3$ at 300 K. Its electron and hole mobilities are 0.39 and 0.19 m$^2$V$^{-1}$s$^{-1}$ respectively. Calculate the conductivity of the sample.
   *Ans.* 2.23 $\Omega^{-1}$m$^{-1}$.

10. Calculate the current produced in a small germanium plate of area 1 cm$^2$ and of thickness 0.3 mm, when a potential difference of 2 volts is applied across its faces. The intrinsic carrier concentration of geranium is $2 \times 10^{19}$/m$^3$ and the mobilities of electron and holes are 0.36 and 0.17 m$^2$V$^{-1}$s$^{-1}$, respectively.
    *Ans.* 1.13 A.

11. Compare the densities of charge carriers in a pure silicon crystal at the two temperatures 300 K and 330 K. The energy gap for silicon is 1.1 eV.    *Ans.* 0.12.

12. Consider a sample of *n*-type silicon with $N_D = 10^{21}$/m$^3$. Determine the electron and hole densities at 300 K. The intrinsic carrier concentration for silicon at 300 K is $9.8 \times 10^{15}$/m$^3$.
    *Ans.* $10^{21}$/m$^3$, $9.6 \times 10^{10}$/m$^3$.

13. If a sample of silicon is doped with $3 \times 10^{23}$ arsenic atoms and $5 \times 10^{23}$ atoms of boron, determine the electron and hole concentrations if the intrinsic charge carriers of silicon are $2 \times 10^{16}$/m$^3$.
    *Ans.* $1.33 \times 10^9$/m$^3$, $2 \times 10^{23}$/m$^3$.

14. Determine the density of the donor atoms which have to be added to intrinsic germanium to make it an *n*-type material of resistivity $0.19 \times 10^{-2}$ $\Omega$m. It is given that the mobility of electrons in the *n*-type semiconductor is $0.325$ m$^2$V$^{-1}$s$^{-1}$.

    *Ans.* $1.01 \times 10^{22}$/m$^3$.

15. An electric field of 100 V/m is applied to a sample of *n*-type semiconductor whose Hall coefficient is $-0.0125$ m$^3$/C. Determine the current density in the sample, assuming the electron mobility to be 0.36 m$^2$V$^{-1}$s$^{-1}$. *Ans.* 2880 A/m$^2$.

16. 5 $\mu$A current flows through a simple *p-n* junction diode at room temperature when it is reverse biased with 0.15 V. Determine the amount of current which will flow when it is forward-biased with the same voltage. *Ans.* 1.66 mA.

# Chapter 14

# Dielectric Properties of Materials

## 14.1 INTRODUCTION

The energy band model of an insulator (dielectric) is similar to that of a semiconductor except that the forbidden gap in dielectric mateials is comparatively larger (section 11.11). In such materials, electrons are very tightly bound to the atoms (i.e. they do not conduct any electric current) so that at ordinary temperatures they cannot be dislodged either by thermal vibrations or with ordinary fields. However, they can only move a bit within the molecule and their cumulative effect account for the characteristic behaviour of dielectric materials. The negative and positive charges in each part of the crystal can be considered to be centered at the same point, and since no conductivity is possible, the localized charges remain practically undisturbed. When an electric field of sufficient magnitude is applied to the crystal, the centres of the positive charges are displaced slightly in one direction (i.e. the direction of the field) and that of the negative charges in the opposite direction,. This produces local electric dipole throughout the crystal, where an electric dipole is an entity in which equal and opposite charges are separated by a small distance.

Dielectric materials include some solids such as glass, porcelain, etc., liquids such as chemically pure water, methyl chloride ($CH_3Cl$), etc., and gases such as hydrogen, nitrogen, carbon tetra chloride ($CCl_4$), ammonia ($NH_3$) etc.

A dielectric is called homogeneous and isotropic if all its properties are the same at any point and in all directions inside it.

If in the absence of an external electric field the centres of mass of the positive and negative charges in a molecule of a dielectric coincide, it is called non-polar. On the other hand, the nuclei and electrons in the molecules of polar dielectrics are arranged in such a way that the centres of mass of the positive and negative charges do not coincide. Such molecules, regardless of the external electric field, behave like rigid dipoles.

## 14.2 DIPOLE MOMENT

If we have two equal and opposite charges, $+q$ and $-q$ as shown in the Fig. 14.1, the moment of this dipole can be defined as

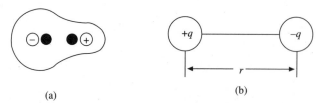

(a)                                    (b)

**Fig. 14.1   An electric dipole**

$$P = qr \qquad (1)$$

and is directed from the negative to the positive charge. The dipole moment is thus equal to one of the charges times the distance between them. The total dipole moment is defined as

$$P = \Sigma\ q_n r_n \qquad (2)$$

where $r_n$ is the position vector of the charge $q_n$. Total sum is independent of the origin chosen for the position vectors, provided that the system is neutral.

## 14.3   POLARIZATION

When a dielectric material is placed in an external electric field, it becomes polarized, i.e. within a small volume of substance the geometric sum of the electric dipole moment vectors of the molecules becomes non zero. The polarization $P$ is thus defined as the dipole moment per unit volume, i.e.

$$P = \frac{p}{\Delta V} \qquad (3)$$

If the number of molecules per unit volume is $N$ and if each has a moment $p$, then the polarization is given by

$$P = Np \qquad (4)$$

The mechanism of polarization differs for non-polar and polar dielectric materials.

*Example*: If the molecular dipoles in a $10^{-3}$ m radius water drop are pointed in the same direction, calculate the polarization. Dipole moment of the water molecule is $6 \times 10^{-30}$ C-m.

*Solution:* Given: $p = 6 \times 10^{-30}$ C-m, $r = 10^{-3}$ m, $P = ?$

We know that the molecular weight of water, $M = 18$, density, $\rho = 10^3$ kg/m$^3$ and the volume $V = M/\rho$. Now, it can be said that

A volume of $\dfrac{18}{10^3}$ m$^3$ will contain $6 \times 10^{26}$ water molecules

or $\quad \dfrac{4\pi}{3}(10^{-3})^3$ will contain $\dfrac{6.02 \times 10^{26} \times 10^3 \times 4\pi \times 10^{-9}}{18 \times 3} = 1.40 \times 10^{20}/\text{m}^3 = N$

Therefore, making use of eq. 4, the polarization can be obtained as

$$P = Np = 1.40 \times 10^{20} \times 6 \times 10^{-30} = 8.4 \times 10^{-10} \text{ C/m}^2$$

## 14.4 THE ELECTRIC FIELD OF A DIPOLE

If we choose the coordinates such that polarization vector $P$ lies at the origin and points in the $z$-direction (Fig. 14.2), then the potential at a point $(r, \theta)$ from the centre of the dipole is given by

$$V_{\text{dip}}(r, \theta) = \frac{\hat{r} \cdot P}{4\pi\varepsilon_0 r^2} = \frac{p \cos \theta}{4\pi\varepsilon_0 r^2} \qquad (5)$$

Taking into account the fact that the electric field is equal to the negative of the potential gradient, we can write various components of the field in the spherical polar coordinate system as:

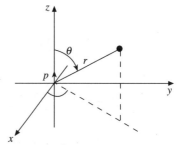

**Fig. 14.2   Electric field of a dipole**

$$E_r = -\frac{\partial V}{\partial r} = \frac{2p \cos \theta}{4\pi\varepsilon_0 r^3}$$

$$E_\theta = -\frac{1}{r} \cdot \frac{\partial V}{\partial \theta} = \frac{p \cos \theta}{4\pi\varepsilon_0 r^3}$$

and

$$E_\phi = -\frac{1}{r \sin \theta} \frac{\partial V}{\partial \phi} = 0$$

Thus,

$$E_{\text{dip}}(r, \theta) = \frac{P}{4\pi\varepsilon_0 r^3}(2 \cos \theta \, \hat{r} + \sin \theta \, \hat{\theta}) \qquad (6)$$

In order to simplify this, let us make the following substitutions,

$$y = r \sin \theta \quad \text{and} \quad z = r \cos \theta$$

The radius vector $r$ lying in the $yz$-plane can then be written as

$$\vec{r} = \hat{j}y + \hat{k}z$$

$$= \hat{j} r \sin \theta + \hat{k} r \cos \theta$$

Therefore,

$$\hat{r} = \frac{\vec{r}}{r} = \hat{j} \sin \theta + \hat{k} \cos \theta$$

Similarly,

$$\hat{\theta} = \hat{j} \cos \theta - \hat{k} \sin \theta$$

where $\hat{r}$ and $\hat{\theta}$ are the unit vectors along their respective axes. Now, substituting the value of $\hat{r}$ and $\hat{\theta}$ in eq. 6, we obtain

$$E_{\text{dip}}(r, \theta) = \frac{P}{4\pi\varepsilon_0 r^3}(2 \cos \theta \, \hat{r} + \sin \theta \, \hat{\theta})$$

$$= \frac{p}{4\pi\varepsilon_0 r^3}\{2 \cos \theta \, (\hat{j} \sin \theta + \hat{k} \cos\theta) + \sin \theta \, (\hat{j} \cos \theta - \hat{k} \sin \theta)\}$$

$$= \frac{p}{4\pi\varepsilon_0 r^3}\{\hat{j}\, 2 \sin\theta \cos\theta + 2\hat{k}\cos^2\theta + \hat{j}\sin\theta\cos\theta - \hat{k}\sin^2\theta\}$$

$$= \frac{p}{4\pi\varepsilon_0 r^3}\{\hat{j}\, 3 \sin\theta\cos\theta + \hat{k}(2\cos^2\theta - \sin^2\theta))\}$$

$$= \frac{p}{4\pi\varepsilon_0 r^3}\{\hat{j}\, 3\sin\theta\cos\theta + \hat{k}(3\cos^2\theta - 1)\}$$

$$= \frac{p}{4\pi\varepsilon_0 r^3}\{3\cos\theta\,(\hat{j}\sin\theta + \hat{k}\cos\theta) - \hat{k}\}$$

$$= \frac{1}{4\pi\varepsilon_0 r^5}\{3\, r^2\cos\theta\, P\,(\hat{j}\sin\theta + \hat{k}\cos\theta) - \hat{k}r^2 P\}$$

$$= \frac{1}{4\pi\varepsilon_0 r^5}\{3\,(\vec{P}\cdot\vec{r})\,\vec{r} - r^2\vec{P}\}$$

## 14.5   LOCAL ELECTRIC FIELD AT AN ATOM

The electric field acting at an atom in a dielectric is known as the polarizing field or the local field, $E_{\text{loc}}$ and is different from the applied external field $E_{\text{app}}$. In order to evaluate this, it is necessary to calculate the total field acting on a certain typical dipole. This was first of all calculated by Lorentz. The reference dipole (Fig. 14.3a) at which the field is to be determined is imagined to be surrounded by spherical cavity (also known as Lorentz sphere) of radius $r$, sufficiently large as compared to the dimension of the dipole. The space outside the cavity may be treated as a continuous medium as far as the dipole is concerned. However, the medium very close to the central dipole inside the cavity is considered to be discrete and the interaction with other neighbouring dipoles is treated microscopically. The local field acting on the reference dipole is given by the sum:

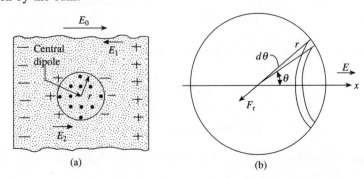

**Fig. 14.3   The procedure for computing (a) the local field and (b) the Lorentz field**

$$E_{\text{loc}} = E_0 + E_1 + E_2 + E_3 \tag{7}$$

where $E_0$ is the applied external field (uniform). When a medium is polarized due to an electric field $E$, the displacment vector $D$ is given by

$$D = \varepsilon_0 E + P$$

As a result of polarization, the electromagnetic properties of the medium changes. The external field is then given by,

$$D = \varepsilon_0 E_0$$

Equating the two equations, we obtain

$$E_0 = E + \frac{P}{\varepsilon_0} \tag{8}$$

$E_1$ is the field due to the polarizing charges lying on the external surface of the dielectric medium, also known as depolarization field.

$E_2$ is the field due to polarization charges lying on the surface of Lorentz sphere (cavity), also known as Lorentz cavity field;

$E_3$ is the field due to other dipoles lying within the sphere (cavity); $E$ is the macroscopic average field, the average being taken over the volume of the specimen, this is the field which enters into the Maxwell's equations and is equal to $E_0 + E_1$.

Now, in order to determine the local field, $E_{\text{loc}}$, let us evaluate the fields appearing in eq. 7.

### Depolarization Field, $E_1$

This field as we know is due to the polarization charges on the external surfaces and hence depends on the geometrical shpae of the dielectrics. This obviously acts in a direction opposite to the external field. For a simple case of an infinite slab, it is given by

$$E_1 = -\frac{NP}{\varepsilon_0} \tag{9}$$

where $N$ is known as depolarization factor and $P$ is the polarization. For some regular geometric shapes the values of $N$ are given in Table 14.1. However, the depolarization factor has a rigorous meaning only for homogeneous ellipsoids in uniform applied field. For this, there exists an important property, i.e.

$$N_x + N_y + N_z = 1$$

where $N_x$, $N_y$, $N_z$ are depolarization factors along the three principal axes of an ellipsoid. The eq. 9 can be confirmed by using Gauss's law.

**Table 14.1   The depolarization factor ($N$) for various shapes**

| Shape | aixs | N (cgs) | N (SI) |
|-------|------|---------|--------|
| 1. Sphere | any | $4\pi/3$ | 1/3 |
| 2. Thin slab | normal | $4\pi$ | 1 |
| 3. Thin slab | in plane | 0 | 0 |
| 4. Long circular cylinder | longitudinal | 0 | 0 |
| 5. Long circular cylinder | transverse | $2\pi$ | 1/2 |

## Lorentz Field, $E_2$

The polarization charges on the surface of Lorentz sphere produce this field (Fig. 14.3a). In order to calculate this at the centre in the direction of the applied field, let us consider an enlarged view of the spherical cavity (Fig. 14.3b). If $\theta$ is the polar angle that an element of area $dA$ is making with respect to the polarization direction (taken as $x$-axis), the induced charge density on the surface of the cavity is equal to the normal component of the polarization times the surface element, i.e.

$$P \cos \theta \times dA$$

According to the Coulomb's law, this charge on the surface element of area $dA$ produces a force $dF_r$ acting on the referred test charge $q$ (assuming at the centre of the cavity) in the direction of $r$ (Fig. 14.3b)

$$dF_r = \frac{q_1 q_2}{4\pi\varepsilon_0 r^2} = \frac{qP \cos\theta \, dA}{4\pi\varepsilon_0 r^2} \tag{10}$$

where $dA = 2\pi r \sin\theta \, rd\theta = 2\pi r^2 \sin\theta \, d\theta$. The force acting in the direction of the applied electric field, $F_x = + F_r \cos\theta$, and therefore from eq. 10, we have

$$dF_x = + \frac{qP \cos\theta}{4\pi\varepsilon_0 r^2} 2\pi r^2 \sin\theta \, d\theta \cos\theta \tag{11}$$

The Lorentz force $F_x$ can be determined by integrating eq. 11 over the range $\theta = 0$ to $\theta = \pi$. Therefore,

$$F_x = + \frac{qP}{2\varepsilon_0} \int_0^r \cos^2\theta \sin\theta \, d\theta \tag{12}$$

Substituting $z = \cos\theta$ in eq. 12, we have $dz = -\sin\theta \, d\theta$, so that

$$F_x = -\frac{qP}{2\varepsilon_0} \int_{+1}^{-1} z^2 dz = -\frac{qP}{2\varepsilon_0} \left|\frac{z^3}{3}\right|_{+1}^{-1} = \frac{qP}{3\varepsilon_0} \tag{13}$$

The Lorentz field, $E_2$ becomes

$$E_2 = \frac{F_x}{q} = \frac{P}{3\varepsilon_0} \tag{14}$$

## Field of Dipoles inside Cavity, $E_3$

The field $E_3$ due to dipoles within cavity is the only term which depends on the crystal structure. In section 14.4, we have seen that the field due to such dipoles (having the moment $p$) at a point $r$ from the centre is given by eq. 6, i.e.

$$E(r) = \frac{1}{4\pi\varepsilon_0 r^5} \{3(\vec{P} \cdot \vec{r})\vec{r} - \vec{P}r^2\}$$

Now, suppose that all the atoms within the cavity are replaced by point dipoles parallel to each other. If the axis of the dipoles is taken as the $z$-axis, then the field due to other dipoles $p_i$ at a reference point can be written as

$$E_3(z) = \sum_i \frac{3 p_i z_i^2 - p_i r_i^2}{r_i^5} \tag{15}$$

By the symmetry of the lattice and the cavity, we have

$$\sum_i \frac{z_i^2}{r_i^5} = \sum_i \frac{y_i^2}{r_i^5} = \sum_i \frac{x_i^2}{r_i^5}$$

so that

$$\sum_i \frac{r_i^2}{r_i^5} = 3 \sum_i \frac{z_i^2}{r_i^5}$$

Thus, for a spherically symmetric case, e.g. a cubic structure, $E_3 = 0$, while, $E_3 \neq 0$ for other crystal structures, e.g. monoclinic, triclinic, hexagonal, etc.

Now, substituting all the above calculated field in eq. 7, the local field acting on the reference dipole is given by

$$E_{\text{loc}} = E_0 + E_1 + E_2 + (E_3 = 0)$$

$$= \left( E + \frac{P}{\varepsilon_0} \right) + \left( -\frac{P}{\varepsilon_0} \right) + \frac{P}{3\varepsilon_0} = E + \frac{P}{3\varepsilon_0} \tag{16}$$

This is known as Lorentz relation. The difference between $E$, the Maxwell's field, and the Lorentz field, $E_{\text{loc}}$ may be understood as follows. The field $E$ is macroscopic in nature and is an average field. In the present situation, this is constant throughout the medium. On the other hand, $E_{\text{loc}}$ is a microscopic field and is periodic in nature (Fig. 14.4). This is quite large at molecular sites indicating that the molecules are more effectively polarized than they are under the average field.

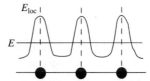

**Fig. 14.4** **The difference between the Maxwell field $E$ and the local feild $E_{\text{loc}}$. Solid circles repesent molecules**

## 14.6 DIELECTRIC CONSTANT AND ITS MEASUREMENT

Dielectric constant (also known as permittivity of the medium) is a measure of the degree to which a medium can resist the flow of charge. It is defined as the ratio for the electric displacement $D$ to the electric field intensity $E$, i.e.

$$\varepsilon = \frac{D}{E} = \varepsilon_r \varepsilon_0 \tag{17}$$

where $\varepsilon_r$ is the relative permittivity of the medium and $\varepsilon_0$ is the permittivity of free space (i.e. vacuum). If $\varepsilon_r = 1$, we have $\varepsilon = \varepsilon_0$.

Fig. 14.5 shows a simple experimental setup for measuring dielectric constant. The plates of a capacitor are connected to a battery which charges them. In the absence of a dielectric inside the capacitor, the field produced by the charges is $E_0$, which can be determined by measuring the potential difference $V_0$ across the capacitor using the relation

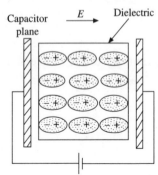

Capacitor plane    $E$    Dielectric

$$E_0 = \frac{V_0}{L} \qquad (18)$$

where $L$ is the distance between the plates. When a dielectric slab is introduced between the plates, the field $E_0$ polarizes the medium, which in turn modifies the field to a new value $E$. Like wise, this field can be determined by measuring the new potential difference $V$ across the capacitor using the relation

**Fig. 14.5   Simple experimental setup for measuring dielectric constant**

$$E = \frac{V}{L} \qquad (19)$$

The dielectric constant in terms of the fields $E_0$ and $E$ is given by the relation

$$\varepsilon_r = \frac{E_0}{E} \qquad (20)$$

From eqs. 18 and 19, it follows that

$$\varepsilon_r = \frac{V_0}{V} \qquad (21)$$

We can thus obtain the dielectric constant by measuring the potential differences across the capacitor with and without a dielectric, and taking their ratio as in eq. 21.

Similarly, it can be shown that the dielectric constant can also be obtained by measuring the capacities of condenser with and without a dielectric and taking their ratio as

$$\varepsilon_r = \frac{C}{C_0} \qquad (22)$$

where $C_0$ and $C$ are the capacities in the absence and presence of a dielectric, respectively.

Further, we know that the capacity of a parallel plate condenser is defined as the ratio for the charge $Q$ on either plate (regardless of sign) to the potential difference between the plates as

$$C = \frac{Q}{V}, \quad \text{or} \quad Q = CV \qquad (23)$$

Equation 23 indicates that the increase in the capacity (after introducing the dielectric medium between the plates) by a factor $\varepsilon_r$ means a decrease in the potential difference as well as in the field by the same factor, i.e. if $C = \varepsilon_r C_0$ (eq. 22) then the decrease in the field in the presence of a dielectric medium is

$$E = \frac{E_0}{\varepsilon_r}$$

This decrease in the field in turn, induces dipoles and the medium gets polarized. The polarization produced in the material is a measure of the charge in the capacitance (or field) such that

$$P = (C - C_0)V$$
$$= (\varepsilon - \varepsilon_0)E$$
$$= (\varepsilon_r - 1)\varepsilon_0 E$$

Rearranging the terms, we get

$$\varepsilon_r = 1 + \frac{P}{\varepsilon_0 E} = 1 + \chi_e \tag{24}$$

where $\chi_e = \dfrac{P}{\varepsilon_0 E}$ is the electric susceptibility.

Equation 24 gives the dielectric constant of an isotropic medium or a solid with cubic structure. This is represented by a scalar quantity, i.e. by a single number. However, for anisotropic medium $\varepsilon_r$ or $\chi_e$ depends on direction of the field and is represented by a tensor of second rank.

## 14.7  POLARIZABILITY

When an electric field is applied to a solid, electric charges are displaced causing polarization in it. The induced dipoles of moments $p$ are proportional to the local field, $E_{Loc}$, i.e.

$$p = \alpha E_{Loc} \tag{25}$$

where $\alpha$ is known as electrical polarizability of the atom. The total polarization of the dielectric containing $N$ atoms is given by

$$P = \sum_{i=1}^{N} N_i \alpha_i E_{Loc}(i) \tag{26}$$

where $N_i$ is the number of $i$ atoms having polarizabilities $\alpha_i$, and $E_{Loc}(i)$ is the local field at the atoms of type $i$.

For an isotropic dielectric medium, the local field inside the crystal is everywhere the same so that it can be taken out of the summation sign from eq. 26. Substituting the value of the local field from eq. 16, the eq. 26 becomes

$$P = \left( E + \frac{P}{3\varepsilon_0} \right) \sum_i N_i \alpha_i$$

After rearranging terms and making use of eq. 24, we have

$$\frac{P}{\varepsilon_0 E} = \frac{\sum_i N_i \alpha_i}{\varepsilon_0 - \frac{1}{3} \sum_i N_i \alpha_i} \tag{27}$$

Now, solving for $\sum_i N_i \alpha_i$, we get

$$\frac{\varepsilon_r - 1}{\varepsilon_r + 2} = \frac{P}{3\varepsilon_0} \sum_i N_i \alpha_i \qquad (28)$$

This is known as Clausius-Mosotti equation. This equation can be used to determine the electrical polarizabilities of the atoms if the dielectric constant is known. Further, since according to eq. 28, the polarizabilities are additive, therefore this relation can also be used to predict the dielectric constant of new materials if the individual polarizabilities of the atoms are known.

Now, the total polarizability $\alpha$ can be written as the sum of three terms representing the most important contributions to the polarization

$$\alpha = \alpha_e + \alpha_i + \alpha_d \qquad (29)$$

where $\alpha_e$, $\alpha_i$ and $\alpha_d$ are the electronic, ionic and dipolar polarizabilities, respectively (Fig. 14.6). Let us discuss them one by one.

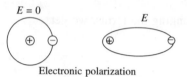

Electronic polarization

Ionic polarization

Diplolar polarization

Space charge polarization

**Fig. 14.6  Atomic contributions to electric polarization**

*Example*: Assuming that the polarizability of Kr atom is $2.18 \times 10^{-40}$ Fm$^2$, calculate its dielectric constant at 0°C and 1 atmosphere.

*Solution:* Given: $\alpha_{Kr} = 2.18 \times 10^{-40}$ Fm$^2$, $T = 0°C$, pressure = 1 atmosphere, $\varepsilon_r$ = ? At NTP, the number of Kr atoms are

$$N = \frac{6.02 \times 10^{26}}{22.4} = 2.69 \times 10^{25} / m^3$$

Now, making use of eqs. 4, 24 and 25, we have

$$\varepsilon_r = \frac{N\alpha}{\varepsilon_0} + 1$$

$$= \frac{2.69 \times 10^{25} \times 2.18 \times 10^{-40}}{8.85 \times 10^{12}} + 1 = 1.00066$$

*Example:* Find the total polarizability of $CO_2$, if its susceptibility is $0.985 \times 10^{-3}$. Density of carbon dioxide is 1.977 kg/m$^3$.

*Solution:* Given: $\chi = 0.985 \times 10^{-3}$, $\rho(CO_2) = 1.977$ kg/m$^3$, $\alpha$ = ?
We know that the molecular weight of $CO_2$ = 44. Therefore, the number of molecules per unit volume will be

$$N = \frac{6.02 \times 10^{26} \times 1.977}{44} = 2.70 \times 10^{25} / m^3$$

Again, making use of the eqs. 4, 24 and 25, we have

$$\alpha = \frac{\varepsilon_0 \chi}{N} = \frac{8.85 \times 10^{-12} \times 0.985 \times 10^{-3}}{2.70 \times 10^{25}} = 3.23 \times 10^{-40} \text{ Fm}^2$$

*Example*: On being polarized, an oxygen atom produces a dipole moment of $0.5 \times 10^{-22}$ C-m. If the distance of the centre of negative charge cloud from the nucleus is $4 \times 10^{-17}$ m, calculate the polarizability of oxygen atom.

*Solution:* Given: $p = 0.5 \times 10^{-22}$ C-m, $d = 4 \times 10^{-17}$ m, $\alpha = ?$
In equilibrium, both the Coulomb interaction and the Lorentz force will be equal, so that for oxygen atom, we have

$$8eE = \frac{(8e) \times (8e)}{4\pi\varepsilon_0 d^2}$$

or

$$E = \frac{8e}{4\pi\varepsilon_0 d^2} = \frac{8 \times 1.6 \times 10^{-19}}{4\pi \times 8.85 \times 10^{-12} \times 16 \times 10^{-34}} = 2.6 \times 10^{24} \text{ V/m}$$

Further, the dipole moment $p = \alpha E$. Therefore,

$$\alpha = \frac{p}{E} = \frac{0.5 \times 10^{-22}}{2.6 \times 10^{24}} = 1.9 \times 10^{-47} \text{ Fm}^2$$

### Electronic Polarizability

The electronic contribution $\alpha_e$ arises as a result of the displacement of electrons in an atom relative to the nucleus. As shown in Fig. 14.6a, the negatively-charged electrons move antiparallel to the field creating an electric dipole parallel to the field. This contribution is common in all solids, since all are made up of atoms. It is the chief contributor in materials such as diamond in which other effects are absent. If we look to the polarizability versus frequency curve (Fig. 14.7), we find that in the optical frequency range the dielectric constant arises almost entirely from the electronic polarizability. The ionic and dipolar contributions are small at high frequencies because of the inertia of the ions and molecules. In the optical range, the eq. 28 reduces to

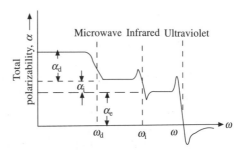

**Fig. 14.7   Schematic representation of frequency dependence of the several contributions to the polarizability**

$$\frac{n^2 - 1}{n^2 + 2} = \frac{P}{3\varepsilon_0} \sum_i N_i \alpha_i \quad \text{(electronic)} \tag{30}$$

This is obtained as follows: we know that the velocity of electromagnetic waves in matter is given by

$$v = \frac{c}{\sqrt{\varepsilon\mu}}$$

where $c$ is the velocity of light in vacuum and $\varepsilon$, $\mu$ are the permittivity and the permeability of the medium, respectively. Also, the refractive index $n$ is given by

$$n = \frac{c}{v} = \sqrt{\varepsilon\mu}$$

Further, for non-magnetic materials $\mu = 1$, therefore, $n = \sqrt{\varepsilon}$. Thus, replacing $\varepsilon_r$ by $n^2$ in eq. 28, we obtain eq. 30.

Now, with the help of eq. 30, it is possible to find the value of electronic polarizability if the refractive index of the material is known.

### Ionic Polarizability

Ionic polarizability arises from the relative displacement of positive and negative ions. The cations are displaced parallel to the local field, and the anions are displaced in the opposite direction (Fig. 14.6b). As expected, such effects are most important in alkali halides and other ionic solids. If the relative displacement of the positive and the negative ions is $d$ and $q$ is the charge on each ion, then the dipole moment per molecule is $\bar{p} = qd$ and the ionic polarization becomes

$$P_{ion} = Nqd \qquad (31)$$

where $N$ is the number of molecules per unit volume.

## 14.8   THE CLASSICAL THEORY OF ELECTRONIC POLARIZABILITY

First of all, let us understand the static polarizability of free atoms or molecules in an external electric field. The term "free" refers to a system in which the mutual interaction between the particles may be neglected, as in gas of low density. In a free atom, in the absence of an electric field the centre of gravity of the electron distribution coincides with the nucleus. When the atom is placed in a static homogeneous external field $E$, the force exerted on the nucleus and on the electrons is oppositely directed. As a result, the external field tends to draw the centre of gravity of the electrons away from the nucleus (Fig. 14.8). On the other hand, the attractive forces between the electrons and the nucleus tend to preserve a vanishingly small dipole moment in the atom. Consequently, under equilibrium situation, the atoms bear a finite dipole moment. The induced dipole moment may be represented by

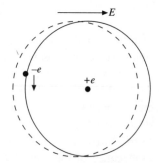

**Fig. 14.8**   Schematic illustration of the displacement of the electron orbit relative to the nucleus for a hydrogen atom under the influence of an external electric field

$$p_{ind} = \alpha_e\, E_{Loc} \qquad (32)$$

where $\alpha_e$ is the electronic polarizability of the atom.

In order to obtain the magnitude of $\alpha_e$, let us assume that the atom is represented by a nucleus of charge $Ze$ and homogeneous negative charge distribution inside a sphere of radius $r$. If the nucleus is displaced over a distance $d$ (as shown in Fig. 14.9), the resulting force is equal to the force exerted on the nucleus by a negative charge $Zex/4\pi\varepsilon_0 r^3$. Under equilibrium condition, we have

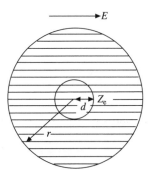

$$ZeE = \frac{(Ze)^2 d}{4\pi\varepsilon_0 r^3}$$

or
$$d = \frac{4\pi\varepsilon_0 r^3 E}{Ze} \qquad (33)$$

**Fig. 14.9 Simplified model for estimating the magnitude of the electronic polarizability of an atom**

The corresponding dipole moment is

$$p = Zed = 4\pi\varepsilon_0 r^3 E \qquad (34)$$

and the electronic polarizability (from eq. 32) becomes

$$\alpha_e = \frac{p_{ind}}{E_{Loc}} = 4\pi\varepsilon_0 r^3 \qquad (35)$$

Note that $\alpha_e$ has the dimension of volume. For $r \simeq 10^{-10}$ m, $\alpha_e$ is of the order of $10^{-40}$ m$^3$.

In order to understand the *ac* polarizability, we assume that the electrons in the atom experience an elastic restoring force corresponding to a resonant frequency $\omega_0 = (K/m)^{1/2}$, where $K$ is the force constant and $m$ is the mass of an electron. Thus, the equation of motion of an electron of mass $m$ and charge $e$ in a local field $E_{Loc} \sin \omega t$ is given by

$$m\frac{d^2x}{dt^2} + m\omega_0^2 x = -eE_{Loc} \sin \omega t \qquad (36)$$

Let $x = x_0 \sin \omega t$ (i.e. the displacement is harmonic) and solve eq. 36 for $x$, we find

$$m(\omega_0^2 - \omega^2)x_0 = -eE_{Loc} \qquad \text{or} \qquad -x_0 = \frac{eE_{Loc}}{m(\omega_0^2 - \omega^2)}$$

The corresponding amplitude of the dipole moment becomes

$$p_0 = -ex_0 = \frac{e^2 E_{Loc}}{m(\omega_0^2 - \omega^2)}$$

Hence, the electronic polarizability becomes

$$\alpha_e = \frac{p_0}{E_{Loc}} = \frac{e^2/m}{(\omega_0^2 - \omega^2)} \qquad (37)$$

If there are $Z$ electrons per atom and $N$ atoms per unit volume, then the resulting electric susceptibility is

$$\chi_e = \frac{NZe^2/\varepsilon_0 m}{(\omega_0^2 - \omega^2)} \tag{38}$$

and hence the index of refraction is given by

$$n^2 = 1 + \chi_e = 1 + \frac{NZe^2/\varepsilon_0 m}{(\omega_0^2 - \omega^2)} \tag{39}$$

The plot between $n^2$ versus $\omega$ shows a strong dispersion at the resonance frequency $\omega = \omega_0$.

## 14.9  DIPOLAR POLARIZABILITY

The dipolar polarizability (also known as orientational polarizability) is important only in materials which contain complex ions having permanent dipole moments. These dipoles are not free to rotate in the solid while they do so in a liquid or a gas. An applied electric field helps orient these dipoles along the direction of the field. Such an orientation is opposed by the thermal agitation which tends to randomize the dipoles. It is because of this reason, the calculation of dipolar polarizability has to be made under thermal equilibrium.

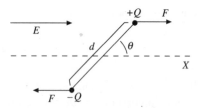

Fig. 14.10  **The turning couple produced on the dipole by the external field**

Now, let us suppose that a dipolar system is placed in a uniform electric field, out of which consider a dipole as shown in Fig. 14.10. Force exerted by the field on the positive and negative charges of the dipole is equal but acts in opposite directions. Thus, a torque exerted by the field on the dipole having a dipole moment $p$ is given by

$$\tau = p \times E \tag{40}$$

The magnitude of the torque is $pE \sin \theta$, where $\theta$ is the angle between the direction of the field and the moment, and the direction of the torque is such that it tends to turn the dipole into the direction of the field, i.e. to reduce $\theta$. The potential energy of the dipole in the field is given by

$$U = -p \cdot E = -pE \cos \theta \tag{41}$$

It is clear from eq. 41, that the energy of the dipole is minimum (equal to -$pE$) when $\theta = 0$, i.e. when the dipole is aligned parallel to the field and is maximum (equal to $pE$) when $\theta = 180°$, i.e. when the dipole is antiparallel to the field. Thus, the potential energy is a function of angle. Despite the minimum energy condition of $\theta = 0$, all the dipoles do not point in the direction of the field because of thermal agitation. A dipole of moment $p$ making an angle $\theta$ with the direction of the field contributes to the polarization a component $p \cos \theta (= p_x$ the $x$ component).

According to the Boltzmann statistics, the probability of finding a dipole within the solid angle $\theta$ and $\theta + d\theta$ or $(d\Omega)$ is proportional to the Boltzmann factor

$$f(\theta) = \exp\left(-\frac{U}{kT}\right) = \exp\left(\frac{pE \cos \theta}{kT}\right) \tag{42}$$

Therefore, the average moment contribution per dipole $\bar{p}$ lying within the solid angle can be determined by integrating over all angles from parallel alignment $\theta = 0$, to antiparallel alignment, $\theta = \pi$, so that

$$\bar{p} = \frac{\int_0^\pi P_x f(\theta) d\Omega}{\int_0^\pi f(\theta) d\Omega} \tag{43}$$

where $p_x = p \cos\theta$, $d\Omega = 2\pi \sin\theta\, d\theta$ and $f(\theta)$ is given by eq. 42. Substituting these values, the eq. 43 becomes

$$\bar{p} = \frac{\int_0^\pi P \cos\theta\, 2\pi \sin\theta \exp(pE \cos\theta/kT) d\theta}{\int_0^\pi 2\pi \sin\theta \exp(pE \cos\theta/kT) d\theta} \tag{44}$$

Now, substituting $a = pE/kT$, $t = \cos\theta$ and $dt = -\sin\theta\, d\theta$, eq. 44 can be written in the form

$$\bar{p} = \frac{p \int_{-1}^{+1} \exp(ta) t\, dt}{\int_{-1}^{+1} \exp(ta) dt} = p \frac{d}{da} \log \int_{-1}^{+1} \exp(ta) dt$$

$$= p\left[ \frac{d}{da} \log(e^a - e^{-a}) \frac{d}{da} \log a \right] = p\left[ \coth(a) - \frac{1}{a} \right] \equiv p L(a) \tag{45}$$

where
$$L(a) = \coth(a) - \frac{1}{a} \tag{46}$$

The function $L(a)$ is known as Langevin function because Langevin first of all derived this formula in 1905 for a paramagnetic gas. In 1912, Debye applied this relation to an electric dipole gas. Fig. 14.11 shows a plot of the Langevin function $L(a)$ as a function of $a$. When $a$ is very large, that is at very high field strength or at low temperatures, the function $L(a)$ approaches

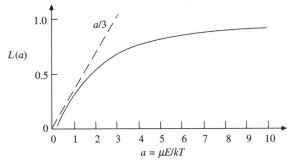

**Fig. 14.11   A plot of the Langevin function L(a) as a function of a**

saturation value at unity. This corresponds to the maximum alignment of the dipoles along the direction of the field. For small values of $a$ (i.e. $a \ll 1$ or $pE \ll kT$), we have

$$\coth{(a)} = \frac{1}{a} + \frac{a}{3} + \frac{a^3}{45} + \ldots$$

so that
$$L(a) \simeq \frac{a}{3} \qquad (47)$$

Actually, in order to approach the value of $a$ to be unity at room temperature, the field strength of about $10^9$ V/m is required. Thus, for a moderate field ($\sim 10^5 - 10^6$ V/m) and moderate temperatures ($\sim 300$K), the value of $a$ is of the order of $10^{-3} - 10^{-4}$, which is much less than unity and hence the above approximation (eq. 47) could be used safely without losing much of accuracy. This assumption may be justified by showing that the magnitude of $kT$ at room temperature is many times larger than the potential energy gain resulting from the alignment of the dipoles at the same temperature. Moreover, the value of $a$ found in most experimental situations is of the same order. Now, substituting the value of $L(a)$ in eq. 45 and replacing back the value of $a$, we obtain

$$\bar{p} = \frac{p^2 E}{3kT} \qquad (48)$$

Therefore, the dipolar polarizability per dipole becomes

$$\alpha_d = \frac{\bar{p}}{E} = \frac{p^2}{3kT} \qquad (49)$$

If $\alpha_0$ denotes the sum of the electronic and ionic polarizabilities, then from eq. 29, the total polarizability may be written as

$$\alpha = \alpha_0 + \frac{p^2}{3kT} \qquad (50)$$

This is known as Langevin-Debye equation and is of great importance to chemists in interpreting molecular structure.

*Example:* Assuming that there are $10^{27}$ molecules/m$^3$ in HCl vapour, calculate the orientational polarization at room temperature if the vapour is subjected to an electric field of $10^6$ V/m. The dipole moment of HCl molecule is $3.46 \times 10^{-30}$ C-m. Show that at this temperature and for such a high field, the value of $a$ (where $a = pE/kT$) is very much small than unity.

*Solution:* Given: $N = 10^{27}$ molecules/m$^3$, $E = 10^6$ V/m, $p = 3.46 \times 10^{-30}$ C-m, $\alpha_d = ?$
From eq. 49, we know that the orientational (or dipolar) polarizability is given by

$$\alpha_d = \frac{p^2}{3kT} = \frac{(3.46 \times 10^{-30})^2}{(3 \times 1.38 \times 10^{-23} \times 300)} = 9.64 \times 10^{-40} \text{ Fm}^2$$

and hence the orientational polarization will be

$$P = Np = N\alpha_d E = 10^{27} \times 9.64 \times 10^{-40} \times 10^6 = 9.64 \times 10^{-7} \text{ C/m}^2$$

Further, the magnetic energy

$$pE = 3.46 \times 10^{-30} \times 10^6 = 3.46 \times 10^{-24} \text{ J}$$

and the thermal energy

$$kT = 1.38 \times 10^{-23} \times 300 = 4.04 \times 10^{-21} \text{ J}$$

Comparing these two energies, we find that

$$a = \frac{pE}{kT} \sim 10^{-3}$$

*Example:* The polarizability of $NH_3$ molecule is found experimentally by the measurement of dielectric constant as $2.42 \times 10^{-39}$ Fm$^2$ at 309 K and $1.74 \times 10^{-39}$ Fm$^2$ at 448 K, respctively. Calculate for each temperature the polarizability due to permanent dipole moment and due to deformation of molecules.

*Solution:* Given: $\alpha(309) = 2.42 \times 10^{-39}$ Fm$^2$, $\alpha(448) = 1.74 \times 10^{-39}$ Fm$^2$, $\alpha_i = ?$ $\alpha_d = ?$

Since the sum of these two polarizabilities is given by

$$\alpha = \alpha_i + \alpha_d = \alpha_i + \frac{p^2}{3kT} = \alpha_i + \frac{\beta}{T}$$

where

$$\beta = \frac{p^2}{3k}$$

Thus polarizability at 309 K will be

$$2.42 \times 10^{-39} = \alpha_i + \frac{\beta}{309} \tag{i}$$

and at 448 K

$$1.74 \times 10^{-39} = \alpha_i + \frac{\beta}{448} \tag{ii}$$

Subtracting (ii) from (i), we have

$$\frac{\beta}{309} - \frac{\beta}{448} = 0.68 \times 10^{-39}$$

On simplifying this, we have

$$\beta = 677 \times 10^{-39}$$

Substituting the value of $\beta$ in eq. (i), we have

$$\alpha_i = 2.42 \times 10^{-39} - \frac{677 \times 10^{-39}}{309} = 2.42 \times 10^{-39} - 2.19 \times 10^{-39}$$

$$= 0.23 \times 10^{-39} \text{ Fm}^2$$

But the orientational (or dipolar) polarizability is given by

$$\alpha_d = \frac{\beta}{T}, \text{ where } \beta = 677 \times 10^{-39}$$

Hence, the orientational polarizability at the two temperatures are:

$$\text{At } 309 \text{ K } \alpha_d = \frac{677 \times 10^{-39}}{309} = 2.19 \times 10^{-39} \text{ Fm}^2$$

and at 448 K $\alpha_d = \dfrac{677 \times 10^{-39}}{448} = 1.51 \times 10^{-39} \text{ Fm}^2$

## 14.10  PIEZO-PYRO-AND FERROELECTRIC PROPERTIES OF CRYSTALS

A material can be either piezoelectric, pyroelectric or ferroelectric only if its crystalline symmetry is inherently asymmetric, i.e. it lacks an inversion centre. A basic principle due to Neumann is that any physical property exhibited by a crystal must have at least the symmetry of the point group of the crystal. Thus, the above properties which are inherently asymmetric can only arise in asymmetric crystals.

Of the thirty-two crystal symmetry classes, eleven exhibit centre of symmetry, in another one case, a combination of symmetries effectively provides such a centre, leaving twenty classes which have asymmetric properties. All the crystals in these twenty classes are piezoelectric. When such a non-centrosymmetric crystal is subjected to a mechanical stress, the ions are displaced from each other in an asymmetric manner and the crystal becomes electrically polarized. This is called piezoelectric effect. The inverse effect of it, i.e an applied field produces strain has also been observed.

The piezoelectric effect is often used to convert electrical energy into mechanical energy, and vice-versa. Quartz is the most familiar piezoelectric substance and the one most frequently used in transducers. The existence of direct effect and its inverse is to be distinguished from a similar property called electro-striction. In the latter case, the material becomes strained in an electric field $E$. Furthr, the electro-striction is proportional to $E^2$. Hence, there does not exist any inverse of this effect.

Crystals in ten of the twenty classes have a unique polar axis (where none of the point group operations turn the axis round) responsible for the appearance of a spontaneous electric polarization even in the absence of an electric field. A change in the temperature ($\Delta T$) of the crystal produces a change in its polarization ($\Delta P$), according to the relation

$$\Delta P = \lambda \Delta T \tag{51}$$

where $\lambda$ is the pyroelectric coefficient and can be measured. This effect is called the pyroelectric effect and can be produced either by heating or cooling the crystal.

Perhaps the simplest pyroelectric crystal is wurtzite, the hexagonal ZnS (Fig. 14.12). The crystal class is 6 mm, for which the polar axis and $P_s$ are parallel to $c$, the 6-fold symmetry axis. When a wurtzite crystal is heated, it undergoes an anistropic thermal expansion. The resulting change in $c/a$ ratio accounts for the fact that wurtzite is pyroelectric as well as piezoelectric. On the other hand, when a non-centrosymmetric sphalerite (cubic ZnS) is heated, four equivalent directions <111> expand uniformaly. Therefore, sphalerite is piezoelectric but not pyroelectric.

In some pyroelectric crystals, the spontaneous polarization can be reversed by an external applied field giving dielectric hysteresis loop. Such crystals are called ferroelectric crystals and the phenomenon of reversing the direction of polarity is called ferroelectric effect.

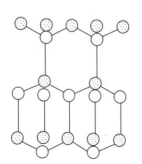

**Fig. 14.12** **Wurtzite (hexagonal ZnS) structure projected on (010) plane**

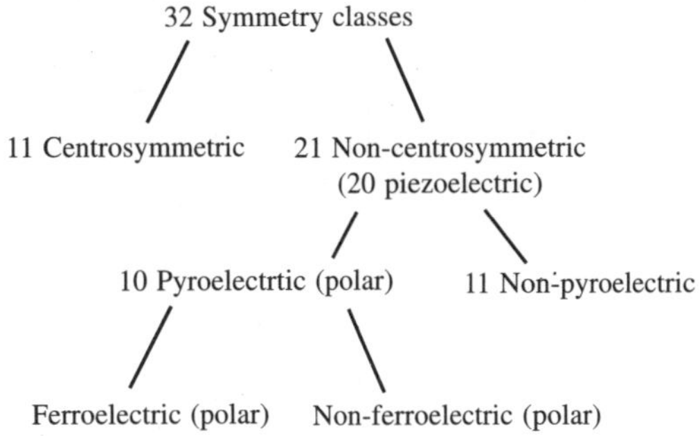

32 Symmetry classes

11 Centrosymmetric    21 Non-centrosymmetric
(20 piezoelectric)

10 Pyroelectrtic (polar)    11 Non-pyroelectric

Ferroelectric (polar)    Non-ferroelectric (polar)

**Fig. 14.13** **Classification of piezoelectric and pyroelectric materials**

It is to be noted that both piezoelectric and pyroelectric are inherent property of a crystal. They are entirely due to crystal structure. Ferroelectricity on the other hand, is an effect produced in a pyroelectric crystal by the application of an external electric field. Classification of these crystals based on symmetry is shown schematically in Fig. 14.13.

## 14.11 FERROELECTRICITY

Ferroelectricity was first of all discovered by J. Valasek in 1921 in Rochelle salt. This phenomenon is analogous to that of ferromagnetism. A ferroelectric material like a ferromagnetic one exhibits spontaneous polarization even in the absence of an external electric field. Similarly, the spontaneous polarization gets destroyed and the ferroelectricity disappears above a certain temperaure called the transition temperature (or the Curie temperature) where the materials become paraelectric. Fig. 14.14 illustrates the temperature dependnce of polarization in ferroelectric crystals. A phase transition from paraelectric to ferroelectric or vice-versa is accompanied by a change in crystal structure, such that the ferroelectric phase is well ordered and has a lower crystal symmetry than the paraelectric one.

The occurrence of ferroelectricity may be understood in terms of either (i) polarization catastrophe, or (ii) transverse optical phonon mode. Let us first discuss the simple form of catastrophe theory in which for some critical condition the polarization becomes very large. Consequently, the local electric field caused by the polarization increases faster than the restoring force on an ion in the crystal, leading to an asymmetrical shift in the positions of the ions.

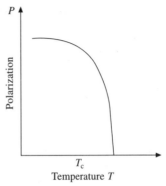

**Fig. 14.14** **Spontaneous polarization versus temperature**

When a transition from paraelectric to ferroelectric phase takes place, it is accompanied by the appearance of spontaneous polarization. In principle, two interactions should occur this transition (i) work down in polarizing the medium and (ii) attractive, dipole-dipole interactions.

In order that the process be spontaneous, the lowering in energy in (ii) should be more than the energy absorbed during (i).

Let us suppose that the work done during the process of polarizing the medium is

$$W_1 = \int F \, dx \tag{52}$$

where $F$ is the force and $dx$ is the macroscopic electric field, then the polarizability is given by

$$\alpha = \frac{p}{E} = \frac{e^2 x}{F} \text{ (since } p = ex \text{ and } E = F/e)$$

Therefore,

$$W_1 = \int F \, dx = \frac{e^2 x^2}{2\alpha} = \frac{p^2}{2\alpha} \tag{53}$$

Further, the attraction energy due to dipole-dipole interactions will be

$$W_2 = -\frac{p^2}{r^3} \tag{54}$$

where the negative sign indicates attraction and "$r$" is the distance between the dipoles. If $W_1 = |W_2|$, then

$$\frac{p^2}{2\alpha} = \frac{p^2}{r^3} \quad \text{or} \quad \alpha = \frac{r^3}{2} \tag{55}$$

For an isotropic system, e.g. cubic dielectric, eq. 53 can be written as

$$W_1 = \frac{P^2}{2 \Sigma N_i \alpha_i} \tag{56}$$

where $P$ is the polarization and $N_i$ and $\alpha_i$ are the atomic concentration and polarizability of the *i*th atom, respectively. In order to calculate $W_2$, we proceed as follows:

The local field at the atomic site in the dielectric is given by eq. 16. For spontaneous polarization, $E$ must be zero. Therefore,

$$E_{\text{Loc}} = \frac{p}{3\varepsilon_0}$$

and

$$W_2 = -\int E_{\text{Loc}} \, dP = -\frac{1}{3\varepsilon_0} \int P \, dP = -\frac{P^2}{6\varepsilon_0} \tag{57}$$

From eqs. 56 and 57, we have

$$\frac{P^2}{2 \Sigma N_i \alpha_i} = \frac{P^2}{6\varepsilon_0} \quad \text{or} \quad \frac{1}{3\varepsilon_0} \Sigma N_i \alpha_i = 1 \tag{58}$$

For an isotropic system, the Claussius-Mosotti equation can be written as

$$\varepsilon_r = \frac{1 + \dfrac{2}{3\varepsilon_0} \sum_i N_i \alpha_i}{1 - \dfrac{1}{3\varepsilon_0} \sum_i N_i \alpha_i} \tag{59}$$

If eq. 58 is satisfied, then the dielectric constant (given by eq. 59) becomes infinite. In practice, although the dielectric constant does become very high ($\sim 10^3 - 10^5$) in many cases, it never becomes infinity. Therefore, let us put

$$\frac{1}{3\varepsilon_0} \sum_i N_i \alpha_i = 1 - \delta \tag{60}$$

where $\delta \ll 1$. Then the dielectric constant becomes

$$\varepsilon_r = \frac{3 - 2\delta}{\delta} \simeq \frac{3}{8} \tag{61}$$

Now, if near the critical temperature, $T_c$ the deviation $\delta$ in eq. 61 varies with the temperature in a linear fashion according to the

$$\delta \cong \frac{3}{C} (T - T_c) \tag{62}$$

where $C$ is the Curie constant. Thus, eq. 61 becomes

$$\varepsilon_r = \frac{C}{(T - T_c)} \tag{63}$$

This indicates that the dielectric constant follows the Curie-Weiss law. Fig. 14.15 shows the dependence of dielectric constant with temperature in a ferroelectric crystal.

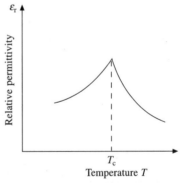

**Fig. 14.15  Relative permittivity versus temperature, showing maximum at $T_c$.**

## 14.12  FERROELECTRIC DOMAIN

Similar to the existence of ferromagnetic domains, the ferroelectric domains are found to exist in ferroelectric materials as shown in Fig. 14.16. As a result, similar to M-H hysteresis curve, the ferroelectric materials also exhibit hysteresis in the polarization when an electric field is applied as shown in Fig. 14.17.

In a particular domain, the atomic dipoles are aligned parallel to one another. Further, the direction of alignment of dipoles varies from one domain to another.

Let us suppose that the net polarization of the specimen is zero in the beginning when no field is applied. When an electric field is applied and gradually increased, the favourably oriented domains (in which the polarization $P$ is parallel or nearly parallel to the electric field $E$) grow at the expense of others (in which $P$ is antiparallel to $E$). As the field is increased further, more and more domains rotate along the direction of the field until the polarization reaches a maximum

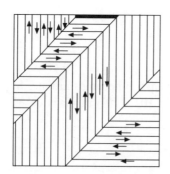

**Fig. 14.16 Ferroelectric domains**

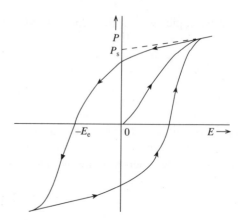

**Fig. 14.17 Ferroelectric hysteresis curve**

value called the saturation value. At this stage, the whole specimen represents a single domain. This is usually accompanied by a distortion in the crystal structure (in the form of elongation) along the polarization direction. An extrapolation of the saturation value to zero field gives the magnitude of the spontaneous polarization $P_s$. This value of $P_s$ is the same as possessed by each domain before the application of the field. When the field is decreased, the polarization also decreases but follows another path and does not become zero for zero field. The remaining polarization at this stage is called remnant polarization $P_r$, where $P_r$ refers to the whole crystal block. In order to destroy the remnant polarization, the polarization of nearly half of the crystal is to be reversed by reversing the direction of the field. The field required to make the polarization zero is called the coercive field, $E_c$. Further increase in the reverse field results in the saturation of polarization in the reverse direction. Reversing the field again, the hysteresis curve will be obtained.

## 14.13 ANTIFERROELECTRICITY AND FERRIELECTRICITY

Antiferroelectricity is an analogue of antiferromagnetism. Hence like antiferromagnets, antiferroelectric materials may possess two equivalent interpenetrating sublattices having equal and opposite polarizations (in the ordered state). A transition to the paraelectric (disordered) state is accompanied by an anomaly in the dielectric constant and a change to higher symmetry. In antiferroelectric materials, each dipole is antiparallel to its neighbouring dipoles, hence has no bulk polarization and do not exhibit hysteresis effect. However, antiferroelectric state may be changed into ferroelectric state under the influence of strong external field or upon cooling to a very low temperature.

Similarly, a ferrielectric is an analogue of a ferrimagnet. If a material consists of two non-equivalent sublattices such that there is net "ferroelectric" behaviour, it is called ferrielectric. Table 14.2 enlists some ferroelectric, antiferroelectric and ferrielectric materials alongwith their transition temperatures.

## 14.14 SUMMARY

1. The polarization $P$ of a dielectric medium is defined as

**Table 14.2** **Some ferroelectric, antiferroelectric and ferrielectric materials and their Curie temperatures**

| Materials | $T_c(K)$ |
|---|---|
| Ferroelectrics | |
| $KH_2PO_4$ | 123 |
| $KD_2PO_4$ | 213 |
| $RbH_2PO_4$ | 147 |
| $RbH_2AsO_4$ | 111 |
| $KH_2AsO_4$ | 96 |
| GeTe | 670 |
| Tri-glycine sulphate | 322 |
| Tri-glycine selenate | 295 |
| $BaTiO_3$ | 393 |
| $SrTiO_3$ | 1 |
| $KNbO_3$ | 712 |
| $PbTiO_3$ | 763 |
| $LiTaO_3$ | 890 |
| $LiNbO_3$ | 1470 |
| Antiferroelectrics | |
| $WO_3$ | 1010 |
| $PbZrO_3$ | 506 |
| $PbHfO_3$ | 488 |
| $NH_4H_2PO_4$ | 148 |
| $NH_4D_2PO_4$ | 242 |
| $NH_4H_2AsO_4$ | 216 |
| $ND_4D_2AsO_4$ | 304 |
| Ferrielectrics | |
| $Na(Nb_{0.7}V_{0.3})O_3$ | 523 |

$$P = Np$$

where $N$ is the number of molecules per unit volume and $p$ is the electric moment of each of these molecules.

2. The electric field of a dipole is defined by

$$E_{dip}(r, \theta) = \frac{1}{4\pi\varepsilon_0 r^5} \{3(\vec{P} \cdot \vec{r})\vec{r} - r^2\vec{P}\}$$

3. For a spherically symmetric dielectric medium (e.g. a medium with cubic structure), the local field acting on a dipole is given by

$$E_{Loc} = E + \frac{P}{3\varepsilon_0}$$

where $E$ is macroscopic average field.

4. Dielectric constant of a (dielectric) medium is defined as the ratio of the electric displacement $D$ to the electric field intensity $E$, i.e.

$$\varepsilon = \frac{D}{E} = \varepsilon_r \varepsilon_0$$

where $\varepsilon_r$ is the relative permittivity of the medium and $\varepsilon_0$ is the permittivity of the free space (vacuum).

5. The relative dielectric constant of an isotropic medium is a scalar quantity and is defind as

$$\varepsilon_r = 1 + \frac{p}{\varepsilon_0 E} = 1 + \chi_e$$

where $\chi_e = \dfrac{p}{\varepsilon_0 E}$ is the electric susceptibility.

6. The electric moment is proportional to the field, and is given by

$$p = \alpha E$$

where $\alpha$ is the molecular polarizability.

7. If the dielectric constant is known, the electrical polarizability can be obtained by using Clausius-Mosotti equation

$$\frac{\varepsilon_r - 1}{\varepsilon_r + 2} = \frac{P}{3\varepsilon_0} \sum_i N_i \alpha_i$$

8. The optical dielectric constant (or the index of refraction) $n^2$, obtained by treating the electron as a classical particle bound to the remainder of the atom by a harmonic force, is

$$n^2 = 1 + \chi_e = 1 + \frac{NZe^2/\varepsilon_0 m}{(\omega_0^2 - \omega^2)}$$

where $\chi_e$ is the electric susceptibility.

9. The total polarizability $\alpha$ (also known as Langevin-Debye equation) is the sum of electronic, ionic and dipolar polarizabilities, i.e.

$$\alpha = \alpha_e + \alpha_i + \alpha_d = \alpha_0 + \frac{p^2}{3kT}$$

where $\alpha_0 = \alpha_e + \alpha_i$ and $\alpha_d = \dfrac{p^2}{3kT}$.

10. A material can be either piezoelectric, pyroelectric or ferroelectric only if it lacks centre of (inversion) symmetry. Piezoelectricity and pyroelectricity are inherent property of a crystal, while ferroelectricity is an effect produced in pyroelectric crystals by applying external electric field.

11. A ferroelectric substance exhibits spontaneous polarization below a certain temperature $T_c$ (called Curie temperature). Above this temperature, the dielectric constant is given by the Curie-Weiss law

$$\varepsilon_r = \frac{C}{(T - T_c)}$$

The ferroelectric property can be explained on the basis of domain theory.

## 14.15  DEFINITIONS

*Dielectric Displacement D*: The vector used to describe the electric field in dielectrics.

*Dielectric Strength (Breakdown):* The limiting voltage gradient required to cause appreciable current flow or failure of a dielectric.

*Electric Field Intensity E:* The force experienced by a unit charge placed in an electric field.

*Electrostriction:* The change in dimensions of a dielectric due to an applied field.

*Ferroelectric*: A material which exhibits spontaneous polarization, and electric hysteresis.

*Permittivity ε*: It is a measure of the degree to which a medium can resist the flow of charge.

*Piezoelectric*: A non-centrosymmetric crystal which becomes polarized when a mechanical stress is applied.

*Polarizability α*: The proportionality constant between the induced dipole moment and the local electric field.

*Polarization*: The total dipole moment per unit volume in a dielectric.

*Relative Dielectric Constant or Relative Permittivity*: The factor by which the capacitance of a vacuum capacitor is increased when a dielectric medium is introduced in the vacuum.

*Relaxation Frequency*: The reciprocal of relaxation time.

*Relaxation Time*: The time required for a disturbed system to reach $1/e$ of the final equilibrium configuration.

## REVIEW QUESTIONS AND PROBLEMS

1. Derive an expression for the local electric field acting at an atom in SI system. Explain the terms, depolarization field and Lorentz field.

2. Derive Clausius-Mosotti equation in SI system. Show that the dielectric constant of a ferroelectric should follow the Curie-Weiss law above the Curie temperature.

3. What are various polarizabilities? Discuss the classical theory of electronic polarizability and obtain corresponding dispersion relation.

4. Discuss orientational polarizability and obtain an expression known as Langevin-Debye equation.

5. Explain the phenomenon of piezoelectricity. Describe any two applications of the piezoelectric effect.

6. What is ferroelectricity? Name any two ferroelectric materials and their applications.

7. The relative permittivity of argon at 0°C and one atmosphere is 1.000435. Calculate the polarizability of the argon atom.  *Ans.* $1.43 \times 10^{-40}$ $Fm^2$.

8. Calculate the induced dipole moment per unit volume (polarization density) of helium gas when it is placed in a field of $6 \times 10^5$ V/m. The atomic polarizability of helium is $0.18 \times 10^{-40}$ $Fm^2$ and the concentration of helium atom is $2.6 \times 10^{25}/m^3$. Also calculate the separation of positive and negative charges in each atom.
   *Ans.* $2.81 \times 10^{-10}$ $C/m^2$, $6.75 \times 10^{-17}$ m.

9. If the density of polarization of dimond is $1.32 \times 10^{-10}$ $C/m^2$, calculate the shift of the centre of negative cloud of 6 electrons on each atom from the nucleus. The density of the carbon is 3500 $kg/m^3$ and the atomic weight is 1.2  *Ans.* $7.8 \times 10^{-17}$ m.

10. There are $1.6 \times 10^{20}$ molecules/$m^3$ in NaCl vapour. Determine the orientational polarization at room temperature if the vapour is subjected to a field of $5 \times 10^6$ V/m. Assume that the NaCl molecule consists of $Na^+$ and $Cl^-$ ions separated by 2.5 Å.
    *Ans* $10.32 \times 10^{-11}$ $C/m^2$.

11. The dielectric constant of helium at 0°C and one atmosphere is 1.000074. Calculate the dipole moment induced in each helium atom when the gas is subjected to an electric field of $3 \times 10^4$ V/m.
    *Ans.* $7.3 \times 10^{-37}$ C-m.

12. The polarizability of $NH_3$ molecule in the gaseous state, from the measurement of dielectric constant is found to be $2.42 \times 10^{-39}$ $Fm^2$ at 309 K and $2 \times 10^{-39}$ $Fm^2$ at 448 K, respectively. Calculate for each temperature the polarizability due to permanent dipole moment and due to deformation of molecules.
    *Ans.* $0.23 \times 10^{-39}$ $Fm^2$, $2.19 \times 10^{-39}$ $Fm^2$ and $1.51 \times 10^{-39}$ $Fm^2$.

# Chapter 15

# Optical Properties of Materials

## 15.1 ABSORPTION PROCESSES

When an electromagnetic radiation passes from one medium to another, three processes can occur, viz reflection, transmission or absorption. The absorption process transforms the electromagnetic radiation into a different form. The nature of the absorption process depends on the frequency of the radiation and on the substance involved.

### 1. The Fundamental Absorption

This process involves a transition of electron from the valence band to the conduction band as shown in Fig. 15.1. Such an electronic transition takes place between occupied (filled) and unoccupied (unfilled) energy states. Let us suppose that these energy states are separated by an energy $\Delta E$, which is greater than the energy gap $E_g$.

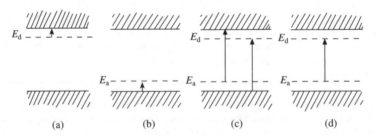

$$\qquad\text{(a)}\qquad\qquad\text{(b)}\qquad\qquad\text{(c)}\qquad\qquad\text{(d)}$$

**Fig. 15.1    Various absorption processes**

An electron in the valence band absorbs a photon of energy $h\nu$ (from the incident beam) and jumps into the conduction band provided

$$h\nu \geq E_g \quad \text{or} \quad \nu \geq \left(\frac{E_g}{h}\right) \tag{1}$$

The critical frequency (corresponds to the minimum energy required for such a transition to take place) and the critical wavelength will be given by

$$\nu_0 = \left(\frac{E_g}{h}\right) \quad \text{or} \quad \lambda_0 = \left(\frac{hc}{E_g}\right) \tag{2}$$

At the critical stage, there appears a sharp absorption in the spectrum. To the long wavelength side of this edge, the material will be transparent.

## 2  Exciton Absorption

In the fundamental absorption process, it is assumed that the excited electron is free in the conduction band and the hole left in the valence band is also free. Alternatively, one can assume that an electron may be excited such that it remains in the vicinity of its nucleus which in turn forms an electron-hole bound state. An electrostatic attraction exists between them and the electron-hole pair revolves around their mutual centre of mass. The bound electron-hole pair is called an exciton. The energy required to form an exciton is less than the band gap energy and is given by

$$hv = E_g - E_{ex} \tag{3}$$

where $E_{ex}$ is the exciton binding energy and is characteristically about 0.01 eV. Fig. 15.2 depicts the exciton levels within the band gap.

Absorption of an exciton introduces complications into the fundamental absorption spectrum, particularly near the edge, which makes the determination of energy gap in semiconductors more difficult. However, exciton absorption is important in discussion of optical properties of insulators in the ultraviolet region of the spectrum.

## 3  Free-carrier Absorption

Free-carriers (both electrons and holes) absorb radiation and instead of getting excited into the other band, they make transitions into another energy states in the same band, as shown in Fig. 15.3. This process is also known as interband transition.

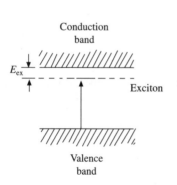

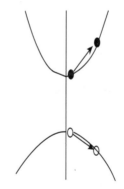

**Fig. 15.2   Schematic representation of exciton energy levels**

**Fig. 15.3   Free Carrier absorption**

Free-carrier absorptions can take place even if $hv < E_g$, and frequently this process dominates below the fundamental edge. However, for $hv > E_g$, both fundamental absorption and free-carrier absorption can occur simultaneously.

## 15.2  PHOTOCONDUCTIVITY

In the absence of light (i.e. in dark), an intrinsic semiconductor or a pure single crystal may exhibit negligible electrical conductivity because the energy of the incident photon is very small as compared to the energy gap (i.e. $hv \ll E_g$) between the top of the valence band and bottom of the conduction band. However, when an electromagnetic radiation including white light is incident, considerable increase in the electrical conductivity may be observed. Thus, photoconductivity is the increase in the electrical conductivity of certain insulating crystalline solids, as a result of exposure to electromagnetic radiation. The increase in the electrical conductivity is due to the production of electron-hole pairs by the absorbed photons. This phenomenon is used in light meters (in cameras) and solid state infrared detectors. A simple experimental setup for measuring the photoconductivity is illustrated in Fig. 15.4. Let us consider a semiconducting slab placed in dark. Since a negligibly small current flows in dark, the dark conductivity is written as

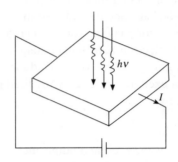

**Fig. 15.4  The generation of photocarriers in a photoconductor**

$$\sigma_d = ne\mu_e + pe\mu_n \simeq 0 \qquad (4)$$

where $n$ and $p$ are free electron and hole concentrations, $\mu_e$ and $\mu_h$ are the electron and hole mobilities, and $e$ is the electronic charge. When the electromagnetic radiation of an appropriate frequency is allowed to fall on the semiconductor slab, the electrical conductivity increases. The change in the conductivity (assuming $\Delta n = \Delta p$) is given by

$$\Delta\sigma = \sigma - \sigma_d = \Delta n \, e(\mu_e + \mu_h) \qquad (5)$$

and

$$\frac{\Delta\sigma}{\sigma_d} = \frac{\Delta n \, e(\mu_e + \mu_h)}{\sigma_h} \qquad (6)$$

If $\tau$ is the carrier lifetime and $f$ is the rate of their generation (i.e. number of electron-hole pairs produced per second by the absorbed photons), then the average photo induced concentration is given by

$$\Delta n = f\tau \qquad (7)$$

where $\Delta n \cong 10^{20}$ m$^{-3}$, for germanium.

In a practical device, the sensitivity is expressed as a gain $G$, which is the ratio of the crrier photocurrent $I$ to the rate of generation of carriers. Thus,

$$G = \frac{I}{ef} \qquad (8)$$

If $t$ is the transit time of the carriers between the electrodes, then,

$$G = \frac{\tau}{t} \qquad (9)$$

Thus, photoconductivity is large when the lifetime is large. A pure material is generally found to have low $\tau\,(\sim 10^{-6}$ s) due to the greater probability of electron-hole recombination, and hence is relatively insensitive. However, a careful doping can supress recombination and hence increase $\tau$ and sensitivity. For example, in CdS, careful doping of iodine increases $\tau$ to $10^{-3}$ s. This process is represented in Fig. 15.5. Iodine, substituting for sulphur, acts as donor. To fit into the divalent ionic lattice, the iodine atom should accept two electrons. However, it shows a strong affinity to one while the second is only weakly bound and can be easily removed thermally. This gives rise to a charge imbalance. In order to compensate this, $Cd^{2+}$ vacancies are generated at the rate of one per two iodine donors. These divalent positive ion vacancies act as efficient hole traps. During

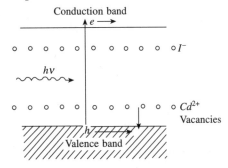

**Fig. 15.5** **Model for increasing the electron lifetime in CdS as a result of doping with iodine**

photoexcitation, holes are readily trapped and electrons have much less chance of recombination and hence average lifetime is increased.

CdS and CdTe single crystals are widely used as photoconductors because of their high sensitivity and response to visible light wavelengths.

## 15.3 PHOTOELECTRIC EFFECT

In the late nineteenth century, a series of experiments revealed that the electrons are ejected from metal surfaces when they are illuminated by radiations like X-rays, ultra-violet rays or even visible light of sufficiently high frequency. This phenomenon is known as photoelectric effect and the electrons so emitted are known as photoelectrons. Fig. 15.6 shows a typical experimental arrangement used to study the photoelectric effect. The apparatus consists of an evacuated glass tube fitted with two electrodes. The metal plate whose surface is to be irradiated acts as a cathode, also called as emitting electrode and is kept at zero potential. On the other hand, the electrode at the other end of the tube acts as an anode, also called the collecting electrode, and may be kept at positive or negative with respect to the cathode. A varying potential difference can be applied across the two electrodes. The potential difference is measured by a voltmeter.

When a suitable monochromatic radiation is allowed to fall on the cathode, photoelectrons are ejected from it. Initially, when the potential at the anode is positive and large, all the ejected photoelectrons are collected at the anode and the current measured by the ammeter reaches maximum value. By decreasing the potential

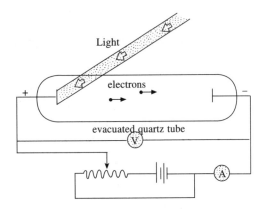

**Fig. 15.6** **Experimental observation of the photoelectric effect**

at the anode, the current is found to decrease slowly. However, if the potential at the anode is made negative with respect to the cathode, the photoelectric current does not immediately becomes zero. This shows that the photoelectrons have certain initial kinetic energies. As it is made more and more negative, the photoelectric current decreases and finally becomes zero at a potential difference say $V_0$. At this potential even the faster moving electrons cannot reach the anode and hence is called the stopping potential. Thus, the work done by the stopping potential is equal to the maximum kinetic energy of the photoelectrons, i.e.

$$eV_0 = T_{max} = \frac{1}{2} mv^2_{max} \qquad (10)$$

Photoelectric current is found to depend on the intensity of light beam. A strong light beam yields more photoelectrons than a weak one of the same frequency. Fig. 15.7 shows the variation of photoelectric current with applied electrode potential for three different intensities of light of same frequency. It is clear from the figure that the stopping potential $V_0$ (or the maximum kinetic energy $T_{max}$) is independent of the intensity of light.

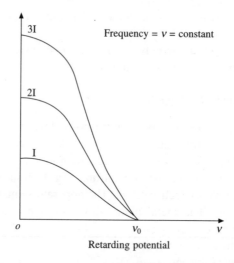

**Fig. 15.7 Photoelectric current as a function of retarding potential for three different intensities (but same frequency) of light**

Like above, the photoelectric current also depends on the frequency of the light employed. Fig. 15.8 shows the variation of photoelectric current with the applied electrode potential for three different frequencies of light of same intensity. It is clear from the figure that the higher the frequency (i.e. the higher the maximum kinetic energy of the photoelectrons), the larger the stopping potential.

In is further observed that the emission of photoelectrons takes place only when the frequency of the incident radiation is above a certain critical value $v_0$, characteristic of a particular metal. Below this frequency, no photoelectrons are emitted whatever may be the intensity of light. This critical frequency is called the threshold frequency and is different for different metals. Fig. 15.9 shows the plot of maximum photoelectron energy $T_{max}$ versus the frequency of incident light. They are related as,

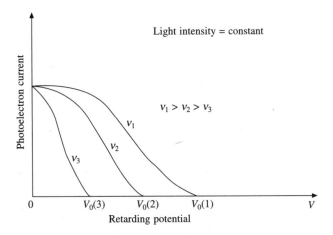

**Fig. 15.8** **Photoelectric current as a function of retarding potential for three different frequencies (but same intensity) of light**

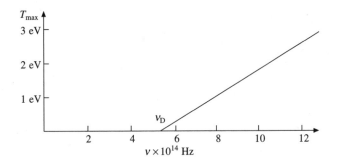

**Fig. 15.9** **Maximum photoelectron energy as a function of frequency of the incident light**

$$T_{max} = h(v - v_0) = hv - hv_0 \tag{11}$$

This equation can further be written as

$$hv = T_{max} + hv_0 \tag{12}$$

$$= T_{max} + W \tag{13}$$

where $W$ is called the workfunction and $h$ is Planck's constant. These equations are known as Einstein's photoelectric equations.

*Example:* A metallic surface, when illuminated with light of wavelength $\lambda_1$ emits electrons with energies upto a maximum value of $E_1$, and when illuminated with a light of wavelength $\lambda_2$ (where $\lambda_2 < \lambda_1$), it emits electrons with energies upto a maximum value of $E_2$. Prove that the Planck's constant $h$ and the workfunction $W$ of the metal are given by

$$h = \frac{\lambda_1 \lambda_2 (E_2 - E_1)}{c(\lambda_1 - \lambda_2)} \quad \text{and} \quad W = \frac{E_2 \lambda_2 - E_1 \lambda_1}{\lambda_1 - \lambda_2}$$

*Solution*: Making use of eq. 11, we have

$$E_1 = h\nu_1 - W = \frac{hc}{\lambda_1} - W \qquad\qquad \text{(i)}$$

Similarly, we have

$$E_2 = h\nu_2 - W = \frac{hc}{\lambda_2} - W \qquad\qquad \text{(ii)}$$

Subtracting eq. (i) from (ii) and simplifying we get

$$h = \frac{\lambda_1 \lambda_2 (E_2 - E_1)}{c(\lambda_1 - \lambda_2)}$$

Further, substituting the value of $h$ either in (i) or (ii) and solving for $W$, we obtain

$$W = \frac{E_2 \lambda_2 - E_1 \lambda_1}{\lambda_1 - \lambda_2}$$

*Example*: A radio transmitter operates at a frequency of 1760 kHz and a power of 10 kW. How many photons does it emit?

*Solution*: Given: $\nu = 1760$ kHz, $P = 10$ kW, No. of photons = ?

Light energy emitted per second = 10 kJ = $10^4$ J. Further, the energy carried by one photon is given by

$$h\nu = 6.626 \times 10^{-34} \times 1760 \times 10^3 \text{ J}$$

Therefore, the number of photons emitted by the transmitter is given by

$$\frac{\text{Light energy emitted per second}}{\text{Energy carried by one photon}} = \frac{10^4}{6.626 \times 10^{-34} \times 1760 \times 10^3}$$

$$= 8.58 \times 10^{30}$$

*Example*: The energy required to remove an electron from sodium metal is 2.3 eV. Does sodium exhibit the photoelectric effect from an orange light having wavelength 2800 Å.

*Solution:* Given: $W = 2.3$ eV = $2.3 \times 1.6 \times 10^{-19}$ J = $3.68 \times 10^{-19}$ J, $\lambda = 280 \times 10^{-9}$ m.

We know that the frequency of radiation is given by

$$\nu = \frac{c}{\lambda} = \frac{3 \times 10^8}{280 \times 10^{-9}} = 1.07 \times 10^{15} /s$$

Therefore, the energy carried by each photon of radiation is

$$h\nu = 6.626 \times 10^{-34} \times 1.07 \times 10^{15} = 7.08 \times 10^{-19} \text{ J} = 4.43 \text{ eV}$$

Since, the energy of the radiation is found to be greater than the workfunction, the photoelectric effect is possible.

*Example*: Calculate the number of photons from green light of mercury ($\lambda = 4961$ Å) required to do one joule of work.

*Solution*: Given: $\lambda = 496.1 \times 10^{-9}$ m, No. of photons required to do one joule of work = ? The frequency of radiation can be found as

$$v = \frac{c}{\lambda} = \frac{3 \times 10^8}{496.1 \times 10^{-9}} = 6.047 \times 10^{14} \text{ /s}$$

Therefore, the energy carried by each photon of radiation is

$$hv = 6.626 \times 10^{-34} \times 6.047 \times 10^{14} = 4.006 \times 10^{-19} \text{ J}$$

Therefore, the number of photons required to do one joule of work is equal to

$$\frac{1}{hv} = \frac{1}{4.006 \times 10^{-19}} = 2.5 \times 10^{18}$$

*Example*: In a photocell, a copper surface was irradiated by light of wavelength 1849Å, the stopping potential was found to be 2.72 volts. Calculate the threshed frequency, the workfunction and the maximum energy of the photoelectrons.

*Solution:* Given: $\lambda = 184.9 \times 10^{-9}$ m, $V_0 = 2.72$ volts, $v_0 = ?$ $W = ?$ $T_{max} = ?$ The frequency of radiation can be found as

$$v = \frac{c}{\lambda} = \frac{3 \times 10^8}{184.9 \times 10^{-9}} = 1.622 \times 10^{15} \text{ /s}$$

Therefore, the energy carried by each photon of radiation is

$$hv = 6.625 \times 10^{-34} \times 1.622 \times 10^{15} = 10.75 \times 10^{-19} \text{ J} = 6.719 \text{ eV}$$

Further, from eq. 10 the maximum energy is given by

$$T_{max} = eV_0 = 2.72 \times 1.6 \times 10^{-19} \text{ J} = 2.72 \text{ eV}$$

Also, from eq. 11 we have

$$T_{max} = hv - hv_0$$

or $W = hv_0 = hv - T_{max} = 6.719 - 2.72 = 4$ eV

Therefore, $\qquad v_0 = \dfrac{W}{h} = \dfrac{4 \times 1.6 \times 10^{-19}}{6.626 \times 10^{-34}} = 9.66 \times 10^{14} \text{ /s}$

## 15.4  PHOTOVOLTAIC EFFECT

When an electromagnetic radiation of frequency $v$ (with $hv > E_g$) is incident on a *p–n* junction, electron-hole pairs are produced. The electrons diffuse into the *n*-region (move downhill) while the holes diffuse into the *p*-region (move uphill) of the crystal as shown in Fig. 15.10. In the absence of an external electric field, the light induced current develops a photovoltage across the *p-n* junction. This phenomenon is called the photovoltaic effect. In section 13.8, we obtained the

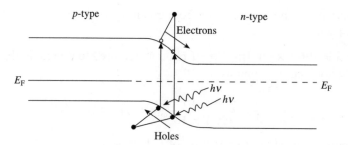

**Fig. 15.10   Photogeneration of electron-hole pair at a p-n junction**

general expression of the net current flowing through the junction under the application of an external voltage as

$$I_v = I_0 \left[ \exp\left(\frac{eV}{kT}\right) - 1 \right] \tag{14}$$

where $V$ may be positive or negative, representing forward or reverses bias, respectively and $I_0$ is called the dark current.

When light is allowed to fall on the junction, photocurrent $I_L$ is produced whose direction is opposite to that of $I_v$. Therefore, the net current in the presence of radiation is

$$I = I_L - I_v \tag{15}$$

When no external voltage is applied to the junction, then the junction acts as a photovoltaic cell and $I = 0$, so that eq. 15 becomes

$$I_L + I_0 - I_0 \exp\left(\frac{eV_{ph}}{kT}\right) = 0 \tag{16}$$

where "$V_{ph}$" represents the photovoltage. Therefore, from eq. 16, we have

$$\exp\left(\frac{eV_{ph}}{kT}\right) = \left(\frac{I_L + I_0}{I_0}\right) = \left(1 + \frac{I_L}{I_0}\right)$$

or

$$\frac{eV_{ph}}{kT} = \ln\left(1 + \frac{I_L}{I_0}\right) \quad \text{or} \quad V_{ph} = \frac{kT}{e} \ln\left(1 + \frac{I_L}{I_0}\right) \tag{17}$$

For very high light intensities $(I_L/I_0) \gg 1$, so that eq. 17 reduces to

$$V_{ph} = \frac{kT}{e} \ln\left(\frac{I_L}{I_0}\right) \tag{18}$$

Thus, the photovoltage varies logarithmically with the photocurrent and hence the intensity of electromagnetic radiation. This is the reason why the photovoltaic cells are so useful in ordinary light meters.

## 15.5   PHOTOLUMINESCENCE

When a crystalline solid absorbs energy (usually in the form of radiation) and re-emits it in the visible (or nearly visible) region of the spectrum, this phenomenon is referred to as luminescence. It is a two step process: (i) excitation of electrons from a lower energy state to a higher energy state as a result of absorption of energy, and (ii) emission of light radiation when the electrons fall back to a lower energy state. When the luminescence is produced by the bombardment of photons of an electromagnetic radiation lying in the range from infrared to X-rays, it is called photoluminescence.

The time during which luminescence be observed, depends on the time interval between the acts of excitation and emission. If the emission takes place within $10^{-8}$ seconds of excitation (as a rule the lifetime of an excited state is $\sim 10^{-8}$ seconds) or if the emission takes place as long as the excitation is maintained, the phenomenon is called fluorescence. On the other hand, if the luminescent emission continues for some time (perhaps hours) even after the excitation has been ceased, it is known as phosphorescence or "afterglow". For example, when kerosene oil is illuminated by light, it emits a faint bluish fluorescence, while a crystalline ZnS when illuminated by X-rays, it displays phosphorescence.

## 15.6   COLOUR CENTRES

Most insulator crystals and pure alkali halide crystals are transparent to visible light. However, when irradiated, these crystals appear to be coloured due to the selective absorption of some component of visible spectrum by certain imperfections, which are usually present in the crystal. Thus a colour centre is a lattice imperfection (or defect) which absorbs visible light. The transmitted beam received by our eyes contains only the complementary (remaining) colours. Table 15.1 shows the spectral colours alongwith their wavelengths and their complementary colours.

**Table 15.1   The spectral colours and their complementary colours**

| Spectral colours | $\lambda(\text{Å})$ | Complementary colours |
| --- | --- | --- |
| Violet | 4100 | Lemon-yellow |
| Indigo | 4300 | Yellow |
| Blue | 4800 | Orange |
| Blue-green | 5000 | Red |
| Green | 5300 | Purple |
| Lemon-Yellow | 5600 | Violet |
| Yellow | 5800 | Indigo |
| Orange | 6100 | Blue |
| Red | 6800 | Blue-green |

## 15.7   TYPES OF COLOUR CENTRES

Broadly speaking, colour centres can be put into two different categories:
(a) Electronic centres and (b) Hole centres.

### (a) Electronic Centres

Electronic centres include: (i) *F* centres, (ii) $F_A$ centres, (iii) *R* centres and (iv) *M* centres

## (b)   Hole Centres

Hole centres are antimorphs of the electronic centres, and are known as $V$ centres. For example, $V_1$ centre is antimorph of the $F$ centre. Similarly, $V_2$ and $V_3$ centres are the antimorphs of $R_1$ and $R_2$ centres, respectively whereas $V_4$ is the antimorph of $M$ centre. Let us discuss them briefly:

*F Centre*

This is the most extensively studied and the simplest of all colour centres. Its name comes from the German word for colour, Farbe. The $F$ centre in alkali halides is a negative ion vacancy (which acts as an effective positive charge) with one excess electron trapped in it as shown in Fig. 15.11a. Its energy level diagram is shown in Fig. 15.11b.

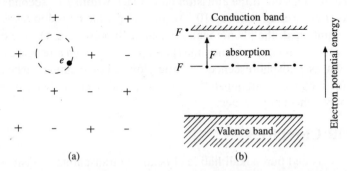

Fig. 15.11   The $F$ centre (a) the lattice configuration (b) the $F$-band transition in KCl

The orbital motion of the trapped electron (which is only weakly bound to the vacant site) is quantized and therefore has a series of discrete permitted energy levels spaced at optical frequencies. The optical absorption bands ($F$-bands) associated with $F$ centres in several alkli halide crystals are shown in Fig. 15.12. According to Mollwo, the frequency corresponding to $F$-band, $\nu_F$ is related to the interatomic separation "$a$" and is given by

$$\nu_F\, a^2 \approx 0.5 \text{ cm}^2\text{s}^{-1}$$

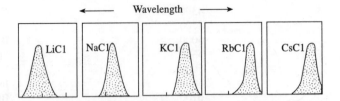

Fig. 15.12   The $F$-bands for several alkali halides; optical absorption versus wavelength for crystals which contain $F$ centres

The $F$ centres are usually produced by heating the crystal in excess alkali (Na or K) vapour or by irradiation. In the process, alkali atoms get ionized as

$$\text{Na} \rightarrow \text{Na}^+ + \bar{e} \quad \text{and} \quad \text{K} \rightarrow \text{K}^+ + \bar{e}$$

While Na$^+$ or K$^+$ ion presumably occupies a normal cation site in the NaCl structure, the electrons get trapped around an anion (chloride) vacancy. This has been verified by esr (electron spin resonance) study and is in agreement with a model suggested by de Boer. The model is found to be consistent with the following experimental facts:

1. The *F* band optical absorption is characteristic of the host crystal and not of the alkali vapour. The role of the vapour is only to produce *F* centres in the host crystal.
2. Chemical analysis shows that the crystal coloured by heating in excess of alkali vapour contains an excess of alkali metal atoms (typically $\sim 10^{16} - 10^{19}$ per $cm^3$)
3. Coloured crystals are less dense than uncoloured crystals. This agrees with the elementary picture that the creation of vacancies should lower the density.

**Other Electronic Centres**

When a crystal already containing *F* centres is irradiated at elevated temperatures by light that is absorbed by these *F* centes, a new absorption band on the long wavelength side of the *F* band appears. The resulting centres are called *F′* centres. Some of the electrons which are being excited by the incident light become free by absorbing heat. These electrons can combine with the existing *F* centres to form an *F′* centre, i.e. an *F′* centre is an *F* centre with two trapped electrons. A reversible process will give rise to an *F* centre, i.e. when a crystal already containing *F′* centre, is similarly irradiated by light that is absorbed by these centres, *F* centres are produced. Besides, some other trapped-electron centres formed by groups of *F* centres are:

1. *M* centres consist of two adjacent *F* centres.
2. *R* centres consist of three adjacnt *F* centres.

*Hole Centres (V Centres)*

Like electrons, holes can also get trapped at vacant lattice site to produce colour centres. When an alkali halide crystal is heated in excess halogen ion, positive ion vacancies are created where holes get trapped. The resulting colour centres are called *V* centres and are antimorphs to the *F* centres. Some of them are as follows:

1. A $V_k$ centre is formed when a hole is trapped by a pair of negative ions.
2. A $V_L$ centre is formed when a neutral $Cl_2$ molecule occupies a negative ion site.
3. An *H* centre is formed when a singly ionised $Cl_2^-$ molecule occupies a negative ion site.

## 15.8   GENERATION OF COLOUR CENTRES

Colour centres may be produced by one of the following methods

1. By additive colouration:

   (i)   by the introduction of chemical impurities
   (ii)  by the introduction of excess of metal ions

2. Colouration by ionising radiation
3. Electrolytic colouration

## Additive Colouration

### Introduction of Chemical Impurities
The imperfections which are responsible for colour centres may be interstitial impurity atoms such as transition-metal ions or simple vacancies in the structure such that there may be excess of positive ions accompanied by negative vacancies or excess of negative ions accompanied by positive vacancies. Thus, when excess Zn are present in ZnO, it becomes yellow, whereas excess of Li in LiF turns the crystal pink and excess K in KCl makes the crystal appear violet.

### Introduction of Excess Metal-ions
When a colourless alkali halide crystal is heated in an atomsphere containing excess alkali metal vapour, it becomes coloured. For example, when a sodium chloride crystal is heated in the presence of sodium vapours, the crystal becomes yellow. Similarly, when potassium bromide and potassium chloride are heated in the presence of excess potassium vapours, potassium bromide becomes blue and potassium chloride becomes magenta. This can be understood as follows: when the alkali halide crystal is heated in the presence of alkali metal vapours, the excess metal atoms get deposited on the surface of the crystal by losing their valence electrons. Halogen ions then may diffuse to the surface and combine with the metal ions. The free electron in turn diffuses into the crystal until it encounters a negative ion vacancy (which has effective positive charge relative to the crystal) with which it combines. A similar result is obtained when excess alkali metal atoms are introduced during crystal growth. Such electrons are weakly bound to the vacant sites and are responsible for absorption in the visible range. The quantum state of such an electron lies somewhere within the energy gap. The exact energy value of this state depends only on the metal atom from which the electron originally came. Therefore, it does not matter whether the excess metal atom present in the crystal is the same as the host metal atom or not.

### Colouration by Ionising Radiations
It is possible to produce colour centres when a crystal is irradiated with high energy radiations such as X-rays, $\gamma$-rays, neutron and electron beams. In this method, the trapped electron and trapped hole centres are produced simultaneously, which can interact during irradiation or even after it. The rate of growth or the efficiency of production of colour centres and the saturation value are observed to depend in a complicated fashion on the following: (i) type of radiation, (ii) dose rate, (iii) temperature, and (iv) purity and mechanical state of the sample.

Intense colouration is achieved when an appreciable amount of soft X-ray component is present in the radiation. When radiating with soft polychromatic X-ray beam, thin crystals should be used. Further, to achieve maximum uniformity of colouration, the crystal should be irradiated from both sides.

### Electrolytic Colouration
In this method, colour centres can be produced as a result of electrolytic conduction when an electric field of about 100 Volts/cm is applied to a crystal held at about 100°C (well below its melting point). In order to produce only trapped electron centres in the crystal, a pointed wire cathode (made of molybdenum or tungsten) on one end of the crystal is used. A thin foil of

platinum is most often used as anode. A cloud of colour centres emege from the pointed cathode and migrate towards anode. Trapped hole centres can be produced in some alkali halide crystals by using pointed anode. Colour centres produced in this case are due to excess of one of the elements as in the case of additive colouration.

## 15.9   MASER AND LASER

The name MASER stands for molecular (formerly microwave) amplification by stimulated emission of radiation. Similarly, the name LASER stands for light amplification by stimulated emission of radiation. Both of them work on the same principle of stimulated emission of radiation but in different region of the electromagnetic spectrum. For their operation they must satisfy the following conditions:

1. There must be an active medium. It may be a collection of atoms, molecules, ions, radicals or atomic nuclei (in liquid or solid form) that can absorb photons of a particular energy and emit radiations in the microwave or the optical regions of the spectrum.
2. There must be a "population inversion" of atoms, molecules, ions, radicals or atomic nuclei. They will be treatd in common under the general term as atom.
3. There must be some form of optical feedback present in the system for the continuous production of laser beam.

### Absorption and Emission

Absorption of photons by the atom and consequent emission of radiation by them in the microwave or the optical regions are important processes for producing very intense monochromatic, and highly collimated beam. Let us suppose that the atoms are characterized by two energy states $E_1$ (may or may not be the ground state) and $E_2$ (where $E_2 > E_1$). When the atoms are illuminated by photons of appropriate frequency, three processes can arise. They are shown in Fig. 15.13.

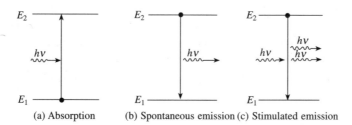

(a) Absorption       (b) Spontaneous emission (c) Stimulated emission

**Fig. 15.13   Processes of absorption and emission: (a) induced absorption (b) spontaneous emission and (c) stimulated emission**

*I. Induced Absorption*
If the atoms are initially in the state $E_1$, as a result of induced absorption they are excited into the higher energy state $E_2$.

*II. Spontaneous Emission*
The excited atoms can return back to the lower energy state spontaneously (without any external

influence) by emitting photons of the same frequency as that of the stimulating photons and travel in the same direction.

### III Stimulated Emission

In this case, the de-excitation of the atoms takes place when they are stimulated (or induced externally) by photons of the same energy as that of the de-excitation. Also, for every incident photon, there are two emitted photons, causing amplifications in the outgoing beam. This process is an essential part in the laser and the maser action.

The three transition processes, viz, the induced absorption, the spontaneous emission and the stimulated emission occur in a collection of atoms. In 1917, Albert Einstein defined the coefficient in each case and showed that the rates of these processes are related mathematically.

For induced absorption to take place, there must be radiation energy present. Further, he postulated that the induced absorption transition rate to be proportional to the number of atoms (say $N_1$) in the lower energy state $E_1$ and to the energy density of radiation $u(v)$ incident on these atoms, i.e.

$$\frac{dN_{12}}{dt} \propto N_1 u(v) \qquad \text{or} \qquad \frac{dN_{12}}{dt} = B_{12} N_1 u(v) \tag{19}$$

where $B_{12}$ is the Einstein coefficient for induced absorption and $u(v)$ is defined such that $u(v)\,dv$ represents the radiation energy per unit volume within the frequncy interval $v$ and $v + dv$.

For spontaneous emission, an atom in the excited state spontaneously drops into the lower energy state. Einstein postulated that the spontaneous emission transition rate is indepenent of the energy density of the radiation and is proportional only to the number of atoms in the excited state (say $N_2$), i.e.

$$\frac{dN_{21}}{dt} \propto N_2 \qquad \text{or} \qquad \frac{dN_{21}}{dt} = N_2 A_{21} \tag{20}$$

where $A_{21}$ is the Einstein coefficient for spontaneous emission. The reciprocal of $A_{21}$ is the time for $(2 \rightarrow 1)$ transition to take place and is called the transition life time for the upper state.

Like induced absorption, the incident radiation energy is required for the stimulated emission to take place. The stimulated emission rate was postulated to be proportional to the number of atoms in the excited state $N_2$ and to the energy density of radiation $u(v)$ incident on these atoms, i.e.

$$\frac{dN_2}{dt} \propto N_2 u(v) \qquad \text{or} \qquad \frac{dN_2}{dt} = B_{21} N_2 u(v) \tag{21}$$

where $B_{21}$ is the Einstein coefficient for stimulated emission.

At thermal equilibrium, the number of upward transitions must be equal to the number of downward transitions Therefore,

$$B_{12} N_1 u(v) = A_{21} N_2 + B_{21} N_2 u(v)$$

or
$$u(v) = \frac{A_{21} N_2}{B_{12} N_1 - B_{21} N_2} \tag{22}$$

Further, from Boltzmann's law, we have

$$\frac{N_1}{N_2} = \exp\left(\frac{E_2 - E_1}{kT}\right) = \exp\left(\frac{h\nu}{kT}\right) \tag{23}$$

Therefore, eq. 22 becomes

$$u(\nu) = \frac{A_{21}}{B_{12} \exp\left(\dfrac{h\nu}{kT}\right) - B_{21}} \tag{24}$$

Now, according to the Planck's law, the energy density of radiation is given by

$$u(\nu) = \frac{8\pi h\nu^3}{c^3} \cdot \frac{1}{\exp\left(\dfrac{h\nu}{kT}\right) - 1} \tag{25}$$

Comparing eqs. 24 and 25, we obtain

$$B_{12} = B_{21} = B \text{ (say)} \tag{26}$$

and

$$\frac{A_{21}}{B_{21}} = \frac{8\pi h\nu^3}{c^3} = \frac{8\pi}{c^3 h^2}(E_2 - E_1)^3 \tag{27}$$

where $(E_2 - E_1)$ is the energy difference between the two states, $h$ is the Planck's constant and $c$ is the velocity of light. These equations are known as Einstein relations.

Further, from eq. 24, at thermal equilibrium the ratio of the spontaneous to stimulated emissions is obtained as

$$\frac{A}{Bu(\nu)} = \exp\left(\frac{h\nu}{kT}\right) - 1 \tag{28}$$

From eq. 28, it is clear that under the condition $h\nu \ll kT$, the stimulated emissions is much greater than the spontaneous emissions. On the other hand, under the condition $h\nu \gg kT$, the reverse is true.

## Population Inversion

According to the Boltzmann statistics, if a sample contains large number of atoms $N_0$ (in the ground state) at a temperature $T$, then in the thermal equilibrium the number of atoms in the state $E_1$ is given by

$$\frac{N_1}{N_0} = \exp\left(-\frac{E_1}{kT}\right)$$

or in general

$$\frac{N_i}{N_0} = \exp\left(-\frac{E_i}{kT}\right) \tag{29}$$

where $N_i$ is the number of atoms in the excited state $E_i$. This equation is known as Boltzmann ratio. The population of several energy states measured relative to the ground state are shown in

Fig. 15.14. From eq. 29, the atomic populations for two arbitrary energy levels $E_2 > E_1$ can be easily obtained as

$$\frac{N_2}{N_1} = \frac{\exp(-E_2/kT)}{\exp(-E_1/kT)} = \exp\left(-\frac{E_2 - E_1}{kT}\right) = \exp\left(-\frac{\Delta E}{kT}\right) \tag{30}$$

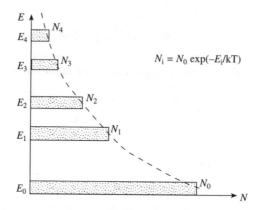

**Fig. 15.14**   **Boltzmann distribution for several energy levels. $N_1, N_2, \ldots$ indicate populations at different energy levels**

There can be three possibilities:

*Case I:* When $\Delta E \gg kT$. It means that the thermal energy is low as compared to the incident energy. Under this condition the Boltzmann ratio is found to be quite small. This indicates that virtually there does not exist any atom in the higher energy states. In other words, in the low temperature region, higher energy states are almost empty.

*Case II:* When $\Delta E \ll kT$. It means that the thermal energy is high as compared to the incident energy. Under this condition the Boltzmann ratio is found to be nearly unity. This indicates that the population at the energy state $E_1$ is nearly equal to the population at the energy state $E_2$. In other words, in the high temperature region, all the states are equally populated.

*Case III:* When $\Delta E = kT$. Under this condition, Boltzmann ratio given by eq. 29, reduces to

$$\frac{N_i}{N_0} = \frac{1}{e}$$

This indicates that the number of atoms in the excited states is reduced by a factor of $1/e$ from its preceding lower states. (may or may not be the ground state). It is taken as a convenient dividing line from the two extreme situations.

From the first two cases, we find that as the temperature is increased in eq. 30, $N_2$ approaches $N_1$ but cannot exceed it. If however, through an artificial means more atoms are excited (or pumped) to the higher energy state then $N_2$ may exceed $N_1$. This artificial pumping causes population inversion. Let us discuss the masers and lasers which employ respectively, two and three-level pumping schemes.

*Example:* What electron energy must be transferred to the atoms of sodium vapour in order to stimulate the emission of the sodium *d*-lines? Given $\lambda_{mean}$ = 5893 Å.

*Solution:* Given: $\lambda_{mean}$ = 5893 Å, $\Delta E$ = ?
The energy of the election which must be transferred to the atoms of sodium vapour to produce stimulated emission is given by

$$\Delta E = h\nu = \frac{hc}{\lambda_{mean}} = \frac{6.626 \times 10^{-34} \times 3 \times 10^{8}}{5893 \times 10^{-10} \times 1.6 \times 10^{-19}} = 2.108 \text{ eV}$$

**Maser**

In 1954, Gordon, Zeiger and Townes constructed the first man made device to amplify the electromagnetic radiation by stimulated emission of radiation based on two-level pumping scheme. They used ammonia ($NH_3$) mlecules as the active medium. An ammonia molecule has the energy states like hydrogen, but the first excited state is only $10^{-4}$ eV (whereas in hydrogen it is 10.2 eV) above the ground state. From eq. 30, the Boltzmann ratio at room temperature ($T$ = 300K) is

$$\frac{N_2}{N_1} = \exp\left(-\frac{\Delta E}{kT}\right) = \exp\left(-\frac{10^{-4} \times 1.6 \times 10^{-19}}{1.38 \times 10^{-23} \times 300}\right) = \exp(-0.00386) \simeq 1$$

This indicates that the two energy states are equally populated. Further, the energy difference of $10^{-4}$ eV corresponds to a transition frequency of

$$\nu = \frac{\Delta E}{kT} = \frac{10^{-4} \times 1.6 \times 10^{-19}}{6.626 \times 10^{-23}} = 24 \times 10^{9} \text{ Hz}$$

which is in the shorter (microwave) region of the spectrum. A schematic view of the ammonia-beam maser is shown in Fig. 15.15. Ammonia molecules obtained from an ammonia source

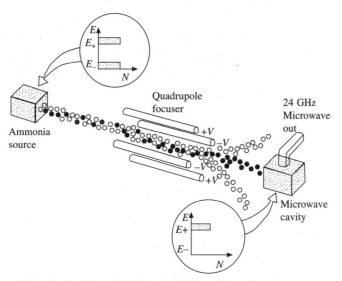

**Fig. 15.15  Schematic representation of amonia-beam maser**

(which produces roughly equal number of excited and unexcited molecules as shown in the top inset) are allowed to pass through an electric field gradient (produced by quadrupole focusser). To differentiate the two types of molecules, the excited ones are designated by solid spheres while the unexcited ones by hollow spheres. The excited molecules with higher energy pass through the electric field directly and enter into the microwave cavity while the unexcited molecules are deflected away by the electric field. Since, the greater majority of the molecules in the molecular beam entering into the cavity belong to the higher energy state, a population inversion is achieved inside the cavity (as shown in the bottom inset) and hence stimulated emission becomes possible. If one molecule makes a transition from its excited state to the ground state, it is likely to stimulate another. This process will continue because the majority of the molecules were in the excited state in the beginning. In order to sustain the process, new excited molecules are introduced continuously.

In general, masers can be used both as oscillators and amplifiers. The ammonia gas maser is used as a stable oscillator while other solid state masers are mainly used as low-noise amplifiers in microwave communication systems and radio-astronomy.

### Laser

As we know that laser is a device for producing very intense, monochromatic, coherent and highly collimated beam of light. The working principle of lasers is the same as that of masers. However, lasers differ from masers broadly on the following aspects:

1. Unlike masers, in lasers the energy difference between the two states is much larger so that the corresponding frequency falls in the visible region of the spectrum.
2. The population inversion is brought about by optical pumping scheme rather than non-optical scheme used in masers.
3. Three and four-level schemes are used in lasers while two level schemes are characteristic of ammonia maser.

There are various types of lasers: (a) gas lasers, (b) dye lasers, (c) solid state lasers, and (d) semiconducting or plastic lasers. However, we shall discuss the working of a solid state laser based on three-level scheme only. The three-level scheme (Fig. 15.16) was first of all proposed by Bloembergen in 1956. Initially, the distribution of state populations obeys the Boltzmann's law as shown in Fig. 15.16a. In the absence of pumping, the transition between the states $E_2$ and $E_1$ is purely absorptive.

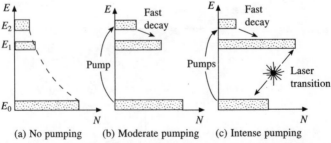

Fig. 15.16 **Population of energy levels by pumping in a three-level system. (a) Boltzmann distribution of energy states with no pumping (b) moderate pumping and (c) intense pumping**

When the ground state atoms are illuminated with a suitable light (e.g. with a xenon flash lamp), a large number of atoms can be excited (through induced absorption) to the highest energy level $E_3$ directly. This process of excitation of atoms is known as optical pumping. From the level $E_3$, they decay to the metastable state level $E_2$ as shown in Fig. 15.16b. If the optical pumping is continued, a significant number of atoms (more than the ground state) can be pumped to the level $E_2$ to obtain a population inversion as shown in Fig. 15.16c.

The first solid state laser to be operated successfully in the year 1960, was a ruby laser. A ruby laser is basically a single crystal of alumina ($Al_2O_3$) doped with 0.01-0.1 percent $Cr^{3+}$ ions. The energy level diagram of the chromium ion is shown in Fig. 15.17. In thermal equilibrium, the number of chromium ions in the three states obey Boltzmann's law as mentioned above. When a beam of photons of energy $h\nu = E_3 - E_1$ is incident on the ruby laser, as a result of induced absorption, the chromium ions get excited from the ground level $E_1$ to the excited level $E_3$ (where the decay from $E_3$ to $E_1$ is forbidden). These ions in turn spontaneously decay to the $E_2$ level (the mean life time of the level $E_3 \sim 10^{-8}$ s). The $E_2$ level is a metastable state with a life time of $3 \times 10^{-3}$ s. Thus, the ions reach the level $E_2$ faster than they leave it. If the optical pumping is continued, the number of ions in the level $E_2$ will increase and a population inversion will be achieved. Now, if the ruby laser is exposed to a beam of photons of energy $h\nu = E_2 - E_1$, the stimulated emission will take place. The stimulating photons in combination with the stimulatd photons can cause further stimulated emission, resulting in a narrow beam of monochromatic radiation, the intensity of which increases exponentially. The beam is coherent and has a very high energy density

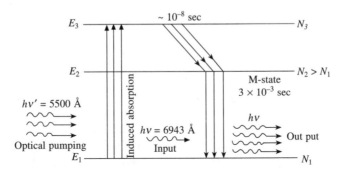

**Fig. 15.17   The energy level diagram of $Cr^{3+}$ ion in ruby laser**

## 15.10   SUMMARY

1. The process of absorption of electromagnetic radiation by a solid substance includes the fundamental absorption, exciton absorption and Free-carrier absorption. Such absorptions take place only if the photon energy is greater than the energy gap, i.e. $h\nu > E_g$. The shape of the absorption curve is a function of the band structure.

2. The photoconductivity of a semiconductor can be increased by shining a light beam on the sample. Such beam excites additional carriers and cause a rise in the conductivity.

3. When a metal (or a semiconductor) surface is illuminated by electromagnetic radiation of certain energy, electrons are ejected. The maximum kinetic energy of the electrons is then given by

$$\frac{1}{2} m v^2_{\text{max}} = h\nu - W$$

where $W$ is the workfunction of the given solid.

4. When an electromagnetic radiation of certain energy $h\nu > E_g$ is incident on a *p-n* junction, the light induced current developes a photovoltage across the junction. For very high light intensities, the resulting photovoltage is given by the equation

$$V_{\text{ph}} = \frac{kT}{e} \ln \left( \frac{I_L}{I_0} \right)$$

where $I_L$ is the photocurrent and $I_0$ is the net current flowing through the junction under the application of voltage $V$.

5. Most insulator crystals and pure alkali halide crystals are transparent to visible light, but when irradiated, they look coloured. Broadly, there are two categories of colour centres. They are electronic centres and hole centres.

6. MASER stands for molecular (formerly microwave) amplification by stimulated emission of radiation, while LASER stands for light amplification by stimulated emission of radiation. Both of them work on the same principle of stimulated emission of radiation. For the sustained operation, there must be an active medium, population inversion and a feedback system.

7. When atoms are illuminated by photons of appropriate frequency, three different processes may take place. They are: induced absorption, induced emission and stimulated emission. Einstein showed that the coefficients of spontaneous and stimulated emissions are related according to the relation

$$A_{21} = \frac{8\pi (E_2 - E_1)^3}{h^2 c^3} B_{21}$$

8. Laser (which is also known as optical maser) is a source of intense, monochromatic and coherent radiation in the visible, ultraviolet and infra-red regions of the spectrum.

9. In 1954, Gordon, Zeiger and Townes constructed first man made device (called Maser) based on two-level pumping scheme. Ammonia molecules obtained from the source are allowed to pass through an electric field gradient. The excited molecules pass through the field and enter into the cavity where population inversion takes place and hence stimulated emission becomes possible.

10. A ruby laser (it is a single crystal of alumina doped with $Cr^{3+}$ ions) is based on a three-level system. The chromium ions are optically pumped to the highest level directly whose lifetime is very short. These ions simultaneously decay to metastable $E_2$ level where population inversion takes place. Exposing the ruby laser with a beam of photons causes stimulated emission.

## 15.11 DEFINITIONS

*Monochromatic Light*: Light of a single wavelength.
*Coherent Radiation*: Cooperative and a single phase radiation.

*Colour Centre (F-Centre):* Electron bound to a negative ion vacancy which introduces additional energy levels in the forbidden energy gap of an insulator crystal.

*Fluorescence:* Light emitted simultaneously or within $10^{-8}$ seconds of its excitation.

*Laser:* Abbreviation of "light amplification by stimulated emission of radiation". A light source which gives coherent radiation. This is also known as optical maser.

*Luminescence:* Absorption of light or other energy by a substance followed by spontaneous emission of light of longer wavelength.

*Maser:* Abbreviation of "microwave (or molecular) amplification by stimulated emission of radiation".

*Phosphorescence:* Light emitted from phosphor at times more than $10^{-8}$ seconds after excitation.

*Spontaneous Emission:* Radiation due to the decay of an excited state which has not been perturbed after excitation.

*Stimulated Emission:* Radiation due to the decay of an excited state, which has been induced to radiate by a photon of the frequency corresponding to the decay emission.

# REVIEW QUESTIONS AND PROBLEMS

1. What is photoconductivity? How does it arise? Mention a few applications of the phenomenon.
2. What is luminescence? Describe in detail the photoluminescence.
3. Several kinds of absorbtion bands can be formed in alkali halide crystals by the introduction of impurities. Discuss the properties of *F*-centres and *V*-centres.
4. Explain the basic princple of MASER and LASER. Discuss the working of ammonia maser.
5. Explain the term (i) stimulated emission, (ii) population inversion as applied to Laser. Discuss the working of ruby laser.
6. Write an essay on Lasers and their applications.
7. Prove that in the photoelectric effect from a metal surface, the maximum velocity of the photoelectron is related to the stopping potential by the equation

$$v_{max} = 5.923 \times 10^5 \sqrt{V_0}$$

8. A metallic surface, when illuminated with light of wavelength 3333 Å emits electrons with energies upto 0.6 eV and when illuminated with light of wavelength 2400 Å, it emits electrons with energies upto 2.04 eV. Calculate Planck's constant and the workfunction of the metal.

   *Ans.* $6.58 \times 10^{-34}$ Js, 3.1 eV.

9. Light of wavelength 4300 Å is incident on (a) nickel surface of workfunction 5 eV and (b) a potassium surface of workfunction 2.3 eV. Find out whether electrons will be emitted, and if so, the maximum velocity of the emitted electrons in each case.

   *Ans.* (a) No electron emission possible (b) electrons are emitted, $v_{max} = 4.59 \times 10^5$ m/s.

10. A photon of wavelength 3310 Å falls on a photocathode and ejects an electron of energy $3 \times 10^{-19}$ J. If the wavelength of the incident photon is changed to 5000 Å, the energy of the ejected electron is 0.972 $\times 10^{-19}$ J. Calculate the value of the Planck's constant, the threshold frequency and the workfunction for the photocathode.

    *Ans.* $6.766 \times 10^{-34}$, $4.63 \times 10^{14}$/s, 1.958 eV.

11. A photon of wavelength 1400 Å is absorbed by cold mercury vapour and two other photons are emitted. If the wavelength of one of them is 1850 Å, what is the wavelength of the other photon?

    *Ans.* 5752 Å.

# Chapter 16

# Magnetic Properties of Materials

## 16.1 INTRODUCTION

Magnetism is perhaps that aspect of solid state physics which has been familiar to man for the longest period of time. The ability of lodestone (magnetite) to attract iron objects was known to ancient Greeks about 3000 years ago. A vast wealth of experimental data on the phenomenon was available long before any conclusive theory of magnetism could be developed. For example, it was known that iron could be magnetized by stroking it with another magnet, by hammering it when placed in the magnetic meridian, or simply by holding it somewhere in the vicinity of a strong magnet. In fact, almost everything known about the magnetic properties of materials have been derived from experimental discoveries and from a few inspired guesses. This is mainly due to the reason that a quantitative description of magnetism requires the knowledge of quantum mechanics and electromagnetic theory of many atom system, which is generally very complex. Therefore, in this chapter we present a simplified description of the phenomenon.

## 16.2 RESPONSE OF SUBSTANCE TO MAGNETIC FIELD

A magnetic field can be described by either magnetic induction $B$ (or magnetic flux density) or the field strength $H$. In vacuum, they are related by the equation

$$B = \mu_0 H \tag{1}$$

where $\mu_0 = 4\pi \times 10^{-7}$ H–m$^{-1}$ and is called the permeability of the free space (vacuum).

When a substance is placed in a magnetic field, it gets magnetized and hence a magnetization $M$ (defined as the magnetic moment per unit volume, i.e $M = \mu_m/\Delta V$) is produced in it. The magnetic induction inside the substance is given by

$$B = \mu_0 H + \mu_0 M = \mu_0(H + M) \tag{2}$$

where the first term on the right side of eq. 2 is due to external field and the second term is due to the magnetization. For an isotropic medium, $M$ and $H$ are parallel vectors and are related to each other according to the relation

$$M = \chi H \tag{3}$$

where $\chi$ is the susceptibility of the medium and is a scalar quantity. Substituting the value of $M$ from eq. 3 into eq. 2, we have

$$B = \mu_0(1 + \chi)H = \mu H \qquad \text{(4)}$$

where
$$\mu = \mu_0(1 + \chi) \qquad \text{(5)}$$

is known as the permeability of the medium. It is often more convenient to use the relative permeability $\mu_r$, which is defined as

$$\mu_r = \frac{\mu}{\mu_0} = (1 + \chi) \qquad \text{(6)}$$

Equation 6 connects the permeability and susceptibility of the medium.

*Example*: The applied magnetic field in copper is $10^6$ A/m. If the magnetic susceptibility of copper is $-0.8 \times 10^{-5}$, calculate the flux density and the magnetization in copper.

*Solution*: Given: $H = 10^6$ A/m, $\chi = -0.8 \times 10^{-5}$, $\mu_0 = 4\pi \times 10^{-7}$ H/m, $B = ?$, $M = ?$ Making use of eq. 3, we have

$$M = \chi H = -0.8 \times 10^{-5} \times 10^6 = -8 \text{ A/m}$$

Further, from eq. 2, we have

$$B = \mu_0 (H + M) = 4\pi \times 10^{-7} (-8 + 10^6) = 1.256 \text{ T}$$

## 16.3 CLASSIFICATION OF MAGNETIC MATERIALS

Magnetic materials can be classified into different categories according to their $\chi$ values and the way in which these vary with the magnetic field strength and temperature. They are: (i) Diamagnetic, (ii) Paramagnetic, (iii) Ferromagnetic, (iv) Antiferromagnetic and (v) Ferrimagnetic.

The Diamagnetic property is the result of an induced magnetic moment. This arises when an atom is placed in a magnetic field. The motion of orbital electrons of the atom (analogous to a current flowing in a circuit) gets modified in such a way that weak magnetic moment opposing the field is induced. Also, if $\chi$ is negative in eq. 3, the direction of magnetization $M$ is opposite to that of the field $H$.

A diamagnetic solid has a tendency to repel the magnetic lines of force due to an external applied field (Fig. 161a). A superconductor which repels all the lines of force, is an example of a perfect diamagnet.

Diamagnetic substances include inert gases (helium, argon, etc.). metals (bismuth, copper, zinc, gold, silver, etc.), mercury, water, glass, marble and many other organic compounds. For a diamagnetic substance, the relative permeability $\mu_r$ (or the susceptibility $\chi$) is independent of temperature.

Unlike diamagnetism, paramagnetism and ferromagnetism are the result of intrinsic magnetic moment. Some atoms and ions do possess permanent magnetic moment. In the absence of an external field, these moments are randomly oriented with respect to one another because of thermal fluctuations and therefore the substance exhibits no net magnetic moment. However, when placed in a magnetic field, the moments tend to align along the direction of field, producing a net magnetization. When the atoms and ions are acted upon individually, with no mutual interaction between them, the effect is called paramagnetism. Since the moments line up in the direction of the field which help enhance the external field, the paramagnetic susceptibility is greater than zero. Further, because of small paramagnetic susceptibility a paramagnetic substance weakly attracts the lines of force (Fig. 16.1b). As thermal energy randomizes the alignment of the dipoles, the paramagnetic susceptibility decreases with the increase of temperature.

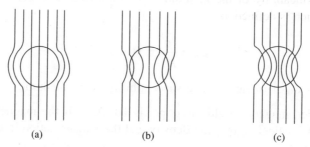

(a)　　　　　　　　(b)　　　　　　　　(c)

**Fig. 16.1**　Behaviour of magnetic lines of force under applied magnetic field in (a) Diamagnet (b) Paramagnet and (c) Ferromagnet

Paramagnetic substances include aluminium, platinum, potassium, manganese, the rare-earth elements, alkali and alkaline earth metals, etc.

A ferromagnetic substance possesses permanent (spontaneous) magnetic moments even in the absence of an external magnetic field. Since, the ferromagnetic susceptibility is very large and positive, so that a ferromagnetic substance strongly attracts the lines of force (Fig. 16.1c). Ferromagnetism exists only below a certain temperature $T_c$, above which the substance becomes paramagnetic.

Ferromagnetic substances include iron, cobalt, nickel and a number of alloys.

In fully magnetized state of a ferromagnet, all the dipoles are aligned in exactly the same direction (Fig. 16.2a). An antiferromagnetic substance has the dipoles with equal moments, but the alternate dipoles point in opposite directions (Fig. 16.2b). As a result, the moments balance each other and result in a zero net magnetization. Another commonly encountered substance is ferrimagnetic, the moments of which are shown in Fig. 16.2c. In this case too,

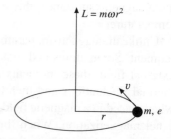

(a)　　　(b)　　　(c)

**Fig. 16.2**　**Magnetic arrangements in (a) Ferromagnet (b) Antiferromagnet and (c) Ferrimagnet**

the neighbouring dipoles point in opposite directions but they are unequal. As a result, they do not completely balance each other and possess finite net magnetization

## 16.4　ATOMIC THEORY OF MAGNETISM

In an atom, we know that the electrons revolve round the nucleus in different circular orbits. Analogous to this situation let us consider an electron of mass $m$, having an electronic charge $(-e)$ moving in a circular orbit of radius $r$ with a velocity $v$ (angular velocity $\omega$) as shown in Fig. 16.3. From the basic knowledge of current

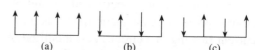

**Fig. 16.3**　**Angular momentum of an orbitting electron**

electricity, we know that a moving electron constitutes an electric current, i.e.

$$I = \frac{dq}{dt} \text{ and } Ids = \frac{dq}{dt} ds = dq \frac{ds}{dt} = -ev \qquad (7)$$

where $dq = -e$ and $v = \frac{ds}{dt}$, the linear velocity. But for a circular orbit, $ds = 2\pi r$ and $v = \omega r$, so that

$$I \times 2\pi r = -e\omega r$$

or
$$I = -\frac{e\omega}{2\pi} \qquad (8)$$

From electromagnetic theory, it is well known that the magnetic field produced by a current, $I$ flowing in a stationary loop of cross sectional area $A$ at right angles to the plane of the current loop is identical with that produced by a magnetic dipole when measured at large distance (as compared to the radius of the loop). The magnitude of the magnetic moment produced by (the circular motion of the electron) such a dipole is

$$\mu_m = I \cdot A \qquad (9)$$

For a circular orbit $A = \pi r^2$, also substituting the value of $I$ from eq. 8 into eq. 9, we obtain

$$\mu_m = -\frac{e\omega}{2\pi} \times \pi r^2$$

or
$$\mu_m = -\frac{e\omega r^2}{2} = -\frac{em\omega r^2}{2m} = -\left(\frac{e}{2m}\right)L \qquad (10)$$

where $L = m\omega r^2$ is the orbital angular momentum of electron and is normal to the plane of the orbital. The minus sign in eq. 10 indicates that the magnetic moment $\mu_m$ is antiparallel to the angular momentum $L$ (Fig. 16.4). This equation is valid only for motion of electron and not for spin of the electron or nucleus. Therefore, to understand the origin of magnetic moments of an atom completely, we have to take into account the spinning motion of electron and nucleus as well. For the purpose, let us introduce the quantum theory of atom, according to which the state of electrons in an atom can be completely specified by four quantum numbers. Let us review them briefly.

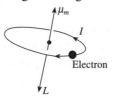

**Fig. 16.4   The magnetic dipole moment and the angular momentum associated with a current loop**

## 16.5   THE QUANTUM NUMBERS

These are integral or half integral numbers used to specify the state of a system in Quantum Mechanics. The four quantum numbers are:

### 1. The Principle Quantum Number, *n*
The principle quantum number determines the energy level of the electron in an atom. It can accept only integer values, i.e. $n = 1, 2, 3, 4 \ldots$ The corresponding electronic levels are called the K, L, M , N, . . . orbits.

## 2.   The Orbital Quantum Number, *l*

This determines the electronic state of an atom and is related to the shape of the electron orbital. The values of orbital quantum number are restricted to

$$l = 0, 1, 2, 3, \ldots (n - 1),$$

where *n* is the principle quantum number. The electrons associated with the states $l = 0, 1, 2, 3,$ ... are called s, p, d, f, ... electrons, respectively. The total angular momentum associated with a given value of *l* is

$$L_l = \hbar[l \, (l + 1)]^{1/2} \tag{11}$$

where                                              $\hbar = h/2\pi,$

## 3.   The Magnetic Quantum Number $m_l$

When an atom is placed in an external magnetic field, the direction of the angular momentum vector and hence the magnetic moment, precesses about the field direction and can have only specific orientation in space. The orentation of the vector $L_l$ in an external magnetic field of induction *B* is characterized by its projection $L_{l,B}$ along the direction of *B* (Fig. 16.5), i.e.

$$L_{l,B} = L_l \cos \alpha \tag{12}$$

The vector $L_l$ can have only such orientations at which the projection $L_{l,B}$ will take on integral values that are multiple of $\hbar$ i.e.

$$L_{l,B} = m_l \hbar = m_l \frac{h}{2\pi} \tag{13}$$

The integer $m_l$ determining the possible values of $L_{l,\,B}$ is called magnetic quantum number. It can have the following values

$$m_l = -l, -(l - 1) \ldots 0 \ldots (l - 1), l$$

or                                    $m_l = 0, \pm 1, \pm 2, \ldots \pm l \tag{14}$

where *l* is the orbital quantum number.

From eq. 14, it is clear that $L_l$ can have $(2l + 1)$ possible values. Fig. 16.6 shows the possible orientations of the vector $L_l$ for an electron in *p* and *d* states, i.e. $l = 1$ and 2.

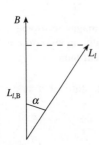

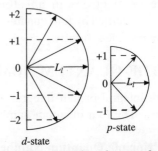

**Fig. 16.5**   **Projection of angular momentum along the field**

**Fig. 16.6**   **Possible orientation of an angular momentum defined by the quantum number *l* in an external magnetic field**

### 4. The Magnetic Spin Quantum Number, $m_s$

As has been pointed out above that the electrons have spinning motion in addition to their orbital motion. According to the quantum theory, the spin is a fundamental property of an electron and thereby has its own angular momentum. In a magnetic field of induction vector $B$, the spin angular momentum is oriented such that its projection along the field direction takes only two values, i.e.

$$S = m_s \hbar = m_s \frac{h}{2\pi} \qquad (15)$$

The angular momentum is pointing either upwards or downwards depending on whether the electron is spinning clockwise or anti-clockwise in the field (Fig. 16.7). The corresponding magnetic spin quantum numbers $m_s$ are $\pm \frac{1}{2}$.

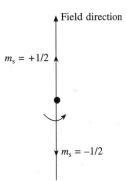

Fig. 16.7 Spin quantization

## 16.6 THE ORIGIN OF PERMANENT MAGNETIC MOMENTS

Permanent magnetic moments can arise from the following three different sources:

1. the orbital magnetic moment of the electrons,
2. the spin magnetic moment of the electrons, and
3. the spin magnetic moment of the nucleus.

### 1. The Orbital Magnetic Moment of the Electrons

Based on the classical consideration of atomic theory of magnetism, we obtained an expression (eq. 10) of magnetic moment in section 16.4. However, quantum consideration tells us that the angular momentum vector can take only specific orientation in space (given by eq. 13) when the atom is placed in an external magnetic field. Therefore, with the help of these equations (eqs. 10 and 13), we obtain

$$\mu_m = -\left(\frac{e}{2m}\right)L_{l,B} = -\left(\frac{e}{2m}\right)m_l \hbar = -\left(\frac{eh}{4\pi m}\right)m_l$$

or $$\mu_m = -m_l \mu_B \qquad (16)$$

where $\mu_B = \dfrac{eh}{4\pi m} = 9.27 \times 10^{-24}$ A-m$^2$, and is called the Bohr magneton. It is the quantum of orbital magnetic moment and is accepted as one unit for measuring the magnetic moments of atomic systems.

In a complex atom whose shells have many electrons, the total orbital magnetic moment is determined by taking the algebraic sum of the magnetic moments of individual electrons in compliance with the rules. The moment of a completely filled shell is zero and hence an atom with partially filled shells will have a non zero orbital magnetic moment.

## 2. The Spin Magnetic Moment of the Electrons

Like orbital magnetic moment, the spin magnetic moment can be determined by substituting the value of magnetic spin angular momentum $S$ from eq. 15 into eq. 10, we obtain

$$\mu_s = \frac{\mu_B}{2} \tag{17}$$

That is, the spin magnetic moment is half of a Bohr magneton. This is only approximately correct because eq. 10 is not valid for electron spins. In fact, the magnetic moment component $\mu_{sz}$ along the field direction is given by

$$\mu_{sz} = g\left(\frac{e}{2m}\right)m_s \hbar = g\left(\frac{eh}{4\pi m}\right)m_s \tag{18}$$

where $g$ is called the spectroscopic splitting factor or the Lande's splitting factor. For the electron spin $g = 2.0023$, i.e. the electron spin gives rise very nearly one Bohr magneton in the direction (or opposite) of an external field. The reason for the name "splitting factor" is the following. Consider an electron having no orbital motion, is placed in a magnetic field of induction $B$. As a result, the electron spin magnet rotates and the potential energy of the magnetic system changes. The potential energy of a magnetic dipole is then given by

$$U = -\mu \cdot B = -\mu B \cos \theta \tag{19}$$

Now, since we know that the magnetic spin quantum number $m_s$ can take two values, either $+\frac{1}{2}$ or $-\frac{1}{2}$. It is reasonable to assume that before the application of the field, the electron is in the higher energy state, i.e. $m_s = +\frac{1}{2}$ and after the application of the field it flips over to the lower energy, i.e. $m_s = -\frac{1}{2}$. For the state $m_s = +\frac{1}{2}$, the angular momentum vector is parallel to the field which is seen as antiparallel to the magnetic moment (angle between $\mu$ and $B$ is 180°). Accordingly, for the state $m_s = -\frac{1}{2}$, the magnetic moment is parallel to the field (i.e. the angle between $\mu$ and $B$ is zero). Making use of this in eq. 19 and substituting $\mu_{sz}$ for $\mu$ (from eq. 18), the change in the energy of the electron spin magnetic moment is

$$\Delta U = 2|\mu_{sz}|B = g\left(\frac{eh}{4\pi m}\right)B = g\mu_B B \tag{20}$$

Thus $g$ determines the amount by which the original level splits up under the influence of magnetic field. This is illustrated in Fig. 16.8.

Sometimes, the orbital angular momentum $L$ and spin angular momentum $S$ may be combined vectorially to get the total angular momentum $J$ of the whole electron system of the atom. For such atoms, the spectroscopic splitting factor $g$ is given by the Lande formula,

$$g = 1 + \frac{J(J+1) + S(S+1) - L(L+1)}{2J(J+1)} \tag{21}$$

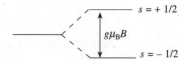

**Fig. 16.8 Splitting of an energy level for an electron with spin 1/2 and zero orbital momentum in a magnetic field**

so that the total magnetic moment of the atomic system becomes

$$\mu = gJ\mu_B \tag{22}$$

The values of $g$ and $J$ are known from the spectroscopic data and thus the total magnetic moment of a free atom or ion, in principle, can be determined.

### 3. The Spin Magnetic Moment of the Nucleus

Just like an electron, the atomic nucleus possesses intrinsic spin (called nuclear spin) and thus a magnetic moment is associated with this. Since the nuclear mass is about $10^3$ times greater than the mass of an electron, therefore the nuclear magnetic moment is approximately three orders of magnitude smaller than the magnetic moment associated with the electron. As the electron magnetic moment is expressed in the unit of Bohr magneton, similarly the nuclear magnetic moment is expressed in the unit of nuclear magneton. A nuclear magneton is defined as

$$\mu_n = \frac{eh}{4\pi M_P} = 5.05 \times 10^{-27} \text{ A} - \text{m}^2 \tag{23}$$

where $M_P$ is the mass of a proton.

## 16.7  LANGEVIN'S CLASSICAL THEORY OF DIAMAGNETISM

As we know that the diamagnetism is the occurrence of negative susceptibility and the magnetization $M$ in this case is antiparallel to the field (eq. 3). There is no electrical counterpart to the negative susceptibility, although it is vaguely analogous to the depolarization field (section 14.5). The negative susceptibility arises from Lenz's law which states that when the flux in an electrical circuit is changed, an induced current is set up in such a direction as to oppose the flux change. For the following discussion, a circuit will mean the circulating electron in an atom, ion or molecule at a lattice site. Let us consider the Bohr model of atom, i.e. consider an electron which revolves round a central nucleus as shown in Fig. 16.9. If $m$ is the mass of the electron, $-e$ is the charge of the electron and $r$ is the radius of the orbit then in the absence of an external field the centripetal force acting on the electron due to the nucleus is given by

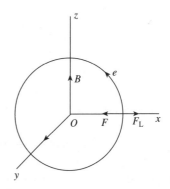

**Fig. 16.9  Motion of an electron in xy-plane**

$$F_0 = \frac{mv^2}{r} = m\omega_0^2 r \tag{24}$$

where $v = \omega_0 r$. When a magnetic field is applied along the $z$-axis (perpendicular to the $xy$-plane), an additional force $F_L$ equal to the Lorentz force starts acting on the electron in a direction away from the centre. The Lorentz force is given by

$$F_L = -e(v \times B) = -eBr\omega \tag{25}$$

where the magnetic field $B$ is perpendicular to $r$. Because of the change in the net force on the electron, there is a change in the angular frequency from $\omega_0$ to $\omega$. The resulting equation can be written as

$$F_0 - eBr\omega = m\omega^2 r \tag{26}$$

Substituting $F_0$ from eq. 24 into eq. 26 and solving for $\omega$, we obtain

$$\omega^2 + \frac{eB}{m}\omega - \omega_0^2 = 0$$

so that

$$\omega = \pm\left[\left(\frac{eB}{2m}\right)^2 + \omega_0^2\right]^{1/2} - \frac{eB}{2m}$$

If $\omega_0 \gg \left(\dfrac{eB}{2m}\right)$ then $\left(\dfrac{eB}{2m}\right)^2$ term can be neglected, therefore,

$$\omega = \pm\omega_0 - \frac{eB}{2m} = \pm\omega_0 - \omega_L \tag{27}$$

where the change of frequency $\omega_L = eB/(2m)$ is called the precessional frequency or Larmour frequency. The ($\pm$) sign on $\omega_0$ implies that those electrons whose orbital moments are parallel to the field are slowed down by $\omega_L$. In this case, $\omega = \omega_0 - \omega_L$. Similarly those electrons whose moments are antiparallel to the field are speeded up by the same amount. In this case, $\omega = -\omega_0 - \omega_L$.

The change in the frequency of the electronic motion as a result of the application of the magnetic field produces magnetization. Actually, in the absence of the field the electron motion being spherically symmetrical and produces no net current or flux. On the other hand, in the field, the electron's motion is no longer spherically symmetric but precesses about the field (i.e. the plane of the orbit does not remain stationary) and produces a net current $I$. Due to the change in frequency $\omega_L$, the current for each electron can be written as

$$I = (\text{Charge}) \times (\text{Revolution per unit time}) = -\frac{e\omega_L}{2\pi} = -\frac{e^2 B}{4\pi m} \tag{28}$$

If each atom contains $Z$ electrons then the current becomes

$$I = -\frac{Ze^2 B}{4\pi m} \tag{29}$$

Making use of eq. 9, the magnetic moment could be written as

$$\mu_m = -\frac{Ze^2 B}{4\pi m}\pi\bar{\rho}^2 \tag{30}$$

where $\bar{\rho}^2$ is the mean square radius of the projection of the orbit on a plane perpendicular to the field axis (Fig. 16.10). As the field is acting parallel to the z-axis, therefore

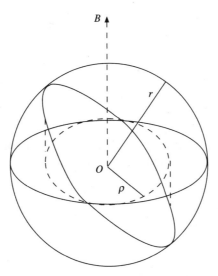

**Fig. 16.10   Great circle and projection of inclined circular orbits in a plane perpendicular to the field**

$$\overline{\rho}^2 = \overline{x}^2 + \overline{y}^2 \tag{31}$$

The mean square distance (average radius) of the electron from the nucleus is

$$\overline{r}^2 = \overline{x}^2 + \overline{y}^2 + \overline{z}^2 \tag{32}$$

Now, for spherically symmetric charge distribution, we have

$$\overline{x}^2 = \overline{y}^2 = \overline{z}^2$$

Here, average is used because all the electrons in an atom do not have the same effective radii, so that

$$\overline{\rho}^2 = \frac{2}{3}\overline{r}^2 \tag{33}$$

This result expresses the fact that the projected area of the great circle tilted with respect to the equatorial plane is less than $\pi r^2$ as shown in Fig. 16.10. Thus from eqs. 30 and 33, we obtain

$$\mu_m = -\frac{Ze^2 B\pi \frac{2}{3}\overline{r}^2}{4\pi m} = -\frac{Ze^2 B\overline{r}^2}{6m} \tag{34}$$

If $N$ is the number of atoms per unit volume, then the magnetization $M$ is given by $M = N\mu_m$ (also making use of the fact that $B = \mu_0 H$), the diamagnetic susceptibility per unit volume is

$$\chi_{dia} = \frac{M}{H} = -\frac{\mu_0 Ze^2 N\overline{r}^2}{6m} \tag{35}$$

This is the classical Langevin equation for diamagnetism. From eq. 35, it is clear that the diamagnetic susceptibility is proportional to $N$ implying that the diamagnetic susceptibility depends on the size of the atom. We also observe that $\chi_{\text{dia}}$ is proportional to $\bar{r}^2$, meaning thereby that the outer electrons make the largest contribution to the diamagnetic susceptibility.

For normal solids, we may take $N \simeq 5 \times 10^{28}$ m$^{-3}$, $\bar{r}^2 = 10^{-20}$ m$^2$ and substituting them into eq. 35 along with the values of other constant quantities, the above equation reduces to

$$\chi_{\text{dia}} \simeq Z \times 10^{-7} \tag{36}$$

This shows the temperature invariance of diamagnetic susceptibility. Diamagnetism is common to all elements, however usually it is too weak to be detected in para and ferromagnetic cases.

*Example*: Estimate the order of the diamagnetic susceptibility of copper by assuming that only one electron per atom makes the contribution. The radius of the copper atom is 1 Å and the lattice parameter is 3.608Å.

*Solution*: Given: $r = 1$ Å $= 10^{-10}$ m, $a = 3.608 \times 10^{-10}$ m, $\chi_{\text{dia}} = ?$
We know that copper is a face centred cubic crystal, so it has 4 atoms per unit cell. The number of electrons per unit volume can be found as

$$N = \frac{n}{a^3} = \frac{4}{(3.608 \times 10^{-10})^3} = 8.5 \times 10^{28} / \text{m}^3$$

Now making use of eq. 35 and substituting the different values, we obtain

$$\chi_{\text{dia}} = -\frac{\mu_0 Z e^2 N \bar{r}^2}{6m} = -\frac{4\pi \times 10^{-7} \times 8.5 \times 10^{28} \times (1.6 \times 10^{-19})^2 \times 10^{-20}}{6 \times 9.1 \times 10^{-31}} = -5 \times 10^{-6}$$

## 16.8   SOURCES OF PARAMAGNETISM

As we know that paramagnetism is the case of a positive magnetic susceptibility. It is the magnetic analogue of the electrical orientational polarizability and is due to the permanent magnetic moment of the atoms. The direction of the magnetization is parallel to the external applied field in paramagnetic substances. Paramagnetism (positive contribution to $\chi$) is found in:

1. Atoms, molecules and lattice defects having an odd number of electrons; that is there should be at least one electron which does not pair. The atoms of the group I, III, V and VII of the periodic Table, gaseous nitric oxide (NO); organic free radicals such as triphenylmethyl $C(C_6H_5)_3$ and $F$-centres in alkali halides, satisfy this criterion.
2. Free atoms with unfilled innershell: transition elements $(Z = 57 - 72)$ and $(Z = 91 - 102)$, rare earth and actinite elements have atoms with unfilled inner shells.
3. A few compounds with an even number of electrons including molecular oxygen and organic biradicals.
4. Metals: The electrons in a metal are considered to be free like molecules in a gas. They tend to pair up but there are always a few unpaired electrons to produce a weak temperature independent paramagnetism known as pauli paramagnetism.

## 16.9 LANGEVIN'S CLASSICAL THEORY OF PARAMAGNETISM

As has been pointed out above that the paramagnetic susceptibility is the magnetic analogue of the electrical orientational polarizability, therefore a similar treatment may be used to calculate this. The following are the points of similarity in the two cases:

(i) There is an assembly of permanent dipoles independent of each other oriented randomly in the absence of an external field.

(ii) The potential energy of the dipoles have the same form:

$$U \text{ (electrical)} = - \text{P} \cdot \text{E, and } U \text{ (magnetic)} = - \mu_m \cdot B$$

Thus, substituting $\mu_m$ for $P$ and $B$ for $E$, we can use the same Langevin-Debye theory (as used in section 14.9) to calculate the magnetization $M$ which is given by

$$M = N\mu_m L(x) \tag{37}$$

where $x \equiv \dfrac{\mu_m B}{kT}$ and the Langevin function $L(x)$ is

$$L(x) = \coth x - \frac{1}{x}$$

For $x \ll 1$, $L(x) \equiv \dfrac{x}{3}$ as before, so that

$$M = \frac{N\mu_m^2 B}{3kT}$$

and

$$\chi = \frac{M}{H} = \frac{\mu_0 N\mu_m^2}{3kT} = \frac{C}{T} \tag{38}$$

where $C = \dfrac{\mu_0 N\mu_m^2}{3k}$ is known as Curie constant. Consequently eq. 38 is known as Curie law. The susceptibility versus temperature curve is shown in Fig. 16.11a.

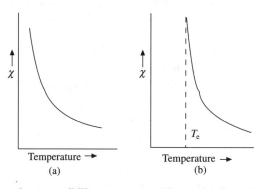

Fig. 16.11   **Paramagnetic susceptibility curve according to (a) Curie law, (b) Curie-Wiess law**

*Example:* Approximately how large must be the magnetic induction for the orientation energy to be comparable to the thermal energy at room temperature? Assume $\mu_m = 5\mu_B$.

*Solution:* Given: $\mu_m = 5\mu_B$, $T = 300$ K, $B = ?$

Here, the magnetic energy $= \mu_m B$ and the thermal energy $= kT$. Now according to the question

$$\mu_m B \simeq kT$$

or

$$B = \frac{kT}{\mu_m} = \frac{kT}{5\mu_B} = \frac{1.38 \times 10^{-23} \times 300}{5 \times 9.27 \times 10^{-24}} = 89.32 \text{ W/m}^2 \simeq 10^2 \text{ W/m}^2$$

*Example:* A paramagnetic salt contains $10^{28}$ ions/m³ with magnetic moment of one Bohr magneton. Calculate the paramagnetic susceptiblity and the magnetization produced in a uniform magnetic field of $10^6$ A/m, at room temperature.

*Solution:* Given: $N = 10^{28}$ ions/m³, $\mu_m = \mu_B = 9.27 \times 10^{-24}$ A/m², $H = 10^6$ A/m, $T = 300$ K, $\chi = ?$ $M = ?$

From eq. 38, we know that the paramagnetic susceptibility is given by

$$\chi = \frac{\mu_0 N \mu_m^2}{3kT} = \frac{4\pi \times 10^{-7} \times 10^{28} \times (9.27 \times 10^{-24})^2}{3 \times 1.38 \times 10^{-23} \times 300} = 0.87 \times 10^{-4}$$

Further, the magnetization is given by

$$M = \chi H = 0.87 \times 10^{-4} \times 10^6 = 87 \text{ A/m}$$

## 16.10 FUNDAMENTALS OF QUANTUM THEORY OF PARAMAGNETISM

The Langevin's classical theory of paramagnetism is incapable of providing a consistent explanation of the magnetic phenomena resulting from the motion of electric charges. The very basis of the classical theory that all orientations of magnetic moments with respect to $B$ are possible, is wrong according to quantum considerations. To overcome various difficulties, let us discuss the essence of quantum theory of paramagnetism based on the following basic facts:

1. For each unit of orbital angular momentum, an electron in an atom has one Bhor magneton ($\mu_B = eh/4\pi m$) of magnetic moment associated with it. The magnetic moment is antiparallel to the angular momentum.
2. For each unit of spin angular momentum ($\hbar/2$), there is also associated one half Bohr magneton ($\mu_B/2$) of magnetic moment to an electron.
3. The total effective angular momentum of an electron is described as the vector sum of orbital and spin contributions, i.e.

$$J = L + S \tag{39}$$

4. The effective magnetic moment is given by $g\mu_B J$, where $g$ and $J$ are respectively given by eqs. 21 and 39.
5. From energy level splitting scheme (Fig. 16.8) for an electron with only spin angular momentum in a magnetic field, the energy difference between the levels is given by eq. 20.

6. According to quantum mechanics, the magnitude of the angular momentum vector is given by $\{J(J+1)\}^{1/2}$ and not by simply $J$. Also there are $2J+1$ ways in which the atomic dipoles may orient relative to the magnetic field. The probability of such orientation is determined by the Boltzmann factor $\exp(-\Delta U/kT)$.

For simplicity, let us consider the atoms with $L = 0$. This gives $g = 2$ (eq. 21), and $J = S = 1//2$ (eq. 39) which in turn provide only two possible states (Fig. 16.8). The lower level ($m_s = m_J = -1/2$) corresponds to the moment parallel to the field, while the upper level corresponds to the moment opposite to the field.

Let $N_1$ and $N_2$ be the concentration of atoms in the lower and upper levels, respectively and that $N_1 + N_2 = N$ the total number of atoms. The difference of these concentrations produces a magnetization

$$M = g\mu_B (N_1 - N_2) \tag{40}$$

where $g\mu_B$ is the $z$-component of the magnetic moment when it is fully aligned with the field. These two concentrations are related by the expression

$$\frac{N_1}{N_2} = \frac{\exp(+\Delta U/kT)}{\exp(-\Delta U/kT)} \tag{41}$$

where $\Delta U = g\mu_B B$ (eq. 20). Now assuming $x = g\mu_B B/kT$, we obtain

$$N_1 - N_2 = N\left(\frac{e^x - e^{-x}}{e^x + e^{-x}}\right) = N\tan h(x)$$

so that

$$M = g\mu_B (N_1 - N_2) = Ng\mu_B \tanh(x) \tag{42}$$

Fig. 16.12 shows a curve between the magnetization $M$ and $x = gm_B B/kT$. At low field, $M$ is proportional to $B$, but at higher fields $M$ begins to saturate and eventually reaches a maximum value $Ng\mu_B$ when all the dipoles turn parallel to the field. Thus, for low field $x << 1$, and hence $\tanh(x) \sim x$, so that eq. 42 becomes

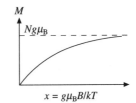

**Fig. 16.12  Magnetization $M$ versus $x$ for a system with $J = 1/2$**

$$M = Ng\mu_B x = \frac{N(g\mu_B)^2 B}{kT} = \frac{\mu_0 N(g\mu_B)^2 H}{kT} \tag{43}$$

Therefore, the paramagnetic susceptibility is given by

$$\chi = \frac{M}{H} = \frac{\mu_0 N(g\mu_B)^2}{kT} \tag{44}$$

Now, in a magnetic field, for a system of atoms with $L = 0$, and $J = S = 1/2$, the projection of magnetic moment is similar to that of spin momentum. In eq. 44, $\mu_B$ is projected value of moment whereas the magnitude of the effective moment of the atom is given by

$$\mu_{\text{eff}} = 2g\mu_{\text{B}}\{J(J + 1)\}^{1/2} = \sqrt{3}g\mu_{\text{B}} \quad \text{for} \quad S = J = \frac{1}{2}$$

or
$$\mu_{\text{eff}}^2 = 3g^2\mu_{\text{B}}^2 \quad \text{or} \quad g^2\mu_{\text{B}}^2 = \frac{\mu_{\text{eff}}^2}{3}$$

Substituting this in eq. 44, we have

$$\chi = \frac{\mu_0 N\mu_{\text{eff}}^2}{3kT} \tag{45}$$

which is in agreement with the classical result. However, for $J > 1/2$ an atom with angular momentum quantum number $J$ has $(2J + 1)$ equally spaced energy levels. The magnetization is then given by

$$M = NgJ\mu_{\text{B}}B_{\text{J}}(x), \text{ with } x \equiv \frac{gJ\mu_{\text{B}}B}{kT} \tag{46}$$

where the Brillouin function $B_{\text{J}}$ is defined as

$$B_{\text{J}}(x) = \frac{(2J + 1)}{2J} \coth\left(\frac{(2J + 1)x}{2J}\right) - \frac{1}{2J} \coth\left(\frac{x}{2J}\right) \tag{47}$$

when $J$ becomes very large, the Brillouin function becomes identical to the Langevin function, i.e.

$$L(x) = \coth x - \frac{1}{x} \equiv \frac{x}{3}$$

Therefore, from eq. 46, the susceptibility becomes

$$\chi = \frac{\mu_0 NJ(J + 1)g^2\mu_{\text{B}}^2}{3kT} = \frac{\mu_0 Np^2\mu_{\text{B}}^2}{3kT} = \frac{\mu_0 N\mu_{\text{eff}}^2}{3kT} \tag{48}$$

where the effective moment of the atom, is now defined as $\mu_{\text{eff}} = p\mu_{\text{B}}$ and $p = g\{J + 1)\}^{1/2}$ is called the effective number of Bohr magneton for the atom. The eq. 48 indicates that the quantum mechanical treatment leads to the same conclusions as the classical treatment.

## 16.11 PARAMAGNETISM OF FREE ELECTRONS

According to Langevin's theory (eq. 38), the paramagnetic susceptibility is inversely proportional to the temperature. However, some metals have been found to exhibit paramagnetism independent of temperature. It was W. Pauli (1927) who demonstrated that this is due to paramagnetism of free electrons (that constitute the electron gas), since they can orient only in two directions, either along the manetic field or against it.

In order to understand the existence of Pauli paramagnetism, let us recall the curve between density of states versus energy (Fig. 10.11) at absolute zero of temperature. That curve may be split into two parts with spins pointing in the +ve z-direction and other with spin in the opposite direction, as shown in Fig. 16.13a. In the absence of an external electric field, the distribution of electrons with spins parallel to $z$-direction is equal to the number of electrons with opposite spins and hence the net magnetic moment of the electron gas is zero. When a field is applied along the z-direction, the energy of the spins aligned parallel to $B$ is lowered by the amount $\mu_B$, while the energy of the spins opposite to $B$ is raised by the same amount (Fig. 16.13b). As a result of this, the Fermi level for the two spin distributions shift with respect to each other and give rise to energetically unstable situation. In order to acquire the stable configuration, the electrons lying near the Fermi level with antiparallel spins flip into the region of parallel spins until the two Fermi levels become equal again (Fig. 16.13b).

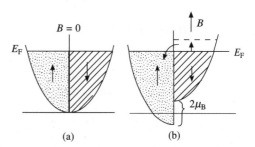

**Fig. 16.13 Fermi-Dirac distribution at (a) $B = 0$, (b) $B \neq 0$**

The number of electrons which effectively change their direction is equal to the density of states at the energy level in one of the spin distribution times the change in energy, i.e.

$$N_{\text{eff}} = \frac{1}{2} g(E_F)\mu_B B \tag{49}$$

where the factor 1/2 is due to the fact that the density of states of one spin distribution is half of the total density of states. Thus after the application of the field, the number of electrons with spins parallel to the field is greater than the electrons with opposite spin by $N_{\text{eff}}$, leading to a net magnetization. Since each flip increases the magnetization by $2\mu_B$ (from $-\mu_B$ to $+\mu_B$), the net magnetization is given by

$$M \simeq N_{\text{eff}} \times 2\mu_B = g(E_F)\mu_B^2 B \tag{50}$$

and hence the Pauli spin susceptibility of the electron gas is

$$\chi_p \simeq \mu_0\mu_B^2 g(E_F) \tag{51}$$

According to eq. 51, $\chi_p$ is essentially temperature independent. This is clear from the fact that temperature has a very small effect on the Fermi-Dirac distribution of the electrons (Fig. 10.13). Making use of the eqs. 20 and 24 of chapter 10, we obtain

$$g(E_F) = \frac{3N}{2E_F}$$

so that

$$\chi_p = \frac{3\mu_0 N\mu_B^2}{2E_F} = \frac{3\mu_0 N\mu_B^2}{2kT_F} \tag{52}$$

where $E_F = kT_F$. This equation can be rewritten in terms of the classical susceptibility as

$$\chi_p = \frac{3}{2}\chi\frac{T}{T_F} \tag{53}$$

where $\chi = \dfrac{\mu_0 N \mu_B^2}{kT}$ for $J = 1/2$. Since, $T_F$ is normally very high, $\chi_p$ is smaller than $\chi$ by about two orders of magnitude, which is in agreement with the experimental results. In transition metals, the paramagnetic susceptibility, $\chi_p$ is exceptionaly high, because $g(E_F)$ is large.

## 16.12 FERROMAGNETISM

In general, when we speak of a magnet we actually mean a ferromagnet. For example, consider a piece of iron, which has the ability to pick up other pieces of iron towards it, possesses permanent magnetic moments and is said to be a permanent magnet. Thus, ferromagnetism is the existence of magnetization even in the absence of the external magnetic field. Phenomenonlogically, it is the magnetic analogue of ferroelectricity. Some of the experimentally observed facts are:

1. Magnetization $M$ increases when an external field is appied to the specimen. Moreover, the relationship between magnetization $M$ and applied field $H$ is nonlinear and shows hysteresis effect similar to that shown by polarization $P$ and the electric field $E$.
2. The strong magnetism is found to disappear at a critical temperature ($T_c$), the specimen becomes demagnetized, behaves like a paramagnet and shows magnetic effects only when an external field is applied.

   In order to explain these experimental facts, Weiss put forward a theory of ferromagnetism based on the following hypothesis.

1. Ferromagnetic materials are made up of large number of 'domains' (each domain contains about $10^9 - 10^{15}$ atoms), which are spontaneously magnetized. The magnitude of spontaneous magnetization (refers to a single domain) of the specimen is determined by the vector sum of the magnetic moments of the individual domains (Fig. 16.14).

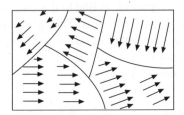

**Fig. 16.14 Ferromagnetic domain**

2. Within a given domain, all the dipoles (spins) are aligned in the same direction, so that magnetization is the maximum possible value for a given material and temperature.

## 16.13 THE WEISS MOLECULAR (EXCHANGE) FIELD

In order to explain the spontaneous magnetization of a ferromagnetic material, Weiss (1907) assumed that there exists an internal molecular field (also called exchange field $H_{ex}$) acting on a given dipole and is given by

$$H_{ex} = H + \lambda M \tag{54}$$

where $\lambda$ is called Weiss constant (it is independent of temperature) and $H$ is applied field. In a ferromagnet the Curie law holds for exchange field as well. Therefore,

$$\frac{M}{H_{ex}} = \frac{C}{T} \tag{55}$$

Simplifying the eqs. 54 and 55, we have

$$M = \frac{CH}{T - C\lambda} \tag{56}$$

Therefore, the ferromagnetic susceptibility becomes,

$$\chi = \frac{M}{H} = \frac{C}{T - C\lambda} = \frac{C}{T - T_c} \tag{57}$$

where $T_c = C\lambda$ is called the Curie temperature and the eq. 57 is known as Curie-Weiss law. The corresponding variation of susceptibility with temperature is shown in Fig. 16.11b. As long as $T \geq T_c$, this curve and the curve shown in Fig. 16.11a (corresponding to Curie law) are similar. However, as $T \to T_c$, Curie Weiss susceptibility tends to infinity and for $T \leq T_c$, there exists a spontaneous magnetization in the material even in the absence of an external field. This can be verified from eqs. 54 and 55.

## 16.14 TEMPERATURE DEPENDENCE OF SPONTANEOUS MAGNETIZATION

As discussed above, the magnetic moments due to orbital motion of free electrons in a metal is negligible in comparison to the spin moments. Therefore assuming only the spin system, it is possible to determine the magnetic behaviour of a ferromagnetic material below the Curie temperature. In the absence of an external field ($H = 0$), eq. 54 reduce to

$$H_{ex} = \lambda M \tag{58}$$

where $M = N\overline{\mu}$ is the spontaneous magnetization at some temperature $T$ less than $T_c$.

According to quantum theory of paramagnetism (eq. 42), the magnetization $M$ for spin half ($S = J = 1/2$) is given by

$$M = Ng\mu_B \tan h(x) \tag{59}$$

where

$$x = g\mu_B B/kT \tag{60}$$

For ferromagnetic case, we must replace the field $B$ by $H_{ex}$ given by eq. 58. Therefore,

$$x = \frac{\mu_0 g\mu_B \lambda M}{kT}$$

or

$$M = \frac{kT}{\mu_0 g\mu_B \lambda} x \tag{61}$$

The equations 59 and 61 can be solved simultaneously by plotting them on $M$ versus $x$ graph (Fig. 16.15). The value of $M$ at a given temperature is obtained from the point of intersection of the two curves. From eq. 61, it

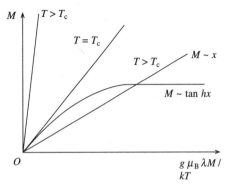

**Fig. 16.15** *M* **versus** *x* **and** *M* **versus tan** *hx* **curves. The point of intersection represents spontaneous magnetization**

is clear that if $T$ increases, the slope of the straight line also increases. For temperatures below a critical value $(T < T_c)$, the two curves intersect at a point, which gives a non vanishing spontaneous magnetization. The maximum spontaneous magnetization occurs at $T = 0$K and is given by (from eq. 59)

$$M_s(0) = Ng\mu_B \qquad (62)$$

At $T = T_c$ the straight line (eq. 61) is tangential to the hhyperbolic˙ curve (eq. 59) at the origin where the spontaneous magnetization just reduces to zero and remains zero for all temperatures above the critical value $(T > T_c)$. Further, at $T = T_c$, for $x \ll 1$, the hyperbolic function can be approximated as

$$\tanh(x) \simeq x$$

Now equating eqs. 59 and 61, we have

$$\lambda = \frac{kT_c}{\mu_0 N (g\mu_B)^2} \qquad (63)$$

In order to describe the temperature dependence of spontaneous magnetization in a convenient manner, let us make use of the eqs. 62 and 63, and rewrite the eq. 59 in the form

$$\frac{M_s(T)}{M_s(0)} = \tanh\left(\frac{T}{T_c}\right) \qquad (64)$$

This expresses the relation between the normalized magnetization $M_s(T)/M_s(0)$ and normalized temperature $T/T_c$. This is called thermomagnetic equation of state for the ferromagnetic phase of materials and is shown in Fig. 16.16 (for Ni and Gd with $J = 1/2$ and 7/2). This curve is universal in the sense that the reduced parameters are common to all ferromagnetic materials for same $J$ value. At 0K, the magnetization is at a maximum and the normalized magnetization $M_s(T)/M_s(0)$ is unity. As the temperature is increased, thermal energy randomizes the system. As a result, the spontaneous magnetization ceases to exist above Curie temperature. This behaviour is quite similar to order-disorder transition in binary alloys in which an ordered array of atoms at low temperature, gradually loses its orderedness

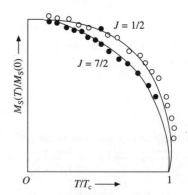

**Fig. 16.16** **A curve between normalized magnetization $M_s(T)/M_s(0)$ and noramlized temperature $T/T_c$ for Ni and Gd with $J$ = 1/2 and 7/2**

with increasing temperature and eventually becomes completely disordered at the transition temperature.

## 16.15 THE PHYSICAL ORIGIN OF WEISS MOLECULAR FIELD

The introduction of Weiss molecular field made it possible to explain a wide range of phenomena observed in ferromagnetism. However, the nature of the field itself remained a mystery for a long time. At first, it was supposed to be due to a simple nearest neighbour dipole-dipole interaction. Such an interaction would give rise to a field of the order of

$$\frac{\mu_B}{a^3} \simeq 10^3 \text{ gausses}$$

where $a$ is the interatomic distance in a ferromagnetic crystal. On the other hand, for a Curie temperature $T_c \simeq 1000K$, the exchange field is approximately found to be

$$H_{ex} \simeq \lambda M_s(0) \simeq 10^4 \times 10^3 \simeq 10^7 \text{ gausses}$$

This discrepancy shows that a simple model based on dipole-dipole interaction cannot account for ferromagnetism. Actually a much stronger type of interaction is needed.

The first attempt to solve the problem was made by Heisenberg in 1982. According to him the large Weiss molecular field can be explained in terms of the so-called exchange interaction between the electron spins. The energy of the interaction (i.e. the exchange energy) for ions $i, j$ bearing spins $S_i$, $S_j$ can be expressed as

$$E_{ex}^{ij} = -2J S_i \cdot S_j \tag{65}$$

and the total exchange energy of spin $i$ with its (nearest) neighbours $J_1, J_2, \ldots$ may be expressed as

$$E_{ex}^{ij} = -2J \sum_{j=1}^{n} S_i \cdot S_j \tag{66}$$

where $J$ is called the exchange integral and is a measure of the strength of interaction.

In general, the exchange integral is negative and hence a non-ferromagnetic state is favoured. However, for a ferromagnet it must be positive. In the above equations, the dot product is used because the exchange energy is governed by the relative orientation of the spins. In ferromagnetism, where parallel orientation of spins is favoured, $E_{ex}$ is minimum and $S_i$, $S_j = S^2$. Similarly, $E_{ex}$ is maximum when spins are antiparallel and therefore $S_i \cdot S_j = -S^2$.

It is possible to determine the exchange integral experimentally as a function of the ratio of the interatomic spacing "$a$" to the unfilled shell of radius $r$. For transition metals this is represented by the curve shown in Fig. 16.17. The ratio $a/r$ for transition element of the iron group is found to be

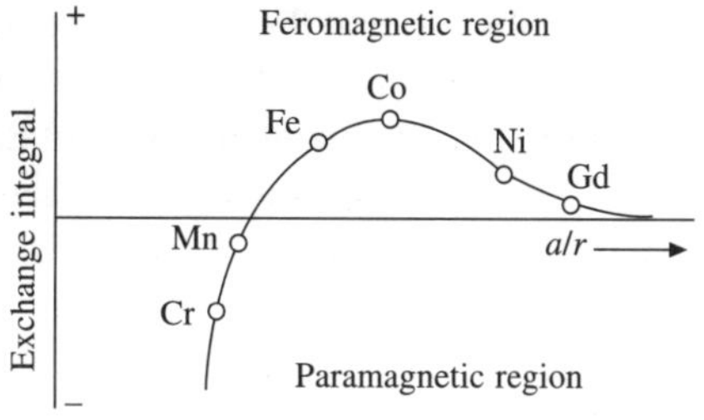

**Fig. 16.17** **Variation of exchange integral with *a/r***

| Elements | Fe | Co | Ni | Cr | Mn | Gd |
|---|---|---|---|---|---|---|
| *a/r* ratio | 3.26 | 3.64 | 3.94 | 2.60 | 2.94 | 3.10 |

According to Slater (1930), the ratio $(a/r) \geq 3$ (but not very large) must be satisfied for the occurrence of ferromagnetism. The substances viz. Fe, Co, Ni and Gd satisfy the above criterion and are found to be ferromagnetic. On the other hand, Cr and Mn fail to satisfy the above criterion and are not ferromagnetic. however, they can also be made ferromagnetic by alloying them with some suitable non-ferromagnetic elements (with slightly higher but comparable interatomic spacings) to form compounds whose ($a/r$) ratio is greater than 3. For example, Mn-As, Cu-Mn, Mn-Sb show ferromagnetic behaviour because of the favourable $a/r$ ratio.

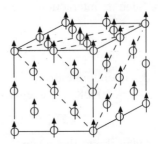

Hence the necessary and sufficient conditions for ferromagnetism are the existence of incomplete internal atomic shells and the positive exchange integral which cause the parallel orientation of the spins as shwon in Fig. 16.18.

**Fig. 16.18** **Spontaneous magnetization of a ferromagnetic substance. Exchange forces cause parallel orientation of the spins of electrons belonging to inner partially filled shells**

## 16.16 FERROMAGNETIC DOMAINS

The above discussion helps us to understand why iron, cobalt and nickel are ferromagnetic. In the following, we shall see why a fresh piece of these materials is non-magnetized (demagnetized) and why they exhibit hysteresis loop when a magnetic field is applied to them. These may be understood by taking into account the Weiss domain hypothesis (section 16.12) according to which ferromagnetic materials contain small domains, each of which is magnetized to saturation, but the net macroscopic magnetization may vary form zero to saturation. A completely demagnetized ferromagnetic specimen, represented schematically by four equal domains (Fig. 16.19a), has no resultant magnetic moment. If a gradually increasing field is applied in some arbitrary direction (as shown in Fig. 16.19b), those domains which have magnetic moments along the direction of the applied field (called favourably oriented domains) will grow at the expense of the others (called unfavourably orientd domains) because of the motion of domain walls. As the field is increased further, the magnetization increases to saturation due to a sudden rotation of unfavourably oriented domains, so that the whole specimen may become one single domain whose moment is directed parallel to the field (Fig. 16.19c). This happens when a large field is applied in any arbitrary direction, the magnetization rotates from "easy" to a "hard" direction. At this stage, the specimen is said to be saturated and possesses maximum achievable magnetization (i.e. a further increase in the field causes no change in the magnetization). At low temperatures, the dependence

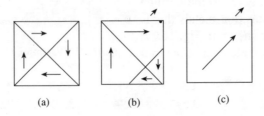

|       |       |       |
|:-----:|:-----:|:-----:|
|  (a)  |  (b)  |  (c)  |

**Fig. 16.19** **The domain structure (a) corresponds to the non-magnetized state, (b) the magnetization is due to wall motion, (c) the magnetization is due to rotation from an easy to hard direction**

of magnetization $M$ on the field strength $H$ is shown by familiar hysteresis curve (Fig. 16.20). This is associated with the motion of domain walls and domain rotation and consequently has three distinct regions as indicated in the figure.

Formation of the hysteresis curve may be described as follows:

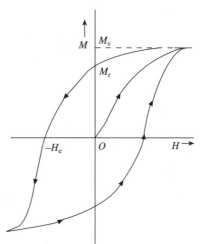

**Fig. 16.20  Hysteresis loop of a ferromagnetic material**

When the applied field is small, the induced magnetization varies linearly with the field and is also reversible. The region within which the magnetization is reversible is called reversible region. When the field is gradually increased, the magnetization shows a non-linear variation with the field and also becomes irreversible. This is the region of irreversible wall motion. If the field is gradually increased further, the magnetization also increases gradually and ultimately attains a saturation value ($M_s$). This is the region where the rotation of domains takes place i.e. all the domains rotate towards the hard direction. A further increase in the field produces no change in the magnetization. However, on the other hand, when the field is gradually decreased, the decrease in magnetization follows a different path and for a zero field, the specimen continues to retain a certain amount of magnetization, called the residual or remnant magnetization ($M_r$). A finite field equal to the coercieve field ($-H_c$) is required to bring the magnetization back to zero. A further increase in the reverse field results in a complete reversal of $M_s$. A second reversal of the field completes the hysteresis curve.

In the crystal specimen, the domains are separated from one another by boundaries (Fig 16.14). These are the regions within which the moments (spins) change their spatial directions. The transition layer between two domains is called a "domain wall" or a "Bloch wall". This is shown in Fig. 16.21 for a transition from a domain with a spin up arrangement to one with a spin down arrangement.

## 16.17  DOMAIN THEORY

The physical origin of domains may be understood from the general thermodynamic principle

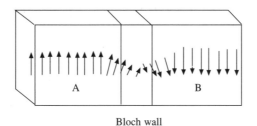

Bloch wall

**Fig. 16.21 Schematic representation of a Bloch wall**

that the free energy $F = E - TS$ of a system (a solid in the present case) is minimum. As we know (from section 16.14) that well below $T_c$, the magnetization $M \rightarrow M_s(0)$ in a ferromagnet and have high degree of order in such a magnetic system, the entropy term from the free energy expression may be neglected. Thus, the minimum free energy means minimum total internal energy $E$ of the system. The knowledge of which should be sufficient to understand of existence of domains.

Landau and Lifshitz have shown that the domain structure is a natural consequence of various energies contributing towards the total energy of a ferromagnet. They are: the exchange energy, the magnetic field energy and the anisotropy energy.

### 1. The Exchange Energy

From section 16.15, we know that the exchange energy, $E_{ex}$ is minimum when the spins are parallel. it is because of this energy, the spontaneous magnetization occurs in such materials. This energy establishes the existence of a single domain in a specimen of ferromagnetic material (Fig. 16.22a). The exchange energy favours an indefinitely large domain (the hole sample), since it is minimum when all spins are parallel.

### 2. The Magnetic Field Energy

In this case, we shall see that by dividing a crystal into two domains, the magnetic energy can be reduced to minimum or even to zero for certain domain structures (Fig. 16.22). Because of the free magnetic poles at the ends of the specimen, having a single domain (Fig. 16.22a) will have highest magnetic energy $(1/8\pi) \int B^2 \, dV$. However, this energy can be reduced to roughly half by dividing the crystal into two domains magnetized in opposite directions as in Fig. 16.22b. Similarly, dividing the crystal into $N$ domains (Fig. 16.22c), reduces the magnetic energy by $1/N$ or more accurately by $0.8525 \, M_s^2 / N$. However, since certain amount of energy is required to create a domain boundary wall, this subdivision process can be continued until the energy required to create an additional interface, the domain (Bloch) wall, between the domains is greater than the reduction in magnetic energy. In fact, for a given size of the sample, the number and the arrangement of domains present is a compromise between these two energy terms. Taking this into account, the domain arrangements shown in Figs. 16.22d and 22e will have zero magnetic field energy. This is achieved by introducing the triangular prism domains near the end faces of the crystal; such domains are called closure domains. Here, it is to be noted that the boundary walls of the closure domains make equal angles (i.e. 45°) with the direction of magnetization each due to closure domains themselves and vertical domains. This means that the

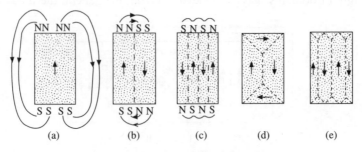

**Fig. 16.22  The origin of domains**

normal component of the magnetization across the boundary wall is continuous. As there are no free poles near the end faces of the crystal, there is no magnetic field energy.

### 3. The Anisotropy Energy

Experimental study of ferromagnetic single crystals show that the magnetic field required to magnetize them depends on direction. Fig. 16.23 shows the magnetization ($M$ versus $H$) curve for a single crystal of iron at 18°C, where the applied field is directed along different crystallographic directions. It is to be noted that a very small magnetic field along <100> direction is sufficient to produce a large (saturation) magnetization while to produce the same magnetization along <111> direction, a large field is required. In other words, it is "easy" to magnetize a single crystal of iron along <100> direction, while it is "hard" to do so along <111> direction. The difference in magnetic energy to produce saturation in an easy and a hard direction is called the anisotropy energy. For a cubic crystal, the anisotropy energy may be expressed as

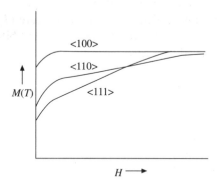

**Fig. 16.23 Magnetization curves for single crystal of iron at 18°C**

$$E_{an} = K_1(\alpha^2\beta^2 + \beta^2\gamma^2 + \gamma^2\alpha^2) + K_2\alpha^2\beta^2\gamma^2 \qquad (67)$$

where $K_1$ and $K_2$ are anisotropy constants and $\alpha$, $\beta$, $\gamma$ are the direction cosines of the magnetization vector with respect to the cube axes.

These three sources of energy are the main determinants of the domain characteristics. The size of the domain is determined by a balance between the exchange energy and the magnetic field energy. On the other hand, the thickness of the domain wall is determined by a balance between the exchange energy and the anisotorpy energy.

## 16.18 ANTIFERROMAGNETISM

In section 16.15, we observed that in ferromagnetism the exchange energy $H_{ex}$ is minimum when the neighbouring spins are parallel and the exchange integral is positive. However, in many solid substances $H_{ex}$ has been found to be minimum when the neighbouring spins are antiparallel and the exchange integral as negative favouring a non-ferromagnetic state. If the neighbouring spins are balanced, the material is said to be antiferromagnetic and if remain ubalanced it is ferrimagnetic. Such systems were first investigated theoretically by Neel and Bitter, and was later extended by van Vleck.

Antiferromagnetism was first discovered in MnO by Bizette, Squire and Tsai in 1938. Since then, a number of other materials have been found to be antiferromagnetic. They include the Mn and Cr metals, many of the rare earth metals, and some compounds of the 3d and 4d transition elements. Neutron diffraction technique is largely responsible for the discovery of many new antiferromagnetic materials.

The susceptibility versus temperature curves in Fig. 16.24 provide us the distinguishing features of para, ferro and antiferromagnetic materials. An enormous increase in ferromagnetic susceptibility is observed at the transition (Curie) temperature, while in antiferromagnetic case the susceptibility increases at first with temperature and reaches a maximum (and gives rise a kink) at a certain temperature called the Neel temperature ($T_N$). Above the Neel temperature, the suceptibility is observed to follow the equation

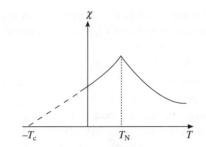

**Fig. 16.24    Mgnetic susceptibility of an antiferro-magnetic material**

$$\chi = \frac{C}{T + T_c} \qquad (68)$$

where $C$ is the Curie constant and $T_c$ is the paramagnetic Curie temperature.

The characteristic feature of antiferromagnetic materials may be explained qualitatively on the basis of two sublattice model. For example, consider a lattice system in which the magnetic atoms are arranged in a body centered cubic structure. One may visualize all the ions at the body centered having "spin up" and all the corner atoms having "spin down" as shown in Fig. 16.25. This is a simple case of magnetic structure with two interpenetrating simple cubic sublattices, such that the spin moment of atoms in one sublattice array are antiparallel with the spin moments of atoms in the other sublattice array as shown in Fig. 16.26.

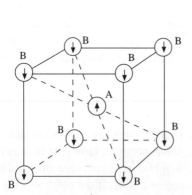

**Fig. 16.25    Representation of two sublattices. *A* and *B*, showing antiparallel spins**

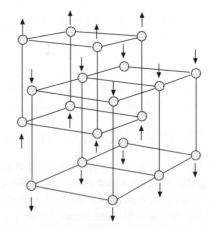

**Fig. 16.26    Two interpenetrating simple cubic sub-lattices with antiparallel spins**

At absolute zero, the spin moments of both sublattice arrays are ordered (as in Fig. 16.26) and mutually compensated so that the net magnetization is zero. As the temperature is raised, the antiparallel arrangement of the spins is gradually disturbed and the magnetization rises and becomes maximum at the Neel point, above whcih the material behaves as paramagnetic.

The simplest antiferromagnetic materials are the crystalline ionic compounds of the transition series in which the metallic ions are arranged in such a way that they can be subdivided into two equivalent interpenetrating sublattices, $A$ and $B$, such that $A$ atoms have only $B$ atoms as the nearest neighbours, and vice versa (Fig. 16.25). Now, following a procedure similar to that in ferromagnetic case, let us introduce an expression for the internla field $H_A$ for the $A$ ions, and $H_B$ for the $B$ ions, respectively. Since the magnetization $M_A$ of the $A$ ions is oposite to the internal field of $B$ ions, we have

$$H_A = H - \lambda M_B$$

and
$$H_B = H - \lambda M_A \tag{69}$$

where $\lambda$ is the internal field constant which determines the strength of exchange interaction. Then as in eq. 59, we have

$$M_A = Ng\mu_B \tanh\left(\frac{\mu_0 g\mu_B}{kT}(H - \lambda M_B)\right)$$

and
$$M_B = Ng\mu_B \tanh\left(\frac{\mu_0 g\mu_B}{kT}(H - \lambda M_A)\right) \tag{70}$$

Again, making use of the approximation $\tanh(x) \approx (x)$ at high temperatures, we have

$$M_A = \frac{N\mu_0(g\mu_B)^2}{kT}(H - \lambda M_B)$$

and
$$M_B = \frac{N\mu_0(g\mu_B)^2}{kT}(H - \lambda M_A) \tag{71}$$

So that the total magnetization is

$$M = M_A + M_B = \frac{N\mu_0(g\mu_B)^2}{kT}(2H - \lambda M) \tag{72}$$

This equation may become a scalar equation if we assume that $M$ and $H$ are parallel. Thus, solving for $M/H$, we find

$$\chi = \frac{M}{H} = \frac{2C}{T + C\lambda} = \frac{2C}{T + T_c} \tag{73}$$

where
$$C = N(g\mu_B)^2\mu_0/k \text{ and } T_c = C\lambda.$$

Comparing eq. 73 and eq. 57, we observe that the antiferromagnetic case contains $T + T_c$ instead of $T - T_c$ and the Curie constant is twice (the Curie constant of the individual $A$ or $B$ lattice) that in the ferromagnetic case.

The Neel temperature $(T_N)$ can be determined by equations under 70, sicne it is the temperature for which $M_A$ or $M_B$ has a finite value in the absence of an external field. Thus, writing equations under 70 for $H = 0$, we have

$$M_A + \frac{C\lambda}{T}M_B = 0 \text{ and } \frac{C\lambda}{T}M_A + M_B = 0 \tag{74}$$

For $T > T_N$, these equations have trivial solutions $M_A = M_B = 0$, i.e. there is no spontaneous magnetization of the sublattices above the Neel temperature. If spontaneous magnetization of the sublattices is supposed to set at $T = T_N$, then eq. 74 must have non-trivial solutions for $M_A$ and $M_B$ at that temperature. This is equivalent to the requirement that the determinant of the coefficient of $M_A$ and $M_B$ is zero. Hence

$$\frac{C\lambda}{T_N} = 1 \quad \text{or} \quad T_N = C\lambda = T_c \tag{75}$$

where the last relationship follows from eq. 73, shows that the Neel temperature is the same as the paramagnetic Curie temperature $T_c$. However experimental results show that $T_N$ is generally less than $T_c$. The discrepancy arises because of the fact that the above two sublattice model is over simplified and the actual situation is more complicated than this.

**Antiferromagnetic Susceptibility**

The magnetic susceptibility behaviour depends on the direction of the external magnetic field. Let us consider two cases of special interest:

1. An external magnetic field is perpendicular to the spin axis.
2. An external magnetic field is parallel to the spin axis.

*Case I: H is perpendicular to both $M_A$ and $M_B$ (spin axis):*
In this case, the two sublattice magnetizations, $M_A$ and $M_B$ tend to align themselves along the direction of the field. This results in the rotation of $M_A$ and $M_B$ through an angle $2\phi$ (where $\phi$ is usually very small) with each other as shown in Fig. 16.27a. Then the molecular field acting on the sublattice B, in the direction parallel to $H$ wil be $-\lambda M_A \times 2\phi$ (for small angles) and at equilibrium, this is equal but opposite to $H$, i.e.

$$2\lambda M_A \phi = H \tag{76}$$

where $\lambda$ is a positive Weiss constant. Since $|M_A| = |M_B|$, the total magnetization along the external field direction is

$$M = (M_A + M_B)\phi = 2M_A \phi \tag{77}$$

From eqs. 75 and 76, we have

$$M = \frac{H}{\lambda}$$

so that

$$\chi_\perp = \frac{M}{H} = \frac{1}{\lambda} \tag{78}$$

which is independent of temperature. Further, it can be shown that $\chi_\perp$ is equal to the susceptibility at Neel temperature.

*Case II: H is parallel to $M_A$ or $M_B$ (spin axis)*
The exact calculation of $\chi_\parallel$ is much more complicated because of the involvement of Brillouin functions. However, this can be understood qualitatively as follows:
When the field is parallel to one sublattice magnetization and antiparallel to other sublattice

magnetization (Fig. 16.27b), the applied magnetic field will produce no resultant moment on them and therefore there is no net magnetization at 0K. Thus

$$\chi_\| = 0 \qquad (79)$$

As the temperature is raised, the spin alignment is upset slightly and the field will be able to produce rotation of spins and hence a small susceptibility is produced. $\chi_\|$ increaes to $\chi(T_N)$ as the temperature increases to $T_N$. The susceptibility curve of an antiferromagnetic crystal is shown in Fig. 16.28. Below Neel temperature, the susceptibility of a material in polycrystalline form is obtained by averaging of the susceptibilities over all directions. At absolute zero, this is given by

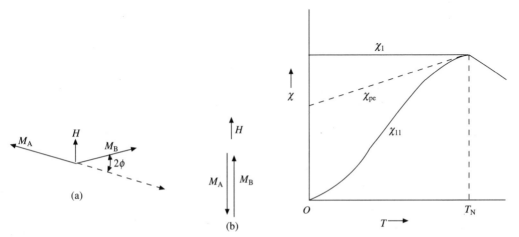

**Fig. 16.27** **Calculation of (a) perpendicular and**
**(b) parallel susceptibilities at 0K**

**Fig. 16.28** **Magnetic susceptibility of an antiferro-**
**magnet as a function of temperature.**
**$T_N$ is the Neel temperature**

$$\chi_{pc} = \frac{1}{3} \chi_\|(0) + \frac{2}{3} \chi_\perp(0) = \frac{2}{3} x_\perp(T_N) \qquad (80)$$

whereas at Neel temperature, it is given by

$$\chi_{pc} = \frac{2}{3} \chi_\perp(0) = \frac{2}{3} \chi_\perp(T_N) = \frac{2}{3} \chi(T_N) \qquad (81)$$

## 16.19   FERRIMAGNETISM AND FERRITES

In the preceding section, we observed that when the antiparallel magnetic moments of the two sublattices are completely compensated (due to this the net magnetization is zero), the material is said to be antiferromagnetic. However, there are cases when they are not compensated for different reasons (e.g. the difference in the number or in the nature of atoms that make up the sublattices). Such an uncompensated antiferromagnetism is known as ferrimagnetism and the corresponding materials are said to be ferrimagnetic or ferrites. They exhibit spontaneous magnetization below the ferrimagnetic Neel temperature ($T_{FN}$).

The external behaviour of a ferrimagnet is similar to that of a ferromagnet. However, because of the difference in their internal structure, the temperature dependence of their spontaneous magnetization may be quite different. For example, the magnetization of a ferrimagnet does not necessarily decrease monotonously with rise in temperature but can pass through zero even before the Neel point is reached. Besides, the ferrite materials have about 10 order of magnitudes higher d.c resistivity than ferromagnetic iron.

The natural ferrite is the iron ore magnetite, $Fe_3O_4$, whose chemical formula is $Fe^{2+}Fe_2^{3+}O_4$. The corresponding general formula is written as $Me^{2+}Fe_2^{3+}O_4$, where Me is the divalent metal such as Mn, Co, Ni, Cu, Mg, Zn, or Cd (may or may not be magnetic). The structure of ferrites are based on the structure of naturally occurring spinel, $MgOAl_2O_3$. Spinel occurs in two forms, normal and inverse. Simple ferrites occur in both forms.

The normal spinel structure $(AB_2O_4)$, can be considered to contain two sublattices A and B. Divalent metal ions on A sublattice (A sites) are surrounded by four $O^{2-}$ ions in a tetrahedral coordination while trivalent metal ions on B sites are surrounded by six $O^{2-}$ ions octahedrally. In normal spinels, the divalent and trivalent metal ions appear only on A sites and B sites, respectively. Zinc ferrite $(Zn^{2+})_A O(Fe^{3+})_B O_3$ is an example of normal spinel.

It is interesting that the majority of ferrites occur in inverse spinel form. In this case, the divalent metal ions occupy octahedral (B) sites while $Fe^{3+}$ metal ions are distributed equally over the tetrahedral (A) sites and octahedral (B) sites. The arrangement may thus be represented by $(Fe^{3+})_A [Fe^{3+} Me^{2+}]_B O_4$. Manganese and nickel ferrites are the examples of inverse spinel.

## 16.20 SUMMARY

1. The magnetic induction $B$ and the magnetic field $H$ in a material medium are related by the equation

$$B = \mu_0 H + \mu_0 M$$

where $M$ is the magnetization vector of the medium and is proportional to the field,

$$M \propto H \quad \text{or} \quad M = \chi H$$

The constant $\chi$ is known as magnetic susceptibility.

2. The different sources of permanent magnetic moment are: the orbital magnetic moment of the electrons, the spin magnetic moment of the electrons and the spin magnetic moment of the nucleus. When the atom is placed in a magnetic field, the orbital magnetic moment of the electrons is quantized. A quantum of magnetic moment of an atomic system is known as Bohr magneton. Similarly, a quantum of magnetic moment obtained from the spin magnetic moment of the nucleus is known as nuclear magneton.

3. When an atom (as considered in Bohr's model) is placed in a magnetic field, the motion of electron does no longer remain spherically symmetric but starts precessing about the field. The resulting diamagnetic susceptibility is given by the equation

$$\chi_{dia} = \frac{M}{H} = -\frac{\mu_0 Ze^2 N}{6m} \cdot \bar{r}^2$$

which depends on the size of the atom.

4. Considering the atom has a net magnetic moment, Langevin showed that the alignment of the moments with the field leads to a classical paramagnetic susceptibility

$$\chi = \frac{M}{H} = \frac{\mu_0 N \mu^2}{3kT} = \frac{C}{T}$$

where $C$ is known as Curie constant. The quantum treatment also leads to the same general result, provide that

$$\mu_{\text{eff}} = 2g\mu_B \{ J (J + 1) \}^{1/2}$$

5. Some metals have been found to exhibit paramagnetism which is essentially independent of temperature. This is known as Pauli paramagnetism and the susceptibility is given by

$$\chi_P = \mu_0 \mu_B^2 g(E_F) = \frac{3\mu_0 N \mu_B^2}{2E_F} = \frac{3}{2} \chi \cdot \frac{T}{T_F}$$

where $E_F = kT_F$. Since $T_F$ is normally very high, $\chi_P$ is smaller than $\chi$ by about two orders of magnitude. In transition metals, $\chi_p$ is exceptionally high, because $g(E_F)$ is large.

6. Ferromagnetism is the existence of spontaneous magnetization below a critical temperature $T_c$, known as Curie temperature. Above this temperature, the substance becomes paramagnetic and obeys the Curie-Weiss law

$$\chi = \frac{M}{H} = \frac{C}{T - C\lambda} = \frac{C}{T - T_c}$$

In order to explain the existence of spontaneous magnetization in a ferromagnet Weiss assumed that there exists an exchange field ($H_{\text{ex}} = \lambda M$) whose origin is due to the exchange interaction between the dipoles of the substance.

7. The molecular field based on simple dipole-dipole interaction was found to be less and hence cannot account for the existence of ferromagnetism. Heisenberg removed this discrepanyc by assuming the exchange interaction between the electrons spins instead of dipole-dipole interaction. The total exchange energy of spin i with its nearest neighbours $J_1, j_2 \ldots$ may be expressed as

$$E_{\text{ex}}^{ij} = -2J \sum_{j=1}^{n} S_i \cdot S_j$$

where $J$ is the exchange integral and is a measure of the strength of interaction.

8. According to Weiss, ferromagnetic materials are made up of a large number of domains, each of which is spontaneously magnetized. Landau and Lifshitz have shown that the domain structure is a natural consequence of contributions from, the magnetic field energy and the anisotropy energy.

9. Like ferromagnetism, antiferromagnetism and ferrimagnetism also owe their existence to exchange interaction between magnetic moments. The characteristic feature of antiferromagnetic materials can be qualitatively explained on the basis of two sublattice model. The susceptibility in the paramagnetic region $T > T_N$ is obtained as

$$\chi = \frac{M}{H} = \frac{2C}{T + C\lambda} = \frac{2C}{T + T_N}$$

where $T_N = C\lambda$ is called the Neel temperature.

10. Ferrimagnetism is an uncompensated form of antiferromagnetism. Ferrimagnetic substances exhibit spontaneous magnetization below ferrimagnetic Neel temperature ($T_{FN}$). The external behaviour of a ferrimagnet is similar to that of a ferromagnet, however, their spontaneous magnetizations are quite different. The structure of ferrites is based on naturally occurring spinel, $MgOAl_2O_3$. However, majority of ferrites occur in inverse spinel form.

## 16.21   DEFINITIONS

*Antiferromagnetism:* The opposite alignment of adjacent atomic magnetic moments in a solid produced by the exchange interaction.

*Bohr Magneton:* The fundamental quantum of magnetic moment and is equal to $9.27 \times 10^{-24}$ A-m$^2$.

*Coercive Field:* The applied field required to reduce the induction of a magnetized material to zero.

*Crystal Anisotropy Energy:* The energy of magnetization which is a function of crystal orientation. The difference in energy between the hard [111] and easy [100] in Fe is about $1.4 \times 10^4$ J/m$^3$.

*Curie Constant:* The proportionality constnat between $\chi$ and $1/T$ in the Curie law.

*Curie Law:* For paramagnetic material $\chi = C/T$.

*Curie Temperature:* If a ferromagnetic material is heated above its Curie temperature, it becomes paramagnetic.

*Diamagnetism:* The magnetic property of material for which $M$ (and therefore $\chi$) is negative.

*Domain:* A region in a ferro-or ferrimagnetic material where all the moments are aligned.

*Domain Wall Energy:* The sum of contributions from exchange and crystalline anisotropy energy in the domain wall region.

*Electron Spin:* A term used to refer the fact that electrons have permanent angular moments and magnetic moments.

*Exchange Energy:* The energy associated with the quantum mechanical coupling that aligns the individual atomic dipoles within a single domain.

*Ferrimagnetism:* A special case of antiferromagnetism, where the opposite moments are of different magnitudes. As a result of this a large amount of magnetization results.

*Ferromagnetism:* The appearance of a very large magnetization due to the parallel alignment of neighbouring magnetic moments by an exchange interaction.

*Hysteresis:* The irreversible $B$-$H$ or ($M$-$H$) characteristic curve of ferromagnetic or ferrimagnetic materials.

*Magnetic Permedability:* Defined by the relation $B = \mu H$.

*Magnetic Susceptibility:* Defined by the relation $M = \chi H$.

*Magnetization:* Defined by the relation $B = \mu_0(M + H)$. $M$ is equal to the dipole moment per unit volume.

*Magnetostriction:* The change in length along the direction of magnetization of a multidomain solid.

*Neel temperature:* The temperature above which a ferrimagnetic or antiferromagnetic material becomes paramagnetic.

*Paramagnetism:* The small positive susceptibility due to weak interaction and independent alignment of permanent atomic and electronic magnetic moments with the applied field.

*Relative Permeability:* Defined by the relation $\mu_r = \mu/\mu_0$, where $\mu$ is the permeability of a material and $\mu_0$ is the permeability of free space.

*Remanence:* The value of $B$ or $M$ in the specimen when $H$ is reduced to zero.

*Weiss Constant:* The proportionality constant between the Weiss field and the magnetization.

*Weiss Field:* A hypothetical internal magnetic field, strong enough to make the spin magnetic moment in a solid line up despite the effect of thermal energy.

# REVIEW QUESTIONS AND PROBLEMS

1. Distinguish clearly between diamagnetism, paramagnetism and ferromagnetism. Derive an expression of diamagnetic susceptibility on the basis of classical theory.

2. Obtain an expression for paramagnetic susceptibility of free electrons on the basis of classical laws. Discuss its shortcomings and show how Pauli modified it.

3. Give an account of Weiss theory of ferromagnetism. On the basis of this theory how will you explain hysteresis effect and Curie point. Explain clearly the basic difference between paramagnetism and ferromagnetism.

4. Draw a typical M–H curve for a ferromagnetic material and explain the different stages of magnetization process on the basis of domain theory.

5. Draw temperature dependence of the susceptibility of all types of magnetic materials. Explain the Heisenberg's exchange interaction in ferromagnetism.

6. Distinguish between ferromagnetism and antiferromagnetism. Explain theoretically the observed variation of susceptibility with temperature for antiferromagnets.

7. What is antiferromagnetic state? Describe the two sub-lattice model and show that it leads to a transition temperature equal to the constant $T_c$ in the Curie-Weiss law. How is this result supported by experiment?

8. Explain Heisenberg's exchange interaction. Show that it explains ferromagnetism. Discuss the difference in the nature of the magnetic susceptibility of a ferromagnetic and antiferromagnetic substance.

9. Describe Heisenberg's interaction of the origin of Weiss molecular field. Relate the exchange integral to the Weiss constant and ferromagnetic Curie temperature.

10. Distinguish between ferromagnetic, ferrimagnetic and antiferromagnetic substances. On the basis of two sub-lattice model, deduce the expression for the susceptibility of an antiferromagnetic material above and below the Neel temperature.

11. A magnetic material has a magnetization of 3300 A/m and flux density of 0.0044 W/m$^2$. Calculate the magnetic field and the relative permeability of the material.

    *Ans.* 203 A/m, 17.26

12. The magnetic field intensity in a piece of ferric oxide is $10^6$ A/m. If the susceptibility of the material at room temperature is $1.5 \times 10^{-3}$, calculate the flux density and the magnetization of the material.

    *Ans.* $1.5 \times 10^3$ A/m, 1.259 T

13. The magnetic susceptibility of copper is $- (0.5 \times 10^{-5})$. Calculate the magnetic moment per unit volume in copper when it is subjected to a field of $10^4$ A/m.    *Ans.* 0.05 A/m.

14. A paramagnetic has $10^{28}$ atoms/m$^3$. The magnetic moment of each atom is $1.8 \times 10^{-23}$ Am$^2$. Calculate the paramagnetic susceptibility at 300 K. What would be the dipole moment of a bar of this material 0.1 m long and 1 sq cm cross-section placed in a field of $8 \times 10^4$ A/m.

    *Ans.* $3.28 \times 10^{-4}$, 2.62 Am$^2$.

# Chapter 17

# Superconductivity

## 17.1 INTRODUCTION

One of the most unusual and interesting properties of solids that certain metals and alloys exhibit is almost zero electrical resistivity (i.e. infinite conductivity) when they are cooled to sufficiently low temperatures. The reduction in the value of electrical resistivity to zero is known as superconductivity. This phenomenon was first of all observed by H.K. Onnes in 1911 while making electrical conductivity measurement of metals at low temperatures. During the process, he observed a sudden decrease in the resistivity (actually it is immeasurably small and for all practical purposes it is taken as zero) when pure mercury was cooled down to below 4K (Fig. 17.1). The temperature at which the transition takes place in the absence of magnetic field is called the critical temperature ($T_c$) or the transition temperature. $T_c$ is found to be different for different substances. Therefore above $T_c$, a given specimen is in the usual normal state, while below $T_c$ it is in the superconducting state.

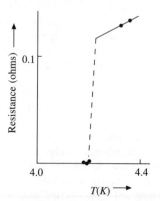

**Fig. 17.1  Resistance versus absolute temperature curve for mercury by K. Onnes which marked the discovery of super-conductivity**

For a chemically pure and structurally perfect specimen, the superconducting transition is usually sharp while for structurally imperfect specimens or the specimens containing some impurity elements, the transition range is broad (about one tenth of a degree or so).

Ever since the discovery of superconductivity by *K.* Onnes and until quite recently it was strictly a low temperature phenomenon. However, with the discovery of new oxide superconductors (having transition temperature of about 125 K or above), there has been a tremendous excitement particularly in the scientific world for two reasons. First, this may open a new age of high temperature superconducting devices, which will have widespread commercial applications. Second, the electron-lattice interaction appears not to be the origin of the superconductivity in these materials, leaving the fundamental physics open to investigation. Many of the properties of these materials appear to be unusual, and a proper understanding of the same requires an overall theoretical development. However, the superconducting state in these materials too appears to be associated with electron pairing and the overall behaviour may be similar to the conventional system in many respects. In fact, most of the important phenomena such as persistent current, Josephson tunneling, etc. have also been observed in the high-$T_c$ superconductors.

## 17.2 SOURCES OF SUPERCONDUCTIVITY

The phenomenon of superconductivity is not common to all but yet it is observed in many substances including metallic elements, alloys and compounds whose transition temperature vary widely. In 1957, B. Mathias proposed certain empirical rules on the basis of which he discovered a number of new superconductors. The rules are:

1. Superconductivity is found to occur in metallic elements in which the number of valence electron $Z$ lies between 2 and 8. In general, superconducting elements lie in the inner columns of the periodic Table.
2. Transition metals having odd valence electrons (Z) such as 3.5 or 7 have higher $T_c$ and are favourable to exhibit superconductivity while metals having even numbers of valence electrons are particularly unfavourable (Fig. 17.2).
3. For elements lying along a given row of the periodic Table (Fig. 17.3), $T_c$ versus $Z^2$ gives straight line.
4. A small atomic volume, accompanied by a small atomic mass favours superconductivity.
5. Materials having high normal resistivities exhibit superconductivity.
6. Materials with the product of number of valence electrons and the resistivity (in electrostatic units at 20°), $n\rho > 10^6$ show superconductivity.

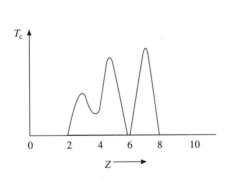

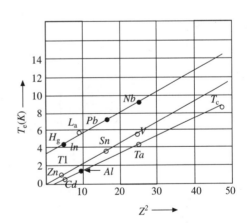

**Fig. 17.2** **Variation of transition temperature with number of valence electrons (Z)**

**Fig. 17.3** **An empirical correlation between transition temperature and $Z^2$**

## 17.3 RESPONSE OF MAGNETIC FIELD

The magnetic field and the superconductivity are found to be mutually exclusive. When a weak magnetic field is applied to a superconducting specimen, below transition temperature it expels the magnetic flux (i.e. lines of force) initially held and acts as an ideal diamagnet. This phenomenon is called the Meissner effect and is shown in (Fig. 17.4). When the applied field is gradually increased to a critical or threshold value, (often denoted by $H_c$), the superconductivity is destroyed (Fig. 17.5). However, this transition is reversible. The critical field ($H_c$) is a function of temperature, and for a given substance decreases gradually with increase in temperature from $T = 0K$ to $T = T_c$. Fig. 17.6 shows the variation of critical field with temperature for several superconducting elements. Further, this variation is empirically found to be represented by the expression

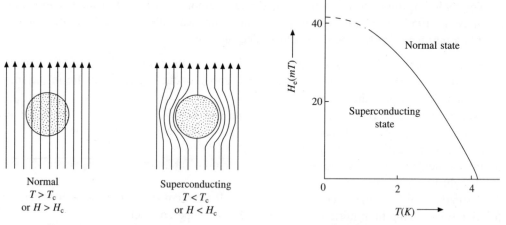

<table>
<tr><td>

**Fig. 17.4   The Meissner effect**
</td><td>

**Fig. 17.5   Schematic representation of the critical magnetic field as a function of temperature for Hg**
</td></tr>
</table>

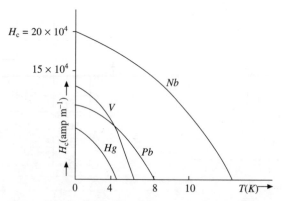

**Fig. 17.6   The critical magnetic field as a function of temperature for different superconducting elements**

$$H_c(T) = H_c(0)\left[1 - \left(\frac{T}{T_c}\right)^2\right] \tag{1}$$

where $H_c(0)$ is the maximum value of the field at $T = 0K$ and $H_c(T_c) = 0$ at $T = T_c$. $H_c(0)$ and $T_c$ are constants and characteristic of the material.

The critical field which destroys superconductivity, need not necessarily be an external field. It may also arise as a result of an electric current flowing through the superconductor specimen itself. For example, a current flowing through a superconducting ring has its own magnetic field, and as the current is increased to a critical value $I_c$ the associated magnetic field becomes $H_c$, which is sufficient for the destruction of superconductivity in the ring. The critical current $I_c$ flowing through a superconducting ring of radius $r$ is given by

$$I_c = 2\pi r H_c \tag{2}$$

This puts a limit on the strength of the current which can flow in a superconductor and hence is the main hurdle in producing high field superconducting magnet.

*Example*: A superconducting tin has a critical temperature of 3.7 K at zero magnetic field and a critical field of 0.0306 Tesla at 0 K. Find the critical field at 2 K.

*Solution:* Given: $T_c = 3.7$ K, $H_c(0) = 0.0306$ $T$, $T = 2$ K, $H_c(T) = ?$
Making use of eq. 1, and substituting different values, we have

$$H_c(T) = H_c(0)\left[1 - \left(\frac{T}{T_c}\right)^2\right] = 0.0306\left[1 - \left(\frac{2}{3.7}\right)^2\right] = 0.0216 \; T$$

*Example:* The magnetic field intensity in the tin material is zero at 3.69 K and $(3 \times 10^5)/4\pi$ at 0 K. Calculate the temperature of the superconductor if the field intensity is measured as $(2 \times 10^5)/4\pi$.

*Solution:* Given: $T_c = 3.69$ K, $B_c(0) = (3 \times 10^5)/4\pi$, $B_c(T) = (2 \times 10^5)/4\pi$, $T = ?$ Writing eq. 1 in terms of magnetic field intensity and substituting the desired values, we have

$$B_c(T) = B_c(0)\left[1 - \left(\frac{T}{T_c}\right)^2\right]$$

or
$$(2 \times 10^5)/4\pi = (3 \times 10^5)/4\pi\left[1 - \left(\frac{T}{3.69}\right)^2\right]$$

Simplifying this equation for $T$, we find

$$T = 2.13 \; K$$

*Example:* Calculate the critical current for a wire of lead having a diameter of 1 mm at 4.2 K. The critical temperature for lead is 7.18 K and $H_c(0) = 6.5 \times 10^4$ A/m.

*Solution:* Given: $T_c = 7.18$ K, $H_c(0) = 6.5 \times 10^4$ A/m, $T = 4.2$ K, $2r = 1$ mm $= 10^{-3}$ m, $I_c = ?$
Again, making use of the eq. 1 and substituting the desired values, we have

$$H_c(T) = H_c(0)\left[1 - \left(\frac{T}{T_c}\right)^2\right] = 6.5 \times 10^4\left[1 - \left(\frac{4.2}{7.8}\right)^2\right] = 4.28 \times 10^4 \; \text{A/m}$$

Further, from eq. 2, we have

$$I_c = 2\pi r H_c = \pi \times 10^{-3} \times 4.28 \times 10^4 = 134.46 \; \text{A}$$

## 17.4  THE MEISSNER EFFECT

In the preceding section, we found that a superconductor expels magnetic flux completely, a phenomenon first observed by Meissner and Ochsenfeld in 1933 and is known as Meissner effect (Fig. 17.4). By measuring the magnetic field in the neighbourhood of the specimen in a number of cases, they established that as the temperature is lowered to $T_c$ the specimen becomes superconducting and the flux is pushed out of it for all temperatures $T < T_c$. They also demonstrated that the effect is reversible, i.e. when the temperature is raised from below $T_c$, the flux suddenly starts penetrating the specimen at $T = T_c$ as a result of which the specimen returns back to the normal state. In this state, the magnetic induction inside the specimen is given by

$$B = \mu_0(H + M) \tag{3}$$

where $H$ is the external applied field and $M$ is the Magnetization produced inside the specimen.

According to Meissner effect the magnetic induction $B = 0$ inside the bulk superconductor. Therefore, eq. 3 becomes

$$\mu_0(H + M) = 0 \quad \text{or} \quad M = -H$$

Since such a material is perfectly diamagnetic whose magnetic susceptibility is given by

$$\chi = \frac{M}{H} = -1 \tag{4}$$

This is an important result which cannot be derived from the simple definition of superconductivity as a medium of zero resistivity. Accordingly, if $\rho$ tends to zero while the current $J$ is held finite, then from Ohm's law $E = J\rho$, $E$ must be zero. Further, from the Maxwell's equation,

$$\nabla \times E = -\frac{dB}{dt}$$

We obtain $dB/dt = 0$ and hence $B$ = constant, i.e. the flux passing through the specimen cannot change on cooling through the transition. The Meissner effect contradicts this result and suggests that perfect diamagnetism is an essential property of defining the superconducting state. They are:

$$E = 0 \text{ (from zero resistivity)} \quad \text{and} \quad B = 0 \text{ (from Meissner effect)}$$

Superconductors are of two types, type I and type II, in accordance with their diamagnetic response as shown in Fig. 17.4. Superconductor exhibiting a complete Meissner effect (perfect diamagnetism) are called type I superconductors (formerly known as soft superconductors). In this case, the diamagnetism abruptly disappears at the critical magnetic field value $H_c$ and the transition from superconducting to normal state is sharp. Pure specimens of many materials exhibit this behaviour. Al, Zn, Hg and Sn are some examples of type I superonductors. On the other hand, in type II superconductors, the magnetic flux starts penetrating the specimen at a field $H_{c1}$, the lower critical field which is lower than $H_c$. The specimen is in a mixed state between $H_{c1}$ and $H_{c2}$ (the upper critical field). Above $H_{c2}$, the specimen is a normal conductor in every respect. The value of $H_{c2}$, is generally 100 times more than the critical field $H_c$. Type II superconductors are also known as hard superconductors. Ta, V and Nb are some examples of this category.

## 17.5 THERMODYNAMICS OF SUPERCONDUCTING TRANSITIONS

Experimental observations show that the transition between the normal and superconducting state is thermodynamically reversible, just like the transition between liquid and vapour phases of a substance. The Meissner effect also suggests the same. Thus we may apply thermodynamics to this phase change and thereby obtain expressions for the difference in entropy and specific heat between normal and superconducting states near absolute zero. In the following, we shall discuss the thermodynamics of type I superconductors only for which $B = 0$ inside the specimen. Further, we shall study the superconducting transition under conditions of constant temperature and pressure when the two phases (normal and superconducting) are in equilibrium.

Since, thermodynamics of the superconducting transition in a magnetic field is analogous to that of any other phase transitions, it is sufficient to consider Gibbs free energy which remains invariant during isothermal isobaric process. The Gibbs free energy per unit volume in the magnetic field is given by

$$G = U - TS - HM \tag{5}$$

where $M$ is the magnetization, $S$ is the entropy and $PV$ term is neglected. Also, from second law of thermodynamics, the internal energy is given by

$$dU = T\,dS + H\,dM \tag{6}$$

where $H\,dM$ is the work done on the superconductor per unit volume. Comparing this value with the standard expression for internal energy $dU = T\,dS - P\,dV$ for a gas, we find that $H$ plays a role of $P$ and $M$ for $-V$ (or $H$ for $-P$ and M for $V$). Now differentiating eq. 5, we obtain

$$dG = dU - T\,dS - S\,dT - M\,dH - H\,dM = -S\,dT - M\,dH \tag{7}$$

Further, at constant temperature, $dT = 0$, so that eq. 7 reduces to

$$dG(H) = -M\,dH \tag{8}$$

Integrating eq. 8 for the superconducting state, we get

$$\int_0^H dG = -\int_0^H M\,dH$$

or

$$G_S(H) - G_S(0) = -\int_0^H M\,dH \tag{9}$$

On the other hand, if the sample is in the normal state, it is a paramagnet (normal state of most superconductors is paramagnetic) and therefore $M \to 0$ or $\chi \to 0$, so that from eq. 9 we can write

$$G_N(H) - G_N(0) = 0 \quad \text{or} \quad G_N(H) = G_N(0) \tag{10}$$

implying that in the normal state the Gibbs function remains invariant under the application of the magnetic field.

Now, if we look at the curve $H_c$ versus $T$ (Fig. 17.5), we find that the normal state and the superconducting state are in equilibrium and therefore the free energies of the two states at the

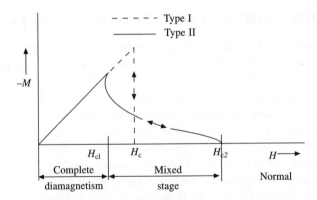

**Fig. 17.7   Magnetization curves for (a) Type (I) and Type (II) superconductors**

boundary must be equal. This gives

$$G_N(T, H_c) = G_S(T, H_c) \tag{11}$$

Combining eqs. 9 and 11, we obtain

$$G_N(T, H_c) = G_S(T, H_c) = G_S(0) - \int_0^H M \, dH \tag{12}$$

and eqs. 10 and 12 give

$$G_N(0) = G_S(0) - \int_0^H M \, dH \quad \text{or} \quad G_N(0) - G_S(0) = - \int_0^H M \, dH$$

or

$$\Delta G = - \int_0^H M \, dH \tag{13}$$

Now, from Meissner effect we known that $M = -H$ ($B = 0$), so that

$$\Delta G = G_N(0) - G_S(0) = - \int_0^H M \, dH = \int_0^{H_c} H \, dH = \frac{H_c^2}{2} \tag{14}$$

**Entropy Difference**

The entropy $S$ of a solid (from eq. 7) is found as

$$S = - \left( \frac{\partial G}{\partial T} \right)_H \tag{15}$$

Now, with the help of eqs. 14 and 15, the entropy difference between the normal and the superconducting state can be obtained as

$$S_N - S_S = - H_c \frac{dH_c}{dT} \tag{16}$$

Since $dH_c/dT$ is always negative, therefore $S_N - S_S$ is always positive, implying that the superconducting state is more ordered than the normal state. Further, at $T = T_c$, $H_c = 0$, therefore $S_N - S_S = 0$, and also at $T = 0K$, $S_N - S_S = 0$ because $dH_c/dT$ tends to zero (from third law of thermodynamics). Between $T = 0K$ and $T = T_c$, $S_N - S_S$ is positive, i.e. $S_N > S_S$. These are illustrated in Fig. 17.8.

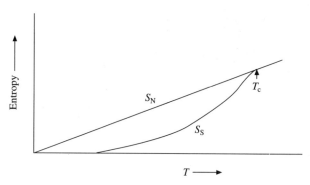

**Fig. 17.8** **Entropy $S$ of Aluminium in the normal and superconducting state as a function of temperature**

The entropy difference is related to the latent heat of the system according to the equation

$$Q = T(S_N - S_S) = -TH_c \frac{dH_c}{dT} \tag{17}$$

As we have seen above that at $T = T_c$, $S_N - S_S = 0$ because $H_c = 0$. Thus, from eq. 17, $Q = 0$. This implies an absence of latent heat when transition occurs at $T_c(H_c = 0)$. However, if $H_c \neq 0$, i.e. in the presence of magnetic field, the transition occurs at some lower temperature $T < T_c$. From eq. 17, this gives us latent heat because between $T_c$ and $0K$ the entropy of the normal state is greater than that of superconducting state, so the required amount of heat must be supplied if the transition is to take place at constant temperature.

**Specific Heat**
The specific heat of a solid is given by the expression

$$C = T \frac{dH}{dT} \tag{18}$$

Again, with the help of eqs. 16 and 17, the specific heat difference between the normal and the superconducting states can be obtained as

$$C_N - C_S = -\left[TH_c \frac{d^2 H_c}{dT^2} + T\left(\frac{dH_c}{dT}\right)^2\right] \tag{19}$$

At $T = T_c$, $H_c = 0$, and as we know that $dH_c/dT$ is always negative, therefore

$$C_N - C_S = -T_c\left(\frac{dH_c}{dT}\right)^2 = -\text{ve} \tag{20}$$

This implies that near $T_c$, $C_N$ is less than $C_S$. But as the temperature $T$ decreases, the first term on the right hand side of eq. 19 increases with negative sign while the second term decreases with positive sign (because of the square term), and hence $C_N - C_S$ is positive, i.e. $C_N$ is greater than $C_S$ at lower temperatures.

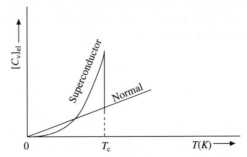

**Fig. 17.9**   **Electric contribution of specific heat of a conductor as a function of temperature in the normal and superconducting state**

Thus, whether a material is cooled or warmed in the absence of a magnetic field, there will be a discontinuity in the specific heat curve at the transition temperature. The electronic specific heat versus temperature curve (for bismuth with 4% tin) is shown in Fig. 17.9. But as we know that the specific heat arises from two different sources, i.e the lattice and the electronic specific heats discussed in earlier chapters. Consequently, the total specific heat is

$$C = C_{\text{lattice}} + C_{\text{el}} \tag{21}$$

so that $\qquad C_N = (C_{\text{lattice}})_N + (C_{\text{el}})_N \quad \text{and} \quad C_S = (C_{\text{lattice}})_S + (C_{\text{el}})_S$

However, it is to be pointed out that the properties of the lattice (crystal structure, Debye temperature, etc.) do not change when a material becomes superconductor, and therefore

$$(C_{\text{lattice}})_N = (C_{\text{lattice}})_S \tag{22}$$

Consequently, $\qquad C_N - C_S = (C_{\text{el}})_N - (C_{\text{el}})_S \tag{23}$

From Fig. 17.9, we find that well below $T_c$, $C_S$ is very small and is difficult to measure accurately. However, careful measurements have shown that well below $T_c$, the electronic specific heat of a metal in the superconducting state varies with temperature in an exponential manner, i.e.

$$(C_{\text{el}})_S = a \exp\left(-\frac{\Delta}{kT}\right) \tag{24}$$

where $a$ is constant and $\Delta$ is the energy gap.

## 17.6   ORIGIN OF ENERGY GAP

The exponential behaviour of the electronic specific heat in the superconducting state implies the presence of an energy gap in the energy spectrum of the electrons (Fig. 17.10) or in the

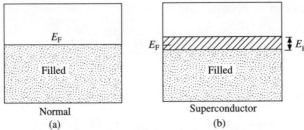

**Fig. 17.10**   **(a) Conduction band in the normal state, (b) energy gap at the Fermi level in the superconducting state**

distribution of density of states (Fig. 17.11). The energy gap is situated at the Fermi level. This gap is a characteristic feature of the superconducting state and differs from the energy gap

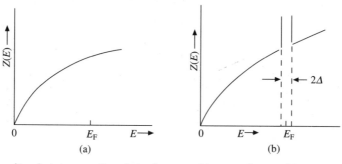

**Fig. 17.11** **Density of states as a function of energy (a) normal state (b) superconducting state**

encountered in insulators. In an insulator, the gap is associated with the lattice while in superconductors the gap is associated with the Fermi gas. In a superconducting state, the width of the gap $2\Delta$ is of the order of $kT_c$ (i.e. $2\Delta \cong kT_c$). This prevents the super electrons from being excited below $T_c$. Only above $T_c$, they behave like normal electrons and may be readily excited. As an example, for a typical value of $T_c = 5$ K, one finds that $2\Delta \cong 10^{-4}$ eV. This energy gap is very small as compared to the gaps encountered in semiconductors or insulators. The variation of energy gap with temperature is shown in Fig. 17.12.

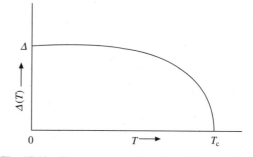

**Fig. 17.12** **Energy gap as a function of temperature**

BCS theory is able to explain the existence and temperature dependence of the energy gap in superconductors. According to this theory, the ratio of the energy gap $2\Delta$, to the thermal energy at the critical temperature ($kT_c$) is same for all superconductors and is equal to 3.53. Table 17.1 presents the energy gap at 0 K, critical temperature $T_c$ and the ratio $2\Delta/kT_c$ for some superconducting elements.

**Table 17.1** **The energy gap at 0K and the critical temperature for some superconductors**

| Elements | $2\Delta$ (*m eV*) | $T_c$ | $\dfrac{2D}{kT_c}$ |
|---|---|---|---|
| Nb | 3.05 | 9.50 | 3.8 |
| Ta | 1.40 | 4.48 | 3.6 |
| Sn | 1.16 | 3.72 | 3.5 |
| Al | 0.34 | 1.20 | 3.3 |
| Pb | 2.90 | 7.18 | 4.3 |
| Hg | 1.65 | 4.16 | 4.6 |

## 17.7 ISOTOPE EFFECT

Experimental study of superconducting materials shows that the transition temperature varies with the average isotopic mass, $M$, of their constituents. In particular,

$$T_c \propto M^{-1/2} \tag{25}$$

For example, in mercury $T_c$ was found to vary from 4.185 K to 4.146 K with the variation of its average isotopic mass from 199.5 to 203.4 atomic mass units. More recent experiments suggest the above variation in the following general form

$$T_c \propto M^{-\alpha} \tag{26}$$

where $\alpha$ is called the isotope effect coefficient and is defined as

$$\alpha = \frac{\partial \ln T_c}{\partial \ln M} \tag{27}$$

On the other hand, according to recent theories $\alpha$ is given by

$$\alpha = 0.5 \left[ 1 - 0.01 \left\{ N(0)V \right\}^{-2} \right] \tag{28}$$

where $N(0)$ is the density of single particle states for one spin at the Fermi level and $V$ is the potential between the electrons.

Since the Debye temperature $\theta_D$ and the velocity of sound $v$ is proportional to $M^{-1/2}$, therefore the transition temperature of superconducting materials is closely related to the corresponding Debye temperature. From eq. 26, we have

$$T_c \propto \theta_D \qquad \text{or} \qquad \frac{T_c}{\theta_D} = \text{constant} \tag{29}$$

Equation 29 implies that the lattice vibrations play an important role in superconductivity and hence the electron-lattice interactions must be taken into account in its theoretical development.

## 17.8 LONDON EQUATIONS

Under the heading "The Meissner effect" in section 17.4 we saw that a superconducting specimen expels magnetic flux completely from its interior. However, the same is not found to be correct in the case of thin films. On the basis of Maxwell's electrodynamic equations alone, it has not been possible to deduce the Meissner effect and field penetration in superconductors. Therefore, based on two fluid model of Gorte and Casimir (1935), London brothers (F. London and H. London) first examined the magnetic aspects quantitatively and showed that it was necessary to introduce two additional equations to explain them completely.

According to two fluid model, a superconductor is supposed to be composed of two distinct types of electrons, i.e. normal electrons and superelectrons. The normal electron behaves in a usual manner as discussed in chapter 10. However, the superelectrons behave in a much different way, such as they experience no scattering, have zero entropy (perfect order), have a long coherence length (~$10^4$ Å), and so on. At $T = T_c$, all the electrons are normal and as the temperature decreases an increasing proportion becomes superelectrons until at $T = 0$K all are superelectrons. Therefore, based on this model, London brothers put forward the idea that at any temperature the total sum of superelectrons and normal electrons is equal to the conduction electron density in the material in the normal state. So that if $n_n$ and $n_s$ respectively are the densities of normal electrons and superelectrons, the conduction electrons $n$ become

$$n = n_n + n_s \tag{30}$$

The normal current and the supercurrent are assumed to flow parallel. Since the supercurrent flows with no resistance whatsoever (on the contrary the normal current cannot flow without resistance and gets dissipated), it will carry the entire current induced by any small transitory electric field. The normal electrons will remain quite inert and are therefore ignored in the following discussion.

Let us suppose that a small transient electric field $E$ arises within a superconductor which freely accelerates the superelectrons (without dissipation). If $v_s$ is the average velocity, $m$ is the mass and $e$ is the charge of a superelectron, then the equation of motion can be written as

$$m \frac{dv_s}{dt} = -eE \tag{31}$$

and the current density of superelectron is

$$J_s = -en_s v_s \tag{32}$$

From eqs. 31 and 32, we obtain

$$\frac{dJ_s}{dt} = \frac{n_s e^2}{m} E \tag{33}$$

This is called the first London equation. This shows that it is possible to have steady state current in a superconductor in the absence of an electric field, because in eq. 33, for $E = 0$, $J$ is finite and constant or vice-versa. The corresponding expression for normal current density is

$$J_n = \sigma E$$

which shows that no current is possible in the absence of an electric field, a usual behaviour of materials in the normal state.

The conclusion $E = 0$ leads to another important result when combined with the Maxwell's equation

$$\nabla \times E = -\left(\frac{dB}{dt}\right) \tag{34}$$

that is

$$\left(\frac{dB}{dt}\right) = 0 \quad \text{or} \quad B = \text{constant} \tag{35}$$

Equation 35 tells us that in steady state $B$ is constant inside a superconductor irrespective of its temperature. This result is not in agreement with the Meissner effect, according to which a superconductor expels magnetic flux completely for all temperatures below $T_c$. In order to remove this discrepancy, London suggested some modifications in the above formalism. For the purpose, let us take curl of eq. 33 and then substitute the value of curl $E$ from eq. 34, we obtain

$$\nabla \times \left(\frac{dJ_s}{dt}\right) = -\frac{n_s e^2}{m} \cdot \frac{dB}{dt} \tag{36}$$

Integrating eq. 36 w.r.t time and putting the constant of integration equal to zero (so that it remains consistent with the Meissner effect), we have

$$\nabla \times J_s = -\frac{n_s e^2}{m} B \tag{37}$$

This is called the second London equation and leads to results that are in agreement with the experiment.

## 17.9 LONDON PENETRATION DEPTH

London brothers successfully explained the Meissner effect and zero resistivity by adding two new equations to the four Maxwell's equations used in electrodynamics. According to the London equations, the flux does not suddenly drops to zero at the surface of Type I superconductors, but decreases exponentially. In order to see the actual variation of flux with distance, let us start with the Maxwell's equation

$$\nabla \times B = \mu_0 J_s \tag{38}$$

Taking curl of this equation, we obtain

$$\nabla \times \nabla \times B = \mu_0 \, \nabla \times J_s \tag{39}$$

Making use of the identity $\nabla \times \nabla \times B = \nabla (\nabla \cdot B) - \nabla^2 B = -\nabla^2 B$, where $\nabla \cdot B = 0$ for a superconductor, eq. 39 becomes

$$-\nabla^2 B = \mu_0 \, \nabla \times J_s \tag{40}$$

Now, from eqs. 37 and 40, we have

$$\nabla^2 B = -\frac{\mu_0 n_s e^2}{m} B = \frac{1}{\lambda^2} B \tag{41}$$

where $\lambda = \left(\dfrac{m}{\mu_0 n_s e^2}\right)^{1/2}$ and is called the London penetration depth. One dimensional form of eq. 41 is

$$\frac{\partial^2 B_z}{\partial x^2} = \frac{1}{\lambda^2} B_z \tag{42}$$

Here it is supposed that the specimen is semi-infinite with its surface lying in the $yz$-plane and the field is applied in the $z$-direction. The solution of this simple differential equation is assumed to be of the form

$$B_z(x) = B_z(0) \exp\left(-\frac{x}{\lambda}\right) \tag{43}$$

The graphical representation of eq. 43 is shown in Fig. 17.13. This indicates that the flux density decreases exponentially inside the superconductor, falling to $1/e$ of its initial value at a distance $\lambda$, the London penetration depth. It further indicates that the flux inside the bulk of superconductor is zero and hence is in agreement with the Meissner effect.

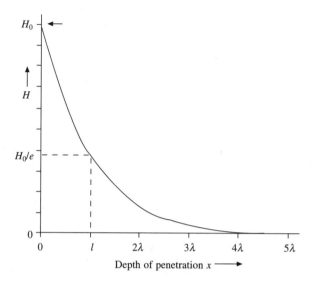

**Fig. 17.13   Exponential decrease of the magnetic field inside a superconductor**

The penetration depth has been verified and measured in a number of cases and is found to be in agreement with the theoretical value which is about 500 Å. The penetration depth is also found to depend on temperature according to the relation

$$\lambda(T) = \lambda(0)\left(1 - \frac{T^4}{T_c^4}\right)^{-1/2} \tag{44}$$

where $\lambda(0) = \lambda$, the penetration depth at $T = 0K$. According to eq. 44, $\lambda$ increases with the increase of $T$ and becomes infinite at $T = T_c$ (Fig. 17.14).

This is expected because at $T = T_c$, the substance changes from superconducting state to normal state when the field can penetrate to the whole specimen, i.e. the specimen has an infinite depth of penetration. Further, since the London penetration depth and the number of superelectrons $n_s$ is inversely related to each other and is also temperature dependent, therefore a similar equation like eq. 44 can be obtained for superelectrons, i.e.

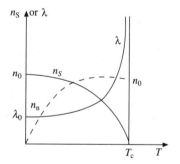

**Fig. 17.14   The penetration depth as a function of temperature**

$$n_s = n_0\left(1 - \frac{T^4}{T_c^4}\right) \tag{45}$$

or

$$w = \frac{n_s}{n_0} = \left(1 - \frac{T^4}{T_c^4}\right) \tag{46}$$

where $w$ is called the order parameter which characterizes the degree of order in the superconducting state. The variation of superelectrons and normal electrons with temperature is also depicted in Fig. 17.14.

*Example*: The penetration depth of mercury at 3.5 K is about 750 Å. Estimate the penetration depth at 0 K. Also calculate the superconducting electron density.

*Solution:* Given: $\lambda(3.5) = 750$ Å, $T_c = 4.12$ K, $T = 3.5$ K, $\lambda(0) = ?$, $n_s = ?$ From eq. 44, we can write

$$\lambda(0) = \lambda(T)\left[1 - \left(\frac{T}{T_c}\right)^4\right]^{1/2} = 750\left[1 - \left(\frac{3.5}{4.12}\right)^4\right]^{1/2} = 519 \text{ Å}$$

The normal electron density in mercury can be found in terms of molecular weight and molecular density. Therefore,

$$n_0 = \frac{N\rho}{M} = \frac{6.02 \times 10^{26} \times 13.55 \times 10^3}{200.6} = 4.06 \times 10^{28}/m^3$$

Now, making use of eq. 45 and substituting the desired values, we have

$$n_s = n_0\left[1 - \left(\frac{T}{T_c}\right)^4\right] = 4.06 \times 10^{28}\left[1 - \left(\frac{3.5}{4.12}\right)^4\right]$$

$$= 4.06 \times 10^{28} \times 0.479 = 1.95 \times 10^{28}/m^3$$

## 17.10   COHERENCE LENGTH

From the preceding two sections, we have come to know that near the surface of a superconductor there exist two types of electrons (i.e. normal electrons and superelectrons) and the transition from normal to superconducting state or vice versa is not abrupt. Pippard (1953) was the first to recognise the idea of a transition length associated with the order parameter $w$. It is a distance within which the order parameter $w$ changes from its maximum value in the bulk superconducting region to zero in the normal region (Fig. 17.15). This distance is known as coherence length ($\xi$) and depends on the purity of the sample. For a pure superconductor, the intrinsic coherence length $\xi_0$ is obtained as follows:

As we know that the electron states which are responsible for superconductivity lie within $kT_c$ of the Fermi surface. From uncertainty principle, their lifetime $\tau$ is given by

$$(kT_c) \simeq \hbar$$

If $v_F$ is the electron velocity at the Fermi surface, then the wave function must extend over a distance $\xi_0 = v_F\tau$. Therefore,

$$\xi_0 \cong \frac{\hbar v_F}{kT_c} \cong \frac{\hbar v_F}{2\Delta} \tag{47}$$

However, a more refined form of this equation is

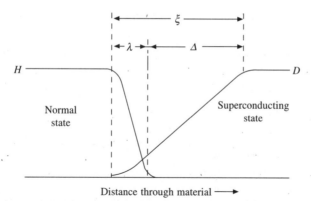

**Fig. 17.15   Variation of magnetic field *H* and the order parameter *w* through an interface between the normal and superconducting regions**

$$\xi_0 = \frac{2\hbar v_F}{\pi \Delta} \cong 10^{-6} \text{ m} \tag{48}$$

Like London penetration depth $\lambda$, the coherence length $\xi$ is also a function of temperature and also vary in the same manner (Fig. 17.14).

## 17.11   ELEMENTS OF BCS THEORY

The modern theory of superconductivity was put forward by Bardeen, Cooper and Schrieffer in 1957 and hence named as BCS theory. This theory successfully explained all observable effects such as zero resistivity, the Meissner effect, isotope effect and so on. The BCS theory is based on advance quantum concept and mathematical techniques and it is not possible to describe a detail formalism here. However, we shall present here the important aspects of the theory in a brief and qualitative manner. They are:

### 1.   Electron-Electron Interaction Via Lattice Deformation

In 1950, Frohlich emphasized that the theory of superconductivity requires a net attractive interaction between a pair of electrons in the neighbourhood of Fermi surface. This is possible only if the interaction between the pair of electrons is taking place via positive ions of the lattice, a direct Coulomb interaction between them always produces a repulsion. In order to understand the direct interaction, let us consider an electron passing through the packing of the positive ions. Because it is negatively charged, it is attracted by the neighbouring positive ions (which form a positive ion core as shown in Fig. 17.16) and gets screened by them. The screening greately reduces the effective charge of this electron, in fact the ion core may produce a net positive charge on this assembly. At the same time, due to the attraction between the electron and the

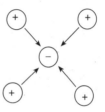

**Fig. 17.16   Positive ions attracted towards an electron forming a positive ion core**

ion core, the lattice gets deformed on local scale. This deformation is greater for smaller mass of positive ion core.

Now, suppose another electron passes by the side of the assembly of the said electron and the ion core. The second electron does not see simply the bare electron but a deformed lattice and gets attracted towards the assembly. Thus, it can be said that the second electron interacts with the first via lattice deformation.

In the language of filed theory, the above interaction is said to be due to the exchange of a virtual phonon, $q$, between the two electrons. In terms of the wave vectors, $k$, of the two electrons, the interaction process can be written as (refer Fig. 17.17)

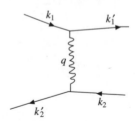

**Fig. 17.17**  **The exchange of virtual phonons between the two electrons (Cooper pair)**

$$k_1 - q = k_1' \quad \text{and} \quad k_2 + q = k_2' \tag{49}$$

This gives $k_1 + k_2 = k_1' + k_2'$, i.e. the net wave vector of the pair is conserved. The process as a whole leaves the lattice invariant and yet the momentum is transferred between the electrons.

### 2. Cooper Pair

From earlier discussions, namely the energy gap and the coherence length, we find that no sharp boundary exists between the normal and the superconducting states. In fact, they are separated by an energy gap, $\Delta \sim 10^{-4}$ eV. In order to understand the mechanism of Cooper pair formation, let us consider the distribution of electrons in metals at absolute zero given by Fermi-Dirac distribuion function

$$F(E) = \frac{1}{\exp\left(\dfrac{E - E_F}{kT}\right) + 1} \tag{50}$$

we know that at $T = 0$ K all the quantum states below the Fermi level $E_F$ are completely filled and all the quantum states above $E_F$ are completely empty as shown in Fig. 17.18. Similarly, the momentum distribution of electrons at absolute zero in $k$-space occupies a sphere (known as Fermi sphere and is shown in Fig. 17.19) of radius

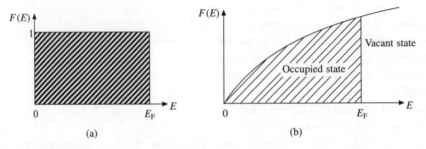

**Fig. 17.18**  **The Fermi-Dirac distribution function and the density of states for $T = 0$ K**

$$k_F = \left( \frac{2mE_F}{\hbar^2} \right)^{1/2} \tag{51}$$

Now, let us see what happens when two electrons are added to a metal at absolute zero. Since all the quantum states with energies $E \leq E_F$ (or $k \leq k_F$) are filled, therefore according to Pauli's exclusion principle they are forced to occupy states having energies $E > E_F$ (or $k > k_F$). In this situation, Cooper showed that if there is an attraction between the two electrons (however weak) they are able to form a bound state (provided they are just above the Fermi surface) so that their total energy is less than $2E_F$. These electrons are paired to form a single system and their motions are correlated. These two electrons together form a Cooper pair and is known as Cooper electron. Pairing between the two electrons can be broken only if an amount of energy equal to the binding energy (also equal to $\Delta$) is supplied to the system. The binding is strongest when the electrons forming the pair have opposite momenta and opposite spins, i.e. $k\uparrow, -k\downarrow$. Therefore, it follows that if there is an attraction between any two electrons lying in the neighbourhood of the Fermi surface then all other electrons lying in that region will form Cooper pairs. These pairs of electrons are in fact superelectrons which are responsible for the superconductivity.

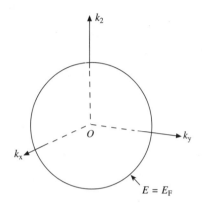

**Fig. 17.19   The Fermi surface in $k$-space**

### 3.   BCS Ground State

Figures 17.17 and 17.18 in the preceding section represent the filled Fermi sea which is the ground state of a Fermi gas of noninteracting Fermi electrons. In normal metals, the excited states lie just above the Fermi surface and even an arbitrarily small excitation energy is sufficient to excite an electron from this surface to the excited state. However, in a superconducting material the situation is entirely different. In this case, when a pair of electrons lying just below the Fermi surface is taken just above it, they form a Cooper pair and their total energy is reduced. If it is done for one pair, it can be done for other pairs until the system can gain no additional energy by pair formation and hence the total energy is further reduced. Fig. 17.11 shows the density of states as a function of energy for normal metals and superconductors at absolute zero. The important feature of the BCS ground state is that even at absolute zero the energy (or momentum) distribution of electrons does not show any abrupt discontinuity as in the case of normal metals. Another feature is that the states are occupied in pairs, i.e. if a state with wave vector $k$ and spin up ($k \uparrow$) is occupied then the state ($-k\downarrow$) also occupied and if ($k\uparrow$) is vacant then ($-k\downarrow$) is also vacant. In other words, a Cooper pair is imagined to be an electron pair in which the two electrons always occupy states ($k\uparrow$, $k\downarrow$), ($k'_\uparrow$, $k'_\downarrow$) and so on with opposite $k$-vectors and spins.

The London penetration depth and coherence length are consequences of the BCS ground state.

## 17.12 FLUX QUANTIZATION

In 1950 Ginzburg and Landau developed a macroscopic theory for superconducting phase transition based on a general thermodynamical approach to the theory of phase transition. They considered the long-range order as fundamental and introduced a complex wave function $\psi$ as an order parameter to describe the superconducting state, where the density of the superconducting electrons $n_s \propto |\psi|^2$. For a given temperature, the "order parameter" $\psi$ is a function of position in the material, i.e. it is not constant and vanishes above $T_c$. It is sometimes helpful to think of $\psi$ as the wave function for a Cooper pair (although the Ginzburg and Landau theory was developed much before the BCS theory). Since all Cooper pairs are in the same two-electron state, a single wave function is sufficient.

If we write the wave function explicitly in terms of the magnitude and a phase as $\psi = |\psi| \exp(i\phi)$, then the current density can be written as

$$J = -\left(\frac{2e^2}{mc} A + \frac{e\hbar}{m} \nabla\phi\right)|\psi|^2 \tag{52}$$

where $A$ is the vector potential.

Let us consider a superconducting material in the shape of a ring as shown in Fig. 17.20 and take a closed path, we find

$$\oint J \cdot dl = |\psi|^2 \oint \left(\frac{2e^2}{mc} A + \frac{e\hbar}{m} \nabla\phi\right) \cdot dl = 0 \tag{53}$$

whereas Stokes theorem gives us

$$\int J \cdot dl = \int \nabla \times A \cdot ds = \int B \cdot ds = \Phi \tag{54}$$

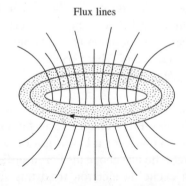

Flux lines

**Fig. 17.20 A ring shaped superconducting material showing the path of integration $C$ through its interior**

where $\Phi$ is the flux enclosed by the ring. Further, since the order parameter is single valued, its phase change around the closed path must be zero or an integral multiple of $2\pi$. Therefore,

$$\oint \nabla\phi \cdot dl = 2\pi n \tag{55}$$

where $n$ is an integer.

Substituting eqs. 54 and 55 in eq. 53 and solving for $\Phi$, we find that the magnetic flux enclosed by a ring must be quantized, i.e.

$$\Phi = \frac{nhc}{2e} = n\Phi_0 \tag{56}$$

where $\Phi_0 = \dfrac{hc}{2e} = 2.07 \times 10^{-7}$ gauss-cm$^2$ is known as fluxoid or flux quantum. The equation 56 does not hold if the flux penetrates the ring itself (particularly when the material of the ring is thin).

Actually, the flux through the ring is the sum of the flux due to the external source and the flux due to the supercurrent flowing through the ring, i.e.

$$\Phi = \Phi_{ext} + \Phi_{sc} \tag{57}$$

It is the flux $\Phi$ which is quantized. Normally, the flux due to the external source is not quantized, therefore, $\Phi_{sc}$ must adjust itself such that $\Phi$ assumes a quantized value.

## 17.13  NORMAL TUNNELING AND JOSEPHSON EFFECT

When a thin insulating layer (normally an oxide layer of about 20 Å thickness) is sandwiched between two metals, it acts as a potential barrier as far as the flow of conduction electrons is concerned. Further, we know that quantum mechanically electrons can tunnel across a thin potential barrier and in thermal equilibrium they continue to do so until the chemical potential of electrons in both the metals become equal. When both the metals are normal conductors (Fig. 17.21a) and if a potential difference is applied across them, the chemical potential of one of them increases with respect to other. As a result, more electrons tunnel through the insulating layer. The current-voltage relation across the tunneling junction is observed to obey Ohm's law at low voltages (Fig. 17.21b). However, when one of the metals is a superconductor (Fig. 17.22a), no current is observed to flow across the junction until the potential reaches a threshold value, eV

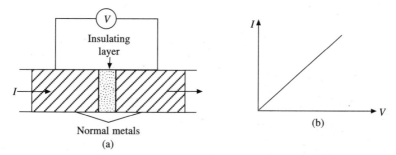

**Fig. 17.21**  (a) A thin insulating layer is sandwiched between two metals and (b) the corresponding current-voltage relation for electron tunneling through the thin barrier

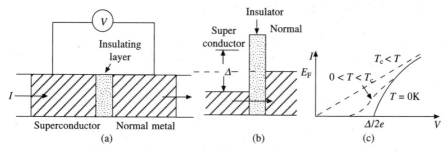

**Fig. 17.22**  (a) A thin insulating layer is sandwiched between a metal and a superconductor and (b) Tunneling in a metal-superconductor junction. Note that the Fermi level is the same throughout the system, and pass through the mid gap of superconductor and (c) current-voltage relationship at the junction at different temperatures

= $\Delta/2$ (half the energy gap in the superconducting state), as shown in Fig. 17.22b. It is because the energy states lying horizontally below $E_F$ in the normal metal are already occupied. Further, since the Fermi level $E_F$ is the same throughout the system and lies in the middle of the energy gap of the superconductor, the knowledge of the threshold voltage helps in determining the energy gap of a superconductor. As the temperature is increased towards $T_c$, the threshold voltage decreases (due to the presence of thermally excited electrons, which require less energy to tunnel. This consequently indicates a decrease in the energy gap itself. The current-voltage relations across the tunneling junction at different temperatures are shown in Fig. 17.22c.

The above discussed tunneling is called the normal tunneling or single electron tunneling, where electrons tunnel in singles through the insulated layer. However, when both the metals are superconductors (Fig. 17.23a), Josephson (1962) predicted that in addition to the normal tunneling of single electrons, the Cooper pairs (superelectrons) not only can tunnel through the insulating layer from one superconductor to another without dissociation, even at zero potential difference across the junction, but also their (quantum) wave functions (order parameter) on both sides would be highly correlated. This is known as Josephson effect. As the two superconductors are only weakly coupled because of the presence of a thin insulating layer in between, the typical tunneling current across the junction will be far smaller than typical critical currents for single specimens. The current-voltage relations across the tunneling junction at different temperatures are shown in Fig. 17.23b.

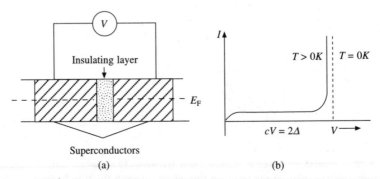

**Fig. 17.23** (a) **Tunneling in a superconductor-insulator-superconductor (SIS) junction, (b) Current-voltage characteristic at $T = 0K$ and $0 < T < T_c$**

Josephson predicted a variety of further effects by assuming that the superconducting ordering on both sides of the junction could be described by a single order parameter $\psi(r)$. The effect of the insulating layer is just to introduce a phase difference $\Delta\phi$ between the two parts of the wave function on opposite sides of the junction, as shown in Fig. 17.24. He showed that the tunneling current would be given by

$$I = I_0 \sin(\phi_0) \qquad (58)$$

where $I_0$ is the maximum current that the junction can carry without a potential difference

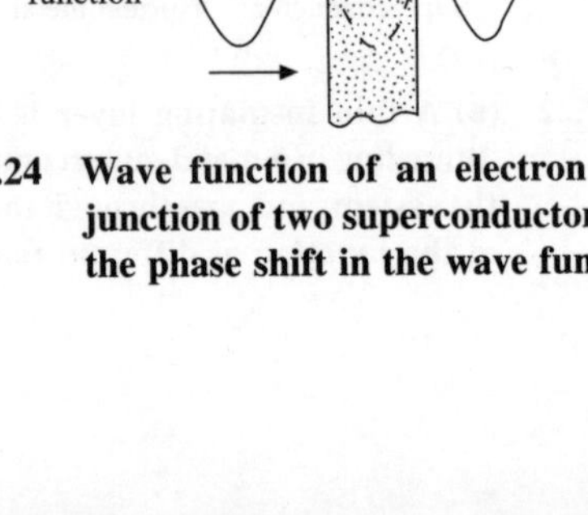

**Fig. 17.24** **Wave function of an electron at the junction of two superconductors; note the phase shift in the wave function**

across it and depends on the temperature and the structure of the junction, e.g. its thickness. With no applied voltage, a dc current will flow across the junction (Fig. 17.25), with a value between $I_0$ and $-I_0$ according to the value of phase difference $\phi_0 = (\phi_2 - \phi_1)$. This is called dc Josephson effect.

Now, let us suppose that a static potential $V_0$ is applied across the junction due to which an additional phase will be introduced by the Cooper pair during tunneling across the junction. In order to calculate the same, let us make use of the phase of the wave function as used in quantum mechanics

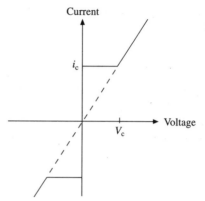

$$\Delta\phi = \frac{Et}{\hbar} \qquad (59)$$

**Fig. 17.25  Current-voltage characteristic of a Josephson junction**

where $E$ is the total energy of the system. In the present case $E = (2e)V_0$, the factor 2 is because a Cooper pair contains 2 electrons. Therefore

$$\Delta\phi = \frac{2eV_0 t}{\hbar} \qquad (60)$$

Introducing this, the eq. 58 takes the form

$$I = I_0 \sin(\phi_0 + \Delta\phi) = I_0 \sin\left(\phi_0 + \frac{2eV_0}{\hbar}t\right) \qquad (61)$$

which represents an alternating current, with an angular frequency

$$\omega = \frac{2eV_0}{\hbar} \qquad (62)$$

This is the ac Josephson effect. Equation 62 states that a photon of energy $\hbar\omega = 2eV_0$ is emitted or absorbed when an electron pair crosses the junction. By measuring the voltage and frequency, it is possible to obtain a precise value of the fundamental constant $e/h$.

## 17.14  HIGH–$T_C$ SUPERCONDUCTIVITY

A real breakthrough in high temperature superconductivity took place in 1986, when Bednorz and Muller discovered metallic, oxygen deficient copper oxide compounds of the Ba-La-Cu-O system with transition temperature of about 35 K and subsequently by Chu and coworkers in Y-Ba-Cu-O system with transition temperature of 90 K. Since then a large number of other oxide superconductors with varied transition temperatures have been discovered by various workers. A vast amount of experimental data is now available and is presented in chronological order in Table 17.2. It may be noted from the table that compounds with the general formula $MBa_2Cu_3O_7$ (where $M = Y$ or rare earth) are superconducting above liquid nitrogen temperature. Because of the lower cooling costs, technological applications of these materials can be easily appreciated.

At present, it is difficult to make any decisive statement about the mechanism of high temperature superconductivity. However, a number of arguments have been put forward to explain high $T_c$ superconductors. For example, it has been realised that the role of oxygen is essential for high $T_c$ oxide superconductors.

The high temperature superconductors discovered so far belong to five chemical systems having the following general formulae.

1. $BaPb_{1-x}Bi_xO_3$
2. $La_{2-x}M_xCuO_{4-x}(M = Ba, Sr)$
3. $Ba_2MCu_3O_{7-x}(M = Y \text{ or rare earth metals such as Gd, Eu, etc.})$
4. $Ba_{2-x}La_{1+x}Cu_3O_\delta$
5. $Bi_2CaSr_2Cu_2O_\delta$

**Table 17.2  High $T_c$ Superconductors**

| Compounds | $T_c(K)$ | Year of discovery |
|-----------|----------|-------------------|
| $SrTiO_{3-x}$ | ~1 | 1964 |
| $AxWO_3$ | 6 | 1965 |
| $LiTi_2O_4$ | 13 | 1974 |
| $Ba(Pb, Bi)O_3$ | 13 | 1975 |
| $(La, Sr)_2 CuO_4$ | 37 | 1986 |
| $YBa_2 Cu_3O_{7-x}$ | 95 | 1987 |
| $NdBa_2 Cu_3O_{7-x}$ | 80 | |
| $SmBa_2 Cu_3O_{7-x}$ | 90 | |
| $EaBa_2 Cu_3O_{7-x}$ | 98 | |
| $GdBa_2 Cu_3O_{7-x}$ | 92 | |
| $DyBa_2 Cu_3O_{7-x}$ | 95 | |
| $HoBa_2 Cu_3O_{7-x}$ | 96 | |
| $YbBa_2 Cu_3O_{7-x}$ | 93 | |
| $LuBa_2 Cu_3O_{7-x}$ | 45 | |

## 17.15  SUMMARY

1. Certain metals and alloys exhibit almost zero electrical resistivity (i.e. infinite conductivity) when they are cooled to sufficiently low temperatures. This phenomenon is known as superconductivity. The critical temperature is different for different substances.
2. The magnetic field and the superconductivity are found to be mutually exclusive. Below $T_c$, a superconducting specimen (in bulk) expels magnetic flux completely and acts as an ideal diamagnet (i.e. $B = 0$). This is the Meissner effect.
3. The critical field ($H_c$) is a function of temperature and is given as

$$H_c(T) = H_c(0)\left[1 - \left(\frac{T}{T_c}\right)^2\right]$$

where $H_c(0)$ is the maximum value of the field at $T = 0$ K and $H_c(T_c) = 0$ at $T = T_c$.

4. There are two types of superconductors, Type-I and Type-II. Superconductors exhibiting a complete Meissner effect are called Type I superconductors (formerly known as soft superconductors). Superconducting state is destroyed at a critical field $H_c$ and above. On the other hand, a type-II superconductor has two critical fields, $H_{c1}$ and $H_{c2}$.

5. Transition between the normal and superconducting states is thermodynamically reversible. The entropy difference between the two states is given by

$$S_N - S_S = -H_c \frac{dH_c}{dT}$$

$S_N - S_S$ is +ve because $\dfrac{dH_c}{dT}$ is −ve

$\Rightarrow$ Superconducting state is more ordered.

The latent heat of the system is related to the entropy difference as

$$Q = T(S_N - S_S) = -TH_c \frac{dH_c}{dT}$$

The difference in the specific heats of the two states is given as

$$C_N - C_S = -T_c \left( \frac{dH_c}{dT} \right)^2 \text{ is −ve} \Rightarrow C_N < C_S \text{ (near } T_c)$$

The electronic specific heat of a superconductor is given by

$$(C_{el})_S = ae^{-\Delta/kT}$$

where $a$ is constant and $\Delta$ is the energy gap $\cong kT_c$.

6. In order to explain the Meissner effect and field penetration in superconductors, based on two fluid model London brothers introduced two additional equations (in addition to the four Maxwell's equations). They are:

$$\frac{dJ_c}{dt} = \frac{n_s e^2}{m} E \quad \text{and} \quad \nabla \times J_S = -\frac{n_s e^2}{m} B$$

According to the London equations, the flux does not drop to zero abruptly at the surface of a Type-I superconductor but decreases exponentially. The penetration depth is found to vary with temperature according to the equation

$$\lambda(T) = \lambda(0) \left( 1 - \frac{T^4}{T_c^4} \right)$$

and consequently

$$n_s = n_0 \left( 1 - \frac{T^4}{T_c^4} \right)$$

7. According to the BCS theory, superelectrons exist as Cooper pairs. They form a bound

state and their motions are highly correlated. The binding is strongest when the electrons forming a pair have opposite momenta and opposite spins, i.e. $k\uparrow$ and $-k\downarrow$. Such pairs form through electron-electron interaction via lattice deformation (phonons).

8. When a thin insulating layer (normally an oxide layer) is sandwiched between a metal and a superconductor or two superconductors, electrons can tunnel through the junction. The current-voltage characteristics of the junction help in determining the energy gap of a superconductor.

For a thin insulating layer, Cooper electrons can tunnel even at zero potential difference, leading to the Josephson effect. A static voltage across the junction produces an alternating current of frequency

$$\omega = \frac{2eV_0}{\hbar}$$

9. The high temperature superconducting materials discovered in the last couple of years belong to five chemical systems.

## 17.16   DEFINITIONS

*Critical current density* ($J_c$): The current density above which superconductivity disappears.
*Critical field* ($H_c$): The magnetic field above which superconductivity disappears.
*Critical temperature* ($T_c$): The temperature above which a superconductor regains its normal electrical resistance.
*Fluxoid*: A microscopic normal region surrounded by circulating supercurrents in a Type-II superconductor at fields between $H_{c1}$ and $H_{c2}$.
*Hard Superconductor*: A substance characterized by irreversible magnetization and a high value of $J_c$, whether Type-I or Type-II.
*Mixed State*: The fine sub-division of normal and superconducting phases in a Type-II superconductor that arises between $H_{c1}$ and $H_{c2}$; the fluxoid configuration.
*Meissner effect*: The complete expulsion of magnetic flux ($B = 0$) inside a bulk superconductor.
*Normal state*: A superconducting solid in the normal state exhibits measurable electrical resistance.
*Penetration depth* ($\lambda$): The effective depth to which the magnetic field penetrates a superconductor.
*Self Superconductor*: A substance which exhibits reversible ideal magnetization and low $J_c$, whether Type-I or Type-II.
*Superconducting State*: A solid in the superconducting state exhibits zero electrical resistance.
*Type-I superconductor*: It is the substance which exhibits complete flux explusion, due to a positive surface energy between the normal and superconducting phases.
*Type-II superconductor*: It is the substance which exhibits partial penetration of flux, due to a negative surface energy between the normal and superconducting phases.

## REVIEW QUESTIONS AND PROBLEMS

1. Give an account of the experimental results which distinguish the superconducting state from the normal state of a metal.
2. Enumerate the properties of type I and type II superconductors. Derive London equations and discuss how do they help in explaining the superconducting state.
3. What is Meissner effect? Obtain an expression for the London penetration depth of magnetic field for a superconductor.
4. Discuss London's phenomenological theory of superconductors. What is London penetration depth? What are Cooper pairs? Derive an expression for energy gap in a superconductor at absolute zero temperature.

5. Explain the formation of Cooper pair in a superconductor. Obtain an expression for the energy gap in a superconductor at absolute zero temperature.

6. Using BCS theory obtain an expression for the magnitude of coherence length in superconductors and explain the physical significance of this length.

7. Give an elementary treatment of BCS theory of superconductivity. How does it explain the energy gap at 0 K and the isotope effect.

8. Calculate the critical current which can flow through a long thin superconducting wire of aluminium of diameter $10^{-3}$ m. The critical field for aluminium is $7.9 \times 10^3$ A/m.

   *Ans.* 24.81 Å

9. A superconducting lead has a critical temperature of 7.26 K at zero magnetic field and a critical field of $8 \times 10^5$ A/m at 0 K. Find the critical field at 5 K. *Ans.* $4.2 \times 10^5$ A/m.

10. The critical temperature for mercury with isotopic mass 199.5 is 4.185 K. Calculate its critical temperature when its isotopic mass changes to 203.4. *Ans.* 4.139 K.

11. The penetration depths for lead are 396 Å and 1730 Å at 3 K and 7.1 K, respectively. Calculate the critical temperature for lead. *Ans.* 7.193 K.

# Chapter 18

# Anisotropic Properties of Materials

## 18.1 INTRODUCTION

The last few chapters of the book deal with the various physical properties of crystalline solids. Some properties, such as density, entropy, enthalpy etc. called scalars are found to be independent of crystallographic directions. On the other hand, there are many other properties, such as thermal and electrical conductivity, dielectric and magnetic susceptibility, peizoelectric effect, refractive indices etc; essentially depend on the direction along which they are measured.

Thus, if the property of a substance does not depend on the direction, or in other words, if the description of a given property is independent of any orientation of the frame of reference, then the substance is said to be isotropic with respect to that property. Accordingly, gases, liquids and polycrystalline solids are isotropic with respect to some properties only. On the other hand, if the properties are direction dependent, their description depends on the orientation of the frame of reference and the substance is said to be anisotropic. All crystals are anisotropic with respect to at least some of their properties. Anisotropy is also exhibited by liquid crystals, natural and synthetic polymers. The extent of this anisotropy depends partly on the nature of the property itself and partly on the macroscopic symmetry of the crystals.

In this chapter, we shall study some of the physical properties defined by measurable physical quantities in terms of tensor of an appropriate type and rank.

## 18.2 CLASSIFICATION OF PHYSICAL PROPERTIES

Based on the nature of relationships between the physical quantities, physical properties can be broadly classified as of the following types:

(i) Equilibrium
(ii) Steady state
(iii) Hysteretic
(iv) Irreversible

Equilibrium, steady state and hysteretic properties relate intensive and extensive parameters such as stress and strain, or entropy and temperature. Under the influence, the intensive parameters produce some sort of response in the materials which are then measured as extensive parameters. For examples, stress produces strain, magnetic field causes magnetization, electric field results in the flow of current.

Equilibrium properties are derived from reversible incremental changes in a material which is in thermal equilibrium with its surroundings. A mechanical stress is applied in incremental steps, allowing the body to establish equilibrium at each stage and the corresponding strain is measured. Decreasing the stress retraces the curve (Fig. 18.1a), showing reversibility. The elastic coefficients relating stress and strain constitute an equilibrium property of the material. Such properties can be formulated as tensors and matrices, and are subject to certain thermodynamic symmetry restrictions.

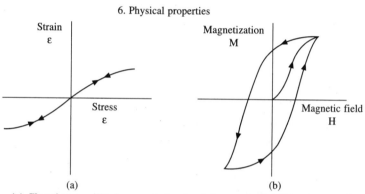

Fig. 18.1 (a) Showing equilibrium and steady state properties (b) a hysteretic property

Steady state properties can also be written as tensors but the thermodynamic relations are more complex. Most transport properties are measured under steady state conditions. The steady state property relating the potential gradient (electric field) to the flow of charge (electric current) is electric resistivity. The parameters such as gradients, flow, etc. differentiate the steady state properties from the equilibrium one. The system is not changing with time but it is not in equilibrium with its surroundings.

Systems exhibiting hysteresis make it impossible to define a unique functional relationship between the intensive and extensive parameters. Consider the relationship between magnetization $M$ and the magnetic field $H$ in a ferromagnetic material. Beginning from the demagnetized state and slowly increasing the field, initial magnetization curve is obtained (Fig. 18.1b). On reaching to a saturation value, the field is slowly reversed but the curve does not retrace itself. Rather it follows a different path leading to remanent magnetization at zero field. A further reversal of the field will produce a hysteresis loop. Such behavior is caused by the presence of metastable domains. Ferroelectric and ferroelastic crystals show similar hysteresis loops.

Irreversible properties are defined in terms of a specific test which generally leaves the specimen in a permanently altered condition. The tests are qualitative in nature. They provide a scale of numbers to rank various materials in regards to the property for which the measurement has been made. For example, MOH's hardness scale is a scratch test which assigns a hardness number from zero to ten. Irreversible properties can be correlated with the crystal symmetry although there are no precise definitions.

## 18.3 DESCRIPTION OF PHYSICAL PROPERTIES

The physical properties of a crystal describe its response to externally applied influence such as force or field. In many cases, the response is directly proportional to the external influence and is defined by a general relation of the type

$$\text{Response} = \text{coefficient} \times \text{External influence} \qquad (1)$$

where the term coefficient represents the measure of the physical properties such as elastic moduli, thermal expansion, etc.

Based on the scalar or directional character of the external influence and response, there can be various different possibilities. In the simplest case, the external influence and the response both are taken as scalars. For example, external influence as temperature and response as heat so that from eq. 1 the coefficient turns out to be specific heat, which is also a scalar. Similarly, the external influence and the response both may be vectors or in general, tensors.

It is to be noted that:

(i) A scalar is a tensor of zero rank. It is specified by a single component without reference to any axial system.

(ii) A vector is a tensor of rank one. It is specified by three components each of which is related to one axis of reference.

(iii) A tensor of rank two is specified by nine components each of which is related to two axes of reference.

(iv) Similarly, in general a tensor of rank $n$ is specified by $3^n$ components each of which is related to $n$ axes of reference.

Further, if the influence and response are tensors of rank $m$ and $n$ respectively then the physical property must be a tensor of rank $(m + n)$. A list of some common physical properties followed by the associated tensor, rank and symbol are provided in Table 18.1.

**Table 18.1   Representation of Physical Properties as Tensors**

| Physical Properties | Associated Tensor | Rank | Transformation equation New = $f$(old) |
|---|---|---|---|
| Density | Scalar | 0 | $\rho' = \rho$ |
| Temperature | Scalar | 0 | |
| Electric field | Vector | 1 | |
| Electric current density | Vector | 1 | $E_i' = a_{ij}E_i$ |
| Electric moment | Vector | 1 | |
| Electric Susceptibility | tensor | 2 | |
| Stress | tensor | 2 | $\chi_{ij}' = a_{ip}a_{jq}\chi_{pq}$ |
| Strain | tensor | 2 | |
| Piezoelectricity | tensor | 3 | |
| Hall effect | tensor | 3 | $T_{ijk}' = a_{ip}a_{jq}a_{kr}T_{pqr}$ |
| Elasticity | tensor | 4 | $T_{ijkl}' = a_{ip}a_{jq}a_{kr}a_{ls}T_{pqrs}$ |

Equilibrium and steady state properties of materials can be represented in tensor notation. Tensors are defined in terms of transformations from one orthogonal axes to another. A zero rank tensor such as temperature, density, etc. is unchanged by the transformation from old to new axes that is

$$\rho'(x_1', x_2', x_3') = \rho(x_1, x_2, x_3) \tag{2}$$

Accordingly, the number of coefficients for a zero-rank tensor is ($3^0 = 1$) only one.

The transformation equation for tensors of rank one is the same as that for the coordinates i.e. $x_i' = a_{ij}x_j$. Electric field, force and other vector quantities are the examples of first rank tensors. The number of coefficients are ($3^1 = 3$) three. The components of electric field transform according to the relation.

$$E_i' = a_{ij}E_j \tag{3}$$

where summation is automatically understood for repeated subscripts. The transformation equation for a second rank tensor is the same as that for the product of two coordinates i.e. $x_{ij}' = a_{ik}a_{jl}x_{kl}$. Electric susceptibility is an example of a second rank tensor, the number of coefficients in this case are ($3^2 = 9$) nine. The components of electric susceptibility transform according to the relation

$$\chi_{ij}' = a_{ip}a_{jq}\chi_{pq} \tag{4}$$

Thus in general, a tensor of rank $n$ has $n$ subscripts and transform as the product of $n$ coordinates.

Tensors in general may be polar or axial. The transformation law for a polar tensor is unaffected by handedness. It remains unchanged whether the old or new axes are both of the same handedness or not. Strictly speaking a polar tensor transforms like a product of coordinates under either proper rotations or rotoinversions. Electric polarization is an example of the first rank polar tensor. On the other hand, in an axial tensor, the sign of the transformation law changes for the change of handedness. That is an axial tensor transforms like a product of coordinates under proper rotations, but like ($-1$) times the product of coordinates under roto inversions. Magnetic field is an example of the first rank axial tensor.

## 18.4 INTRINSIC SYMMETRY OF PHYSICAL PROPERTIES

There are certain physical properties which possess inherent symmetry elements. The existence of such symmetry is generally manifested as the symmetry of the tensor representing them.

For example, tensile stresses possess cylindrical symmetry $\left(\dfrac{\infty}{m} m\right)$ while shear stresses have orthorhombic symmetry (*mmm*). However, both of them are centrosymmetric. Electric field can be represented by a vector with polar cylinderical symmetry, $\infty m$. Magnetic fields have an axial cylinderical symmetry, $\dfrac{\infty}{m} m'$. Temperature is a scalar quantity with spherical symmetry $\dfrac{\infty}{m}\infty$. Likewise, there may be a number of other physical quantities having their inherent symmetry elements.

The considerations that are responsible for the existence of an intrinsic symmetry of physical properties are mainly thermodynamical in nature. For equilibrium properties which are described with respect to a thermodynamically reversible system, the intrinsic symmetry is determined in terms of thermodynamic potentials. Similarly, for steady state systems, the intrinsic symmetry of the transport properties is a result of Onsager's principle.

## 18.5 TRANSFORMATION LAW FOR SECOND RANK TENSOR

In general, physical properties can be represented as tensors of different rank. In turn, a tensor is defined in terms of transformations from one orthogonal axial system to another. To understand the problem, let us first specify the transformation of axes and then examine how the values of the tensor components $T_{ij}$ transform when the axes are transformed.

For the purpose, let us suppose that $x_1, x_2, x_3$ be the old axes and $x_1', x_2', x_3'$ be the new axes mutually perpendicular to one another with the same origin as shown in Fig. 18.2. The angular relations between the axes are:

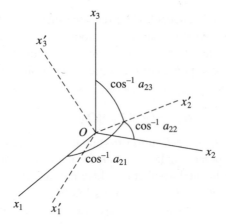

**Fig. 18.2　Transformation of axes**

Old

|  Axes | $x_1$ | $x_2$ | $x_3$ |
|---|---|---|---|
| $x_1'$ | $a_{11}$ | $a_{12}$ | $a_{13}$ |
| $x_2'$ | $a_{21}$ | $a_{22}$ | $a_{23}$ |
| $x_3'$ | $a_{31}$ | $a_{32}$ | $a_{33}$ |

New (5)

Eq. 5 can be written in the matrix form as

$$\begin{pmatrix} x_1' \\ x_2' \\ x_3' \end{pmatrix} = \begin{pmatrix} a_{11} & a_{12} & a_{13} \\ a_{21} & a_{22} & a_{23} \\ a_{31} & a_{32} & a_{33} \end{pmatrix} \begin{pmatrix} x_1 \\ x_2 \\ x_3 \end{pmatrix} \tag{6}$$

This can further be written in short as

$$x_i' = a_{ij} x_j \tag{7}$$

where
$$a_{ij} = \begin{pmatrix} a_{11} & a_{12} & a_{13} \\ a_{21} & a_{22} & a_{23} \\ a_{31} & a_{32} & a_{33} \end{pmatrix} \qquad (8)$$

Such a matrix is generally known as transformation matrix whose elements $a_{ij}$ are referred to as the direction cosines between the new and old axes. The first suffix in the symbol $a_{ij}$ refers to the new axes, and the second to the old ones. In a right handed coordinate system, the angle of rotation is assumed positive if the rotation from the old axis to the new axis, observed from the positive end of the axis (of rotation) towards the origin, occurs in the counterclockwise direction. Thus, for example, the direction cosines of $x_2'$ with respect to $x_1, x_2, x_3$ are $a_{21}, a_{22}, a_{23}$, respectively.

According to the Einstein summation convention, the suffix $i$ in eq. 7 is called a free suffix (since it can take any numerical value), while the suffix $j$ is called the dummy suffix because any suffix except $i$ could be used without changing the meaning of the equation. For example, one can write

$$x_i' = a_{ij}x_j = a_{ik}x_k = a_{il}x_l, \text{ etc.} \qquad (9)$$

Now, let us consider a physical property representing a second rank tensor $T$, which relates two mutually orthogonal vectors $p = (p_1, p_2, p_3)$ and $q = (q_1, q_2, q_3)$ in such a way that

$$p_1 = T_{11}q_1 + T_{12}q_2 + T_{13}q_3$$
$$p_2 = T_{21}q_1 + T_{22}q_2 + T_{23}q_3$$
$$p_3 = T_{31}q_1 + T_{32}q_2 + T_{33}q_3 \qquad (10)$$

then $T_{11}, T_{12} \ldots T_{33}$ are referred to as the components of the second rank tensor. In matrix notation, the components are

$$T_{ij} = \begin{bmatrix} T_{11} & T_{12} & T_{13} \\ T_{21} & T_{22} & T_{23} \\ T_{31} & T_{32} & T_{33} \end{bmatrix} \qquad (11)$$

Eq. 10 can also be written as

$$p_i = T_{ij}q_j \quad (i, j = 1, 2, 3) \qquad (12)$$

In eq. 12, the components $T_{ij}$ determine how the three components $p_i$ vary with the variation of the components $q_i$ in general in a crystal. However, in an isotropic body, the corresponding equation becomes

$$p_i = Tq_j \qquad (13)$$

where $T$ is a single constant.

Now suppose we have a certain vector $p$ whose components with respect to the axes $x_1, x_2, x_3$ are $p_1, p_2, p_3$ as shown in Fig. 18.3. Similarly, let the components with respect to the axes $x_1', x_2', x_3'$ are $p_1', p_2', p_3'$, then from eq. 5 we obtain

$$p_1' = a_{11}p_1 + a_{12}p_2 + a_{13}p_3$$

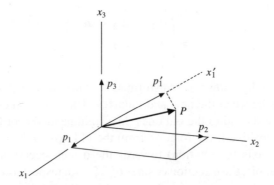

**Fig. 18.3   Transformation of the components of a vector**

$$p'_2 = a_{21}p_1 + a_{22}p_2 + a_{23}p_3$$

$$p'_3 = a_{31}p_1 + a_{32}p_2 + a_{33}p_3 \qquad (14)$$

In short, this can be written as

$$p'_i = a_{ij}p_j \qquad (15)$$

Making use of eq. 5 a reverse transformation will provide us

$$p_i = a_{ji}\, p'_j \qquad (16)$$

Similarly, the reverse transformation for the vector $q$ will give us

$$q_i = a_{ji}\, q'_j \qquad (17)$$

In eqs. 16 and 17, we find that the vectors $p$ and $q$ have the components $p'_i$ and $q'_i$. Now let us find out a relationship between these new components. To do this, let us use the following series of equations

$$p' \xrightarrow{(15)} p \xrightarrow{(12)} q \xrightarrow{(17)} q'$$

where the arrow ($\rightarrow$) stands for 'in terms of '. The respective equation number is also written on top of the arrows. Making suitable changes in the free and dummy suffixes, the equations 15, 12 and 17 can be rewritten as

$$p'_i = a_{ik}p_k \text{———}(15)'$$

$$p_k = T_{kl}q_l \text{———}(12)'$$

and

$$q_l = a_{il}\, q'_j \text{———}(17)'$$

Combining these equations, we obtain

$$p'_i = a_{ik}p_k$$

$$= a_{ik}T_{kl}q_l$$

$$= a_{ik}T_{kl}a_{jl}q'_j$$

$$= T'_{ij}q'_j \tag{18}$$

where
$$T'_{ij} = a_{ik}a_{jl}T_{kl} \tag{19}$$

This is the required transformation law for second rank tensors. In eq. 19, we observe that $i$ and $j$ are free suffixes, while $k$ and $l$ are dummy suffixes. Let us write eq. 19 in expanded form which can be helpful in understanding the higher rank tensors. Let us expand this in two stages, first for one (dammy) suffix and then for the second (the order is immaterial). Thus expanding first for $l(= 1, 2, 3)$, we have

$$T'_{ij} = a_{ik}a_{j1}T_{k1} + a_{ik}a_{j2}T_{k2} + a_{ik}a_{j3}T_{k3}$$

Similarly, expension for $k(= 1, 2, 3)$, is

$$T'_{ij} = a_{i1}a_{j1}T_{11} + a_{i1}a_{j2}T_{12} + a_{i1}a_{j3}T_{13}$$
$$+ a_{i2}a_{j1}T_{21} + a_{i2}a_{j2}T_{22} + a_{i2}a_{j3}T_{23}$$
$$+ a_{i3}a_{ji}T_{31} + a_{i3}a_{j2}T_{32} + a_{i3}a_{j3}T_{33} \tag{20}$$

## 18.6  EFFECT OF CRYSTAL SYMMETRY ON PHYSICAL PROPERTIES

The classical method of studying the effect of crystal symmetry on physical properties is that the symmetry elements constituting the point group of the crystal are successively applied on the tensor representing the property and each time it is demanded that the tensor should remain invariant. The effect of the crystal symmetry makes many of the tensor components either equal to one another or to zero and hence the number of independent components decreases drastically. Before we discuss the effect of crystal symmetry on physical properties as tensors of various ranks, it is important to note that all tensors with which we will be dealing are inherently centrosymmetric. That is for a second rank tensor

$$T_{ij} = T_{ji} \tag{21}$$

consequently, the independent components of the tensor (eq. 11) reduces from nine to six. They are represented in the following manner

$$T'_{ij} = \begin{bmatrix} T_{11} & T_{12} & T_{13} \\ T_{12} & T_{22} & T_{23} \\ T_{13} & T_{23} & T_{23} \end{bmatrix} \tag{22}$$

In the following, we shall discuss the effect of crystal symmetry on the property tensor in eq. 22 for all crystal systems and crystal classes with increasing symmetry.

### 1.  Triclinic Crystal System
Crystal Classes: 1, $\bar{1}$

This crystal system has effectively no symmetry. It has the point group 1 (which is completely unsymmetrical) and $\bar{1}$ (the centre of symmetry already possessed by the property tensor), which are unable to put any restriction on the symmetry of the property tensor. Thus the property tensor will remain the same as in eq. 22.

## 2. Monoclinic Crystal System

Crystal Classes: 2, $m$, $\dfrac{2}{m}$

A monoclinic crystal system is characterized by the presence of a 2-fold symmetry parallel to $OX_2$ axis. The transformation matrix $a_{ij}$ for this symmetry operation is given by

$$2[010] = \begin{pmatrix} -1 & 0 & 0 \\ 0 & 1 & 0 \\ 0 & 0 & -1 \end{pmatrix} \tag{23}$$

Making use of eqs. 19 and 23 we can write the six components of the transformed tensor as

(i) $T'_{11} = a_{11}a_{11}T_{11}$ (all other products containing $a_{1k}a_{1\ell} = 0$)
$= T_{11}$

(ii) $T'_{12} = a_{11}a_{22}T_{12}$ (all other products containing $a_{1k}a_{2\ell} = 0$)
$= -T_{12}$

(iii) $T'_{13} = a_{11}a_{33}T_{13}$ (all other products containing $a_{1k}a_{3\ell} = 0$)
$= T_{13}$

(iv) $T'_{22} = a_{22}a_{22}T_{22}$ (all other products containing $(a_{2k}a_{2\ell} = 0$)
$= T_{22}$

(v) $T'_{23} = a_{22}a_{33}T_{23}$ (all other products containing $a_{2k}a_{3\ell} = 0$)
$= -T_{23}$

(vi) $T'_{33} = a_{33}a_{33}T_{33}$ (all other products containing $a_{3k}a_{3\ell} = 0$)
$= T_{33}$

Inspection of the transformed tensor components reveals that all remain unchanged except (ii) and (v) which change sign. According to Neumann's principle this is possible only if both $T'_{12} = T_{12} = 0$ and $T'_{23} = T_{23} = 0$. The property tensor for monoclinic system therefore reduces to the form

$$T'_{ij} = \begin{bmatrix} T_{11} & 0 & T_{13} \\ 0 & T_{22} & 0 \\ T_{13} & 0 & T_{33} \end{bmatrix} \tag{24}$$

where the number of independent components reduces from six to four.

A similar result (eq. 24) is obtained corresponding to the crystal classes—$m$ and $\dfrac{2}{m}$.

## 3. Orthorhombic Crystal System

Crystal Classes: 222, mm2, mmm

The characteristic symmetry of an orthorhombic crystal system is three mutually perpendicular

2-fold axes or mirror planes. We have already considered 2[010] in monoclinic system and derived eq. 24. However, applying further the symmetry element 2[100] or 2[001] in eq. 24, we obtain,

(i) $T'_{11} = a_{11}a_{11}T_{11} = T_{11}$

(ii) $T'_{13} = a_{11}a_{33}T_{13} = -T_{13}$

(iii) $T'_{22} = a_{22}a_{22}T_{22} = T_{22}$

(iv) $T'_{33} = a_{33}a_{33}T_{33} = T_{33}$

In (ii) we observe a change of sign, implying that $T'_{13} = T_{13} = 0$, from Neumann's Principle. This further reduces the number of independent components of the property tensor from four to three. They are represented as

$$T'_{ij} = \begin{bmatrix} T_{11} & 0 & 0 \\ 0 & T_{22} & 0 \\ 0 & 0 & T_{33} \end{bmatrix} \tag{25}$$

A similar result is obtained corresponding to the crystal classes—mm2 and mmm.

## 4. Tetragonal, Trigonal and Hexagonal Crystal System

Crystal Class: 3, $\bar{3}$, 32, 3m, $\bar{3}$m; 4, $\bar{4}$, 4/m, 42, 4mm, 4/mmm, $\bar{4}$2m; 6, $\bar{6}$, 6/m, 62, 6mm, 6/mmm, $\bar{6}$2m.

We know that tetragonal, trigonal, and hexagonal crystal systems are characterized by a single 4-, 3- or 6-fold axis, respectively. In all the three cases, one crystallographic axis (usually the $x_3$-axis) is taken parallel to the unique axis (except for the primitive rhombohedral), other two axes are perpendicular to it and equal to each other. Therefore, for these crystal systems, the components of the property tensor

$$T_{11} = T_{22}$$

For example, Let us consider the tetragonal case. This is characterized by the presence of a 4-fold symmetry parallel to $OX_3$ axis. The corresponding transformation matrix $a_{ij}$ is given as

$$4[001] = \begin{pmatrix} 0 & 1 & 0 \\ -1 & 0 & 0 \\ 0 & 0 & 1 \end{pmatrix} \tag{26}$$

Making use of eqs. 19 and 26, we can write the six components of the transformed tensor as

(i) $T'_{11} = a_{12}a_{12}T_{22}$ (all other products containing $a_{1k}a_{1\ell} = 0$)

$\quad = T_{22}$

(ii) $T'_{12} = a_{12}a_{21}T_{21}$ (all other products containing $a_{1k}a_{2\ell} = 0$)

$\quad = -T_{21}$

(iii) $T'_{13} = a_{12}a_{33}T_{23}$ (all other products containing $a_{1k}a_{3\ell} = 0$)

$\quad = T_{23}$

(iv) $T'_{22} = a_{21}a_{21}T_{11}$ (all other products containing $a_{2k}a_{2\ell} = 0$)

$\quad = T_{11}$

(v) $T'_{23} = a_{21}a_{33}T_{13}$ (all other products containing $a_{2k}a_{3\ell} = 0$)

$\qquad = -T_{13}$

(vi) $T'_{33} = a_{33}a_{33}T_{33}$ (all other products containing $a_{3k}a_{3\ell} = 0$)

$\qquad = T_{33}$

Inspection of the transformed tensor components reveals that $T_{11} = T_{22}$, $T'_{12} = T_{21} = 0$ and $T'_{13}$ $= T_{23} = T'_{23} = T_{13} = 0$.

The property tensor for tetragonal system therefore reduces to

$$T'_{ij} = \begin{bmatrix} T_{11} & 0 & 0 \\ 0 & T_{11} & 0 \\ 0 & 0 & T_{33} \end{bmatrix} \qquad (27)$$

Similarly, it can be shown that other crystal classes of tetragonal and the crystal classes of trigonal and hexagonal will give rise to the same (eq. 27) property tensor. This way there are only two independent coefficients corresponding to these crystal systems.

**5. Cubic Crystal System**

Crystal classes: 23, *m*3, 43, $\overline{4}$3*m*, *m*/3*m*

Cubic crystal system is the most symmetric out of all crystal systems. In this case,

$$T'_{ij} = \text{constant} \quad \text{when } i = j$$

$$= 0 \qquad\qquad \text{when } i \neq j$$

Thus, in cubic crystals, the symmetry requires that the physical properties of materials shall be the same along all the three crystallographic axes. That is, $T_{11} = T_{22} = T_{33}$. The only component of the property tensor for cubic system is

$$T'_{ij} = \begin{bmatrix} T_{11} & 0 & 0 \\ 0 & T_{11} & 0 \\ 0 & 0 & T_{11} \end{bmatrix} \qquad (28)$$

The number of independent components of the property tensor corresponding to various crystal systems are provided in Table 18.2.

## 18.7 PHYSICAL PROPERTIES OF ZERO AND FIRST RANK TENSORS

As pointed out in section 18.3 that the scalar peroperties (a tensor of rank zero) such as temperature, density, specific heat etc. are specified at a point by a single component. They are independent of any coordinate system and also of crystal symmetry. They are said to be invariant under transformation of coordinate system (eq. 2).

There are other physical quantities which can not be specified by a single number like the scalars. They may require 3, 9, 27 numbers and so on. The vector properties (a tensor of rank one) such as velocity, electric moment, force etc. are specified by three components each of

Table 18.2    Effect of crystal Symmetry on Property Tensors

| Crystal System | Crystal class | Rank of Property Tensor | | | |
|---|---|---|---|---|---|
| | | One | Two | Three | Four |
| Triclinic | 1 | 3 | 6 | 18 | 21 |
| | $\bar{1}$ | 0 | 6 | 0 | 21 |
| Monoclinic | 2 | 1 | 4 | 8 | 13 |
| | *m* | 2 | 4 | 10 | 13 |
| | 2/m | 0 | 4 | 0 | 13 |
| Orthorhombic | 222 | 0 | 3 | 3 | 9 |
| | mm2 | 1 | 3 | 5 | 9 |
| | mmm | 0 | 3 | 0 | 9 |
| Trigonal | 3 | 1 | 2 | 6 | 7 |
| | $\bar{3}$ | 0 | 2 | 0 | 7 |
| | 32 | 0 | 2 | 2 | 6 |
| | 3/m | 1 | 2 | 4 | 6 |
| | $\bar{3}/m$ | 0 | 2 | 0 | 6 |
| Tetragonal | 4 | 1 | 2 | 4 | 7 |
| | $\bar{4}$ | 0 | 2 | 4 | 7 |
| | 4/m | 0 | 2 | 0 | 7 |
| | 422 | 0 | 2 | 1 | 6 |
| | 4mm | 1 | 2 | 3 | 6 |
| | $\bar{4}2m$ | 0 | 2 | 2 | 6 |
| | 4/mmm | 0 | 2 | 0 | 6 |
| Hexagonal | 6 | 1 | 2 | 4 | 5 |
| | $\bar{6}$ | 0 | 2 | 2 | 5 |
| | 6/m | 0 | 2 | 0 | 5 |
| | 622 | 0 | 2 | 1 | 5 |
| | 6mm | 1 | 2 | 3 | 5 |
| | $\bar{6}2m$ | 0 | 2 | 1 | 5 |
| | 6/mmm | 0 | 2 | 0 | 5 |
| Cubic | 23 | 0 | 1 | 1 | 3 |
| | m3 | 0 | 1 | 0 | 3 |
| | 432 | 0 | 1 | 0 | 3 |
| | $\bar{4}3/m$ | 0 | 1 | 1 | 3 |
| | m3m | 0 | 1 | 0 | 3 |

which is related to one axis of reference. The pyroelectric effect is an example of this category where the three pyroelectric coefficients ($p_i$) relate the polarization components ($P_i$) to temperature change ($\Delta T$) according to the equation

$$P_i = p_i\,\Delta T \tag{29}$$

Equation 30 is a modified form of eq. 51 (chapter 10).

The pyroelectric effect in a crystal is thus specified by the pyroelectric vector $p$. According to Neumann's principle, $p$ must conform to the point group symmetry of the crystal, using a direct inspection method, it can be shown that the centrosymmetric crystals are non pyroelectric. As we know that a centre of symmetry transforms the reference axes $x_1 \rightarrow -x_1$, $x_2 \rightarrow -x_2$ and $x_3 \rightarrow -x_3$. Since the transformation equation for the first rank tensors is the same as that for the coordinates, the transformation of the pyroelectric components are $p_1 \rightarrow -p_1$, $p_2 \rightarrow -p_2$ and $p_3 \rightarrow -p_3$. However, according to Neumann's principle, $p_1 \rightarrow -p_1 = p_1$ etc. are possible only if $p_1 = p_2 = p_3 = 0$.

Now, let us examine the direction of the pyroelectric vector $p$ and the effect of crystal symmetry (non-centrosymmetric point groups) on its components as per the procedure described in sec. 18.6.

### 1.   Triclinic Crystal System
Crystal Class: 1
    As pointed out earlier that the crystal class 1 does not put any restriction on the direction of $p$. Thus the components are: $(p_1, p_2, p_3)$.

### 2.   Monoclinic Crystal System
Crystal Class: 2 (∥ to $OX_2$)
    In this case, the direction of polarization $p$ is parallel to diad axis. The only component is: $(0, p, 0)$.
Crystal Class: $m$ ($\perp$ to $OX_2$)
    In this case, $p$ takes any direction in the plane. The corresponding components are: $(p_1, 0, p_3)$.

### 3.   Orthorhombic Crystal System
    In this case, orthorhombic axes $x_1, x_2, x_3$ are respectively parallel to the crystallographic axes $x, y, z$.
Crystal Class: 222
    Considering the monoclinic case (crystal class: 2) here and taking into account the three mutually perpendicular axes, we have $p = 0$
Crystal Class: mm2
    Again from monoclinic case (point group, $m$) $p$ will be parallel to the diad axis only, while other components vanish. Thus, the only component is: $(0, 0, p)$.

### 4.   Trigonal, Tetragonal and Hexagonal Crystal System
    In these crystal systems, the orthogonal axis $x_3$ is parallel to z-crystallographic axis.
Crystal Class: 3, 3$m$, 4, 4$m$, 6, 6$m$
    Under these crystal classes, the polarization $p$ is parallel to the 3-, 4- and 6- fold axis, respectively. Thus the only component is: $(0, 0, p)$.
Crystal Class: 32, $\bar{6}$, $\bar{4}$, $\bar{4}2m$, 422, 622, $\bar{6}2m$
    Under these classes, the polarization $p = 0$, either due to inversion symmetry or mutually perpendicular even-fold symmetry.

## 5. Cubic Crystal System

In cubic crystal system, the non-centrosymmetric point groups 432, $\overline{4}3m$, 23, give rise to $p = 0$ because the crystallographic axes are symmetrical and equivalent.

Thus, from the above discussion, it can be said that the pyroelectricity is exhibited by the crystals having the following ten non-centrosymmetric point groups:

| 1 | 2 | 3 | 4 | 6 |
|---|---|---|---|---|
| m | mm2 | 3m | 4mm | 6mm |

*Example:* In a pyroelectric tourmaline crystal of class $3m$ the polarization $p$ varies according to the composition of the crystal and the temperature. The value of $p$ at room temperature is $4.0 \times 10^{-6}$ cm$^{-2}$ $(^\circ C)^{-1}$ in the rationalized m.k.s unit. Determine the value of the electric field which produces the same polarization when temperature changes through $1^\circ C$. The dielectric constant parallel to the triad axis is 7.1.

*Solution:* Given: $p = 4.0 \times 10^{-6}\ C\ m^{-2}(^\circ C)^{-1}$, direction of polarization-triad axis, $\in_3 = 7.1$
We know that the electric susceptibility is given by

$$\chi_3 = \in_3 - 1$$
$$= 7.1 - 1$$
$$= 6$$

Hence, the necessary electric field parallel to $x_3$ within the crystal is

$$E_3 = \frac{p}{\in_0 \chi_3} = \frac{4.0 \times 10^{-6}}{8.85 \times 10^{-12} \times 6.1}$$

$$= 7.4 \times 10^4 \text{ volt/m.}$$

## 18.8 PHYSICAL PROPERTIES OF SECOND RANK TENSOR

Physical properties of second rank tensor arise from a vector-vector combination. The electrical conductivity, resistivity, thermal conductivity, permeability, permittivity, electric susceptibility or polarizability etc. are some examples of the property tensors of second rank. Let us consider the case of electric polarizability, which relates the components of polarization and electric field according to the following equations

$$P_1 = \alpha_{11}E_1 + \alpha_{12}E_2 + \alpha_{13}E_3$$
$$P_2 = \alpha_{21}E_1 + \alpha_{22}E_2 + \alpha_{23}E_3$$
$$P_3 = \alpha_{31}E_1 + \alpha_{32}E_2 + \alpha_{33}E_3 \tag{30}$$

where the polarizability tensor $\alpha_{ij}$ is given by

$$\alpha_{ij} = \begin{bmatrix} \alpha_{11} & \alpha_{12} & \alpha_{13} \\ \alpha_{21} & \alpha_{22} & \alpha_{23} \\ \alpha_{31} & \alpha_{32} & \alpha_{33} \end{bmatrix} \tag{31}$$

This describes the dielectric behaviour of the crystal completely. However, we know that the property tensors of second rank are centrosymmetrical, the eq. 31 can be written as

$$\alpha_{ij} = \begin{bmatrix} \alpha_{11} & \alpha_{12} & \alpha_{13} \\ \alpha_{12} & \alpha_{22} & \alpha_{23} \\ \alpha_{13} & \alpha_{23} & \alpha_{33} \end{bmatrix} \tag{32}$$

Now applying crystal symmetry corresponding to all 32 crystal classes on property tensor $\alpha_{ij}$ (eq. 32), we can easily obtain the respective independent components following the procedure discussed in sec. 18.6.

### 1.   Triclinic Crystal System
Crystal Class: 1
    It has no effect on property tensor ($\alpha_{ij}$) and hence it remains as in eq. 32.

### 2.   Monoclinic Crystal System
Crystal Classes: 2, $m$, $\dfrac{2}{m}$
    Application of any of these symmetry elements has the same effect and reduces the number of independent components of the polarizability tensor from six to four. They are given by

$$\alpha'_{ij} = \begin{bmatrix} \alpha_{11} & 0 & \alpha_{13} \\ 0 & \alpha_{22} & 0 \\ \alpha_{13} & 0 & \alpha_{33} \end{bmatrix} \tag{33}$$

### 3.   Orthorhombic Crystal System
Crystal Classes: 222, mm2, mmm
    Like monoclinic case, they also have the same effect and the application of any one reduces the components from four to three they are given as

$$\alpha'_{ij} = \begin{bmatrix} \alpha_{11} & 0 & 0 \\ 0 & \alpha_{22} & 0 \\ 0 & 0 & \alpha_{33} \end{bmatrix} \tag{34}$$

### 4.   Trigonal, Tetragonal and Hexagonal Crystal System
Crystal Classes: 3, $\bar{3}$, 32, 3$m$, $\bar{3}m$; 4, $\bar{4}$, $\dfrac{4}{m}$, 42 4mm, 4/mmm, $\bar{4}2m$; 6, $\bar{6}$, 6/$m$, 62, 6mm, 6/mmm, $\bar{6}2m$
Symmetry element corresponding to the above crystal classes have the same effect and for these crystal systems the number of independent coefficients reduces to two only. They are given as

$$\alpha'_{ij} = \begin{bmatrix} \alpha_{11} & 0 & 0 \\ 0 & \alpha_{11} & 0 \\ 0 & 0 & \alpha_{22} \end{bmatrix} \tag{35}$$

### 5. Cubic Crystal System

Crystal Classes: 23, *m*3, 43, $\bar{4}3m$, *m*3*m*

Cubic crystal is the most symmetric of all crystal systems. In this case, symmetry requires that all the three diagonal tensor components are equal. That is

$$\alpha'_{ij} = \begin{bmatrix} \alpha_{11} & 0 & 0 \\ 0 & \alpha_{11} & 0 \\ 0 & 0 & \alpha_{11} \end{bmatrix} \tag{36}$$

*Example:* If the 2-fold axis in a monoclinic crystal is parallel to the z-axis, determine the scheme of second rank property tensor.

*Solution:* We know that the transformation matrix of 2-fold rotation parallel to z-axis is given by

$$2[001] = \begin{pmatrix} -1 & 0 & 0 \\ 0 & -1 & 0 \\ 0 & 0 & 1 \end{pmatrix}$$

Making use of this and the eq. 19, we can write the components of the transformed tensors as

(i) $T'_{11} = a_{11}a_{11}T_{11}$ (all other products containing $a_{1k}a_{1\ell} = 0$)
   $= T_{11}$

(ii) $T'_{12} = a_{11}a_{12}T_{12}$ (all other products containing $a_{1k}a_{2\ell} = 0$)
   $= T_{12}$

(iii) $T'_{13} = a_{11}a_{33}T_{13}$ (all other products containing $a_{1k}a_{3\ell} = 0$)
   $= -T_{13} \Rightarrow T'_{13} = T_{13} = 0$

(iv) $T'_{22} = a_{22}a_{22}T_{22}$ (all other products containing $a_{2k}a_{2\ell} = 0$)
   $= T_{22}$

(v) $T'_{23} = a_{22}a_{33}T_{23}$ (all other products containing $a_{2k}a_{3\ell} = 0$)
   $= -T_{23} \Rightarrow T'_{23} = T_{23} = 0$

(vi) $T'_{33} = a_{33}a_{33}T_{33}$ (all other products containing $a_{3k}a_{3\ell} = 0$)
   $= T_{33}$

Thus the property tensor becomes

$$T'_{ij} = \begin{bmatrix} T_{11} & T_{12} & 0 \\ T_{12} & T_{22} & 0 \\ 0 & 0 & T_{33} \end{bmatrix}$$

As pointed out earlier, according to Neumann's principle if the tensor component changes sign after transformation, it must be zero, others will be non zero. Accordingly, the tensor has only four independent components.

## 18.9  PHYSICAL PROPERTIES OF THIRD RANK TENSOR

As pointed out in section 18.3 that a third rank tensor is specified by $3^3 = 27$ components each of which is related to three axes of reference. The piezoelectric effect and the Hall effect are examples of this category, In the direct piezoelectric effect, the piezoelectric coefficients $(d_{ijk})$ relate the components of electric polarization $(P_i)$ to the stress tensor $(\tau_{jk})$ according to the relation

$$P_i = d_{ijk}\tau_{jk} = d_{il}\tau_l \tag{37}$$

Similarly, a converse piezoelectric effect will give us

$$\tau_{jk} = d_{ijk}E_i = d_{il}E_i \tag{38}$$

where $ijk$ take the values 1, 2, 3 and $l$ takes the values 1 to 6. In general, $d_{ijk} = d_{ikj}$ symmetrical in $j$, $k$. This reduces the number of independent components from 27 to 18. This also makes it easy to use a more concise form of the notation known as the matrix notation. The relationship between the tensor notation and the matrix notation are as follows:

| tensor notation | 11 | 22 | 33 | 23, 32 | 31, 13 | 12, 21 |
|---|---|---|---|---|---|---|
| matrix notation | 1 | 2 | 3 | 4 | 5 | 6 |

Making use of this conversion, the array of the piezoelectric coefficients $d_{il}$ can be written as

$$d_{il} = \begin{pmatrix} d_{11} & d_{12} & d_{13} & d_{14} & d_{15} & d_{16} \\ d_{21} & d_{22} & d_{23} & d_{24} & d_{25} & d_{26} \\ d_{31} & d_{32} & d_{33} & d_{34} & d_{35} & d_{36} \end{pmatrix} \tag{39}$$

It is clear that the matrix notation has the advantage over the tensor notation in representing the components with greater compactness and display them easily on a plane diagram. However, it is to be remembered that inspite of their representation with two suffixes, the $d_{il}$ do not transform like the components of a second rank tensor.

### Effect of Crystal Symmetry

Before we discuss the effect of crystal symmetry on piezoelectric coefficients, let us see the effect of inversion symmetry on it. As we know that inversion symmetry changes the sign of piezoelectric tensor. However, according to the Neumann's principle this is possible only if the piezoelectric tensor is zero. Since inversion symmetry is a property of the crystal, we conclude that a crystal with centre of symmetry cannot be piezoelectric. In other words, piezoelectric effect is possible only in non-centrosymmetric crystals.

We know that out of 32 crystal classes 11 are centrosymmetric and 21 are non-centrosymmetric. Let us see the effect of 21 crystal classes on piezoelectric property tensor with increasing symmetry following the procedure discussed in sec. 18.6. The symmetry transformation for the third rank property tensor is obtained as discussed in sec. 18.5. This is given by

$$d'_{ijk} = a_{il}a_{jm}a_{kn}d_{lmn} \tag{40}$$

## 1. Triclinic Crystal System

Crystal Class 1:

This does not put any restriction on the property tensor and thus the independent coefficients remain the same as in eq. 39.

## 2. Monoclinic Crystal System

(i) Crystal Class: 2, 2 ∥ $OX_2$ (standard orientation)

$$d'_{il} = \begin{pmatrix} 0 & 0 & 0 & d_{14} & 0 & d_{16} \\ d_{21} & d_{22} & d_{23} & 0 & d_{25} & 0 \\ 0 & 0 & 0 & d_{34} & 0 & d_{36} \end{pmatrix} \tag{41}$$

(ii) Crystal Class: $m$, $m \perp OX_2$ (standard orientation)

$$d'_{il} = \begin{pmatrix} d_{11} & d_{12} & d_{13} & 0 & d_{15} & 0 \\ 0 & 0 & 0 & d_{24} & 0 & d_{26} \\ d_{31} & d_{32} & d_{33} & 0 & d_{35} & 0 \end{pmatrix} \tag{42}$$

## 3. Orthorhombic Crystal System

(ii) Crystal class: mm2

$$d'_{il} = \begin{pmatrix} 0 & 0 & 0 & 0 & d_{15} & 0 \\ 0 & 0 & 0 & d_{24} & 0 & 0 \\ d_{31} & d_{32} & d_{33} & 0 & 0 & 0 \end{pmatrix} \tag{43}$$

(i) Crystal Class: 222

$$d'_{il} = \begin{pmatrix} 0 & 0 & 0 & 0 & d_{15} & 0 \\ 0 & 0 & 0 & d_{24} & 0 & 0 \\ d_{31} & d_{32} & d_{33} & 0 & 0 & 0 \end{pmatrix} \tag{44}$$

## 4. Tetragonal Crystal System

(i) Crystal Class: 4

$$d'_{il} = \begin{pmatrix} 0 & 0 & 0 & d_{14} & d_{15} & 0 \\ 0 & 0 & 0 & d_{15} & -d_{14} & 0 \\ d_{31} & d_{32} & d_{33} & 0 & 0 & 0 \end{pmatrix} \tag{45}$$

(ii) Crystal Class: $\bar{4}$

$$d'_{il} = \begin{pmatrix} 0 & 0 & 0 & d_{14} & d_{15} & 0 \\ 0 & 0 & 0 & -d_{15} & d_{14} & 0 \\ d_{31} & -d_{31} & 0 & 0 & 0 & d_{36} \end{pmatrix} \tag{46}$$

(iii) Crystal Class: 4mm

$$d_{il}' = \begin{pmatrix} 0 & 0 & 0 & 0 & d_{15} & 0 \\ 0 & 0 & 0 & d_{15} & 0 & 0 \\ d_{31} & d_{32} & d_{33} & 0 & 0 & 0 \end{pmatrix} \tag{47}$$

(iv) Crystal Class $\bar{4}2m$, $2 \parallel OX_1$ (standard orientation)

$$d_{il}' = \begin{pmatrix} 0 & 0 & 0 & d_{14} & 0 & 0 \\ 0 & 0 & 0 & 0 & d_{14} & 0 \\ 0 & 0 & 0 & 0 & 0 & d_{36} \end{pmatrix} \tag{48}$$

(v) Crystal Class: 422

$$d_{il}' = \begin{pmatrix} 0 & 0 & 0 & d_{14} & 0 & 0 \\ 0 & 0 & 0 & 0 & -d_{14} & 0 \\ 0 & 0 & 0 & 0 & 0 & 0 \end{pmatrix} \tag{49}$$

## 5. Trigonal Crystal System

(i) Crystal Class: $3m$, $m \perp OX_1$ (standard orientation)

$$d_{il}' = \begin{pmatrix} 0 & 0 & 0 & 0 & d_{15} & -2d_{22} \\ -d_{22} & d_{22} & 0 & d_{15} & 0 & 0 \\ d_{31} & d_{31} & d_{33} & 0 & 0 & 0 \end{pmatrix} \tag{50}$$

(ii) Crystal Class: 32

$$d_{il}' = \begin{pmatrix} d_{11} & -d_{11} & 0 & d_{14} & 0 & 0 \\ 0 & 0 & 0 & 0 & -d_{14} & -2d_{11} \\ 0 & 0 & 0 & 0 & 0 & 0 \end{pmatrix} \tag{51}$$

## 6. Hexagonal Crystal Systems

(i) Crystal Classes: 6, 6mm, 622—same as crystal classes 4, 4mm and 422.

(ii) Crystal Class: $\bar{6}$

$$d_{il}' = \begin{pmatrix} d_{11} & -d_{11} & 0 & 0 & 0 & -2d_{22} \\ -d_{22} & d_{22} & 0 & 0 & 0 & -2d_{11} \\ 0 & 0 & 0 & 0 & 0 & 0 \end{pmatrix} \tag{52}$$

(iii) Crystal Class: $\bar{6}2m$, $m \perp OX_1$ (standard orientation)

$$d'_{il} = \begin{pmatrix} 0 & 0 & 0 & 0 & 0 & -d_{22} \\ -d_{22} & d_{22} & 0 & 0 & 0 & 0 \\ 0 & 0 & 0 & 0 & 0 & 0 \end{pmatrix} \tag{53}$$

## 7. Cubic Crystal System

Crystal Classes: 23 and $\bar{4}3m$

$$d'_{il} = \begin{pmatrix} 0 & 0 & 0 & d_{14} & 0 & 0 \\ 0 & 0 & 0 & 0 & d_{14} & 0 \\ 0 & 0 & 0 & 0 & 0 & d_{14} \end{pmatrix} \tag{54}$$

*Example:* If the 2-fold axis in a monoclinic crystal is parallel to the z-axis, determine the scheme of piezoelectric moduli.

*Solution:* We know that the transformation matrix of 2-fold rotation parallel to z-axis is given by

$$2[001] = \begin{pmatrix} -1 & 0 & 0 \\ 0 & -1 & 0 \\ 0 & 0 & 1 \end{pmatrix}$$

Making use of this and eq. 41, we can write the components of the transformed tensor as

1. $d'_{11} = d'_{111} = a_{11}a_{11}a_{11}d_{111} = -d_{111} = -d_{11} = 0$
2. $d'_{12} = d'_{122} = a_{11}a_{22}a_{22}d_{122} = -d_{122} = -d_{12} = 0$
3. $d'_{13} = d'_{133} = a_{11}a_{33}a_{33}d_{133} = -d_{133} = -d_{13} = 0$
4. $d'_{14} = d'_{123} = a_{11}a_{22}a_{33}d_{123} = d_{123} = d_{14}$
5. $d'_{15} = d'_{113} = a_{11}a_{11}a_{33}d_{131} = d_{131} = d_{15}$
6. $d'_{16} = d'_{112} = a_{11}a_{11}a_{22}d_{112} = -d_{112} = -d_{16} = 0$
7. $d'_{21} = d'_{211} = a_{22}a_{11}a_{11}d_{211} = -d_{211} = -d_{21} = 0$
8. $d'_{22} = d'_{222} = a_{22}a_{22}a_{22}d_{222} = -d_{222} = -d_{22} = 0$
9. $d'_{23} = d'_{233} = a_{22}a_{33}a_{33}d_{233} = -d_{233} = -d_{23} = 0$
10. $d'_{24} = d'_{223} = a_{22}a_{22}a_{33}d_{223} = d_{223} = d_{24}$
11. $d'_{25} = d'_{213} = a_{22}a_{11}a_{33}d_{213} = d_{213} = d_{25}$
12. $d'_{26} = d'_{212} = a_{22}a_{11}a_{22}d_{212} = -d_{212} = -d_{26} = 0$
13. $d'_{31} = d'_{311} = a_{33}a_{11}a_{11}d_{311} = d_{311} = d_{31}$
14. $d'_{32} = d'_{322} = a_{33}a_{22}a_{22}d_{322} = d_{322} = d_{32}$
15. $d'_{33} = d'_{333} = a_{33}a_{33}a_{33}d_{333} = d_{333} = d_{33}$

16. $d'_{34} = d'_{323} = a_{33}a_{22}a_{33}d_{323} = -d_{323} = -d_{34} = 0$

17. $d'_{35} = d'_{331} = a_{33}a_{33}a_{11}d_{331} = -d_{331} = -d_{35} = 0$

18. $d'_{36} = d'_{321} = a_{33}a_{22}a_{11}d_{321} = d_{321} = d_{36}$

The components of the piezoelectric moduli in the matrix (two suffix) notion are given by

$$d'_{ij} = \begin{pmatrix} 0 & 0 & 0 & d_{14} & d_{15} & 0 \\ 0 & 0 & 0 & d_{24} & d_{25} & 0 \\ d_{31} & d_{32} & d_{33} & 0 & 0 & d_{36} \end{pmatrix}$$

## 18.10   PHYSICAL PROPERTIES OF FOURTH RANK TENSOR

We know that a fourth rank tensor is specified by $3^4 = 81$ components each of which is related to four axes of reference. Elastic stiffness constants (or the moduli of elasticity) or elastic compliance constants (or the compliances) are the example of this category. The moduli of elasticity ($C_{ijkl}$) relate the stress and strain components according to the Hooke's law

$$\tau_{ij} = C_{ijkl}\gamma_{kl} \tag{55}$$

where *ijkl* takes the values 1, 2, 3.
Similarly, we have the inverse relation as

$$\gamma_{ij} = S_{ijkl}\tau_{kl} \tag{56}$$

However, because of the symmetric nature of both stress and strain components, i.e. $\tau_{ij} = \tau_{ji}$ and $\gamma_{kl} = \gamma_{lk}$, the components of moduli of elasticity ($C_{ijkl}$) or elastic compliance ($S_{ijkl}$) reduce from 81 to 36 and could be represented in the matrix notation. Like earlier, the relationship between the tensor notation and the matrix notation is as follows:

| tensor notation | 11 | 22 | 33 | 23, 32 | 31, 13 | 12, 21 |
|---|---|---|---|---|---|---|
| matrix notation | 1 | 2 | 3 | 4 | 5 | 6 |

At the same time, a factor of 2 or 4 is introduced for $S_{ijkl}$ as follows:

$S_{ijkl} = S_{mn}$ when *m* and *n* are 1, 2 or 3

$2\,S_{ijkl} = S_{mn}$ when either *m* or *n* are 4, 5 or 6

$4\,S_{ijkl} = S_{mn}$ when both *m* and *n* are 4, 5 or 6

However, for $C_{ijkl}$ no 2 or 4 are necessary. For this, we can simply write as

$C_{ijkl} = C_{mn}$ ($i, j, k, l = 1, 2, 3; m, n = 1, \ldots, 6$)

Accordingly, the expansion of the equation 55 can be written as

$$\tau_1 = C_{11}\gamma_1 + C_{12}\gamma_2 + C_{13}\gamma_3 + C_{14}\gamma_4 + C_{15}\gamma_5 + C_{16}\gamma_6$$

$$\tau_2 = C_{21}\gamma_1 + C_{22}\gamma_2 + C_{23}\gamma_3 + C_{24}\gamma_4 + C_{25}\gamma_5 + C_{26}\gamma_6$$

$$\tau_3 = C_{31}\gamma_1 + C_{32}\gamma_2 + C_{33}\gamma_3 + C_{34}\gamma_4 + C_{35}\gamma_5 + C_{36}\gamma_6$$

$$\tau_4 = C_{41}\gamma_1 + C_{42}\gamma_2 + C_{43}\gamma_3 + C_{44}\gamma_4 + C_{45}\gamma_5 + C_{46}\gamma_6$$

$$\tau_5 = C_{51}\gamma_1 + C_{52}\gamma_2 + C_{53}\gamma_3 + C_{54}\gamma_4 + C_{55}\gamma_5 + C_{56}\gamma_6$$

$$\tau_6 = C_{61}\gamma_1 + C_{62}\gamma_2 + C_{63}\gamma_3 + C_{64}\gamma_4 + C_{65}\gamma_5 + C_{66}\gamma_6 \tag{57}$$

Similarly, from eq. 56 six strain components can be written in terms of 36 stress components. However, they are of similar nature and hence are not written separately.

## 18.11 THE STRAIN ENERGY

We know that when an elastic body undergoes a deformation, the external forces causing deformation do a certain amount of work. This work done against the forces between the particles is stored as potential energy of deformation. This is called the strain energy. In order to calculate this, let us consider a one dimensional system dealing with the longitudinal stress and longitudinal strain. Let us assume that a force $\tau_i$ per unit area acting on a one dimensional crystal which produces a change in the length per unit length $\gamma_i$. Let the crystal is further deformed by an amount $d\gamma_i$ in the same direction. Then the change in the elastic energy is equal to the work done.

$$d\phi = \tau_i d\gamma_i \tag{58}$$

In an extended form, this can be written as

$$d\phi = \tau_i d\gamma_1 + \tau_2 d\gamma_2 + \tau_3 d\gamma_3 + \tau_4 d\gamma_4 + \tau_5 d\gamma_5 + \tau_6 d\gamma_6 \tag{59}$$

Writing eq. 59 in terms of partial differentiation, we have,

$$d\phi = \frac{\partial \phi}{\partial \gamma_1} d\gamma_1 + \frac{\partial \phi}{\partial \gamma_2} d\gamma_2 + \frac{\partial \phi}{\partial \gamma_3} d\gamma_3 + \frac{\partial \phi}{\partial \gamma_4} d\gamma_4$$

$$+ \frac{\partial \phi}{\partial \gamma_5} d\gamma_5 + \frac{\partial \phi}{\partial \gamma_6} d\gamma_6 \tag{60}$$

Compairing eqs. 59 and 60, we obtain

$$\tau_1 = \frac{\partial \phi}{\partial \gamma_1}, \tau_2 = \frac{\partial \phi}{\partial \gamma_2}, \dots \tau_6 = \frac{\partial \phi}{\partial \gamma_6}$$

Further, differentiating eq. 57 partially, w.r.t $\gamma$'s, we obtain,

$$\frac{\partial \tau_1}{\partial \gamma_1} = C_{11}, \frac{\partial \tau_1}{\partial \gamma_2} = C_{12}, \dots \frac{\partial \tau_1}{\partial \gamma_6} = C_{16}$$

$$\frac{\partial \tau_2}{\partial \gamma_2} = C_{21}, \frac{\partial \tau_2}{\partial \gamma_2} = C_{22}, \dots \frac{\partial \tau_2}{\partial \gamma_6} = C_{26}$$

$$\dots\dots\dots\dots\dots\dots\dots \text{etc} \tag{61}$$

Now substituting the values of $\tau_1$, $\tau_2$ etc. in eq. 61, we obtain,

$$C_{12} = \frac{\partial \tau_1}{\partial \gamma_2} = \frac{\partial}{\partial \gamma_2}\left(\frac{\partial \phi}{\partial \gamma_1}\right) = \frac{\partial^2 \phi}{\partial \gamma_1 \partial \gamma_2}, \; C_{21} = \frac{\partial \tau_2}{\partial \gamma_1} = \frac{\partial}{\partial \gamma_1}\left(\frac{\partial \phi}{\partial \gamma_2}\right)$$

$$= \frac{\partial^2 \phi}{\partial \gamma_1 \partial \gamma_2} \ldots C_{44} = \frac{\partial \tau_4}{\partial \gamma_4} = \frac{\partial}{\partial \gamma_4}\left(\frac{\partial \phi}{\partial \gamma_4}\right) = \frac{\partial^2 \phi}{\partial \gamma_4 \partial \gamma_4}$$

or $$C_{44} = \frac{\partial^2 \phi}{\partial \gamma_4 \partial \gamma_4}, \text{ etc.}$$

However, as we know that in general,

$$C_{ij} = C_{ji}$$

Since the matrix elements $C_{ij}$ are symmetrical, therefore the number of independent elastic constants is reduced further from 36 to 21 (6 diagonal elements and 15 off diagonal elements). They are represented in the following manner

$$
\begin{array}{cccccc}
C_{11} & C_{12} & C_{13} & C_{14} & C_{15} & C_{16} \\
 & C_{22} & C_{23} & C_{24} & C_{25} & C_{26} \\
 & & C_{33} & C_{34} & C_{35} & C_{36} \\
 & & & C_{44} & C_{45} & C_{46} \\
 & & & & C_{55} & C_{56} \\
 & & & & & C_{66}
\end{array}
\tag{62}
$$

Now integrating eq. 57, we find that the work done to produce the longitudinal strain $\gamma_i$ (the so called strain energy) is equal to

$$\phi = \frac{1}{2} C_{ij}\gamma_i\gamma_j \tag{63}$$

## 18.12    EFFECT OF CRYSTAL SYMMETRY ON ELASTIC CONSTANTS

We know that the elastic constant ($C_{ijkl}$ or $S_{ijkl}$) belong to a fourth rank tensor and the presence of crystal symmetry imposes certain conditions on them. The number of elastic constant are found to decrease with the symmetry of the crystal. The Symmetry transformation of the fourth rank property tensor is obtained as discussed in sec. 18.5. This is given by

$$C'_{ijkl} = a_{ip}a_{jq}a_{kr}a_{ls}C_{pqrs} \tag{64}$$

where *pqrs* takes the values 1, 2, 3. In the following, we shall analyse the effect of crystal symmetry on elastic constants for all crystal systems with increasing symmetry following the proceduer discussed in sec. 18.6.

### 1.   Triclinic Crystal System
Crystal Classes: 1, $\bar{1}$

This crystal system is unable to impose any restriction because two point group 1 is completely unsymmetrical and $\bar{1}$ is already possessed by the property tensor. Thus the property tensor remain same as in eq. 63.

## 2. Monclinic Crystal System

Crystal Classes: 2, $m$, $\dfrac{2}{m}$; 2 ‖ $OX_2$ (standard orientation)

Application of these symmetry elements impose the same condition on the elastic constants. They affect only those coefficients which contain suffixes $\geq 4$ such that the coefficients with digit 4 or 5 each appearing only (not in pair or together) once vanish. Therefore, the number of independent non-vanishing elastic constants further reduces from 21 to 13. They are given as

$$
\begin{matrix}
C_{11} & C_{12} & C_{13} & 0 & C_{15} & 0 \\
 & C_{22} & C_{23} & 0 & C_{25} & 0 \\
 & & C_{33} & 0 & C_{35} & 0 \\
 & & & C_{44} & 0 & C_{46} \\
 & & & & C_{55} & 0 \\
 & & & & & C_{66}
\end{matrix}
\tag{65}
$$

## 3. Orthorhombic Crystal System

Crystal Classes: 222, mm2, mmm

The application of three mutually perpendicular 2-fold axes or mirror planes produce the same result. Like monoclinic case, they also affect the coefficients containing suffixes $\geq 4$. In this case, the non-vanishing coefficients contain each suffix in pairs. Thus the nine remaining non-vanishing elastic constants are

$$
\begin{matrix}
C_{11} & C_{12} & C_{13} & 0 & 0 & 0 \\
 & C_{22} & C_{23} & 0 & 0 & 0 \\
 & & C_{33} & 0 & 0 & 0 \\
 & & & C_{44} & 0 & 0 \\
 & & & & C_{55} & 0 \\
 & & & & & C_{66}
\end{matrix}
\tag{66}
$$

## 4. Tetragonal Crystal System

The point group symmetries of the tetragonal crystal system are such that they give rise to two sets of elastic constants, one each for the crystal classes 4, $\bar{4}$, $\dfrac{4}{m}$ and 422, 4mm, $\bar{4}2m$, $\dfrac{4}{mmm}$. Therefore,

(i) Crystal Classes: 4, $\bar{4}$, $\dfrac{4}{m}$

They give rise to the following 7 non-vanishing elastic constants

$$
\begin{matrix}
C_{11} & C_{12} & C_{13} & 0 & 0 & C_{16} \\
 & C_{11} & C_{13} & 0 & 0 & -C_{16} \\
 & & C_{33} & 0 & 0 & 0 \\
 & & & C_{44} & 0 & 0 \\
 & & & & C_{44} & 0 \\
 & & & & & C_{66}
\end{matrix}
\tag{67}
$$

However, it has been found that for an appropriate choice of axes $C_{16}$ no longer remains independent.

(ii) Crystal Classes: 422, 4mm, $\bar{4}2m$, $\dfrac{4}{mmm}$

Under these symmetry operators, $C_{16} = 0$. Therefore, the number of independent elastic constants reduces to 6.
They are as follows

$$
\begin{array}{cccccc}
C_{11} & C_{12} & C_{13} & 0 & 0 & 0 \\
 & C_{11} & C_{13} & 0 & 0 & 0 \\
 & & C_{33} & 0 & 0 & 0 \\
 & & & C_{44} & 0 & 0 \\
 & & & & C_{44} & 0 \\
 & & & & & C_{66}
\end{array} \tag{68}
$$

## 5. Trigonal Crystal System

Like tetragonal, trigonal crystal system also gives rise to two sets of elastic constants, one each for the crystal classes 3, $\bar{3}$ and 3m, 32, $\bar{3}m$.

(i) Crystal Classes: 3, $\bar{3}$

They give rise to the following 7 non-vanishing elastic constants

$$
\begin{array}{cccccc}
C_{11} & C_{12} & C_{13} & C_{14} & C_{15} & 0 \\
 & C_{11} & C_{13} & -C_{14} & -C_{15} & 0 \\
 & & C_{33} & 0 & 0 & 0 \\
 & & & C_{44} & 0 & -C_{15} \\
 & & & & C_{44} & C_{14} \\
 & & & & & \frac{1}{2}(C_{11} - C_{12})
\end{array} \tag{69}
$$

(ii) Crystal Classes: 3m, 32, $\bar{3}m$

Further restrictions are imposed under these classes. Hence, the number of non-vanishing elastic constants reduces to six. They are given as

$$
\begin{array}{cccccc}
C_{11} & C_{12} & C_{13} & C_{14} & 0 & 0 \\
 & C_{11} & C_{13} & -C_{14} & 0 & 0 \\
 & & C_{33} & 0 & 0 & 0 \\
 & & & C_{44} & 0 & 0 \\
 & & & & C_{44} & C_{14} \\
 & & & & & \frac{1}{2}(C_{11} - C_{12})
\end{array} \tag{70}
$$

## 6. Hexagonal Crystal System

In this crystal System, a simultaneous existence of a 2-fold and a 3-fold proper rotation give rise to the elastic constants satisfying both monoclinic and trigonal systems. Therefore, the elastic constants are given as

$$
\begin{matrix}
C_{11} & C_{12} & C_{13} & 0 & 0 & 0 \\
 & C_{11} & C_{13} & 0 & 0 & 0 \\
 & & C_{13} & 0 & 0 & 0 \\
 & & & C_{44} & 0 & 0 \\
 & & & & C_{44} & 0 \\
 & & & & & \frac{1}{2}(C_{11} - C_{12})
\end{matrix}
\qquad (71)
$$

## 7. Cubic Crystal System

Crystal Classes: 23, $m3$, 43, $\overline{4}3m$, $m3m$

This is the most symmetric crystal systems out of all systems. All three crystallographic axes are indistinguishable in this case. Therefore, considering an orthorhombic system (eq. 66) and applying suitable symmetry operations, we find that only three independent elastic constant. They are given as

$$
\begin{matrix}
C_{11} & C_{12} & C_{12} & 0 & 0 & 0 \\
 & C_{11} & C_{12} & 0 & 0 & 0 \\
 & & C_{11} & 0 & 0 & 0 \\
 & & & C_{44} & 0 & 0 \\
 & & & & C_{44} & 0 \\
 & & & & & C_{44}
\end{matrix}
\qquad (72)
$$

## 18.13  SUMMARY

1. Many physical properties show anisotropic behaviour. They can be represented by tensors of appropriate type and rank.
2. In general, a tensor of rank $n$ is specified by $3^n$ components each of which is related to $n$ axes of reference.
3. Physical properties in general can be classified into four categories: equilibrium, steady state, hysteretic and Irreversible.
4. Physical properties of a crystal describe its response to the externally applied influence. They can be defined according to the relation

$$\text{Response} = \text{Coefficient} \times \text{External influence}$$

5. If the influence and the response are tensors of rank $m$ and $n$ respectively then the physical property must be a tensor of rank $(m + n)$.
6. Certain physical properties possess inherent symmetry element. For example, tensile stress has cylindrical symmetry while shear stress has orthorhombic symmetry.
7. Crystal Symmetry imposes certain conditions on the components of the property tensor. The number of independent components have been found to decrease with the increase of crystal symmetry.
8. The strain energy produced in a deformed body is given by the work done against the forces between the particles. This is stored as potential energy.

## 18.14   DEFINITIONS

Anisotropy: The variation of physical properties with direction.

Centrosymmetry: Symmetry with respect to a point. Centrosymmetric crystals have their faces arranged in pairs which are parallel and enantiomorphous.

Conductivity: The reciprocal of resistivity. It is defined as the current density divided by the electric field strength.

Elastic deformation: A change in the relative position of points in a solid body that disappears when the deforming stress is removed.

Elasticity: The property of a body by which it tends to resume its original size and shape after being subjected to deforming force.

Hooke's Law: It states that under the elastic limit the strain produced in the body is proportional to the applied stress.

Neumann's Principle: According to this principle the symmetry elements of any physical property of a crystal must include the symmetry element of the point group of the crystal.

Piezoelectric effect: In some non-centrosymmetric crystals the surfaces become oppositely charged when subjected to pressure. These charges are proportional to the applied tension. The sign of the charges changes when tension is changed into compression.

Polar axis: A crystal axis of rotation which is not normal to a reflection plane and which does not contain a centre of symmetry. Certain crystal properties are dissimilar at opposite ends of such axis.

Polarizability: When a molecule is subjected to an electric field there is a small displacement of electrical centres which induces a dipole in the molecule. If $\mu = \alpha E$, then the constant $\alpha$ is called the polarizability.

Pyroelectricity: The development of opposite electric charges at the end of the polar axes in crystals which do not possess a centre of symmetry when the temperature is changed.

Refractive index: It is the ratio of the sine of angle of incidence to the sine of angle of refraction.

Stress Components: They are the internal forces arising between continuous part of a body due to applied surface and body forces.

Tensor: Vector notation is not always sufficiently general to express the relationships between physical quantities. Tensor notation is a general form of notation. A vector is a tensor of rank one and has three components. In general, a tensor of rank $n$ has $3^n$ components.

## REVIEW QUESTIONS AND PROBLEMS

1. How would you define physical properties of crystals? Discuss the mode of their classification. Explain each of them with examples.

2. Explain the description of physical properties as tensors of different rank. Discuss their intrinsic symmetry.

3. What do you understand by the transformation of axes? Discuss the transformation of the components of a second rank tensor and determine the required formula.

4. Obtain general expressions of transformation law corresponding to third and fourth rank tensors.

5. What is the difference between the transformation matrix $a_{ij}$ and the tensor $T_{ij}$? Discuss the effect of crystal symmetry on physical property of a second rank tensor.

6. For a property tensor of first rank if the 2-fold rotation axis in a monoclinic crystal is parallel to z- axis. What is the direction of polarization?                           Ans: $(0, 0, p_3)$.

7. For a property tensor of first rank if the mirror plane is perpendicular to $OX_2$ axis. Find the direction of polarization components.                           Ans: $(p_1, 0, p_3)$

8. If the 2-fold axis in a monoclinic crystal is parallel to $x$-axis, determine the scheme of conductivity tensor.

$$\text{Ans: } \sigma'_{ij} = \begin{bmatrix} \sigma_{11} & 0 & 0 \\ 0 & \sigma_{22} & \sigma_{23} \\ 0 & \sigma_{23} & \sigma_{33} \end{bmatrix}$$

9. Examine the effect of orthorhombic crystal symmetry on a second rank conductivity tensor. Show that there are only three independent components.

$$\text{Ans: } \sigma'_{ij} = \begin{bmatrix} \sigma_{11} & 0 & 0 \\ 0 & \sigma_{22} & 0 \\ 0 & 0 & \sigma_{33} \end{bmatrix}$$

10. Show that there are only two independent components of conductivity possible under trigonal, tetragonal and hexagonal crystal systems.

$$\text{Ans: } \sigma'_{ij} = \begin{bmatrix} \sigma_{11} & 0 & 0 \\ 0 & \sigma_{11} & 0 \\ 0 & 0 & \sigma_{22} \end{bmatrix}$$

11. Show that there exists a unique component of conductivity tensor in cubic crystal system

$$\text{Ans: } \sigma'_{ij} = \begin{bmatrix} \sigma_{11} & 0 & 0 \\ 0 & \sigma_{11} & 0 \\ 0 & 0 & \sigma_{11} \end{bmatrix}$$

12. In a monoclinic crystal, if the mirror plane is perpendicular to $OX_3$ axis, determine the scheme of piezoelectric moduli

$$\text{Ans: } d'_{ij} = \begin{pmatrix} 0 & 0 & 0 & d_{14} & d_{15} & 0 \\ 0 & 0 & 0 & d_{24} & d_{25} & 0 \\ d_{21} & d_{22} & d_{23} & 0 & 0 & d_{26} \end{pmatrix}$$

13. Determine the scheme of piezoelectric moduli for crystal class $3m$ when the mirror plane is perpendicular to $OX_2$ axis.

$$\text{Ans: } d'_{ij} = \begin{pmatrix} d_{11} & -d_{11} & 0 & 0 & d_{15} & 0 \\ 0 & 0 & 0 & d_{15} & 0 & -2d_{11} \\ d_{31} & d_{31} & d_{33} & 0 & 0 & 0 \end{pmatrix}$$

# Bibliography

A. Beiser, *Concept of Modern physics*, McGraw-Hill Kogakusha Limited (1973).

A. Cottrell, *An Introduction to Metallurgy*, ELBS (1975).

A.H. Cottrell, *Theory of Dislocations,* Gordon and Breach Science Publishers (1964).

A. Hart-Davis, *Solids: An Introduction*, McGraw-Hill Book Company (1975).

A.J. Bondi, *Phys. Chem.*, **68** (1964), 441.

A.J. Dekker, *Solid State physics,* The Macmillan Press Ltd. (1981).

A.J. Dekker, *Electrical Engineering Materials*, Prentice Hall of India Pvt. Ltd. (1994).

A.O.E. Animalu, *Intermediate Quantum Theory of Crystalline Solids*, Prentice Hall, Inc. (1977).

A.R. Verma and O.N. Srivastava, *Crystallography for Solid State Physics*, Wiley Eastern Limited (1987).

A.R. Verma and P. Krishna, *Polymorphism and Polytypism in Crystals,* John Wiely & Sons (1966).

A.R. West, *Solid State Chemistry and its Application*, John Wiley & Sons (1984).

B. Henderson, *Defects in Crystalline Solids*, Crane, Russak & Company (1972).

B. Palosz, *Z. Krist.*, **151** (1980), 31.

B. Palosz and J. Przedmojski, *Z. Krist.*, **153** (1980), 51.

Charles Kittel, *Introduction to Solid State Physics*, Wiley Eastern Limited 5th ed. (1976).

C.M. Kachhava, *Solid State Physics*, Tata McGraw-Hill Publishing Company Limited (1990).

C.A. Wert and R.M. Thomson, *Physics of Solids*, McGraw-Hill Kogakusha Limited (1970).

C.N.R. Rao and J. Gopalakrishnan, *New Directions in Solid State Chemistry*, Cambridge University Press (1986).

C.S. Barrett and T.B. Massalski, *Structure of Metals*, McGraw-Hill Book Company (1996).

C.S. Cook, *Structure of Atomic Nuclei*, Affiliated East-West Press Private Limited (1972).

D. Hull, *Introduction to Dislocations*, Pergamon Press (1965).

D.M. Adams, *Inorganic Solids*: *An Introduction to Concepts in Solid State Structural Chemistry*, John Wiley & Sons Limited (1974).

D. Mapother, H. Crooks and J. Maurer, *Chemical Physics*, **18** (1950), 1231.

E. Mooser and W.B. Pearson, *Acta Cryst.*, **12** (1959), 1015.

F.C. Philips, *An Introduction to Crystallography*, John Wiley (1963).

G. Burns, *Solid State Physics,* Academic Press, Inc. (1985).

G.C. Trigunayat and G.K. Chadha, Pogress in the Study of Polytypism in Crystals (I) *Phys. Stat. Sol.* (a) **4** (1971), 9.

G.I. Epifanov, *Solid State Physics*, Mir Publishers (1979).

H. Clark, *Solid State Physics*: *An Introduction to its Theory*. Macmillan (1968).

H.C. Gupta, *Solid State Physics*, Vikas Publishing House Private Limited (1995).

H.E. Hall, *Solid State Physics*, ELBS and John Wiely & Sons Limited (1978).

H.J. Brophy, M.R. Rose and J. Wulff, *Thermodynamics of Structure*, Wiley Eastern Limited (1980).

H.W. Schamp, Ph.D. Thesis, University of Michigan (1951).

H. Ibach and H. Luth, *Solid State Physics: An Introduction to Theory and Experiments*, Narosa Publishing House (1992).

H.M. Rosenberg, *The Solid State: An Introduction to the Physics, Materials Science and Engineering*, Clarendon Press, Oxford, II ed. (1978).

H.V. Keer, *Principle of the Solid State*, Wiley Eastern limited (1993).

J.C. Philips, *Bonds and Bonds in Semiconductors*, Academic Press (1973).

J.D. Morrison, *Rev. Pure Appl. Chem.*, 5 (1995), 46.

J.D. Ryder, *Electronic Fundamentals and Applications*, Prentice Hall of India Private Limited (1971).

J.F. NYE, F.R.S, Physical Properties of Crystals, Oxford University Press (1985).

J.P. Herth and J. Lothe, *Theory of Dislocations*, McGraw-Hill Book Company (1968).

J.R. Manning, *Diffusion Kinetics for Atoms in Crystals*, D. Van Nostrand Company, Inc. (1968).

J.W. Lynn, *High Temperature Superconductivity*, Springer-Verlag (1990).

J.S. Blackmore, *Solid State Physics*, Cambridge University Press, II ed. (1974).

K. Fichtner, *Z. Krist.*, **159** (182), 311.

K. Fichtner, *Cryst. Res Tech.*, **19** (1984), 49.

L. Pauling, *The Nature of Chemical Bonds*, Cornel University Press (1960).

L.S. Darken and R.W. Gurg, *Physical Chemistry of Metals*, McGraw-Hill, 1953.

L.S. Dent Glasser, *Crstallography and its Applications*, VNR Company Limited (1977).

L.S. Ramsdell, *Am. Miner.*, **32** (1974), 64.

L.V. Azaroff, *Introduction to Solids*, McGraw-Hill Book Company (1960).

L.V. Azaroff, *Elements of X-ray Crystallography*, McGraw-Hill Book Company (1968)

L.V. Azaroff and J. Brophy, *Electronic Processes in Materials*, McGraw-Hill Book Company, Inc. (1963).

M.A. Omar, *Elementry Solid State Physics: Principles and Applications*, Addison-Wesley Publishing Company (1975).

M.A. Wahab and R. Kant, *Cryst. Res. Tech.*, **21** (1986), 239.

M.C. Bansal, R.C. Madhani and M.P. Singh, *Modern Physics*, Pragati prakashan (1982).

M.C. Lovell, A.J. Avery and M.W. Vernon, *Physical Properties of Materials*, ELBS and VNR Company Limited (1983).

M. Husain et al., *Polyhedron*, **8** (1989), 1233.

M.H.B. Stiddard, *The Elementary Language of Solid State Physics*, Academic Press (1975).

M.J. Buerger, *X-ray Crystallography*, John Wiley & Sons (1966).

M.N. Rudden and J. Wilson, *Elements of Solid State Physics*, John Wiley & Sons Limited (1980).

M.P. Tosi, *Solid State Physics: Advances in Research and Applications*, Vol. 16, Academic Press (1964).

N.B. Hanny, *Solid State Chemistry*, Prentice-Hall of India Private Limited (1976).

N.F. Mott and R.W. Gurney, *Electronic Processes in Ionic Crystals*, Oxford (1950).

N. Ruddenn and J. Wilson, *Elements of Solid State Physics*, John Wiley and Sons (1980).

N.V. Perelomova and M.M. Tagieva, Problems in Crystal Physics with Solutions, Mir Publishers Moscow (1982).

N.W. Ashcroft and N.D. Mermin, *Solid State Physics*, CBS Publishing Asia Limited (1988).

P.B. Dorain, *Symmetry in Inorganic Chemistry*, Amrind Publishing Company Private Limited (1964).

P.C. Jain and G.C. Trigunayat, *Acta Cryst.*, **A33** (1977), 256.

P.G. Shewmon, *Diffusion of Solids*, McGraw-Hill (1963)

R.C. Evans, *Introduction to Crystal Chemistry*, Cambridge University Press (1964).

R.M. Rose, L.A. Shepard and John Wulff, *Structure and Properties of Materials*, Vol. IV. Wiley Eastern Limited (1980).

R. Ramaswamy, *Elementry Solid State Physics*, Published by Mrs. Laxmi Ramaswamy, Madurai (1969).

S.L. Kakani and C. Hemarajani, *Solid State Physics*, Sultan Chand and Sons (1992).

T.P. Orlando and K.A. Dalin, *Foundation of Applied Superconductivity*, Addison-Wesley Publishing Company (1991).

T.S. Hutchison and D.C. Baird, *The Physics of Engineering Solids*, John Wiley & Sons, Inc. (1963).

V. Raghavan, *Materials Science and Engineering: A First Course*, Prentice-Hall of India Private Limited (1988).

V. Schomaker and D.P. Stevenson, *J. Am. Chem. Soc.*, **63** (1941), 37.

W.G. Moffatt, G.W. Pearsall and J. Wulff, *Structure and Properties of Materials*, Vol. I (Structure), Wiley Eastern Limited (1980).

W. Hayden, W.G. Moffatt and J. Wulff, *Structure and properties of Materials*, Vol. III (Mechanical Behaviour), Wiley Eastern Limited (1980).

W. Jost, *Diffusion in Solids, Liquids, Gases*, Academic Press (1952).

W.W. Porterfield, *Inorganic Chemistry: A Unified Approach*, Addison-Wesley Publishing Company (1984).

# Subject Index